PROOFREADERS' MARKS FOR ROUGH DRAFTS AND REVISES

ABBREVIATIONS OF STATES, TERRITORIES, AND POSSESSIONS OF THE UNITED STATES

AL	Alabama	Ala.	KY	Kentucky	Ky.	ND	North Dakota	N. Dak.
AK	Alaska	...	LA	Louisiana	La.	OH	Ohio	...
AZ	Arizona	Ariz.	ME	Maine	...	OK	Oklahoma	Okla.
AR	Arkansas	Ark.	MD	Maryland	Md.	OR	Oregon	Oreg.
CA	California	Calif.	MA	Massachu-		PA	Pennsylvania	Pa.
CZ	Canal Zone	C.Z.		setts	Mass.	PR	Puerto Rico	P.R.
CO	Colorado	Colo.	MI	Michigan	Mich.	RI	Rhode Island	R.I.
CT	Connecticut	Conn.	MN	Minnesota	Minn.	SC	South	
DE	Delaware	Del.	MS	Mississippi	Miss.		Carolina	S.C.
DC	District of		MO	Missouri	Mo.	SD	South Dakota	S. Dak.
	Columbia	D.C.	MT	Montana	Mont.	TN	Tennessee	Tenn.
FL	Florida	Fla.	NE	Nebraska	Nebr.	TX	Texas	Tex.
GA	Georgia	Ga.	NV	Nevada	Nev.	UT	Utah	...
GU	Guam	...	NH	New		VT	Vermont	Vt.
HI	Hawaii	...		Hampshire	N.H.	VI	Virgin Islands	V.I.
ID	Idaho	...	NJ	New Jersey	N.J.	VA	Virginia	Va.
IL	Illinois	Ill.	NM	New Mexico	N. Mex.	WA	Washington	Wash.
IN	Indiana	Ind.	NY	New York	N.Y.	WV	West Virginia	W. Va.
IA	Iowa	...	NC	North		WI	Wisconsin	Wis.
KS	Kansas	Kans.		Carolina	N.C.	WY	Wyoming	Wyo.

Use the two-letter abbreviations on the left when abbreviating state names in addresses. In any other situation that calls for abbreviations of state names, use the abbreviations on the right.

Business
English
and
Communication

Business English and Communication

Seventh Edition

This edition is dedicated to the late Marie M. Stewart, Ph.D., the original author of the *Business English and Communication* program. For more than 25 years, her brilliant teaching methods and learning materials set the standards for instruction in business English and communication both here and abroad.

Lyn R. Clark, Ed.D.
Professor of Business
Los Angeles Pierce College
Woodland Hills, California

Kenneth Zimmer, Ed.D.
Professor Emeritus of Business Education and
    Office Administration
California State University
Los Angeles, California

Joseph Tinervia, B.A.
Former Editor in Chief
Business Communication and Typing
Gregg Division/McGraw-Hill Book Company
New York, New York

GREGG DIVISION/McGRAW-HILL BOOK COMPANY
NEW YORK · ATLANTA · DALLAS · ST. LOUIS ·
SAN FRANCISCO · AUCKLAND · BOGOTÁ ·
GUATEMALA · HAMBURG · LISBON · LONDON ·
MADRID · MEXICO · MILAN · MONTREAL · NEW DELHI ·
PANAMA · PARIS · SAN JUAN · SÃO PAULO · SINGAPORE ·
SYDNEY · TOKYO · TORONTO

Business English and Communication, Seventh Edition
INTERNATIONAL EDITION 1988

Exclusive rights by McGraw-Hill Book Co — Singapore, for
manufacture and export. This book cannot be re-exported
from the country to which it is consigned by McGraw-Hill.

3 4 5 6 7 8 9 0 KKP 9 3 2 1

The letters and memos in this book were created electronically.

Library of Congress Cataloging-in-Publication Data

Clark, Lyn.
    Business English and communication.

    Rev. ed. of: Business English and communication/
Marie M. Stewart, Kenneth Zimmer, Lyn R. Clark.
6th ed., Teacher's ed. c1984.
    Includes index.
    Summary: Emphasizes the English and communication skills that are necessary in the business world, including speaking, listening, reading, and writing.
    1. English language-Business English.   2. Language
arts (Secondary) [1. English language-Business English.   2. Language arts] I. Zimmer, Kenneth, date.
II. Tinervia, Joseph, date.   III. Stewart,
Marie M., date. Business English and communication.   IV. Title.
PE1115.C46   1987   428.2'02465   86-18501
ISBN 0-07-061432-6 (pupil's ed.)

Sponsoring Editor: Marie Orsini Rosen
Editing Supervisor: Suzette André
Production Supervisor: Kathleen Donnelly
Design and Art Supervisor: Frances Conte Saracco
Photo Editor: Rosemarie Rossi
Photo Researcher: Betsy Horan

Photographs on chapter-opening spreads appear courtesy of the following: Chapters 1, 6, and 9: Jules Allen; Chapters 2-5, 7, 8, 10, and 11: Richard Hackett.

Line illustrations and excerpted material appearing on the following pages were reprinted or adapted courtesy of the following: pages 43-44: Walt Disney Productions, Burbank, California; pages 74-75: Merriam-Webster, Inc., Springfield, Massachusetts; page 78: Houghton Mifflin Company, Boston, Massachusetts; page 278: *Wordwatching*, Bryn Mawr, Pennsylvania; page 415: The Franklin Mint, Porcelain Division, Franklin Center, Pennsylvania; page 427: University of Illinois College of Medicine, Chicago, Illinois; page 437: Carnation Company — Health and Nutrition Division, Los Angeles, California; page 461: JC Penny Company, Inc., Northridge, California; page 468: Dow Jones & Company, Inc., New York, New York; page 480: California Federal Savings & Loan Association, Los Angeles, California; page 485: Xerox Corporation, Warner Center, Woodlawn Hills, California; page 497: Creative Travel Planners, Inc., Woodland Hills, California.

When ordering this title use ISBN 0-07-100171-9

Printed in Singapore

Contents

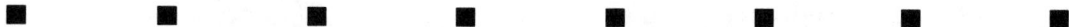

Contents

Contents

Contents

Contents

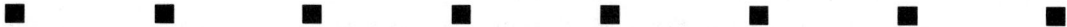

■   ■   ■   ■   ■   ■   ■   ■

Contents

Contents

Contents

Contents

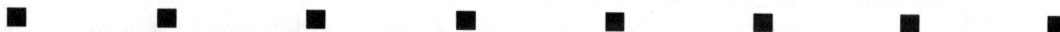

Preface

Think about all the time you spend communicating. You may not even realize how much of your day is spent this way. Whether you are the secretary to the president of a company, a word processing operator, a marketing representative, an information systems manager, or a corporate executive, much of your work involves reading, writing, listening, and speaking. Even though technology helps you function more efficiently and across long distances, you must still have polished communication skills to succeed at what you do. In fact, your value as an employee and your very promotability may depend, in large part, on your ability to communicate.

The *Business English and Communication* program has been designed to provide you with the broad, thorough training necessary to develop competence on the job in each of the communication skills: reading, writing, speaking, and listening.

The Seventh Edition

The Seventh Edition begins by introducing you to the fundamentals of business communication skills and describing the impact of communication psychology, human relations, and electronic office technology on these skills. Then, after you have learned how to develop good reading, proofreading, *and editing* skills, you will start to improve your general word skills and study how mastery of grammar, punctuation, and style can make the difference between effective and ineffective communication. Next, you will start to develop your written and your oral communication skills. Finally, you will learn how to apply *all* your communication skills and talents toward getting a job. In addition to having developed your communication skills, you will also have been introduced to the language of business, for the textbook emphasizes business vocabulary throughout.

Business Communication, Human Relations, and Technology.   The Seventh Edition addresses some of the most interesting aspects of business communication: human relations and office technology. Right away, in Chapter 1, the communication skills of reading, writing, speaking, and listening are identified and illustrated through practical examples. Then you are shown what motivates us all to act. You will see how applying the principles of communication psychology and human relations will help you communicate more effectively. You will learn that technology in the electronic office—an astounding productivity aid—does not eliminate the need to master your fundamental language and human relations skills; technology only makes communicating faster and easier. Throughout the text, photographs depict business communicators using these skills in both the traditional and the electronic office.

Reading and Proofreading.   Your reading and—more important—proofreading skills are developed early in the text, in Chapter 2. This way, you may apply these skills throughout the course. Also, starting in Chapter 2 and continuing throughout the editing, grammar, punctuation, and style coverage (Chapters 3, 4, and 5), you will find oral Class Practice and Editing Practice exercises. Special class Proofreading Practice exercises will be found in Unit 6 and then in Chapters 3, 4, and 5. These short exercises are designed to provide immediate reinforcement of principles just learned.

Editing and Word Skills.   Because messages can always be improved, Chapter 3 concentrates on developing editing skills. In addition, Chapter 3 offers a broad overview for developing word skills. You learn how to expand your vocabulary and how to use a dictionary and other word references. Of special interest in Chapter 3 is Unit 9, on spelling, which offers a three-step approach for mastering a basic business vocabulary. In addition, you learn to distinguish differences in meaning of many of the most commonly confused words.

Grammar and Punctuation.   A solid foundation in English grammar is essential for successful communication, and Chapters 4 and 5 offer you all the grammar and punctuation know-how you will need to succeed on the job. Developed over several editions, these chapters stress the practical principles of grammar and punctuation—the ones that you *must* know. Much of the confusing, complex terminology has been eliminated. Moreover, Quick Trick sections are frequently offered immediately after those rules that are most confusing. These Quick Tricks take difficult principles and change them into easy-to-remember rules. Many practice exercises are provided throughout each unit in the grammar and punctuation chapters—after every Quick Trick section, for example—to help you understand each principle and to reinforce your understanding.

Writing—The Building-Block Approach.   Expert writers do more than write messages that are correct. They create messages that are explicit and polished, and their ability to do so is what distinguishes their messages from everyday, routine messages. Chapter 6 uses a unique building-block approach to the writing process, beginning with word selection and moving onto sentence and paragraph writing. Of special interest in Chapter 6 is Unit 38, which covers writing 50-word messages at the computer—concisely and correctly.

Letters.   Chapter 7 offers you a thorough training program on business letters, from the general to the specific. It begins with general business letter formats and proceeds to cover almost every specific type of letter, each in an individual unit. You learn to write not only routine letters such as transmittals and requests, which would be assigned to beginning employees, but also more specialized letters such as sales and credit letters. Especially interesting are Units 46 and 47, which cover using paragraph libraries and shell documents.

Memos.   Memos are the primary means of written communication within an organization. Therefore, in Chapter 8 you are given expanded coverage on how memos are used in business. Because memos are used in so many ways, techniques for tailoring memos for special purposes—including the use of graphics and readability devices—are included.

Reports.   Chapter 9 includes a thorough treatment of report writing. It also covers the use of commonplace form messages, minutes, and news releases.

Listening and Speaking Skills.   In Chapter 10, the important skills of becoming a good listener and a good speaker are discussed. You will learn techniques that will help you master these crucial skills. In addition, ways that listening may bear on your job are discussed. Chapter 10 also prepares you to speak effectively by offering practical guidance on planning and giving a talk, meeting the public in person and by telephone, and participating in group discussions. In this chapter you will also learn some of the common pitfalls of enunciation and pronunciation and how to avoid them. New coverage offers techniques for speaking with *and* without electronic equipment.

Résumés and Job Applications.   The effectiveness with which you can prepare résumés and employment letters will have an immediate, direct impact on your success in seeking employment. Chapter 11 prepares you for all the employment messages you may write—application letters, résumés, reference letters, acceptance letters, and so on. In addition, it offers helpful suggestions— many of them provided by professional recruiters—that will prepare you for employment interviews.

Communication Laboratory

At the end of every unit within the text is a Communication Laboratory section, which provides exercises that will help you apply the principles learned in the unit. Each Communication Laboratory offers a series of three different exercises.

Application Exercises.   These exercises test your understanding of the principles presented in the current unit and review those presented in previous units.

Vocabulary and Spelling Studies.   This section of each Communication Laboratory emphasizes the development of spelling and vocabulary skills.

Communicating for Results.   Each Communication Laboratory ends with Communicating for Results, a thought-provoking exercise that tests your ability to apply communication skills in realistic business situations. Not only do these exercises require you to apply the principles of language usage, but they also test your ability to solve problems in human relations, social-business etiquette, and so on.

Supporting Materials

In addition to this text, the *Business English and Communication* program includes a workbook of projects and activities for students; a set of objective, printed tests; a computerized test bank; and teacher's editions of both the textbook and the workbook.

The Workbook.   A complete teaching-learning aid, *Student Projects and Activities for Business English and Communication* provides application exercises closely correlated with the principles covered in each of the corresponding units of the textbook. These worksheets offer enrichment, reinforcement, and review exercises covering spelling and vocabulary development, reading comprehension, listening comprehension, proofreading, editing, rewriting, note-taking, and composition of letters and other types of business communications. All the exercises offered in this workbook differ from those given in the text.

Teacher's Edition of the Textbook. *Business English and Communication* offers a unique and popular page-for-page teacher's edition of the textbook. Short teaching suggestions and short exercise solutions appear, in a second color, right on the page of the text to which they refer. In addition, grouped at the back of the teacher's edition are explanations of how to use the program; additional detailed unit-by-unit teaching suggestions; schedules and grading guidelines; and longer solutions to exercises in the text, carefully cross-referenced to the actual exercises.

Teacher's Edition of the Workbook. Another teaching aid is the teacher's edition of the workbook. Not only does it include a page-for-page facsimile key of all the workbook exercises, it also includes objective tests for the students (see below).

Tests. Forty-eight pages of test masters are included at the back of the teacher's edition of *Student Projects and Activities for Business English and Communication*. Ten progress tests cover all the units of the textbook. In addition, an inventory test for use at the beginning of the course and a final examination for the end of the course are included. A facsimile key to the tests follows the tests at the back of the teacher's edition of *Student Projects and Activities for Business English and Communication*.

Computerized Test Bank. The computerized test bank allows you to create, edit, and print (randomly or nonrandomly) your own tests. Another feature of the computerized test bank allows you to modify and print, randomly or nonrandomly, already existing tests.

Acknowledgments

We would like to thank the following educators for their invaluable review comments on our program: **Martha Dominquez,** Ysleta Independent School District, El Paso, Texas; **Gary Gebhart,** Great Oaks Joint Vocational School District, Cincinnati, Ohio; **Cindy George,** Central Cambria High School, Ebensburg, Pennsylvania; **Arthur Goldstein,** Mabel Dean Bacon High School, New York, New York; **Jacquelyn Griffin,** Delta School of Business, Lake Charles, Louisiana; **Eva Lewis,** formerly of Foothills Adult Education Center, El Cajon, California; and **Arlene Sinding,** Hillsborough High School, Belle Mead, New Jersey.

Lyn R. Clark
Kenneth Zimmer
Joseph Tinervia

Chapter

1

Think about how much time you spend sending ideas *to* others or receiving ideas *from* others. When you are reading a report, listening to instructions, filling out an application form, or speaking about your interests, you are spending your time communicating.

Communication activities take skill. When you send a message to others, you want to be sure that the receiver of your message understands exactly what you mean. When you are receiving a message from someone, you want to be sure *you* understand what that person means.

To be an effective communicator, you need to know the importance of communication skills, both in your personal life and in your career. You also need to know how communication psychology and evolving technologies can affect your communication skill. Given a situation requiring speaking, listening, reading, and writing skills, you will be able to do the following when you master the units in this chapter:

1. *Identify the kinds and levels of communication skills needed for success in your personal life, your personal-business activities, and your chosen career.*

2. *Select and use verbal and nonverbal communication to make your message effective.*

3. *Demonstrate your understanding of how the levels of human needs and how human relations affect the communication process.*

4. *Describe the impact that communication technology has made and will further make on all your roles as a communicator.*

5. *List ways that office technology—such as word processing, information processing, telecommunications, and networking— affects the communication process.*

U · N · I · T

Communicating On and Off the Job

The ring of the telephone—someone wishes to speak with you. A knock at the door—the person on the other side is asking you to open it. The utterance of your name—the person speaking wants your attention. All these sounds are signals that someone wishes to communicate with you. That person has a message to convey.

The exchange of messages between and among human beings is known as communication. We send and receive messages in a variety of ways. The examples given above rely on sounds to send messages; other methods of message transmission include speaking, writing, gestures, and facial expressions. Listening, reading, and observing are the means we use to receive the messages sent. The most difficult task involved in the communication process is ensuring that the receiver interprets the message as the sender meant it to be interpreted.

This process is not so simple as it seems. Take, for example, the following case. Scott, a seventeen-year-old high school junior, received a telephone call from his friend Bob. Bob informed Scott, "I can't go swimming with you tomorrow because I have to look for another job." "OK," responded Scott, "give me a call when you can go." So ended the conversation! When Scott hung up, he told his parents that Bob had lost his job at Hathaway's Grocery Store and had to look for another one. It was not until a few days later that the true circumstances were uncovered. Bob had not lost his job at the grocery store; he was just looking for *another* part-time job to supplement the too-few hours he was working at Hathaway's.

Why did this breakdown in communication occur? Both the sender and the receiver were at fault. The sender, Bob, gave too little information; he was not specific or concrete in conveying his message. Too many details were left to the imagination of the receiver. Scott, the receiver, was at fault too because he reached an unwarranted conclusion based upon the information given. Just because Bob was looking for another job, Scott should not have assumed that Bob had lost his previous one.

Miscommunication can occur easily in any situation—especially in our electronic age, where even the pressing of a button can send an incorrect message. That is why it is important for you to study the entire communication process and sharpen your verbal skills. To communicate effectively, you need to develop your abilities in speaking, writing, listening, reading, and observing. You also need to understand the principles of communication psychology. This unit begins your study of the communication concepts necessary for success in your personal and business life.

Your Personal Communication

Communication begins early in life. The baby's cry provokes the parents' response. Is the baby hungry? Does he or she need to have a diaper changed? Is the cry for attention? The fact that the baby has a need is communicated by a simple cry. As children grow older, however, they use a more complex communication process. Words become the means of communication, and to a considerable degree the extent of a person's vocabulary governs his or her ability to send and receive messages. Besides communicating with family members and friends, the child must learn to communicate effectively in school in order to prepare properly for later life.

Verbal Skills for Everyday Life. Communication skills are not important just for functioning among family members and friends and in school; they are also essential for functioning in everyday life. Reading, writing, speaking, and listening all play an integral part in our contemporary lifestyle. Take, for example, the communication involved in obtaining a driver's license.

Reading plays a prominent role. You must read the directions to fill in the application form. You must also read the driving manual issued by the motor vehicle department, since a knowledge of the rules and regulations of the road is essential to pass the written test. Reading skills are also necessary for actually taking the written test. Complicated questions, sometimes with tricky choices for answers, require critical reading skills. Road signs, too, not only require interpretive skills but may also require reading skills.

Writing skills are needed to fill out the license application form. Correct information must be supplied clearly. Speaking skills come into play in asking questions, providing answers, and following through in the application process. Listening plays an especially important role in the practical test. If the examiner were to instruct you to turn left at the next intersection and you instead turned into the first driveway, you would decrease your likelihood of passing the examination. If you did not hear the instruction and continued to drive straight ahead, points would be deducted from your score. Equally serious results would occur if you were to misinterpret the instruction to turn left and instead turned right. Careful listening and appropriate interpretation govern your success in this and many other endeavors.

Skills to Avoid Misunderstanding. As you can see, the entire communication process plays a vital role in acquiring a driver's license. Communication skills are essential in many other aspects of the young adult's world. As an additional example, note the difficulties that can result from a communication breakdown in applying for a social security card.

Cindy Brooks, a sixteen-year-old high school sophomore, went to her local social security office to apply for a card. She already had obtained her first part-time job but needed the card to begin work. As instructed, Cindy brought with her a copy of her birth certificate. She carefully filled out the application, using the name shown on her birth certificate, Cynthia Jean Brooks. Satisfied that she had completed all the requirements, Cindy signed her application and went home.

A week later Cindy's application was returned to her by mail with the request to resubmit it. You see, Cindy had signed her application "Cindy Brooks" instead of "Cynthia Jean Brooks." Yet the instructions had clearly stated, "Sign name as shown on application." If Cindy had signed her name correctly, she could have started her job a week earlier. Not reading the instructions carefully had cost Cindy the wages she would have earned if she had signed the application correctly and begun work the prior week.

Your Personal Communication in the Business World

Even though you may never work in a business organization, you cannot escape communicating with business and government in conducting your personal business. Routine purchases of food, clothing, gas, and household supplies require reading, listening, and speaking skills. Reading labels and instructions carefully enables you to make proper and economical selections. Asking questions, making requests, giving instructions, and describing your needs all require precise and distinct speaking skills. Listening, too, is required to follow directions in meeting your personal purchasing needs.

Satisfying Your Needs as a Consumer. Purchasing a car, a home, life insurance, medical insurance, or a major home appliance requires communication skills. So do contractual agreements for home improvements, installment buying, or investment. Solving problems generated by faulty merchandise, insurance claims, legal matters, and medical concerns requires even more advanced communication skills. Not only will you rely on speaking, listening, and reading, but you also will draw on your writing skills for such tasks.

Notice how Dave Friedman, a twenty-eight-year-old bank clerk, solved this problem. The Mitsubi electronic game he had purchased nearly two years ago was no longer working; one of the circuit boards was broken. Mitsubi had no authorized repair stores in the city where he lived, so Dave had to write a business letter to solve his problem. This meant writing to Mitsubi, explaining the nature of the problem, requesting shipment of the appropriate replacement part, and making arrangements for payment. This information needed to be stated simply, exactly, and clearly in his letter. To do this, Dave called upon his knowledge of spelling, grammar, writing style, message organization, and business-letter format—all areas you will be studying in this textbook.

Communicating With Government. Writing skills are essential for solving problems that may arise with government. Isabel Granadino, a twenty-six-year-old nurse's aide, was shocked when she opened a letter that stated, "If the enclosed parking ticket is not paid within 30 days, a warrant will be issued for your arrest." Upon examining the enclosed parking ticket, Isabel saw that it had been issued in a city more than 90 miles from her home on a day that she had been working. After a closer reading she noticed that the cited vehicle had the license plate number 1DSE438. Isabel's license number was 1DSE439! Evidently someone had made an error in entering the license number into the computer to locate the owner's name and address—a perfect example of miscommunication in our electronic age.

Nevertheless, Isabel was still faced with the problem of having to correct this situation. She could take a day off from work and drive 90 miles to the courthouse to correct the situation, but why waste so much time and money when a well-written letter could achieve the same results? Isabel chose to write the letter. Again, skillful and clear expression was needed to ensure that the reader understood the circumstances and took the action requested.

Business Communication in the World of Work

No matter what occupation you select—accountant, electronic technician, office worker, business executive, nurse, construction worker, mail carrier, flight attendant, or computer programmer—you will need to deal with communication in the world of work.

Interactions in the Work Environment. In your work environment you will interact with coworkers, superiors, subordinates, customers, suppliers, and machines. You will be involved with face-to-face dialogues, telephone conversations, conferences, and committee meetings. All these activities will require you to exercise your speaking and listening expertise.

Media such as forms, letters, memorandums, reports, bulletins, news releases, meeting minutes, newsletters, and employee handbooks require reading and writing skills. At this point you may view yourself only as a reader of these documents, but your job may also involve your writing some of them. You may be asked to generate letters to customers and suppliers, memos to coworkers or subordinates, reports to superiors, or any of the other written documents that an organization produces.

Responsibilities for Written Communications. Take, for example, the array of written communiqués originating at the desk of a secretary. Simple phone messages may not seem too important; but think of the communication breakdowns that could occur if the secretary forgot to ask the name of the caller, jotted down the phone number incorrectly, misinterpreted the message, or even neglected to place the message on the recipient's desk.

One Monday a secretary took a phone message for a clothing department manager that read, "The shipment of dresses you inquired about should arrive by next Wednesday." Well, "next Wednesday" was too late for the weekend sale planned by the store, so the department manager removed this item from the newspaper ads announcing the bargains to be offered during the coming weekend.

When the dresses arrived on Wednesday in time for the sale, the department manager was confused. That is when she discovered that "next Wednesday" to her secretary meant "the next Wednesday occurring." To the department manager "next Wednesday" meant "not this immediate Wednesday but the one following it." Are you confused? Then there is little wonder that this message was misinterpreted. If the message had been written to say, "The shipment of dresses you inquired about should arrive by Wednesday, May 12," surely there would have been no doubt about the day in question.

Besides being responsible for preparing all kinds of written communiqués, a secretary sometimes must originate letters, memorandums, bulletins, and meeting minutes. The types of letters a secretary is asked to write frequently include acknowledging receipt of a document while the supervisor is away on a business trip, answering a routine inquiry or request, and writing a nonroutine order. A memo to the personnel department requesting a replacement for a terminating employee or a bulletin to other staff members informing them of telephone directory changes might be initiated by a secretary. And meeting minutes are more often than not the total responsibility of the secretary.

Persons in other occupations, too, are faced with originating a variety of written documents. Salespeople draft letters to customers and suppliers, accountants prepare reports for clients, nurses chart patients' progress, insurance agents complete claims, and engineers write specifications. Almost all occupations require some kind of writing skill, and virtually all occupations require oral communication skills. Your success as a communicator may well measure your success in a chosen field. That is why it is important for you to improve your personal communication skills constantly.

COMMUNICATION LABORATORY

APPLICATION EXERCISES

A. Select a person you know whom you would classify as an expert communicator. In your opinion what skills does this person possess that make him or her successful?

B. Select a well-known local, national, or international personality. Describe why you feel this individual is a good or a poor communicator. Give concrete examples to substantiate your judgment.

C. Select a friend, family member, or coworker whom you have the opportunity to observe frequently. Evaluate that person's ability to communicate effectively. Give specific incidents to justify your opinion.

D. Describe a situation, humorous or otherwise, in which you were involved and miscommunication occurred. What were the consequences? How could the misunderstanding have been prevented?

E. Search your local newspaper for an article that cites a language barrier or misinterpretation as the cause of a problem (or at least a contributory cause). Summarize and report the circumstances to your class.

F. Keep a log of your significant communication activities for a day, two days, or a week. Prepare it in tabular format, using headings such as the following: "Date," "Time," "Persons Involved," "Summary of Content," "Communication Processes," and "Evaluation." Under "Evaluation" rate the effectiveness of the communication in the incident by using terms such as *Excellent, Good, Fair,* and *Poor.* The log can best be kept on 8½- by 11-inch paper, writing across the 11-inch side as the width. Note the details of any important conversations, telephone calls, business transactions, written materials, social encounters, or instructional programs in which you were involved. For each activity determine which processes (listening, speaking, reading, writing) were used, and evaluate your success in completing the communication process.

G. Choose two activities in which you are presently involved—one that usually attracts your interest and one that rarely does so. Analyze the factors that contribute to making one activity interesting and the other less so. Which of these factors can be related to the presence or absence of effective communication?

H. Interview a member of your family or a member of a family close to you. Discuss the kinds of personal-business correspondence written by this family and the circumstances that prompted the correspondence. Inquire specifically about claim letters, inquiry letters, order letters, and letters to correct problems. Describe in detail at least two situations that resulted in specific letters or that could be resolved through letters.

I. Communication skills are essential for job success. Choose one of the following occupations and discuss the various kinds of written communications needed to carry out the duties and responsibilities of this job classification.

1. salesperson
2. manager
3. nurse
4. electrician
5. accountant
6. word processor

J. Select an occupation in which you are interested. Discuss the oral and written communication skills necessary for success in that job.

VOCABULARY AND SPELLING STUDIES

A. The following words were used in the text in this unit. Locate them in the dictionary and write the definition that relates to each word as it was used in the unit. Then construct a sentence using each word to show that you understand its meaning and use.

1. transmission
2. expertise
3. generate
4. subordinates
5. superiors
6. array
7. communiqués
8. recipient
9. originate
10. terminating

B. Words are not always spelled as they sound. For example, the sound of *f* in our language may be spelled *f*, *ff*, *ph*, or *gh*. The sound of *s* is prefaced with a silent *p* in *psychology*. Likewise, a number of other sounds use different letters in the formation of words. Complete the spelling of the following words. Use the correct letter or combination of letters to complete the sound shown in parentheses.

1. al (*f*) abet
2. (*n*) eumonia
3. le (*j*) er
4. (*f*) enomenon
5. (*a*) rial
6. (*f*) armacy
7. bu (*j*) et
8. h (*i*) giene
9. (*s*) issors
10. s (*i*) ndicate

COMMUNICATING FOR RESULTS

Avoid a Mistake. You overhear the new salesclerk promise that a customer's new dress will be delivered the following evening. As an experienced clerk you know that the alterations will not be completed for three days and that still another day will be for delivery. How can you convey the correct information to the customer without embarrassing the new salesclerk?

2 Principles of Communication Psychology

Communication is involved in every part of our lives, from the time we wake up until the time we go back to sleep. When we are talking with family or friends, other students or our teachers, other employees or our supervisors; when we are listening to the radio or watching TV; when we are buying or selling products or services; when we are speaking, writing, listening, or "sizing up" a situation—when we do any of these things, we are involved in communication. Since communication has such a major effect on all our lives and since everyone is a communicator, it is very important for us to understand what happens when people communicate. If we look at people who are successful communicators, we find that they apply effectively the principles of human behavior.

What Do We Know About Human Behavior?

Many problems from communication mishaps are caused by a lack of understanding of human behavior. If we compare what we know about computer technology, space travel, and medicine, we can easily see that we are far ahead in these last areas. The inner workings of a giant mainframe computer are more easily explained than the inner workings of the human brain and mind!

There are many reasons why our breakthroughs in understanding human behavior have not been as remarkable as those in computer technology, space travel, and medicine. The most obvious reason is that the study of human behavior as it relates to business is only about as old as the century. If that sounds very old to you, remember that some of the science and technology fields—chemistry, physics, and engineering, for example—are *centuries* old! Obviously, much more time and research are needed for us to catch up in our understanding of human behavior.

Continued research in psychology, sociology, and anthropology contributes to our understanding of human behavior and helps us to apply its principles to communication psychology. Psychologists study individual behavior; sociologists, group behavior; anthropologists, cultural behavior. Their studies provide us with theories that are useful in understanding human behavior. However, we must remember that theories are useful only to understand how and why *most* people behave as they do—there are always exceptions. Throughout history, for instance, we find examples of people who have overcome almost insurmountable obstacles in reaching their goals. So while you are studying behavior theory in an attempt to improve your communication skills, remember that we are generally talking about the behavior of most people and that there are exceptions.

A Look at Our Needs

As a communicator you must recognize that all human beings have certain needs at certain times. These needs determine our behavior and the goals we set for ourselves. A successful communicator has the ability to understand the needs of those who will receive his or her message. A successful communicator speaks and writes with the receiver's needs in mind at all times.

According to Abraham Maslow, a famous psychologist, most people will respond positively to messages that will meet their particular needs at particular times.* Maslow theorizes that human needs are based on a system of priorities, similar to the rungs of a ladder. Once a person's foot is securely balanced on the first rung—that is, once that person's first-rung needs are met—he or she may be willing and ready to ascend to the second rung. And once that person's second-rung needs are met, he or she may be willing and ready to ascend to the third rung, and so on. The point is that until the primary needs (those associated with the first rung) have been reasonably well satisfied, most of us will reject messages that focus on fulfilling higher-level needs.

Maslow uses five "rungs," or classifications, to describe the hierarchy of human needs. These rungs are illustrated on page 13. Keep them in mind as you attempt to send messages to potential receivers.

Rung 1—Basic Physical Needs. What basic things do we need before we can turn our attention to other things? We need food, shelter, and clothing—physical needs. Until these needs are reasonably well met, we think of little else.

Rung 2—Safety and Security Needs. Next we think about keeping ourselves free from physical harm or mental abuse. Most of us try to avoid situations that could cause us physical harm or people that threaten our peace of mind.

The first two rungs represent lower-level needs. Once we have met these needs, we can turn our attention to our upper-level needs.

Rung 3—The Need to Belong. Most of us want to feel that we are part of a group. During our teen years, we place great importance on being "one of the gang." Our families also provide us with a sense of belonging. When we finally go to work full time, we will want to have friends and enjoy being with our coworkers.

*Abraham H. Maslow, *Motivation and Personality*, 2d ed., Harper & Row, New York, 1970.

Rung 5—The Need to Help Others and to Be Creative

Rung 4—The Need to Be "Somebody"

Rung 3—The Need to Belong

Rung 2—Safety and Security Needs

Rung 1—Basic Physical Needs

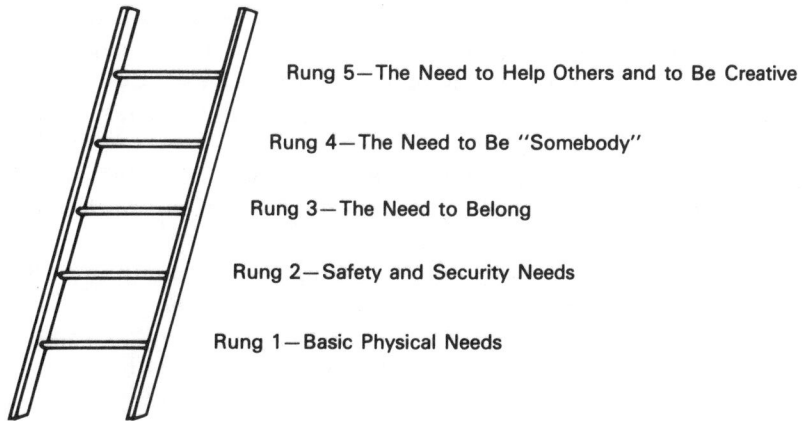

According to Maslow, human needs are based on a system of priorities, similar to the rungs of a ladder.

Rung 4—The Need to Be "Somebody.   Once we have met the needs of Rung 3, feeling comfortable in the society in which we live, most of us want to feel that we are good at doing something. If we are good at swimming or bowling or some of our school subjects, we feel very pleased with the recognition we receive. We feel that we are "somebody." We have met the needs of our ego.

Rung 5—The Need to Help Others and to Be Creative. If we are reasonably able to meet all the previous needs, we seem to lose our anxieties and fears. Two things then happen: (1) we are more willing to help people who are still struggling on the lower rungs of the ladder, those still striving to meet their physical, safety, and security needs; and (2) we become more creative, and creative people improve the quality of life for us all.

Our Needs Determine Our Reaction

To be a successful communicator, you must try to determine the needs of the people to whom you are writing or speaking. You can do this by noticing which goals seem to motivate them. But remember that goals may change rapidly. For example, when you arrive at school in the morning, you have had a good breakfast, so you are not hungry (Rung 1). You feel safe and comfortable in your surroundings (Rung 2), and you have enjoyed visiting with friends before class (Rung 3). You have just finished a class that you enjoy and do well in, so you have satisfied the need to be "somebody" (Rung 4). However, 11:30 a.m. comes and you get hungry. The lunch hour doesn't begin till 12 noon. You shift in your chair and keep looking at your watch. You find concentrating very difficult because you now have a basic physical need, the need for food (Rung 1). Until that need is satisfied, the only really meaningful messages you will receive concern food.

Have you ever been invited to someone's office for what you thought would be an interesting conference? Maybe you felt flattered (Rung 4) and were looking forward to the meeting. Yet while you were there, telephone calls and other interruptions were permitted. Soon you began to feel very unimportant and perhaps even wanted to leave (Rung 3). We react favorably to a situation or a person who helps us satisfy our needs, but we react negatively to a situation or a person who hurts us and our ability to meet our needs.

An example of sending a positive message directed toward our needs is our government's appeal to us to use car pools. Although the main reason for car pools would be to conserve energy and to control traffic congestion, we are also told that riding to work with a group is more fun (Rung 3). Our reaction is favorable because the message also appeals to our personal needs.

Thus we can learn to identify these levels of needs and relate them to all our communications. Whether we are looking for a job, buying or selling products or services, ordering supplies, or asking for information—we must always put ourselves in the place of our receiver, decide what our receiver's needs are, and then phrase our message to meet those needs. In this way we go a long way toward getting the reaction we want.

Nonverbal Communication

When we speak or write, we send our receivers two types of messages: those expressed in words and those *not* expressed in words. For example, if your teacher says to you, "Don't be late for class tomorrow," you could surmise that the message asks you to be on time. The sentence does not state in words but may, through your teacher's stern facial expression, imply such additional messages as "You are frequently late" or "I am upset that you may not be on time." These messages *not* expressed in words are called *nonverbal communication*.

Nonverbal communication—facial expressions, gestures, posture, body movements, attire, grooming—contribute greatly to the meaning of a message. Keep in mind that cultural and environmental differences often determine how these nonverbal messages will be interpreted. On the one hand, people from all cultures seem to turn up the corners of their mouths to show amusement. On the other hand, people from some cultures require less "personal space" than people from other cultures.

Learning to use nonverbal communication can help us make the meanings of our oral messages clearer. The following information on personal space, gestures and posture, and facial expressions can help us become better communicators.

Personal Space. All of us, as human beings, maintain our own environment. This means that we all need a certain amount of "space" in which to operate. The amount of space that we require depends upon our particular culture, the circumstances in which we find ourselves, and the specific actions expected of us at the time.

The next time you sit with your friends at a table in the cafeteria, notice how each of you generally seems to use the same amount of space in which to eat. You have all unconsciously occupied approximately the same amount of space at the table.

In the United States people usually stand about 2 feet apart when they talk with each other. If someone moves too close to us and invades our personal space, we begin to exhibit uncomfortable and unnatural kinds of behavior. We may give signals of tension (uneasy movements) to get the intruder to move, or we may start to back up in an attempt to maintain the distance needed between the person speaking and ourselves.

Space violations occur not only in conversations. Picture yourself stepping into a crowded elevator on your way up to the twenty-third floor. As the elevator rises, everyone peers up at the floor indicator. Why? Because each person's personal space has been invaded, he or she feels uncomfortable and is unable to carry on a conversation. The abnormal or uncomfortable behavior exhibited at this point is looking up at the floor indicator.

Notice, however, how comfortable we feel when we step into an elevator with only one or two other persons in it. We might even exchange a casual "Hello," "Good morning," or some other kind of greeting. If the ride is lengthy, the discussion might even continue with some additional small talk, provided the spatial distance that is comfortable for everyone in the elevator can be maintained.

An understanding of personal space can certainly help you communicate more successfully. If you back away from people because they have invaded your personal space, they may perceive this behavior as a sign that you don't like them. On the other hand, if you invade others' personal space, how much information can be assimilated when they are backing up, feeling uneasiness, or displaying discomfort? Ask yourself, "How much information has been lost during this stage of discomfort and uneasiness?" Obviously, a communicator who relies on oral communication must be conscious of proper spatial relationships under varying circumstances.

Gestures and Posture. People can communicate many moods through gestures and posture. Keeping your head down and hunching your shoulders may be your way of telling people to leave you alone. Crossing your arms may indicate that you do not accept what someone is saying. Sliding down in your chair may convey that you are bored. Shrugging your shoulders may mean that you no longer have any interest in a situation. If you do not wish to convey these kinds of negative ideas, you need to monitor your body language in communicating with others.

As a receiver of messages in the communication process, you should keep in mind that nonverbal communication does not always tell the whole story.

Interpret gestures, posture, and body movements in conjunction with what is being said and the whole context of the situation.

Facial Expressions. Looking *away* from a person can convey as much meaning as looking *at* a person. Looking away may tell people that we would not invade their privacy. Or it may mean that we are not comfortable with what they are saying. Or it may mean that we are trying to hide something. We know that facial expressions can convey a whole range of meanings—joy, hate, love, sorrow—but as with gestures and posture, we need to consider the entire situation.

Our Language Affects Our Behavior

The words we use can make us behave in different ways. To communicate successfully, we must remember that words are only symbols; meaning is added by people. Two people may interpret the same word differently. At the same time, words also have different kinds of meanings. The *denotative* meaning, the one that appears in the dictionary, is one kind; the feelings and impressions the word invokes, the *connotative* meaning, is another. The total meaning you get from a word is a combination of its denotation and connotation.

Consider these words: *slender*, *slim*, *thin*, *skinny*, and *scrawny*. These words essentially mean the same denotatively. If one of these words were being used to describe you, however, would you react the same to *scrawny* as you would to *slender*?

If a supervisor wished to describe an employee who did not give up easily, that supervisor could use terms such as *persistent*, *tenacious*, *persevering*, *obstinate*, *stubborn*, or *unyielding*, depending upon how the supervisor felt about the person being described. All these words have essentially the same denotation—*following through regardless of the obstacles*. These words, however, are not interchangeable because they differ substantially in connotation.

A noted semanticist coined the terms *purr words* and *snarl words* to refer to words that affect people's emotions either positively or adversely.* Purr words are ones such as *beautiful*, *kindness*, *freedom*, *successful*, *persevering*, and *slender*. People usually respond warmly to words such as these because of their strong connotation of goodness. Snarl words such as *cheap*, *negligent*, *fraud*, *delinquent*, *obstinate*, and *scrawny* stimulate distasteful images. Effective business communicators generally rely on purr words and avoid snarl words to convey their messages. They are also aware that the same words can convey different meanings to different people.

*S. I. Hayakawa, *Language in Thought and Action*, 3d ed., Harcourt Brace Jovanovich, Inc., New York, 1972.

COMMUNICATION LABORATORY

APPLICATION EXERCISES

A. Visit a department store and note five ways that appeals are made to your physical and safety needs (Rung 1 and Rung 2) through advertising, displays, and pricing.

B. Tell which need levels the following items would appeal to: (1) a gold necklace, (2) a school sweatshirt, (3) taking class notes for a fellow student whose hearing is impaired, (4) exercising daily, and (5) a home smoke-detector alarm.

C. Prepare an oral account of a newspaper or magazine advertisement or of a television or radio commercial that made a direct appeal to your need to be "somebody."

D. Analyze the following advertisement, using your knowledge of the various levels of needs: "When you drive up in a Faunta XT80, the car itself says everything that can be said. From the bold hood ornament to the gold-plated rear bumper, the car proclaims success. All you need do is to quietly acknowledge the knowing glances."

E. Analyze the impact of body language on your own communication experiences. Summarize in writing on a single sheet one incident where personal space, gestures, facial expressions, or posture may have interfered with message transmission or caused miscommunication.

F. Suppose you wished to describe another person's personality. Words such as *aggressive, dynamic, forceful, assertive,* and *pushy* come to mind. Basically, these words have similar denotative meanings. Based on their connotative meanings, however, which words would you classify as "purr" words and which ones would you consider "snarl" words?

VOCABULARY AND SPELLING STUDIES

A. Do you really know the exact order of the letters of the alphabet? Locate the following words in your dictionary, taking each one in the sequence in which it is shown. Note the exact time you start your search and the exact time you finish. How many minutes did you need? Then write the words in alphabetic order.

1. genuine
2. regional
3. articulate
4. extensive
5. definition

6. inflation
7. appreciate
8. withhold
9. condense
10. evidence

11. deliberate
12. essential
13. ingenious
14. periodic
15. condominium

B. Among the following words are several common misspellings. Find and correct any words that are misspelled.

1. preparation
2. corespondence
3. exagerated
4. seperately
5. accidentally
6. beneficial

7. dispair
8. disatisfied
9. technical
10. commiting
11. briliant
12. chosing

C. The following words were used in the text of this unit. Locate each word in the unit to determine how it was used in the sentence; then use your dictionary to find and write down the appropriate definition. Write your own sentence using the word as it was used in the unit.

1. mishaps
2. insurmountable
3. obstacles
4. ascend
5. hierarchy
6. surmise

7. assimilated
8. denotation
9. connotation
10. tenacious
11. semanticist
12. adversely

COMMUNICATING FOR RESULTS

Positive and Friendly. Positive statements are more likely to win friends than negative ones. Rewrite the statements below so that they will accomplish something in a positive way.

1. All our products work well when they are used by intelligent people.
2. If you will return your toaster to us at once, we will think about giving you an adjustment.

U · N · I · T

3

Applying Psychology to Human Relations

Knowledge of any kind is of little value unless it can be used. For example, men and women who succeed in business are knowledgeable people—but it is not knowledge alone that makes them successful; it is the intelligent *use* of what they know. There are fewer crippled children today because Dr. Jonas Salk gave the world the benefit of his research on the problem of infantile paralysis. There are fewer companies treating their employees like machines because Dr. Lillian Gilbreth gave the world the benefit of her research on the problems of increasing production. Logically, then, your success as a communicator depends not only on your understanding of the principles of communication psychology but also on your use of that knowledge.

In the preceding unit you studied the human behavior factors that must be known by any communicator who desires to rise to the top. Unless you know how to apply what you have learned, however, this knowledge is wasted. Your study of this unit links the principles of communication psychology to promoting goodwill and preventing ill will on the job.

Promoting Goodwill

Goodwill is difficult to define because it is a feeling, an emotion. We know that in business it is listed as an asset and therefore can be sold—but nobody can see or touch it. Perhaps the nearest we can come to a definition is to say that *goodwill* is the favor or prestige that a business has which causes people to trade with—and keep coming back to—that company.

We know that goodwill results from satisfying people's needs. Whenever we do or say anything that causes people to like *themselves* better, they like *us* better. Keep in mind the workings of the needs ladder as you learn how to promote goodwill in the categories being discussed.

Customer Goodwill. A business, of course, continually seeks to gain new customers. Equally important, however, is the need to keep old customers. How will a firm profit if it gains new business but, at the same time, loses current business? Promoting customer goodwill, then, must be concerned with both the new and the old.

Most people who come into our place of business and most people with whom we correspond are either customers or potential customers. Therefore, you need to know the following essentials of goodwill building. Apply these basics to your oral as well as to your written communications, and you will be sure to satisfy your customers' needs.

Be Courteous. To most people *courtesy* means saying "Please" and "Thank you." Of course, saying these words is important when dealing with all people, not just customers—but "Please" and "Thank you" merely scratch the surface of the courtesy needed to promote customer goodwill.

The basis of true courtesy is consideration for the other person. Some of us seem to develop this quality easily; others must develop it by constantly saying to themselves, "How would I feel if this were said or done to me?" For example, you would immediately greet a client who came into your office, and by doing so you would meet the client's need to feel comfortable around others. But your prompt recognition of the client could also be based on your instinctive knowledge of how *you* would feel if *you* were kept waiting.

If you were talking to a customer and your telephone rang, would you excuse yourself before lifting the receiver? Would you keep taking calls while you had someone in your office? If people are behind you when you reach a closed door, do you hold the door for them or even let them precede you? These instances are but a few of the courtesies that mark a person whose good manners come from sincere consideration for others.

Another aspect of consideration for others is a genuine desire to be of help. Suppose, for instance, a customer asks if your company sells Coldtemp refrigerators. You know that Coldtemp is an exclusive Modern Appliances brand. Although a simple "no" would answer the question, a wish to help would prompt you to say something like this: "No, Coldtemp is carried by Modern Appliances on Broad Street. But perhaps you'd like to see and compare our General refrigerator over here on the right." And who knows? Maybe you'll gain a new customer. Even if you don't sell the General, you will have shown that you want to be of help and made a potential customer feel warm and important; and quite possibly, you will have created an atmosphere that will lead the customer back to you for future purchases.

Be Pleasant and Cordial. Feeling welcome and wanted builds morale and satisfies our need to belong. We can give a customer that satisfaction by being pleasant and cordial not only in the words we say but also in our facial expressions and our tone of voice. If we have a professional attitude at work, we don't allow our personal troubles to show. No matter how warm and gracious our words may be, they fall flat when they come from the lips of a deadpan or indifferent face. If we really are pleased to see a customer, our facial expression and tone will project that pleasure.

Use the Customer's Name. Everyone considers his or her name very important; therefore, a person is pleased when recognized and called by name. Many customers favor certain stores, cleaners, restaurants, and so on, even though these stores are *not* the ones that are located closest to them. If asked why, they might say that their favorites are superior. But often the real reason is that the business people with whom they deal show a personal interest in their customers and give them individual service, an impression created partly because they are known and greeted *by name*.

One of the ways in which you can promote customer goodwill, therefore, is to make a determined effort to learn and use your customers' names (taken, for example, from credit cards, checks, or sales slips). Be sure to check spelling, and if it is an unusual name, like *Tarnowski*, be sure to check pronunciation. After the customer leaves, make a note like this: *Tarnowski (Tar-'nov-skē)*. When you make a cash sale, find a tactful way of learning that customer's name. Then the next time the customer comes in, you can say, "Good morning, Mrs. Tarnowski, and how are you today?" instead of the less personal "May I help you?"

Listen Attentively. An attentive listener boosts the speaker's ego; an inattentive listener deflates it. Therefore, since ego satisfaction helps build customer goodwill, we must be concerned with how to listen, as well as with how to talk. Attentive listening will also help you to identify and correct any real problems that the customer may have.

When listening to customers, regardless of the importance or the triviality of what is said, look directly at them. Show that you are following their every word; don't interrupt or try to change the subject. Even if they are talking about an uninteresting subject, your listening techniques will make them feel so warm and important that they may very likely think of your firm first the next time they need your products or services.

If what customers say affects you or your employer, you may be able to increase goodwill, turn ill will into goodwill, or learn how to improve your products or services. For example, suppose you are listening to Mr. Torti, an angry customer who has a just complaint. You show that you are interested and concerned. You let him express his entire complaint with no comment except an occasional, "Oh, that's too bad, Mr. Torti." When he finishes, his anger will be considerably reduced because he was able to tell his entire story to a sympathetic audience—*you*. Then if you have the authority to right the wrong, you should do so immediately. If not, you should make arrangements for the customer to see whoever does have the authority to help him.

Give Prompt Service. We of this generation are a "now" people. We want everything right away; we are always in a hurry. Customers expect, even demand, quick service, and their trade goes to the companies that do not keep them waiting. Merely giving speedy service, however, is not enough to promote customer goodwill. After all, customers expect prompt service and therefore take it for granted. So what must we do to increase goodwill?

Without being obvious we must impress upon customers the fact that we give "super" service. For instance, if a customer hands you a change of address, you shouldn't just say, "Thank you." Instead say, "Thank you, Ms. Erhardt, I'll attend to this right away." As you make out the sales slip for a dinette, you might say to the customer, "You can expect your dinette on Tuesday, our very first delivery day to your section of the city." Take every opportunity to point out the prompt service your company gives. Make each customer feel deserving of your special attention.

Vendor Goodwill. *Vendors* are individuals or companies from whom we buy in wholesale quantities; we pay them to supply us with goods that we in turn resell to our customers. If we didn't have vendors, we wouldn't be able to do business. We need them; consequently, their goodwill is important to us. Yet many people do not recognize the importance of vendor goodwill. Because they pay the vendor, they see no reason for trying to cultivate a friendly relationship. They see no need to be gracious or even courteous to vendors.

For example, there are executives who would drop everything to attend to a customer but who would think nothing of keeping other firms' sales representatives waiting for an hour before getting around to seeing them. And there are sales representatives who, when the roles are reversed and they are the buyers, treat others like second-class citizens.

If a customer arrives while a vendor is talking with you, the vendor may encourage you to serve the customer while the vendor waits. Watch for cues from vendors, as they may be interested in seeing and hearing how a customer reacts to their merchandise.

Failure to give the same courteous treatment to everyone is not just unkind but also unintelligent. Consider some of the benefits that will come our way when suppliers are made to feel like friends. Our orders will receive prompt attention; and if we are in urgent need of a special order, we can depend on the vendor to get it to us without delay. In addition, we will be among the first to know of any special discounts or of any possible future price increases. Thus having vendor goodwill helps us to promote customer goodwill, for we can give customers the best of service only if we ourselves receive top service.

Coworker Goodwill. Football coaches stress the need for teamwork. Social organizations emphasize the necessity of having cooperation among their members. The armed forces aim for *esprit de corps*, a common feeling of enthusiasm among members of a group. Business managers try to develop high employee morale. All of them know that a spirit of loyalty, willingness, and friendliness produces the best results whenever two or more people are engaged in a common enterprise. As a member of an office team, you also have a financial stake in promoting coworker goodwill. When the company profits, you profit; and to make a profit, the company must have the backing of a smooth-running, harmonious staff.

Consequently, you should make a conscious effort to be pleasant, courteous, friendly, and helpful—but above all, tactful and considerate. To be thoughtful and promote coworker goodwill, you can (1) avoid listening to or spreading gossip, (2) put away materials correctly when you have finished with them, (3) return what you borrow, and (4) be tactful in the remarks you make to others. In other words treat others as you would like to be treated.

Credibility and Goodwill. If you are dealing with established customers and vendors, much of your credibility is based on your past performance—your "track record." Maintaining your track record includes keeping the same high-quality goods and/or services. You must also keep your established customers and vendors well informed and reassure them about changes that occur in all successful businesses—new merchandise, new employees, new owners, new facilities. Rumors often precede such changes. To avoid the dangers of rumors, be sure to share complete and accurate information with your established customers and vendors.

In dealing with new customers, your appearance may affect your credibility. *You* know the kind of person you really are, but the fact is that to other people you are what they perceive you to be. Banks, for example, are run essentially on goodwill, as banking services are about the same for all banks. Have you ever noticed that bank employees are generally neat and well groomed? Since bank employees handle people's money, people want to have a secure feeling about the bank employees with whom they leave their money.

All businesses want a prospective customer to have a secure feeling about their ability to give the customer quality service. Vendors, too, have much concern for the image presented by the businesses that handle their goods. Thus it is important to develop credibility and goodwill with all customers and vendors.

Some Personal Qualities. If you flare up easily or if you are short on patience or if you lack tact, you need to do some self-training. Temper control, patience, and tact are high on the list of personal qualities that are "musts" if goodwill is to be maintained.

Control Your Temper. Expressing anger is a luxury that business people cannot afford because it interferes with good human relations. Whether you receive an insulting, rude letter or are faced with direct verbal abuse, always try to get a grip on yourself *before* responding. Remember that although a sharp answer may relieve *your* feelings, it definitely will not foster goodwill with others.

Be Patient. Patience in answering questions can be one of your most valuable assets. Your customers and clients should be able to depend on you for information because they are paying for your merchandise or services. Without them you would have no job. You must expect to be asked the same questions by many customers even though there may be no apparent necessity for asking. For instance, suppose there is a sign right in plain view that reads "Cash and personal checks only." Customer after customer, though, asks, "Do you take VISA?" "Do you take MasterCard?" "Do you take American Express?" Each time the question is asked, you should answer as though it were the first time. After all, for this customer *it is*. You should also keep your tone of voice friendly; any answer that shows your impatience would be sure to lose a customer.

Be Tactful and Have a Positive Tone. Very few people would be so blunt and rude as to say, "Well, you certainly did a lousy job." On the other hand, very few people understand that what they write or say may *imply* equally rude criticism. Study the following examples and learn how to avoid even hinting at carelessness, negligence, or dishonesty.

Suppose a customer who places an order by October 1 is entitled to a 5 percent discount for ordering before the holiday season rush. One customer submits his order on October 11 but still deducts the discount; therefore, we must write a letter to correct the situation. Look at these possible ways of conveying the same message:

POOR: You are not entitled to the special discount because you did not order in time. *(Are you trying to take advantage of us?)*

BETTER: You probably overlooked the fact that the discount was available only to those who ordered by October 1. *(This is a mistake that anyone could make.)*

Suppose you are writing to a vendor to order goods that you need very soon. Note the implications in each of the following closing sentences:

POOR: We want this order right away. *(We can't wait for your usual slow service.)*

BETTER: Your rapid delivery will allow us to keep our customers happy. *(Happy customers lead to continual sales.)*

BEST: Since we have immediate buyers, your rapid delivery will allow us to keep our customers happy. *(Take advantage of this opportunity to increase your sales by delivering this order as soon as you can.)*

Now that you are alerted to the dangers of implied criticism, your written communications will take on an added polish; you will see your messages as your readers see them and will have second thoughts about your wording. But what about oral communication? The moment words are spoken, they cannot be recalled or revised. Despite the fact that we speak more often than we write, training in this area of oral communication is often neglected. But you will know the fundamentals of such training if you give careful attention to the following discussion.

Mr. Rustin selects some items in a retail store and goes to a register to pay for them. Because he has gone to a closed checkout line, a salesclerk must ask him to come to another register. Note the different ways of making the request.

POOR: Hey, come over here. Can't you see that register is closed? *(Tells the customer to do something that he or she should have been alert enough to do in the first place.)*

BETTER: Sir or Madame, if you will step over here, I will serve you at once. *(Ignores the customer's lack of attention and emphasizes immediate service.)*

When a service technician receives a call about a home appliance, he or she knows that something basic could have been overlooked. The technician's response can cause or prevent ill will.

POOR: Of course you did plug in the machine. *(Is it possible that you made this stupid error?)*

BETTER: We will be happy to look at the machine. But check to be sure that it's plugged in. Some of those plugs slip out easily. *(The plug itself might be at fault.)*

Then there is the secretary who gives the supervisor a message that Miss McKinney called and asked to be called back. Time passes, and the supervisor still has not made the call. Various reminders might be:

POOR: Didn't you call Miss McKinney yet? *(Is it possible that you could be so forgetful?)*

BETTER: Miss McKinney really wanted to talk to you. Did you remember to call her? *(A little more positive.)*

BEST: Would you like me to place that call to Miss McKinney? *(I am not criticizing. I merely want to be of service.)*

Tact and positive tone when communicating orally depend not only on *what is* said but also on *how* it is said. That is why expert communicators think before they speak and mentally rephrase any words that might be construed as criticism.

COMMUNICATION LABORATORY

APPLICATION EXERCISES

A. Calling people by name and pronouncing their names correctly are ways of promoting customer goodwill. Gain skill here by canvassing your school, community, and social groups for names with unusual spellings or pronunciations. Bring these names to class and share them with your fellow students. Be sure that you can pronounce these names correctly so that you share only correct pronunciations.

B. To maintain customer goodwill, you need to be able to listen attentively to customer complaints, criticisms, and suggestions. Select a class partner. Decide on a fictitious company and product or service. Have one person assume the role of a customer and the other one the role of a salesperson. The "customer" should then explain in detail a situation that has caused inconvenience or problems with the product or service offered by the "salesperson's" company. Then the salesperson should summarize briefly in writing the customer's complaint. Have the customer verify for accuracy the salesperson's written statement. Switch roles and go through the exercise again.

C. Keeping in mind the importance of promoting customer, vendor, and colleague goodwill, rate each of the following sentences as *Good* or *Poor*.

1. We very much appreciate the immediate attention given to our special order.
2. Whenever you have a problem with service, please let me know right away.
3. Drop into our showroom sometime soon.
4. I would be most happy to see you on Wednesday, April 8, at 3 p.m.
5. You will have to give us more information if you expect us to act on your complaint.
6. You had better pick up at once the lawn mower that you mistakenly delivered to us.
7. Since it took you so long to deliver our order, we don't want it anymore.
8. It is very easy to understand why the delivery delay upset you.
9. Unfortunately, your line of sweaters would not fit in with our other merchandise.
10. This watch has obviously been abused, so we won't take it back.

D. Now rewrite the sentences that you rated *Poor*, wording them in such a way that they will promote goodwill or prevent ill will.

E. Using your knowledge of communication psychology, write four suggestions that you would give to salespeople.

VOCABULARY AND SPELLING STUDIES

A. These words are often confused: *receipt, recipe; vein, vain, vane*. Explain the differences.

B. Each of the following sentences contains slang or an incorrect expression. Substitute a more formal word or expression for each.

1. I could of told you that this customer would complain.
2. We will really have to hustle to meet their competition.
3. I sort of think that we can improve our advertising.
4. Our salespeople should of featured the less expensive model.
5. I can't get a handle on the shipping problem.

C. Should *ei* or *ie* appear in the blank spaces in these sentences?

1. We bel__ve you will find this to be a conven__nt way to rec__ve the magazines you want each month.
2. It is a real ach__vement to become ch__f of police in a large city in such a br__f period of time.
3. Th__r fr__ght was misdelivered to a n__ghboring warehouse.

COMMUNICATING FOR RESULTS

What Should Have Been Said? Some examples of poor human relations are shown in the following incidents. Suggest (**a**) what the probable reaction was in each situation and (**b**) what should have been said to maintain or further good human relations.

1. Secretary on the telephone: "Ms. Costellano is not here. I have no idea where she is. Try calling tomorrow."
2. Salesperson to customer: "I told you that the more expensive camera was a better deal. Maybe you'll listen to me next time."
3. Customer to salesclerk: "Don't you know I'm in a hurry? I've been here 20 minutes watching you fool around."
4. From a letter to a customer: "If you had read the guarantee, you would not have returned the watch to us."
5. Customer to supplier: "We would like some real speed on this order, not your usual leisurely pace."

U · N · I · T

4

Using Communication Technology

Modern technology makes it possible to send oral and written messages around the world in just a matter of seconds. Computers and electronic transmission systems have enabled business and government to speed up and improve the communication process. As a result communicators today must be able to apply communication psychology as well as use communication technology to develop their oral and written messages.

Data, voice, and graphic networks supply the technology for rapid communication and decision making. These networks are composed of computer-based systems that "talk" to each other so that voices, images, and written data can be transmitted electronically and instantaneously.

Within the last three decades, this emerging new technology has caused a revolution in human communications. Think about the pace of human progress during past centuries and compare it with the developments that have taken place during the last thirty years—even the last ten years.

Early Communication

Human beings have communicated from the beginning of time. Communication probably began with grunts, gestures, and expressions. The origins of speaking and writing are unknown, but signs and symbols were added very early in the time line of human development.

Even in early times people kept records. The Egyptians developed a picture language called *hieroglyphics;* at the same time the Sumarians were writing on clay tablets with a system that used wedge-shaped signs. The Semites were the first to devise an alphabet, around 1500 B.C., and the Assyrians and Babylonians established libraries around 600 B.C.

Many historians relate the invention of writing to the priests in these early societies. The need to recall the rituals and the secrets of healing prompted the development of written records. Writing also allowed messages to be sent over considerable distances without revealing their contents to the messengers.

In early societies writing was once taught only to scribes and priests. It was such a laborious and time-consuming process that only a privileged few were allowed to learn to write. Even with the development of the pen and quill, writing was such a chore that few people had ever seen a book, let alone owned one. Just imagine how long it would take you to copy by hand the pages of this textbook!

Not until the invention of the printing press in the fifteenth century was knowledge opened to everyone. Printing provided a more rapid and easy way to communicate. Although type needed to be set by hand, multiple copies could be run once the type had been set. Then, in the middle of the nineteenth century, a vehicle appeared that would speed up the printing process. Little did Christopher Scholes realize when he invented the typewriter that this machine would be the forerunner of the sophisticated equipment used in publishing and modern offices today. Some contemporary typewriters permit materials to be revised easily during and after the typing process, have printers that produce copies at thousands of words a minute, and are connected with duplicating systems that reproduce copies in seconds.

The New Technology

Civilization has progressed from tediously chiseling into rock signs and symbols to instantaneously communicating messages by machine. Human beings, however, must still generate the messages processed by these machines. People are responsible for the content, organization, wording, and format of the information processed. Therefore, users of modern technology must be skilled in the communication process. Your study of the principles and concepts in this textbook will prepare you to make effective use of the communication technology found in modern offices today.

The advanced technologies that have emerged during the last three decades include word processing, information processing, telecommunications, and networks. Each is defined and briefly described for you in the following sections.

The Word Processing Concept

People have been processing words since the Semites developed the first known alphabet, but the concept of word processing as we know it today was introduced by the IBM Corporation in the early 1960s.

Word processing began with the release of the IBM typewriter known as the MT/ST. Since then IBM and many other companies have introduced more sophisticated and advanced versions of this original design. Today the MT/ST may be viewed in the word processing industry as the Model T Ford is viewed in the automobile industry. The Model T Ford got you where you were going, but the modern-day Lincoln Continental will get you there faster, more comfortably, and with greater ease. Modern-day *word processing* now involves the use of a standardized set of procedures combined with text-editing equipment to produce written documents.

What Word Processors Can Do. To obtain a better understanding of word processing, let us first look at some word processing equipment. Word processors have a typewriter keyboard. As data is entered into the word processor, each keystroke is recorded on a magnetic medium, much in the same manner as a voice is recorded on a cassette tape. If you wish to make a change on a cassette tape, all you need to do is back up and record over the present material. Similarly, if you make a keyboarding or typing error, all you need to do is backspace to erase the error from the magnetic medium and then retype the correct stroke in its spot.

With word processors you can also easily add and delete complete sentences and paragraphs. Once you have made all the corrections and revisions you wish in a letter, memorandum, report, or other document, you are ready to prepare the finished copy. Word processing printers read the magnetic medium and type out its contents error-free at speeds ranging from hundreds of words a minute to over a thousand words a minute.

What are the advantages of using word processing equipment to record typewritten material for playback to obtain finished copy? The equipment saves time in the production of business documents. Word processing operators can type at fast rates, just backspacing and retyping to correct keyboarding errors. No longer does a typist who makes a so-called uncorrectable error during the typing process have to start over. Business writers, too, may save time by creating their documents at the keyboard. With the revision capabilities of word processing, writers can easily produce final copy or just prepare their documents for final editing and formatting by a secretary.

Many times the same originally typed document must be sent to a number of different people or the same paragraph must be repeated in different documents. By using word processing to record these materials, you may play back as many times as necessary to obtain the number of originally typed copies needed.

Reports provide information that is often the basis for important decisions. The person who writes a report may rewrite it several times before it is ready for distribution. In the past the report had to be retyped with each rewrite, thereby necessitating the tedious process of keyboarding and proofreading the entire document. By using word processing to prepare a report, you keyboard and proofread only the changes; the remainder of the report remains unaltered, just waiting to be played out with the changes or additions to form a revised final copy.

Word processing offers reduced costs and improved quality in written communications. Because they eliminate repetitive keystroking, reduce the time needed for proofreading, and print error-free copy at hundreds of words a minute, word processors are playing a dominant role in American business and industry.

Word Processing at Work. Who uses word processing equipment? For what purposes is it used? Frequent users include law firms, where many documents that require precise wording are produced. In addition, many legal documents contain large sections of wording that do not need to be changed for each new client. These standardized paragraphs are recorded on disks or other electronic media and recalled for the preparation of contracts, wills, trusts, agreements, dissolutions, testimonies, and many other legal documents.

Banks and savings and loan associations use word processing to communicate with their current and prospective customers. Standardized form letters are entered into and stored by the word processing equipment. When a single letter needs to be sent to a list of customers, the standardized form can be retrieved and merged with the list of names to produce an originally typed letter for each name on the list. Similarly, many companies use word processing equipment to send collection letters to their overdue accounts.

Hospitals and other health care facilities use word processing to prepare patients' files and to compile reports of diagnoses and examinations. Standardized examination reports are stored for each specialty, so doctors can immediately cite any abnormal conditions that may exist. Word processing is also used for preparing government and insurance reports, professional papers presented by staff members, public service bulletins, applications for special projects, and a variety of other documents.

Insurance companies use word processing to communicate with their large number of clients. Specialized types of communication are sent to those clients who carry certain kinds of insurance. Personalized letters prepared on word processors are also used to solicit additional business.

Businesses such as those in the aircraft industry, whose major revenue comes from government contracts, use word processing equipment to prepare proposals. Volumes of paperwork describing specifications, costs, and procedures need to be prepared before a contract can be awarded. Thousands of hours of editing and revision are required to prepare a proposal for submission. Word processing eases the typewriting and proofreading burden and fosters accuracy.

These are just a few applications of word processing currently in use. With the increasing popularity of the microcomputer, word processing is now within the reach of small as well as large businesses. Word processing programs such as WordStar, MultiMate, DisplayWrite, Microsoft Word, WordPerfect, Samna, Applewriter, Appleworks, and IBM Writing Assistant, to name a few, have enabled microcomputers to assume full-fledged roles as word processors. Consequently, word processing is steadily becoming a way of life in modern businesses as managers use it to increase office productivity and business writers use it to make their jobs easier.

Information Processing—A Broader Perspective

In most instances *word processing* refers to the process of creating, editing, formatting, storing, retrieving, revising, and printing text materials electronically. *Information processing* is the movement of words, symbols, or numbers from the origination of an idea to its destination. It is the manipulation of data by electronic means to collect, organize, record, and store information for decision-making purposes. Information processing retains the text-editing and revision function but has the capability to use the data in a wider range of applications.

Information Processing at Work. The hospital that uses word processing to prepare and maintain patients' records can use information processing technology many ways. For example, it can obtain a list of patients by any one of many different categories—by specific disease or disorder, by admitting doctor, by admission date, or by age. Expanded applications and capabilities can be achieved by *interfacing* (connecting) word processing programs and equipment with other computer programs and/or equipment.

Picture the checkout stand of a modern supermarket. Notice how the clerk skims each product over a certain section of the counter top. Listen for the high-pitched beep as the name of the item and its price are recorded on the cash register tape. You, as a customer, may like this new procedure because it provides you with an itemized tape listing the specific product purchased and its price. To the grocery store, however, the new system provides information that was not as readily available before information processing technology. Now the store has complete inventory records on which to make purchasing decisions. How many frozen turkeys should be purchased for Friday? How many cases of a certain brand of canned peas are needed to restock its shelves? What products move slowly and should be discontinued? These questions and many more can be answered accurately and quickly to cut costs and increase profit—all through information processing technology.

A Revolution in Technology. Since the early 1980s the flood of microcomputers entering business and industry has revolutionized business's ability to use information processing for management decision making. No longer must a company invest in expensive mainframe computer time or acquire costly minicomputers to take advantage of this tool. Reasonably priced microcomputers coupled with spreadsheet, data base, and graphics programs provide information processing capabilities to large and small companies alike.

Business writers charged with preparing reports for management decision making may organize, enter, and store information in computerized data files. From this data base they may easily transfer information into a spreadsheet for either preparing analyses or making projections. Spreadsheet data can then be converted into graphic form for ease of understanding and interpretation through any one of a number of graphics software programs.

Integrating software programs allow the modern business communicator to combine word processing technology with information processing technology so that charts and tables derived from data bases and spreadsheets may be entered directly into reports prepared through word processing programs. The popularity of microcomputers and these kinds of programs is growing rapidly because of their relatively inexpensive cost in comparison with minicomputers and mainframes. Now even the small company or business can afford to use computer technology to increase its profit potential.

The World of Telecommunications

The documents produced by word and information processing equipment discussed so far have been printed on paper and carried to their destinations by intracompany mail systems, the U.S. Postal Service, and private mail carriers. Since paper is associated with slow delivery and high costs, more companies are turning to electronic methods for transmitting information. Distributing information electronically over telephone lines is called *telecommunication.*

You already know that information can be sent electronically through voice communications. Every time you make a telephone call, you are using a form of telecommunication. Perhaps you did not know, though, that printed words can also be sent electronically through telephone lines. You can type a document on a terminal at one location, transmit it over telephone lines to another location miles away, and have it play back on a terminal at the destination. In just seconds data can be communicated from city to city and from coast to coast.

Like printed words graphic data may also be sent electronically. Copies of charts, graphs, maps, and diagrams may be sent from one location to another. An electronic device called a *facsimile* scans the copy to be sent, sends it over telephone wires, and produces a replica at the destination.

Teleconferencing is a type of video communication that involves sending pictures of people as well as voice and print communications. Once a teleconferencing room with the proper electronic equipment is rented, people in various locations can exchange ideas with gestures and facial expressions as well as through speaking, listening, and writing.

Presently the major carriers of telecommunication in business are telephone lines. However, scientists are continually experimenting with new technologies to move information more rapidly. Lasers, fiber optics,* and satellites are all being explored further to speed up such business applications as teleconferencing and facsimile transmission.

Networking in the Business Environment

Computer communication is and will continue to be a key factor in information exchange. You have already learned that written messages can be transmitted electronically over telephone lines from one computer terminal to another. Almost all kinds of computer-based equipment—word processors, microcomputers, minicomputers, mainframes, and mainframe terminals—are capable of exchanging messages. Those computers that are linked together and are able to communicate with one another are components of a network.

Local Area Networks. *Networking* is a way of connecting various kinds of computerized equipment so that data may be transferred from one location to another or from one piece of equipment to another without having to reenter the data. *Local area networks* link machines that are close, that is, machines that are within a building, several adjacent buildings, or the same geographical area.

Local area networks, often referred to as LANs, may use telephone wires, radio waves, coaxial cables, or fiber optics to connect the stations within the network. Dissimilar machines can work together as a team through one of these means and a series of interfaces that connect the machines to the data transportation medium used. In this way information can be transmitted from one machine to another in a matter of seconds or minutes.

Wide Area Networks. Local networks can be linked to larger networks that enable individuals and companies to send and receive information throughout the United States and other countries in the world. Networks that connect distant machines are known as *wide area networks* or *global networks* and

---

* Fiber optics are thin, transparent fibers of glass or plastic used to transmit light through internal reflections.

use combinations of telephone wires, satellites, and microwave radio links to send information.

Electronic Mail. Electronic mail services provide faster delivery than the U.S. Postal Service, private mail carriers, and intracompany mail delivery services. This machine-to-machine method of communication is accomplished through networks and permits immediate or same-day delivery.

Large computer systems are evolving as the directors of electronic mail traffic. A communicating word processor, microcomputer, or computer terminal serves the user as a keyboard device for outgoing messages and a receptacle for incoming messages. Messages can be sent immediately or stored and forwarded at a time when transmission rates are less expensive.

To participate in an electronic mail system, each user must have communicating equipment, a number (known as an *electronic mail address*), a computer file to contain incoming and outgoing messages (known as an *electronic mailbox*), and a directory of user names and addresses.

Implications for the Business Communicator. Networking is the newest dimension in communication technology. It opens up to the business communicator avenues never before explored. With such expanded access to information, however, the business person of the future must develop keen skills of analysis, organization, and verbalization to sort through the resources being made available by technology. Your study of the communication skills and knowledge in this textbook will better prepare you to deal with the communication technology of today and tomorrow.

COMMUNICATION LABORATORY

APPLICATION EXERCISES

A. Visit your local public library or school library. Locate from a business periodical an article on any phase of word processing or information processing. Summarize in writing the important points brought out by the author of this article. Be prepared to share this article orally with the rest of the class.

B. Visit a local business or industry that uses microcomputers or word processing equipment. Prepare a short written summary of your visit that describes briefly the equipment in use and the purposes for which it is used. Analyze whether the equipment is performing only word processing functions or whether it has been expanded to include information processing functions.

C. Visit your local Western Union office to inquire about telecommunication services. List and briefly describe the kinds of services offered by Western Union.

D. Collect mail samples prepared on word processing equipment or computers that have been sent to your home or to the homes of neighbors and friends. Although these materials have been prepared through electronic means, analyze their effectiveness as communication devices. Which of these devices were effective in accomplishing their purposes?

E. Visit your local public or school library. Locate at least one magazine article that discusses personal or home computers (microcomputers). Summarize the contents of this article. What impact do you foresee these computers having on your personal life?

VOCABULARY AND SPELLING STUDIES

A. Many computer terms are fast becoming everyday words. Because a knowledge of certain terms will be necessary for successful communication, you should incorporate them into your vocabulary. Locate the definitions of the following terms; copy each term and its definition on a separate sheet of paper.

1. communicating computer
2. microcomputer
3. minicomputer
4. interface
5. program
6. software
7. compatibility
8. mainframe

B. What letter should appear in the blank space in each of these words?

1. perc__late
2. attend__nce
3. sep__rate
4. controver__y
5. p__rsuade
6. vet__ran

C. The following words are spelled as they are often incorrectly enunciated. A letter or syllable has been added or dropped. Respell all words correctly.

1. Wednesdy
2. canidate
3. filum
4. labratory
5. strenth
6. sophmore
7. probly
8. libary
9. naturly

COMMUNICATING FOR RESULTS

Urgent Message. You receive this telephone message: "Tell Ms. Takei I've been called out of town and can't see her until Thursday." Ms. Takei, your boss, is on the way to the airport to board a plane to the city of the caller. The plane is to leave in 45 minutes. How would you relay this urgent message to your boss? List alternative methods in case your first attempt fails.

Chapter

2

Reading many types of written communications will be part of your business experience, no matter what your job may be. As a reader you will be judged by how quickly you understand written messages. But reading written communications will be only part of your business experience. You will have to write many communications as well. As a writer you will be judged by how well you communicate your ideas. Since errors—even typographic ones—reduce your message's effectiveness, your skill in proofreading what you write relates directly to your success as a communicator.

You can easily see, then, why improving your reading and proofreading abilities will improve your effectiveness at your job. Given a situation that requires reading and proofreading, you will be able to do the following when you master the units in this chapter:

1. *Judge and explain which reading technique most benefits the purpose for which you are reading.*

2. *Increase your reading speed through timed practices.*

3. *Improve your reading comprehension.*

4. *Develop techniques to remember better what you have read.*

5. *Apply a systematic method for proofreading typewritten or printed documents.*

6. *Use proofreaders' marks to indicate corrections in rough-draft materials.*

U · N · I · T

5

Reading for Professional Results

You already know the importance of reading in your personal life. Take a moment to reflect how your life would be if you were not able to read. You would be unable to drive a car, read your favorite magazine, understand your mail, or even follow instructions to play the latest video games. The pleasure found in books, newspapers, and magazines would not be available to you. You wouldn't be able to install parts to repair your car, follow a new recipe, or select a menu item at your favorite restaurant.

As a student you are aware that there is a close connection between school success and the ability to read well—but have you taken the time to consider that your reading ability may be even more important to you *after* you have completed your formal education? Whether you continue your education by attending college or decide to accept a business position after high school, reading will still contribute significantly to your life. Successful business and professional people spend much of their time reading all types of material—books, magazines, notices, bulletins, reports, memorandums, and letters, as well as other written materials that provide them with information that is essential to performing their jobs. Therefore, the greater your reading skill, the better equipped you will be to succeed in your chosen career.

Purpose Determines Reading Technique

The way in which you read should be determined primarily by your purpose in reading. When you read for pleasure alone, your reading is different from those situations in which you read to absorb information, as in studying. Therefore, you should always know your reading purpose so that you can better determine *how* you should read. Among the many purposes in reading, the following are probably the most used.

Reading for Pleasure. When reading for pleasure, you need not absorb every detail, remember all facts, or read critically. Therefore, you may read such materials as most novels, biographies, and magazine articles at a rapid rate. Try to target your pleasure reading at 400 words a minute.

Reading for Specific Information. When hunting for information such as a name or date that is somewhere within a block of reading material, you should skip and skim in order to make the best use of your reading time.

Skipping merely means jumping over large portions of material that are not needed to serve your reading purpose. *Skimming* means moving your eyes rapidly down a page of type, stopping to read only significant facts and phrases. When you wish to gain the main ideas and details of an article but are not sure beforehand what the article contains, you should both skim and skip. Most people read newspapers largely by skipping and skimming. They simply can't take the time to read every single word.

Reading to Absorb Information. Reading to study—to absorb information—is always required of you as a student, whether the reading is from a textbook or from some resource material. It calls for your active participation, since you must read for meaning and must remember what you read.

Reading for Copying and Checking. Most business writers, secretaries, typists, accountants, and clerical workers do a great deal of this kind of reading. Every prepared business document or typing job, every set of inventory figures that must be checked, and every invoice that must be compared with receiving reports and purchase orders requires careful reading. When such reading is done without concentration and without attention to meaning, errors may not be detected and corrected. This type of reading is so important to the student and the business worker that it will be discussed fully in the next unit.

Setting the Stage

Research has shown that the average executive spends half the business day reading, and reading experts say that two hours could be cut from this load by learning to read faster and with greater understanding. What about you? Does it take you longer than it should to read your assigned work? Do you dread reading because you have a feeling of plowing your way through? Do you have to spend so much time reading for some courses that you do not have enough time for others? If you said "yes" to any of these questions, then you *can* and *should* do something to improve your reading skills, beginning now. The suggestions in the remaining part of this unit will help you to get off to the right start.

Your Eyes. The first step in your reading improvement program is to make certain that your eyes are in good condition. There are many differences in different people's ability to see. One person may have difficulty seeing objects that are close, whereas another may find it difficult to see objects that are some distance away. If you must hold ordinary written material either very close to your eyes or at arm's length to read it, if the material you are reading seems blurred, or if your eyes tire easily, then you should consult an eye doctor. You may need to wear glasses, perhaps only for reading. If you already wear glasses, you may need to have them changed.

Whether or not you wear glasses, you should practice eye hygiene. Here are a few suggestions:

1. Rest your eyes every half hour or so by looking into the distance or by closing your eyes for a few minutes.
2. Exercise your eyes from time to time, particularly after doing close work. One good eye exercise is to rotate the eyes slowly, without moving your head. Move your eyes far to the right; then to the left; then up; and finally, down. These exercises will help to strengthen your eye muscles.
3. Avoid reading in bright sunlight or while riding in a car, train, or other vehicle.
4. Have eye injuries or sties attended to at once by a doctor.

Reading Conditions. Poor lighting contributes to eye fatigue and blurry vision. Of course, nonglaring daylight provides the best light for reading, and light-colored walls help reflect daylight. Indirect lighting, rather than semidirect or direct lighting, is the best artificial lighting. Therefore, make certain that there are no glaring light bulbs visible to the eyes or any other glaring spots anywhere near where you are reading.

For the best reading conditions, sit comfortably in a well-ventilated (not overheated) room that is free from distracting sights and sounds. Above all, do not attempt to do serious reading with the radio, television, or stereo on.

Increasing Your Speed

As discussed earlier, how rapidly you should read depends upon the type of material you are reading and the purpose for which you read. Most "light" reading should be at a rate of at least 400 words a minute. Most studying and other serious reading should be at a rate of at least 200 to 250 words a minute.

There are technical aids for improving reading speed, and reading specialists may be consulted for assistance. However, there are a number of things you can do on your own to improve your reading speed. If you follow these six suggestions, you should soon note an increase in your reading speed. (If you already are a fast reader, these suggestions will help you to read still faster.)

Read in "Thought Units. When you read in phrases, or thought units, rather than word by word, your eyes take in more words before each pause. Since you make fewer pauses on each line, you automatically read faster. To illustrate, read these short lines and notice the difference in your reading time for each line:

1. f d z r t m
2. climbing of spell
3. read for meaning

You probably read each line with ease, but reading the first line took longer than reading the second line, and the second line took longer than the third. Why? Because in the first line you read *six* individual letters; in the second you read *three* individual words; but in the third you read *one* entire phrase.

You should be able to read a newspaper column line with one or two eye pauses and a book-width line with not more than four or five pauses. Now read the following sentence, noticing the difference in speed when you read it word by word from when you read it in phrases.

You / are / more / likely / to / understand / and / remember / what / you / read / if / you / actively / participate / in / what / you / read.

You are more likely / to understand and remember / what you read / if you actively participate / in what you read.

Reading in phrases means reading in *units of thought*. Reading this way enables you to understand better what you read, because sentences—complete thoughts—are made up of these smaller thought units.

Because slow readers usually *think* much faster than they can read, their thoughts often wander. On the other hand, phrase readers receive ideas from the printed page more rapidly and thus keep their minds so busy that they do not have time to let their thoughts wander. Therefore, the fast reader—the phrase reader—usually gets better results from reading.

Keep Eyes Moving From Left to Right. Once you have read a phrase, do not allow yourself to go back and read it a second time. Such backward movements of the eyes are called *regressions,* and they slow the reader considerably. For the untrained reader these regressions become a habit. Force yourself to get the meaning of a phrase the first time; force yourself to concentrate. This forcing yourself calls for practice and discipline, as well as for eliminating all distractions that might interfere with your reading.

Keep Lips and Tongue Motionless. Don't spell or pronounce the words you are reading, not even inwardly. Such vocalization slows down your reading; it makes you read silently only as fast as you can read aloud.

Read Word Beginnings. You can identify the following portions of words without seeing the entire word: *undoub——, remem——, partici——.* (You can tell from the rest of the sentence whether the last word should be *participate, participating,* or *participation.*)

Keep Building Vocabulary. Try to increase your vocabulary. The more words you have at your command, the fewer pauses you will have to make to check the meanings of words and the faster you will read. Also, when your mind instantly recognizes words, you will better understand what you are reading.

Constantly Practice. Continual increase in reading speed means exercising your willpower and continually practicing rapid reading. If you force yourself always to read a little faster than is comfortable, rapid reading soon will become a habit.

Increasing Your Understanding

Reading speed is very important to both students and business workers. However, even more important than speed is understanding (comprehension) and remembering (retention) what you have read. Some of the suggestions made for increasing your reading speed will also contribute to your greater understanding. Developing a wide vocabulary is one example. Reading in thought units is another. Both contribute a great deal to understanding and to speed. The following suggestions will further help to improve your reading comprehension as well as your ability to remember what you read.

Scan or Preview the Material. First, look over the material to be read, noting the main headings and subheadings, looking at the illustrations, and reading captions and numbered sections. This preliminary survey will help you to determine your purpose in reading, and it will also reinforce important points that you want to remember.

Think As You Read. You will understand more fully what you read if you read actively—if you try to relate what you are reading to what you already know. You must also constantly keep in mind the problem you want to solve when you started to read. This takes a high degree of concentration. It demands that you be on the lookout for main ideas and also for the way in which the author arranges these ideas to reach a conclusion.

Study all visual aid material, such as pictures, graphs, and charts, as well as the footnotes; all these are designed to explain and to expand the main ideas. Be sure, too, to read examples presented by the author. Often these examples will help to clarify an idea that at first may seem hazy to you. They will also help you to remember main ideas.

Make Brief Notes. If you own the book or magazine you are reading, you may wish to underline, highlight, or circle some key words or phrases. Or you may wish to make marginal notes. If the publication is not yours, make your notes in a notebook to use for future reference.

How do you select the essential material for notes? Just record main ideas and related ideas. Never take verbatim (word-for-word) notes, even if you know shorthand.

How do you find the main ideas? Usually writers convey only one idea in each paragraph. Often this main idea is in the first sentence, but sometimes it may be in the last sentence. Occasionally there may be two central ideas expressed in a key phrase or sentence within the paragraph. If you have difficulty in finding a central idea, you may need to read the paragraph carefully two or three times.

Reread and Review. How often you reread or review the material will depend upon its difficulty and the use you plan to make of the material. Often a quick skimming of the material or a reading of your notes will be adequate for review if the first reading was done carefully.

If you immediately put into practice the suggestions made in this unit, not only will you reap dividends in terms of improved schoolwork but also you will see these dividends assist your professional growth.

COMMUNICATION LABORATORY

APPLICATION EXERCISES

A. Everyone does some reading every day. Make a list of your typical reading activities, including reading for school and reading that you do for your own personal reasons. After each activity indicate the approximate percent of total reading time you spent on that particular activity. An example of a reading activity with a percent of total reading time would be "Textbook reading for school—40 percent."

B. On another sheet of paper, indicate your professional goal (for example, word processing operator, medical secretary, carpenter, and so on). Then write a short essay (about 350 words) telling how you will use reading in your professional life and how your reading can contribute to your professional growth.

C. To get an idea of your reading speed, have someone time you with a stopwatch as you read the following excerpt from a report issued by the Disney Corporation to introduce its popular feature at Disney World, Epcot Center.

Disney World's Epcot Center—Spaceship Earth

The architecturally unique Spaceship Earth globe forms a breathtaking entrance to Epcot Center. Entering Future World, visitors pass directly beneath this glistening geosphere which reaches a height surpassing that of the Walt Disney World Contemporary Resort Hotel. Within this theme structure, a swirling time journey retraces the increasingly important role of communications in mankind's survival.

Upon entering Spaceship Earth, guests become time travelers taken back to the age of Cro-Magnon man. The caveman's attempts to record his experiences are seen as the earliest contribution to the development of written communication. We'll survey other communication milestones such as the Egyptians' development of hieroglyphics and the Phoenician alphabet which established the foundation for modern alphabets.

Dramatic communication is born in the Greek theater, becoming a poetic expression of ideas and philosophy. Another stopping point in the journey, Gutenberg's 15th century print shop, is the setting for a communications revolution.

More centuries pass and we're propelled into the Age of Invention. A stream of inventions—the telegraph, telephone, radio, motion pictures, television—brings the dream of instant communication to reality.

Accelerating into space-age technology, we find ourselves within a maze of computer impulses and are electronically transmitted into space aboard a burst of telemetry. Momentarily suspended in the heavens, we gaze down upon our small planet, our Spaceship Earth, adrift in the midnight sky. Having relived our past and eyed our future, we time passengers are ready to become captains, to chart our earth's course toward tomorrow and determine our own destinies.*
(250 words)

Note the time it took you to read the above selection. Then locate this time in the following chart. Your reading speed will be opposite the time. For example, if you read the above paragraphs in 50 seconds, your reading speed is 300 words a minute (wam); if it took you 1 minute, your speed is 250 words a minute. Most material such as this should be read at a rate no slower than 300 words a minute. How does your speed compare?

Reading Time	Reading Rate
30 seconds	500 wam
40 seconds	375 wam
50 seconds	300 wam
1 minute	250 wam
1 minute 10 seconds	215 wam
1 minute 20 seconds	190 wam
1 minute 30 seconds	165 wam
1 minute 40 seconds	150 wam
1 minute 50 seconds	135 wam
2 minutes	125 wam

D. Without rereading the paragraphs in Exercise C, write a brief synopsis of them. Use your own words. Then compare your summary with the selection. Were you accurate? complete?

E. Be prepared to read aloud in class the paragraphs in Exercise C, thus demonstrating your ability to read for meaning.

F. One good reading habit that will help you gain speed is to look only at the beginnings of familiar words rather than at the entire words. Test your ability to do so by reading as rapidly as possible the following paragraphs in which the endings of some familiar words have been omitted.

Your abil___ to read is of___ taken for gran___. Aren't you, there___, surp___ when you hear someb___ make the state___ that read___ is and prob___ always will be one of the most useful and most impor___ skills taught in sch___?

* Copyright © 1982, Walt Disney Productions.

Your work in elem___ school, high sch___, and col___ is great___ affec___ by your abil___ to read. As a stu___ you must be able to read qui___ and thoro___. You must be ab___ to read fast enough so that you will have ti___ for some pers___ relax___.

In busi___ you will have to read corres___ and other writ___ mater___ rela___ to the busi___ activ___ in which you eng___ ev___ day.

VOCABULARY AND SPELLING STUDIES

A. A skillful reader should have a well-developed vocabulary. Indicate whether the italicized word has been used correctly in each of the following sentences. If not, what is the correct word?

1. The committee *past* the motion quickly.
2. No one will *except* the responsibility for the error.
3. I drove 15 kilometers *further* than you did.
4. Joan and Phil followed the *recipe* for making that dip.
5. We need your *presents* at the meeting today.

B. Should *ance* or *ence* be added to the following?

1. accord___
2. dilig___
3. experi___
4. resembl___
5. appli___

6. remembr___
7. correspond___
8. abund___
9. evid___
10. assist___

C. Should *er, or,* or *ar* be added to the following?

1. counsel___
2. gramm___
3. betray___
4. collect___
5. propell___

6. advertis___
7. supervis___
8. profess___
9. prosecut___
10. calend___

COMMUNICATING FOR RESULTS

Reducing Reading Time. Larry managed to get through high school, but when he got to college, Larry began to have difficulty passing his courses. He had a great many reading assignments and often had to stay up until after midnight. Even then, he often could not complete all the required reading. What advice would you give Larry so that he will not have to spend so much time on reading assignments and neglect both his much-needed sleep and some opportunity for recreation?

6

Proofreading for Professional Results

In business writers are responsible for their own communications. If an error appears that results in misunderstanding, it is the fault of the business writer, regardless of who may have typed the letter, memorandum, report, or other written communication. The ultimate responsibility for the content and presentation of a document lies with the business writer. That is why it is important for the document originator to be able to proofread accurately.

Just because business writers carry the major responsibility for the documents they generate, this does not mean that secretaries, typists, word processing operators, or clerks who assist with the preparation are blameless for any errors that are not corrected. Such administrative support personnel will not hold their jobs for long if they allow many errors to go undetected. They, too, must become expert proofreaders to ensure that the communication process will function smoothly, efficiently, and professionally.

Imagine the consequences of a simple typing transposition. What if you worked for a computer consulting firm and wrote to a client that you would be able to install a loan-processing computer system for $134,500? The client accepts your offer. However, when you check your original records containing your calculations, you find that the correct quotation for this particular job should have been $143,500—$9000 more than the cost you submitted! A simple transposition error not caught in the proofreading process can result in a substantial financial loss.

Other errors may not have such direct consequences. Incorrect spellings, strikeovers, improper formatting, typographical errors, capitalization errors, and other such mistakes, though, can create a poor image in the mind of the receiver. Errors in written documents lower the reader's confidence in the writer and create communication barriers. You, as a business communicator, always need to present your most positive image. By developing keen proofreading skills, your documents will be error-free and assure the reader of your abilities.

Proofreading skills can be acquired through study and practice. A thorough knowledge of grammar principles, correct spelling, proper punctuation, capitalization, number-usage rules, and word division principles is needed to exercise precise proofreading techniques. These principles are all part of your study of business English and communication and are thoroughly covered in the units that follow. In addition to having the needed knowledge, the expert proofreader must approach the task in an organized and methodical fashion. A recommended procedure includes the following steps: (1) skim and check for format errors, (2) read carefully for typographical and content errors, and (3) review for inconsistencies. Each of these important steps is discussed fully in the following sections.

Skim and Check for Format Errors

The first step in the proofreading process is to skim the document for any format errors. For example, if you were proofreading a business letter, you would need to check the placement of the various letter parts: the date, the inside address, the complimentary close, the signature lines, the reference initials, and any enclosure or copy notations. Are the margins even? If indented paragraphs were used, are all new paragraphs indented uniformly? Is the letter placed properly on the page? These questions could be answered quickly by skimming the document.

All the parts separate from the body of a document need to be checked individually. In a report the title, subtitles, and footnotes need to be reviewed. Introductory "To," "From," and "Subject" lines in the memorandum require special attention, and in the business letter the inside address must be scrutinized carefully. To illustrate the appropriate approach, examine a method for checking the following business-letter inside address:

Ms. Ann Thomsen
922 Shasta Drive
Phoenix, AZ 85351

Ask yourself the following questions:

1. Has the correct courtesy title been used?
2. Is the name spelled correctly (*Ann* or *Anne; Thompsen, Thompson,* or *Thomsen*)?
3. Are the numbers in the street address and ZIP Code accurate?
4. Are the street and city names spelled correctly?
5. Have you used the correct two-letter abbreviation for the state?

By verifying step by step all the information in the inside address, you can ensure that it is correctly written.

Read for Typographical and Content Errors

The second step in the proofreading process is to read the body of the document for a variety of typographical and content errors. You need to develop an awareness of the kinds of errors for which you are looking and a skill in spotting them during a single reading.

Typographical Errors. Probably one of the easiest kinds of typographical errors to recognize is the transposition error. Notice how this type of error stands out in the following sentence.

Please answer hte following questions:

As a proofreader you need to indicate that the letters *h* and *t* must be reversed. Standard proofreaders' marks provide the tool to show easily the adjustments needed, and these symbols should be learned by the business writer. See how the transposition error in the previous sentence is marked for correction.

Please answer the following questions:

The transposition symbol may be expanded in use to indicate a reversal of words, phrases, clauses, or even sentences.

We have asked all our clients to immediately inform us of any address corrections.

Other obvious typographical errors include omitted letters, extra letters, and incorrect letters. Corrections for these kinds of errors are shown below:

omit*t*ed letter

e*x*tra letter

in*c*orrect letter

To show an insertion, use a caret ($\wedge$) to indicate where the additional letter should be placed. This mark may also be used to show the insertion of entire words or word groups. For letter deletions use a forward-slanting diagonal line ($\diagup$) through the unwanted letter; close up the extra space with loops above and below ($\supset$). Incorrect letters can be changed easily by running the forward-slanting diagonal through the incorrect letter and then writing the correct letter directly above the diagonal.

Less obvious typographical errors can be hidden because they seem to blend in with the rest of the typewritten material. Read the following sentences carefully:

Your last three bank statement have shown an incorrect balance.

As soon as we hear form you, we will ship your order.

Only by reading for meaning can you locate the errors in the above examples. That is why the accurate proofreader not only must look at the words but also must read the content for meaning and make the necessary corrections. Would you have changed the sentences like this, based on your knowledge of proofreaders' marks?

Your last three bank statement*s* have shown an incorrect balance.

As soon as we hear *from* you, we will ship your order.

PROOFREADING PRACTICE 1

In this unit and throughout the grammar, punctuation, and style units, Proofreading Practice exercises are provided to help you master the principles you are studying.

Check your understanding of the proofreading techniques discussed so far. On a separate sheet of paper, write the numbers from 1 to 8. Read the following sentences and locate any typographical errors; write the incorrect word as it is shown in the sentence. Then use the appropriate proofreaders' marks to show the needed change. If a sentence is correct as shown, write *OK* on your paper.

1. Please sign adn date the application before returning it.
2. Do you stilll wish us to reinvest your dividends?
3. We are pleased to establish an acount for you at Nash's Department Store.
4. If you will return the enclosed bussiness reply card, one of our experienced salespeople will call you.
5. You should receive our signed contract within the next few days.
6. Do you wish to resckedule your appointment time from 9:30 a.m. to 2:30 p.m.?
7. May we have you reply by October 1.
8. Have all our customers been sent copies of thier monthly statement?

Omitted Words and Lines. As you are reading for content, be alert for omitted words. Make sure that each sentence makes sense.

For further information please your local sales representative.

This sentence does not make sense without the missing word; the reader does not know what action is to be taken. Should the reader write, telephone, see, contact, or ask the local representative? Notice how this error of omission can be corrected.

For further information please *contact* your local sales representative.

Sometimes errors cannot be detected just by reading the copy. The finished typewritten copy needs to be compared with the rough draft. Can you locate the error in the following sentence?

The balance in your account will earn interest at the rate of 7 percent compounded daily.

Probably not! You see, the omitted word does not obviously cloud the meaning. The sentence was supposed to have read, "The balance in your *checking* account will earn interest at the rate of 7 percent compounded daily." The word *checking* is necessary because it clarifies which account, but this error might not have been discovered unless the proofreader checked the final copy against the rough draft. Therefore, in the proofreading process, be sure to check the revised copy against the original copy for errors of omission. Do not limit this check to single-word omissions, but look for omissions of word groups, a complete line of type, and sentences as well.

Repeated Words and Lines. Delete repeated words and lines by drawing a straight horizontal line through them. Some single repeated words may appear within the same line, but they generally occur at the end of one line and at the beginning of another. Notice the corrected example that follows.

> Next week we will meet with you to select word processing, spreadsheet, and ~~and~~ data base programs for our new microcomputers.

Repeated lines are usually caused by an identical word appearing elsewhere in the copy. Study the following example to see how this error occurred and how the correction was handled.

> Line repetition errors usually occur when vocabulary in a document is repeated. The typist often shifts focus and returns to the inappropriate spot. The document is ~~repeated. The typist often shifts focus and returns to the inappropriate spot. The document is~~ then typed with an extra line, one repeated from an earlier copy.

PROOFREADING PRACTICE 2

On a separate sheet of paper, copy the following sentences. Use the proper proofreaders' marks to show your corrections.

1. For further details please your instruction booklet.
2. Who will be manufacturing the movable parts for our new line of exer- exercise equipment?
3. Your computer desk and printer table are both scheduled for delivery on on June 28.
4. Please the contract and mail it to us in the enclosed envelope.
5. As soon we receive approval from our central office, we will notify you.
6. Two of our older stores and our new warehouse need to have more up- up-to-date security systems installed.

Number Errors. All figures should be checked for accuracy. First, ask yourself, "Does the number make sense?" If you saw the weight of a newborn infant stated as 70 pounds, you might suspect that this was an error and that the typist may have meant to type 7 pounds. If the price of a 25-inch color television set was stated as $195, you might conclude that the first digit had been mistyped. Likewise, if a ZIP Code appeared as 911135, you would know that an error had occurred; ZIP Codes contain five or nine digits, not six. Reading for sense helps you locate obvious numerical errors.

Other errors need to be checked against copy to be identified. To make sure the numbers in the rough draft and final copy coincide, follow these procedures. For a long number, count the digits in the original copy and make sure the same number of digits appears in the copy being checked.

Then compare in groups of three the digits in the original with the digits in the copy.

In some cases it may be necessary to verify computations and recalculate totals. Be sure to think through each calculation so that errors in reasoning will not be duplicated. Approach the verification process as if it were a new problem. This outlook will enable you to find errors that otherwise might be overlooked.

PROOFREADING PRACTICE 3

On a separate sheet of paper, write the numbers from 1 to 12. Compare the figures in Column A with those in Column B; use proofreaders' marks to make any necessary corrections in the figures appearing in Column B. If no corrections are needed, write *OK* on your paper.

A	B
1. 3624 West 59 Place	1. 3626 West 59 Place
2. (212) 873-5669	2. (213) 873-5669
3. San Diego, CA 92143-1896	3. San Diego, CA 921143-1896
4. 567-44-7478	4. 567-44-7748
5. December 13, 1973	5. December 31, 1973
6. XT 954782643	6. XT 954782543
7. (818) 365-3827	7. (818) 365-3837
8. $17,923.81	8. $17,932.81
9. KRT647934648	9. KRT84793648
10. Serial No. 965468325679	10. Serial No. 965468325679
11. 7463901743	11. 746390173
12. 432-82-8987	12. 423-882-8987

Spelling Errors. Keep an up-to-date dictionary handy as you proofread, and look up any word whose spelling you doubt. Use the appropriate proofreaders' marks to show any corrections that need to be made.

Sometimes spelling errors may be viewed as typographical errors and vice versa. It does not matter what kind of error has occurred; the important consideration is that the error is noted and corrected. See how the following error was changed:

Use your MAGNA-CHARGE to send flowers for this special occasion.

Punctuation Errors. Internal punctuation marks may be added to copy by using the insertion mark; just place the comma, semicolon, or colon inside the caret at the point of insertion. Closing punctuation marks (periods, question marks, and exclamation marks) may be added to copy without insertion marks; periods are circled to make them more visible.

Vans, campers, and trucks are prohibited from parking in Lot A.

Three packages of crystal arrived today, when may we expect the remaining four

Extra or incorrect punctuation marks may be deleted by using the forward-slanting diagonal (╱). If another punctuation mark must be substituted, just delete or change the incorrect mark and follow the procedures for inserting the correct one.

ORIGINAL: This apartment complex will be converted to condominiums, therefore we must notify all tenants by October 1?

REVISION: This apartment complex will be converted to condominiums⁄therefore⁄ we must notify all tenants by October 1⁄⊙

ORIGINAL: Would you be able to assume responsibility for the following duties; locating a restaurant, selecting a menu, and coordinating the arrangements.

REVISION: Would you be able to assume responsibility for the following duties⁄ locating a restaurant, selecting a menu, and coordinating the arrangements?

Grammar Errors. Pay close attention to the grammatical construction of sentences in the copy you are proofreading. Watch for errors in subject-verb agreement, noun plurals and possessives, compound adjectives, and other such commonly misused principles of grammar. Use the proofreaders' marks you have learned so far to make any necessary changes.

PROOFREADING PRACTICE 4

Copy the following sentences on a separate sheet of paper. Then make any necessary corrections using the proofreaders' marks presented in this unit.

1. We do not want to loose this opportunity to thank you for your patronage during the past year.
2. July 11, will mark our twenty-fifth anniversary serving the residents of Springfield.
3. We was disappointed to learn that you will be moving your offices.
4. Did you notify your insurance company of your address change.
5. Unfortunately, we cannot acommodate you on February 14.
6. Please provide us with the name address and telephone number of your family physician.
7. Both switchs on this computer monitor are defective.
8. Did you recieve the information I sent you?

Capitalization Errors. While you are proofreading, look for those words that should be capitalized and are not. At the same time be alert for those words that have been capitalized but should appear in lowercase letters. A good source for determining whether a word should be capitalized is *The Gregg Reference Manual*, Sixth Edition, by William A. Sabin (Gregg Division, McGraw-Hill Book Company, New York, 1985).

To show that a letter should be capitalized, place three short lines under it; to capitalize entire words, underline the word or word group three times.

You may buy copies of The Lundberg Letters at Dalton's bookstore.

Ms. Deschiff will be transferred to our east coast office next month.

Use a forward-slanting diagonal through a capital letter that should appear in lowercase form. Words appearing in all-capital letters that should be written in a combination of capital and lowercase letters may be changed by using the forward-slanting diagonal in conjunction with a straight horizontal line.

Your Century Living Room Suite will be delivered by Z-EXPRESS AIR FREIGHT SERVICES the week of December 17.

Number-Usage Errors. Number-usage rules dictate that some numbers be written in figure form and others be written in word form. When proofreading copy, check to see that each number is expressed in the proper format. If a figure should be spelled out, merely circle it. If a number in word form should be expressed in figure form, draw a horizontal line through the incorrect expression and above it write the correct figure or figures.

Last week 5 of our sales personnel each sold over ~~thirty thousand dollars~~ $30,000 in video recording accessories.

PROOFREADING PRACTICE 5

Proofread the following sentences. On a separate sheet of paper, write the error or errors as they are shown in each sentence. Use proofreaders' marks to make the necessary corrections.

1. These prices will be in effect 1 day only, October 25.
2. How many english classes have been scheduled for next semester?
3. Our division sells Copiers, COMPUTERS, and Electronic Typewriters.
4. Because Marisa's new job requires a security clearance, the fbi is interviewing her references.
5. Only one hundred twenty-seven of the five hundred questionnaires were returned.
6. Please send your claim directly to amalgamated life insurance company.

Review for Inconsistencies

Once a document has been proofread carefully, it should be checked an additional time for any inconsistencies. Some of these inconsistencies may have been recognized in the initial reading. Less obvious ones, though, need to be located through a separate inspection after the document has been read thoroughly.

Titles. Check to make sure that courtesy titles have been used consistently throughout. If "Dr. Guffey" is used in one place, "Mrs. Guffey" in another, and "Ms. Guffey" in still another, then revisions are in order. More than likely, "Dr. Guffey" is correct and should be used in all three places.

Spelling. Spellings of names and references to companies and associations should be consistent. Is the spelling Guffey or Guffy? Clark or Clarke? McDonald or MacDonald? Whichever one it may be, be sure it is correct consistently throughout the document. If California State University, Los Angeles, is generally referred to as CSULA, then make sure that any "Cal State" references are changed to CSULA. Similarly, if a company called Midwest Medical Equipment and Supply is generally referred to as Midwest Med, then any attempt to also call this company MMES would be incorrect. Be consistent in the use of shortened forms for the same company, group, association, or government body.

Number Usage. Check for inconsistencies in number usage. For example, if a certain set of numbers is presented in figure form in one section, be sure that similar sets of data are presented in figure form also. Double-check the accuracy of dates and times. If you plan to meet someone on Monday, August 10, be sure your calendar shows August 10 to be on a Monday. If you will arrive at your hotel by eleven on Thursday, June 24, be sure to let the reservations clerk know whether you mean 11 a.m. or 11 p.m.

Once you have checked the document for inconsistencies, the proofreading process has been completed. The material is now ready to be prepared in final form if you have followed the procedure recommended in this unit.

Proofreaders' Marks

Proofreaders' marks provide a concise, organized method for noting changes on rough drafts, manuscripts, and other documents. By consistently using the same symbols to indicate certain changes, you are minimizing the opportunities for communication failure with the preparer of the final document. Whether the preparer is a printer, a typist, or even you, these symbols will convey a uniform set of instructions that will result in error-free copy.

The proofreaders' marks you have learned so far, as well as several others you will need as a proofreader, are shown below. Learn them and practice using them as often as you can.

Transpose letters	thier
Transpose words	to directly call you
Insert letter or letters	convient (en)
Insert word or words	a customer (charge account)

Delete stroke	reduces
Delete stroke and close up space	electronic
Delete punctuation mark	On May 5/ we . . . .
Change stroke	correspond*e*ance
Omit word or word group	a ~~charge account~~ customer
Change word or word group	. . . book ~~which~~ *that* we sent you.
Capitalize letter	bushnell corporation
Use all capitals	stop sign
Use lowercase letter	the Company
Use a series of lowercase letters	FDI CORPORATION
Insert semicolon, comma, or colon	. . . today,therefore,please send us the following:
Insert period, question mark, or exclamation mark	. ? !
Insert apostrophe or quotation marks	. . . the companys innovative policies.
Spell out	3 . . . 20% . . . 4 doz.
Close up space	sales person
Insert a space	in addition
Hyphenate	up to date files
Underscore	The word receive is often . . . .
Restore word or words deleted	stock ~~and bond~~ certificates
Start new paragraph	¶ May we have your
Do not start new paragraph	no ¶ This information is
Indent five spaces	5 In the future
Single-space	When we receive your report, we will submit it to . . . . *ss*
Double-space	One of our sales representatives will call on you within . . . . *ds*
Move as indicated	at your discretion
Move to the left	Send in your report
Move to the right	Send in your report
Center	January 25, 1989

COMMUNICATION LABORATORY

APPLICATION EXERCISES

A. On a separate sheet of paper, write the numbers from 1 to 20. Proofread the following sentences. If a sentence contains an error, write the error on your paper. Then use the appropriate proofreaders' marks to make the necessary correction. If a sentence does not contain an error, write *OK* on your paper.

1. Please send us this information by December seventh.
2. Have all the tenants their rent for this month?
3. When may we expect delivery of this order.
4. Your apointment with Dr. Eckles has been changed to May 3.
5. Copies of your transcript and test scores have been sent to michigan state university.
6. Be sure to save your signed reciept for this payment.
7. We do not except coupons from any other markets.
8. Checks will be honored for the ammount of purchase only.
9. You may submit the report to John Ellen or Chris.
10. Our local High School is sponsoring a number of fund-raisers to help finance the new auditorium.
11. Only three of our salespersonnel have met their quotas for this month.
12. Obtain three copies of these forms from the CALIFORNIA FRAN-CHISE TAX BOARD.
13. Please specify the amt. of your payment on the enclosed stub.
14. If you can not attend this meeting, please let us know by March 10.
15. Only 1 office in our building, is available for lease.
16. How many of your staff members have completed the questionnaire?
17. Two irs officials will audit the company books next week.
18. In response to you advertisement, I am requesting a copy of your free booklet on lawn care.
19. You are one of our valued customers, and we appreciate the the business you have given us in the past.
20. Please include with your reservation a deposit for the first night

B. Reading carelessly when checking amounts of money and other figures often leads to problems. Compare the following two lists. On a separate sheet of paper, indicate which pairs of numbers do not agree by writing *X* next to the appropriate number. Write *OK* if the item is correct.

List A	List B	Do *Not* Agree
0. 7654321	7653421	0. _X_
1. $846,783	$846,873	1. _____
2. 8734972390	8724972390	2. _____
3. $382,479.23	$382,479.23	3. _____
4. 1DSE479-6843	1DSE479-6843	4. _____
5. 437-81-9823	437-881-9823	5. _____
6. R6243778109TT	R642377810TT	6. _____

C. Test your proofreading skill by comparing the following letter with the copy that appears directly below it. On a separate sheet of paper, number and list the errors that appear. Then use proofreaders' marks to show the needed corrections.

Copy to Be Proofread

Dear Msr. Andrews:

We welcome you as a charge acount customer of field's department store. Enclosed is your charge card and a broshure discribing our charge plan. We hope that you will take advantage of our many bargins and use you card often.

This month we are featuring a sale on famous-brand stainless steel cookware. All pots and frying pans inthis line have been from 25 to 50 persent. If you need to replace your cookware now is the time to do so. Also, if your need a wedding gift for the June bride, consider giving this fine cookware.

What ever your needs in the department store line maybe, be sure to visit field's first. We are eager to to serve you with our complete line of high quality merchandize.

Sincerly,

Correct Copy

Dear Mrs. Andrews:

We welcome you as a charge account customer of Field's Department Store. Enclosed are your charge card and a brochure describing our charge plan. We hope that you will take advantage of our many bargains and use your card often.

This month we are featuring a sale on famous-brand stainless steel cookware. All pots and frying pans in this line have been reduced from 25 to 50 percent. If you need to replace your cookware, now is the time to do so. Also, if you need a wedding gift for the June bride, consider giving this fine cookware.

Whatever your needs in the department store line may be, be sure to visit Field's first. We are eager to serve you with our complete line of high-quality merchandise.

Sincerely,

D. Proofread the following excerpt from a business letter, and on a separate sheet of paper, make a list of the errors. Then rewrite the excerpt, correcting the errors.

We received you letter of Febuary 14 and the check for $182 enclosed. Every store appreciate the patronage of it's customers. We have credit your account for $182 and hope that their will be many more opportunity to serve you.

VOCABULARY AND SPELLING STUDIES

A. Without consulting your dictionary, indicate which of the two spellings shown for the following words is preferable. Then check your selections in the dictionary.

1. judgement, judgment
2. realize, realise
3. usable, useable
4. desireable, desirable
5. accidently, accidentally
6. acknowledgment, acknowledgement
7. instalment, installment
8. quartet, quartette

B. The following brief definitions indicate frequently used words that contain silent letters. Spell the words. To help you, the number of letters in each word is given.

1. The opposite of right (5 letters).
2. A visitor (5 letters).
3. A twenty-fourth part of a day (4 letters).
4. A body of land surrounded by water (6 letters).
5. The opposite of day (5 letters).
6. Unruffled; still (4 letters).
7. The branch of medicine that deals with mental disorders (10 letters).
8. To strike or rap on a door (5 letters).
9. A religious song (4 letters).
10. A lien on property by which the property is made security for a loan (8 letters).

COMMUNICATING FOR RESULTS

Following Instructions. Laura got into difficulty because she failed to read correctly the memorandums that came from her supervisor regarding changes in procedures. When her supervisor finally had to speak to Laura regarding her failure to follow instructions, Laura replied, "Oh, we get so many memos that I can't keep all of them straight in my mind." If you were Laura's supervisor, what advice would you give to help keep the memorandums "straight"?

There are 5 words not in the dictionary. Do you w
L54..t....t....t....t....t....t....t

January 17, 1986◄

Mr.Jeromy Dunlap◄
1505 Elm Lane◄
New York, NY 20000◄

Dear Mr. Dunlap:◄

It has come to our attention that youracc
now thirty days overdue.◄

We must ask that you remit your payment t
possible. If you have already done so, p
any inconvenence this may have caused.◄

Thank you.◄

Sincerely,

Press Ctrl-Break to exit the Terminal option.

Expressing yourself well is the key to communicating effectively with others. Think about how a situation can cause confusion and hostility because someone does not understand your messages. In business such misunderstandings can be costly.

The words you select will determine whether you can communicate your ideas *exactly as you intended.* An expanded vocabulary will provide you with accurate and precise words, which can only help promote the understanding that is critical to effective communication. Given a situation that requires you to express yourself, you will be able to do the following when you master the units in this chapter:

1. *Edit your messages so that they include the most accurate, effective, and meaningful words possible.*

2. *Use reference books such as a dictionary, a thesaurus, and a word division manual to increase your knowledge of words.*

3. *Use commonly confused words in sentences to show that you understand their different meanings and spellings.*

4. *List, with their correct spelling, many of the words frequently used in business writing.*

U · N · I · T

7 Editing for Professional Results

In Unit 6 you learned a procedure for proofreading typewritten documents. As part of this process, you used proofreaders' marks to indicate changes in prepared material. These same proofreaders' marks will also play an important role during the editing function.

What is the difference between proofreading and editing? Aren't these terms interchangeable? Although at first glance proofreading and editing may seem synonymous, they are quite different. The proofreader compares prepared copy with a model, one that is presumed to be correct, complete, and well written. His or her job is to ensure that there are no deviations from the "model." Should the proofreader note any discrepancies during the proofreading process, they are carefully and clearly marked with proofreaders' marks.

The editor's task, though, is actually quite different. No models tell him or her if the copy is complete, correct, or well written. Editors must make their own decisions. They must determine *for themselves* if a sentence is ungrammatical, if a word is misspelled, or if a comma is in the incorrect position. The editing process requires decisions not only regarding correctness but also whether a document is complete, clear, consistent, and concise. The editor bears responsibility for ensuring that a document accomplishes its purpose, is easily read and understood, and is as nearly perfect as possible in correctness of expression.

As you develop and refine your communication skills, you will take on the role of an editor. Your first editing experiences will be in your study of the grammar units, where you will learn to recognize and correct grammar errors. Later, in the punctuation and style units, you will have the same opportunity with punctuation, capitalization, number-usage, and writing style errors.

Why do you need such practice? As a business communicator you will be called upon to write letters, memorandums, bulletins, reports, and other documents. Because few writers produce perfect copy with their first drafts, you will need to rely upon your editing skills to review and revise what you have written. No model is available with which you can compare *your* letter, *your* memorandum, or *your* report. Your work is original and must be evaluated by you with the "editor's" eye.

Documents that are well written are more likely to accomplish their purpose. Those that are *correct, clear, complete, concise, consistent, concrete*, and *courteous* transmit ideas readily; they tend to inform accurately or to motivate readers to take a specific action. That is why you need to inspect—*edit*—the documents you write for these qualities. In this unit you will learn how to revise written materials with the seven Cs in mind.

Correctness of Expression and Content

Many of the errors you spotted as a proofreader will require your attention as an editor. As an editor, though, you must know how to recognize and remedy these errors on the original copy *without the aid of a correct example*. For some people, finding their own errors is a more difficult task than finding the errors of others. In this text you will begin your editing practice by finding others' errors and then learning to revise your own written work.

Grammar. In your everyday conversations you more than likely would not say, "We *was* late for class yesterday" or "*Me* and Bill have already finished our homework assignments." Such obvious grammar errors would also probably not appear in your writing. More subtle oversights, though, such as the following, may occur, and these are the ones that you as an editor need to correct. They are ones that you will learn to identify and <u>elude</u> in your study of the grammar units.

INCORRECT: I have always wanted to work for a organization such as yours.
CORRECT: I have always wanted to work for a_norganization such as yours.

INCORRECT: A large supply of double-sided, double-density computer disks have arrived at our central warehouse.
CORRECT: A large supply of double-sided, double-density computer disks ~~have~~ *has* arrived at our central warehouse.

INCORRECT: Between you and I, perhaps we can convince Ms. Hardesty to purchase another computer for our department.
CORRECT: Between you and *me*, perhaps we can convince Ms. Hardesty to purchase another computer for our department.

Spelling. Use the dictionary, a word division manual, or any other spelling aid to assist you with detecting any misspelled words in the copy you are editing. Your study of the dictionary and word division manuals in Unit 8 and of spelling in Unit 9 should help you correct spelling errors.

Five words in the following paragraph have been misspelled. Can you identify them without checking the corrected copy that follows?

INCORRECT: We are pleased to be able to accomodate you and the members of your staff for this ocassion. You will find our location to be convient to restaurants and shopping centers in the Denver area. In addition, our rates are lower than other hotels offering similiar services in this location.

CORRECT: We are pleased to be able to accommodate you and the members of your staff for this ocassion. You will find our location to be convient to restaurants and shopping centers in the Denver area. In addition, our rates are lower than other hotels offerying similiar services in this location.

Punctuation. Errors in punctuation can often cause confusion and impede clarity. Business writers should check their documents to ensure that commas, semicolons, colons, periods, dashes, question marks, apostrophes, quotation marks, and exclamation marks have not been either overused or omitted. Note how the following omission of a comma causes the reader to reread the sentence to obtain the appropriate meaning.

INCORRECT: In the past editions of this dictionary have distinguished standard English usage from slang.

CORRECT: In the past, editions of this dictionary have distinguished standard English usage from slang.

Errors such as the one illustrated waste the reader's time and cause confusion. By not using a comma to signal a pause, the writer forced the reader to reread the sentence to obtain its intended meaning. During the editing process you will want to make sure that the correct punctuation marks have been used in their appropriate places.

Capitalization. Capitalized letters introduce significant words. Words that begin a sentence and those nouns that refer to *specific* people, places, events, things, or concepts need to be capitalized. The conventions established for capitalization place emphasis on those words that deserve special consideration because of their distinct identity. You, as a business communicator, will wish to follow these conventions closely.

If your name were Joyce Mooneyhan, how would you feel if a correspondent wrote your name as "joyce mooneyhan"? Likewise, if you wrote to the Des Moines Chamber of Commerce for a donation, what kind of an impression would you make if you referred to this organization as the "Desmoines chamber of commerce"? Obviously, such abuses of capitalization principles would result in communication distortions.

Overcapitalization, too, can lead to miscommunication by distracting the reader from ideas contained in the document. Compare the following two sentences:

INCORRECT: One of your Company officials must contact our Attorney about this provision in the Agreement.

CORRECT: One of your company officials must contact our attorney about this provision in the agreement.

Check your documents carefully so that those words that *name* specific nouns are capitalized; avoid capitalizing general nouns, even though they may take the place of a specific name.

Number Usage. Through the years business writers have developed guidelines on the effective expression of numbers. Amounts of money, dates, weights and measures, percentages, mixed fractions, and large numbers are generally expressed in figures. Numbers at the beginning of a sentence, whole numbers *ten* and below, and general time periods usually appear in word form. Other kinds of numbers are sometimes written in figures and then at other times written in words. You will study the principles governing correct number expression in Unit 35.

Content. In addition to checking for correctness of expression, the editing process requires scrutinizing the contents for accuracy—accuracy in numeric data, dates, and information presented. Are all figures and dates correct? Are all the facts and circumstances represented accurately? No matter how well written a document may be, if its data is inaccurate, the document is ineffective.

EDITING PRACTICE 1

In this unit and in all grammar, punctuation, and style units, Editing Practice exercises are provided to help you master the principles you are studying. For this first exercise locate and correct the following errors in the paragraphs that appear below.

1. Two grammar errors
2. One punctuation error
3. Three spelling errors
4. Three capitalization errors
5. One number-usage error

Copy the paragraphs on a separate sheet of paper, and then use the proofreaders' marks you learned in Unit 6 to make your corrections.

Congradulations! You have aquired the Wilson House Reference Set, a powerful reference tool. We feel that our Dictionary and Thesaurus functions will be of use to anyone who uses a word processor. 5 additional options enhance the program even further.

If the program is incompatible with your system or you is disatisfied with its performance please complete the enclosed form and return it with the program to our chicago office within 30 days. A immediate refund will be sent.

Clarity

Clearly worded and organized messages enable the receiver to understand easily the contents and purpose of a message. Such messages use comprehensible sentences free from misplaced modifiers and rambling thought patterns. These sentences are organized so that one thought grows naturally from another and paragraphs contain only a single major idea. Paragraphs, too, must take the reader along a continuum of ideas so that the entire message portrays an intelligible picture for the reader. In reviewing written documents, the editor must look for these qualities.

Sentence Construction. Sentences must be constructed so that the reader can easily identify who is doing what. Related words placed in a logical and consecutive order enable the reader to follow the writer's thought patterns. By placing word groups that describe other thought units as closely as possible to the words they modify, business writers can avoid ambiguity and confusion. Notice how the correct versions in the following examples promote an understanding of who does what.

INCORRECT: The contract should be signed by Mr. Chapman on the dotted line. (Can't you just picture "Mr. Chapman on a dotted line"?)

CORRECT: The contract should be signed on the dotted line by Mr. Chapman. (Now the phrase *on the dotted line* has been placed correctly next to the words it modifies—*should be signed.*)

INCORRECT: As newcomers to our community, the merchants of San Dimas wish to make available to you a variety of complimentary products and services. (Here it appears that the merchants are the newcomers, which is highly unlikely.)

CORRECT: As newcomers to our community, you are invited to take advantage of a variety of complimentary products and services offered by the merchants of San Dimas. (Now the modifier *As newcomers to our community* appears next to the word it describes—*you.*)

Paragraph Coherence. Isolated sentences do little to develop concepts, convey information, or persuade readers. Only by bundling sentences into meaningful thought units can the business writer expect to communicate effectively. Sentences related to a specific unit of thought are contained in a paragraph, with each paragraph dealing only with a single theme. Paragraphs containing more than one idea violate the writing principle of paragraph unity. In editing your written work, you will want each of your paragraphs to deal with a single concept and all the sentences in this paragraph to relate to that concept.

Not only must each paragraph deal with one major idea but also each sentence in that paragraph must be placed logically so that it flows naturally from the sentence that precedes it. Paragraphs with sentences that flow smoothly from one thought to another are coherent. They lead the reader carefully through the writer's thought processes.

Coherence, the quality of hanging together, is like the chocolate in a chocolate peanut cluster. It pulls together the isolated units and enhances the flavor of the outcome. Editors have at their disposal several techniques for achieving coherence:

1. Make sure the sentences are placed in logical order.
2. Make sure that a following sentence relates to the previous sentence.

3. Substitute pronouns and synonyms to refer to previously mentioned nouns and pronouns.
4. Add transitional expressions such as *therefore, of course, meanwhile,* or *as a consequence* to move smoothly from one point to another.
5. Signal a turning point with words such as *but, however,* or *on the other hand.*

Compare the following two examples by noting how the second one achieves the quality of paragraph coherence.

> POOR: As soon as we receive another shipment of Oxford crystal, your order will receive top priority. We are doing everything possible to restock our inventory. The 10-inch Lismore vase is presently out of stock. We appreciate receiving your recent order for Oxford crystal.

> BETTER: We appreciate receiving your recent order for Oxford crystal.
> The 10-inch Lismore vase you requested is presently out of stock. However, we are doing everything possible to restock our inventory. As soon as we receive another shipment of Oxford crystal, filling your order will be our top priority.

Message Organization. The editor's task does not end with a scrutiny of individual paragraphs. Indeed, the editor must evaluate the entire message in terms of coherence, the quality of hanging together. Just as each sentence in each paragraph must flow smoothly from its predecessor, so each paragraph must grow naturally from the previous one.

To achieve its purpose, a message must be organized appropriately. Paragraphs must be ordered in a logical manner and written so that the transition between each one contributes to the overall objective of the message.

EDITING PRACTICE 2

On a separate sheet of paper, copy the following paragraphs. Use proofreaders' marks to correct two sentence construction errors and two errors in paragraph coherence.

> A family invests money, starts to earn more money, and then suddenly faces financial disaster because a family member is hospitalized by an unexpected illness. Underwritten by Continental Life Insurance Company, we feel this supplemental hospital insurance protection is essential for every family's welfare. That is why we are pleased to announce the Group Hospital Supplemental Insurance Plan.

> As a customer of Valley Federal Savings and Loan, we guarantee your acceptance. You cannot be turned down. For only pennies a day, you can ensure your financial security.

Completeness

As you read your document to determine whether all important ideas have been included, check the content for any possible omissions in detail. If you are sending a meeting announcement, have you included the date, time, and exact place of the meeting? If the meeting is to be held at the Wilshire Hotel, remember to give the street address and room location. Information on directions and parking might prove useful too.

The successful business writer always provides the reader with *all* the necessary details. The easier it is for the reader to react to the writer's message, the more fruitful the communication effort will be. During the revision process editors must take the place of their anticipated readers and assume *they know nothing* about the information contained in the document being edited. In this way editors can spot omissions of both major ideas and essential details.

Conciseness

Too often writers and editors equate *conciseness* with *brevity*. Granted, the message should be as short as possible—but without omitting any significant ideas or details.

The following message is short: "Meet me at 3 p.m." Yet, without knowing the date or place, the reader would be unable to respond to the message. A more effective version of this sentence would be "Please meet me on Monday, June 30, at 3 p.m. in Room 312 of the Towers Building." Although this sentence is considerably longer than our first example, it is a better one because it provides all the necessary details.

Messages should be concise but not sacrifice the qualities of completeness and courtesy. Conciseness means that only relevant ideas appear in the document and that these ideas have been expressed in as few words as possible. The communication is free from rambling sentences, redundant phrases, and an abundance of prepositional phrases. Notice how the quality of conciseness has been achieved in the second versions of the following examples:

POOR: Our marketing director thinks that perhaps next week or the following one we will find ourselves in the appropriate position to announce to the industry and to the public our newly developed and inexpensive scanner, the All-Print Reader.

BETTER: Our marketing director anticipates that within the next two weeks we will be ready to announce our new, inexpensive scanner—the All-Print Reader.

POOR: Please raise the top of the table another 3 inches.

BETTER: Please raise the tabletop another 3 inches.

POOR: The two twins work in the same department.

BETTER: The twins work in the same department.

Consistency

Like the proofreader, the editor must check for consistency. Check to make sure that courtesy titles have been used consistently throughout. If "Ms.

Henry" is used in one place, then "Mrs. Henry" should not be used in another, *even though both titles for the same person may be correct.* Spellings of names and references to companies and associations should also be consistent. Headings and subheadings in a long letter, memorandum, or report should be parallel; that is, similar headings should be expressed in the same word format.

Take extra care with figures. Check for inconsistencies in number usage. If certain sets of numbers are presented in figure form, be sure that similar sets of data are also presented in figure form. Double-check the accuracy of dates and times so that the "Monday" referred to is indeed January 25 or the "Thursday" is February 6.

Concreteness

The use of explicit, tangible language promotes reader understanding. Vague, abstract writing only interferes with clarity and the reader's ability to visualize what the writer has in mind. See for yourself in the following example how the communication process could have been improved with a single sentence expressed in concrete terms.

> "I bought a dog yesterday."
> "Oh yeah! What kind?"
> "St. Bernard."
> "Full grown or puppy?"
> "Puppy."
> "Male or female?"
> "Male."
> "What color?"
> "Brown and white."
> "Why didn't you say in the first place that you bought a brown-and-white male St. Bernard puppy yesterday?"

Check the messages you edit to make sure that instead of describing "a dog" they project the image of "a brown-and-white male St. Bernard puppy." The use of concrete nouns and precise verbs enables the reader to picture and grasp more easily the ideas presented.

Courtesy

Words such as *please, thank you,* and *appreciate* connote (imply) a courtesy that creates goodwill and understanding. The use of "purr" words and the avoidance of "snarl" words, discussed in Unit 2, sets the stage further for establishing rapport with the reader so that he or she is receptive to our messages.

Successful editors rid documents of offensive words or innuendos. These editors strive to ensure that the message reflects as much as possible the reader's viewpoint. This "you" attitude promotes understanding, avoids antagonism, and increases message effectiveness.

EDITING PRACTICE 3

Assume the following paragraphs were written as part of a letter to invite an applicant for an interview. The applicant applied for an accounting position at White Brothers, an office furniture manufacturing company. The paragraphs contain violations of completeness, conciseness, consistency, concreteness, and courtesy. On a separate sheet of paper, rewrite the paragraphs to improve them in terms of these five qualities.

Meet me next Wednesday to discuss the possibility of your working for our company. Dr. Haswell, the president of our company, has in the last few months expressed an interest, both orally and in writing, in hiring an additional person to work in this department because our company is growing. Mr. Haswell will be joining us for the interview next Wednesday.

Let me know if you will be able to meet with us by calling my office within the next few days.

COMMUNICATION LABORATORY

APPLICATION EXERCISES

A. Copy the following paragraphs on a separate sheet of paper; then edit them for correctness of expression. Locate the errors listed below, and use proofreaders' marks to make the appropriate corrections.

3 grammar errors
3 punctuation errors
4 capitalization errors
6 spelling errors
4 number-usage errors

You are amoung a prefered group of Brereton charge customers who is being invited to save 25 to 50% on our collection of fine furniture. For 2 days you will have a opportunity to chose from furniture, that has been gathered from all our stores just for this exciting sale. This event will not be advertized to the public.

This is your chance to save hundreds of dollars on living room dinning room and bedroom suites. Mark october second and third on your calender, and join us in the Furniture Department of Brereton's at the sherman oaks mall. We hope to see you their.

B. On a separate sheet of paper, copy the following paragraphs. Make the changes necessary to correct two sentence construction errors, one error in paragraph unity, and two errors in paragraph coherence.

Effective March 1, employees will be assigned specific parking spaces for their vehicles. Based on seniority with the company, spaces will be allocated. Too many employees have been parking their cars in spaces reserved for our customers. Therefore, we are instituting a new parking policy for all personnel.

Each person's space will be numbered, and he or she will receive a decal that corresponds to the assigned number. Any employee who parks in a space other than the one assigned will be cited for a municipal code parking violation. These decals must be placed in the lower corner on the passenger side of the vehicle of the front windshield.

C. The following paragraphs contain violations of correctness, clarity, completeness, conciseness, consistency, concreteness, and courtesy. On a separate sheet of paper, rewrite the paragraphs to improve them in terms of these qualities. Assume any information necessary to complete this assignment.

We are in the process of planning a money-raising project in which the alumni of Dorsey High School can participate to raise funds for the school's extracurricular activitys. A luncheon is being planned for the third Saturday in Febuary at the century plaza hotel.

Do plan to attend this luncheon and bring your wife, husband or friend. Tickets are reasonably priced. Remember that the proceeds from this luncheon will benefit your alma mater and the students who are following in your footsteps.

Send in your reservation card today. Discounts are available for those who wish to reserve a full table.

VOCABULARY AND SPELLING STUDIES

A. The following words were used in the text in this unit. Locate them in the dictionary and write the definition that relates to the word as it was used in the unit. Then construct a sentence using each word to show that you understand its meaning and use.

1. synonymous
2. discrepancies
3. elude
4. impede
5. scrutinizing
6. comprehensible
7. continuum
8. intelligible
9. ambiguity
10. predecessor
11. abundance
12. innuendos

B. Using standard spellings, respell these well-known brand names that manufacturers have devised for their products.

1. Ry-Krisp Crackers
2. Spic and Span Cleanser
3. Cut-Rite Waxed Paper
4. My-T-Fine Pudding Mix
5. Pepomint Lifesavers
6. Sunkist Oranges

COMMUNICATING FOR RESULTS

Helping a New Employee. A new employee is assigned to the desk next to yours. Your supervisor, Bob Bradley, was called to a meeting before he could introduce the new employee to you or to any of the other employees. Courtesy demands that you take action. What are your responsibilities? Enact a typical introduction. Make a list of other things you could do to introduce this person to the new situation.

U · N · I · T

8

Using the Dictionary and Other Word References

Is the noun *advice* or *advise*? Is the plural of *radio* formed by adding *s* or by adding *es*? When word division is necessary at the end of a line, should *describe* be divided into *des-cribe* or *de-scribe*? What does *moratorium* mean? Is it correct to pronounce *adult* either 'ad-ult (with emphasis on *ad*) or a-'dult (with the emphasis on *dult*)? If you end a sentence with *in*, is *in* a preposition or an adverb? These are the kinds of questions that often confront even the most accomplished speakers and writers. The answers to such questions about words are to be found in the dictionary and other word references. You will find out more about these references in this unit.

The Alphabet—A Useful Tool

There are many extremely fine word references available and most—if not all—are arranged in alphabetic order. Although we all "know" the alphabet, we must all develop the ability to find words *quickly* using the alphabet. Have you ever suffered from "alphabet blackout"? To test yourself, try finding in the dictionary at least ten words that you already know how to spell. You should be able to find each of those words in not more than 20 seconds. When taking this self-test or when using the dictionary at any time, be sure to make use of the guide words (the first and last words on each page) appearing at the top of the page.

Authoritative References

Today there are many authoritative references available in both hardback and paperback. Because our language is constantly growing and changing, our references should be up to date. You can depend on your library to have the large, expensive, up-to-date references.

Occasionally, references may differ as to the spellings, pronunciations, or syllabications for some words. Regardless of the reasons for such differences, you should remember that language is constantly changing in all respects and that differences among references do not make one reference wrong and the other one right. Any established, up-to-date reference can properly be cited as the authority for acceptable word usage.

Dictionaries

Many of the differences among dictionaries are of little consequence to the ordinary user. For example, one dictionary may show abbreviations, biographical names, and geographic names in separate sections at the end of the book; another dictionary may include all this information arranged alphabetically with the words in the main vocabulary list. Also, different dictionaries use different systems for indicating pronunciation and for showing definitions, word origins, and other information about words. See pages 74–75 for the system used in one popular dictionary.

The most nearly complete dictionaries are unabridged, such as *Webster's Third New International Dictionary* and *Funk & Wagnalls New Standard Dictionary of the English Language*. These comprehensive works contain approximately 450,000 words in the main vocabulary list.

For personal use at home, in the office, or at school, a good standard desk dictionary is the best choice. Among these are *Webster's New Collegiate Dictionary*,* *The American Heritage Dictionary of the English Language*, *The Winston Dictionary for Schools*, *The American College Dictionary*, *Funk & Wagnalls Standard College Dictionary*, *Webster's New World Dictionary of the American Language*, *The Random House College Dictionary*, *Chambers Twentieth Century Dictionary*, *The Doubleday Dictionary: For Home, School, & Office*, and *The Thorndike/Barnhardt Advanced Dictionary*.

Every dictionary, no matter how small or how large, whether paperback or hardback, shows the spelling, word division, pronunciation, and meaning or meanings of each word listed. A good standard desk dictionary also gives the part of speech of a word, its origin, the ways in which it is used, any synonyms, and certain irregular forms; for example, the principal parts of the verb (*did, done, do, doing*), the plural of the noun (*alumna, alumnae*), and the comparative and superlative forms of the adjective (*gluey, gluier,*

---

* *Webster's Ninth New Collegiate Dictionary* (Merriam-Webster, Inc., Springfield, Massachusetts, 1986) is the source for spelling and syllabication for all words in this book as well as for the definitions and pronunciations given.

Parts of speech (in abbreviated form) label each main entry.

Principal parts of verbs are often listed, especially when the verb ending changes or when the verb is irregular.

Variant spellings are preceded by the word *also.*

Pronunciations—even of foreign terms—are listed for each main entry.

Syllable breaks for word division are shown for main entries.

Synonyms offer words that are similar in meaning to the main entry. **Antonyms** (words that mean the opposite) are sometimes listed as well.

re·peat·er \ri-'pēt-ər\ *n* (1598) : one that repeats: as **a** : one who relates or recites **b** : a watch or clock with a striking mechanism that upon pressure of a spring will indicate the time in hours or quarters and sometimes minutes **c** : a firearm having a magazine that holds a number of cartridges loaded into the chamber by the action of the piece **d** : an habitual violator of the laws **e** : one who votes illegally by casting more than one ballot in an election **f** : a student enrolled in a class or course for a second or subsequent time **g** : a device for receiving electronic communication signals and delivering corresponding amplified ones

re·peat·ing *adj, of a firearm* (1824) : designed to load cartridges from a magazine

repeating decimal *n* (1773) : a decimal in which after a certain point a particular digit or sequence of digits repeats itself indefinitely — compare TERMINATING DECIMAL

re·pe·chage \,rep-ə-'shäzh, rə-,pesh-'äzh\ *n* [F *repêchage* second chance, reexamination for a candidate who has failed, fr. *repêcher* to fish out, rescue, fr. *re-* + *pêcher* to fish, fr. L *piscari* — more at PISCATORY] (ca. 1928) : a trial heat (as in rowing) in which first-round losers are given another chance to qualify for the semifinals

re·pel \ri-'pel\ *vb* **re·pelled; re·pel·ling** [ME *repellen,* fr. L *repellere,* fr. *re-* + *pellere* to drive — more at FELT] *vt* (15c) **1 a** : to drive back : REPULSE **b** : to fight against : RESIST **2** : TURN AWAY, REJECT ⟨*repelled* the insinuation⟩ **3 a** : to drive away : DISCOURAGE ⟨foul words and frowns must not ~ a lover —Shak.⟩ **b** : to be incapable of adhering to, mixing with, taking up, or holding **c** : to force away or apart or tend to do so by mutual action at a distance **4** : to cause aversion in : DISGUST ~ *vi* : to cause aversion — **re·pel·ler** *n*

re·pel·len·cy \ri-'pel-ən-sē\ *n* (1747) : the quality or capacity of repelling

¹re·pel·lent *also* **re·pel·lant** \ri-'pel-ənt\ *adj* [L *repellent-, repellens,* prp. of *repellere*] (1643) **1** : serving or tending to drive away or ward off — often used in combination ⟨a mosquito-*repellent* spray⟩ **2** : arousing aversion or disgust : REPULSIVE **syn** see REPUGNANT — **re·pel·lent·ly** *adv*

²repellent *also* **repellant** *n* (1661) : something that repels; *esp* : a substance used to prevent insect attacks

¹re·pent \ri-'pent\ *vb* [ME *repenten,* fr. OF *repentir,* fr. *re-* + *pentir* to be sorry, fr. L *paenitēre* — more at PENITENT] *vi* (13c) **1** : to turn from sin and dedicate oneself to the amendment of one's life **2 a** : to feel regret or contrition **b** : to change one's mind ~ *vt* **1** : to cause to feel regret or contrition **2** : to feel sorrow, regret, or contrition for — **re·pent·er** *n*

²re·pent \'rē-pənt\ *adj* [L *repent-, repens,* prp. of *repere* to creep — more at REPTILE] (1669) : CREEPING, PROSTRATE ⟨~ stems⟩

re·pen·tance \ri-'pent-²n(t)s\ *n* (14c) : the action or process of repenting esp. for misdeeds or moral shortcomings **syn** see PENITENCE

re·pen·tant \-²nt\ *adj* (13c) **1** : experiencing repentance : PENITENT **2** : expressive of repentance — **re·pen·tant·ly** *adv*

re·per·cus·sion \,rē-pər-'kəsh-ən, ,rep-ər-\ *n* [L *repercussion-, repercussio,* fr. *repercussus,* pp. of *repercutere* to drive back, fr. *re-* + *percutere* to beat — more at PERCUSSION] (1536) **1** : REFLECTION, REVERBERATION **2 a** : an action or effect given or exerted in return : a reciprocal action or effect **b** : a widespread, indirect, or unforeseen effect of an act, action, or event — usu. used in pl. — **re·per·cus·sive** \-'kəs-iv\ *adj*

rep·er·toire \'rep-ə(r)-,twär\ *n* [F *répertoire,* fr. LL *repertorium*] (1847) **1 a** : a list or supply of dramas, operas, pieces, or parts that a company or person is prepared to perform **b** : a supply of skills, devices, expedients ⟨part of the ~ of a quarterback⟩; *broadly* : AMOUNT, SUPPLY ⟨an endless ~ of summer clothes⟩ **c** : a list or supply of capabilities ⟨the instruction ~ of a computer⟩ **2 a** : the complete list or supply of dramas, operas, or musical works available for performance ⟨our modern orchestral ~⟩ **b** : the complete list or supply of skills, devices, or ingredients used in a particular field, occupation, or practice ⟨the ~ of literary criticism⟩

rep·er·to·ry \'rep-ə(r)-,tōr-ē, -,tȯr-\ *n, pl* **-ries** [LL *repertorium* list, fr. L *repertus,* pp. of *reperire* to find, fr. *re-* + *parere* to produce — more at PARE] (1593) **1** : a place where something may be found : REPOSITORY **2 a** : REPERTOIRE **b** : a company that presents several different plays, operas, or pieces usu. alternately in the course of a season at one theater **c** : a theater housing such a company **3** : the production and presentation of plays by a repertory company ⟨acting in ~⟩

rep·e·tend \'rep-ə-,tend\ *n* [L *repetendus* to be repeated, gerundive of *repetere* to repeat] (1904) : a repeated sound, word, or phrase; *specif* : REFRAIN

rep·e·ti·tion \,rep-ə-'tish-ən\ *n* [L *repetition-, repetitio,* fr. *repetitus,* pp. of *repetere* to repeat] (1526) **1** : the act or an instance of repeating or being repeated **2** : MENTION, RECITAL — **rep·e·ti·tion·al** \-'tish-nəl, -ən-²l\ *adj*

rep·e·ti·tious \-'tish-əs\ *adj* (1675) : characterized or marked by repetition; *esp* : tediously repeating — **rep·e·ti·tious·ly** *adv* — **rep·e·ti·tious·ness** *n*

re·pet·i·tive \ri-'pet-ət-iv\ *adj* (1839) **1** : containing repetition : REPEATING **2** : REPETITIOUS — **re·pet·i·tive·ly** *adv* — **re·pet·i·tive·ness** *n*

re·pine \ri-'pīn\ *vi* (1530) **1** : to feel or express dejection or discontent **2** : to long for something — **re·pin·er** *n*

re·place \ri-'plās\ *vt* (1595) **1** : to restore to a former place or position ⟨~ cards in a file⟩ **2** : to take the place of esp. as a substitute or successor **3** : to put something new in the place of ⟨~ a worn carpet⟩ — **re·place·able** \-'plā-sə-bəl\ *adj* — **re·plac·er** *n*

syn REPLACE, DISPLACE, SUPPLANT, SUPERSEDE mean to put out of a usual or proper place or into the place of another. REPLACE implies a filling of a place once occupied by something lost, destroyed, or no longer usable or adequate; DISPLACE implies an ousting or dislodging preceding a replacing; SUPPLANT implies either a dispossessing or usurping of another's place, possessions, or privileges or an uprooting of something and its replacement with something else; SUPERSEDE implies replacing a person or thing that has become superannuated, obsolete, or otherwise inferior.

re·place·ment \ri-'plā-smənt\ *n* (1790) **1** : the action or process of replacing : the state of being replaced : SUBSTITUTION **2** : something that replaces; *esp* : an individual assigned to a military unit to replace a loss or complete a quota

re·plant \(')rē-'plant\ *vt* (1575) **1** : to plant again or anew **2** : to provide with new plants **3** : to subject to replantation

Every dictionary shows the spelling, word division, and meaning or meanings of each word listed. A good standard desk dictionary also gives the part of speech of the word, its origins, the ways in which it is used, and certain of the irregular

Word origins help with understanding the meaning of a main entry.

Run-on entries list words that are derived from the main entry.

Different entries that are spelled the same way are indicated by numbers.

Plurals of nouns are given when the main entry's plural is formed irregularly.

Example phrases show how the main entry is commonly used.

Pronunciation guides are handy charts that explain pronunciation symbols.

re·plan·ta·tion \,rē-(,)plan-'tā-shən\ n (1870) : reattachment or reinsertion of a bodily part (as a limb or tooth) after separation from the body
¹re·play \(')rē-'plā\ vt (1884) : to play again or over
²re·play \'rē-,plā\ n (1895) 1 a : an act or instance of replaying b : the playing of a tape (as a videotape) 2 : REPETITION, REENACTMENT ⟨don . . . . . . of our old mistakes⟩
re·plead·er \(')rē-'plēd-ər\ [replead (to plead again) + -er (as in misnomer)] (1607) 1 : a second legal pleading 2 : the right of pleading again granted usu. when the issue raised is immaterial or insufficient
re·plen·ish \ri-'plen-ish\ vb [ME replenisshen, fr. MF repleniss-, stem of replenir to fill, fr. OF, fr. re- + plein full, fr. L plenus — more at FULL] vt (14c) 1 a : to fill with persons or animals : STOCK b archaic : to supply fully : PERFECT c : to fill with inspiration or power : NOURISH 2 a : to fill or build up again ⟨~ed his glass⟩ b : to make good : RE-PLACE ~ vi : to become full : fill up again — re·plen·ish·able \-ə-bəl\ adj — re·plen·ish·er n — re·plen·ish·ment \-ish-mənt\ n
re·plete \ri-'plēt\ adj [ME, fr. MF & L; MF replet, fr. L repletus, pp. of replēre to fill up, fr. re- + plēre to fill — more at FULL] (14c) 1 : fully or abundantly provided or filled ⟨a book ~ with . . . delicious details —William Safire⟩ 2 a : abundantly fed b : FAT, STOUT 3 : COMPLETE syn see FULL — re·plete·ness n
re·ple·tion \ri-'plē-shən\ n (14c) 1 : the act of eating to excess : the state of being fed to excess : SURFEIT 2 : the condition of being filled up or overcrowded 3 : fulfillment of a need or desire : SATISFACTION
¹re·plev·in \ri-'plev-ən\ n [ME, fr. AF replevine, fr. replevir to give security, fr. OF, fr. re- + plevir to pledge, fr. (assumed) LL plebere] (15c) 1 : the recovery by a person of goods or chattels claimed to be wrongfully taken or detained upon the person's giving security to try the matter in court and return the goods if defeated in the action 2 : the writ or the common-law action whereby goods and chattels are replevied
²replevin vt (1678) : REPLEVY
¹re·plevy \ri-'plev-ē\ n, pl re·plev·ies [ME, fr. AF replevir, v.] (15c) : REPLEVIN
²replevy vt re·plev·ied; re·plevy·ing (1596) : to take or get back by a writ for replevin — re·plevi·able \-ē-ə-bəl\ adj
rep·li·ca \'rep-li-kə\ n [It, repetition, fr. replicare to repeat, fr. LL, fr. L, to fold back — more at REPLY] (1852) 1 : a close reproduction or facsimile esp. by the maker of the original 2 : COPY, DUPLICATE syn see REPRODUCTION
rep·li·case \'rep-li-,kās, -,kāz\ n [replication + -ase] (1963) : a polymerase that promotes synthesis of a particular RNA in the presence of a template of RNA
¹rep·li·cate \'rep-lə-,kāt\ vb -cat·ed; -cat·ing [LL replicatus, pp. of replicare] vt (1607) : DUPLICATE, REPEAT ⟨~ a statistical experiment⟩ ~ vi : to undergo replication : produce a replica of itself ⟨virus particles replicating in cells⟩
²replicate \-li-kət\ adj (1922) : MANIFOLD, REPEATED
³rep·li·cate \-li-kət\ n (1929) : one of several identical experiments, procedures, or samples
rep·li·ca·tion \,rep-lə-'kā-shən\ n (14c) 1 a : ANSWER, REPLY b (1) : an answer to a reply : REJOINDER (2) : a plaintiff's reply to a defendant's plea, answer, or counterclaim 2 : ECHO, REVERBERATION 3 a : COPY, REPRODUCTION b : the action or process of reproducing 4 : performance of an experiment or procedure more than once; esp : systematic or random repetition of agricultural test rows or plats to reduce error
rep·li·ca·tive \'rep-li-,kāt-iv\ adj (ca. 1890) : of, relating to, involved in, or characterized by replication ⟨the ~ form of tobacco mosaic virus⟩
rep·li·con \'rep-li-,kän\ n [replicate + ²-on] (1963) : a linear or circular section of DNA or RNA which replicates sequentially as a unit
¹re·ply \ri-'plī\ vb re·plied; re·ply·ing [ME replien, fr. MF replier to fold again, fr. L replicare to fold back, fr. re- + plicare to fold — more at PLY] vi (14c) 1 a : to respond in words or writing b : ECHO, RESOUND c : to make a legal replication 2 : to do something in response; specif : to return gunfire or an attack ~ vt : to give as an answer syn see ANSWER — re·pli·er \-'plī(-ə)r\ n
²reply n, pl replies (1560) 1 : something said, written, or done in answer or response 2 : REPLICATION 1b(2)
re·po \'rē-,pō\ n, pl repos [by shortening & alter.] (1963) : REPURCHASE AGREEMENT
re·po·lar·iza·tion \,rē-,pō-lə-rə-'zā-shən\ n (1958) : polarization of a muscle fiber, cell, or membrane following depolarization — re·po·lar·ize \(')rē-'pō-lə-,rīz\ vb
¹re·port \ri-'pō(ə)rt, -'pò(ə)rt\ n [ME, fr. MF, fr. OF, fr. reporter to report, fr. L reportare, fr. re- + portare to carry — more at FARE] (14c) 1 a : common talk or an account spread by common talk : RUMOR b : quality of reputation ⟨a witness of good ~⟩ 2 a : a usu. detailed account or statement ⟨a news ~⟩ b : an account or statement of a judicial opinion or decision c : a usu. formal record of the proceedings of a meeting or session 3 : an explosive noise — on report : subject to disciplinary action
²report vt (14c) 1 a : to give an account of : RELATE b : to describe as being in a specified state ⟨~ed him much improved⟩ 2 a : to serve as carrier of (a message) b : to relate the words or sense of (something said) c : to make a written record or summary of d (1) : to watch for and write about the newsworthy aspects or developments of : COVER (2) : to prepare or present an account of for broadcast 3 a (1) : to give a formal or official account or statement of ⟨the treasurer ~ed a balance of ten dollars⟩ (2) : to return or present (a matter referred for consideration) with conclusions or recommendations b : to announce or relate as the result of investigation ⟨~ed no sign of disease⟩ c : to announce the presence, arrival, or sighting of d : to make known to the proper authorities ⟨~ a fire⟩ e : to make a charge of misconduct against ~ vi 1 a : to give an account : TELL b : to present oneself c : to account for oneself ⟨~ed sick on Friday⟩ 2 : to

\ə\ abut \ᵊ\ kitten, F table \ər\ further \a\ ash \ā\ ace \ä\ cot, cart
\aů\ out \ch\ chin \e\ bet \ē\ easy \g\ go \i\ hit \ī\ ice \j\ job
\ŋ\ sing \ō\ go \ò\ law \òi\ boy \th\ thin \t̲h̲\ the \ü\ loot \ů\ foot
\y\ yet \zh\ vision \à, ᵏ, ⁿ, œ, œ̄, ue, ūe, ᴇ̄\ see Guide to Pronunciation

forms. By permission. From *Webster's Ninth New College Dictionary,* copyright © 1986 by Merriam-Webster, Inc., Springfield, Massachusetts, publishers of the Merriam-Webster dictionaries.

gluiest). In addition, the dictionary helps you determine whether a word should be capitalized.

Determining Capitalization and Noun Plurals. The dictionary is an important source for capitalization and noun plurals. Suppose you are writing advertising copy for a sale of women's bathing suits—one-piece, skirted, and bikini types. You happen to know that Bikini is an *atoll* (a coral reef surrounding a lagoon) of the Marshall Islands, so you think you should capitalize the word. You check to make sure.

As you open the dictionary, you recall that each word entry is printed in small letters unless the word almost always, or more often than not, begins with a capital letter. Therefore, when you see *bikini* and read the definition, you know that the word, as you are using it, does *not* begin with a capital letter. The main part of your dictionary will help you with capitalization. You may also get further help from the rules for capitalization in the dictionary reference section.

The dictionary supplies any out-of-the-ordinary plural forms. It does not show most regular plurals—those formed by adding *s* or *es* or by changing a final *y* to *i* and adding *es*. If you need to know the plural of *stadium*, for example, you would look in the dictionary and see this information after that word: "*n, pl* **stadia** or **stadi•ums.**" And if it is the plural of *brother-in-law* that bothers you, you would find after that word: "*n, pl* **broth•ers-in-law.**"

Following the Pronunciation Guide. As we have said, not all dictionaries agree on preferred pronunciations. Since the standard of English pronunciation is based on the usage that prevails among educated people, this collective usage is hard to measure. When a word has more than one pronunciation, the "preferred" pronunciation is generally the first one listed. In one dictionary you may find two pronunciations for *lever:* 'lev-ər, 'lē-vər. In another you may find the opposite arrangement. Thus it is essential that you know how your dictionary denotes pronunciation.

Each dictionary offers a pronunciation guide that explains the use of stress marks (') (,) for accented syllables and the meaning of the vowel and consonant symbols that stand for all the sounds in our language. This pronunciation guide usually appears at the front of the dictionary. To help users quickly find the meanings of these symbols, most dictionaries offer a short list of the most frequently used symbols at the bottom of every two-page spread:

\ə\ **abut** \ᵊ\ **kitten,** F **table** \ər\ **further** \a\ **ash** \ā\ **ace** \ä\ **cot, cart** \au̇\ **out** \ch\ **chin** \e\ **bet** \ē\ **easy** \g\ **go** \i\ **hit** \ī\ **ice** \j\ **job** \ŋ\ **sing** \ō\ **go** \ȯ\ **law** \ȯi\ **boy** \th\ **thin** \t̲h̲\ **the** \ü\ **loot** \u̇\ **foot** \y\ **yet** \zh\ **vision** \à, k̲, ⁿ, œ, ꭤ̄, ue, u̅e, ᴧ\ *see* Guide to Pronunciation

Assume that you want to know how to pronounce the noun *datum*. Is the *a* long (as in *ace, ape, cape*), or is it short (as in *cap, at, happy*)? By referring to the mark above the vowel and then checking the handy guide at the bottom of the page, you would find that the *a* has the sound of the long *a*, as in *ace*.

Understanding the Explanatory Notes. To save you time and promote accuracy, study the explanatory notes before you use your dictionary. These notes explain the different typefaces and labels, the significant symbols and punctuation, and the other means by which a dictionary can achieve compactness. Take just one example, that of word division.

Suppose you want to know if the noun *goodwill* is one word, two words, or a hyphenated word. When you look it up, you see *good•will.* The explanatory notes tell you that a centered period denotes a syllable break only; therefore, *goodwill* is one word. If you looked up the adjective *self-addressed,* you would find *self-ad•dressed.* This word, then, is hyphenated after *self* and syllabicated after the hyphen and after *ad*.

Knowing the Abbreviations and Symbols. So much information must be packed into a dictionary that abbreviations and symbols frequently are necessary. To get full use of your dictionary, you should read and know where to find the explanations of these abbreviations and symbols. For example, it is important for you to know that *obs* stands for *obsolete,* which means that the word or the meaning listed is no longer in current usage. Knowing the abbreviations for the parts of speech—*n., v., adj., adv.,* and so on—may save you from making embarrassing errors when you speak and write.

Although you need not memorize all the abbreviations, you should learn those most commonly used. You should also know where to find the meanings of those used less often.

Finding Synonyms. Your writing will be more interesting if you can use a varied supply of words. To do so, you will frequently have to use synonyms.

A synonym is a word that has the same or nearly the same meaning as another word. Although a dictionary is not primarily a book of synonyms (like a synonym dictionary or a thesaurus), it does offer synonyms for some words. Therefore, when you have a synonym problem, you ordinarily reach first for that good old reliable reference, the dictionary. Suppose you are writing a memo recommending a "new plan." Since you have already used the word *new* twice, you don't want to repeat it a third time. Looking in a dictionary, you might find these four substitutes listed: *novel, modern, fresh, original.* For a more detailed list of synonyms, see a thesaurus or a synonym dictionary.

The Thesaurus

A thesaurus is a collection of words and phrases arranged according to ideas. The function that it serves is different from that of a dictionary. A dictionary gives the meaning of the word that one has in mind. A thesaurus enables one to find the best word with which to express an idea one has in mind.

In other words, a thesaurus goes one step further than a dictionary. In using the dictionary or a book of synonyms, you must have at least one word in mind; in using a thesaurus, you can start with a general idea from which comes one word that will start you on the hunt for the exact word you need.

Suppose, for example, that you want to change your job and job location. You know very little about the area to which you want to move. To find out what businesses are there, you decide to write to the local chamber of commerce. When writing the letter, you find that you are using the word *employment* so often that your language sounds repetitious. So you turn to a thesaurus for help.

A thesaurus usually gives three types of information about a word: which part of speech it is, its definition(s), and synonyms. Sometimes it will even give you an example of how the word is used in a phrase or sentence. When you look up the noun *employment* in a thesaurus, you will find something like this:

employment   *noun*

1. The act of employing for wages: *investigated the company's methods of employment.*
2. The act of putting into play.
3. The condition of being put to use.
4. A specific use.
5. The state of being employed: *No person in our employment will betray trade secrets.*
6. Activity pursued as a livelihood.

1. **Syns:** engagement, engaging, hire, hiring.
2. EXERCISE *noun*.
3. DUTY.
4. APPLICATION.
5. **Syns:** employ, hire.

6. BUSINESS.*

You can readily see that definition 1 and its synonyms are helpful. Using *engaging* or *hiring* at times instead of *employment* in your letter is an improvement in style. However, you would like to have even more words to use than *employment* and its synonyms, and you would like to use the word in a slightly different context. Therefore, you look up the word *job* in a thesaurus and you find something like this:

job   *noun*

1. Activity pursued as a livelihood.
2. A post of employment.
3. The proper activity of a person or thing.
4. A piece of work that has been assigned.
5. A difficult or tedious undertaking.

1. BUSINESS.
2. POSITION *noun*.
3. FUNCTION *noun*.
4. TASK *noun*.
5. TASK *noun*.*

* By permission. From *Roget's II: The New Thesaurus*, copyright © 1980 by Houghton Mifflin Company, Boston, Massachusetts.

Now you have several more words that you can use to help your letter sound less redundant and boring. You can use *business, position, function,* and/or *task* as well as *job.*

Other References

Biographical and Geographical Names. Suppose you need some information about a famous person. For example, say you read or hear the name Thomas Edison and want to know more about him. For fast identification you might check the Biographical Names section of your dictionary and find under *Edison:* "Thomas Alva 1847–1931 Am. inventor." For more information you would check *Webster's Biographical Dictionary* (Merriam-Webster, Inc., Springfield, Massachusetts) or other comprehensive list of biographical names.

Have you ever been confused as to the pronunciation of faraway places and strange-sounding names? Suppose your boss asks you to make travel arrangements to Montreal and Beauport, Canada, and neither you nor your boss knows how to pronounce *Beauport.* Checking the Geographical Names section of your dictionary or a source such as *Wesbster's New Geographical Dictionary* (Merriam-Webster, Inc., Springfield, Massachusetts), you would learn that Beauport, pronounced 'bō-pərt, is a city in southern Quebec; it has a population of 55,339.

Abbreviations and Acronyms. Commonly used abbreviations such as *COD* (for cash on delivery) and *PBX* (for private branch exchange) are usually listed in standard desk dictionaries. To find the meaning of abbreviations that are not listed in your dictionary, refer to a reference such as *Abbreviations Dictionary, Sixth Expanded Edition,* by Ralph DeSola (American Elsevier Publishing Co., Inc., New York, 1981).

An acronym is a word formed from the initial letter (or letters) of other words. *Radar* is an acronym derived from the words "*ra*dio *d*etecting *a*nd *r*anging"; *sitcom* is formed from "*sit*uation *com*edy." To find the meaning of an acronym, see a reference such as *Acronyms, Initialisms, and Abbreviations Dictionary, Eighth Edition,* edited by Ellen T. Crowley (Gale Research Company, Detroit, Michigan, 1982).

Foreign Words and Phrases. Foreign terms often become popular in our language. For example, we often see the words *par avion* on some international mail. To understand what these words have to do with our mail, we need to know what *par avion* means. It means "by airplane"— that is, airmail. To find the meaning of a puzzling foreign term that is not listed in your dictionary, you should use a reference such as *The Dictionary of Foreign Phrases and Abbreviations, Third Edition,* translated and edited by Kevin Guinagh (Wilson Publishing Co., New York, 1982).

Style Manuals. Everyone who writes or types will occasionally require a style manual to answer the common (and uncommon) questions that arise in ordinary written communications. Should you use a period at the end of a polite request, or should you use a question mark? When do you spell numbers? When do you use numerals? How do you set up personal or confidential notations, mailing notations, and postscripts? The answers to these and many more questions can be found in a good style manual.

Among the style manuals available today are *The Gregg Reference Manual, Sixth Edition,* by William A. Sabin (Gregg Division, McGraw-Hill Book Company, New York, 1985); and *HOW: A Handbook for Office Workers, Fourth Edition,* by James Clark and Lyn Clark (Kent Publishing Company, Inc., Boston, Massachusetts, 1985).

Word Division Manuals. Like the users of style manuals, everyone who writes or types documents will occasionally need some quick information. That information might be the spelling of a word without its definition or the proper syllabication or end-of-line division. The answers to these questions can be found in a good word division manual like *20,000 + Words* by Charles Zoubek, Gregg Condon, and Louis Leslie (Gregg Division, McGraw-Hill Book Company, New York, 1986).

COMMUNICATION LABORATORY

APPLICATION EXERCISES

A. Do you really know the exact order of the letters of the alphabet? In your dictionary, locate the following 15 words, taking each one in the sequence shown. Note the exact time you start your search for the words and the exact time you finish.

1. computation	6. fiscal	11. consolidate
2. expenditure	7. executive	12. submission
3. envelope	8. writ	13. insurance
4. amendment	9. clause	14. courteous
5. truly	10. computer	15. monitor

How many minutes did you take? If you took more than five minutes, you should practice the alphabetic sequence.

B. Now write the words listed in Exercise A in alphabetic order, without consulting a dictionary.

C. The words below and on the top of the next page are found on consecutive pages of a dictionary. Without using a dictionary, write them in alphabetic order. Note your starting and finishing times. How long did it take?

1. manufacture	4. manual	7. marmalade
2. maple	5. manor	8. marigold
3. market	6. masonry	9. marriage

10. mankind	13. margarine	16. maroon
11. mariner	14. mantel	17. marry
12. manner	15. marrow	18. maritime

D. Several of the following words are misspelled, and a few are spelled correctly. Rewrite the misspelled words as they should be spelled.

1. accamadate	6. message
2. receive	7. libary
3. ninety	8. prefered
4. truely	9. cieling
5. servise	10. communication

E. The following words were used in this unit. If you are not already familiar with them, try to guess their meaning from the context of the sentences in which they are used. Then check your guesses in the dictionary.

1. accomplished	4. significant
2. standard	5. function
3. superlative	6. repetitious

F. Here are ten common words. You should know how to break them down into syllables. Without consulting your dictionary, indicate all syllable divisions for each word. In words of more than one syllable, place a primary stress mark (') *before* the accented syllable. Check your decisions in the dictionary.

1. reference	6. insurance
2. impossible	7. contract
3. service	8. desirable
4. opportune	9. table
5. primary	10. frequent

COMMUNICATING FOR RESULTS

Using the Dictionary. Your supervisor leaves a note on your desk. In the note are several abbreviations and acronyms. Use your dictionary to find the meaning of each one.

As you know, later this year we will participate in state computer shows throughout the country—in CA, NC, TN, OK, MI, NJ, VT, and FL. For each meeting I would like you to ship a min. of 600 flyers that we have printed for various societies and organizations, especially the latest journals for the AMA, ANA, NEA, LWV, and NCAA.

Package the samples in boxes that can withstand NTP.

Make sure the boxes arrive five days bef. each show.

U · N · I · T

9 Learning the Correct Spelling

One of the keys to successful communication is correct spelling. In business writing a misspelled word can detract the reader from the content of the message and cause misunderstanding. Incorrect spelling may also cause embarrassment because it lowers the writer's image in the reader's mind. Proper spelling, therefore, is basic to effective communication.

What spelling skills are needed to communicate effectively? How can a person learn to become a good speller? The purpose of this unit is to help you gain those skills needed to spell correctly as you write.

To become a good speller, you should be able to spell automatically those words used frequently in business writing. Your basic spelling vocabulary should include some of those "tricky" words that often cause problems—those that are used frequently enough to warrant your memorizing them.

You should also have an awareness of the basic spelling rules commonly used in our language. These rules will help you distinguish among common confusions.

Finally, you should have a knowledge of the common spellings of word beginnings and commonly used secondary sounds. Then you can use your dictionary effectively to locate the spellings of words you do not readily know.

In this unit the following three-step process will be your basis for study to improve your spelling of business vocabulary: (1) memorizing a basic vocabulary, (2) reviewing important spelling rules, and (3) learning the various spellings of word beginnings and frequently used secondary sounds.

Mastery of a Basic "50"

Even if most commonly used words do not cause you any spelling difficulties, there may be a few tricky ones that do. Some of these tricky words, however, are so frequently used in business writing that you should master their spelling for your minimum vocabulary.

Double-Letter Combinations. Some words are misspelled because one or more of their double-letter combinations are not written in their entirety. Study the following words and note that each word has *two* or more sets of double letters.

accommodation   occurring
bookkeeper   succeeded
committee   embarrassing

Note the single set of double letters in the following words:

occasional   proceedings
questionnaire   dissatisfaction
offered   professor
recommendation

One Word or Two Words? Some words are misspelled because they are written as separate words instead of as a single word; other words are misspelled because the reverse is true.

Single Words	Separate Words
cannot	all right
nevertheless	home owner
percent	a lot

EDITING PRACTICE 1

Use your editing skill to complete this Practice exercise. In each of the following sentences, select the correct spelling of the words shown in parentheses.

1. Can you (accamadate, accommodate, acomodate) another guest?
2. We (can not, cannot) attend the meeting next week.
3. We understand your (disatisfaction, dissatisfaction) with our product.
4. We have had no (occasion, ocassion) to distrust our attorney.
5. What (per cent, purcent, percent) of total sales does this represent?
6. The only (profesor, professor, proffesor) I disliked was fired.
7. When do you plan to mail the (questionnairre, questionnaire)?
8. They (offerred, offered) more than I ever expected.

Dropped Letters or Sounds. Some words are misspelled because letters or syllables in the words are omitted. Such words often include the following:

convenient	(*not* convient)	thorough	(*not* through)
sincerely	(*not* sincerly)	Wednesday	(*not* Wenesday)
interest	(*not* intrest)	mortgage	(*not* morgage)
knowledge	(*not* knowlege)	bankruptcy	(*not* bankrupcy)
column	(*not* colum)	acquire	(*not* aquire)
manufacturers	(*not* manufacters)	ninety	(*not* ninty)
guarantee	(*not* garantee)	library	(*not* liberry)
February	(*not* Febuary)		

EDITING PRACTICE 2

Select the correct spelling of the words shown in parentheses.

1. We will (acquire, acqire, acwire) another postage meter machine.
2. The company is ready to file for (bankrupcy, bankruptcy) at present.
3. It is not (convenient, convient) for us to write today.
4. We start manufacturing this product in (Febuary, February).
5. We drove (ninty, ninety) miles to tour the new convention center.
6. We had no (nowledge, knowlege, knowledge) of your difficulties.
7. Can you meet with me on (Wensday, Wednesday, Wenesday)?
8. We are glad you have an (interest, intrest) in this project.

Additional Letters. Sometimes words are misspelled because letters are added. Here are some words commonly misspelled for this reason.

realty	(*not* reality)
usable	(*not* useable)
privilege	(*not* priviledge)
regarding	(*not* reguarding)
similar	(*not* similiar)
ninth	(*not* nineth)

Changed Letters. Words are also misspelled because one vowel is substituted for another or letters are *transposed* (reversed). Some words commonly misspelled because of changed letters are shown below.

separate	(*not* seperate)
superintendent	(*not* superintendant)
likelihood	(*not* likelyhood)
congratulations	(*not* congradulations)
describe	(*not* discribe)
definite	(*not* definate)
currency	(*not* currancy)
grateful	(*not* greatful)
finally	(*not* finely)
verify	(*not* varify)

EDITING PRACTICE 3

Select the correct spelling of the words shown in parentheses.

1. (Congradulations, Congratulations) are in order, don't you think?
2. We have a (definite, definate) commitment from the company.
3. Is there any (likelyhood, likelihood) that you will leave?
4. I will be most (greatful, grateful) for any help you can give.
5. We are (privileged, priviledged) to have you on our side.
6. We contacted our (realty, reality) company today.
7. The new machine is not at all (useable, usable).
8. Can you telephone the (superintendent, superintendant) today?

**Three Basic
Spelling Rules**

There are many spelling rules that can help you improve your spelling. Only three rules are discussed in this unit because they are the ones that can be applied most consistently. These three basic rules do have some exceptions, but they are few, as you will see. Whenever you doubt the spelling of any of these words, be sure to consult a dictionary.

IE or *EI*? Generally speaking, use the *ie* combination to represent the sound of long *e* (the sound in *meet*).

chief	yield	piece
field	niece	grief
believe	thief	pierce

EXCEPTIONS: either, neither, weird, seize, leisure.

After *c*, however, use the *ei* combination.

receive	conceit	deceit
ceiling	receipt	deceive

EXCEPTION: financier

The *ei* is also used when the combination is sounded like long *a* (the sound in *may*).

weigh	freight	vein
neighbor	their	heir
veil	sleigh	eight

EDITING PRACTICE 4

Use *ie* or *ei* to complete the correct spelling of the words in the following sentences.

1. Did you get the rec__pt for the repair work?
2. We did not w__gh the package before mailing it.
3. Mr. Jones is our n__ghbor on the left.
4. I cannot bel__ve you are correct.
5. How much did your stock y__ld?
6. N__ther he nor she is correct.
7. What f__ld of work are you in?
8. Do not try to dec__ve the owner of the business.

Double the Final Consonant. When adding an ending to a one-syllable word ending in a consonant, double the final consonant if it is *preceded* and *followed* by a single vowel.

ship + ed	shipped		ban + ed	banned
bag + age	baggage		trim + est	trimmest
plan + ing	planning		wrap + er	wrapper

EXCEPTION: The final consonant of a word ending in *x* or *w* is not doubled.

tax + ed   taxed   saw + ing   sawing
wax + ing   waxing   bow + ed   bowed

Drop the *E* or Keep the *E*? Words that end in silent *e* usually drop the *e* before an ending that begins with a vowel (such as *able* or *ing*).

desire + able   desirable   use + ag   usage
decorate + or   decorator   advise + ing   advising
enclose + ure   enclosure

EXCEPTIONS:

shoe + ing   shoeing   acre + age   acreage
mile + age   mileage   eye + ing   eyeing
dye + ing   dyeing

When adding an ending that begins with a consonant (such as *ful* or *ment*), retain the silent *e*.

entire + ty   entirety   cease + less   ceaseless
use + ful   useful   bare + ly   barely
state + ment   statement   tire + less   tireless
gentle + ness   gentleness   absolute + ly   absolutely

EXCEPTIONS:

wise + dom   wisdom   acknowledge + ment   acknowledgment
whole + ly   wholly   judge + ment   judgment

EDITING PRACTICE 5

Select the correct spelling of the words shown in parentheses.

1. His (judgement, judgment) is usually correct.
2. It would not be (adviseable, advisable) to make this investment now.
3. Is the work (absolutely, absolutly) necessary at this time?
4. Jean was (holely, wholely, wholly) correct in this matter.
5. I will be (adviseing, advising) you regarding your investment.

Spellings of Common Sounds

All the words that may cause you spelling difficulties are listed in your dictionary. Even though these words are included in the dictionary, they may not be found easily because many sounds have a variety of spellings. Thus the business writer who is not familiar with these spellings will not know where to look in the dictionary.

By learning the various spellings for commonly used word sounds, you can become a better speller. Your dictionary will become a more valuable tool to help you locate the correct spelling of all the words you use. This section focuses on the spellings of commonly used word sounds that appear at the beginning or in the middle of words.

Double Letters. Sometimes certain consonant sounds are expressed with single letters; other times these same sounds are expressed with double letters. In looking up words in your dictionary, remember that a consonant sound may be expressed with either a single letter or a double one. Study the following examples:

Single Consonant	Double Consonant
apologize	appoint
inoculate	innocent
imitate	immediate
elate	ellipse
acoustic	accordion
operation	opposite
melody	mellow
galoshes	gallon
deference	deferred

Vowel Variations. Words are often misspelled because they are mispronounced. Word beginnings that have identical consonant sounds but different vowel sounds fall into this category. When trying to locate such words in the dictionary, keep in mind the possibility that the word may be spelled with a vowel other than the one you have in mind. Notice, for example, the similarity within the following groups.

des	des/cription	mon	mon/ey
dis	dis/tribute	mun	mun/dane
fer	fer/ocious	per	per/suade
for	for/eign	pur	pur/sue
fur	fur/lough	pre	pre/cision
def	def/inite	in	in/sure
dif	dif/ferent	en	en/large
dev	dev/astate	un	un/pleasant
div	div/idend	im	im/prove
men	men/ace	em	em/ploy
min	min/eral		

EDITING PRACTICE 6

Select the correct spelling of the words shown in parentheses. Use your dictionary, if necessary, to locate the correct spelling.

1. We recently established an (indowment, endowment) fund in his name.
2. This site is more (desirable, desireable, disireable) for us.
3. What is your legal (oppinion, opinion) regarding this case?

4. Is your decision based on (realty, reality) or supposition?
5. We intend to (persue, pursue) this matter to its limit.
6. I was (devastated, devestated) by the sad news.
7. I am not allowed to (devulge, divulge) that kind of information.

Common Beginning Sounds. To locate words in the dictionary, you must know the different possible spellings for the common sounds used at the beginning of words—that is, the most common first and second sounds. See below and page 89 for a list of these sounds and their spellings.

SOUND	SPELLINGS	SOUND	SPELLINGS	SOUND	SPELLINGS
a	a (*a*bout)	e	ae (*ae*sthetic)	i	e (*e*nlist)
	ai (pl*ai*d)		e (*e*stimate)		i (*i*diom)
	au (l*au*gh)		ea (br*ea*kfast)		ie (s*ie*ve)
	ea (h*ea*rt)		ei (h*ei*fer)		y (m*y*stery)
			eo (l*eo*pard)		
ā	a (*a*ble)		ie (fr*ie*nd)	ī	ai (*ai*sle)
	ai (*ai*lment)				eigh (sl*eigh*t)
	au (g*au*ge)	ē	ae (*ae*on)		i (*i*dentical)
	ea (br*ea*k)		e (*e*gotist)		ie (l*ie*)
	ei (n*ei*ghbor)		ee (st*ee*l)		igh (fl*igh*t)
	eigh (sl*eigh*)		ei (perc*ei*ve)		y (h*y*peractive)
			eo (p*eo*ple)		
ä	a (f*a*ther)		i (m*a*chine)	j	dg (bu*dg*et)
	eau (bur*eau*cracy)		ie (rel*ie*ve)		g (*g*enerate)
	o (*o*bligation)				gg (exa*gg*erate)
		er	ar (li*ar*)		j (in*j*ure)
ak	ac (*ac*robat)		ear (*ear*nest)		
	acc (*acc*laim)		er (*er*osion)	k	c (*c*riminal)
	ack (*ack*nowledge)		err (*err*oneous)		cc (oc*c*ur)
	acq (*acq*uire)		ir (*ir*ksome)		ch (*ch*emistry)
	aq (*aq*ueduct)		or (w*or*thless)		k (*k*imono)
			our (j*our*nal)		q (l*iq*uidation)
är	ar (*ar*ea)		ur (*ur*gency)		
	aer (*aer*ial)			m	lm (ca*lm*)
	air (*air*port)	f	f (*f*easible)		m (*m*edicine)
			ff (e*ff*ective)		
as	as (*as*bestos)		gh (lau*gh*ter)	n	gn (*gn*arled)
	asc (*asc*end)		ph (*ph*otograph)		kn (*kn*itwear)
	ass (*ass*embly)				mn (*mn*emonic)
		g	g (*g*rievance)		n (*n*atural)
aw	aw (*aw*kward)		gh (*gh*etto)		pn (*pn*eumonic)
	au (*au*dience)		gu (*gu*arantee)		
	augh (t*augh*t)			o	o (*o*rdinary)
	ough (th*ough*t)	h	h (*h*oliday)		oa (b*oa*rd)
			wh (*wh*olesale)		

SOUND	SPELLINGS	SOUND	SPELLINGS
ō	eau (*beau*)	sh	ch (ma*ch*ine)
	o (n*o*table)		ci (spe*ci*al)
	oa (thr*oa*t)		s (*s*ure)
	oe (t*oe*)		sc (con*sc*ious)
	ou (s*ou*l)		sch (*sch*illing)
	ough (th*ough*)		se (nau*se*ous)
	ow (kn*ow*)		sh (*sh*ampoo)
			si (ten*si*on)
oi, oy	oi (f*oi*l)		ss (i*ss*ue)
	oy (env*oy*)		ti (par*ti*al)
o͞o	eu (man*eu*ver)	t	pt (*pt*omaine)
	ew (thr*ew*)		t (*t*arnish)
	ieu (ad*ieu*)		
	o (rem*o*ve)	u	u (*u*pper)
	oo (f*oo*lish)		
	ou (s*ou*)	ū	eau (b*eau*tiful)
	ough (thr*ough*)		eu (f*eu*d)
	u (r*u*le)		ew (p*ew*ter)
	ue (bl*ue*)		u (*u*seful)
	ui (fr*ui*t)		ue (c*ue*)
			yu (*yu*le)
ow	ou (pron*ou*nce)		
	ough (b*ough*)	w	o (ch*o*ir)
	ow (br*ow*se)		u (q*u*artile)
			w (*w*edding)
r	r (*r*elaxation)		wh (*wh*arf)
	rh (*rh*etoric)		
	wr (*wr*inkle)		
s	c (*c*ivil)		
	ps (*ps*ychology)		
	s (*s*table)		
	sc (*sc*enic)		
	ss (pe*ss*imist)		

EDITING PRACTICE 7

Use the preceding chart to find the various spellings for the sounds in parentheses. Then find the correct spelling in your dictionary, and rewrite each word.

1. Do you enjoy your study of (s)(i)chology?
2. I took the gift in l(oo) of cash.
3. I prefer a natural spray over the (ar)osol can.
4. That was a strange man(oo)ver on his part.

5. I walked up the (i)sle briskly.
6. Helga (ak)wired her accent in Norway.
7. She is a most con(sh)ien(sh)ous employee.
8. I always buy (n)eumatic tires.
9. I asked the butcher to w(a) the ham.
10. There was a great deal of ten(shun) in the office.

COMMUNICATION LABORATORY

APPLICATION EXERCISES

A. On a separate sheet of paper, write the correct spelling of any words misspelled in the following sentences. If a sentence does not contain a misspelled word, write *OK* on your paper.

1. Our account will acrue interest at the rate of 10 percent.
2. The accountant is hospitalized with numonia.
3. What information reguarding my automobile is necessary?
4. I was greatful for your assistance in handling the matter.
5. Mr. Nestle has innate physical skills.
6. When do you expect to recieve the merchandise?
7. We regret having to forclose on your property.
8. It is doutful that the report will be ready on time.

B. On a separate sheet of paper, provide the correct spellings for the sounds shown in parentheses. Then rewrite each word.

1. I loved that science fiction movie about mar(sh)ian life.
2. Did they include the fr(a)t charges in the price?
3. How large is the mor(g)age on your home?
4. Ms. Kline is pe(s)imistic about the potential of the new employee.
5. It is difficult to dec(e)ve the IRS.
6. The clerk complained about the (mun)otony of his job.
7. How much mil(e)ge did you accumulate on that delivery?
8. What amount was a(p)lied to my account?
9. The loss o(k)u(r)ed during last month's sale.
10. They were not given permission to proc(e)d with the purchase.
11. There were ni(n)ty applicants for the remaining homes.
12. It is a privile(j)e doing business with your firm.
13. We rec(e)ved your letter in today's mail.

14. We would like to (i)nlist your help with our overdue accounts.
15. We have a heavy a(j)enda this morning.

C. On a separate sheet of paper, correctly spell the underlined word in each of the following sentences.

1. Children should not loyter in the mall.
2. The story was highly egzagerated by the witness.
3. You heard a destorted view of the event, I am sorry to say.
4. The erban renewal project took most of the time at the meeting.
5. We were unable to excede the budgeted amount for the computer.
6. The dammage was greater than we expected.
7. The witness pergured himself at the trial.
8. Their pronounciation of the word was so unusual.
9. They have a color monitur for the computer.
10. Do they also have a modum for telecommunication?

D. Correct all the spelling errors you find in the following paragraph.

We excepted the offer we recieved from the comittee at the meeting this mourning. We must, however, reequest a larger ammount for our next bujet. The larger amount is needed because we must perchase severl new computors, at least two of which must have greater capacitys.

VOCABULARY AND SPELLING STUDIES

A. Some commonly used words may not be easily located in the dictionary because the spellings of their sounds do not follow usual spelling patterns. Look up in your dictionary the pronunciation and meaning of the following words:

1. quay
2. scenic
3. indictment
4. pneumatic
5. rendezvous
6. rhetoric

B. These words are often confused: *extent, extant, extinct; collision, collusion.* Explain the meaning of each.

C. To each of the following, add the ending pronounced *shun.*

1. frustra___
2. collec___
3. conven___
4. politi___
5. coer___
6. provi___

COMMUNICATING FOR RESULTS

Poor Speller. Assume that you work in a word processing center as a correspondence secretary. Most of your typing involves letters that are sent to customers. Another correspondence secretary with whom you work has the same reference initials as you. He is careless and a poor speller, and since he does not consult a dictionary, the letters he types are full of mistakes. This is the third time this week you have been blamed for spelling errors made by your coworker. What would you do to correct this situation?

U · N · I · T

10

Identifying the Right Word

An amazing number of words in the English language are confused because they sound alike or look alike but have different spellings and different meanings. Some words are pronounced exactly alike, as *great* (many, large) and *grate* (to grind; a part of a furnace). Some sound somewhat alike, as *respectively* (in the order given), *respectfully* (courteously), and *respectably* (in a conventionally correct manner). Others look somewhat alike. They may contain the same letters but in different order, as *liar* (a teller of untruths) and *lair* (an animal's den). One word may have one letter where the other has two, as *ad* (the shortened form of *advertisement*) and *add* (to increase). Or they may have other superficial resemblances, as *viable* (relevant) and *visible* (able to be seen).

How to Study Word Confusions

In this unit are groups of words that are often confused because they either sound or look exactly alike or sound or look similar. You will easily distinguish between these kinds of words if you will do the following:

1. Examine carefully how each word is spelled, noting whether the same letters occur but in different order, whether a letter is doubled in one word but not in another, and so on.
2. Learn how each word is pronounced. Consult the dictionary to be sure. Note the phonetic spelling, which indicates the correct sounds, together with the stress marks that tell you which syllables are to be accented.
3. Determine the part of speech of each word. This will save you time in locating the precise meaning in the dictionary. It is very important to do this when words are spelled alike, as *desert* (barren land) and *desert* (to abandon).
4. Study how the word is used in a sentence. This method of finding meaning from context often reveals the distinctions between words more easily than do dictionary definitions.
5. If you have any doubt about the meaning of a word, always look it up in a dictionary. Sift through the various meanings; become acquainted with the word's possibilities for use.
6. Make a habit of entering in your personal notebook any new group of words that are often confused. Head one section of your notebook "Word Confusions" and include brief definitions for each entry. Enter any sentences you find that illustrate how these words are used. Some students find it helpful to underscore the letters that are the keys to the differences in meaning of the words in a group; for example, a<u>cc</u>ept, ex<u>c</u>ept, ex<u>p</u>e<u>c</u>t.

Words Commonly Confused

The spelling or meaning of the following combinations of words are commonly confused. Study them carefully. Be sure to look up the pronunciation of any word that is unfamiliar.

accede (*v.*) To comply with. "We must *accede* to this customer's request."
exceed (*v.*) To surpass. "Our sales this quarter will *exceed* our projections."

accent (*n.*) A stress in speaking or writing. "Where is the *accent* in the word *profit*?" (*v.*) To stress; emphasize. "The manager's remarks *accented* the need to control expenses."
ascent (*n.*) A rising or climbing. "Her *ascent* in the department was swift because of her qualifications."
assent (*n.*) Agreement. "The customer's written *assent* is necessary before we can charge an account." (*v.*) To agree. "Did Ms. Mendoza *assent* to your request?"

accept (*v.*) To approve; receive with favor. "We *accept* your decision."
except (*prep.*) Other than. "All employees must work this Saturday *except* those with over ten years of service." (*v.*) To exclude. "We can *except* no one from the need to arrive at work on time."

expect (*v.*) To look forward to. "I *expect* our sales to increase soon."

all ready (*adj.*) Prepared. "The reports are *all ready* for the meeting."
already (*adv.*) By this time. "I have *already* met my quota."

advice (*n.*; rhymes with *ice*) A recommendation regarding a course of conduct. "Mr. Sims' *advice* will help your career."
advise (*v.*; rhymes with *skies*) To counsel. "What do you *advise* me to do about this overdue account?"

affect (*v.*) To influence. "How will the new procedures *affect* our budget?" (*v.*) To pretend. "He *affects* busyness and overwork."
effect (*v.*) To bring about. "We expect this new computerized system to *effect* an upturn in our business." (*n.*) A result. "What *effect* has the new word processing system had upon efficiency?"

altar (*n.*) Table used in worship. "The *altar* dominated the cathedral."
alter (*v.*) To change. "If we *alter* the schedule, our customers will be glad."

assistance (*n.*) Support. "Do you need *assistance* with the payroll?"
assistants (*n. pl.*) Those who help. "Our company president has three *assistants*."

bare (*adj.*) Uncovered. "This report looks *bare* without graphs and charts."
bear (*v.*) Carry. "She *bears* the responsibility for the entire department."
bear (*n.*) Large mammal. "The *bear* wandered freely in a protected part of the park."

capital (*adj.*) Chief; principal. "Carson City is the *capital* city of Nevada." (*n.*) The value of accumulated goods. "We used all our *capital* to start this company."
capitol (*n.*) The building in which a legislature meets; capitalized when it refers to the building in which the U.S. Congress meets. "Industry representatives will testify in the Capitol on August 4."

chews (*v.*) Masticates. "I noticed that our dog *chews* his food very well."
choose (*v.*) To select; to prefer. "We must *choose* a word processing system that will serve our needs."
chose (*v.*; past tense of *choose;* chōz) Selected. "You *chose* the best system."

cite (*v.*) To quote; to refer to. "She *cited* our poor delivery record."
site (*n.*) A location. "This is the new *site* for our company headquarters."
sight (*n.*) Vision. "Jane's well-kept ledgers are a *sight* to see." (*v.*) To see. "If all goes well, we will *sight* land tomorrow morning."

close (*v.*; klōz) To shut. "The office will *close* at noon tomorrow." (*n.*) The end. "We balance all accounts at the *close* of the business day."
close (*adj.*; klōs) Stuffy. "The air in this room is *close*." (*adj.*) Tight. "It will be a *close* fit, but the copy machine will go in that corner." (*adv.*) Near. "The water cooler is too *close* to my office."
clothes (*n.*) Wearing apparel. "Appropriate *clothes* should be worn in an office."
cloths (*n.*) Fabrics. "Are there any more *cloths* in the supply room?"

commence (*v.*) To begin. "We shall *commence* contract negotiations today."

comments (*n. pl.*) Remarks. "Your *comments* on our marketing problems are most helpful." (*v.*) To mark distinctly. "My supervisor always *comments* on my performance."

complement (*n.*) Something that completes. "Without a full *complement* of workers, we can't handle that contract." (*v.*) To make whole. "The new employees *complement* our staff nicely."
compliment (*n.*) A flattering remark. "A *compliment* for a job well done is most welcome." (*v.*) To express approval. "A wise supervisor always *compliments* good workers."

correspondence (*n.*) Letters. "We answer all *correspondence* immediately."
correspondents (*n. pl.*) Persons conducting correspondence or commercial relations. "Each of our sales *correspondents* works for five representatives."

council (*n.*) An assembly that deliberates. "An advisory *council* sets industry guidelines."
counsel (*n.*) Advice. "The company's legal staff provides management with good *counsel.*" (*v.*) To give advice, especially on important matters. "Our personnel department will *counsel* employees on career choices."
consul (*n.*) A government official who represents a nation in a foreign country. "If you need help in negotiating with companies in Germany, notify the American *consul* in Bonn."

defer (*v.*) To postpone. "May I *defer* my payment until next month?" To yield. "When it comes to a knowledge of procedures, I always *defer* to the older workers."
differ (*v.*) To disagree; to be unlike. "Successful salespeople often *differ* in their approach to a customer."

dense (*adj.*) Thick. "The *dense* smoke drove us from the building."
dents (*n. pl.*) Depressions in a surface. "This old file cabinet has a lot of *dents.*"

dependence (*n.*) Reliance; trust. "The company's *dependence* upon a single supplier frightened the purchasing department."
dependents (*n. pl.*) Persons who rely on others for support. "The tax withheld from your check will depend on the number of *dependents.*"

desert (*n.*; 'dez-ərt) Arid, barren land. "The new agricultural company hoped to make the *desert* bloom."
desert (*v.*; di-'zərt) To abandon. "This is a good financial plan, and we will not *desert* it." (*n.*; usually plural) Deserved reward or punishment. "He got his just *deserts* for being too greedy."
dessert (*n.*) A sweet course at the end of a meal. "We had chocolate cake for *dessert.*"

dye (*n.*) A stain or color. "Will this *dye* run when it is washed?" (*v.*) To stain or color. "I *dyed* this coat last month."
die (*n.*) A tool for molding or shaping. "We will need new *dies* if we change the product's design." One of a pair of dice. "One *die* is red." (*v.*) To cease living. "That tree will *die* unless it is fertilized."

formally (*adv.*) In a formal manner. "She has not *formally* accepted."
formerly (*adv.*) Previously. "He *formerly* worked for a competitor."

lead (*n.*; rhymes with *bed*) A heavy metal. "It took three people to lift that large *lead* pipe."
lead (*v.*; past *led*) To guide. "She will *lead* the company into new markets."
To guide. "She will *lead* the company into new markets."

loose (*adj.*) Unfastened; not compact. "The *loose* parts will get all mixed up." (*v.*) To set free. "Don't let the dog *loose*."
lose (*v.*) To mislay; to fail to win. "Please don't *lose* that important report."

patients (*n. pl.*) Persons under medical care. "The physician examined the *patients* carefully."
patience (*n.*) The quality of enduring without complaint. "If you have *patience*, you can work with and for anyone."

personal (*adj.*) Belonging to a particular person. "Never leave your *personal* belongings on the top of your desk."
personnel (*n.*) Staff of people. "All our *personnel* know how to use a desktop computer."

precede (*v.*) To go before. "My name should *precede* Ms. Castella's in the company telephone directory."
proceed (*v.*) To advance. "After the meeting in Denver, we will *proceed* to the conference in Seattle."

precedence (*n.*) Priority in time or rank. "That rush project takes *precedence* over everything else."
precedents (*n. pl.*) Established rules; things done that may serve as examples for later actions. "There are several *precedents* to guide us in this kind of sales campaign."

principle (*n.*) General truth. "The basic *principle* of finance does not change." Rule of conduct. "His company has always been guided by the highest *principles*."
principal (*adj.*) Chief. "Electronic computers are the company's *principal* product." A chief person or thing. "She is one of the *principals* in the company." Money on which interest is paid or income received. "We can spend the interest, but we cannot touch the *principal*." One who hires another to act for him or her. "An agent has power to make contracts for a *principal*."

reality (*n.*) That which is real. "The *reality* is that certain skills are more in demand."
realty (*n. and adj.*) Real estate. "Our *realty* company is looking for a new office site for us."

residence (*n.*) A house; dwelling place. "Is your *residence* close to where you work?"
residents (*n. pl.*) Those living in a place. "The *residents* of the apartment started a bowling league."

right (*adj.*) Correct. "After weeks of searching, he found the *right* job." (*n.*) Privilege. "You have the *right* to find a better job."

rite (*n.*) Ceremony. "We observe the *rite* of opening each meeting with the Pledge of Allegiance."

write (*v.*) To inscribe. "Please *write* your account number on each check."

stationary (*adj.*) Fixed in position. "A *stationary* lamp gives better light."

stationery (*n.*) Writing paper and envelopes. "Our company *stationery* was redesigned last year."

superintendence (*n.*) Management. "We work directly under the *superintendence* of a district manager."

superintendents (*n. pl.*) Supervisors. "The *superintendents* of our company's power plants spoke at the energy conference."

COMMUNICATION LABORATORY

APPLICATION EXERCISES

A. Since you have studied the meanings of the words most commonly confused, you should be able to apply these meanings correctly. Select from the list of words given here the appropriate words to insert in the blank spaces within the sentences. Write those words on a separate sheet of paper, using each word only one time.

accept–except	principal–principle	complement–compliment
advice–advise	already–all ready	formally–formerly

1. No one _____ Jack was opposed to the new organization plan.
2. Ms. Aarons _____ served as treasurer in our firm.
3. Mr. Pringle was _____ in the office when I arrived.
4. Your award was a distinct _____ to your ability.
5. What would you _____ Marie to do about her problem?
6. What amount is due on the _____ of your mortgage?
7. Are you _____ to go to the office reception?
8. This product is an excellent _____ to our other products.
9. The _____ of law that applies in this case is quite clear.
10. We cannot _____ the responsibility for the damage to your order.

B. Follow the instructions used in Exercise A.

assistants–assistance	dependence–dependents	precede–proceed
stationary–stationery	cite–site	desert–dessert

1. We cannot find a better _____ for the location of our business.
2. That was an excellent _____ you selected for the banquet.
3. What color ink have you selected for our letterhead _____?
4. We need your _____ to complete the report on time.
5. How many _____ are you claiming on your withholding tax form?
6. The president of the company has two _____ working in his office.
7. We cannot move the desk because it is _____.
8. The calculation of labor costs must _____ the writing of a letter.
9. He will _____ the law that applies in this case.
10. I hope you will not _____ the company now that it needs you.

C. Follow the instructions used in Exercise A.

residents–residence   accede–exceed   basis–bases
altar–alter   bare–bear   led–lead

1. We can only afford _____ necessities in our office now.
2. This is the _____ of our decision, as is evident in my report.
3. We find it impossible to _____ to the union demands.
4. We expect them to _____ their demands if we are to do so.
5. Mr. Kemp will _____ the company out of its troubled state.
6. Will your _____ be on State Street or Market Street?
7. The costs will certainly _____ the benefits we will receive.
8. Service and quality are the _____ of our success.
9. Who will _____ the cost of the changes is a problem to resolve.
10. Most of the _____ oppose an increase in taxes.

D. Follow the instructions used in Exercise A.

precedence–precedents   personnel–personal   affect–effect
comments–commence   council–counsel   patients–patience

1. We welcome your _____ on our plan for remodeling.
2. Our company will _____ a change in the policy immediately.
3. The company _____ will handle this legal matter for us.
4. Mr. Atkins is in charge of hiring new _____.
5. Higher costs always _____ the profits.
6. The accountant says that there are no _____ for the action.
7. We expect the construction to _____ next month.
8. The doctor had no _____ with Mrs. King and her problems.
9. The city _____ will discuss all the items on the agenda.
10. I went to Chicago with my family on _____ business last week.

COMMUNICATING FOR RESULTS

Using the (Right, Rite, Write) Word. The following sentences were taken from an office report. Rewrite the sentences, using correctly spelled words for those that have been used incorrectly or misspelled.

We must comments to investigate the rite cite for our new factory building. We have the necessary capitol to chose any location. Our dependents on your council is evident; we will altar any part of the plan you feel would benifit us.

More than ever before, job applicants today must have superior grammar skills, because employers are aware that an understanding of grammar provides an excellent basis for good writing, speaking, listening, and reading skills—skills that help businesses succeed.

This chapter will help you choose the correct words and put them together expressively and meaningfully, thereby enhancing your ability to communicate well and making you an attractive prospective employee. Given a situation that requires polished grammar skills, your mastery of the units in this chapter will enable you to do the following:

1. *Construct complete sentences that will describe your ideas fully.*

2. *Use verbs correctly to give your writing the proper direction.*

3. *Use nouns and pronouns precisely, so that who does what is always clear.*

4. *Choose the correct verb form to agree with any noun or pronoun so that your sentences are always easy to understand.*

5. *Select exact descriptive words—adjectives and adverbs that will convey your thoughts.*

6. *Use conjunctions and prepositions to join words clearly and correctly.*

U · N · I · T

11

An Overview of Grammar

If you have not already been exposed to word processing equipment, you may not be familiar with words such as *cursor, wraparound,* and *scroll.* These words are mysterious to those who have not had the opportunity to use a word processor. But those who have know that a *cursor* is only a blinking light on a television screen. *Wraparound* is simply the machine's ability to start a new line without being told to do so. And *scroll* is just a way of saying "turn the page."

The concepts behind this jargon, as you can quickly see, are not in any way mysterious or difficult to understand. These words are difficult to understand *only if they are unfamiliar.*

Likewise, the principles of grammar and punctuation are not difficult to understand. Some grammatical terms, however, may be unfamiliar. Others you may have heard of but may not fully understand. The best way to understand such jargon is simply to learn what the words mean—which, of course, is the goal of this introductory unit.

The Parts of Speech

The many thousands of different words that we use can be categorized into just eight groups, called the *parts of speech.* The parts of speech are:

1. nouns
2. pronouns
3. verbs
4. adjectives
5. adverbs
6. prepositions
7. conjunctions
8. interjections

Knowing the eight parts of speech will simplify your understanding of the rules of grammar and punctuation, so be sure to study the following pages carefully.

Nouns and Pronouns. The names of people, places, and things are called *nouns.*

PEOPLE:	manager	Ellen Rodriguez
	coach	Walter
	neighbor	Janet
	supervisor	Martin Strand

PLACES:	city	Dallas
	store	Route 22 Auto Mart
	state	Oregon
	county	Greene County
THINGS:	car	Buick
	television	Zenith
	bike	Schwinn

You can easily add hundreds of words to these lists because nouns are *very* commonly used. In fact, almost all sentences contain nouns.

Our *manager* bought a *car* at *Route 22 Auto Mart*.
Her *coach* borrowed her *bike*.
Greene County is where *Janet* lives.

Words that substitute for nouns are called *pronouns*.

Singular	Plural	Singular	Plural	Singular	Plural
I	we	me	us	my	our
you	you	you	you	your	your
he		him		his	
she	they	her	them	her	their
it		it		its	

In the following sentences, note how pronouns are used to replace nouns.

Beatrice went to the seminar with *James*.
She went to the seminar with *him*.

Hugh and Diane purchased the *property*.
They purchased *it*.

Remember that *pro* means "for," and you will be sure to remember that pronouns are substitutes *for nouns*.

Verbs. You may have heard verbs referred to as *action words*, because verbs do indeed indicate the motion or the activity of a sentence.

Patricia *signed* the check.
Mr. Lamont *is interviewing* applicants.
We *will be going* to Los Angeles tomorrow.

Besides showing action, however, verbs also show condition or state of being.

Jason *is* tired.

Ms. Vance *has been* away on a business trip.

I *am* the assistant director.

Verbs can be just a single word, or they can consist of several words.

Our company *has* a pool on the fourth floor. (*Has* is the verb in this sentence.)

Grace *has been swimming* during her lunch hours. (The verb is *has been swimming*.)

Arthur *should have been* here for this meeting. (The verb is *should have been*.)

Arthur *should have been asked* to this meeting. (The verb is *should have been asked*.)

CLASS PRACTICE 1

In this unit and in all the grammar, punctuation, and style units, Class Practice exercises are provided to help reinforce the principles you learn in each unit.

To test your skill in identifying nouns, pronouns, and verbs, label each word in parentheses in the following sentences *N*, *P*, or *V*. Use a separate sheet of paper.

1. The (supervisors) at the conference (rejected) the proposal after (they) discussed it.
2. My two assistants (have been working) on the (outline) for the report (they) are writing.
3. As you know, (she) and (I) already (have submitted) the manuscripts to our (editor in chief).
4. The suggestion (I) submitted to the committee (has been accepted), according to the (chairperson).
5. (She) and (Henry) (might be going) to the meeting; if (they) decide to attend, I will call your (office).

Now fill in a word for each blank (marked *a* and *b*) in the sentences below. Identify whether your choices are nouns, pronouns, or verbs.

6. Our ___*a*___ obviously ___*b*___ more money.
7. Please give ___*a*___ a copy of the summary sheet that I ___*b*___.
8. Alex ___*a*___ extra copies of the ___*b*___.
9. ___*a*___ retyped the entire ___*b*___.
10. Only ___*a*___ has returned the completed ___*b*___.

Adjectives. *Adjectives* are words that modify, describe, or define a noun or a pronoun. They tell what kind, which one, or how many. Note how adjectives change the descriptions of nouns in the following sentences.

The *first* draft was a *wordy, boring* proposal. (*First* tells which draft; *wordy* and *boring* describe the noun *proposal*.)

BetteJean is a *successful, creative* architect. (The adjectives *successful* and *creative* describe the noun *architect*.)

She is *successful* and *creative*. (Here, the adjectives *successful* and *creative* modify the pronoun *she*.)

Note how the italicized adjectives in the following phrases clarify or describe the nouns that they modify.

this company	*these* applicants
that agency	*those* groups
Mexican food	*New Jersey* politics
three books	*first* client
two-week vacation	*up-to-date* information

REMEMBER: Adjectives modify only nouns or pronouns. Now let's review another kind of modifier, the adverb.

Adverbs. Like adjectives, adverbs are also modifiers. But adverbs modify only adjectives, verbs, or other adverbs.

1. Adverbs modify adjectives:

   his *nearly* fatal accident (The adverb *nearly* modifies the adjective *fatal.*)

   a *fairly* long table (The adverb *fairly* modifies the adjective *long.*)

   her *obviously* expensive car (The adverb *obviously* modifies the adjective *expensive.*)

2. Adverbs modify verbs:

   Jack ran *quickly.* (The adverb *quickly* modifies the verb *ran.*)

   The committee *unanimously* approved the plan. (The adverb *unanimously* modifies the verb *approved.*)

3. Adverbs modify other adverbs:

   Jack ran *very* quickly. (The adverb *very* modifies the adverb *quickly.*)

   The committee *almost* unanimously approved the plan. (The adverb *almost* modifies the adverb *unanimously.*)

Perhaps you noticed that except for *very* and *almost,* all the adverbs above end in *ly.* Indeed, many adverbs are formed by adding *ly* to adjectives:

Adjective	Adverb
quiet	quietly
bad	badly
sudden	suddenly
careful	carefully

But there are others that do not end in *ly,* including *very, almost, never, here, there,* and many, many more.

To identify adverbs, remember that adverbs answer such questions as "How?" "When?" "Where?"

Put that carton *there.* (Where? There. *There* is an adverb.)

Joanne draws *beautifully.* (Draws how? Beautifully.)

Ms. Clemson will arrive *soon.* (Arrive when? Soon.)

CLASS PRACTICE 2

A. Identify the words in parentheses as either adjectives or adverbs.

1. Ms. Hamilton (quickly) reviewed the (four) résumés.
2. Leonard decided to open the (sealed) cartons and (carefully) checked their contents.
3. We need some (basic) information to complete our analysis; we expect to receive the data (soon).
4. Charles (obviously) objects to raising these (high) prices.
5. The (replacement) parts will be shipped (there) before Friday.

B. On a separate sheet of paper, rewrite the following sentences, filling in the blanks as you do so. Identify each of your fill-ins as an adjective or an adverb.

6. My assistant always submits _____ work.
7. My assistant always works _____.
8. Steven generally arrives _____.
9. All of us were _____ happy about Pamela's promotion.
10. We were considering buying a _____ printing machine.

Prepositions. Prepositions are words that connect and describe relationships. They include these very commonly used words:

in	to	for	about	except
by	from	with	above	between
of	after	before	behind	into
out	on	over	before	until

Prepositions are always used in prepositional phrases such as the following:

in the morning	in April
by the door	by Hills Department Store
of the owners	of Mrs. Henson
to the company	to Collins Chemical Company
from her	from Rebecca
for him	for Scott
with them	with Rebecca and Scott

Now read the following pairs of sentences and notice the prepositional phrases in the second sentence in each pair.

We plan to meet.
We plan to meet *in the morning*.

Please give me the package.
Please give me the package *by the door*.

The request was to provide an itemized estimate.
The request *of the owners* was to provide an itemized estimate.

The price was 10 percent higher than we anticipated.
The price *to the company* was 10 percent higher than we anticipated.

The letter did not include a purchase order.
The letter *from her* did not include a purchase order.

A gift was delivered early this morning.
A gift *for him* was delivered early this morning.

We went later.
We went *with them* later.

In each case, the preposition helps to connect words in the form of a prepositional phrase, and it serves to connect that prepositional phrase to the rest of the sentence.

Conjunctions. Conjunctions are the most commonly used connectors. The words *and*, *but*, *or*, and *nor* are conjunctions.

Robert *and* Paula will be promoted. (The conjunction *and* joins two nouns, *Robert* and *Paula*.)

Robert, Paula, *and* Daniel are attending the workshop. (Here the conjunction *and* joins three nouns.)

We have extra brochures in the storeroom *and* on those shelves. (The conjunction *and* joins two prepositional phrases, *in the storeroom* and *on those shelves*.)

The compact, light, *and* attractive computer has helped us increase our productivity. (The conjunction *and* joins three adjectives, *compact*, *light*, and *attractive*.)

Owen always types quickly *but* accurately. (The conjunction *but* joins two adverbs, *quickly* and *accurately*.)

In later units, you will learn about other conjunctions that have special uses.

CLASS PRACTICE 3

On a separate sheet of paper, identify the words in parentheses as prepositions (*P*) or as conjunctions (*C*). For each preposition identify the prepositional phrase.

1. Mr. Reynolds (and) Ms. McGrath went (to) the auditorium.
2. Vouchers must be signed (by) your supervisor.
3. The discount (on) sale items is valid (until) June 30.
4. We divided the invoices (between) Jack (and) me.
5. (For) the annual sales meeting, we developed special awards (and) prizes (for) the top sales representatives.

6. Sheila sent copies (of) the report (to) everyone (in) the department (except) Myrna.
7. (In) March, most (of) the secretaries (and) clerks will attend the workshop.
8. Although Amy (and) Rachel were (against) the suggestion, the committee voted to increase the budget (for) promotional brochures.
9. Lewis Annucci was scheduled to be one (of) the speakers, (but) he had to cancel.
10. Don (or) Melanie will be (at) the convention center (in) the afternoon.

Interjections. Interjections are words that express strong feeling; they are usually independent of the rest of the sentence.

Great! Joan succeeded in getting the Wilson account.

No! We certainly cannot approve the terms of this agreement.

Subjects and Predicates

Sentences consist of subjects and predicates. Simply put, the *subject* is that part of the sentence that tells (1) who is speaking, (2) who is spoken to, or (3) who or what is spoken about.

1. Who is speaking:

   I prefer an afternoon flight.   (The subject *I* identifies the person speaking.)

   We prefer an afternoon flight.   (*We* identifies the persons speaking.)

2. Who is spoken to:

   You are one of the best salespeople in our company, Betty.   The subject *you* identifies the person spoken to.)

   You are two of the best salespeople in our company.   (Here the persons spoken to are two people, identified by the subject *you*.)

3. Who or what is spoken about:

   Mae Nichols is the person in charge of sales promotion.   (Who is spoken about? *Mae Nichols*, the subject of the sentence.)

   She is the person in charge of sales promotion.   (Who is the person spoken about? *She*, the subject of the sentence.)

   Now notice how these sentences can be rephrased:

   The person in charge of sales promotion is Mae Nichols. *The person in charge of sales promotion* is she.   (In both sentences, the subject is now *The person in charge of sales promotion*.)

   This text editor performs a global search in just a few seconds.   (What is spoken about? *This text editor*, the subject of the sentence.)

It performs a global search in just a few seconds. (What is spoken about? *It*, the subject of the sentence.)

Now notice how the person or thing spoken about can be compounded—that is, notice how two or more people or things can be spoken about:

Mae and Gerald are in charge of this office. (The subject is *Mae and Gerald*, the people spoken about.)

Mae, Gerald, and Vera are in charge of this office. (Now three people are spoken about. The subject is *Mae, Gerald, and Vera*.)

Once you have identified the subject correctly, remember that the predicate is simply the rest of the sentence.

CLASS PRACTICE 4

On a separate sheet of paper, identify the subjects in the following sentences. Can you tell whether the subject is the person speaking, the person spoken to, or the person or thing spoken about?

1. Anne Ford will probably conduct the class on Tuesday.
2. The computer equipment will be delivered on July 1.
3. Sarah, Elaine, and Katherine are among the candidates for promotion to supervisor.
4. I enjoyed meeting Mr. and Mrs. Kline this morning.
5. You wrote an excellent proposal for revising our old operations manual.
6. Karen and Paul, you did a very good job of organizing this conference.
7. All these invoices and bills must be processed before we leave today.
8. We really should have developed a plan before we began this project.

Phrases and Clauses

When words are grouped together, those word groups may be categorized as phrases or as clauses. A *clause* is a group of words that has both a subject and a predicate. A *phrase* does *not* have a subject and a predicate. Let's look at clauses first.

Independent Clauses. As we have seen, a complete sentence is a clause. Because the clause in a complete sentence can stand alone, we call that clause an *independent clause*.

Mae Nichols is the person in charge of sales promotion. (The subject is *Mae Nichols*. The predicate is the rest of the sentence. This is an independent clause. It can stand alone as a sentence.)

This text editor can perform a global search in a few seconds. (The subject is *This text editor*. The predicate is the rest of the sentence. This clause is independent; it can stand alone as a sentence.)

Dependent Clauses. Not all clauses can stand alone as a sentence. Clauses that are incomplete—that cannot stand alone as sentences—are called *dependent clauses.*

> if you need more information (The subject is *you;* the predicate is the rest of the clause. Read the clause aloud. Does it make sense by itself? No—it is missing a complete thought. What should you do *if you need more information?*)

> when Ms. Block returns the merchandise (Is this a clause? Does this group of words have a subject and a predicate? Yes. The subject is *Ms. Block,* and the predicate is *returns the merchandise.* But what will happen *when Ms. Block returns the merchandise?* This is a dependent clause.)

Because they cannot stand alone as sentences, dependent clauses must be joined to independent clauses, as in the following sentences.

> If you need more information, you should call your regional benefits office. (Here the dependent clause, *If you need more information,* is joined to an independent clause, *you should call your regional benefits office.*)

> Henry will give Ms. Block a credit voucher when she returns the merchandise. (Again, the dependent clause, *when she returns the merchandise,* is joined to an independent clause.)

EDITING PRACTICE 1

Some of the following groups of words are sentences. Others are dependent clauses that are incorrectly treated as sentences. Identify each (*I* for independent clause and *D* for dependent clause), and then add independent clauses to the dependent clauses to create sentences.

1. Before Mr. Conklin goes to Allied Corporation headquarters.
2. Walter has submitted the specifications for the new laboratory.
3. If Ms. Roseborough decides to cancel the workshop next week.
4. They expect the stock to reach at least $75 a share by November.
5. When Jessica was promoted to store manager.
6. She purchased extra supplies to take advantage of the superb discount.
7. Because the workload has increased as a result of the new billing system.
8. Ms. Gibson has accepted a transfer to our Detroit office.

Phrases. Unlike clauses, phrases have neither subjects nor predicates. Three kinds of phrases are discussed below: prepositional phrases, infinitive phrases, and verb phrases.

    Prepositional Phrases. Prepositional phrases such as *in the office, with them, to the store, at the meeting,* and *on the plane* generally serve as adjectives or adverbs.

> The morale *in the office* has improved since Janet O'Toole became our supervisor. (*In the office* describes the noun *morale.* Because it describes a noun, this prepositional phrase must be an adjective.)

Harry went *with them.* (Went where? *With them.* The prepositional phrase *with them* answers the question "*Where?*" and therefore serves as an adverb.)

Infinitive Phrases. An infinitive is the *to* form of a verb: *to run, to go, to write, to be, to see, to have,* and so on. Infinitive phrases include the infinitive plus its subject, object, or modifiers. Infinitive phrases are most often used as nouns or as adjectives.

To complete this report on time is our objective. (The complete infinitive phrase is *To complete this report on time.* The phrase is the subject of the verb *is.*)

In our opinion, Ellen Redmond is the person *to hire as a consultant for this department.* (The infinitive phrase *to hire as a consultant for this department* modifies the noun *person* and therefore serves as an adjective.)

One pitfall in identifying infinitives is to confuse an infinitive with a prepositional phrase that begins with *to.* To avoid this trap, study the following Quick Trick.

QUICK TRICK	**INFINITIVE OR PREPOSITIONAL PHRASE?**

Compare the following infinitives with the prepositional phrases next to them.

Infinitive	Prepositional Phrase
to run	to the store
to type	to them
to control	to us
to write	to many customers

Now try to use each infinitive as a verb: *I run, you type, we control, they write,* and so on. Using these infinitives as verbs works because infinitives are verbs! Prepositional phrases do not include any verbs. Thus if you were to try to use any of the words in the prepositional phrase as a verb, you would get nonsense. Try it to see for yourself.

Verb Phrases. Verb phrases consist of two or more verbs—a main verb plus one or more helping verbs—joined to function as one verb within a sentence. (REMEMBER: The main verb is always the last verb in the verb phrase.)

Darren *has been revising* the old procedures manual. (*Has been revising* is a verb phrase. The main verb in the phrase is *revising;* the helping verbs are *has* and *been.*)

We *should have gone* to the workshop on Thursday. (*Should have gone* is the verb phrase. *Gone* is the main verb, and *should* and *have* are the helping verbs.)

The report *will have been completed* by the time Ms. Simpson returns. (The verb phrase is *will have been completed*. Which is the main verb? Which is the helping verb?)

When words interrupt the verb phrase, the complete phrase may be confused.

Darren *has* already *been revising* the old procedures manual. (The adverb *already* interrupts the verb phrase *has been revising*.)

The report *will* certainly *have been completed* by the time Ms. Simpson returns. (The adverb *certainly* interrupts the verb phrase *will have been completed*.)

CLASS PRACTICE 5

Identify the words in parentheses in the following sentences. On a separate sheet of paper, write *PP* for each prepositional phrase, *IP* for each infinitive phrase, or *VP* for each verb phrase.

1. The brochure (has been designed) and (has been approved) by our manager, who (will discuss) the marketing strategy with us tomorrow.
2. She is working (on the summary) (of the questionnaires).
3. Our supervisor divided all the letters (between Matthew and me) and asked us (to write replies) (to all of them).
4. Paulson Auto Parts has several plants (on the West Coast), but its headquarters is (in New Orleans).
5. Please be sure (to apologize for our error) and (to respond quickly).
6. Discuss these points (with the accountant) (to get her opinions).
7. Jerome said that he wants (to begin working) (for an advertising agency) (in New York City).
8. Pamela (has worked) (for Greene & Ford) (for nearly five years).

COMMUNICATION LABORATORY

APPLICATION EXERCISES

A. Identify the words in parentheses in the following sentences. On a separate sheet, for each choice write the part of speech (*noun, verb, conjunction, preposition, adverb, adjective,* or *pronoun*) or the kind of phrase (*VP, IP,* or *PP*).

1. We sent two (of the cartons) (to St. Louis) (by airfreight).
2. The proposal is (very) interesting, (but) it (would be) expensive.
3. One (of) the reasons for changing the (policy) is that our advisers (have recommended) tightening our credit.

4. The (executive) who (is) in charge of manufacturing is (Clara Poole).
5. The (discount) (will be offered) (until December 31).
6. Of course, we do believe the (plan) (will be) effective, (but) we (will need) time (to prove that it will work).
7. Brenda is (obviously) happy (about her promotion) to (district manager).
8. One of the (best) designers (on) our staff is (Caryl).
9. Yes, (they) finally decided (to test these products).
10. The (meeting) should be over (soon); (I) will call (you) as soon as Joan leaves the meeting.
11. I am sure that she (will want) a copy of the (new) pamphlet; will (you) please send her a (copy)?
12. Tom (and) Ron (have been developing) the (next) campaign (for) this product.
13. All of (us) want (to see Gregory) when (he) returns (from) England.
14. If you want (to share a copy) (with Mr. Jenkins), I (will be) glad (to bring it to him).
15. Martin has (already) left for the (airport) because (he) had an (early) flight.

B. Which of the following clauses are dependent, and which are independent? On a separate sheet, write *D* or *I* to identify each clause. (REMEMBER: Independent clauses can stand alone as complete sentences; dependent clauses cannot.)

1. That we should get Ms. Deere's approval.
2. Because the price of all chemicals has increased drastically.
3. Al said that he would discuss the changes in the benefits program with someone in the Personnel Department.
4. The new supervisor of the Manufacturing Department is Louisa D'Amato.
5. Since the company started distributing its own product lines.
6. As our regional managers agreed when they were here for the national sales meeting.
7. She quickly approved the idea.
8. The site for the new plant will be near Buffalo, New York.
9. While we were discussing ways to resolve the budget cuts.
10. Kyle and Diana did an excellent job.
11. We discussed ways to cut the budget.
12. Before the offer expires on December 31.
13. Whenever our manager gives us the approval to proceed with the production of these items.
14. We sent the original contracts to the Legal Department.
15. Until the estimated budget is formally authorized by the committee.

VOCABULARY AND SPELLING STUDIES

A. Distinguish between the meaning and the spelling of each of the following groups of words, which are often confused: *recent, resent; reference, reverence.*

B. Add a short prefix to each of the following words to change the meaning of the word to a negative one.

 1. polite
 2. pure
 3. certain
 4. reliable
 5. perfect
 6. logical
 7. productive
 8. rational
 9. precise
10. available

COMMUNICATING FOR RESULTS

A Matter of Publicity. You work for Lockhart Productions, a large company with an excellent reputation for high-quality products and for fairness to its employees. Lockhart, through its supervisors, always encourages its employees to take advantage of tuition-refund programs, supports employees' favorite charities, makes available a physical fitness center after work and on weekends, and has an annual Christmas party and a summer picnic for employees and their families. Because of these policies, Lockhart is generally regarded as a good place to work.

Recently there have been various rumors concerning a possible merger of Lockhart with another company. One day you receive a phone call from a local newspaper editor who asks you what you know about the merger. You have heard quite a bit.

A lot of the information you have heard is unflattering to Lockhart and its management. You have heard this information from many different sources and feel confident that most of it is true. You and your family have been very friendly with your Lockhart colleagues and with some of Lockhart's management. Given this and your satisfaction in working at Lockhart, you don't know what to do.

What should you tell the editor?

12

The Sentence

When speaking to someone, we can sometimes communicate clearly without using complete sentences. For example, if a friend asks, "Are you going to the game tomorrow?" a one-word reply such as "Yes" is complete and clear. In this case your one-word answer includes some understood words. "Yes" really means "Yes, *I am going to the game tomorrow.*" But one short word conveys the entire message!

When writing, however, we must take extra efforts to make sure that each sentence is complete. We can seldom use a one-word sentence to express a complete thought. To express our thoughts precisely and completely, we must know how to use sentences expertly. The first step, of course, is to learn what a sentence is.

Definition of a Sentence

You have probably heard a *sentence* defined as "a group of words that expresses a complete thought." Note the word *complete.* If the thought is not complete, then the group of words is not a sentence but a fragment.

It is important that you learn to write and speak in sentences—that is, learn to express yourself in complete thoughts, not in fragments or dependent clauses. To be able to distinguish between complete thoughts and incomplete thoughts, look at the Quick Trick below.

QUICK TRICK | NO SENSE, NO SENTENCE

Whenever you must decide whether a group of words is a sentence, consider whether the words make sense. If they do make sense, then the group of words is a sentence. If they do not make sense, the group of words is not a sentence.

We will receive a 10 percent discount for early payment. (These words make sense; they express a complete thought. Therefore, they make up a sentence.)

Jessica Owens is planning to attend the seminar next week. (Again, the words make sense. They express a complete thought; therefore, this is a sentence.)

If we do not receive the equipment within the next ten days. (This group of words is not complete; it doesn't express a complete thought. This is *not* a sentence.)

EDITING PRACTICE 1

In the following groups of words, tell which ones are sentences and which ones are not. Just say "sense" or "no sense." Then, for additional practice, take each group of "no sense" words and add words as necessary to make sense of them.

1. The Dallas store will open in June or July.
2. Ms. Purcell has been named Director of Marketing.
3. Since the Benefits Department improved the dental coverage.
4. If you need more information.
5. Mr. Bentley sent the bid to the architect.
6. Knowing that the committee had many issues on the agenda.
7. When Donna returns from her trip to the San Diego office.
8. You will need two copies.

Subjects and Predicates

The subject is that part of the sentence that shows (1) who is speaking, (2) who is spoken to, or (3) the person or thing spoken about. In the following examples, note that the complete subject may be one word or several words. Also notice that all the other words in the sentence make up the predicate of the sentence.

The predicate is that part of the sentence that tells you what the subject does or what is done to the subject. The core of the predicate is the verb, which can also be one word or more than one word.

Study these examples:

1. The person speaking is generally *I* or *we*, as shown in these examples:

Complete Subject	Complete Predicate
I	am revising the schedules for the production meeting.
	Verb

Complete Subject	Complete Predicate
We	will reject the bid that Ulster Metals submitted.
	Verb

2. The person *spoken to* is generally addressed *you:*

| Complete | Complete |
| Subject | Predicate |

You   should inform your supervisor of the change in schedule.
                Verb

3. The person or thing *spoken about* can be any number of subjects, two of which are shown here:

| Complete | Complete |
| Subject | Predicate |

One accountant whom we consulted was especially helpful.
                                Verb

| Complete | Complete |
| Subject | Predicate |

Our new training materials will be delivered later today.
                           Verb

Once you identify the subject, you know that the rest of the sentence is the predicate. As you can see, then, identifying subjects and predicates is not a difficult task, but it will become simpler yet with practice.

CLASS PRACTICE 1

Identify the *complete subject* of each sentence below. (Remember that the rest of the sentence must, of course, be the *predicate*.)

1. The manual that we now use to train new employees is being revised.
2. The cartons on the loading platform must be shipped to the warehouse.
3. Betty Russo is the person who coordinates these projects.
4. One of these word processors should be moved to the seventh floor.
5. The discounts that we now offer for cash purchases may be discontinued.
6. I prefer establishing a committee to analyze the results of the ads.
7. Most of the customers named "courtesy" as the most important trait in salesclerks.
8. One of the main reasons for changing the schedule was that Ms. O'Brien will be out of town.

Simple and Compound Subjects

The complete subject of a sentence is a shell within which is another subject—the *simple* subject or the *compound* subject of the sentence. Now that you are able to identify the complete subject, let's see how to find the simple or the compound subject within this complete subject. As you will see later, your skill in finding the simple or the compound subject is very important for correct verb choice.

A *simple subject* is the single most important word in the complete subject.

> The *plaintiff* in this suit did not appear in court today. (The complete subject is *The plaintiff in this suit*. The most important word in this complete subject is *plaintiff*, which is the simple subject of this sentence.)

A *compound subject* consists of two or more words that are *equally* important. The words are usually joined by *and, or,* or *nor.*

> The *plaintiff and* her *attorney* did not appear in court today. (The complete subject is *The plaintiff and her attorney*. In this complete subject the most important words are *plaintiff* and *attorney*. The compound subject, therefore, is *plaintiff and attorney*.)

> The *plaintiff,* her *attorney, and* the main *witness* did not appear in court today. (The complete subject is *The plaintiff, her attorney, and the main witness*. It has three words that have equal importance—*plaintiff, attorney,* and *witness*. Thus the compound subject is *plaintiff, attorney, and witness*.)

CLASS PRACTICE 2

Select the simple or the compound subject in each sentence below. (HINT: Identify the complete subject first.)

1. A revised inventory statement and an updated sales report were sent to the executive vice president.
2. James or Laura will probably be assigned to handle this account.
3. Ms. Carole P. Quentin is the senior counselor of our firm.
4. A microcomputer and a duplicator were damaged in the fire.
5. The opinion of each of the attorneys is that we should sue for libel.
6. The issue of copyright infringement was the topic of greatest interest at the convention.
7. A new hotel near the ocean has been selected for the sales representatives' meeting.
8. The folders on her desk contain all the information that you will need.

Sentence Order

The *normal order* of the sentence is complete subject followed by complete predicate, as in all the examples that you have seen so far.

None of the customers were aware of the special discount for cash payments. (The complete subject is *None of the customers;* it is followed by the complete predicate, *were aware of the special discount for cash payments.* This sentence is in *normal* order.)

Whenever the complete subject does *not* precede the complete predicate, the sentence is said to be in *inverted order.*

During the third-quarter sales period two representatives in our division received cash bonuses of $5000 each. (This sentence is in inverted order because part of the predicate appears before the complete subject. The complete subject is *two representatives in our division.* As you see, part of the complete predicate, *During the third-quarter sales period,* appears before the complete subject. Therefore, this sentence is in *inverted* order.)

The normal order of the sentence is as follows:

Two representatives in our division received cash bonuses of $5000 each during the third-quarter sales period.

Some of the most common—and the most serious—errors in grammar occur because writers and speakers are not able to identify the simple subjects of sentences, especially in inverted sentences. Thus the ability to recognize normal order is important. Likewise, it is important to be able to change inverted order to normal order.

To change inverted sentences to normal order, simply find the complete subject and then rearrange the sentence so that the complete subject is first and is followed by the complete predicate.

When she bought this property, Elvera originally planned to build a store. (Inverted order.)

Elvera originally planned to build a store when she bought this property. (Normal order.)

During the airline strike we delivered cargo by truck. (Inverted order.)

We delivered cargo by truck during the airline strike. (Normal order.)

Have you ever noticed that questions are usually phrased in inverted order? Note these examples:

Will you be going to the convention in Puerto Rico? (Inverted order.)

You will be going to the convention in Puerto Rico. (Normal order.)

Where have all the cartons been placed? (Inverted order.)

All the cartons have been placed where? (Normal order.)

Some sentences will sound odd when you change them to normal order, but do not let this bother you. You are merely using this as a technique to identify subjects of sentences.

EDITING PRACTICE 2

Which of the following sentences are in normal order, and which ones are in inverted order? Identify each; then change the inverted-order sentences to normal order. In addition, identify the complete subject of each sentence.

1. Is this envelope for Mr. Byrd?
2. The file copy of the agreement is on my desk.
3. When she arrives, you should give Sylvia this memo.
4. Were all the proofs corrected and returned?
5. We discussed various ways to solve the temporary backlog of orders.
6. Next summer our department will test a new computerized billing system.
7. As soon as Lyn calls, we will leave for the airport.
8. Our new supervisor was formerly with the Fitch & Scranton Advertising Agency.

COMMUNICATION LABORATORY

APPLICATION EXERCISES

A. On a separate sheet of paper, number from 1 to 15. For each of the following sentences (a) change to normal order any sentence that is inverted, (b) write the complete subject, and (c) draw a line under the simple or the compound subject.

1. By tomorrow afternoon we should have all the information we need.
2. Will Brad Hamilton be able to speak at next week's conference?
3. Lunch and dinner are included in this flat rate.
4. All employees who are interested may sign up for this insurance coverage.
5. At the end of each session, my assistants will collect the evaluation forms.
6. As you know, all raises will be delayed until September 1.
7. I have not yet proofread the price list that we will include in our mailing.
8. You should really wear a safety mask whenever you enter the lab area.
9. Whenever you enter the lab area, you should really wear a safety mask.
10. Has Eric completed the first draft of the annual marketing strategy report?
11. He has not completed it.
12. Tomorrow evening Marion and John will host the dinner for Mr. and Mrs. Smyth.
13. Do you have any vacation time left?

14. Ms. Bertoli generally presides at the monthly production status meetings.
15. At the monthly production status meetings, Ms. Bertoli or Mr. Cohen generally presides.

B. On a separate sheet of paper, (a) identify each fragment or complete sentence below, and (b) add the words necessary to make any sentence fragment a complete sentence. Then (c) indicate the normal order of any inverted sentence, and (d) identify the complete subject and the simple or compound subject for each sentence, labeling each as simple or compound.

1. Gold and silver are subject to price changes, of course.
2. Will Mr. Horne visit our Tennessee office too?
3. One of the most successful franchises.
4. Susan or Bill can probably help you with these programming errors.
5. Leonard said that the Securities and Exchange Commission is now studying the issue.
6. One of the managers at the meeting wants to extend the deadline until April or May.
7. April or May is usually the best month for television sales, according to these analyses.
8. According to these analyses, April or May is the best month for television sales.
9. Superior Inks is the company that submitted the highest bid.
10. Have you decided whom you will hire as your assistant?
11. You have already interviewed several applicants, haven't you?
12. The manager in charge of the Customer Relations Department.
13. The principal reason for moving the factory to Atlanta is that we lost the lease on the old property.
14. One of the applicants whom I interviewed this morning.
15. Will one of your assistants be able to help me proofread all these advertisements?

VOCABULARY AND SPELLING STUDIES

A. Because the following groups of words are so similar, they are often confused: *device, devise; precede, proceed, proceeds; mood; mode; command, commend.*

Distinguish between the meaning and the spelling of the words in each group; then write a sample sentence using each word.

B. Which of the following words are misspelled?

1. apologize
2. merchandize
3. realise
4. advertise
5. exercise
6. analyse

COMMUNICATING FOR RESULTS

Understanding Industry Jargon. During his first day at work for the World-Wide Film Corporation, Rick Taggart is asked by his supervisor to "get two *OKs* and send them to Deborah Theobold." Rick is embarrassed to ask, but he does not know what an *OK* is. What should he do?

U · N · I · T

13

Verbs and Verb Phrases

Verbs are the core of the sentence. Because they describe what the subject is doing or what is being done to the subject, verbs convey the action or movement that sparks a sentence and brings it to life.

Skill in using verbs correctly is essential to good writing and speaking. To ensure that you avoid some of the most common and the most serious errors in speaking and writing, pay special attention to this unit.

Verbs—The Motors of Sentences

A verb describes a subject's action, condition, or state of being. Therefore, you may find it helpful to think of verbs as the "motors" of sentences. Find the subject and ask "subject what"?

Denise *announced* the changes to the staff. (*Announced* is a verb; it describes Denise's action.)

Denise *looks* tired. (*Looks* is the verb; it tells Denise's condition.)

Denise *is* in the conference room. (*Is* is the verb; it tells Denise's state of being.)

Now read the above sentences *without* the verbs. Do you see how the verbs serve as motors—how they describe an action, a condition, and a state of being? Here are some sentences without verbs. Note how they are incomplete without their motors.

Jack and Rosemary the workshop on real estate investing.

Ross Plastics the contract with the labor unions.

Mr. Grant someone from the Word Processing Department.

Do you understand these messages? Without verbs the above groups of words express no message because they are incomplete. Now watch how these words come to life with the addition of verbs:

Jack and Rosemary (*teach, enjoyed, attended, will coordinate*) the workshop on real estate investing.

Ross Plastics (*signed, negotiated, rejected, reviewed, revised*) the contract with the labor unions.

Mr. Grant (*hired, wants, promoted, accepted, prefers*) someone from the Word Processing Department.

CLASS PRACTICE 1

Underline the verb in each of the following sentences. If the sentence has no verb, supply a verb for it.

1. Ms. Glynn presented the award to Howard during the luncheon.
2. They gave each staff member an instructive booklet.
3. My supervisor the monthly inventory report.
4. Jerry and Lyn the catalog copy for these products.
5. The batteries are in the supply room.
6. Elise the new sales representative for this region.
7. Owen the agenda for next week's training sessions.
8. Helen Munch has the price list and the discount chart.
9. Bettejean completed the sketches this morning.
10. Your assistant the meeting for Monday, March 29.

Verb Phrases

Two or more verbs are sometimes joined in a sentence. Two or more verbs that work together as one verb are called a *verb phrase*. Verb phrases such as *will be, will be going, has been asked, is working, has been working*, and *will have been approved* allow speakers and writers to express their meanings exactly.

In a verb phrase the last verb is the main verb; any other verbs are considered *helping* (or *auxiliary*) verbs.

Frances *should have* a duplicate key to this cabinet. (Main verb: *have*, the last verb in the phrase. Helping verb: *should*.)

We *should have asked* him for more information. (Main verb: *asked*, the last verb in the phrase. Helping verbs: *should* and *have*.)

In the examples on the previous page, note that *have* is the main verb in the first sentence, but *have* is a helping verb in the second sentence. Remember that the main verb is always the last verb in the phrase and you will have no difficulty finding the main verb in any phrase.

The following chart gives some typical verb phrases. Note that in all cases the main verb is the *last* verb in each phrase.

Helping Verb	Main Verb
is	walking
are	dancing
do	deliver
will	be
will be	finished
has been	accomplished
did	explain
should have	insisted
might have	listened
had been	returned
will have	received
will have been	budgeted

In questions a verb phrase is often separated.

Has Jacqueline *returned* from her vacation yet? (The verb phrase *has returned* is separated by the subject *Jacqueline*. The normal order is *Jacqueline has returned . . . .*)

Will an order blank *be included* in each catalog? (The verb phrase *will be included* is split by the complete subject *an order blank*.)

Adverbs also split verb phrases, as shown in these examples:

Charles *has* always *been* on time for our morning meetings. (The verb phrase *has been* is separated by the adverb *always*.)

Sharon and I *have* often *visited* the Museum of Modern Art. (The verb phrase *have visited* is separated by the adverb *often*.)

CLASS PRACTICE 2

In each of the following sentences, identify the verb phrase and the main verb in each phrase. (HINT: Be on the lookout for split verb phrases!)

1. Only Lee has already reserved his hotel room for the convention.
2. Maria has often requested a transfer to our San Diego office.
3. The union meeting for Thursday has been canceled.
4. Does Kim have all the photographs for the catalog?
5. Can Milton assist us with these sketches?
6. Her vacation plans have already been made.
7. These errors should have been corrected in the first printing.
8. Will Eric have time to help us with these invoices?

9. Next March Dorothy will have been with our company for ten years.
10. Joanne should have asked us for help with these orders.

Principal Parts of Regular Verbs

The principal parts of verbs are the forms we use to express the time of action, or *tense*, of a verb. The four parts are the present, the past, the past participle, and the present participle. For most verbs these parts are very easily formed, as shown in the table here.

PRESENT	PAST	PAST PARTICIPLE	PRESENT PARTICIPLE
type	typed	typed	typing
prepare	prepared	prepared	preparing
use	used	used	using
return	returned	returned	returning
answer	answered	answered	answering

PRINCIPAL PARTS OF SOME REGULAR VERBS

Verbs that end in *e* just add *d* to form the past tense and the past participle. The present participles of verbs ending in *e* are formed by dropping the *e* and then adding *ing*.

For verbs that do not end in *e*, add *ed* to form both the past tense and the past participle. Add *ing* to form the present participle.

Because most of the verbs in our language form their principal parts in one of the ways described above, such verbs are called *regular verbs*.

Present Tense and Past Tense. Study the present tense and past tense forms of the verb *type* below:

Present Tense		Past Tense	
I type	we type	I typed	we typed
you type	you type	you typed	you typed
he, she, it types	they type	he, she, it typed	they typed

As you can see, there are only two present tense forms—*type* and *types*. There is only one past tense form—*typed*. This pattern is standard for all regular verbs.

I *type* my own weekly summaries. Alan *types* his monthly status reports. (*Type* and *types* are present tense forms.)

Diana *typed* the first draft of our proposal. (Past tense.)

Past Participle and Present Participle. In verb phrases participles are always the main verbs—the last verbs in the phrases.

Gail *has typed* all her notes from the meeting. (The past participle *typed* is the main verb; *has* is the helping verb.)

Matthew *has been typing* for the past two hours. (The present participle *typing* is the main verb; *has* and *been* are the helping verbs.)

CLASS PRACTICE 3

In the sentences below identify the present tense and past tense forms and the present participles and past participles. (REMEMBER: Past tense and present tense forms never have helping verbs.)

1. Ms. Andrews has accepted our invitation to the luncheon.
2. Yes, Pedro always completes his sales analyses on time.
3. Has Mr. Jacobs mailed his check yet?
4. The final copy has been completed.
5. Since 1981 she has worked for National Metals Inc.
6. Yes, Jean is accepting a transfer to our Mexico City branch.
7. We are now completing our work on the Loomis project.
8. Are you still working for an advertising agency?
9. Jeremy works part-time for us in the summer.
10. He wants more brochures for all our charge-card customers.

Principal Parts of Irregular Verbs

You have seen that regular verbs form their past tense and past participle forms by adding *d* or *ed* to their present tense forms. A number of other different verbs form their principal parts in various ways—often by changing to a different word. Note, for example, the verbs in the table here.

PRINCIPAL PARTS OF SOME IRREGULAR VERBS

PRESENT TENSE	PAST TENSE	PAST PARTICIPLE	PRESENT PARTICIPLE
am	was	been	being
begin	began	begun	beginning
do	did	done	doing
go	went	gone	going
have	had	had	having
write	wrote	written	writing

Obviously, these verbs deserve special attention, as do all the irregular verbs in the table on pages 127–128. Study these irregular verbs. Memorize them if you don't already know them. Always consult the dictionary for those verbs whose forms you do not know. (The dictionary lists at least the past tense and past participle forms of irregular verbs.)

PRINCIPAL PARTS OF IRREGULAR VERBS

PRESENT	PAST	PAST PARTICIPLE	PRESENT PARTICIPLE
am	was	been	being
become	became	become	becoming
begin	began	begun	beginning
bid (to offer)	bid	bid	bidding
bite	bit	bitten	biting
blow	blew	blown	blowing
break	broke	broken	breaking
bring	brought	brought	bringing
burst	burst	burst	bursting
buy	bought	bought	buying
catch	caught	caught	catching
choose	chose	chosen	choosing
climb*	climbed	climbed	climbing
come	came	come	coming
do	did	done	doing
drag*	dragged	dragged	dragging
draw	drew	drawn	drawing
drink	drank	drunk	drinking
drive	drove	driven	driving
drown*	drowned	drowned	drowning
eat	ate	eaten	eating
fall	fell	fallen	falling
fight	fought	fought	fighting
find	found	found	finding
flee	fled	fled	fleeing
fly	flew	flown	flying
forget	forgot	forgotten	forgetting
freeze	froze	frozen	freezing
get	got	got	getting
give	gave	given	giving
go	went	gone	going
grow	grew	grown	growing
hang	hung	hung	hanging
hang (to put to death)*	hanged	hanged	hanging
hide	hid	hidden	hiding
hold	held	held	holding
know	knew	known	knowing
lay	laid	laid	laying
leave	left	left	leaving
lend	lent	lent	lending
lie	lay	lain	lying
lose	lost	lost	losing

* These are regular verbs, but their past tense and past participles are often misused.

PRINCIPAL PARTS OF IRREGULAR VERBS

PRESENT	PAST	PAST PARTICIPLE	PRESENT PARTICIPLE
pay	paid	paid	paying
read†	read‡	read‡	reading
ride	rode	ridden	riding
ring	rang	rung	ringing
rise	rose	risen	rising
run	ran	run	running
see	saw	seen	seeing
set	set	set	setting
shake	shook	shaken	shaking
shine	shone	shone	shining
shine (to polish)*	shine	shined	shining
shrink	shrank	shrunk	shrinking
sing	sang	sung	singing
sit	sat	sat	sitting
speak	spoke	spoken	speaking
spring	sprang	sprung	springing
stand	stood	stood	standing
steal	stole	stolen	stealing
strike	struck	struck	striking
swear	swore	sworn	swearing
sweep	swept	swept	sweeping
swim	swam	swum	swimming
take	took	taken	taking
teach	taught	taught	teaching
tear	tore	torn	tearing
tell	told	told	telling
think	thought	thought	thinking
throw	threw	thrown	throwing
wear	wore	worn	wearing
win	won	won	winning
write	wrote	written	writing

* These are regular verbs, but their past tense and past participles are often misused.
† Pronounced "reed."
‡ Pronounced "red."

As with regular verbs, always be sure to use a helping verb with the past participle. On the other hand, *never* use a helping verb with the past tense. Note, for example, the correct uses of the verbs below.

Past Tense	Past Participle
She *went*.	She has *gone*.
He *did* a good job.	He has *done* a good job.
We *broke* the vase.	We have *broken* the vase.
I *flew* to Denver.	I had *flown* to Denver.
They *gave* us a discount.	They have *given* us a discount.

In each case note again that the past participle always has a helper and that the past tense never has a helper. Thus it is always wrong to say or write *she gone, he done,* and so on, because these past participles must have helping verbs.

EDITING PRACTICE 1

In the following sentences, correct all errors in the use of verb forms.

1. Sara has already spoke with Ms. Roosevelt concerning the new procedures.
2. Apparently, the merchandise had been broke before delivery.
3. We had began revising the policy manual before we met with the committee.
4. Do you know whether Mr. VanHooten has already went to the airport?
5. Yes, I seen both of them before this morning's production meeting.
6. Have you already did your monthly inventory summary?
7. We have wrote only a first draft of our proposal, but we will complete the final draft before the end of the day.
8. As soon as we had ate lunch, we began discussing marketing strategies.
9. If we had chose this sample, we would have saved hundreds of dollars in manufacturing costs.
10. Has the messenger already took all the cartons to our headquarters office?

COMMUNICATION LABORATORY

APPLICATION EXERCISES

A. Find the verb or verb phrase in the following sentences. Then identify the main verb in each phrase. Supply a verb or verb phrase for any group of words that has none.

1. Frankly, I do prefer the panel's suggestion about lowering prices and increasing discounts.
2. Does Mr. Boynton have the commission checks for our sales representatives?
3. By the end of next year our annual revenue will be approximately $3.6 million.
4. Our company will be earning about 30 cents a share.
5. Several assistants next year.
6. Yes, Ms. Cooper's name has been added to the list of guests.
7. Fred, have you corrected all the errors in this printout?
8. Did you already ask Marie for instructions for using this equipment?

9. Mr. Perez and I have interviewed all the candidates.
10. All the candidates have been interviewed by Mr. Perez and me.
11. The incentive-compensation plan for sales representatives.
12. No, Edward has not yet decided.
13. Several of our important clients have been complaining about the change in our credit policy.
14. Have you and Samantha approved the budget for printing these pamphlets?
15. The new computer program has improved the speed and the accuracy of our billing system.

B. Correct any errors in the following sentences. If a sentence has no error, write *OK*.

1. Through her work on the Profit Committee, Harriett become very adept at handling budgets.
2. The first session had began a few minutes before we arrived.
3. If the older machine is broke, Ken, use the newer duplicator on the sixth floor.
4. As soon as we had wrote all our suggestions, we shared them with the panel leader.
5. Anna been very busy with several clients who are visiting this week.
6. Obviously, Bill had forgotten about his 1:30 appointment with Mr. Harrington.
7. Although the package had fell from the top shelf, the containers were not broken.
8. Our consultants had already knew about the changes in specifications.
9. The solutions had froze overnight because the temperature suddenly dropped.
10. Yes, I seen Ms. Marx just a few minutes ago; she was in the conference room.
11. Has Mr. Reynolds gave you all the signed contracts?
12. Have you flew to Los Angeles recently?
13. I had driven only a few miles when I noticed the sign to the railroad station.
14. Has she took any of the excellent courses offered by the Training Department?
15. Had Jeanette already went by the time you arrived?

C. The blanks within the following sentences should contain some form of these verbs: *begin, break, drink, drive, go, grow, know, see, speak,* or *write.*

1. Ms. Weathers has already _____ her speech, hasn't she?
2. During the break this morning, we _____ all the cold juices on the coffee wagon.

3. Helen and I have _____ each other since we graduated from high school.
4. We _____ Mr. Hansen earlier today when he was keyboarding information at this terminal.
5. The delivery will be late, but we have already _____ to the dispatcher.
6. Market research has shown that consumer demand for software has _____ tremendously.
7. Our interest in buying word processors such as this one _____ a few months ago.
8. After we have _____ Ms. Mackenzie to the airport, we will return to the hotel.
9. Unfortunately, this equipment has been _____ for several weeks.
10. Edna generally _____ to work on Saturdays during the busy season.

VOCABULARY AND SPELLING STUDIES

A. Distinguish between the meaning and spelling of the following words, which are often confused: *fineness, finesse; leased, least.* Then write a sample sentence using each word.

B. Some of the following words contain silent letters: *listen, strength, night, island, candidate, doubt.* List the words and tell which letters (besides *e*) are silent. Use the pronunciation guide in your dictionary.

C. Should *ancy* or *ency* be added to the following words to complete the correct spellings?

1. effici__
2. hesit__
3. emerg__
4. flu__
5. buoy__
6. occup__

COMMUNICATING FOR RESULTS

Remembering Names. Business people often meet several new clients or coworkers at a time. How well can you remember names when several people are introduced to you at the same time? Have six of your classmates assume fictitious names; then introduce yourselves to one another. As you meet each person, ask a question of each that will help you fix that person's name in your memory. (HINT: Try to associate face, appearance, dress, speech, and so on, with each name.)

14

Common Verb Errors

The "being" verbs are the most commonly used verbs in our language. Unfortunately, they are also among the most misused. In this unit you will have an opportunity to master the forms of the verb *to be* in a simple and practical way. In addition, as you will see later, understanding the difference between transitive and intransitive verbs will help you avoid errors in a few other commonly misused irregular verbs. Therefore, this unit will focus on (1) "being" verbs, (2) transitive verbs, and (3) intransitive verbs.

"Being" Verbs

The "being" verbs are all the forms of the verb *to be: am, is, are, was, were, been,* and of course, *be.* Now let's see how they are used. To begin, make sure you know the present tense and the past tense forms of the verb *to be:*

Present Tense		Past Tense	
I am	we are	I was	we were
you are	you are	you were	you were
he		he	
she } is	they are	she } was	they were
it		it	

As you can see, then, the verb *to be* is unique. Its present tense has three forms—*am, are,* and *is.* Its past tense has two forms—*was* and *were.* Memorize these forms, because you will certainly use them often.

I *am* responsible for this project. Sam *is* one of the artists assigned to the project. We *are* still on schedule. (Present tense forms.)

You *were* not at the committee meeting, *were* you? Henry *was* there. (Past tense forms.)

Past Participle and Present Participle. The past participle *been* can be used as a main verb with a helper, as in *has been, have been, had been, should have been, will have been, could have been, might have been,* and so on. In addition, *been* can be used as a helping verb. Note that a verb *phrase* is not considered a "being verb" unless the *main* verb is the "being" verb.

132

Joe Paul *should have been* here by noon. (*Been* is the main verb; *should* and *have* are helping verbs. Therefore, this verb phrase *is* a "being" verb.)

He *should have been told* about the change in departure time. (Now the main verb is *told*, and the helping verbs are *should, have,* and *been*. This verb phrase is *not* a "being" verb.)

Likewise, the present participle *being* can be used as a main verb, as in *am being, is being, are being, was being,* and *were being*. It can also be used as a helping verb, as in *is being planned, are being reviewed, was being discussed,* and so on. Again, to find out whether *being* is the main verb in a verb phrase, be sure to isolate the entire phrase; then see whether *being* is the *last* word in that phrase.

We *are being* very careful about storing chemicals at our plants. (The main verb is *being;* the helping verb is *are.*)

We *are being trained* to handle chemicals carefully. (Now the main verb is *trained; are* and *being* are helping verbs.)

Are you *being trained* to handle chemicals carefully? (In this inverted sentence the verb phrase *are being trained* is separated by the subject *you.*)

Be. The last form is the word *be* itself. *Be* can also be used as a helper or as a main verb.

Beatrice *will be* in charge of the newly formed group. (In the verb phrase *will be, be* is the main verb and *will* is the helping verb.)

She *will be promoted* soon. (The main verb is *promoted,* and the helping verbs are *will* and *be.*)

CLASS PRACTICE 1

In each of the following sentences, identify the verb or the verb phrase. Then determine whether that verb or verb phrase is a "being" verb. (HINT: Remember that a verb phrase is a "being" verb only when the *last* verb in the phrase is a "being" verb.)

1. You really should have been at our last panel discussion.
2. The merchandise was shipped to San Francisco on March 30.
3. When are you planning to make the new price list effective?
4. Each of these payments must be acknowledged, of course.
5. In your opinion, is this product worth so much money?
6. Kristen has been selected chairperson of the policy committee.
7. Kristen has been the chairperson of many committees within the past two years.
8. Frankly, we were not expecting this many orders from just one small ad.

9. By the end of the year, we will be the nation's largest distributor of computer peripherals.
10. Bernard should have been advised about the discount policy changes.

Transitive and Intransitive Verbs

A *transitive* verb is a verb that has an *object*—a word that tells what or who receives the action expressed by the verb.

> Mario *typed* the *report*. (The object of *typed* is *report*, so *typed* is a transitive verb.)

> Mario *travels* to the West Coast once a month. (The verb *travels* has no object; therefore, it is intransitive.)

For a shortcut in identifying transitive and intransitive verbs, study the following Quick Tricks.

QUICK TRICK   ## ASK "WHAT?" OR "WHOM?"

After saying the verb, ask the question "What?" or "Whom?" If you can supply a noun or a pronoun that makes sense, then the verb is transitive.

> Neil Torre asked me for a revised expense budget. (Asked what? No answer. Asked whom? Answer: *me*. *Asked* is a transitive verb because it has an object.)

> Angela Bryan sells office equipment in the metropolitan area. (Sells what? Answer: *office equipment*. *Sells* is a transitive verb.)

> Lori Clayton frequently speaks at sales conventions. (Speaks what? No answer. Speaks whom? No answer. *Speaks* is an intransitive verb.)

QUICK TRICK   ## ALWAYS TRANSITIVE

Whenever you see a past participle that has a "being" verb helper, the verb phrase is automatically transitive. Remember this rule:

Being Verb Helper + Past Participle = Transitive Verb Phrase

This combination automatically makes the subject the receiver of the action. Because there is always a receiver of the action, such verbs must therefore be transitive.

> Ms. Diaz *should have been promoted* a long time ago. (*Promoted* is a past participle, and *should have been* is a phrase with a "being" verb helper. Thus *should have been promoted* is automatically a transitive verb.)

CLASS PRACTICE 2

Identify the verbs and the verb phrases in the following sentences; then label each as *transitive* or *intransitive*. (REMEMBER: Use the "always transitive" formula as a shortcut.)

1. Keri has been training lab assistants for the entire company.
2. Mr. Goode, my manager, explained the reasons for his decision.
3. Mrs. Trumbell worked especially quickly this morning.
4. Of course, the check was signed by our treasurer.
5. Our Rochester, New York, office was built in 1984.
6. Ms. Gurr has been traveling for the past three weeks.
7. She has carefully analyzed the contents of both chemical containers.
8. We should have been warned of the possible hazard.
9. Has Mrs. Wayne been informed about the budget cuts?
10. We should have tried harder.

Lie and *Lay; Sit* and *Set; Rise* and *Raise.* Your knowledge of transitive and intransitive verbs will help you avoid errors in using these verbs: *lie* and *lay, sit* and *set,* and *rise* and *raise.* As you will see in the following Quick Trick, the secret is to remember that *lie, sit,* and *rise* are *intransitive.*

QUICK TRICK | **THE _I_ VERB IS INTRANSITIVE**

First study the principal parts of these pairs of verbs. As you do so, note that the three verbs with the short or long sound of the letter *i* are *lie, sit,* and *rise.*

Present	Past	Past Participle	Present Participle
lie	lay	lain	lying
lay	laid	laid	laying
sit	sat	sat	sitting
set	set	set	setting
rise	rose	risen	rising
raise	raised	raised	raising

Now let's review them one pair at a time.

LIE–LAY. Which verb has the *i* sound? Answer: *lie.* Let the *i* sound in *lie* remind you that the word *intransitive* begins with *i. Lie* is intransitive.

SIT–SET. Which verb has the *i* sound? Answer: *sit.* Let the *i* sound in *sit* remind you that the word *intransitive* begins with *i. Sit* is intransitive.

RISE–RAISE. Which verb has the *i* sound? Answer: *rise.* Let the *i* sound in *rise* remind you that the word *intransitive* begins with *i. Rise* is intransitive.

This simple, foolproof method will help you remember that *lie, sit,* and *rise* are *in*transitive. Also remember that the other verb in each verb pair (that is, *lay, set,* and *raise*) is transitive. Now let's see how you can put this knowledge to use in choosing the right verb.

I will (lie, lay) the briefcase on your desk tomorrow.

To decide whether the intransitive *lie* or the transitive *lay* is correct, just ask whether the verb in this sentence has an object. Answer: Yes, *briefcase.* Therefore, a transitive verb is required. Which verb is transitive? Answer: *lay.*

Let's try another example:

Paul (lay, laid) the papers on my desk.

This is the tricky part, so pay strict attention. Here, *lay* is the past tense form of *lie; laid* is the past tense form of *lay.* Thus in this example *lay* is intransitive and *laid* is transitive. Now let's proceed with our analysis of this sentence.

Does the verb in this sentence have an object? Answer: Yes, *papers.* Which verb is required: a transitive verb or an intransitive verb? Answer: a transitive verb is required. Which is the transitive form, *lay* or *laid?* Answer: *laid.*

As you can see, then, you must know the forms of these troublesome verbs—especially the forms of *lie* and *lay. Lie* and *lay* are particularly tricky because it is so easy to confuse the present tense of the transitive verb *lay* with the past tense of the intransitive verb *lie.*

Present Tense of *Lie*	**Past Tense of *Lie***
I *lie* down after work.	I *lay* down after work yesterday.
You *lie* down after work.	You *lay* down after work yesterday.
He *lies* down after work.	He *lay* down after work yesterday.
We *lie* down after work.	We *lay* down after work yesterday.
They *lie* down after work.	They *lay* down after work yesterday.

Present Tense of *Lay*	**Past Tense of *Lay***
I *lay* packages on this table.	I *laid* packages on this table.
You *lay* packages on this table.	You *laid* packages on this table.
She *lays* packages on this table.	She *laid* packages on this table.
We *lay* packages on this table.	We *laid* packages on this table.
They *lay* packages on this table.	They *laid* packages on this table.

As with *all* verbs except *to be, lie* has only two present tense forms (*lie* and *lies*) and one past tense form (*lay*). Likewise, *lay* has only two present tense forms (*lay* and *lays*) and one past tense form (*laid*). The same is true of *sit, set, rise,* and *raise.*

I usually *sit* near the window.   (Present.)
Yolanda always *sits* in the front of the room.   (Present.)
Yesterday we *sat* in different places.   (Past.)

You generally *set* the prices for these products, don't you?   (Present.)
Sometimes Ms. Greer *sets* the prices.   (Present.)
We *set* these prices last May.   (Past.)

We always *rise* to applaud the speaker.   (Present.)
Gene *rises* to greet all his visitors.   (Present.)
They *rose* in order to see the screen more clearly.   (Past.)

I often *raise* money for charitable causes.   (Present.)
Fran still *raises* money for the United Fund.   (Present.)
Together we *raised* several thousand dollars last year.   (Past.)

EDITING PRACTICE 1

Select the correct verb for each of the following sentences. (Be sure to determine whether a transitive or an intransitive verb is required.)

1. Do you know when the foundation will be (lain, laid)?
2. The alarm sounds when the water has (risen, raised) to a certain level.
3. The production manager has already (sat, set) a new schedule for completing this project.
4. How much money have they (risen, raised)?
5. I really enjoy (lying, laying) in the sun on summer mornings.
6. Did you know that all these sketches had (lain, laid) here in the storeroom for months?
7. She instructed us to sell the stock when the price (rises, raises) to $25 a share.
8. The printing calculator is (lying, laying) on the file cabinet in my office, Dick.
9. A special panel, according to Ms. Hayworth, is responsible for (sitting, setting) promotion policies.
10. This question has been (risen, raised) often during our monthly meetings.

If I Were . . . .

Sometimes it is correct to use *were* where ordinarily you would expect to use *was*. Usually this use of *were* occurs after *if, as if, as though,* and *wish.* Follow this rule: If the expressed condition is not true, is not possible, or is highly doubtful, use *were.*

Steven sometimes acts *as if he were* from another planet! (He is not "from another planet"; because the condition expressed is not true, *were* is correct.)

If I *were* you, I would explain this situation to the company attorneys. (I am not "you.")

Ms. Dunlop is in England. If she *were* here in St. Louis, she would probably accept your invitation. (But she is *not* in St. Louis.)

However, use *was* if the condition *could be true.*

If the check *was* delivered this morning, then perhaps Ellen signed for it. (The condition *could be true.*)

If Mr. Naldi *was* at the conference center, he probably left before I arrived. (The condition *could be true.*)

EDITING PRACTICE 2

Which is correct in the following sentences, *were* or *was?*

1. Both of us wish that Ralph (was, were) still in charge of this department.
2. If Margaret (was, were) in the office this morning, she must have left with Anne to attend the early training session.
3. We wish that it (was, were) possible to refund the full amount, but the warranty period expired last December.
4. Our office manager sometimes acts as if she (was, were) the president of the corporation.
5. If the former president (was, were) still managing this company, she would certainly object to these changes.

COMMUNICATION LABORATORY

APPLICATION EXERCISES

A. On a separate sheet of paper, write the complete verb in each of the following sentences and indicate whether each verb is transitive, intransitive, or a "being" verb. Use *T* for *transitive,* *I* for *intransitive,* and *B* for *"being."*

1. Louise Taylor has been the supervisor of this department for more than five years.
2. Mr. Quicker and Ms. d'Amato are coordinating the entire sales convention.
3. In our opinion, Andrew should have been in charge of the entire project.
4. He should have been appointed director of production.
5. Francine was transferred to San Diego in February.
6. Before the transfer she was the manager of Telecommunications.
7. Thanks to our employees' efforts, more than $5,000 has been raised for local charities.
8. Has Ms. Lendman returned from her trip to London?
9. The Blue Star product line has been one of our most successful moneymakers.
10. Obviously, June and Barry prefer the first sample.
11. Both of us sat quietly throughout the presentation.

12. Three new terminals will be installed within the next week or so.
13. Yes, this microcomputer uses 5¼-inch diskettes.
14. Tara and Joyce should have been at this morning's orientation.
15. They should have been informed of the address changes last month.

B. Correct any errors in the following sentences and identify the transitive and intransitive verbs. Write *OK* on your paper if the sentence is correct.

1. The actual budget (not counting the effect of inflation) has been risen only 2 percent.
2. If this was last month, we would have plenty of time to help you!
3. The contractors promise that the foundation will have been lain by September 13.
4. The masons who have been lying bricks for the warehouse addition are union workers.
5. John, will you please help me sit these cartons on that pallet?
6. The nurse immediately asked him to lay down.
7. Because the chemicals had laid in the storeroom too long, we discarded all the containers.
8. I wish that I was in our Honolulu office!
9. As a result of our group meeting, we rised some serious questions about our marketing strategy.
10. The best way to proceed is to lay all the parts on a table or a flat surface.
11. The cost of living has been rising steadily for the past seven months.
12. If it was earlier, Karen and I would also go with you to the seminar.
13. When the carpenters have laid the new flooring, we will move the furniture back into that office.
14. Are there any extra brochures lying on the table in the reception area?
15. If it was possible, we would gladly trade places with the Sandersons.

C. For each sentence write the correct form of the verb in parentheses.

1. The photographs are usually (hang) to dry for several minutes.
2. The reference materials that you'll need are (lie) on the credenza.
3. While recuperating from the accident, Morgan had (lie) in bed for over three weeks.
4. We (lay) the handouts on a table in the front of the room.
5. Last night I (lie) in bed for hours before I finally fell asleep.
6. Of course, I do wish that I (was) earning more money so that I could return to school.
7. I (set) all the graphs on the conference room table, just as Ms. Wilson had requested.
8. Dave has already (speak) to his staff about the increase in work load that he expects next year.

9. Although all of us were careful, the new monitor for the word processor (break).
10. After several years of hard work and long hours of study, Agnes finally (become) a department head.
11. The sun was (set) as we drove through the campground gates in Rocky Mountain National Park.
12. The rainfall was so heavy in May that the local water table (rise) to a record high.
13. Ray (sit) quietly in his study, each and every day before the national sales manager's meeting, to practice his speech.
14. Ms. Monroe (lay) the official documents on my desk early last Monday.
15. We were (raise) our hands to volunteer our time even before the community organizers asked for our help.

VOCABULARY AND SPELLING STUDIES

A. The spellings and meanings of word pairs such as *feet/feat* and *aisle/isle* are often confused. Give the meaning of each of these four words; then write a sample sentence using each correctly.

B. Which of the following words is *mis*spelled: *signify, testify, liquify, classify?*

C. Which of the following words is spelled correctly: *accomodate, privelege, embarrass, aquiesce?*

COMMUNICATING FOR RESULTS

Business Courtesy. Read each of the following statements to judge whether it is correct. Explain your answer.

1. To save time when placing a telephone call, the caller should always ask a secretary to get the other party on the line first.
2. An employee who must be out for sick leave should call the office to let the supervisor know.
3. After completing the required work for the day, an employee may then visit coworkers.

U · N · I · T

15

Plural Nouns

The words *managers, manager's,* and *managers'* are all pronounced precisely the same. In speaking, therefore, we need not specify which of these three forms we intend to use. But in writing, errors in using such forms of nouns are obvious because these three words cannot be used interchangeably. We must know whether the plural form *managers* is correct or whether one of the possessive forms, *manager's* or *managers',* is correct.

In this unit you will review forming plurals of nouns. Then, in the next unit, you will review forming possessives of nouns. Together, these two units will help you avoid many of the obstacles to correct spelling.

Forming Routine Plurals

Most Nouns. Most plural nouns end in *s*. To form these plurals, we simply add *s* or *es* to the singular forms.

Add *S*

clerk	clerks	Smith	Smiths
building	buildings	Brown	Browns
car	cars	Freid	Freids
attorney	attorneys	Donnelly	Donnellys
machine	machines	John	Johns

Add *ES*

boss	bosses	Adams	Adamses
tax	taxes	Marx	Marxes
bench	benches	Lidz	Lidzes
blitz	blitzes	Tench	Tenches
wish	wishes	Walsh	Walshes

As you can see, for nouns that end in *s, x, z, ch,* and *sh,* you must add *es* to the singular form. For all other nouns (exceptions are discussed later in this unit), just add *s*. Note that the same rule applies to common nouns and to proper nouns. A *common noun* is the name of a person, place, or thing, such as *accountant, street,* and *company*. A *proper noun* is the name of a *specific* person, place, or thing, such as *Louella Carter, Himrod Street,* and *General Motors*.

141

Nouns Ending in *Y*. In the list on the previous page, the plural of *attorney* is *attorneys*, and the plural of *Donnelly* is *Donnellys*. But not all nouns that end in *y* form their plurals by adding *s*. Note the following rules:

For Common Nouns. For common nouns, if the final *y* is preceded by a vowel (*a, e, i, o,* or *u*), then just add *s* to the singular form. If the final *y* is preceded by a consonant (that is, by any letter other than *a, e, i, o,* or *u*), then change the *y* to *i* and add *es:*

Add *S*		Change *Y* to *I* and Add *ES*	
day	days	quantity	quantities
valley	valleys	secretary	secretaries
toy	toys	company	companies
ray	rays	facility	facilities
key	keys	territory	territories
relay	relays	factory	factories

For Proper Nouns. For proper nouns ending in *y*, just add *s* to form the plural, regardless of whether the *y* is preceded by a vowel or not.

Connelly	Connellys
Delaney	Delaneys
Haggerty	Haggertys
Pauly	Paulys

There are very few exceptions to this rule, but note the following three common ones:

Complete Name	**Shortened Name**
Allegheny Mountains	the Alleghenies
Rocky Mountains	the Rockies
Smoky Mountains	the Smokies

Both the complete and the shortened names are plural forms, but for the shortened names change the *y* to *i* and add *es*.

EDITING PRACTICE 1

On a separate sheet of paper, write the numbers 1 through 15. Next to each number, write the plural of the following words.

1. Delaney
2. Jones
3. Mary
4. lunch
5. tax
6. Conroy
7. Roosevelt
8. business
9. warehouse
10. Blainy
11. gas
12. factory
13. wrench
14. ruby
15. subsidiary

Now correct any errors in the use of plurals in the following sentences. If a sentence has no error, write *OK*.

1. We asked several companys to send us catalogs.
2. Neither of the Haggerties was able to attend our seminar.
3. One of the territorys above quota is our Lexington, Kentucky, office.
4. The attornies did not agree on the amount of the settlement.
5. Several of our franchises are located in the Alleghenies.
6. According to the shareholders' report, the Cassidies own 32 percent of the company.
7. Perhaps the Doughertys will sell both their factories.
8. Of all the propertys that we inspected, only the plot of land on Sunset Street is worth the price.

Forming Special Plurals

In addition to the routine plurals that you learned to form earlier in this unit, you must learn how to form the plurals of such special words as *woman, man,* and *child.* You already know that they do not form their plurals in any regular way. You must also learn to form the plurals of compound nouns and of titles used with names. Finally, there are a few plurals that are formed using the apostrophe, and you must also master these.

Vowel Changes. Some nouns form the plural by vowel changes.

man	men	woman	women
tooth	teeth	mouse	mice
foot	feet	goose	geese

Note, however, that the plural of *German* is *Germans.*

Compound Nouns. A compound noun is a noun in which two or more words have been combined. When the compound is written as one word (no hyphen), then form the plural at the end of the word.

cupful	cupfuls
toothbrush	toothbrushes
textbook	textbooks
stepchild	stepchildren
courthouse	courthouses
letterhead	letterheads

EXCEPTION:

passerby	passersby

When the compound is written with either a space or a hyphen between the words, make plural the *main word* in the compound. (REMEMBER: The main word is the *most important* word in the compound.)

bulletin board	bulletin board_s_
general manager	general manager_s_
editor in chief	editor_s_ in chief
vice president	vice president_s_
daughter-in-law	daughter_s_-in-law
court-martial	court_s_-martial
notary public	notar_ies_ public
attorney-at-law	attorney_s_-at-law
lieutenant colonel	lieutenant colonel_s_

When there is no main word in the hyphenated compound, form the plural at the end of the noun.

follow-up	follow-up_s_
write-in	write-in_s_
hand-me-down	hand-me-down_s_
tie-up	tie-up_s_
trade-in	trade-in_s_

Titles With Names. Sometimes it is necessary to form the plural of a name with a title such as *Miss, Ms., Mrs.,* or *Mr.* In such cases make either the title or the name plural—not both. Note the plurals of these common titles:

Singular	**Plural**
Miss	Misses
Ms.	Mses. or Mss.
Mrs.	Mesdames (*Mesdames* is a French word, meaning "more than one *Mrs.*")
Mr.	Messrs. (*Messrs.* is the abbreviation for *messieurs,* the French word for "*misters.*")

Now compare the alternative ways to make a name with a title plural. In each case note that only one word, the title *or* the name, is made plural.

Singular (One Person)	Plural (Two or More People With the Same Name and Title)
Miss Jensen is the owner of this apartment building.	The *Misses* Jensen are the owners of this apartment building.
	The Miss *Jensens* are the owners of this apartment building.
Inform Ms. Oliver of the price changes.	Inform the *Mses.* Oliver of the price changes.
	Inform the Ms. *Olivers* of the price changes.
Yes, Mrs. Root coordinated the charity drive.	Yes, the *Mesdames* Root coordinated the charity drive.
	Yes, the Mrs. *Roots* coordinated the charity drive.

Please invite Mr. Feinberg to Saturday's event.

Please invite the *Messrs.* Feinberg to Saturday's event.

Please invite the Mr. *Feinbergs* to Saturday's event.

Plurals With Apostrophes. As you will see in Unit 16, apostrophes are used in possessive forms of nouns. In rare instances, however, an apostrophe prevents possible misreading of certain plurals—for example, plurals of capital or lowercase letters that could be misread.

No Apostrophe Needed	Apostrophe Prevents Misreading
several M.D.s	learning your abc's
two CPAs	counting the c.o.d.'s
all Bs	earned three A's

Plurals such as *pros* and *cons*, *ins* and *outs*, and *dos* and *don'ts* are not likely to be misread.

EDITING PRACTICE 2

Correct any errors in the following sentences. Write *OK* for any sentence that has no error.

1. What is the store's policy concerning trades-in?
2. Have you already posted all the announcements on the bulletins board?
3. By all means, please be sure to include the Messrs. Smiths on your list.
4. Several of the woman in this department are excellent candidates for promotion.
5. All the researchers in our group have earned their Ph.D.s.
6. The Mesdames Cassidys have approved the sale of the building and the land.
7. Of course, we consulted two attorney-at-laws before we made our final decision.
8. The Medical Department has three full-time M.D.'s on staff.

Forming Tricky Plurals

Because there are so many exceptions to the rules for forming plurals for nouns ending in *o* and *f* or *fe*, you should develop the habit of using the dictionary to check the spellings of such plurals. In addition, you will find the dictionary especially helpful for checking nouns that originated in foreign languages and nouns that have only one form for both the singular and the plural. All these troublesome plurals are covered on pages 146 and 147.

Nouns Ending in O. When a singular noun ends in *o*, its plural is usually formed by adding *s*. In the examples on the next page, note that all musical terms ending in *o* are included in this category.

dynamo	dynamo<u>s</u>	tobacco	tobacco<u>s</u>
studio	studio<u>s</u>	Eskimo	Eskimo<u>s</u>
zero	zero<u>s</u>	ratio	ratio<u>s</u>
radio	radio<u>s</u>	memento	memento<u>s</u>
piano	piano<u>s</u>	soprano	soprano<u>s</u>
solo	solo<u>s</u>	banjo	banjo<u>s</u>
trio	trio<u>s</u>	alto	alto<u>s</u>

However, some nouns ending in *o* preceded by a consonant form the plural by adding *es:*

echo	echo<u>es</u>	motto	motto<u>es</u>
tomato	tomato<u>es</u>	veto	veto<u>es</u>
hero	hero<u>es</u>	cargo	cargo<u>es</u>
embargo	embargo<u>es</u>	potato	potato<u>es</u>

Nouns Ending in *F* or *FE*. For some singular nouns ending in *f* or *fe*, change the *f* or *fe* to *v* and add *es*. For others, simply add *s*.

Change *F* or *FE* to *V*; Then Add *ES*

wi*fe*	wi<u>*ves*</u>	shel*f*	shel<u>*ves*</u>
li*fe*	li<u>*ves*</u>	loa*f*	loa<u>*ves*</u>

Just Add *S*

plaintiff	plaintiff<u>s</u>	belief	belief<u>s</u>
proof	proof<u>s</u>	chef	chef<u>s</u>

Foreign Nouns. Nouns of foreign origin such as *agenda* and *prospectus* may form their plurals by adding *s* (*agendas*) or *es* (*prospectuses*). But many foreign nouns have both an "English plural" and a "foreign plural," as shown below.

Singular	Plural	English Plural
addend*um*	addend*a*	
alumn*a*	alumn*ae*	
alumn*us*	alumn*i*	
analys*is*	analys*es*	
ax*is*	ax*es*	
bacteri*um*	bacteri*a*	
bas*is*	bas*es*	
cris*is*	cris*es*	
criteri*on*	criteri*a*	criteri*ons*
curricul*um*	curricul*a*	curricul*ums*
dat*um*	dat*a**	
formul*a*	formul*ae*	formul*as*

* *Data* is now also considered "correct" in a singular construction, as in "The data *is* summarized on page 121."

Singular	Plural	English Plural
fung*us*	fung*i*	
hypothes*is*	hypothes*es*	
ind*ex*	ind*ices*	ind*exes*
medi*um*	medi*a*	medi*ums*
memorand*um*	memorand*a*	memorand*ums*
nucle*us*	nucle*i*	nucle*uses*
oas*is*	oas*es*	
parenthes*is*	parenthes*es*	
stadi*um*	stadi*a*	stadi*ums*
stimul*us*	stimul*i*	
vertebr*a*	vertebr*ae*	vertebr*as*

In some cases the preferred form is the English plural (for example, *memorandums*); in other cases the preferred form is the foreign plural (for example, *criteria*). Obviously, there is no one rule that will simplify your using these words correctly. Be sure to consult your dictionary whenever you are uncertain about the plural form of a noun of foreign origin. If two different plural forms are given, use the form that appears first, since this is the preferred plural.

For this and other usage principles, learn to use a comprehensive, up-to-date reference manual.

Always Singular	Always Plural	One Form for Both Singular and Plural	
news	thanks	deer	salmon
genetics	trousers	fish	politics
mathematics	proceeds	odds	economics
aeronautics	pants	sheep	statistics
	riches	corps	shrimp
	tidings	Chinese	spaghetti
	credentials	moose	
	belongings	Japanese	
	scissors		

The news about the merger *is* certainly encouraging. (Not *news are.*)

Lilly's credentials *are* quite impressive.

A Japanese *is* the inventor of this instrument.

Several Japanese *have* bought the firm.

Note, too, how words such as *hundred, thousand,* and *dozen* are used in the following sentences.

One *hundred* people are expected.

Three *hundred* customers requested credit cards.   (Not *Three hundreds.*)

Several *dozen* complaints were received.   (Not *Several dozens.*)

EDITING PRACTICE 3

Select the correct word in each of the following sentences.

1. The news that we heard this morning (is, are) quite optimistic about fourth-quarter interest rates.
2. According to the reports, Ivan and Paulette are the (heros, heroes) of the day.
3. His (analysis, analyses) of the new financial situation was concise but informative.
4. Blue Star Industries manufactures and distributes (pianos, pianoes) all over the world.
5. The numbers in (parenthesis, parentheses) represent metric equivalents, don't they?
6. All the (datum, data) that we gathered will be compiled in tables at the end of this report.
7. The top and bottom (shelfs, shelves) contain all the file copies that you are looking for.
8. Bart and Jeff are going to the dinner tonight; their (wifes, wives) are meeting them there.
9. According to this suggestion, all revenue obtained from taxing the (casinos, casinoes) will be used for educational purposes.
10. Avery Pharmaceuticals claims that the new drug will save thousands of (lifes, lives) each year.

EDITING PRACTICE 4

Correct any errors in the following sentences. If a sentence has no error, write *OK*.

1. The United States threatened embargoes against both nations.
2. The proceeds from the special drive is expected to top $1 million!
3. Economics have always been a required course for all business students.
4. The company choir is seeking two more altoes for the upcoming Christmas show.
5. Increased prices of potatos and tomatos will affect the consumer price index.
6. In both cases the plaintives claimed high damages.
7. The formulas they developed were remarkably similar.
8. To avoid such crisis in the future, our security staff is taking special precautions.
9. Has Rory completed the many addendum he was typing?
10. Only one analyses has been completed as of this morning.

COMMUNICATION LABORATORY

APPLICATION EXERCISES

A. On a separate sheet of paper, write your corrections for any errors in the following sentences. Write *OK* for any sentence that has no error.

1. Most of the radioes that we import are sold through direct-mail advertising.
2. Did you know that the owners of Watts Enterprises are the Franklin's?
3. Nearly 70 percent of the alumnuses of Fitch University live within the tristate area.
4. Needless to say, we gladly reimbursed the Shermans for the defective merchandise.
5. Thursday's interview with two senator-elects should draw a large television audience.
6. Only one of the countys in the northern part of the state has already put the new system into effect.
7. Mr. and Mrs. Bunch have coordinated this charity drive in the past, but the Bunchs moved to Arizona last month.
8. Before we have this office painted, let's remove all those books from the shelfs.
9. According to the executor, the entire estate will be divided among Mrs. Gordon's four stepchilds.
10. Please be sure to file these letters, reports, and memorandums before we leave for the airport, Leonard.
11. The only important criteria, in our opinion, is the safety of all employees in the plant.
12. We are now waiting to hear from our attornies concerning the validity of the documents.
13. The company is owned by two brothers—the Messrs. Smiths—who have managed to make Smith Enterprises a million-dollar business in a very short time.
14. Because of various government embargoes, we do not ship computer equipment to certain nations.
15. Only countrys listed on this sheet are permitted to place orders for computers with our firm.

B. Beginning with this exercise and continuing through Unit 25, each Application Exercise B will be a review. The following sentences will help you review the grammar principles you have studied so far. Correct sentences with errors; write *OK* for any sentence that has no error.

1. Both office's are being moved to the ninth floor, according to this chart.
2. Here are the instructions for merging both halfs of the manuscript onto one diskette.
3. If these figures represent thousands, then please be sure to add three zeroes to each numeral as you retype these columns.
4. Use parenthesis to enclose metric equivalents; for example, 10 yards (9.14 meters).
5. In the past three years, our assets have grew an average of 20 percent a year.
6. Please be very careful as you lie these delicate pieces on the countertop.
7. The Hamiltons have owned the firm for three generations.
8. Yes, both my daughter-in-laws are designers for this advertising agency.
9. Two of the bidders are the Mesdames Marxes, who want to build garden apartments on the property.
10. Two sales territorys that are now open are in Rochester, New York, and Boston, Massachusetts.
11. The news that we heard from Ms. Peterson confirms the rumors we had heard.
12. If the Donnellys purchase the land, they will try to resell it quickly for a fast profit.
13. The pipes had froze because the walls are not insulated properly.
14. We have carefully tested all these waxs to make sure that they contain no harmful ingredients.
15. Mr. Claridge been with the Legal Department since 1981, hasn't he?

C. Correct the errors in the following paragraph.

To make sure that all agreements with foreign countries are legal, we asked the attornies and the CPA's in the Tax Department to inspect the documents carefully. Their analyses will be completed within the next few week's. Then, when the various embargos against these countrys are lifted by our government, we will be able to resume our business in Europe and Asia.

VOCABULARY AND SPELLING STUDIES

A. These words are often confused: *adverse, averse; preposition, proposition.* Distinguish between the pairs, and write a sentence using each word.

B. What does the suffix *ish* (as in *bookish, bluish,* and *devilish*) mean: (1) "resembling," (2) "full of," or (3) "made of"?

C. What does the suffix *ee* (as in *employee, lessee, mortgagee,* and *nominee*) mean: (1) "a native of," (2) "state or quality of," (3) "the recipient of an action," or (4) "having the characteristics of"?

D. How do you spell:

1. The verb meaning "to be before"?
2. The number that follows *one?*
3. The adverb formed from *full?*

COMMUNICATING FOR RESULTS

Judgment Calls. Your employer, Carolyn Watts, is in Chicago on a business trip. While her secretary is away from the desk, you answer Ms. Watts' phone. The caller is a good customer, Mr. Jeffries, who asks for a number where he can call Ms. Watts. Assuming that you know Ms. Watts' number at her hotel in Chicago, what should you tell Mr. Jeffries?

U · N · I · T

16 Possessive Nouns and Possessive Pronouns

The pronunciation of both singular and plural possessives is the same for most nouns—*boy's/boys', manager's/managers',* and so on. Furthermore, because the simple plurals are also pronounced the same (*boys, managers*), writing these forms often results in misspellings.

You already know how to form plurals correctly, so we will now concentrate on possessives. Study this unit carefully to make sure that you can always avoid errors in using possessive forms.

Possessive Nouns—Basic Uses

When used with a noun, the apostrophe is the symbol of possession: one *woman's* briefcase, several *employees'* records, *Katherine's* promotion. The apostrophe helps us take a shortcut from the longer possessive expressions "the briefcase of one woman," "the records of several employees," and "the promotion of Katherine."

Follow these three rules for using apostrophes to form noun possessives:

1. Add an apostrophe plus *s* to a noun that does not end in *s:*

    One *woman's* suggestion developed into a new product.

    Five *women's* handbags were turned in to the police.

    Because neither *woman* nor *women* ends in *s*, add an apostrophe plus *s* to form the possessive of these nouns. This rule applies to all nouns, singular and plural, that do not end in *s*.

2. Add only the apostrophe to a plural noun that ends in *s:*

    The *Smiths'* franchise is in Tampa, Florida.

    Several *clients'* contracts expire on December 31 of this year.

    We'll need about two *years'* time to renovate this old plant.

    A *students'* lounge will be constructed in one corner of the floor.

    To form the possessives of *Smiths, clients, years,* and *students,* add only the apostrophe.

3. **a.** Add an apostrophe plus *s* to a singular noun ending in *s* if the resulting possessive form is pronounced with an additional syllable.

    One *actress's* script did not have the revised pages.   (*Actress's* has one more syllable than *actress.*)

    His *boss's* solution was to file a lawsuit against the manufacturer.   (*Boss's* has one more syllable than *boss.*)

    b. Add only the apostrophe to a singular noun ending in *s* if the possessive form is *not* pronounced with an additional syllable. The key to this rule is to determine whether the possessive form would sound awkward if pronounced with the additional syllable. This rule applies mainly to proper names.

    Of course, we checked to make sure that it was Ms. *Saunders'* signature.   (The pronunciation of *Saunders's* would be awkward.)

    To help remember these rules, study this Quick Trick.

| QUICK TRICK | **FIND THE OWNER!** |

Reword the possessive phrase to be sure that you know which word is the "owner" and which word is the object of ownership:

> that customer's account (the account of that customer: object, *account;* owner, *customer*)

> several manufacturers' bids (the bids of several manufacturers: object, *bids;* owner, *manufacturers*)

the boys' gymnasium (the gymnasium of the boys: object, *gymnasium*; owner, *boys*)

With this method, you will be sure to locate the correct object and the correct owner. When you know the owners, of course, you will then know that *customer, manufacturers,* and *boys* are the words that you must make possessive.

NOTE: In the official names of certain organizations, banks, or buildings, apostrophes may be omitted from the possessive forms; for example, *the Woman Executives Association, Manufacturers Bank,* and *The Theatrical Agents Building.* In all cases, however, always use the official spelling.

EDITING PRACTICE 1

Once you are confident that you can apply the rules for forming noun possessives, select the correct word in parentheses in the following sentences.

1. Do you have a copy of Jim (Hastings', Hastings's) contract?
2. She received only one (applicant's, applicants') résumé in response to yesterday's ad.
3. If Mr. (Walters', Walters's) bid is accepted, we will sell the Chicago warehouse by the end of the year.
4. Several (representative's, representatives') cars will be affected by the new lease agreement.
5. Is your (boss's, bosses') office still on this floor?
6. A new (woman's, women's) clothing store will open in the Anderson Mall on June 1.
7. Ask Ms. (Jenkins', Jenkins's) assistant for an appointment to discuss these problems.
8. One (agent's, agents') commission check was delayed at our headquarters office.
9. You should give the store at least ten (day's, days') notice in such cases.
10. Take all the (applicant's, applicants') employment forms to Ms. Lopez's office.

EDITING PRACTICE 2

Do the following sentences have any errors in the use of apostrophes? Find and correct each error. If a sentence has no error, write *OK.*

1. Is that Jims' car—the car parked near Tom's?
2. Carl Young is handling the estate for the Kellys' children.
3. As you know, the treasurers' signature is required on all checks over $500.
4. Jessica's new computer will be delivered in about ten days or so.

5. One store owners' suggestion was to provide added security for the entire shopping area.

6. The mayors' naming Mr. Broderick to the commission came as a surprise to all of us.

7. As you know, the nations' financial center is Wall Street, which is in New York City.

8. Striker's demands for higher wages will be discussed later this afternoon.

9. In an effort to help needy people in the area, our company has established a childrens' fund.

10. Is Gregorys' new office located in the new Host Building?

Possessive Nouns—Special Uses

Here are some additional rules for using the apostrophe with nouns to show possession. Study them carefully.

Compound Nouns. Form the possessive of a compound noun on the last word of the compound.

> my *editor in chief's* budget   (The budget of my *editor in chief*. Because editor in chief does not end in *s*, add an apostrophe and *s* to form the possessive.)

> both *homeowners'* policies   (The policies of both homeowners. Because *homeowners* is a plural noun ending in *s*, add only an apostrophe.)

> my *brother-in-law's* new business   (The new business of my brother-in-law. Because *law* does not end in *s*, add an apostrophe and *s* to form the possessive.)

Joint Ownership. When two or more "owners" possess something jointly, place the apostrophe (or the apostrophe plus *s*) on the last owner's name.

> Jack and *Dorothy's* original bid was for $25,000.   (One bid, jointly "owned" by both Jack and Dorothy. Place the apostrophe plus *s* only on the second name, *Dorothy's*.)

> New York and *New Jersey's* plan to clean the Hudson will begin on April 11.   (A shared plan, as indicated by placing the 's on the second term, *New Jersey's*.)

Separate Ownership. When two or more owners possess things individually or separately, place the apostrophe (or the apostrophe plus *s*) on the name of *each* owner. (REMEMBER: Make *separate* possessives to indicate *separate* ownership.)

> *Jack's* and *Dorothy's* assistants are experienced auditors.   (Jack's assistant and Dorothy's assistant—*both* are experienced auditors.)

> *New York's* and *New Jersey's* governors were fully supportive of the plan.   (In other words, "New York's governor and New Jersey's governor . . . ." Separate ownership, separate possessive forms.)

The key to using possessives correctly to show joint ownership and separate ownership is to analyze the context of each sentence.

EDITING PRACTICE 3

Select the correct word in parentheses for each of the following sentences.

1. (Lurkin & Crowell's, Lurkin's & Crowell's) sales for this year are estimated at $4.2 million.
2. The annual tax on (Stephen and Edna's, Stephen's and Edna's) property is $42,500.
3. I think that we should get (someone's else, someone else's) opinion on which computers to lease.
4. The projected revenue from (Lord and Wilson's, Lord's and Wilson's) foreign operations is about $5 million.
5. (Ray and Carole's, Ray's and Carole's) joint income tax statement was submitted past the April 15 deadline.

EDITING PRACTICE 4

Read the following sentences to correct any errors in the use of possessives. Write *OK* if the sentence is correct.

1. Her brother's and her sister's shares in the new business are equal.
2. Her brother and her sister's business was recently incorporated.
3. Karen's and Maria's new restaurant will open December 1.
4. Andrew's and Fred's new supervisor will start on Friday, March 3.
5. Yes, Andrew's and Fred's daughters also work for Munch Enterprises.

Possessive Personal Pronouns

The personal pronouns are *I, we, you, he, she, it,* and *they*. In the following chart, note the possessive forms of these personal pronouns—and note that they do *not* have apostrophes.

Personal Pronouns	Possessive Forms
I	my, mine
you	your, yours
he	his, his
she	her, hers,
it	its, its
we	our, ours
they	their, theirs

The first pronoun in each pair of possessives—*my, your, his, her, its, our,* and *their*—is used as an adjective.

My plane leaves at 2 p.m. *His* flight is scheduled to leave at 3 p.m., but *her* flight may be delayed until 4:30.

The pronouns *mine, yours, hers, his, ours,* and *theirs* replace possessive phrases such as *my book, your desk, her car,* and so on.

This is *my book.* OR: This is *mine.*

Is this *your pen?* OR: Is this *yours?*

She parked *her car.* OR: She parked *hers.*

As you see, the pronouns *mine, yours, hers, his, ours,* and *theirs* may never be used as modifiers; they always stand alone. Using personal pronouns correctly is tricky not because their usage is confusing (the opposite is true) but because some of the possessive forms of personal pronouns sound precisely like other words. Review the following pairs, remembering that personal pronouns never have apostrophes. The first word in each heading is the personal pronoun. (The Quick Trick on the next page can also help you.)

Its, It's. The possessive pronoun *its* means "of it" or "belonging to it." *It's* is a contraction—a shortened form of "it is."

The Willis Corporation is well known for *its* generosity to *its* employees.   (*Its generosity*—the generosity of it. *Its employees*—the employees of it. *Its* is a possessive form of a personal pronoun.)

It's exceptionally generous to employees.   (*It's*—a contraction meaning "it is." *It's* is not a personal pronoun.)

NOTE: There is no such word as *its'.*

Their, They're, There. *Their* means "of them" or "belonging to them." *They're* is a contraction, a shortened form of "they are." *There* may mean "in that place"; it may also be used as an introductory word and in some other ways.

Find out which one of *their* warehouses will be open on Saturday.   (Warehouses *belonging to them.*)

They're now in the conference room on the fifth floor.   (*They are* now . . . .)

Please leave the disks *there* when you are finished.   (Leave them *in that place.*)

There are only a few more invoices to process.   (Introductory word.)

Your, You're. *Your* means "belonging to you." *You're* is a contraction, a shortened form of "you are."

When *you're* traveling, be sure to have *your* SuperCard with you.   (When *you are* traveling. The SuperCard *belonging to you.*)

Whose, Who's. *Whose* is a possessive pronoun meaning "belonging to whom." *Who's* is a contraction for "who is" or "who has."

Whose badge was found in the hallway?   (Badge *belonging to whom.*)

Who's working on the late shift tonight?   (*Who is* working . . . .)

Who's been named to the committee?   (*Who has been* . . . .)

QUICK TRICK **TEST THE CONTRACTION**

To choose between *its/it's, their/they're,* and so on, test the sentence by reading it with the full form of the contraction. If the sentence makes sense, then the contraction is correct. If the sentence does not make sense, then the pronoun is correct.

Do you know when (they're, their) supposed to arrive?   (Read the sentence with the full form of the contraction: Do you know when *they are* supposed to arrive? Does the sentence make sense? Yes, so *they're* is correct.)

Please give me (they're, their) new address.   (Again, read the sentence with *they are:* Please give me *they are* new address. Does the sentence make sense? No, so the personal pronoun *their* is correct.)

EDITING PRACTICE 5

In the following sentences find all the errors in the use of possessive personal pronouns. If a sentence has no error, write *OK.*

1. While you're working at the microcomputer, please make a backup copy of this diskette.
2. Who's voice is that on the loudspeaker?
3. When you're ready to distribute your handouts, just let me know.
4. According to the report, there van was damaged only slightly.
5. As soon as you're ready to leave, just call me.
6. No, its not too late to order the Screen Writer II program for your word processor.
7. Their is one easy way to check this release date: call the West Coast office.
8. One benefit of this equipment is that its easy to operate.
9. Do you know whether this diskette is her's?
10. Alan, who's signature is on this check?

Possessive Before a Gerund

A *gerund* is a verb form ending in *ing* and used as a noun. A noun or a pronoun before a gerund should be in the possessive case.

I heard about *Jack's* winning the monthly sales contest.   (Not *Jack winning.*)

I heard about *his* winning the monthly sales contest.   (Not *him winning.*)

We appreciated *Bob's* calling us and *his* sending us the new text on BASIC programming.   (Not *Bob calling.* Not *him sending.*)

EDITING PRACTICE 6

Select the correct word in parentheses.

1. She was angry, of course, at (him, his) leaving early on Friday afternoon.
2. Mrs. VanNostrand appreciated (us, our) volunteering to help her staff with the backlog of orders.
3. (You, Your) informing us of these changes has saved us a lot of time.
4. We are happy to hear about (you, your) accepting a new job offer closer to your home.
5. Thanks to (them, their) helping us with all the invoices, we were able to complete our work on time.

COMMUNICATION LABORATORY

APPLICATION EXERCISES

A. Choose the correct word in each of the following sentences. HINT: For each possessive noun, make sure that you know which word is the owner.

1. Please be sure to inform customers that there will be a (months, month's, months') delay in filling all orders for Bethel products.
2. We appreciated (Bob, Bob's, Bobs') helping us plan the outline for our report.
3. Most of the (secretaries, secretary's, secretaries') in the training program rated the courses "Excellent."
4. The (Lutzes, Lutz's, Lutzes') have franchise operations in four different states.
5. The (Nelsons, Nelson's, Nelsons') holdings in General Metals Inc. have been drastically reduced in the last two years.
6. With two (weeks, week's, weeks') notice, we can ship and install any of the machines listed in this catalog.
7. Because business has been exceedingly slow, we have cut all (managers, manager's, managers') expense budgets by 20 percent.
8. (Tim's and Laura's, Tim and Laura's) suggestion was to hire part-time help during the months of July and August.
9. Before we attend this afternoon's meeting, be sure that (your, you're) prepared to answer any questions concerning the manufacturing schedules.
10. The (Consolinos, Consolino's, Consolinos') newest store—their fifth—will be located in the Pheasant Run Shopping Mall.
11. Roberta, will you please find out (whose, who's) recording equipment this is?
12. Do you know (whose, who's) recording in Studio A right now?

13. One (districts, district's, districts') goal is to exceed its last year's revenue by 32 percent.
14. One of our (districts, district's, districts') has set very ambitious sales goals for next year.
15. Do you know whether (its, it's) possible to get a discount for quantity orders?

B. On a separate sheet of paper, write your corrections for any errors in the following sentences. Write *OK* if a sentence has no error.

1. The marketing director, according to Margaret, has chose Tampa, Florida, as the site of our annual sales convention.
2. She been asking about transfer opportunities because she enjoys living in the Boston area.
3. Randy said, "If I were you, I would ask one of the manager's to approve these purchase orders."
4. One editor in chief's retirement is scheduled for May; another's, for September.
5. How long have you knew about the potential sale of the property to Rasmussen Homes?
6. The documents that you're looking for have been laying on the reception desk for several days.
7. Paul's and Al's wives always join them on their business trips.
8. Have you heard about him helping us with the annual report?
9. If the contract was lying on the conference room table, I probably just didn't notice it.
10. Of course, if its necessary to submit a claim to our insurance company, we will do so.
11. When my assistant's finish this training course, they will begin a special two-week computer-training program in Dallas.
12. You must complete this form if your changing the beneficiaries of your life insurance policy.
13. Mr. Langan asked two clerks to work on Saturdays during the summer months.
14. Do you know whether there planning to bring their families with them to this year's convention?
15. Several companies' now participate in and donate to this community drug-awareness program.

C. Write the correct plural or possessive form of each word or phrase in parentheses.

1. Luxor Fashions, Inc., is a well-known manufacturer of (woman) clothing.
2. This request for information was received from the (attorney general) office.

3. Ms. Nugent is the researcher (who) study is now receiving much nationwide publicity.
4. Try to use (someone else) terminal to see whether you have the same problem.
5. Dr. (Hastings) account is handled by Gordon Moses.
6. We plan to sign a (year) lease for the district office.
7. All (executive) stock options must be exercised before December 31.
8. Among the (CPA) in our office is Lillian Demarest.
9. All the (Nash) have already returned their response cards.
10. Miriam received all (A) last semester.

VOCABULARY AND SPELLING STUDIES

A. These words are often confused: *finely, finally, finale; expensive, expansive.* Explain the differences.

B. Do you know the difference between the following homonyms: *overdo, overdue; prophet, profit; hear, here?* Define each.

C. The following words can have either one *l* or two, but most American dictionaries list one spelling as preferred. Write the preferred spelling of each word.

1. cancellation
2. cancelled
3. traveler
4. skilful
5. marvellous
6. installment

COMMUNICATING FOR RESULTS

Conflicting Interests. You are a member of the advertising staff at Bentley Toys. One of your close coworkers, Louise Cooper, an advertising copywriter in the same department, confides that in order to save money to buy a car, she is doing free-lance writing for Nu-Day Toys and Novelties, one of Bentley's competitors.

Do you see a conflict of interest in working for two different companies that are in the same business? What advice do you have for Louise about working for a competitor?

U · N · I · T

17

Other Forms of Pronouns

Errors in pronoun use may quickly label a person as a poor business communicator. Therefore, avoiding errors such as "Him and I went to the seminar" and "Between you and I" is very important to effective communications and to your business future.

You already studied possessive case forms of personal pronouns. In this unit and the next, you will study the other case forms of personal pronouns so that you will be able to avoid *all* the common errors of pronoun use and communicate effectively both in speaking and in writing.

Case Forms of Pronouns

The pronoun cases are *nominative*, *objective*, and *possessive*. *Case* refers to the relationship of a word to other words in the sentence. You have already learned, for example, that a noun or pronoun in the possessive case shows ownership. A pronoun in the nominative case shows a different relationship to the other words in the sentence, and a pronoun in the objective case shows yet another relationship.

Compare the following pairs of sentences.

Nominative

Henry asked for this pamphlet.   (*Henry* is a nominative case noun.)

He asked for this pamphlet.   (*He* is a nominative case pronoun. *He* substitutes for *Henry* in the sentence above.)

Objective

Give *Henry* this pamphlet.   (*Henry* is an objective case noun, object of the verb *give*.)

Give *him* this pamphlet.   (*Him* is an objective case pronoun, object of the verb *give*.)

Possessive

This is *Henry's* pamphlet.   (*Henry's* is a possessive case noun.)

This is *his* pamphlet.   (*His* is a possessive case pronoun.)

These sentences show the basic relationships of the nominative, the objective, and the possessive cases of nouns and pronouns to other words

161

in the sentence. Note that nouns have the same form for the nominative and the objective cases. Note, too, how pronouns substitute for nouns—*he* for *Henry* in the first pair of sentences, *him* for *Henry* in the second pair, and *his* for *Henry's* in the third pair.

Here is a list of nominative and objective pronouns. Review them before you continue.

Nominative Pronouns		Objective Pronouns		Examples
I	we	me	us	*I* gave; *we* went; for *me*; hired *us*
you	you	you	you	*you* are; with *you*
he she it	they	him her it	them	*he* has; *she* has; *it* will be; *they* know; to *him*; promoted *her*; on *it*; gave *them*
who	who	whom	whom	*who* has; appointed *whom*

Nominative Case

The most common uses of the nominative case are as subjects of verbs and as complements of "being" verbs.

Subject of a Verb. Pronouns that are the subjects of verbs must be in the nominative case.

> *I* asked Renee and Frank to attend the meeting, but *she* will be out of town, and *he* has made vacation plans.   (*I, she,* and *he* are nominatives. *I* is the subject of the verb *asked. She* is the subject of *will be. He* is the subject of *has made.*)

Complement of a "Being" Verb. A noun or a pronoun that completes the meaning of a "being" verb is called a *complement.* As you know, of course, the "being" verbs are *am, is, are, was, were, be, being,* and *been.* A pronoun that follows a "being" verb must be in the nominative case.

> It was *I* who recommended changing these procedures.   (*I* completes the meaning of the "being" verb *was.* As a complement of a being verb, the nominative *I* must be used.)

> The vice president in charge of marketing is *she.*   (*She* completes the meaning of the "being" verb *is;* therefore, the nominative case is required.)

> Could it have been *they* in the auditorium?   (*They* completes the meaning of the "being" verb *could have been;* therefore, the nominative case is required.)

Complement of Infinitive *To Be* When *To Be* Has No Subject. Any pronoun that follows and completes the meaning (is a complement) of the infinitive *to be* when *to be* has no subject of its own is in the nominative case. To apply this rule, remember:

1. This rule applies only to the infinitive *to be.* Do not try to use the rule in any other situation.

2. The infinitive *to be* will have a subject *only when a noun or a pronoun immediately precedes it.*

Look at two sentences where the infinitive *to be* does *not* have a subject.

I would not wish to be *he*.   (Is there a subject—a noun or pronoun—immediately preceding *to be?* No. Then this *to be* has no subject and the complement *he* is correct, because the pronoun must be in the nominative case.)

The owners appeared to be *they*.   (Since *to be* has no subject immediately preceding it, the complement of the infinitive *to be* must be *they*, not *them*, because *they* is in the nominative case.)

In these sentences the infinitive *to be* does have a subject.

Stanley thought *her* to be me.   (*Her* is the subject of *to be*.)

The receptionist mistakenly believed the *visitors* to be us.   (*Visitors* is the subject of *to be*.)

The following Quick Trick can help you with the *to be* rule.

NO SUBJECT—NOMINATIVE CASE

For a memory hook on which to hang the *to be* rule, make this connection:

NO subject—*NO*minative case.

NO is the word you must remember, and *NO* starts the word *NOminative*. Think this over. You will be amazed to see that the Quick Trick will help you to apply the *to be* rule.

EDITING PRACTICE 1

Choose the correct pronoun in parentheses.

1. Didn't you realize that it was (I, me) at the front of the room?
2. Yes, she was in the bank this morning, so perhaps the woman you saw was (she, her).
3. No, I would not choose to be (he, him).
4. Daniel said that (we, us) would not have the approval of the committee until Monday.
5. As you heard, Robert, (they, them) are going to reject our offer.
6. Under these circumstances, I certainly would not wish to be (she, her).

EDITING PRACTICE 2

Now correct any errors in the use of the nominative case in the following sentences. Write *OK* if the sentence is correct.

1. The instructor thought him to be me.
2. Next November, according to Betty, them will completely revise our procedures manual.
3. Teach your staff members to say "This is he" or "This is she" when a caller asks for them.
4. The executives who voted in favor of expanding the medical and dental benefits were they.
5. I do not believe it could have been him at the railroad station.
6. Are you sure that it was her who made these excellent suggestions?

James and I or James and Me?

Nouns and pronouns are commonly joined by *and* or *or* in compound subjects and compound objects.

Compound Subject	Compound Object
James and *I* will go . . .	. . . to James and *me*
Dr. Keller or *he* is . . .	. . . for Dr. Keller and *him*
She and *I* wrote . . .	. . . written by her and *me*

To be sure that you always use the correct pronoun in compounds such as these, follow this Quick Trick:

QUICK TRICK   USE THE PRONOUN BY ITSELF

For compounds that include pronouns, test the pronoun *by itself*, as shown here:

Louis and (I, me) may go with Mr. Keating.   (Omit *Louis and* and the answer becomes clear: "*I* may go . . . .")

Mr. Keating invited Louis and (I, me).   (Again, test the pronoun by itself. Omit *Louis and:* "Mr. Keating invited . . . *me*.")

Note that pronoun choice in the following constructions can be tested in a similar manner:

(We, Us) proofreaders enjoy working overtime.   (Read the sentence omitting the noun *proofreaders* and the answer becomes clear: "(We, Us) . . . enjoy working overtime." Obviously, you would say "*We* enjoy," not "*Us* enjoy."

They have asked (we, us) proofreaders to work overtime.   (To decide between *we proofreaders* and *us proofreaders*, omit the noun *proofreaders*: "They have asked *us* . . . to work overtime.")

EDITING PRACTICE 3

Choose the correct pronoun in the following sentences.

1. Is Randall or (she, her) among the possible choices for district manager?
2. Yes, (we, us) auditors always double-check one another's work.
3. The lab technicians and (they, them) have thoroughly reviewed the safety procedures.
4. The marketing staff members give (we, us) sales representatives very good support.
5. Early this morning she asked Roberta and (I, me) to substitute for her at tomorrow's inventory meeting.
6. She was very thoughtful in telling the president that the booklets were written by Richard and (I, me).

EDITING PRACTICE 4

Correct any errors in the use of pronouns in the following sentences.

1. Please be sure to give we proofreaders enough time to check the galleys carefully.
2. Erica and him will conduct the training program.
3. Only Marsha and her have the authority to sign these documents.
4. Needless to say, we were very surprised to hear that Ms. Crawford had appointed Frances and I district managers.
5. My vice president, Jessica Rosen, informed Larry and I of her decision only this morning.
6. As you requested, I sent additional copies to Mr. Owens, Ms. Cohn, and he.

Objective Case   The objective case of personal pronouns is used when a pronoun is the object of a preposition or the object of a verb. The following rules also apply to *whom* and *whomever*, the objective case forms of the pronouns *who* and *whoever*.

Object of a Preposition. A preposition is always used in a *prepositional phrase*. Every prepositional phrase has a noun or a pronoun as an object.

Preposition	Prepositional Phrase	Examples
to	to the director to her	Give the film *to the director*. (The noun *director* is the object of the preposition *to*.)
		Give the film *to her*. (The pronoun *her* is the object of the preposition *to*.)

Preposition	Prepositional Phrase	Examples
from	from the budget director from them	The message *from the budget director* was vague. (The compound noun *budget director* is the object of the preposition *from.*) The message *from them* was vague. (The pronoun *them* is the object of the preposition *from.*)
against	against the proposal against it	We heard comments *against the proposal.* (The noun *proposal* is the object of the preposition *against.*) We heard comments *against it.* (The pronoun *it* is the object of the preposition *against.*)
for	for Joe, Gloria, and me for us	Get copies *for Joe, Gloria, and me.* (The object of the preposition *for* is *Joe, Gloria, and me*, which includes the nouns *Joe* and *Gloria* and the pronoun *me.*) Get copies *for us.* (The pronoun *us* is the object of the preposition *for.*)

Object of a Verb. Now notice how objective pronouns are used as objects of verbs.

Irwin trained *them.*   (The pronoun *them* is the object of the verb *trained.*)

Agnes told Leo, Vincent, and *her* the news about the warehouse closing.   (The pronoun *her* is the object of the verb *told.* The nouns *Leo* and *Vincent* are also the objects of the verb *told*, of course.)

COMMUNICATION LABORATORY

APPLICATION EXERCISES

A. From the choices in parentheses, select the correct form. For each nominative form you select, give the reason for your choice—write *sub* for subject of a verb and *comp* for complement of a "being" verb.

1. The company depends on (we, us) messengers to deliver merchandise quickly and dependably.
2. If you are ordering additional catalogs, please get three copies for Vera, Thomas, and (I, me).
3. From now on Phyllis and (he, him) will supervise the Sheldon account.

4. Be sure to say "This is (she, her)," not "This is (she, her)," whenever a caller asks for you.
5. Yes, I am sure that it was (he, him) who ordered all this merchandise.
6. Our supervisor, Gail Hendricks, asked Allan and (I, me) to help her with this special assignment.
7. Ms. Calandro asked, "If you were (I, me), what would you do in this situation?"
8. We were surprised, of course, to hear that the annual sales awards will be given to Sarah and (I, me).
9. (We, Us) telemarketing specialists work extra hours during the busy season.
10. Frankly, between you and (I, me), I hope that the merger is approved by the shareholders.
11. Although that gentleman really does look like Mr. Simpson, I'm not sure that it is indeed (he, him).
12. Early this morning Marcella and (I, me) interviewed more applicants.
13. Ms. Whitebook and (he, him) decided to extend their service contracts as a result of the discount.
14. The applicants were interviewed by Marcella and (I, me).
15. The additional copies are to be sent to Mr. Castagna, Ms. Schwartz, and (she, her).

B. Correct any errors in the following sentences. Write *OK* for any sentence that has no error.

1. Ms. Blackmore appreciated me helping her with her "Rush" projects.
2. Ms. Birdsong has already spoke with Mr. Ferris about computerized billing.
3. There are two folders marked "Confidential"; one is ours, and the other is there's.
4. Did you know that Glen and her are moving to our headquarters office?
5. Yes, Glen and her assistant are moving to New York.
6. The person whose responsible for the research laboratory in our Denver plant is Peter Rogalin.
7. The building that you are referring to is co-owned by the Moser's and the Moore's.
8. If the Spiegels return from Miami on Monday, we'll meet with them on Tuesday afternoon.
9. All the professional recruiters did an excellent job of explaining career opportunities in their respective companies.
10. I am not sure whether he been to our Atlanta warehouse before; perhaps you should call his secretary.
11. The company's clinic is on the second floor; there, we have four nurses and two M.D.'s available during working hours.

12. Because the top half of the copy had been tore, the attorneys asked us for the original agreement.
13. John's and Clara's father is one of the executive vice presidents of the Claremont Bank & Trust Company.
14. We sent him a gift to express our thanks for him helping us operate the printing equipment.
15. When we seen Marion, she was returning from her weekly staff meeting.

C. Select the correct pronoun. Then indicate whether this pronoun is in the nominative or the objective case by writing *N* or *O*.

1. Perhaps it was (I, me) who forgot to return the contracts to the company's legal staff.
2. The general manager and (we, us) district managers are concerned that economic conditions will seriously affect sales.
3. Dr. Crowe, the head of our research staff, has asked (we, us) to draft a marketing survey.
4. The people who are responsible for meeting this tight schedule are (we, us) engineers.
5. Gregory enjoys working with either Margaret or (he, him).
6. Just between you and (I, me), do you really believe that this sales goal is realistic?
7. Frankly, Jack, if I were (she, her), I would not invest in such high-risk stocks.
8. Do you have the software that Angela and (I, me) need to draft this report?
9. Whenever you're ready to discuss this agenda, call Carla and (I, me) to set up an appointment.
10. If you should have any problems understanding these complicated instructions, just ask (we, us) programmers for assistance.

VOCABULARY AND SPELLING STUDIES

A. Explain the differences between these words, which are often confused: *sale, sail; intelligent, intelligible.*

B. What are the plural forms of the following words?

1. teaspoonful   4. mouse
2. gas   5. memorandum
3. facility   6. ratio

C. Which of the following possessives are singular, and which are plural?

1. manager's   4. women's
2. Walshes'   5. hotel's
3. children's   6. Smiths'

COMMUNICATING FOR RESULTS

Being on Time. Robert Weldon has been employed by Poole & Travis Data Systems for over four years. He has established an excellent reputation for completing all his assignments on time and within budgeted costs, and he knows that he is a valued employee.

However, although Robert works long hours, he is seldom in the office on time. The official working hours are from 9 a.m. until 5 p.m. Robert usually works until 7 p.m. or 8 p.m. most days, but he arrives between 10 and 10:30 each morning.

Recently Robert's new supervisor politely discussed with him the need to arrive at work on time, but Robert simply thought the supervisor was trying to establish authority. Robert feels that doing his work is all that matters, regardless of what time he arrives.

Is Robert correct in his thinking?

U · N · I · T

18 Common Pronoun Errors

You are now able to use pronouns correctly in almost all situations. This final unit on pronouns will put the finishing touches on your skill. This unit will cover some troublesome uses of pronouns, including the correct uses of the pronouns *who* and *whom*.

More Than I or More Than Me?

Correct pronoun choice is sometimes clouded because of the shortcuts we take in speaking and writing. For example, in the following sentences we generally omit the words in parentheses because these words are understood in the context of the sentence.

MaryBeth prefers working on microprocessors more than *I* (prefer working on microprocessors). (By completing the sentence, you can easily see that *I*, not *me* is correct, because *I* is the subject of the understood verb *prefer*.)

The new policy pleases Adam more than (I, me).   (To choose between *I* and *me*, supply the understood words: "The new policy pleases Adam more than *the new policy pleases me* [or *more than it pleases me*]." *Me* is the correct form.)

Choosing the correct pronoun in such sentences often requires an understanding of the meaning of the sentence, because sometimes both the nominative and the objective pronoun could be correct.

Allison enjoys working with Sam as well as (she, her).   (Depending on the meaning, either pronoun could possibly be correct. "Allison enjoys working with Sam as well as *she enjoys working with Sam*." "Allison enjoys working with Sam as well as *Allison enjoys working with her*." The correct sentence depends on the context, so pay special attention to the meaning of such sentences.)

EDITING PRACTICE 1

Choose the correct pronoun in the following sentences. Be sure to supply the missing words in order to make your choices. (HINT: In some sentences italics provide the emphasis you will need to understand the meaning of the sentence.)

1. In your opinion, is she as interesting a speaker as (he, him)?
2. Generally, Stu and I work on more projects than (they, them).
3. I usually open as many new accounts each year as (she, her).
4. Has *Marla* been as satisfied working with Jeanne as (she, her)?
5. Has Marla been as satisfied working with *Jeanne* as (she, her)?
6. Does Tim have as much experience as (he, him)?

Self-Ending Pronouns

Myself, yourself, herself, itself, ourselves, yourselves, and *themselves* are pronouns. They are used (1) to emphasize and (2) to reflect a noun or pronoun already expressed.

To Emphasize. Note how the *self*-ending pronouns add force to the following statements.

Ms. Jacoby corrected the debit statements *herself*.   (The sentence reads correctly without *herself*. But do you see how *herself* adds emphasis to the statement?)

I requested those printouts *myself*.   (Again, *myself* can be omitted from the sentence, but without *myself* the sentence is a statement without emphasis.)

Be sure that the placement of the *self*-ending pronoun is correct, so that it does not change the meaning of the message.

Bruce *himself* realized that the chemicals were phosphorescing.   (The placement of *himself* is correct, but many may have said or written "Bruce realized that the chemicals were phosphorescing *himself*." Quite a different meaning!)

To Reflect. The *self*-ending pronouns are also used to refer to nouns or pronouns that have already been identified in sentences.

> The sales representatives convinced *themselves* that the new product would not be successful.   (Here, *themselves* refers to *sales representatives*, the subject of the sentence.)

> Warren asked *himself* whether he should continue with the project.   (*Himself* refers to the subject, *Warren*.)

Self-ending pronouns are often incorrectly used as replacements for nominative and objective pronouns, as in the following examples.

> Yes, Mr. Diaz, Roland and *myself* would be delighted to assist you.   (The sentence should be "Roland and *I* would be . . . .")

> Mr. Diaz asked Roland and *myself* for help.   (The sentence should be "asked Roland and *me* . . . .")

EDITING PRACTICE 2

Select the correct pronoun in the following sentences.

1. Ms. Roth explained to Lena and (I, me, myself) that NOI means "net operating income."
2. Before the meeting concluded, the board members voted (they, them, themselves) a 10 percent salary increase.
3. Sheila Poloski and (I, me, myself) will conduct the survey.
4. Sean and I have taught (we, us, ourselves) to type much faster.
5. If you need help, ask Manuel or (I, me, myself).
6. John and (I, me, myself) will work the night shift next weekend.

EDITING PRACTICE 3

Correct any errors in the following sentences. Write *OK* if the sentence is correct.

1. Milton said that he would leave himself at noon.
2. The district manager himself does not want to delay the negotiations further.
3. Apparently, Linda Gibson and myself were not on the mailing list.
4. When we heard the rumors, we convinced ourselves that our plant would soon be closed.
5. Our physical education teacher taught me to drive himself.
6. Please be sure to get two tickets for Carla and myself.

Pronouns in Appositives

In writing and speaking we often use an appositive, a word or a group of words that explains or gives additional information about a preceding word or phrase.

Ms. Reilly, *my colleague,* is an acknowledged expert in this area. (The words *my colleague* give additional information about the subject, *Ms. Reilly. My colleague* is an appositive.)

The Austin Corporation, *a leader in oil exploration,* is backing the research study. (The appositive is *a leader in oil exploration;* it gives additional information about the subject, *the Austin Corporation.*)

Errors in the use of appositives frequently occur when an appositive includes a pronoun. Remember that the case of the pronoun is the same as the case of the noun with which the pronoun is in apposition. Thus:

Only two agents, Bruce and *she,* sell thermoplastics. (*Bruce and she* is in apposition with the subject, *only two agents.* Therefore, *she* is correct.)

We sell thermoplastics through only two agents, Bruce and *her.* (*Bruce and her* is in apposition with *only two agents,* which is the object of the preposition *through.* Therefore, *her* is correct.)

Apply the Quick Trick below to these two examples.

QUICK TRICK	**USE ONLY THE APPOSITIVE**

To test whether the pronoun in the appositive should be nominative or objective case, just omit the word or words with which the pronoun is in apposition. The correct answer will then be obvious.

Our most successful engineers, Susan and (he, him), have been assigned to the Hong Kong project. (Cross out *Our most successful engineers* and the sentence then reads: "Susan and (he, him) have been assigned . . . ." Obviously, *he* stands out as the correct pronoun.)

The Hong Kong project has been assigned to our most successful engineers, Susan and (he, him). (Again, cross out the words with which the pronoun is in apposition and the sentence then reads: "The Hong Kong project has been assigned to Susan and (he, him)." The answer is now clear. *Him* is correct; it is the object of the preposition *to.*)

EDITING PRACTICE 4

Select the correct answers to these sentences.

1. Ms. Simmons plans to present a special award to the three supervisors, Leonora, Harold, and (she, her).
2. Only one of the assistants, Inez or (he, him), will accompany Ms. Loomis.
3. Please explain to the auditors, Ronald and (she, her), why we had to change our schedule.
4. The brochures, which were written by two of our staff members, Laura and (he, him), have been very effective marketing tools.

5. Ask either of my typists, Walter or (she, her), to revise this first draft for you.
6. The trainees, Nancy Hardwick and (he, him), will complete their program by the end of this week.

Who and Whom, Whoever and Whomever

The pronouns *who* and *whoever* are nominative forms. *Whom* and *whomever* are objective forms.

> *Who* is the supervisor of the information processing staff?   (*Who* is the subject of the sentence.)

> *Whom* did she appoint supervisor?   (*Whom* is the object of the verb *did appoint*.)

The following Quick Trick will help you find the correct pronoun form immediately in any sentence. (NOTE: The use of *he/him* is strictly a pneumonic, or a sound, technique.)

QUICK TRICK   SUBSTITUTE *HE* AND *HIM*

As you know, *he* is a nominative pronoun and *him* is an objective pronoun. Therefore, when faced with a choice between *who* and *whom* (or *whoever* and *whomever*), mentally substitute either *he* and *him*. If *he* could be used, then *who* or *whoever* (the nominative form) is correct. If *him* could be used, then *whom* or *whomever* (the objective form) is correct. To make this even simpler, just let the *m* in *him* remind you of the *m* in *whom* or *whomever*!

> (Who, Whom) has the expense report summary?   (Substitute *he*: "He has the expense report summary." Thus *who* is correct because *he* can be substituted.)

> You gave the expense report summary to (who, whom)?   (Substituting *he* obviously does not work. Substitute *him*: "You gave the expense report summary to him?" Because *him* works, then *whom* is correct.)

Who and *Whom* in Questions. Most questions containing *who* or *whom* are in inverted order. To apply the Quick Trick, you must (1) change inverted order to normal order and then (2) substitute *he* and *him*. (Review Unit 12 if you do not remember how to change inverted order to normal order.)

1. Change to normal order if necessary.

> (Who, Whom) has the most recent price list?   (Normal order? Answer: Yes.)

> (Who, Whom) should I ask for the most recent price list?   (Normal order: "I should ask (who, whom) for the most recent price list.")

2. Substitute *he* and *him*.

(Who, Whom) has the most recent price list? (Would you say "*He* has," or would you say "*Him* has"? As you see, "*He* has the most recent price list" is correct. If the nominative *he* is correct, then the nominative *who* is correct.)

I should ask (who, whom) for the most recent price list. (Substituting *he* and *him* shows that "I should ask *him*" is the only choice. Therefore, if *him* can be substituted, *whom* is correct: "*Whom* should I ask for the most recent price list?")

EDITING PRACTICE 5

Before you select the answers in the following sentences, be sure (1) to check whether each sentence is in normal order and (2) substitute *he* and *him*. As a double check, give your reason for each answer.

1. (Who, Whom) did you recommend as the main speaker next Friday?
2. (Who, Whom) will serve as the consultant to the owner of this property?
3. (Who, Whom) is the new analyst on the corporate planning staff?
4. (Who, Whom) has Ms. LaMotta selected to replace Otto?
5. (Who, Whom) writes these so-called "boilerplate clauses"?

EDITING PRACTICE 6

Find and correct any errors in the following sentences. Again, be sure to check for normal order before substituting *he* and *him*. If a sentence has no error, write *OK*.

1. Whom did Theresa suggest as the senior project manager?
2. Whom has been interviewed for the inventory clerk position?
3. Who would you invite to make this presentation?
4. Whom has Mr. Cahill hired to replace Susan Rymer?
5. Whom is the present leader in the monthly sales contest?

Who and *Whom* in a Clause. When *who* or *whom* is used in a clause within a sentence, the first step in determining which one is correct is to isolate the clause from the rest of the sentence. Then, as before, check the clause for normal order and substitute *he* and *him*.

1. Isolate the clause. The clause to which the pronoun belongs always begins with *who, whom, whoever,* or *whomever.* Thus your clue is that the pronoun is the first word in the clause.

The receptionist is not sure (who, whom) the caller could have been. (Isolate the clause: "(who, whom) the caller could have been.")

Dave Haggerty is a manager (who, whom) we all respect. (Isolate the clause: "(who, whom) we all respect.")

Hand out these brochures to (whoever, whomever) asks for warranty information. (Isolate the clause: "(whoever, whomever) asks for warranty information.")

Give this file to (whoever, whomever) you have assigned to the Salinger account. (Isolate the clause: "(whoever, whomever) you have assigned to the Salinger account.")

Why isolate these clauses? Because the choice between *who* or *whom* (or *whoever* and *whomever*) depends on its use *within that clause*. It has nothing to do with any of the other words in that sentence.

2. Change to normal order if necessary.

(who, whom) the caller could have been   (Normal order: "the caller could have been (who, whom).")

(who, whom) we all respect   (Normal order: "we all respect (who, whom).")

(whoever, whomever) asks for warranty information   (This clause is in normal order.)

(whoever, whomever) you have assigned to the Salinger account   (Normal order: "you have assigned (whoever, whomever) to the Salinger account.")

3. Substitute *he* and *him* in each clause.

the caller could have been (he, him)   (The pronoun *he* is correct, because *he* "completes" the "being" verb *could have been*. Therefore, the correct choice is "The receptionist is not sure *who* the caller could have been.")

we all respect (he, him)   (*Him* is correct; it is the object of the verb *respect*. Therefore, *whom* is correct: "Dave Haggerty is a manager *whom* we all respect.")

(he, him) asks for warranty information   (*He* is correct; it is the subject of the verb *asks*. Therefore, *whoever* is correct in the sentence "Hand out these brochures to *whoever* asks for warranty information.")

you have assigned (he, him) to the Salinger account   (*Him* is correct; it is the object of the verb *have assigned*. Therefore, *whomever* is correct: "Give this file to *whomever* you have assigned to the Salinger account.")

CLASS PRACTICE 1

A. Isolate the *who* or *whom* clauses in the following sentences.

1. The additional funds, in our opinion, should be allocated to (whoever, whomever) will be in charge of the Planning Committee.
2. The additional funds, in our opinion, should be allocated to (whoever, whomever) Ms. Ransome appoints to head the Planning Committee.
3. Robert Gosdeck, (who, whom) established this company in 1975, is still the major stockholder.
4. We intend to give the contract to (whoever, whomever) will provide the best service.
5. Did Mr. Weaver tell anyone (who, whom) he has selected as national sales manager?

B. Using the clauses that you isolated in the exercise above, change to normal order any clause that is inverted.

C. Again using the same sentences, select the correct pronoun for each sentence. Be sure to mentally substitute *he* and *him* before you make your choices.

EDITING PRACTICE 7

Now you should easily be able to find errors in the use of *who, whom, whoever,* and *whomever.* Apply your skill by finding errors in the following sentences. Write *OK* if the sentence is correct.

1. Generally, we distribute these complimentary consumer guides to whomever asks us for one.
2. As you know, Joel, the award will be presented to whoever sells the greatest number of new cars through December 31.
3. I attended college with one of the attorneys who Mrs. Robson hired.
4. Of course, I'd be delighted to work with whoever you assign to this project.
5. Yes, Mark, I think I know who will be appointed director of research.
6. Agnes asked, "Does anyone in the office know who Ms. Williams was referring to?"

Clause Within a *Who, Whom* Clause. Parenthetical clauses such as *I think, we believe,* and *she says* sometimes interrupt the *who, whom* clause, clouding the choice of *who* or *whom.* To make the choice correctly every time, just omit the parenthetical clause and follow the usual procedure for selecting *who* or *whom.*

Is Debra the representative (who, whom) he said I should see?

1. Isolate the clause: (who, whom) he said I should see.
2. Omit the parenthetical clause: (who, whom) I should see.
3. Change to normal order if necessary: I should see (who, whom).
4. Substitute *he* and *him:* I should see (he, him). If *him* works as a substitute, then *whom* is correct. "Is Debra the representative *whom* he said I should see?"

EDITING PRACTICE 8

Select the correct pronouns for the following sentences. (HINT: Omit any parenthetical clauses that obscure your selection, and be sure to change the *who, whom* clause to normal order if necessary.)

1. The sales representatives in this region selected Elena DeCapo, (who, whom) I suspect they consider their best spokesperson.

2. Is Marvin the trainee (who, whom) you thought I wanted to transfer to the Sales Department?
3. She is a supervisor (who, whom) all of us think has great executive potential with this company.
4. Janice is the writer (who, whom) most of us think creates the most effective sales brochures and ads.
5. Mike Harrison is one of the engineers (who, whom) I think you should invite to these special planning meetings.

COMMUNICATION LABORATORY

APPLICATION EXERCISES

A. Select the correct pronoun for each of the following sentences. Be sure to know the reasons for your choices.

1. Gary Handler, (who, whom) we hired as a consultant, has excellent credentials in the field of electrical engineering.
2. Has Diane been a manager as long as (he, her)?
3. As you know, Ms. Abrams is a person (who, whom) everyone trusts.
4. Frankly, John Lester knows more about this computer than (I, me).
5. Anthony gave the checks directly to the clients, Mr. Abernathy and (she, her).
6. No, Myron and Dennis are not as careful in their work as (we, us).
7. Carole and (I, me, myself) will discuss these benefits with someone in the Personnel Department.
8. When will he announce (who, whom) the contest winner is?
9. Among the most successful sales representatives in the company are Cheryl and (he, him).
10. Give these discount coupons to (whoever, whomever) requests them.
11. Do you know (who, whom) Donald asked to complete the analysis?
12. Donna is not sure (who, whom) the caller could have been.
13. Has Ms. Conrad told you (who, whom) she has chosen to attend the convention?
14. Two of our brokers, Dominick and (he, him), will explain the SEC's rules and regulations.
15. The new dental program benefits full-time workers more than (we, us).

B. On a separate sheet of paper, correct any errors in the following sentences. Write *OK* for any sentence that has no error.

1. After you revise this report, send a copy to Mr. Rodgers and save one copy for myself.
2. As a result of the budget cuts, each departments' expenses will be reduced by 15 percent.

3. Does anyone know whom this check should be sent to?
4. Two trainees, Roseanne and he, have been assigned to the Advertising Department.
5. The money that we rised for the annual employees' dinner-dance was deposited in a special account.
6. Who should I ask for an explanation of this clause in this insurance policy?
7. Who has Ms. Bodner named as the new liaison with our headquarters office?
8. Ron been very helpful to us in setting up this new accounting system.
9. The movers have already took all the furniture and equipment from this floor.
10. Most of those packages have laid there since we moved from our Fifth Street office.
11. As usual, Mitchell and myself will coordinate the sales meetings.
12. Please ask Penny if there's any reason for the additional shipping charge on this order.
13. One of the companys that rent space in this building is Elder Plastics.
14. Did you say that you seen Roland this morning?
15. Because he felt faint, we told Dan to lie down for a few minutes.
16. After we had spoken with a tax expert, we understood how to maintain our records.
17. Bill and me are confident that we can complete this study before March 15.
18. I gave one manual to Mark, and I kept one for myself.
19. If your planning to go to the Atlanta office, be sure to visit Charles Spivak.
20. We have not yet received Mikes' vacation schedule, have we?

C. Read the following paragraph, correcting any errors you find.

The primary business of Ballentine & Dalton is the marketing of municipal, corporate, and government securitys. The firm has developed a computerized system for handling portfolioes to help its' customer's take advantage of market change's instantly. The firms' network system helps investors' get access to up-to-the-minute financial information.

VOCABULARY AND SPELLING STUDIES

A. These words are often confused: *lean, lien; deference, difference.* Explain the distinctions between them.

B. Complete these analogies:

1. *True* is to *false* as *perfect* is to _____.
2. *Familiar* is to *strange* as *major* is to _____.

3. *Abundant* is to *scarce* as *natural* is to _____.
4. *Conservative* is to *liberal* as *valuable* is to _____.

C. Words ending in *able*, *ible*, *ance*, and *ence* often cause writers problems. Which of the following are spelled correctly? Correct the misspelled words.

1. intelligible
2. correspondance
3. incapable
4. collectable
5. intelligence
6. grievence

COMMUNICATING FOR RESULTS

Dressing for Results. Henry and Edward are good friends who work together in the Collins Leasing Corporation's new suburban office. One major area of disagreement between the two is the right way to dress for work. Henry believes that dressing for work should be fun; it doesn't really matter what you wear unless you are a sales representative. Why dress up for coworkers?

Ed disagrees. He often tells Henry to wear a suit, dress shirt, and tie rather than jeans and sport clothes because clients often pass through their work area, sometimes stopping to ask for information. In addition, both Henry and Ed often meet with people from other departments within the corporation.

Who is correct?

U · N · I · T

19 Predicate Agreement With Simple Subjects

Nonstandard English is now commonly used in movies, television shows, popular songs, and conversation. In fact, errors such as "he don't" and "it don't" are heard so frequently that *they begin to sound correct to listeners.* They are *not* correct, of course: Standard English requires us to say "he doesn't" and "it doesn't."

Standard English is still firmly used as *the* language of business. Grammatical errors such as "he don't" and "it don't" may not affect the chances of success for a movie, television show, or song, but they can certainly damage a business career!

In previous units you have learned enough about subjects and predicates to make it easier to master the agreement principles in this unit and in Units 20 and 21. As you proceed through these units on agreement principles, remember that you *must* be able to make subjects and predicates agree if you are to write and to speak correctly.

The Basic Agreement Rule

The principle of subject-predicate agreement is this: *A predicate must agree with its subject in number and in person.* Specifically, those words in the predicate that must agree with the subject are any verbs and pronouns that refer to the subject. Thus you must pay attention to (1) agreement of verbs with the subject and (2) agreement of pronouns with the subject.

Agreement of Verb With Subject. Notice how the verb agrees with its subject in each of these sentences:

Kristen Pembroke *has* the salary guidelines.   (The verb *has* agrees with the subject *Kristen Pembroke.* Both are *singular* forms.)

Kristen Pembroke, one of the new executives in the Personnel Department, *has* the salary guidelines.   (The subject and the verb are the same. Do not be misled by the words that separate the subject, *Kristen Pembroke,* from the verb, *has.*)

One executive *reviews* all salary guidelines.   (The verb *reviews* agrees with the singular subject *executive.*)

Several executives *review* all salary guidelines.   (Now the subject is *executives.* The verb *review* agrees with the plural subject *executives.*)

When applying the rules of subject-verb agreement, remember that plural nouns usually end in *s* or *es*, but an *s* ending on a verb indicates that it is a *singular* verb. Thus, in the above examples, "one executive reviews" and "several executives review" both illustrate correct subject-verb agreement. Note the following examples:

Singular Noun and Verb	Plural Noun and Verb
the woman is	the women are
an editor in chief has	both editors in chief have
one person says	two persons say
Mr. Quinn does	Mr. and Mrs. Quinn do
one person writes	two persons write

Agreement of Pronoun With Subject. When the predicate includes any pronouns that refer to the subject, those pronouns must agree with the subject.

Mr. Quinn has signed and returned *his* contract.   (The pronoun *his* refers to and must agree with the subject *Mr. Quinn.*)

Mrs. Quinn has signed and returned *her* contract.   (Because the subject is now *Mrs.* Quinn, the correct pronoun is *her.*)

Mr. and Mrs. Quinn have signed and returned *their* contract.   (The pronoun *their* agrees with the subject *Mr. and Mrs. Quinn.*)

I decided to take *my* vacation in August.   (The pronoun *my* refers to and agrees with the subject *I.*)

Do you know yet whether *your* proposal has been accepted by the committee?   (The pronoun *your* refers to and agrees with *you.*)

Making such pronouns agree with the subject is usually a simple matter, especially when the subject is so easily identified, as in the above sentences.

EDITING PRACTICE 1

Select the correct verbs and pronouns in the following sentences. Assume that the pronoun refers to the subject.

1. Each X ray (has, have) been placed in (its, their) original folder.
2. Maureen (wants, want) to change (his, her, their) reservations for tomorrow's flight to Chicago.
3. The technicians (does, do) agree that (his, her, their) new procedures will ensure safety in the plant.
4. One young woman (was, were) interviewed already; (his, her, their) résumé is on my desk.
5. If Beverly (needs need) another manual for (his, her, their) department, send a copy by messenger.
6. The man who asked for a refund (do, does) not know (his, her, their) account number.

EDITING PRACTICE 2

Now correct any agreement errors in the following sentences. Write *OK* if the sentence is correct.

1. Anna prefer answering her own phone.
2. One manager at the meeting forgot their briefcase.
3. That client called to say that they want to change the order.
4. It really don't make sense to retype all these pages.
5. These apartments has intercoms in its foyers.
6. Customers who have used our credit plan have reported that they find the rates reasonable.

Agreement Problems

Understanding troublesome agreement problems will help you avoid falling into traps as you write. Four specific problems are discussed: inverted sentences; words separating subject from verb; *each, either,* and other indefinite pronouns; and common-gender nouns.

Inverted Sentences. As you know, the normal order of a sentence is subject first, then predicate. In inverted sentences part of the predicate precedes the subject. Thus inverted sentences sometimes conceal agreement errors.

Inverted sentences often begin with "there" or are phrased as questions. Here are some examples.

(Do, Does) the manager have the original contract?   (Change to normal order to find the correct verb: "The manager *does* have . . . .")

(Do, Does) the managers have the original contract?   ("The managers *do* have . . . .")

On my desk (is, are) the pamphlet you want.   (Normal order: "The pamphlet you want *is* on my desk.")

On my desk (is, are) the pamphlets you want.   ("The pamphlets you want *are* on my desk.")

Sentences and clauses that begin with *there* and *here* deserve special attention. (HINT: In these cases look for the subject *after* the verb.)

There (is, are) only one way to proceed with these estimates.   (The subject of the sentence is *way,* a singular noun, so the choice must be "There *is* only one way . . . .")

Here (is, are) several ways to correct these problems.   (*Ways* requires the plural verb *are:* "Here *are* several ways . . . .")

In speaking, many people seem to begin sentences with *there's* or *there is* almost automatically, without considering whether the subject that follows is singular or plural. Similarly, *here's* and *here is* and *who's* and *who is* are often used instead of *here are* and *who are.* Beware of these traps in subject-verb agreement.

Words Separating Subject From Verb. When a phrase or a clause separates the subject from its verb, the subject may not be obvious. (HINT: Mentally eliminate the prepositional phrase when you are looking for the subject.)

The building at the corner of Randall and Elm Streets (is, are) a possible site for our new store.   (The prepositional phrase *at the corner of Randall and Elm Streets* separates the subject, *building,* from its verb, *is.* "The building *is* . . . .")

EDITING PRACTICE 3

Choose the correct words for each of the following sentences. Be sure to identify the subjects that your choices agree with.

1. In her office, on the shelf along the left wall, (is, are) the summary of the last meeting.

2. She asked, "(Is, Are) one of the regional managers coming to the evening session?"
3. As you know, the reason for conducting this survey (is, are) to discover what users like best and least about our products.
4. Irene Clemson, who was the manager of the Denver office for nearly ten years, (has, have) been named national sales manager.
5. Where (is, are) the newest patches of material that Allied Distributors sent us?
6. The analysis that we sent to our sales representatives (explains, explain) the reason for all our territory changes.
7. (Does, Do) the new personnel manager know about these classified ads?
8. There (is, are) perhaps only two or three experienced technicians in our foreign offices.

EDITING PRACTICE 4

Correct any errors in the following sentences. If a sentence has no error, write *OK.*

1. Carla, who generally writes all the copy for these brochures and pamphlets, have developed a style manual for all of us to follow.
2. Don't Phyllis know that all these vouchers must be approved by Ms. D'Amato?
3. The proposals that are on my desk, in my opinion, offers no creative solutions to our warehousing problems.
4. Yes, there's only one more month for us to take advantage of the discount offer.
5. "Where's all the new booklets that we ordered to hand out at our display booth?" asked Tara.
6. In the van parked at the receiving desk at the back of the warehouse is the monitors that we must return to the manufacturer.
7. The price list for these new products are now being printed.
8. A manual explaining all these procedures are being developed by the Training Department.

Each, Either, and Other Indefinite Pronouns. The following words are always singular: *each, every, either, neither, everyone, everybody, someone, somebody, anyone, anybody, nobody,* and *no one.* Note that whether they are used as subjects or as subject modifiers, they are always singular and their predicates must be singular.

> Each of the monitors *has its* own antiglare screen. (*Has* and *its* are singular, to agree with the singular subject *each.*)

> Each monitor *is* now on sale. (Here *each* modifies the subject *monitor.* Both *each* and *monitor* are singular, and the singular *is* agrees with the subject *monitor.*)

Neither of the factories *has* had *its* annual inspection yet.   (*Has* and *its* agree with the singular subject *neither*.)

Everyone in the Medical Department *has* also been scheduled for *his or her* checkup.   (*Has* and *his or her* agree with the singular subject *everyone*.)

Common-Gender Nouns. Whenever the gender of a noun is obviously masculine (*father, brother, man, boy*) or obviously feminine (*mother, sister, woman, girl*), choosing a pronoun to agree with it is no problem. *Common-gender nouns* are those that can be either masculine or feminine, such as *instructor, supervisor, customer, president, attorney, nurse, secretary, employee, clerk,* and *coworker*. To agree with singular common-gender nouns, pronoun combinations such as *he or she, his or her,* and *him or her* must be used.

Each supervisor has guidelines that *he or she* must follow.   (*He or she*, singular, to agree with the singular subject *supervisor*, a common-gender noun.)

Each supervisor has already received *his or her* guidelines.   (*His or her*, to agree with *supervisor*.)

Ask each supervisor to bring the guidelines with *him or her* to tomorrow's meeting.   (*Him or her*, to agree with *supervisor*.)

When *he or she* and similar combinations are used too often—especially within the same sentence—the message will be awkward. In such cases the sentences could easily be revised by changing the subjects and the pronouns that agree with them to plurals.

The supervisors have guidelines that *they* must follow.

All the supervisors have already received *their* guidelines.

Ask all the supervisors to bring the guidelines with *them* to tomorrow's meeting.

EDITING PRACTICE 5

Choose the correct words in the following sentences.

1. An executive must rely on the information that (he, she, he or she, it, they) (receives, receive) from (his, her, his or her, its, their) subordinates.
2. Someone in the Atlanta office (has, have) submitted some excellent suggestions.
3. The president of each of these three companies (agrees, agree) that (his or her, their) most important task is to listen carefully to (his or her, their) employees and customers.
4. Anyone who (wishes, wish) to increase (his or her, their) life insurance coverage is encouraged to do so, of course.
5. Every broker in the entire organization (has, have) indicated (his or her, their) interest in joining this retirement plan.
6. Yes, each manager in our district offices (does, do) receive a bonus based on (his or her, their) salary.

EDITING PRACTICE 6

Correct any agreement errors in the following sentences. If no corrections are needed, write *OK*.

1. Anyone in these departments who want to discuss these safety procedures further should make an appointment with their supervisor.
2. The committee members want an assistant who knows how to organize and who can manage his or her own time well.
3. In our opinion, no one should invest in these less-conservative bonds unless they fully understand the risk.
4. Every executive in the country will surely benefit from having his own personal copy of this informative magazine.
5. No, Herman, neither of the executors have reviewed this agreement yet.
6. A customer who is dissatisfied with our products should write to the Customer Service Center nearest their home.

COMMUNICATION LABORATORY

APPLICATION EXERCISES

A. Choose the correct verbs and pronouns in the following sentences. Also, identify the nouns and pronouns with which your choices agree.

1. (There's, There are) several good candidates for the position advertised in our Denver branch office.
2. One of the articles that she quoted (was, were) reprinted from this magazine.
3. As you know, some word processing operators in our headquarters office (is, are) developing an excellent procedures manual for all employees.
4. Where (is, are) the new full-color brochures that were recently printed?
5. On the computer table in my office (is, are) some samples that may help you.
6. Each client that we surveyed in the past few months (is, are) interested in our new service.
7. She said that each word processing operator must follow closely the original copy that (he, she, he or she, they) is keyboarding and must place (his, her, his or her, their) initials next to any editorial changes.
8. One of the men who helped draw these sketches (is, are) here with (his, her, his or her, their) assistant.
9. Every technician (has, have) indicated an interest in the new payroll-savings plan.

10. For maximum safety we encourage everyone who enters the laboratory to wear (his, her, his or her, their) helmet.
11. Sherry asked, "(Doesn't, Don't) every visitor need to show (his, her, his or her, their) guest pass to the guard before (he, she, he or she, they) (enters, enter) this restricted area?"
12. Each of the terminals in this room (has, have) a users' manual next to (it, them).
13. One of the executives (suggests, suggest) that we lease rather than buy this equipment.
14. In the conference room on the fifth floor (is, are) a revised, completely updated price list that you may duplicate.
15. Each trainee will be given a test to determine (his, her, his or her, their) executive potential before (he, she, he or she, they) (begins, begin) the program.

B. Correct the errors in the following sentences. Write *OK* if the sentence is correct.

1. Needless to say, it don't matter which duplicator Ms. Simms selects as long as it can reduce large-size originals.
2. Of course, us programmers reviewed the manual carefully before it was printed and distributed.
3. She gave us permission to share the prize money with whoever contributed to the project.
4. Has Mrs. D'Acosta spoke with Al yet about the proposed changes in the employee discount policy?
5. Every manager in our district offices throughout the country have been asked to send their marketing strategy reports to the home office.
6. Do you know whether Mr. Salvatore has wrote to the IRS for clarification of this new tax law?
7. If your sure that Ms. Wendell approves, I will send the photographs to the studio immediately.
8. No, we weren't surprised to hear about George asking for a transfer to the main office.
9. If Mary and myself are on the convention team, then we will fly to San Jose on Friday morning.
10. Victor done all the invoice processing by himself!
11. The purpose of the various committees is to promote employee participation in the decision-making process.
12. Are these charts and graphs ours, or are they there's?
13. Yes, its true that Allied Industries has indicated an interest in buying our company.
14. Apparently, Catherine enjoys speaking before groups more than him.
15. Whom do you think will be selected to head the negotiations team?

C. What is needed to complete these sentences, a singular or a plural verb? Choose the correct verb for each sentence.

1. A manager who (has, have) good communication skills (is, are) an asset to this company.
2. Where (is, are) the expense vouchers for this month?
3. Fran's credentials in the area of computer programming (is, are) impressive.
4. She said that one of the languages she is currently learning (is, are) COBOL.
5. Each seminar that he has conducted in the past three months (has, have) been extraordinarily successful.

VOCABULARY AND SPELLING STUDIES

A. These words are often confused: *staid, stayed; facilitate, felicitate.* Explain the differences.

B. Select the letter that correctly completes each question.

1. What does the French word *résumé* mean: (**a**) something resumed, (**b**) a conversation, (**c**) a summary, (**d**) the main dish of a meal?
2. What does the Latin term *pro rata* mean: (**a**) professional rates, (**b**) according to the rates, (**c**) concerning, (**d**) proportionately?
3. Which of the following means "for each year": (**a**) per capita, (**b**) per diem, (**c**) per annum, (**d**) per se?

C. Which completes the following correctly, *ie* or *ei?*

1. conc_t
2. bel_ve
3. for_gn
4. ach_ve
5. s_ze

6. n_ce
7. fr_nd
8. L_sure
9. fr_ght
10. ch_f

COMMUNICATING FOR RESULTS

First Day on the Job. Georgia Delaney was hired to work for a large bank. On her first day she spent two hours in an orientation class; then she was to report to her department head, Ms. Carruthers.

Unfortunately, Ms. Carruthers was out on sick leave. What should Georgia do in this situation?

UNIT
20 Predicate Agreement With Special Subjects

This unit presents four "special" subjects—four cases that require some analysis to decide whether the subject is singular or plural. In all cases, however, the basic rule of agreement that you learned will apply: *A predicate must agree with the simple subject in number and in person*. Therefore, if the subject is singular, the verb must be singular; and if the subject is plural, the verb must be plural.

Collective Nouns

A *collective noun* is a word that refers to a group or a collection of persons or things, such as *class, faculty, committee, jury, company, audience,* and *herd*. When a collective noun indicates that the group is acting *as a whole*, the subject is considered singular and takes a singular verb. On the other hand, when a collective noun indicates that the members of the group are acting *as individuals*, the subject is plural and takes a plural verb.

> The jury *are* arguing over several issues concerning this case. (To argue, more than one person is needed. The plural verb *are* is correct because the jury members are acting *as individuals*.)

> The jury *has* reached *its* decision. (Here the jury is acting collectively; because the group is acting as a whole, the subject is singular and the singular verb *has* is correct. Note, therefore, that the singular pronoun *its* is also correct—to agree with the singular *jury*.)

EDITING PRACTICE 1

Determine whether the collective nouns are singular or plural in the following sentences. Then select the verbs and the pronouns that agree with the collective-noun subjects.

1. The audience (was, were) pleased to participate in the questionnaire, as we could tell by (its, their) reaction.
2. The class (is, are) arguing among themselves whether the annual class trip should be canceled.
3. Her new company (has, have) offices throughout the South.
4. According to Professor Simpson, the faculty (wants, want) to ask (its, their) spokesperson to attend the salary negotiations meeting.

188

5. Mr. Edwards said that a new committee (has, have) been established to develop a code of ethics for all employees.

EDITING PRACTICE 2

Make any necessary corrections in the following sentences. If a sentence has no error, write *OK.*

1. The committee is now working on their individual reports to the treasurer.
2. The city council have been arguing over this ruling since the members met this morning.
3. Our union have filed a grievance against Allied Equipment Inc.
4. Each department must submit their financial statements to the city auditors by June 30.
5. That company have their headquarters in Knoxville, Tennessee.

Foreign Nouns

Many nouns of foreign origin form their plurals in special ways, as you learned in Unit 15. Note, for example, the plurals in the following list.

Singular	Plural
alumnus	alumni
alumna	alumnae
criterion	criteria
parenthesis	parentheses
stimulus	stimuli

To determine whether a singular or a plural predicate is required, you must be able to identify accurately both the singular and the plural forms of nouns of foreign origin. Review them carefully—and use your dictionary whenever you need help.

The *basis* for increasing our discount *is* to spark customer buying.   (*Is* is correct because *basis* is singular.)

The *bases* for increasing our discount *are* to spark customer buying and to push out old inventory.   (*Are* is correct because *bases* is plural.)

EDITING PRACTICE 3

Are the foreign nouns in the following sentences singular, or are they plural? Choose the words that agree with the foreign-noun simple subjects.

1. Parentheses (is, are) used to enclose the date of each publication in this report.
2. As you probably heard, the technicians' analyses (proves, prove) that the chemicals were mislabeled.
3. Our criteria for selecting vendors (is, are) service, price, and dependability.

4. The thesis that she submitted (has, have) already been duplicated.
5. The serious crisis that Ms. Hines referred to (was, were) a fire in the main plant.

A Number, The Number

A *number* is a plural subject, and *the number* is a singular subject. Be sure to make their predicates agree accordingly. Note that any modifier immediately before the word *number* (as in *a large number* or *the significant number*) does not affect this rule.

> *The number* of applicants *was* encouraging.   (*Was* agrees with the singular *the number*.)

> *A number* of word processing operators *have* submitted *their* résumés.   (*Have* and *their* agree with *a number*.)

> *A surprising number* of word processing operators *have* submitted *their* résumés.   (The modifier *surprising* does not affect *a number*, which is still plural.)

Use the following Quick Trick to help you with this agreement rule.

QUICK TRICK | **REMEMBER *P·A·S·T***

Use the word *past* to remember the following:

PLURAL: a   SINGULAR: the

If you can remember ***P-A-S-T,*** you can recall the *P*lural term *A* number and the *S*ingular term *T*he number.

EDITING PRACTICE 4

Correct any agreement errors in the following sentences. Write *OK* if the sentence is correct.

1. The stimuli that is used to speed up the chemical reactions will be discussed in the seminar.
2. As Harold pointed out, the number of invitations that we sent was quite small.
3. Ellen said, "All the parentheses that is in this bibliography should be changed to brackets."
4. The alumnae of Central Women's College have supported this charity for many years.
5. A number of interested land developers has submitted preliminary bids on the property.

"Part," "Portion," or "Amount" Subject

Words such as *all, any, most, half, some, two-thirds,* and *none* are used in subjects to indicate a part or a portion of something. Consider such subjects plural when they are followed by plurals; consider them singular when they are followed by singulars. Study these examples:

Half this room *has* already been painted.   (The singular *has* is correct because *room* is singular.)

Half these rooms *have* already been painted.   (The plural *have* is correct because *rooms* is plural.)

All of the office *is* being redecorated.   (The singular *is* is correct because *office* is singular.)

All of the offices *are* being redecorated.   (The plural *are* is correct because *offices* is plural.)

CLASS PRACTICE 1

Are the following "part," "portion," or "amount" subjects singular, or are they plural? Choose the correct verb for each sentence; be sure to indicate the key word in the complete subject with which each verb agrees.

1. Two-thirds of the payment (is, are) due in advance.
2. Most of this building (contains, contain) valuable store fixtures.
3. All of the engine (has, have) been rebuilt.
4. Three-quarters of these payments (is, are) due in advance.
5. Half the supplies (has, have) been stored in this room.
6. None of the building (requires, require) repainting.
7. None of these buildings (requires, require) repainting.

EDITING PRACTICE 5

Identify and correct any agreement errors in the following sentences. Write *OK* for any sentence that has no error.

1. Two-thirds of the storeroom space have been converted to a new office.
2. Half the area that we originally leased are now sublet to another photography studio.
3. All the printing and binding machines in both plants have been reconditioned within the past two years.
4. "Unfortunately," said Ms. Casper, "most of the statues was damaged during the fire."
5. As we expected, about three-tenths of the forms was lost during the move to our new quarters.
6. None of the inventory that we checked last week are included in this report.

COMMUNICATION LABORATORY

APPLICATION EXERCISES

A. Select the correct verbs and pronouns in the following sentences. On your paper indicate the key word in the subject with which each choice agrees.

1. All the criteria that we use to evaluate proposals (is, are) clearly explained in this report.
2. Mr. Smyth-Evans said, "The basic reason for these acquisitions (is, are) to expand our product line to include consumer goods."
3. Only one of the topics to be discussed at the convention (is, are) especially interesting, in my opinion.
4. The number of employees who signed up for the additional health benefits (represents, represent) about 25 percent of the total work force in both plants.
5. According to the suit, a number of tenants (is, are) claiming that (he, she, he or she, they) (does, do) not have to pay the most recent rent increase.
6. Their analyses of the chemicals (leaves, leave) no doubt in our minds that we must carefully dispose of these containers.
7. The alumni who contributed most to the charity drive (is, are) from the Class of '85.
8. The alumnae who contributed most to the charity drive (is, are) from the Class of '85.
9. The alumna who contributed most to the charity drive (is, are) from the Class of '85.
10. The alumnus who contributed most to the charity drive (is, are) from the Class of '85.
11. The data that they compiled from their studies (is, are) summarized at the end of the report.
12. The bases of the union's decision to strike (is, are) listed clearly in this newspaper article.
13. A number of clients who responded to the survey (is, are) eager to hear how the policy change will affect (his, her, his or her, their) credit.
14. Mr. Hanson said that a committee (is, are) to be established to suggest ways to avoid discrimination against the elderly.
15. "None of the original manuscript (has, have) been duplicated yet," said Gregg.

B. Correct any errors in the following sentences. Write *OK* if the sentence is correct.

1. Do you know whether everyone has already gave Emile his or her payment for the theater tickets?
2. Although we had some initial difficultys in setting up the new system, the equipment is now functioning smoothly.
3. One managers' idea was to approve flextime for some of the staff.
4. Although we knew that Alvin was in Baltimore, for a moment we really thought the man we saw was he.
5. The customer had fell because a floor tile was loose; fortunately, however, he was not hurt at all.
6. Yes, there's blank videotapes in Mr. Marshall's office, Frank.
7. If Renee and myself are asked to attend the seminar, we will probably drive to the conference center over the weekend.
8. No, Sam, I do not know who's microfilm this is.
9. Marion and Peter's print shop, which is located in the Perry Building, will be closed for renovation during the week of September 6.
10. Her new assistants' home is only two or three blocks from hers.
11. Yes, its necessary to have either cash or a bank check because that store doesn't accept credit cards.
12. Thank you, Rachel. I really do appreciate you driving me to the airport on such short notice.
13. Frankly, if I were him, I certainly would not accept their offer to buy the property.
14. Jennifer, ask whomever is at the reception desk to give you the key to the supply room.
15. Each of the salesclerks who sell $1000 worth of skis during this special promotion are eligible for a special cash prize.

C. Write one sentence with each of the following: (1) *there is*, (2) *there are*, (3) *neither*, (4) *none*, (5) *a number*, and (6) *the number*.

VOCABULARY AND SPELLING STUDIES

A. These words are often confused: *billed, build; deduce, deduct*. Explain the differences.

B. An *agenda* is: (a) a list of company officers, (b) a special financial statement, (c) a list of topics to be discussed at a meeting, (d) a legal agent.

C. Spell the following as directed.

1. The plurals of *alumnus, parenthesis, basis, criterion*.
2. The past tense of *take, grow, write, know, buy*.
3. The past participle for each verb in the item above.

COMMUNICATING FOR RESULTS

A Time and a Place for Everything. Your friend and coworker Rosalind has just returned from a two-week vacation. Early on Monday morning she begins to give you a detailed description of everything that happened, but you have a deadline to meet.

What should you say to Rosalind?

U · N · I · T

21

Predicate Agreement With Compound Subjects

To complete your study of predicate agreement, you will review some potentially troublesome agreement situations. The first concerns agreement with compound subjects (that is, subjects joined by *and*, *or*, or *nor*). The second concerns agreement in relative-pronoun clauses.

Subjects Joined by *And*

A compound subject joined by *and* is clearly a plural subject and takes a plural predicate.

> One disk drive *and* one video display monitor *are* included in this sale price.   (The two parts of the compound subject are *disk drive* and *monitor*. *Are* is the correct verb to agree with this plural compound subject.)

> Lisa *and* Otis *have* been coordinating the word processing seminars.   (Again, two subjects are joined by *and*. The plural verb *have* is correct.)

EXCEPTIONS: Certain subjects can be joined by *and* to identify *one* person or thing. When both parts of the subject identify the same person or thing, the subject is singular and its predicate must be singular.

> My coauthor *and* business partner *receives* half the royalty on these books.   (Here the subject refers to one person, who is both coauthor and business partner to the speaker. The singular verb *receives* is correct.)

My coauthor *and* my business partner *receive* half the royalty on these books. (This is a genuine compound subject because two different people are referred to.)

Ham *and* eggs *is* the breakfast that will be served. (*Ham and eggs* is *one* breakfast; thus the singular verb *is* correct.)

Another exception to the compound subject rule occurs when a compound subject joined by *and* is modified by *each, every,* or *many a.* In such cases the subject is considered singular and takes a singular predicate.

Each diskette *and* cassette *is* on sale until August 30. (*Is* is correct because *diskette and cassette* is modified by *each*.)

Every district manager *and* regional manager *has* been invited to dinner with *his or her* spouse. (The singulars *has* and *his or her* are correct because the compound subject is modified by *every*.)

Many an author *and* agent has asked for more information about the play. (The singular *has asked* is correct because the compound subject is modified by *Many an*.)

EDITING PRACTICE 1

Apply the agreement rules concerning compound subjects to the following sentences.

1. Many a driver and dispatcher in this company (has, have) made a small fortune by investing (his or her, their) money in company stock.
2. Every teller and cashier (has, have) been carefully selected and trained.
3. Did you know that Emil's agent and adviser (is, are) his sister?
4. No, Jeffrey and Agnes (does, do) not agree that these municipal bonds are safe investments.
5. The word processing operators and their supervisor (is, are) developing a training brochure.
6. Every man and woman in these three district offices (wants, want) to know how (he or she, they) can take advantage of the tuition-refund program.

Subjects Joined by *Or* or *Nor*

Whenever a compound subject is joined by *or* or *nor,* make the predicate agree with that part of the subject that is closer to the verb.

Neither *Marilyn* nor her *assistants have* the master diskette. (Which part of the subject is closer to the verb? Answer: *assistants.* Therefore, the verb *have* is correct.)

Her *assistants or Marilyn has* the master diskette. (Which subject is closer to the verb? Answer: *Marilyn.* Therefore, the verb *has* is correct.)

Are you or Lee responsible for the inputting error? (Which part of the subject is closer to the verb? Answer: *you.* Therefore, the verb *are* is correct.)

Remember to find that part of the subject that follows *or* or *nor* and you will be sure to simplify predicate agreement in such cases.

EDITING PRACTICE 2

The following sentences have compound subjects joined by *or* or *nor*. Choose the words in parentheses that correctly agree with the subjects.

1. According to this manual, an independent auditor or the company treasurer (receives, receive) the official rebate from the government, but (he or she, they) must claim the total amount as income.
2. Of course, the president or the vice presidents (has, have) the authority to approve all vouchers and sign all checks.
3. Deborah or Valerie (has, have) discussed this alternative with (her, their) supervisor.
4. Either a branch manager or an executive vice president (is, are) supposed to sign all releases.
5. Needless to say, neither Mr. VanBrock nor we (prefers, prefer) canceling the entire order.
6. Generally, Suzanne or Vernon (places, place) all orders for supplies.

EDITING PRACTICE 3

Correct the predicates in the following sentences to make sure that they agree with their compound subjects. Write *OK* for any sentence that has no error.

1. Either platinum or nickel is used in such alloys.
2. Bettejean or her assistants usually does double-check all invoices.
3. I think that Ray, Andrew, and Sara has already made his or her reservations.
4. This computer and that printer was leased from General Equipment Inc.
5. Either her daughter or her son are coming to the office to pick up this envelope; please give it to them if I am out.
6. Perhaps the master diskette or the tape drive were damaged.

Relative-Pronoun Clause

The last agreement rule that you will study concerns agreement in clauses that begin with the relative pronouns *who*, *which*, and *that*. To begin, review these few statements:

1. A clause is a group of words having a subject and a verb.
2. The relative pronouns are *who*, *which*, and *that*. They are called *relative* because they *relate to* another word in the sentence. This other word is called an *antecedent*.
3. The *antecedent* is a noun or a pronoun usually occurring immediately before the relative pronoun.

Study the following examples to make sure that you are able to recognize a relative pronoun and to identify its antecedent. In each sentence the relative pronoun is in italics, and an arrow points to its antecedent.

The inspector *who* checks these machines is Mr. Pomeroy.   (The relative pronoun *who* begins the clause *who checks these machines*. What is the antecedent of *who?* Answer: *inspector*.)

Send the printouts by Monday, *which* is the deadline.   (The relative pronoun *which* begins the clause *which is the deadline*. What does *which* refer to? Answer: *Monday*.)

Please give me the catalog *that* is on my desk.   (What does *that* refer to? Answer: *catalog*.)

Notice that in each sentence the verb in the relative-pronoun clause agrees with the antecedent. (REMEMBER: The predicate of a clause that is introduced by a relative pronoun *agrees with the antecedent of that pronoun*, not with the relative pronoun itself. For an easy way to apply this rule, study this Quick Trick.)

QUICK TRICK | **OMIT THE PRONOUN**

By omitting the relative pronoun *who, which,* or *that*, you can quickly make the predicate agree with the antecedent of that pronoun. All you must do is *use the antecedent as the subject of the clause.*

Our Denver office is the one that (is, are) now having (its, their) inventory audited.   (Omit the relative pronoun *that* and use its antecedent, the pronoun *one*, as the subject of the clause: *one is* now having *its* inventory audited. *Is* and *its* are correct, to agree with *one*.)

Our Denver office is one of those offices that (is, are) now having (its, their) inventories audited.   (Again, omit *that* and use its antecedent, the noun *offices*, as the subject of the clause: *offices are* now having *their* inventories audited. *Are* and *their* are correct, to agree with *offices*.)

An employee who (wants, want) to have (his or her, their) vacation schedule changed must see Mr. Helms.   (Again, use the antecedent as the subject of the clause: an *employee wants* to have *his or her* vacation schedule changed.)

Employees who (wants, want) to have (his or her, their) vacation schedule changed must see Mr. Helms.   (Again, use the antecedent as the subject of the clause: *employees want* to have *their* vacation schedule changed.)

CAUTION: *Who, which,* and *that* are not always *relative* pronouns. In the following sentences, note that *who, which,* and *that* do not relate to anything. They have no antecedents.

Who is the woman talking to Ms. Steinberg?   (*Who* has no antecedent in this sentence. It is not a relative pronoun.)

Do you know which restaurant has been selected?   (*Which* has no antecedent.)

Please be sure to treat that microprocessor carefully.   (*That* has no antecedent.)

Also beware of clauses that are preceded by "*the only* one." Such clauses always take a singular predicate.

Did you know that Olga is the only one of the agents who *has* exceeded *her* sales budget?

CLASS PRACTICE 1

In the following sentences identify the relative pronouns and their antecedents before you make your selections of verbs and pronouns. (Be sure to omit the relative pronoun and use the antecedent as the subject of the clause to make your choice.)

1. Her partner is one of those people who (enjoys, enjoy) (his or her, their) work.
2. Jean, please be sure to complete all these notifications before the deadline, which (is, are) Saturday, December 8.
3. Is this the training course that (has, have) become famous for (its, their) effective selling techniques?
4. Leah is one of those product managers who always (completes, complete) (his or her, their) marketing plans on schedule.
5. This is one material that (is, are) worth the extra expense because of (its, their) strength and durability.
6. Ms. Kylish is one of those designers who (is, are) very creative despite the pressure of deadlines.

EDITING PRACTICE 4

Now correct any agreement errors in the following sentences. Again, be sure that you are able to identify the relative pronouns and their antecedents.

1. Have you seen all the promotion notices that was posted in the lobby?
2. One of the programmers who is working on this project is Ivan Templeton.
3. Do you think that we should order one of those terminals that is on sale?
4. Mr. Sarafian is one of those people who insists that he will not retire.
5. Ms. Fredericks is the only one of the district managers who are permitted to sign company checks.
6. Sheldon Supplies is one of the most dependable business forms companies that is in the metropolitan area.

COMMUNICATION LABORATORY

APPLICATION EXERCISES

A. Select the correct verbs and pronouns in each of the following sentences. Also, identify the subjects with which your choices agree.

1. Mr. Elander or Mr. Weymouth (has, have) an appointment with Ms. Clarkson this afternoon, doesn't (he, they)?
2. Many a programmer and instructional designer (has, have) worked on this award-winning educational software package.
3. Mr. Netherland is one of those chauffeurs who always (arrives, arrive) promptly.
4. According to the ad, each monitor, disk drive, and printer (is, are) to be sold at a 30 percent discount.
5. Rhythm and blues (is, are) the kind of music that Advance Records and Tapes distributes.
6. Gerry needs one of those language programs that (teaches, teach) conversational Spanish in just a few hours.
7. Jules is one of those CPAs who always (works, work) very carefully.
8. I'm sure that either Lyn or Susan (finances, finance) (her, their) car through the credit union.
9. Neither Jeffrey nor his brothers (owns, own) any interest in the company as of last December.
10. Phil and Marie generally (reads and approves, read and approve) all copy for ads and promotional materials.
11. Phil or Marie usually (gets, get) executive approval for expenses over $5000.
12. Perhaps Mr. Landau or his daughters still (does, do) own part of the company.
13. We need one of those computer programs that (makes, make) it possible to pay expenses electronically.
14. Fitch Telephone Supplies is one of those stores which (is, are) currently offering special discounts in an effort to build up (its, their) mail order business.
15. Timothy or his two assistants (is, are) going to discuss (his, their) recommendations with the committee next Thursday.

B. On a separate sheet of paper, correct any errors in the following sentences. Write *OK* if a sentence has no error.

1. There's only about two dozen more orders for us to process.
2. After she interviews these six applicants, Caryl will select the one whom she thinks has the best potential.

3. Edna done all she could to complete the order and ship it to the Orlando office as soon as possible.

4. If the Grant's send their check before December 1, they are eligible for a 2 percent discount, aren't they?

5. "The Grants' check arrived this morning," Anthony said.

6. Two or three CPA's on our staff have been assigned to the Gordon account.

7. Do you know whom will be the first speaker at this afternoon's conference?

8. Neither Leo nor the other comptrollers was sure that Ms. Weathers, the executive vice president, would approve purchasing the equipment.

9. If you want Larry and myself to help you with this, Ms. Perez, please let us know.

10. No, us cashiers haven't been told of these changes yet.

11. She is one of those branch managers who want to increase the advertising budget.

12. Has Mr. Cooper said whom he plans to promote to regional manager yet?

13. Jerry been with Braverman Plastics for nearly ten years before he joined our firm.

14. The Harrison's are among the major stockholders in Verg Chemicals, aren't they?

15. Each sales representative is trained to establish goodwill with their clients.

C. Identify whether a singular or a plural verb is required in each of the following phrases.

1. either the manager or her assistants _____
2. one of the people who _____
3. Cliff and Lorraine _____
4. ham and eggs _____
5. the two clerks or their supervisor _____
6. Colleen or Douglas _____

VOCABULARY AND SPELLING STUDIES

A. These words are often confused: *fair, fare; undo, undue.* Explain the differences.

B. How well can you define the following word processing terms?

1. *Delete* means (a) to indent, (b) to represent, (c) to omit, (d) to input copy.

2. *Wraparound* describes the ability of word processing equipment to (**a**) automatically place a word at the beginning of a new line, (**b**) print copy on both the front and the back of a sheet at the same time, (**c**) bind a report in a special wrapper, (**d**) type around the full area of any size sheet.

3. *Hardware* refers to (**a**) the tools that operators must use to adjust or fix equipment, (**b**) the diskettes or disks that are used to store data, (**c**) the mechanical or electronic equipment used in word processing, (**d**) an alternative name for software.

C. Identify the word that is spelled correctly in each of the following groups.

1. wholy, accommodate, symetry
2. specificaly, recolect, Wednesday
3. remembrence, statistical, retreival
4. withold, occasional, aprroximately
5. amateur, expendible, consientious
6. hindrence, necesitate, knowledgeable
7. wraper, baggage, menice
8. neighbor, wiegh, eigth
9. cieling mileage, greif
10. seperate, calender, deceive
11. likelihood, advising, useage
12. nineth, piece, greatful
13. definate, verify, liesure
14. garantee, aquire, Wednesday
15. offerred, convenient, can not

COMMUNICATING FOR RESULTS

To Gossip or Not to Gossip? At lunch with a group of coworkers, you hear the conversation suddenly turn to the looks, dress, and other personal characteristics of Bob, the manager of your department. Someone mentions how poorly he dresses, how unfriendly he is, and other equally negative remarks. Because Bob works in your department, everyone is now waiting to hear what you have to say.

What would you say?

U · N · I · T

22

Adjectives

The better you understand the fundamentals that have been presented in the preceding units, the easier you will find this unit on adjectives and all subsequent units. This unit presents the basic uses of adjectives—namely, to make sentences *specific* and *lively*—and their most common *misuses*. Let's begin, then, with the first step; let's be sure that you can *identify adjectives* correctly.

Identifying Adjectives

Remember that any word that modifies a noun or a pronoun is an adjective. An adjective answers the following questions: "What kind?" "Which one?" "How many?" Now look at the following kinds of adjectives to be sure that you can identify them.

Articles. The words *a* and *an* are called *indefinite articles*. The article *a* is used before a word that begins with a consonant sound, a long *u* sound, or an *h* that is pronounced, as in *a building*, *a union*, and *a hallway*.

Use *an* before a word that begins with a vowel sound (except long *u*) or an *h* that is not pronounced, as in *an airline*, *an essay*, *an item*, *an odor*, *an umbrella*, *an honor*, *an hour*.

The word *the* is also an article (called the *definite article*). Obviously *the* is one of the most commonly used words in our language.

The instructor brought *the* projector to *the* classroom.

Descriptive Adjectives. When most people think of adjectives, they think of words that describe—descriptive adjectives such as *famous, interesting, intensive,* and *new.*

A *famous* speaker, Leslie Wardlaw, gave an *interesting* presentation.   (*Famous* and *interesting* are descriptive adjectives.)

She took an *intensive* course in business management at a *new* school near her home.   (*Intensive* and *new* are descriptive adjectives.)

Possessive Adjectives. The possessive pronouns *my, your, his, her, its, our,* and *their* are used to modify nouns. In addition, possessive nouns (such as *manager's* and *John's*) are used to modify nouns. Therefore, these possessive forms function as adjectives.

Your new assistant asked for *our manager's* approval to order *John's* equipment. (*Your, our, manager's,* and *John's* are all possessive adjectives.)

Limiting Adjectives. Adjectives that tell "how many" or "how much" are called *limiting adjectives.* Notice how numbers and words serve to limit the nouns they modify in the following sentences.

One representative in our division was the *first* person to win the award. (*One* and *first* are limiting adjectives.)

Pour *2.6* liters into each of these *four* metal containers. (*2.6* and *four* are limiting adjectives.)

Proper Adjectives. Proper nouns, too, can be used to describe. When they are used as adjectives, they are called *proper adjectives.*

A *New York* hotel advertised special rates for all *West Coast* travelers. (*New York* and *West Coast,* as used here, are proper adjectives.)

Note that words derived from proper nouns are also proper adjectives.

A *European* cruise attracted many *American* tourists. (*European* and *American* are proper adjectives.)

Compound Adjectives. A compound adjective consists of two or more words that act together as a single thought unit to modify a noun or a pronoun.

an *easy-going* person
a *first-class* trip
my *data processing* text
a *high school* student

EDITING PRACTICE 1

A. Choose *a* or *an,* whichever is correct, in each of the following sentences.

1. One of the representatives had (a, an) unique idea for spurring holiday sales.
2. Do you know whether (a, an) union delegate has been invited to this meeting?
3. More than (a, an) hour after the first speech had ended, (a, an) question-and-answer session was still in progress.
4. Has she received (a, an) answer to her question?
5. In our opinion, this law gives our competitors (a, an) unfair advantage.

B. Identify the adjectives in the following sentences as *descriptive* ("D"), *possessive* ("P"), *limiting* ("L"), *proper* ("PR"), or *compound* ("C"). Disregard the articles *a, an,* and *the.*

1. We asked three or four new supervisors for their suggestions for reorganizing our division.

2. One attorney from our Tax Department gave her opinions about the high taxes.
3. A large number of cold ticket holders waited in the icy rain outside our new office building.
4. Two American companies and one Japanese firm have been selected as distributors of our high-speed printers.
5. The complete inventories of the duty-free shops at six Italian airports were purchased by our firm.

Comparison of Adjectives

Degrees of Comparison of Adjectives. Adjective forms such as *new, newer, newest* represent three different degrees of a certain quality. The three degrees are called *positive, comparative,* and *superlative.*

Positive Degree. This form is used when the person or thing is not compared to anyone or anything else.

a new car, an expensive stereo

Comparative Degree. This form is used to express a higher or a lower degree than expressed by the positive degree when comparing two items.

a newer car, a more expensive stereo

Superlative Degree. This form is used to denote the highest or the lowest degree when comparing three or more items.

the newest car, the most expensive stereo

Forms of Comparison of Adjectives. Adjectives may be compared in one of three ways:

1. By adding *er* or *est* to the positive form:

Positive	Comparative (Two Items)	Superlative (Three or More Items)
large	larger	largest
friendly	friendlier	friendliest

2. By using *more* or *most* (or *less* or *least*) with the positive form:

Positive	Comparative (Two Items)	Superlative (Three or More Items)
interesting	more interesting less interesting	most interesting least interesting
intensive	more intensive less intensive	most intensive least intensive
successful	more successful less successful	most successful least successful

3. By changing the form of the word completely:

Positive	Comparative (Two Items)	Superlative (Three or More Items)
good	better	best
bad	worse	worst
little	less	least
much	more	most
many	more	most

(NOTE: Comparatives and superlatives are formed by using *one* of the three methods just discussed.) Do not apply more than one method at a time.

This package is *larger* than yours.   (Not *more larger*.)

In the *simplest* terms possible, Jean explained to all of us how to use the new word processor.   (Not *most simplest*.)

Selection of Correct Forms. Adjectives of one syllable are compared by adding *er* or *est;* adjectives of three or more syllables, by adding *more* or *most*. However, adjectives of two syllables may be compared either by adding *er* or *est* or by adding *more* or *most*. Sometimes the sound of the word will guide you in making a choice; often both methods are equally acceptable. If you are in doubt, remember that those two-syllable adjectives not taking *more* or *most* are irregular comparisons. These irregular comparisons are shown in the dictionary under the positive form of the adjective.

Arthur is *more ambitious* than Martin.   (You cannot add *er* to *ambitious*.)

Iris is one of the *most courteous* agents in the company.   (You cannot add *est* to *courteous*.)

This word processor is the *costliest* one on the market. OR: This word processor is the *most costly* one on the market.   (Both forms are acceptable.)

Choice of Comparative or Superlative Degree. The comparative degree (*newer, more tired, better,* and so on) is used to compare two persons, places, or things.

Helene is tired, but Bert appears *more tired* than she.

Joe's report was good; however, I really consider Claire's report *better*.

The superlative degree (*newest, most tired, best,* and so on) is used to compare *more than two* persons, places, or things.

Steven appears to be the *most tired* of all the brokers.

Of all the reports that were submitted, Joan's was the *best*.

EDITING PRACTICE 2

Make the correct choice in each of the following sentences.

1. Mr. Jacobi's suggestion was (good, better, best), but Mr. Antuono's idea was (good, better, best).
2. In our opinion the (logicalest, most logical) method is the one described by Mrs. Kofax.
3. The product managers are arguing among themselves as to which of the many alternatives is the (most good, more better, most best, best) of all.
4. Try to select the plastic that is the (clearest, most clear, most clearest) among these samples.
5. Her flight is (late, more late, later, most late) than mine, but Richard's flight is (early, more early, earlier, most early) than mine.
6. Our San Diego store is (successful, successfuler, more successful, most successful), our Seattle store is even (successful, successfuler, more successful, most successful), but our Rochester store is the (successful, successfuler, more successful, most successful) of the entire chain.

Other and *Else* in Comparisons. When the comparative degree is used to compare a person or a thing with *other* members of the same group, use the word *other* or *else* as shown in these sentences:

> Peter is *more* ambitious than any *other* broker in our company.   (Without the word *other*, the meaning of the sentence would be that Peter does not work in our company but that he works for another company.)

> Peter is *more* ambitious than all the *other* brokers in our company.   (Again, the word *other* makes it clear that Peter and the other brokers work for the same company. Without the word *other*, the meaning would be that Peter works for a different company than the brokers work for.)

> Peter is *more* ambitious than anyone *else* in our company.   (Without the word *else*, the sentence would again imply that Peter does not work in our company.)

With the superlative degree, *other* or *else* is not needed, but *all* is often used.

> Peter is the *most* ambitious of all the brokers in our company.   (Note that *other* or *else* is not used in the sentence because the *of* phrase makes it clear that Peter belongs to the group compared.)

Adjectives That Cannot Be Compared. The positive degree of some adjectives already states a quality that cannot be compared. For example, "a *full* glass" tells it all; you cannot have another glass that is *fuller* or a third glass that is *fullest*. *Full* is the absolute degree, so this adjective cannot be compared. Other absolute adjectives are:

absolute	flat	sound
accurate	immaculate	spotless
circular	level	square
complete	perfect	straight
correct	perpendicular	supreme
dead	perpetual	unanimous
empty	right	unique
even	round	universal
final		

To indicate the degree to which a person or thing approaches the state of being full or complete or correct, use *more nearly* for two items or *most nearly* for three or more items.

Louise's estimate ($4500) proved to be correct. Except for Louise's, Joe's estimate ($4350) was *more nearly correct* than any of the others.

Only yesterday's vote was unanimous; however, last week's vote was *more nearly unanimous* than any of the others had been.

EDITING PRACTICE 3

Choose the correct words in the following sentences. How well do you understand when to use *other*, *else*, and *all* in comparisons? How well can you handle adjectives that cannot be compared?

1. Adrian is the most experienced of (all the, all the other) word processing operators in the department.
2. Alex Wesler, one of our senior programmers, conducts training sessions better than (any, any other) programmer in the entire company.
3. The West Coast district has more franchises than (any, any other) district in the country.
4. All the specifications that were submitted are inaccurate, unfortunately; however, Mr. Ruck's specifications are the (most accurate, more accurate, most nearly accurate) of all those which we have reviewed.
5. In my opinion Gail gives clearer instructions than (anyone, anyone else) in her department.
6. Yes, Mario types faster than (anyone, anyone else) in his division, but Gladys is the fastest of (all the, all the other) typists in the company.

EDITING PRACTICE 4

This Editing Practice will provide you with a cumulative review of this unit. Correct any errors in the following sentences.

1. In order for this equipment to work accurately, it must be placed on a table that is very level.
2. A union demand that has caused a strong reaction from management is to have a hourly rate of $10.

3. Our manager's knowledge of accounting is far more comprehensive than that of anyone in her department.
4. Has Mr. Jenkins ever indicated which of the two New York State branches he considers best—the Albany branch or the Manhattan branch?
5. We asked the messenger to bring an handcart for the heavy cartons.
6. With the heater off, the room quickly became slightly more cold.

Adjective Pitfalls

Compound Adjectives. As you saw in the beginning of the unit, a *compound adjective* consists of two or more words that act together as a single thought unit to modify a noun or a pronoun. Certain compound adjectives are hyphenated; others are not. Observe these rules:

1. Do not hyphenate compound adjectives that have become very familiar from long use and are considered a single unit. Do not hyphenate compound proper nouns used as adjectives.

    a high school classroom
    charge account customers
    life insurance policies
    data processing texts
    social security benefits
    real estate contracts
    an East Coast convention
    Los Angeles suburbs

2. Hyphenate most other compound adjectives when they precede a noun:

    air-conditioned offices
    first-class tours
    up-to-date equipment
    a 10-mile drive
    one-hour intervals
    well-known speakers

    BUT: person who is *well known*, an interval of *one hour*

See the Quick Trick below to help you identify compound adjectives.

QUICK TRICK   **TWO ADJECTIVES ACTING AS ONE**

To help you decide whether two words that precede a noun *do* act together as a single unit, try this simple test.

Use *long range plans* for an example. The noun modified is *plans*. Ask yourself, "What kind of plans?" *Long* plans? *Range* plans? No, neither one makes sense. The two words work as a single unit: *long-range plans*—plans that are long-range.

EDITING PRACTICE 5

Decide whether the compound adjectives in the following sentences should be hyphenated.

1. Mr. Norton, a (well known, well-known) tax expert, will discuss some popular (Wall Street, Wall-Street) investing techniques.
2. There is generally no more than a (10 minute, 10-minute) delay in transmitting data by this method.
3. Leonia has become quite (well known, well-known) as a result of her conducting investment seminars throughout the country.
4. Many of the (high interest, high-interest) bonds that she recommends are listed in this (four page, four-page) booklet.
5. A (San Francisco, San-Francisco) corporation has bid on this property, according to Ms. Skelton.
6. We have budgeted several (60 second, 60-second) commercials to introduce this new product.

Those, Them. *Them* is never an adjective and should not be used in place of the adjective *those*.

> Will you be able to help me carry *those* packages to Ms. Lopez?   (Not *them packages*. The noun following *those* helps you see that the adjective *those* is needed.)

Note that *those* is the plural of *that; these* is the plural of *this*. Use *that* and *those* to refer to objects that are at a distance from you; use *this* and *these* for objects that are closer to you.

Either, Neither, Any, Any One, No One, Not Any, None. *Either* and *neither* are used to refer to one of two persons or things. *Any, any one, no one, not any,* and *none* are used to refer to one of *three or more* persons or things.

> *Either* mechanic should be able to help you.   (There are two mechanics.)

> *Any* mechanic should be able to help you.   (Because *any* is used, there must be three or more mechanics.)

Repeated Modifier. Repeating a modifier such as *a, an, the,* or *my* (as in the following example) shows that two different people are referred to:

> The vice president and the general manager approved this addendum to the contract.   (Two different people—one, the vice president, the other, the general manager—approved the addendum.)

Omitting the modifier *the* before *general manager* shows that one person is referred to:

> The vice president and general manager approved this addendum.   (Here, one person is referred to. This one person simply has two titles, *vice president* and *general manager*.)

EDITING PRACTICE 6

Select the correct words in the following sentences.

1. Are you sure that Ms. Campbell wants (this, these) negatives sent to the studio by messenger?
2. According to the lease agreement, we must return (those, them) training films to the distributor by Friday, March 19.
3. If those (kind, kinds) of monitors are on sale, we will probably buy three or four of them.
4. Please tell Terri that she may use (either, any) of these three terminals to retrieve and revise her report.
5. These two word processing programs are both very easy to use because they are menu-driven; you may use (either, any) of them, if you wish.
6. We looked at several (kind, kinds) of VCRs, but (neither, none) really met our requirements.

COMMUNICATION LABORATORY

APPLICATION EXERCISES

A. Select the correct words in the following sentences.

1. We were surprised to see that the smaller package was (heavier, more heavy) than the larger package.
2. If you prefer, you may buy (continuous form, continuous-form) paper for your printer.
3. The paper is available in both (11 inch, 11-inch) lengths and (14 inch, 14-inch) lengths.
4. Kathy is developing (a, an) uniform procedure for handling rejected merchandise.
5. The assistant manager of the Finance Department, Holly Rosen, works harder than (anyone, anyone else) in the department.
6. Be sure to send all (this, these) cartons to the warehouse this afternoon.
7. The lease of the store in the (Park Grove, Park-Grove) Mall expires December 31.
8. To introduce this new line of products, we've planned several (60 second, 60-second) commercials during selected sports events.
9. The comptroller and the vice president (is, are) now reviewing the proposed bid.
10. The antiglare screen on this monitor is better than (any, any other) that we have seen.
11. The book lying on that table is one of the (rarest, more rare) volumes in this library.

12. His three sisters are all successful business people, but Connie is clearly the (successfulest, more nearly successful, most successful) of them.
13. Connie is (more successful, more nearly successful, most successful) than her sisters.
14. The company that submitted the (highest, most high) bid was Miller & Freund Inc.
15. Dexter Industries is now constructing a (ten story, ten-story) building on Elm Street.
16. Agnes prefers (this, these) kind of paper for her sketches.
17. Kent, please return (those, them) items to inventory if they are not damaged.
18. Janice Naldi is considered a better branch manager than (anyone, anyone else) in her company.
19. Our (San Francisco, San-Francisco) office has been moved from Ames Street to Canal Street.
20. Henry is one of the (most tactful, tactfulest) people in the Credit Department.

B. Correct any errors in the following sentences. Write *OK* for any sentence that has no error.

1. Jennifer said that she wants us to take them agendas to the hotel before the luncheon begins.
2. Yes, theirs enough money left in the budget to print more advertising circulars.
3. James been in the conference room with Mr. Mathewson since 9 o'clock this morning.
4. Ms. Abbate said, "Please call the Katzs to see whether they have received the stock certificates yet."
5. Although these checks cannot be cashed, they should not be left to lay on the desk overnight.
6. The checks have lain there on Ken's desk since yesterday morning.
7. Who did Ms. Melner say that she wanted to talk with?
8. Our company pays higher wages for part-time help than any company in this area.
9. Thelma sent two trainees, Louis and she, to the accounting seminar at the Temple Hotel.
10. Both Ray and Paul type very fast, but Paul is more accurate.
11. Either Theodore or Martin, technicians in the Research Department, represent Dr. Wynn when he is away.
12. Mario submitted sketches that were very unique.
13. Ivan said he seen Leonard immediately before the speech began.
14. Yes, Danielle and myself will definitely have enough time to process these invoices before we leave today.
15. "Send one extra copy of both contracts to each of the attornies," Ellen said.

16. Could you please ask Ms. Mackenzie's executive assistant whether he has the documentation to run the software program?
17. Our staff designers prefer these kind of assignment because it is more challenging.
18. The management staff assured us that we employees would benefit from them new benefits.
19. The New-York office of International Inventors Inc. is one of the most sophisticated buildings in the midtown area.
20. The Ferraro's will had laid in the attorney's vault from the day that the will had been signed.

VOCABULARY AND SPELLING STUDIES

A. These words are often confused: *shoot, chute; desolate, dissolute.* Explain the differences.

B. In which of the following words is the *u not* pronounced as in *human?*

1. gratitude
2. utterance
3. student
4. revenue

C. In which of the following words is the *ou not* pronounced like the *oo* in *noon?*

1. souvenir
2. cantaloupe
3. acoustics
4. coupon

COMMUNICATING FOR RESULTS

Sexist Language. "A Woman's Place Is in the House—and in the Senate Too!" This saying appeared on some signs and bumper stickers across the country. It may be humorous on the surface, but it has a deep, important meaning.

U · N · I · T

23 Adverbs

In Unit 22 you learned that *adjectives* are modifiers. Like adjectives, *adverbs* are also modifiers. As you study adverbs in this unit, you will see that many adverbs are formed simply by adding *ly* to an adjective—for example, *carefully, quickly,* and *patiently.* In addition, you will note that adverbs, like adjectives, can also be compared. Study adverbs carefully so that you will be able to use both these modifiers correctly.

Simple Adverbs

An *adverb* is a word that modifies an adjective, a verb, or another adverb. Adverbs answer questions such as "When?" "Where?" "How?" "Why?" "How much?" "How little?" Many adverbs are formed by adding *ly* to adjectives:

Adjective	Adverb
random	randomly
quiet	quietly
poor	poorly
sole	solely
simple	simply
lazy	lazily
defensive	defensively
productive	productively

Although many adverbs end in *ly,* remember that not all adverbs end in *ly.* Look at the following adverbs:

always	here	now	too
soon	often	then	up
late	there	very	sometimes

Now notice how these adverbs answer questions such as "When?" "Where?" "How?" "Why?" "How much?" "How little?" in the following examples:

arrived late   (Arrived when? Answer: *late.*)

sent there   (Sent where? Answer: *there.*)

selected often   (Selected how? Answer: *often.*)

Remember that *not all* adverbs end in *ly.*

Comparison of Adverbs. The same general rules that apply to comparison of adjectives (see page 204) also apply to comparison of adverbs. Adverbs are compared in one of three ways:

1. By adding *er* or *est* to an adverb containing one syllable:

Positive	Comparative	Superlative
fast	faster	fastest
late	later	latest
soon	sooner	soonest

2. By using *more* or *most* (or *less* or *least*) with an adverb ending in *ly:*

Positive	Comparative	Superlative
slowly	more slowly	most slowly
	less slowly	least slowly
quietly	more quietly	most quietly
	less quietly	least quietly
poorly	more poorly	most poorly
	less poorly	least poorly

3. By completely changing the form of the adverb:

Positive	Comparative	Superlative
well	better	best
badly	worse	worst
much	more	most

Adverbs That Join Clauses

Certain adverbs can be used to join clauses. For example, the following adverbs (called *conjunctive adverbs*) are used to join independent clauses, as illustrated in the sentences below.

consequently	moreover
however	accordingly
then	therefore
thus	furthermore
yet	

The cost of the equipment is estimated at $6500; *consequently,* this expense must be approved by our branch manager. (The adverb *consequently* joins two independent clauses—that is, two clauses that can stand alone as complete sentences.)

All expenses over $5000 must be approved by a branch manager; we have, *therefore,* asked Ms. Danforth to approve this purchase. (Here, the adverb *therefore* joins two independent clauses, although it does not appear at the beginning of the second clause but elsewhere in that clause.)

Other adverbs (called *subordinating conjunctions*) join subordinate clauses to independent clauses. Among the commonly used adverbs in this category are:

after	because	since
although	before	when
as	if	while

When Ms. Danforth signs the purchase order, we will quickly schedule a shipping date.   (*When* introduces the clause *When Ms. Danforth signs the purchase order* and joins it to the independent clause *we will quickly schedule a shipping date.* The adverb *quickly* answers the question "will schedule *when?*")

Before you quote any prices, please check the revised discount rates for distributors.   (*Before* introduces the subordinate clause *Before you quote any prices* and joins this clause to the independent clause *please check the revised discount rates for distributors.*)

CLASS PRACTICE 1

Identify the adverbs in the following sentences.

1. Barry works more productively under pressure, doesn't he?
2. Marion explained the issues clearly, and she summarized the alternatives thoroughly.
3. Trent and Edna will work together on the inventory report; at the end of the week, therefore, they will meet here with the auditors.
4. Before we leave for Memphis, we must completely revise this procedures manual.
5. Both clients arrived later than we expected.
6. Anthony and Audrey both speak well, but Christine speaks best of all.

EDITING PRACTICE 1

Correct any errors in the use of adverbs in the following sentences. Write *OK* for any sentence that has no error.

1. Mr. McMahon speaks well; Ms. Vernon, however, speaks more well.
2. Helen said that she thinks AnneMarie writes most clearly than the other account executives.
3. Unfortunately, the machines are operating worse than we had thought.
4. These two duplicators are inexpensive, but they make copies slowlier than the machines we now have.
5. All three district managers are doing a good job, but Ellen is working most well of all.
6. From now on we must be sure to check these invoices more carefully.

Adverb or Adjective?

Should an adjective follow linking verbs such as *look, seem, appear, sound, feel, taste,* and *smell,* or should an adverb follow them? Answer: *Always an adjective!*

This food *tastes* delicious.   (*Tastes* is a linking verb—a no-action verb. Therefore, the adjective *delicious* is correct—not the adverb *deliciously.*)

The cool water *feels* good.   (*Feels* is a linking verb. Therefore, the adjective *good* is correct—not the adverb *well.*)

What, then, is the problem? The problem is that verbs such as *look, taste,* and *feel* are not always linking verbs. A linking verb is a no-action verb. Therefore, in the sentence *This food tastes delicious,* the verb *tastes* merely links the adjective *delicious* to the noun it describes, *food.* Of course, an adjective (not an adverb) must be used to modify a noun, so *delicious* is obviously correct.

In the sentence *The water feels good,* the verb *feels* is a linking verb; it describes no action. *Feels* merely links the adjective *good* to the noun it modifies, *water.* Again, only an adjective can modify a noun, so *good* is correct.

Now let's see some examples in which these verbs *do* describe action.

Martha *tastes* her food slowly before she swallows it.   (*Tastes* is obviously an action verb; it describes something Martha is doing actively—*tasting. Tastes* does not link an adjective to a noun or a pronoun. Tastes how? Answer: *slowly.* The adverb *slowly* modifies the verb *tastes.* Only an adverb, not an adjective, can modify a verb.)

You should *feel* the cloth carefully.   (Feel how? Answer: *carefully.* The adverb *carefully* modifies the verb *should feel.* Here, *feel* is obviously an action verb. It does not link an adjective to a noun or pronoun. Therefore, the adverb *carefully* is correct.)

CLASS PRACTICE 2

Determine whether the verbs in the following sentences are action verbs and therefore require adverbs to modify them. If they are linking verbs, of course, adjectives will follow. Then make your choices.

1. When he realized that he had made a mistake, David seemed (angry, angrily).
2. When the alarm sounded, the security guards appeared (sudden, suddenly).
3. Of course, all of us felt (bad, badly) about the closing of the plant.
4. The auditors checked (immediate, immediately) to find the error.
5. The supervisors seemed rather (worried, worriedly) about possible danger to employees in the factory.
6. As he read the announcement, Mark's voice sounded (nervous, nervously).

EDITING PRACTICE 2

Correct the following sentences. Write *OK* if the sentence is correct.

1. As they discussed the plan with the staff, the managers seemed confidently.
2. Yes, the food did taste well, but the service was poor.
3. The flowers in her office made the air smell sweetly.
4. Although Maria seemed angrily at the dispatcher, she was simply concerned with delivering the merchandise on time.
5. Jack and I feel bad about Mr. Alzado's retiring.
6. The investigators questioned the man who looked suspicious.

Adverb Pitfalls

The adverb errors that occur most often are (1) positioning the adverb incorrectly in a sentence, (2) misusing *never* for *not*, and (3) using double negatives. All three errors are discussed below.

Position of Adverbs. An adverb should be positioned near the word it modifies. As the following sentences show, misplacing the adverb can change or obscure the meaning of the sentence.

Only my assistant read these computer printouts yesterday. (My assistant was the only one who read them—I didn't; my boss didn't; my secretary didn't.)

My *only* assistant read these computer printouts yesterday. (I have only one assistant. Here the word *only* functions as an adjective meaning "sole.")

My assistant *only* read these computer printouts yesterday. (He didn't do anything else to them. He didn't duplicate them; he didn't mail them; he didn't approve them. He only read them.)

My assistant read *only* these computer printouts yesterday. (He read no other computer printouts, no reports, no magazines, no letters, only these printouts.)

My assistant read these computer printouts *only* yesterday. (He read these computer printouts as recently as yesterday: not the day before, not last week, but yesterday.)

My assistant read these computer printouts yesterday *only*. (He didn't read them on any other day; just yesterday.)

EDITING PRACTICE 3

Are adverbs correctly placed in the following sentences? Correct any misplaced adverbs.

1. As of this morning we had only invoiced about 30 new orders.
2. By the end of the afternoon they had hardly received any credit applications.
3. The branch manager and her assistant have the combination to the safe only.

4. The revised estimate for renovating the building was not even estimated for $100,000.
5. We just expect Marisa to call in a few minutes.
6. In just one morning we nearly received 500 inquiries about our newest product line.

Never and *Not.* *Never* means "not ever; at no time; not in any way." Obviously, it is a strong word.

> Since Brandon Metals was established in 1948, the company has *never* laid off employees.

The word *not* simply expresses negation. Do not use *never* when a simple *not* will do.

> We have *not* received the check that is due from Scotch Plains Printers.   (Not "We *never* received . . . .")

> Mr. Durham did *not* deliver the materials to us last week.   (Not "Mr. Durham *never* delivered . . . .")

Double Negatives. Do not use two negatives to express one negation. Errors occur most often with the negative statements *scarcely, only, hardly, but, never,* and *not.*

> Dr. Hood had but one suggestion for us.   (Not *had not but one.*)

> Our manager can hardly believe that we completed all the billing on time.   (Not *cannot hardly believe.*)

EDITING PRACTICE 4

Make the correct selections in the following sentences.

1. Agnes (did not say, never said) that she was changing her vacation schedule.
2. As you know, we can't (help but worry, help worrying) about rising inflation.
3. The Order Department (has, hasn't) hardly any backlog at this time.
4. Lawrence (did not say, never said) whether he would attend next Saturday's banquet.
5. These municipal bonds (did not but earn, never earned more than, earned only) 6.75 percent, but all the interest is tax-free.
6. Sam and Frank (have, haven't) hardly any new accounts this week.

Adverb and Adjective Confusions

Certain word pairs (*sure, surely; real, really; good, well; some, somewhat;* and *most, almost*) deserve special attention. As you study them, remember that the first word in each pair is the adjective; the second is the adverb.

Sure, Surely; Real, Really. The most common errors in using these word pairs occur when the adjectives *sure* and *real* are used instead of the adverbs *surely* and *really.* Study this Quick Trick to choose the right word every time:

QUICK TRICK | **SUBSTITUTE *VERY* OR *CERTAINLY***

When faced with a choice between *real* and *really* (or between *sure* and *surely*), substitute the adverb *very* or *certainly* to test whether an adverb is needed.

Meg (sure, surely) did a great job in landing the Harkovy account. (Substitute *certainly* and you will see that *Meg certainly did* makes sense. Therefore, the adverb *surely* is correct because the adverb *certainly* can be substituted.)

Lawrence did a (real, really) thorough analysis of competitive products. (Substitute *very:* Lawrence did a *very* thorough analysis . . . . Therefore, the adverb *really* is correct.)

Good, Well. Good is the adjective; *well* is the adverb. As an adjective *good* modifies nouns and pronouns. As an adverb *well* should answer the question How?

Margaret really did a *good* job. (The adjective *good* modifies the noun *job.* It does not answer the question How?)

Margaret works very *well* under pressure. (Works how? Well. The adverb *well* modifies the verb *works.*)

EXCEPTION: *Well* can also be an adjective, *but only when referring to health.*

Scot didn't feel *well,* so he left early. (Refers to Scot's health.)

Some, Somewhat. To decide when to use the adjective *some* and the adverb *somewhat,* use the following Quick Trick.

QUICK TRICK | **SUBSTITUTE *A LITTLE BIT***

When you can substitute the words *a little bit,* use the adverb *somewhat.*

Brendan was *somewhat* nervous about the upcoming licensing exam. (He was *a little bit* nervous.)

They requested *some* help to complete their end-of-month paperwork. (*A little bit* help makes no sense; thus *some* is correct.)

Most, Almost. The adjective *most* is the superlative of *much* or *many*. The adverb *almost* means "not quite" or "very nearly."

> *Most* employees are delighted with the additional coverage this policy provides.   (*Many, more, most* employees.)

> The draft of the annual report is *almost* finished.   (*Very nearly* finished.)

EDITING PRACTICE 5

Select the correct word from the choices given.

1. Dean was (sure, surely) happy to hear the (good, well) news.
2. Carlton has received (some, somewhat) résumés and application letters, but he is (some, somewhat) disappointed in their quality.
3. In my opinion, Lindhurst Autos treated us (good, well), and its Service Department is certainly (good, well).
4. Harry was (real, really) excited about moving to Boston.
5. We were (sure, surely) upset that we had not received the contract.
6. Tom always does (good, well) work, but today he isn't feeling very (good, well).

EDITING PRACTICE 6

Read the following sentences and correct any errors in the use of adverbs. Write *OK* for any sentence that has no error.

1. Needless to say, Andrea and I were sure happy to hear that we had been selected to speak at the convention.
2. When Susan was presented with the trophy, she couldn't help but smile.
3. Everyone who works with Rose comments on how good she writes.
4. One aspect that respondents said was really important was the quality of the appliances.
5. No, we haven't hardly heard any news about the construction of our new office in Mexico City.
6. The staff members agree that meeting the schedule is the real issue.

COMMUNICATION LABORATORY

APPLICATION EXERCISES

A. Select the right answer for each of the following sentences.

1. Ms. Weems appeared rather (cautious, cautiously) when she discussed the terms of the union agreement.

2. As you can imagine, Sandra (could, couldn't) hardly wait to travel to Honolulu for the convention.

3. (Most, Almost) of the engineers were (some, somewhat) disappointed to hear that the project had been canceled.

4. Because this report will be sent to all shareholders, we recommend using a (more formal, most formal) tone.

5. When she was asked to substitute for Ms. Quimby, Adelaide (had, hadn't) but two hours to prepare her speech.

6. Please review both columns of figures (careful, carefully) before you send this chart to the Duplicating Department.

7. Rona and her staff always submit (good, well) ad copy because she and her assistants proofread very (good, well).

8. Naturally, we were (real, really) excited to hear that we are tied for first place in the sales contest.

9. Cynthia prefers (only buying, buying only) from Excelsior Computer Equipment.

10. Henry was (sure, surely) delighted to be appointed to the special committee.

11. As Joan proved quite (clear, clearly), the cost of leasing all the computer equipment is prohibitive.

12. After working a double shift, Janice didn't feel (good, well).

13. We knew the food would taste (good, well) because we have often eaten at that restaurant.

14. Mr. Humphreys, our supervisor, plans all projects (good, well) and credits his employees for their (good, well) work.

15. Ted was (real, really) surprised to learn that he is a candidate for the open position.

B. Find and correct any errors in the following sentences. If a sentence has no error, write *OK*.

1. Do you know who Louise appointed to head the department during her absence?

2. Jerome enjoys working on technical projects more than I.

3. Both assistants and myself will work overtime to ensure that the analysis is complete and accurate.

4. Mr. Johnsons' suggestion is to hire a consultant with experience in marketing consumer products.

5. In the conference room on the large table is the samples that we reviewed and approved at this morning's meeting.

6. Do not leave all these documents laying on your desk.

7. Although the new process sounds rather complicated, it is really more simpler than our old process.

8. Some of the clerks been asked to attend special workshops to help them become familiar with the new computer keyboards.

9. Of course, it's very important for an executive to learn to use their time wisely and efficiently.

10. The criteria for hiring supervisory personnel is clearly detailed in this booklet.

11. Yes, its already been decided that both plants will be closed during the week of August 14.

12. Patricia is one of those account executives who always listen carefully to their clients' suggestions.

13. Beth and Gene, both of whom are CPA's, are now working on a presentation to explain the new tax laws to the staff.

14. Us attorneys have been asked to review the federal regulations concerning hiring practices.

15. Most of the sales representative's cars are leased from United Car Leasing.

C. Select the correct word from the choices in parentheses.

1. Suzanne was obviously (real, really) excited to win the Employee of the Year Award.

2. Read the figures in each column (slow, slowly); as you do so, I will check these charts (careful, carefully).

3. Vera hasn't (any, no) money to invest in these stocks.

4. Nina feels (bad, badly) about the closing of the Remsen Avenue plant, especially because she has so many friends there.

5. Maxine acted (wise, wisely) in referring the caller to the Legal Department.

6. Mr. Ford said, "Don't look at the audience so (angry, angrily) while you're speaking."

7. When asked to suggest solutions, Paul rose (immediate, immediately) and cited two good possibilities.

8. Phil always leads the committee meetings very (good, well); he is considered a (good, well) group leader.

9. A benefit of using the new word processor is that you can draft and revise correspondence much more (quick and accurate, quickly and accurately).

10. We became more (confident, confidently) when we were told that we had two months to complete the detailed analysis.

VOCABULARY AND SPELLING STUDIES

A. These words are often confused: *disburse, disperse; equable, equitable.* Explain the differences.

B. Match each word in Column A with the term in Column B that is nearest in meaning.

A	B
1. repetitious	a. with rainbowlike colors
2. iridescent	b. enduring
3. obscure	c. unreal
4. permanent	d. transitory
5. axiomatic	e. monotonous
	f. indistinct
	g. self-evident

C. How are the following words spelled when *ed* is added?

1. admit
2. acquaint
3. develop
4. appall
5. refer
6. embarrass
7. appear
8. worry
9. taste
10. respond
11. fit
12. plan
13. correspond
14. address
15. succeed

COMMUNICATING FOR RESULTS

Business Dress and Grooming. You work for United Banks. Today you have been asked to substitute for Joan Peterson, the assistant director of training and development, who is out of the office. Joan was supposed to address a group of ten new employees who are attending an orientation session during their first day working for United Banks. The topic of Joan's speech was to be "Business Dress."

As Joan's substitute, what would you say to these new employees to impress them with the importance of good grooming and appropriate dress on the job?

U · N · I · T

24 Prepositions

Prepositions often go unnoticed as we write and as we speak, but they do important jobs. As you will see, prepositions serve to join words—and joining words is what writing and speaking is all about! Study prepositions carefully so that you will be able to identify them and to use them correctly in your writing and your speaking.

Prepositional Phrases

A preposition is always followed by a noun or a pronoun. In fact, as you look at the word *preposition* you see the word *position* and the prefix *pre*, which means "before." Thus a preposition is a word that is *positioned before* a noun or a pronoun.

Of course, not *every* word positioned before a noun or a pronoun is a preposition. Look at the following list of commonly used prepositions and the examples of prepositional phrases:

Prepositions			Prepositional Phrases
about	between	off	*after* the meeting
above	by	on	*against* the wall
after	down	out	*between* those cars
against	except	over	*by* that building
among	for	through	*except* one manager
at	from	to	*from* her
before	in	under	*in* the summer
behind	into	until	*on* credit
below	like	up	*to* them
beside	of	with	*with* us

Now let's see how prepositions are used in the following sentences.

They plan to return *after the convention.*   (Return when? After the convention. Because this prepositional phrase answers the question When? it is an adverbial phrase—that is, it does the job of an adverb.)

The man *with her* is the new district manager.   (The prepositional phrase *with her* modifies the noun *man*. Because it modifies a noun, this prepositional phrase serves as an adjective.)

A representative *from Walden Industries* made an appointment with Ms. Dykstra. (Here the prepositional phrase describes the noun *representative*. Which representative? Answer: The representative *from Walden Industries*. Because it modifies a noun, this prepositional phrase is an adjective phrase.)

In the above examples you see that prepositions do indeed join words. They join words to make phrases that can then serve as adjectives or as adverbs. Note, too, that the *object of the preposition* is a noun or a pronoun and is the last word in the phrase.

after the convention   (the noun *convention* is the object of the preposition *after*)

with her   (the object of the preposition *with* is the pronoun *her*)

from Walden Industries   (the noun *Walden Industries* is the object of the preposition *from*)

Preposition Combinations

Certain prepositions must be combined with specific nouns or verbs, as shown below:

abide *by* a decision
abide *with* a person

conform *to* regulations
in conformity *with* regulations

enter *on* the record
enter *into* an agreement

wait *for* someone
wait *on* a customer

Now study the following preposition combinations, which are very commonly used. Whenever you have trouble remembering which preposition is correct in a specific instance, refer to a business writer's manual or to a dictionary.

Agree. *Agree* is used as follows: (1) agree *on* or *upon*—reach a mutual understanding, (2) agree to *(accept)* another's plan, (3) agree *with* a person or his or her idea.

They *agreed upon* a solution to the dispute.

Our directors *agreed to* the offer from Wembly Associates.

Barry *agreed with* the other programmers.

Angry. Be sure to say "angry *with*" a person, "angry *at*" a thing, or "angry *about*" a condition.

Is Lucy still *angry with* us for delaying her project?

Both of us were *angry at* the machine because we lost so much time.

Everyone was *angry about* the mess the contractors left behind.

Discrepancy. Use (1) *discrepancy in* when the object of the preposition is singular, (2) *discrepancy between* when the object denotes *exactly two* in number, and (3) *discrepancy among* when there are *three or more* things.

I found a *discrepancy in* Eileen's report.

There is a *discrepancy between* Eileen's analysis and mine.

There is a *discrepancy among* our three reports.

In Regard To. The phrases *in regard to, with regard to,* and *as regards* are all correct and interchangeable. But be sure not to say "in regard*s* to" or "with regard*s* to."

Ms. Delaney wants to talk with us (in regard to, with regard to, as regards) our policy for reprinting copyrighted materials.   (Which one is correct? All are!)

Miscellaneous Phrases. Memorize the following phrases because they are very commonly used:

different from (not *different than*)
identical with (not *identical to*)
plan to do something (not *plan on* doing something)
retroactive to (not *retroactive from*)
try to do something (not *try and* do something)

This chart is *different from* the one I expected.

Your car is *identical with* mine.

Does Melanie *plan to* join us in Detroit?

Is it true that these increases are *retroactive to* January 1?

Let's *try to* exceed our sales predictions this quarter.

EDITING PRACTICE 1

Select the appropriate words in the following sentences.

1. The itemized estimate that was originally submitted is identical (with, to) this revised estimate.
2. Please be sure to ask Martha and John whether they plan (to attend, on attending) either of the sessions.
3. Does Sam want to schedule a meeting with the staff (in regards, in regard) to the proposed changes?
4. She claims that there is a discrepancy (in, between, among) one section of the report.
5. The specifications for the new laboratory are different (from, than) the specifications for the old one.

6. We selected a staff of experts to ensure that the employment practices manual is in conformity (to, with) government regulations.
7. When they had thoroughly reviewed and discussed the proposal, all the panel members agreed (with, to) the plan.
8. Obviously, Claire was angry (at, with, about) us for the error we made.
9. Ms. Hendricks assures us that the raise will be retroactive (from, to) March 1.

EDITING PRACTICE 2

Correct any errors in the following sentences. Write *OK* for any sentence that has no error.

1. As you know, Mr. Perez is rather strict with regards to accuracy in all sales reports.
2. Ask one of the attorneys to review these contracts in an effort to ensure that they conform with corporate policies.
3. According to one of the sales managers, the total credits for the sales contest will be retroactive to June.
4. Needless to say, all of us will abide with the decision of the panel.
5. Mr. Elliot, please let us know whether you agree to the terms of the enclosed revised agreement.
6. The new sample appears different than the one we originally approved.
7. Yes, I agree with Jerry that this packaging is too expensive for this product.
8. Apparently, the Training Department is planning on offering several new marketing programs next fall.
9. Review Fred's and Maria's reports carefully, please, to see whether there is any discrepancy between them.

Troublesome Prepositions

Choosing between certain pairs of prepositions causes writers and speakers some difficulty. Study the following troublesome pairs to make sure that they will cause *you* no difficulty.

Between, Among. Ordinarily, use *between* when referring to *two* persons, places, or things; use *among* when referring to *more than two.*

> *Between* you and me, I am confident that we can finish this assignment at least one week early.

> All commissions will be divided *among* the three agents.

Beside, Besides. Remember that *beside* means "by the side of" and that *besides* means "in addition to" or "except."

> Place these cartons *beside* the credenza.   ("By the side of" the credenza.)

Besides pads and pencils, what other supplies will we need for the meeting?   ("In addition to" pads and pencils.)

No one *besides* Gail has the authority to sign checks over $500.   ("No one except" Gail.)

Inside, Outside.

Do not use *of* after *inside* or *outside*. When referring to time, use *within*, not *inside of*.

The duplicating machine is just *inside* that door.   (Not *inside of*.)

Our company frowns upon employees' working *outside* regular office hours.   (Not *outside of*.)

Please send your check *within* 10 days after you receive the shipment.   (Not *inside of*.)

All, Both.

After *all* or *both* use *of* only when *all* or *both* is followed by a *pronoun*. Omit *of* if either word is followed by a *noun*.

In March *all of* us will meet to develop the medium-range plan for our division. *All* managers will participate in that meeting.   (*All of* is followed by the pronoun *us*, but *all* precedes the noun *managers*.)

At, To; In, Into.

At and *in* denote position. *To* and *into* signify motion.

Sarah is *at* the production meeting.   (No action.)

Sarah went *to* the meeting at 9 a.m.   (Action—she *went* to the meeting.)

When I saw the computer *in* the store window, I went *into* the store.   (The computer was *in* position—no action. I went *into* the store—action.)

NOTE: When either *at* or *in* refers to a place, use *in* for larger places; *at* for smaller places.

He lives in Fargo and works *at* the Gormky Agency.

Behind, In Back Of.

Use *behind*, not *in back of*. However, *in front of* is correct.

I sat *behind* Mr. Simmons while the representative displayed the products *in front of* him.

From, Off.

Use *from* when referring to persons or places; *off*, when referring to things.

Thomas received the completed applications *from* Helene.   (Not *off*.)

We want customers to take these applications *off* the countertops.   (*Off* things—correct.)

EDITING PRACTICE 3

How well can you now use prepositions?

1. Was Paula (at, in, to) her desk when the main office called?
2. Let's see whether (all, all of) the auditors agree with this proposal.
3. Do you have any monthly reports (beside, besides) the reports for June and July?
4. I'm sure that the large map you're looking for is (behind, in back of) the supply cabinet.
5. Make sure that you take all the charts (from, off) the table before we leave the conference room.
6. John said, "(Both, Both of) the expense vouchers were approved and sent to the Accounting Department."
7. Has anyone (beside, besides) AnneMarie registered for this financial seminar?
8. Let Frank know when you have divided all the extra brochures (between, among) the sales representatives.
9. If you need a revised price list, you can get one (off, from) Anna or Bill.

Preposition Pitfalls

The following are examples of common errors in using a preposition when none is needed or where another word is required.

Of, Have. In speaking, some people tend to pronounce *have* as if it were *of*, as in "I *shoulduv* called earlier." You may hear this from time to time. When you do, remember that the correct phrase is *should have called*, not *should of called*.

At and *To* With *Where.* It is incorrect to use *at* or *to* following *where*.

> *Where* is Maryanne?   (Not *Where is Maryanne at?*)

> I do not know *where* she *went.*   (Not *where she went to.*)

Help, Help From. The word *from* should not follow *help* in sentences such as this:

> We cannot *help* being concerned about the situation.   (Not *help from being.*)

Opposite, Opposite To. Do not use *to* after *opposite*.

> A new office building will be built *opposite* ours.   (Not *opposite to ours.*)

Off. Do not use either *of* or *from* with the word *off*.

> Please ask the maintenance people to take these machines *off* these tables.   (Not *off of.*)

> You can probably borrow a calculator *from* Renee.   (Not *off from Renee* or *from off Renee.*)

EDITING PRACTICE 4

Choose the correct word or words to avoid the preposition pitfalls in the following sentences.

1. Lily said, "We should (have, of) ordered extra copies of the article and distributed the copies to all branch offices."
2. Does anyone here know where Greg (went, went to)?
3. Because we were so near the door, we could not (help, help from) hearing the conversation.
4. Did Sheila take the newsletter (off, off of) my desk?
5. Where are you (going, going to) after the luncheon?
6. Please ask Rae if she knows where Tom (is, is at).
7. If you need an order form, you can probably get one quickly (off, from, off of) Ms. D'Amato.
8. As soon as the seminar ended, we went to the restaurant (opposite, opposite to) our building.

EDITING PRACTICE 5

Correct any preposition errors in the following sentences. Write *OK* if a sentence has no error.

1. Do you think Nancy and Ed will be able to complete all these invoices inside of two days?
2. Yes, there were several agents beside Tyler and Maureen who questioned the marketing strategy.
3. As Ms. Diaz suggested, we should simply divide all the new accounts between Karen, Monty, and Sean.
4. The costs we received were inaccurate; therefore, we could not help from bluntly stating our opinions.
5. We borrowed some pamphlets off of Mary Lou because the printer did not deliver ours.
6. We are looking for Ms. Wilkinson. Does anyone know where she is at?
7. If you need more blank forms, you'll find some in the cabinet opposite to my secretary's desk.
8. According to Frances, both of the vice presidents plan to attend tomorrow's meeting.

COMMUNICATION LABORATORY

APPLICATION EXERCISES

A. On a separate sheet of paper, write the correct selections for the following sentences.

1. Briefly describe the discrepancy you found (in, between) the two market surveys.

2. No, the total for each column is not identical (to, with) yours.

3. Do you know whether Ms. Brill plans (on submitting, to submit) the report to the committee at this afternoon's meeting?

4. (Beside, Besides) Jeff McDonald and Francine Pugh, only one other supervisor was present.

5. Jack, will you please help me stack all these cartons (in back of, behind) those shelves?

6. As you suggested, Mr. Mobley, we shared copies of the findings with (all, all of) our field managers.

7. If the price had been lower, we would (have, of) bought two printing machines for this office.

8. Adam, is this sample any different (from, than) the one we received from Kellogg Fabrics?

9. Following the advice of our attorney, we did not enter (into, upon) the agreement with Central Leasing.

10. When the completed forms are delivered, divide them (between, among) our four clerks for processing.

11. Please tell Judy that we will wait for her if she plans to arrive (inside of, within) an hour.

12. Our attorney clearly communicated our intention to abide (with, by) the panel's ruling.

13. As you can imagine, we were somewhat angry (at, with) our supervisor for not informing us earlier of the mandatory overtime.

14. If you'd like a sample, you can get one (from off, from) your local distributor at the Harmony Clothing Center.

15. No, Bill said he does not know where Jane (went, went to).

B. Correct any errors in these sentences. Write *OK* if a sentence has no error.

1. Charles and Valerie are both excellent traffic managers, but Valerie has more experience than him.

2. We try to provide each district manager with the support they need to do their jobs well.

3. We try to provide all district managers with the support they need to do their jobs well.

4. Is Andrew Abbate the man who you want to hire for the product manager position?

5. Frankly, Jim, I think that your wise to renew this service contract.

6. As soon as Richard had wrote his first draft, he asked Anne for her opinion of the report.

7. Mr. Henley sent two of our best engineers, Michael and she, to the headquarters office for the special workshop.

8. There's certainly more than three qualified candidates for this position, in my opinion, Susan.

9. According to the shareholders' report, the Carringtons' own approximately 11 percent of the stock in the company.

10. Who is the supervisor in charge of the Customer Service Department?

11. Is the supervisor of the department her?

12. The people who asked for more information on these investments are the Spiegel's.

13. Please try to find out where Mr. Adams went to, Mary Lou.

14. No one beside Jessica was assigned to the Quentin account.

15. Did you know that Denise been with the company since 1978?

C. Write one sentence using each of the following phrases:

1. different from
2. identical with
3. angry at
4. retroactive to
5. in regard to

VOCABULARY AND SPELLING STUDIES

A. These words are often confused: *pact, packed; facetious, fictitious.* Explain the differences.

B. Give at least one synonym for each of the following:

1. liable
2. ostentation
3. punctual
4. delineate
5. prodigious

C. Correct any misspelled words in the following sentences.

1. Robert recomended a reputable supplier who has an office nearby.
2. For older investors we strongly suggest buying goverment bonds.
3. One of the acountants with whom we conferred is Marilyn Blumenthal.
4. We considered it a privilige to be asked to coordinate this year's charity drive.
5. Bertha is just begining to draft her monthly status report.

COMMUNICATING FOR RESULTS

Just 15 Minutes. A coworker tells you that your supervisor, Leroy Webster, has warned her not to be late again. "Next time," he said, "you may lose part of your pay." She thinks Mr. Webster is being unfair, but you have always found him to be very fair.

Your coworker asks for your opinion. What would you tell her?

25 Conjunctions

Conjunction Review

A *conjunction* is a word that joins sentences or parts of sentences. You have already seen some uses of conjunctions. For example, in Unit 23 you learned how conjunctive adverbs and subordinating conjunctions are used.

In this unit you will review these uses; in addition, you will learn the uses of coordinate conjunctions and correlative conjunctions. Also, you will learn how to achieve *parallel structure*—one of the requisites for clear writing.

Conjunctive Adverbs. In Unit 23 you saw how conjunctive adverbs join independent clauses:

Hunter Ski Equipment purchased more than $10,000 worth of products this month; consequently, HSE has earned a 3 percent discount. (*Consequently* joins two clauses that can stand alone as independent sentences.)

Helen and I have not yet completed the agenda for the sales convention; *however*, we have more than two weeks' time to prepare the final copy. (*However* is a conjunctive adverb; it joins two clauses that are independent.)

Other conjunctive adverbs are:

accordingly	moreover
furthermore	then
thus	yet
nevertheless	likewise
therefore	

As you can see, the conjunctive adverbs serve not only to *join* two independent clauses but also to *modify* the second clause.

Subordinating Conjunctions. Conjunctions that join an independent clause to a dependent (or *subordinate*) clause are called *subordinating conjunctions*.

Ms. Spano will call us *if she is delayed at the client's office.* (The subordinating conjunction *if* begins a subordinate—or dependent—clause, *if she is delayed at the client's office,* and joins this dependent clause to an independent clause, *Ms. Spano will call us.*)

Although sales dipped slightly in August, we expect September and October to establish new monthly records.   (The independent clause is *we expect September and October to establish new monthly records*. The subordinate conjunction *although* begins the subordinate, or dependent, clause *although sales dipped slightly in August* and joins it to the main clause.)

The most commonly used subordinating conjunctions are:

after	since
although	than
as	that
as if	though
as soon as	till
as though	unless
because	until
before	when
even if	whenever
for	where
how	wherever
if	whether
inasmuch as	while
otherwise	why

CLASS PRACTICE 1

Can you recognize the conjunctive adverbs and the subordinating conjunctions in the following sentences? Label each conjunction that you find.

1. Please let me know whenever you need more copies of these brochures, Ms. Wilson.
2. Only six people have registered for the Elements of Accounting course; nevertheless, we do not plan to cancel the course.
3. Our manager said that he will reduce expenses even if he must personally approve all vouchers.
4. Dan said he will call us as soon as he receives the signed contract.
5. We should send courtesy copies of this report to the branch managers; therefore, please make ten extra copies, David.
6. Stan promised to complete the entire project before he left on vacation.
7. Melissa and I think that Mr. DiBartolo will be selected; however, there are three or four other excellent candidates for the position.
8. If Ms. Patterson approves this purchase order, rush the order to the supplier.

Coordinating Conjunctions

The coordinating conjunctions are *and, but, or,* and *nor,* and they are used to connect *similar* grammatical elements—two or more words, phrases, or clauses.

1. Two or more words:

   Matthew *or* Susan

   quickly *but* carefully

   Pamela, Jeanne, *and* Vincent

2. Two or more phrases:

   in the morning *or* in the afternoon

   on land, on sea, *and* in the air

3. Two or more clauses:

   We did not complete the project on schedule, *nor* did we complete it within the budget.

   Mary created the idea, Bill wrote the copy, *and* Jack designed the ad.

   She said that we should revise the specifications *and* that we should then ask the panel to review the new specifications.

Correlative Conjunctions

Correlative conjunctions are used in pairs:

both . . . and	not only . . . but also
either . . . or	whether . . . or
neither . . . nor	

Correlatives, too, are used to connect *similar* grammatical elements. (Note that *or* is used with *either* and that *nor* is used with *neither*.)

Both Mr. Dempsey *and* Mr. Liston attended the workshop.

Neither Boyd *nor* Ramsey is ready to assume more responsibility.

Our president *not only* authorized the new product line *but also* authorized manufacturing to begin on March 1.

CLASS PRACTICE 2

Identify the coordinating and the correlative conjunctions in the following sentences and label each.

1. Neither Bill Nolan nor Dave Dawkins had been told about the change in schedule.
2. Both the Seattle office and the Denver office have requested more information on this new policy.
3. She asked not only Curt but also Leonard to work on the Anderson account.
4. Write to the personnel manager in our headquarters office, or discuss the problem with your supervisor.

5. Whether we order 10,000 booklets or we order 110,000, the cost per booklet is the same.

6. Not only has Arnold completely revised the entire operations manual, but also he has keyboarded and printed all the copy.

Parallel Structure

As used in the term *parallel structure*, the adjective *parallel* means "similar" or "equal." Sentences are considered as having parallel structure (or *parallelism*) when matching ideas are expressed in similar ways. For example, in the parallel sentences below, note how the coordinating conjunctions connect similar elements.

POOR: This product is sturdy, light, and costs very little.   (The coordinating conjunction *and* connects three elements: (1) the adjective *sturdy*, (2) the adjective *light*, and (3) the phrase *costs very little*. Do the three items match? No!)

PARALLEL: This product is sturdy, light, and inexpensive.   (Now that the conjunction joins three *adjectives*, the sentence *is* parallel.)

POOR: Mr. Morris said to check the value of the property and that our insurance should be increased.   (There are two items after *said*, and both are joined by *and*. The two items are (1) *to check the value of the property* and (2) *that our insurance should be increased*. To be parallel, both should start with *to* or with *that*.)

PARALLEL: Mr. Morris said to check the value of the property *and* to increase our insurance.   (The two elements joined by *and* are parallel.)

PARALLEL: Mr. Morris said that the value of the property should be checked and that our insurance should be increased.   (Again, the two elements connected by *and* match.)

Now let's see how parallelism is achieved in sentences with correlative conjunctions.

POOR: You need *both* a completed medical form *and* to get your supervisor's approval.   (The elements that follow *both* and *and* should match. As the sentence now reads, a noun, *form*, follows *both*, and a verb, *to get*, follows *and*. Compare this with the next two examples.)

PARALLEL: You need *both* a completed medical form *and* your supervisor's approval.   (Now what follows *both* and *and*? Two nouns—*form* and *approval*.)

PARALLEL: You need *both* to complete a medical form *and* to get your supervisor's approval.   (Both elements following the two parts of the correlative *both/and* do match.)

CLASS PRACTICE 3

In the following pairs of sentences, one sentence illustrates parallelism; the other does not. Select the parallel sentence and explain why it is parallel.

1. a. She said that you will need both a down payment and an approved loan form.
   b. She said that you will need both a down payment and to have a loan form approved.
2. a. Ethel has neither the dedication nor does she have the management experience for that job.
   b. Ethel has neither the dedication nor the management experience for that job.
3. a. The training director told us to improve our spelling and that our grammar skills needed improvement.
   b. The training director told us to improve our spelling and our grammar skills.
4. a. Our receptionists not only greet visitors but also handling mail is their responsibility.
   b. Our receptionists not only greet visitors but also handle mail.
5. a. Gathering sales information and presenting all the statistics in well-written reports are part of her job.
   b. Gathering sales information and to present all the statistics in well-written reports are part of her job.
6. a. Before Tuesday either call Mrs. Mackenzie or meet with her to discuss these stocks.
   b. Before Tuesday either call Mrs. Mackenzie or we should meet with her to discuss these stocks.
7. a. The insurance policy neither covers fire nor theft.
   b. The insurance policy covers neither fire nor theft.
8. a. The most important part of this job is to analyze consumer trends and reporting such trends to our Sales Department.
   b. The most important part of this job is to analyze consumer trends and to report such trends to our Sales Department.

EDITING PRACTICE 1

Correct any errors in parallelism in the following sentences. Write *OK* for any sentence that has no error.

1. Tell Ida that she should confirm her hotel reservations and to allow an extra half hour for the trip to the airport.
2. Either Marisa will fly to Dallas or drive there.
3. All of us agree that Della is efficient, hard-working, and ought to be promoted.
4. Return the enclosed card to get your free subscription, or our toll-free number may be called.
5. Caryl has been not only successful as a photographer but also as an advertising copywriter.
6. Gregory has earned a reputation for being both creative and to be efficient.

7. Irma will tell us when the final report is due, Jack will write the first draft, and Daniel and I will proofread the final copy.

8. We have an all-day meeting both on Wednesday and Friday.

Conjunction Pitfalls

Avoiding the following four pitfalls will not only help you use conjunctions correctly but also improve the quality and style of your writing.

1. Use *but*, not *and*, to *join and contrast* two elements.

    I immediately called Lauren, *but* she was not in her office.

    Andy had an ample supply of these brochures, *but* I think that he distributed most of them yesterday.

2. Say "the reason is *that*," not "the reason is *because*." Say "read in the paper *that*," not "read in the paper *where*." Say "pretend *that*," not "pretend *like*."

    The reason he called is *that* he needs the latest prices for the catalog.

    Yesterday I read in a magazine *that* the average interest rate in money markets is now about 8.9 percent.

    Because she works so well under pressure, Nora often pretends *that* every job is a rush job.

3. There is no such conjunction as *being that*. Instead, use *since, because,* or *as*.

    Because Ms. Syms was in town, we did not mail the contracts to her.   (Not *being that Ms. Syms . . . .*)

    I accomplished a lot today, *since* the office was nearly empty.   (Not *being that the office . . . .*)

4. *Like* is a verb or a preposition, not a conjunction. Yet you will often hear people say "*Like* I was telling Jim . . . ." Use *as, as though,* or *as if* when a conjunction is needed, not *like*.

    We *like* the new design.   (Here *like* is a verb.)

    Sharon needs a modem *like* mine to transmit data via telephone lines.   (The preposition *like* is always followed by a *noun* or a *pronoun*.)

    This morning Mike looks *as if* he is ill.   (Not *like he is ill*.)

    Gregory said that it does not look *as though* our loan will be approved.   (Not *like our loan will be approved*.)

EDITING PRACTICE 2

Review the uses of conjunctions and conjunction pitfalls before you tackle the following sentences. Then select the correct choice for each sentence.

1. (Being that, Because) we had so little time, we decided to send the carton airfreight.
2. The Policy Committee was supposed to meet this afternoon, (and, but) Ms. Kowolski, the chairperson, had to reschedule the meeting.
3. On the bulletin board I read (where, that) employees' travel insurance has been increased.
4. The reason for these training sessions is (because, that) the company intends to expand its marketing staff.
5. When speaking to someone on the phone, pretend (like, that) he or she is standing before you.
6. Ms. Sands said to proofread all checks (like, as if) they were written for one million dollars!

EDITING PRACTICE 3

Make any corrections needed in the following sentences.

1. We read in the policy manual where hiring consultants must be approved by the executive vice president, Marsha Gurr.
2. Sherry rescheduled the meeting being that Mr. Noa is out of town.
3. I would very much like to attend that training session, and unfortunately I will be in Milwaukee all week.
4. It looks like sales are beginning to increase as a result of our recent ads.
5. The reason for the price increase is because shipping costs have increased.
6. Mr. Shannon said that it appears like we will win the Funtime Products account.

COMMUNICATION LABORATORY

APPLICATION EXERCISES

A. Choose the words that make each sentence parallel.

1. Making appointments with sales prospects is sometimes more difficult than (to sell, selling) products to them!
2. (Because, Being that) the construction of the building is two months behind schedule, we will remain in these quarters until November.
3. Allied Office Supplies no longer delivers orders free of charge, (and, but) Allied's shipping charges are very reasonable.
4. According to the illustration in the operating manual, these two keys control the movement of the cursor either to the left or (the right, to the right).
5. Each applicant knows how to type and (writing shorthand, to write shorthand).

6. Whenever she returns from an exercise class, Alicia looks (like, **as if**) she is completely exhausted.

7. In such situations we generally return the merchandise or (a deduction is noted on the invoice, deduct the amount from the invoice).

8. Gathering sales statistics is easier than (to analyze them, analyzing them).

9. If you need more information, either write to our Customer Service Department or (our local sales representative should be asked, ask our local sales representative) for help.

10. Simply insert the diskette into the disk drive (like, as) the illustration shows.

11. Next Friday (we must either, either we must) call our headquarters office or send a telex.

12. One adviser suggested buying tax-free municipal bonds or (wants us to buy corporate bonds, corporate bonds).

13. She asked one of our attorneys to draw up a standard contract and (to explain its terms to our staff, an explanation of its terms to our staff).

14. The swatches that we received were neither the right materials nor (the right colors, of the right colors).

15. As a result of our discussion, we decided neither to renew our lease nor (to expand our office space, expand our office space).

B. Correct the following sentences. Write *OK* for any sentence that has no error.

1. Although the Paulson's are not able to attend the March 1 banquet, they will ask one of their partners to attend.

2. The computer store is located in back of the Trenton Building.

3. Because we knew the actual dates, we could not help from correcting Bill's report.

4. Are you sure that the woman you saw was Emily Shatner?

5. Yes, I am sure that the woman was her.

6. Cathleen is intelligent, tactful, and works very efficiently.

7. Apparently, its true that the Sales Department will be hiring five more representatives.

8. Frankly, between you and I, Bob, I cannot believe that the stock will reach 50 by the end of the year.

9. Ms. Edmundson said that it looks like Bertha will be promoted to senior auditor.

10. The Smiths real estate holdings are estimated to be worth more than $2.3 million.

11. Mr. Owens and Ms. Klaus, the supervisors of these two departments, has responsibility for hiring and training all new employees. .

12. We discovered that neither the service contract nor the warranty is still in effect.

13. You were correct: The reason for my error was because I had not initialized the diskette properly.
14. Phyllis been in charge of the Purchasing Department since 1982.
15. Theirs really no reason for these orders to be delayed.

C. Edit the following excerpt from a business memorandum.

> A comparison of sales through the first six month's of this year with sales thorough the first six month's of last year show that we are approximately 15 percent ahead of last year. Among the major reasons for this increase are the obvious success of our newest product, Vita-Chews. Parent's are delighted with the high quality and the low price, and children are equal satisfied with the delicious flavor of these chewable vitamins. Indeed, they do taste real well!

VOCABULARY AND SPELLING STUDIES

A. These words are often confused: *fate, fete; census, senses.* Describe the differences.

B. Each of the phrases below can be replaced by one word that has the same meaning. For each phrase, name that word.

1. Without meaning to
2. Of his or her own free will
3. With great emphasis
4. Without thinking
5. From time to time
6. Lost consciousness

C. Give at least one synonym for each of the following:

1. prohibit
2. lucid
3. homogeneous
4. fortitude
5. diminish

COMMUNICATING FOR RESULTS

Chronic Complainers. Emma and Jerry are two of your coworkers at a very successful firm, World Movie Company. From the time they arrive to the time they leave, Emma and Jerry spend most of the day complaining—about the company, your manager, their wages, other employees, the amount of work, and so on, and so on, endlessly throughout each day.

You've tried to overlook their complaints, of course, but after a while their negativism is starting to get to you.

What should you do?

Pauses, gestures, body language, volume—these and many other tools available to us in speaking are not available to us in writing. Instead, as we write, punctuation marks allow us to tell our readers when to pause, which words go where, and so on.

The following units will teach you how to give your readers clear messages by using the appropriate punctuation marks. Given a situation that requires polished punctuation skills, you will be able to do the following when you master the units in this chapter:

1. *Use periods, question marks, and exclamation points to end sentences correctly.*

2. *Use commas, semicolons, colons, and dashes to provide pauses for your readers and guide them through your message.*

3. *Identify the exact words of other writers and speakers by using quotation marks to set off quotations.*

4. *Separate and identify additional information by using parentheses.*

5. *Form possessives, contractions, and special plurals correctly by using apostrophes.*

6. *Capitalize words according to accepted standards.*

7. *Use correct abbreviations and symbols when they are appropriate.*

8. *Write numbers in words or in figures, whichever is appropriate.*

U · N · I · T

26

Commas—Basic Uses

The comma is certainly the most versatile and the most often used punctuation mark. In some ways the comma leads the reader along a map, and comma errors force the reader to take a detour.

Master the uses of the comma in this and the following two units to make sure that you can guide your reader smoothly—*without* detours.

In a Compound Sentence

A *compound sentence* is one that has two or more independent clauses (main clauses, each of which could stand alone as an independent sentence). Use a comma between independent clauses joined by *and, but, or,* or *nor.*

Carla bought this property in 1985, and she plans to build on it in the future.   (Note the comma before the conjunction *and.*)

Our supervisor always approves these purchase orders, but he is out of the office this week.   (Again, note the comma before the conjunction *but.*)

When the second clause is not *independent,* omit the comma. For instance, let's take the above sentences and change the second clause by omitting the subject (*she* in the first sentence; *he* in the second sentence).

Carla bought this property in 1985 and plans to build on it in the future.   (The second clause no longer has a subject; it is no longer independent.)

Our supervisor always approves these purchase orders but is out of the office this week.   (What follows the conjunction *but* is *not* an independent clause.)

Now the rule about using a comma to separate two *independent* clauses does not apply because the second clause in each sentence is not independent. Be sure that you do not confuse such sentences with sentences that *do* have two independent clauses joined by *and, but, or,* or *nor.*

CLASS PRACTICE 1

Where are commas needed in the following sentences? Explain each answer. Write *OK* if the sentence is correct.

1. Myron handles the Johnson account but is on jury duty this week.

2. An Italian export firm supplies these products and it offers excellent credit terms.
3. An Italian export firm supplies these products and offers excellent credit terms.
4. Richard Johnson is eligible for this position but he does not want to leave the Chicago area.
5. Our manager searched the files for the original specifications but was not able to find them.
6. You may get your free brochure at your local Rent-All store or you may call our toll-free number.

In a Series

A series consists of a minimum of *three* words, phrases, or clauses. For clarity always use a comma after each item in the series except the last. Thus the last comma should be immediately before the conjunction that comes before the last item in the series.

Valuable books, periodicals, and directories were destroyed in the fire. (A series of words. Note the comma before *and*.)

We spent the entire week on the telephone, in our hotel rooms, and at meetings. (A series of three prepositional phrases: (1) *on the telephone*, (2) *in our hotel rooms*, and (3) *at meetings*.)

Jim spent most of the week meeting prospective clients, showing them our products, and describing our services. (A series of phrases.)

Jim introduced the program, Jan gave a slide presentation, and Greta made the closing remarks. (A series of clauses.)

If the conjunction is repeated before each item, then no comma is needed to separate the items.

Our number-one sales office may be Denver or Houston or Manchester.

When *Etc.* Ends a Series. Whenever the abbreviation *etc.* ends a series, be sure to use a comma before and after it (unless, of course, *etc.* ends the sentence).

Sales, profits, revenues, *etc.*, were discussed at this morning's session.

She gave several reasons for increasing the budget estimate—higher costs, overhead, declining market, *etc.*

Always remember that *etc.* (*et cetera*) means "and so forth" and that, therefore, you must not write *and etc.* (the equivalent of *and and so forth*).

CLASS PRACTICE 2

Where are commas needed in the following sentences? Explain your reason for inserting each comma. Write *OK* if the sentence is correct.

1. Companies that have shown an interest in the building are Spectrum Industries Scotchwood Real Estate and Lincoln Bank of Commerce.
2. Purchase orders invoice records important contracts etc. will be stored on microfiche.
3. Joyce Sean Tara and Tim conduct all the training sessions.
4. In only two weeks we wrote the script recorded a master tape and duplicated copies for all branch offices.
5. The only store that is open late on Mondays and Wednesdays and Fridays is the Greenbrook Mall store.
6. Allen wrote the script Betty edited the copy and Charles narrated all the tapes.

After an Introductory Word, Phrase, or Clause

To signal the reader to slow down, use a comma after an introductory word, phrase, or clause.

Introductory Word. Among the most commonly used introductory words are the following. Use a comma after each.

accordingly	moreover
actually	namely
also	naturally
besides	nevertheless
consequently	next
finally	no
first	now
fortunately	obviously
further	otherwise
however	personally
indeed	therefore
meanwhile	yes

Now notice how they are used as introductory words:

First, we must discuss the change in buying patterns. *Second,* we must survey typical customers. (*Fortunately,* we have an excellent mailing list; *however,* the cost of a survey is very high.) *Finally,* we must choose an advertising agency to represent us.

Be sure that you recognize when these words are introductory and when they are not.

Ellen enjoys a challenging project, *however* difficult it may be. (Here, *however* modifies *difficult;* it is not an introductory word.)

She *personally* delivered the films to the studio. (Here, *personally* modifies *delivered.*)

Introductory Phrase. A comma is needed after an infinitive phrase or a participial phrase that introduces an independent clause.

To qualify, you must be a resident of this state. *To get your copy*, just complete and return the enclosed form.   (Introductory infinitive phrases.)

Knowing the exact cost, Karen tried to correct Bill. *Believing he was right*, Bill kept insisting his prices were correct.   (Introductory participial phrases.)

Overwhelmed by the project, the director requested more assistance. *Alerted to the problem*, management assigned help right away.   (Introductory participial phrases.)

A comma is also used after an introductory *prepositional* phrase unless it is a short phrase. Most writers omit commas after *short* introductory prepositional phrases to make the transition to the following clause smoother.

In July we will move to the Dexter Building.   (*In July* is a short prepositional phrase. Read this aloud to see how smoothly the thought flows without a comma.)

During the next month she plans to travel to Europe.   (This phrase, too, flows smoothly into the following clause.)

With the additional clerical help now available to us, our department should no longer have such backlogs.   (This longer prepositional phrase does require a comma after it.)

Introductory Clause. Use a comma after a subordinate clause that introduces the main thought.

After Ms. Stephenson arrives, we will discuss the sales promotion campaign.

Whenever you have time to review these proposals, I will share copies with you. *If your balance is under $5000*, you may charge the entire cost to your account.

The following conjunctions introduce subordinate clauses and, therefore, signal you when to use a comma.

after	since
although	so that
as	unless
as soon as	until
because	when
even if	whenever
if	where
in order that	wherever
inasmuch as	while
provided	

NOTE: When these same subordinate clauses *follow* main clauses, a comma may or may not be needed. Use a comma only if the subordinate clause provides extra information—that is, nonessential information.

You may charge the entire cost to your account *if your balance is under $5000*. (The subordinate clause *if your balance is under $5000* is obviously essential; it restricts the possibility stated in the first clause, "You may charge the entire cost to your account.")

You may charge the entire cost to your account, *if you prefer to do so.*   (The clause *if you prefer to do so* is not essential; it does not restrict the first clause in any way.)

CLASS PRACTICE 3

Where are commas needed in the following sentences? Write *OK* if the sentence is correct.

1. If the messenger does not arrive by noon please let me know.
2. You cannot mail this purchase order until it has been signed by your supervisor.
3. To find out more about this special introductory offer complete and mail the enclosed reply card.
4. We had predicted an increase in sales for the month of July although we frankly did not expect such a large increase over June sales.
5. Whenever a customer pays by check be sure to have the check approved by the department manager.
6. Because the negotiations lasted two extra days Ms. Bronson has not yet returned from London.
7. Using audiovisuals skillfully the instructor clearly described and explained all the features of our new word processing system.
8. Unless anyone has an objection we will skip items 2 and 3 on this agenda for today's meeting.

EDITING PRACTICE 1

Are the following sentences correctly punctuated? Correct any errors. If a sentence has no error, write *OK*.

1. Knowing that the discussion would require at least two hours Robert decided to continue the meeting on Thursday.
2. Do not approve such returns until all the forms have been approved and signed by Mr. Wendall or Ms. Clarke.
3. As you probably heard at this morning's meeting there is a chance that the merger may not be approved by the board.
4. To be eligible for the 2 percent discount you must pay the total invoice within ten days.
5. If you need any additional information call us toll-free at (800) 555-1010.
6. You must pay the total invoice within ten days to be eligible for the 2 percent discount.
7. When you have proofread the catalog copy send your corrections to Martin Janal in the Advertising Department.
8. After we have met with the attorneys and accountants we will discuss the new policy in detail.

COMMUNICATION LABORATORY

APPLICATION EXERCISES

A. On a separate sheet of paper, correct any punctuation errors in the following sentences. Write *OK* for any sentence that is correct.

1. Ms. Harte is a CPA, and has been with our firm for nearly 12 years.
2. To purchase this equipment we must first get Mr. Fowler's approval.
3. Lucille will be assigned to the Gorton account, and Carole will be assigned either to the Harrod account or to the Smyth account.
4. To change your vacation schedule you must complete a Vacation Requisition form and submit it to your supervisor.
5. Having received four estimates from reputable contractors Ms. Danforth selected Embassy Construction for the renovation project.
6. The owner of this property is Barry Hughes, and he has indicated that he plans to build on it in the near future.
7. Barry Hughes owns this property and has indicated that he plans to build on it in the near future.
8. Because the insurance policy had lapsed a few months ago we were not covered for the damage caused by the storm.
9. Jerry, Phil, and Andrea, have been named to the Policy Committee.
10. Personally we consider Lisa Mendez the better candidate for the supervisory position.
11. Wendy is leaving for Toronto later this afternoon, Tom will leave on Thursday morning and Charles will leave on Saturday.
12. We will use this room to store the extra brochures, pamphlets, fliers, etc. that we will need for the sales meetings.
13. Naturally we were happy to hear that we would receive a special bonus.
14. Knowing that the project had to be completed by Friday Ken and I decided to work late all week.
15. You may change your vacation schedule, only if you get your supervisor's approval.

B. Correct the errors in the following sentences. Write *OK* if a sentence has no error.

1. You know that Christopher and me will be happy to help you complete these forms.
2. Have Mark or Anthony arrived yet?
3. There are, in my opinion, no better proofreader on our staff than Marion Fordyce.
4. Our stores in Amarillo, Austin, Dallas, and Houston, are the most profitable ones in the entire chain.
5. These monitors are more easy to read, according to the experts.

6. If you need more of them sales brochures, you may get some from Roger or Anne.

7. Sheila will create a survey form send it to the branch managers and analyze the results.

8. Typing as quickly as possible Bob completed the draft copy by noon.

9. To get your free copy of this new magazine complete and mail the enclosed card today!

10. Has Ed wrote his speech for the sales conference yet?

11. Please call me, when Mr. Hines arrives.

12. Yes the check to Hanson Real Estate was mailed yesterday afternoon.

13. If we receive your order by February 9 you will receive an additional 10 percent discount.

14. Leon been the supervisor of this department for more than 15 years, hasn't he?

15. Knowing the importance of accurate inventories JoAnne and I proofread the reports very carefully.

C. You have been promoted! Beginning with this lesson, the third set of Application Exercises will require you to edit for all kinds of errors—errors in grammar, spelling, punctuation, and vocabulary. Now that you have this added responsibility, be sure to give your editing special attention. Begin with the following excerpt from a memorandum.

> Each customers' opinion of our sales representatives are important to us. Therefore we try to give full attention to the human relations skill, the grooming habits and the speaking ability of our sales representative's. Accordingly we have developed a training program for our sales staff.

VOCABULARY AND SPELLING STUDIES

A. These words are often confused: *lightening, lightning, lighting; respectively, respectfully.* Explain the differences.

B. Which nouns ending in *ty* are related to the following adjectives?

1. rare   4. anxious
2. real   5. facile
3. entire   6. notorious

C. How do you spell the "shun" ending for each of the following?

1. expan___   4. func___
2. connec___   5. discus___
3. comple___   6. suspi___

COMMUNICATING FOR RESULTS

Accepting Criticism. Gloria Ruskin, one of your coworkers, was severely criticized by your supervisor for consistently submitting the weekly sales report late. The report is due at 4 o'clock every Friday afternoon, but Gloria does not usually complete it until midmorning on Mondays. The main reason that Gloria is late is that she always waits for the district offices to call her, and they often call very late in the afternoon with the statistics that she needs for her report. Gloria has not told this to your supervisor, and now Gloria is angry because she has been scolded. What should she do?

U · N · I · T

27 Commas—Special Uses

As we speak and write, for various reasons we interrupt our main thought— our basic sentence—in midstream to add other related thoughts. In speaking, we signal the listener of such interruptions by pauses, by gestures, by voice changes, etc. In writing, we must use other tools to signal our reader when such interrupting expressions are *not* essential to the main thought. The basic tool in such cases is the comma.

Interrupting Elements

Words, phrases, and clauses that interrupt the flow of the sentence and do not contribute essential information to the message should be set off by commas. Such *interrupters* are not absolutely necessary to the meaning of the sentence. These elements provide *extra* information, help contrast ideas, or connect thoughts more smoothly.

> *Therefore,* Anne Kilbride proposed that we sponsor a course on computer graphic arts. (The word *therefore* provides a transition from the preceding thought.)

The agent, *of course*, expected to receive her usual commission.   (The phrase *of course* interrupts the sentence.)

Mr. Jefferson has been elected to the board, *as you probably have heard*.   (The clause *as you probably have heard* provides additional information at the end of the sentence.)

As you see from the above examples, when such elements appear at the beginning or at the end of the sentence, *one* comma is needed to separate the words from the main part of the sentence. When such elements appear in the middle of the sentence, of course, *two* commas are needed to set them off.

Words. As you saw in Unit 26, words such as *accordingly, moreover, therefore, however, nevertheless,* and *consequently* are used at the beginning of sentences as transitions—that is, as bridges between sentences. Review the list of introductory words on page 246. Such words are also commonly used elsewhere in a sentence—as interrupting words.

Francine decided, *consequently*, to table the proposal.

We know that there is a market demand for this product; we are concerned, *however*, about the tremendous investment it would require.

Purchasing this equipment will deplete our capital expense budget for the year, and the purchase requires, *therefore*, very careful consideration.

Phrases. In our everyday speech we use many phrases such as the ones that follow:

to say the least	in the meantime
so to speak	on the other hand
after all	in my opinion
for instance	according to
for example	in the first place

Such phrases often help to make a sentence smoother, to add more information, or to show a contrast; however, these phrases are not *necessary* to complete the meaning of the sentence, and therefore they are separated by commas.

Many of the supervisors, *not just Martin*, prefer the old procedures.   (The interrupting expression provides a contrast.)

There are several districts that promote new products well; both the Denver and the Seattle district offices, *for example*, consistently exceed their sales budgets for new products.   (The words *for example* help provide a smooth transition.)

The reason for the problem, *in my opinion*, is that the operators have not been thoroughly trained.   (The interrupting words offer extra information.)

Clauses. Among the elements that are commonly used as interrupters are all clauses beginning with subordinating conjunctions such as *when, if, as, before, since,* and *because*. See page 247 for a complete list.

> *As soon as the technician completes the installation,* we can begin using the equipment.

> We will, *if our supervisor approves,* delay the completion date by one week.

> Nancy will send the check by November 15, *when the lease is scheduled to expire.*

Note that like words and phrases, subordinate clauses can also appear at the beginning, in the middle, or at the end of sentences. The key point is to remember to separate such words, phrases, and clauses with commas when they add extra information (as in the examples above). But *omit* commas when the subordinate clauses contain essential information:

> Martha said that she will leave *when she completes her report.* (The clause provides essential information—she will not leave before she meets the condition stated in the clause.)

> We will gladly analyze these statistics *if Clarence is still out of the office tomorrow.* (Essential information.)

> Send these contracts to the Legal Department *before you leave for lunch.* (Essential information.)

CLASS PRACTICE 1

Identify the words, phrases, and clauses that should be set off by commas in the following sentences. Remember that such elements may be transitional words or may be interrupters.

1. We were able to convince Mr. Martinez nevertheless of the need to get additional estimates.
2. Let's meet on Friday rather than on Thursday to continue this discussion.
3. Daniel decided to purchase the less-expensive keyboard and monitor as you suggested.
4. Since the Pheasant Run Mall store was opened in 1984 it has steadily increased in profitability.
5. Monica and Kevin recommended consequently that we hire consultants to find an ideal site for the warehouse.
6. Because none of the executives were in the office we could not have the check signed.
7. The Acme model is more expensive but is nevertheless the better buy in the long run.
8. Eric and I must work on July 4 when our store is having its special Independence Day sale.

EDITING PRACTICE 1

Correct any errors in the following sentences. Write *OK* if a sentence has no error.

1. You may return the merchandise in person if you prefer by visiting any of our convenient stores.
2. Ms. Jenkins as you probably already heard is the most likely person to replace Mr. Helmsley.
3. The most important factor of course, is the safety of all our employees.
4. Audrey's "professionalism," so to speak, qualifies her for the negotiating committee.
5. All raises according to Ms. Booker will become effective June 1.
6. All of us are concerned as you can well imagine about the practicality of buying this expensive equipment.
7. One of the reasons for delaying our decision as you know is that we expect inflation to drop drastically within the next year.
8. The terms of the service contract are to say the least far below industry standards.

Appositives and Similar Constructions

Appositives. You have already learned how to choose case forms of pronouns in appositives. At that time you probably realized that all the appositives illustrated were separated by commas.

My supervisors, *Daniel Brawley and she*, are in charge of salary administration. (The words *Daniel Brawley and she* are an appositive.)

Now note that an appositive that is very closely related to the preceding noun is *not* separated by commas.

Her brother *Martin* was also graduated from Pine Bluff Academy. (No commas needed to separate *brother* and *Martin*, which are very closely related.)

In the year *1994* Weber Oil will celebrate its 100th anniversary in this town. (*Year* and *1994* are very closely related. No commas needed.)

The term *user friendly* is used to describe the degree to which automated equipment is easy to use.

Degrees, Titles, and Similar Terms. Abbreviations such as *Ph.D.* and *M.D.* following a person's name should be set off by commas. Likewise, abbreviations of courtesy titles such as *Esq.* and of the names of religious orders following a person's name should also be set off by commas.

Brother Arthur James, *F.S.C.*, is scheduled to be the keynote speaker.

Leonora Hopkins, *M.D.*, is the new doctor in our corporate medical department.

Terms such as *Jr.* and *Sr.* and *Inc.* and *Ltd.* are commonly written without commas. However, writers should always follow the style that individuals or companies prefer.

Jason K. Whitman *Sr.* has been named president of Cooperative Research.

The headquarters building for Time *Inc.* is located in Rockefeller Center in New York City. (The actual company name is *Time Inc.*—no comma.)

BUT: Rorden Products, *Ltd.*, has been bought by Giant Brand Toys, *Inc.* (The actual letterheads of these two companies show commas before *Ltd.* and *Inc.*)

Calendar Dates. No comma is needed when a month and a year are given as dates (for example, *May 1998*). But when a day is included, set off the year with commas:

On May 3, *1998*, the president of our company is scheduled to retire. (At the end of a sentence, of course, the comma after *1998* would be replaced by a period.)

City and State Names. Whenever a city and state name are given in consecutive order, commas are needed to separate the state name.

The auditors are now working in our Seattle, *Washington*, office and our Chicago, *Illinois*, warehouse. (Commas separate the state names.)

The auditors are now working in our Seattle office and our Chicago warehouse. (Without the state names no commas are required.)

Direct Address. When we speak directly to someone, we often use that person's name as we address him or her. Such use is called *direct address*. Note how commas are used to separate names in direct address in the following sentences.

Mr. Klein, will you be able to submit your revised specifications to us by March 15?

If you need help, *Wayne*, please let me know.

I will have the final report ready for distribution on Friday, Miss Wilansky.

CLASS PRACTICE 2

Where are commas needed in the following sentences? Write *OK* if the sentence is correct.

1. His sister Claire is a senior vice president in our headquarters office.
2. Ryan Benson Ph.D. is the person in charge of the Research Department.
3. We were surprised, of course, to hear that Judd Daly Sr. voted in favor of the proposal.
4. Although we won the bid on March 10 1987 we did not formally close on the property until January 6 1988 because of certain technicalities.

5. The former president of this company Carole P. Lombardi was recently named to the mayor's special panel.
6. Be sure to specify clearly whether orders are to be sent to Kansas City Kansas or Kansas City Missouri whenever you complete these forms.
7. Pamela Kenyon one of our financial advisers explained the benefits of these government-guaranteed bonds.
8. His wife Marie is a stock analyst with a company in San Antonio Texas.

EDITING PRACTICE 2

Correct any errors in the following sentences. Write *OK* if a sentence has no error.

1. Both contracts were signed by Robert Weathers Esq. on June 10 1987.
2. George and Rosemary in the meantime were meeting with some clients in the conference room.
3. Marisa Owens CPA has been retained as a consultant for Cantor Advertising since 1985.
4. One of the shipping clerks as you know mistakenly sent the cartons to Albany New York instead of Albany Georgia.
5. Mr. Amaranti, an experienced interpreter, helped us translate all the proposals we submitted to South American companies.
6. One of the applicants Lou Anne Clifford will be offered a position in our headquarters office.
7. Edwardian Productions the European distributor of our films is located in London England.
8. Evelyn suggested that we discuss these marketing strategies with Thomas Bentley our Eastern Regional Manager.

COMMUNICATION LABORATORY

APPLICATION EXERCISES

A. Use commas to separate words, phrases, and clauses as necessary in the following sentences. Correct any errors in comma usage, and write *OK* for each sentence that has no error.

1. Our branch offices in Rochester, New York and Ames, Iowa are now seeking qualified clerical and sales personnel.
2. One of our subsidiaries Manchester Catering plans and operates all banquets and special events.
3. Yes, Time Inc. is the publisher of this series of books.
4. The expense costs listed on this summary as Renee mentioned include estimated (not actual) costs for the last quarter of the year.

5. Bert and Ernie in the meantime have been busily working on a new marketing plan for the next two-year period.

6. Our president decided consequently to increase the advertising budget for the new product lines.

7. Labor costs have dropped slightly; shipping costs on the other hand have increased dramatically over the past six months.

8. We realize, of course that we must hire additional clerical help in order to process all these orders.

9. After we discussed our concerns with our supervisor we felt somewhat relieved.

10. We felt somewhat relieved after we discussed our concerns with our supervisor.

11. Clark P. Grove Jr., has been appointed director of marketing for this division.

12. Two technicians, Gerald Waters and Kristen Dubrow have been working with our staff to get the new equipment on-line as soon as possible.

13. Because the investment is capitalized over several years the cost of the machinery will be kept on the books until October 1995.

14. The original agreement was signed on May 12, 1987 by the former president of our firm.

15. Jessica please arrange a meeting with a representative of Compu-U-Systems to discuss the problems we are having with the new teleconferencing system.

B. Read the following sentences carefully to correct any errors. Write *OK* for any sentence that has no error.

1. Who did Mr. Austin invite to the luncheon?

2. If the cartons are delivered while I'm out, please ask the messengers to lie them along that wall.

3. I think that we should ask each supervisor for their suggestions before we revise the procedures manual.

4. As soon as Ms. Brooks arrives call me.

5. Frank and myself have been working with Ms. DellaCroce on the new television commercials.

6. Does your sister Janice also work for the same company?

7. Since we won the Justerini account, we been exceptionally busy writing storyboards.

8. To receive your free copy of this informative booklet write to our Research Department at the above address.

9. I would like to invite our entire staff to the luncheon but we can accommodate only 20 to 25 people.

10. Ms. Josephson do you prefer a cash refund, or shall we credit your account?

11. The Josephson's were here earlier today to discuss an error in last month's invoice.
12. There's more copies of this newsletter in the Human Resources Department, Ivan.
13. His wife, Alicia Quentin Denmore, is a partner in an engineering consulting firm.
14. Send a copy of this report if you wish to the Personnel Department.
15. On September 6, 1987 we moved our headquarters to Spokane, Washington.

C. Edit the following excerpt from a business letter.

Are you interested in saving money on your car insurance? If you are Union Mutual has a new plan and it is scheduled to take effect on January 1, of next year.

To find out more about the details of this plan read the enclosed brochure. After you have read this pamphlet complete the attached card and return it to us. An agent will call you to discuss the plan, but you will be under no obligation of course.

VOCABULARY AND SPELLING STUDIES

A. These words are often confused: *quiet, quite; explicit, implicit.* Explain the differences.

B. Match the choices in Column B with the correct words in Column A.

A	B
1. absurd	a. unstable
2. artificial	b. ridiculous
3. careless	c. inharmonious
4. discordant	d. negligent
5. incessant	e. abusive
	f. diffident
	g. unnatural
	h. unceasing

C. Add the "uhble" sound to each of the following. Be sure to spell each word correctly.

1. detest___
2. indestruct___
3. inexhaust___

4. unspeak___
5. siz___
6. reduc___

COMMUNICATING FOR RESULTS

Crediting Others Fairly. Bob Masterson, your supervisor, leaves a note on your desk to thank you for the great job you did in gathering quickly all the information he needed for his weekly report. He said that he "sincerely appreciated your efforts." But it was really Agnes DePalma, not you, who did the work for Bob's report. What would you say to Bob?

U · N · I · T

28 Common Comma Errors

To complete your study of commas, this unit presents the last few important principles and covers some of the most common errors of comma use. Study this unit carefully so that you will be sure to write clear, effective messages.

With Two or More Adjectives

When you use two or more adjectives and *each* modifies the same noun, use a comma to separate the adjectives.

> The *small, sturdy, inexpensive* cabinet is ideal for storing these cassettes. (Each adjective modifies the noun *cabinet:* a cabinet that is small and sturdy and inexpensive. Note that the commas are used *between adjectives;* no comma is used between the last adjective, *inexpensive,* and the noun, *cabinet.*)

> Liza needs a *trustworthy, reliable* assistant to help manage her branch office. (An assistant who is trustworthy *and* reliable.)

If you are not sure whether to use a comma between adjectives, apply the following Quick Trick.

QUICK TRICK

SUBSTITUTE *AND*

To test whether adjectives do indeed modify the same noun, substitute the word *and* between the adjectives:

The small *and* sturdy *and* inexpensive cabinet is ideal for storing cassettes.

Liza needs a trustworthy *and* reliable assistant at the branch office.

Note that the word *and* can obviously be used in place of each comma in the above examples. However, do not use a comma before an adjective that is part of a compound noun.

Marilou just recently bought a red sports car. (Here, *red* modifies the compound noun *sports car*. You would not say "a car that is red *and* sports.")

Likewise, do not use a comma before the last adjective when this adjective is very closely connected to the noun or is thought of as part of the noun.

Arthur is now working on his monthly income statements. (No comma between *monthly* and *income* because they do not separately modify *statements*. You would not say "statements that are monthly *and* income." Here, the adjective *monthly* modifies the compound *income statements*.)

A contractor estimated the costs of renovating that old brick building. (No comma between *old* and *brick* because *old* modifies the compound *brick building*. The meaning is not "a building that is old *and* brick.")

CLASS PRACTICE 1

Use commas as needed to separate adjectives in the following sentences. Write *OK* if the sentence is correct.

1. Phillip submitted a lively interesting theme for our sales meeting.
2. Be sure to store these solutions in large plastic jars.
3. Proofreading these statistical reports is certainly a difficult tiresome job.
4. We invested in some low-cost high-risk stocks.
5. She developed a detailed comprehensive analysis of our sales patterns.
6. There is a large well-defined market for these products.

EDITING PRACTICE 1

Test your editing skill by correcting comma errors in the following sentences. If a sentence has no error, write *OK*.

1. We always receive fast efficient friendly service from Speedy Messengers.
2. Everyone agrees that Ms. Quigley's patient, positive, helpful, attitude is an important factor in the high morale in this department.

3. Our sales manager considers her a very intelligent, hard-working, ambitious representative.

4. Mr. Halmy has recommended expensive, word processing equipment for each branch office.

5. The panel received several, innovative suggestions from the staff.

6. Buy-All is one of the more successful discount stores in this area.

That, Which, and *Who* Clauses

Clauses that begin with *that, which,* and *who* deserve special attention. The following discussion simplifies the use of commas with such clauses.

That **and** *Which* **Clauses.** Careful writers use *that* to begin a clause with *essential* information and *which* to begin a clause with *nonessential* information. In the following examples note that *which* clauses are separated by commas because they give extra information.

> We sent Ann Carter our latest sales report, *which* shows sales by units. (Because there is only *one* sales report, the *which* clause can obviously give only extra information about it. Compare the following example.)

> We have two different sales reports. One shows sales by units; the other shows sales by dollars. We sent Ann Carter the sales report *that* shows sales by units. (Now the *that* clause does not give extra information; it gives *essential* information. Without the *that* clause we would not know which of the two different sales reports were sent to Ann Carter.)

Let us look at another set of examples.

> I read Paige Prescott's latest book, *which* was on the best-seller list for six months. (Prescott has only one "latest book," so the *which* clause must give extra information about the book. Compare the next example.)

> Paige Prescott's book *that* was on the best-seller list was her most interesting account of World War II. (She has written several books about World War II. The *that* clause identifies one specific book of all the books that she has written.)

Be sure to use *that* when the clause gives essential information and *which* when the clause gives *non*essential information. Consequently, because a *which* clause gives extra information, separate it with two commas if it interrupts a sentence and one comma if it ends a sentence.

Who **Clauses.** Question: When should a *who* clause be separated by commas? Answer: When it gives extra information, that is, when it is *non*essential.

> Bertha Cartwright, *who* is the vice president in charge of production, is very well respected in the movie industry. (The *who* clause simply provides additional information about one person who is clearly identified.)

> We have two vice presidents. The vice president *who is in charge of production* is very well respected in the movie industry. (Now the *who* clause gives *essential* information; it identifies one of the two vice presidents. Without the *who* clause

this sentence would be confusing because the *who* clause provides necessary information.)

Use commas to let a reader know when a *who* clause gives nonessential information: (1) one comma if the clause ends a sentence and (2) two commas if the clause interrupts a sentence.

NOTE: The pronouns *who* and *whom* refer only to people. The pronoun *which* refers only to things. The pronoun *that* can be used to refer either to people or to things.

The person with *whom* you should speak is Ms. D'Amato.   (*Whom* refers to a person.)

My new personal computer, *which* was on sale for $895, has a 512K memory.   (*Which* refers to a thing.)

He is the kind of person *that* adjusts well.   (Here, *that* refers to a person.)

The personal computer *that* I bought has a 512K memory.   (Here, *that* refers to a thing. Compare this essential *that* clause with the nonessential *which* clause in the second sentence.)

CLASS PRACTICE 2

Where are commas missing in the following sentences? Find the nonessential clauses, and use commas to separate them from the rest of the sentence. Write *OK* if the sentence is correct.

1. In the November issue which is on my desk Dr. Owens' investment tips are discussed in detail.
2. Mr. Winger who has developed many successful advertising campaigns for Benton Products Inc. is coordinating this campaign.
3. The copywriter who generally handles all technical products is Louise Albright.
4. The person who wrote this letter is one of our important clients.
5. If you want a manual that explains these procedures, ask Mr. Gleason.
6. Our new supervisor who was formerly our word processing consultant teaches business courses in a nearby college.

To Indicate Omissions

Writers sometimes omit words in order to be brief. Omitting words is fine as long as the meaning is still clear. In the following sentences, for example, note how the commas tell the reader where the *understood* words belong.

Lena Kutsher was assigned to the Sheilds account; Bill Quince, the J&R account; and Dorothy Franciosa, the Hanover Funds account.   (Each comma substitutes for the words *was assigned to.*)

**To Separate
Repetitions**

The comma also serves to separate words or phrases that are deliberately repeated for emphasis.

> Last week we received *many, many* requests for more information about municipal bonds.

> When she discussed her project, Margaret was obviously *enthusiastic, very enthusiastic.*

In Numbers

Commas are generally used to separate thousands, millions, billions, and so on, in numbers of five digits or more.

> 17,460   43,649 $2,846,094

However, the comma is not used in the following numbers:

> four-digit numbers: 3500, 7818
> years: 1987, 1989
> page numbers: pages 1324 and 1343
> house numbers: 1301 Rockaway Parkway
> phone numbers: (201) 555-6547
> ZIP Codes: 91324
> serial numbers: Policy 98475

In addition, the comma is not used in weights and measurements that express *one* total unit: *11 pounds 3 ounces, 3 hours 23 minutes,* and so on.

Unrelated numbers that are written together should be separated by a comma to avoid misreading.

> By 1992, 34 foreign-language editions will be available.   (The comma prevents the possibility of the reader's seeing *199234* or otherwise confusing these two numbers.)

NOTE: In special cases numbers may get special treatment. For example, in metric terms a space (not a comma) is used to separate groups of three numbers *on both sides of the decimal point!*

> 21 435 kilometers
> 13 432.875 445 liters

But a four-digit metric number is written with no space (for example, *3425 kilograms*) unless it appears in a table with numbers that have five digits or more.

**In Company
Names**

Many law firms, stock brokerage houses, accounting firms, and other companies are known by the names of the firm's principal partners. Generally, such company names are written in either of these two styles:

O'Malley, Schwartz, Vernon and Jones

O'Malley, Schwartz, Vernon & Jones

As you see above, one style is to use the word *and* before the last partner's name; the other style is to use the symbol & (called an *ampersand*) before the last partner's name. In either case, however, no comma appears before either the symbol & or the word *and*.

The "short form" for such company names, generally used only for informal messages, consists of the first two partners' names:

Let me know as soon as *O'Malley, Schwartz* submits its final report.   (Note that no comma follows *Schwartz.*)

In addition, there are other companies that choose to write their official names without commas:

O'Malley Schwartz Vernon and Jones

O'Malley Schwartz Vernon & Jones

The short form, in both examples, is simply *O'Malley Schwartz.*

In any case remember that the full, official name is the correct name.

Comma Pitfalls

Including a comma when it is not needed can slow your reader's progress and cause confusion. Observe these rules:

1. Do not separate a compound by *one* comma. When a compound subject, compound object, or compound verb is interrupted, use *two* commas to set off the interrupting element.

   The sales representatives and the district managers are very happy with the new commission schedule.   (Do not separate the compound subject with a comma.)

   The sales representatives and, *of course,* the district managers are very happy with the new commission schedule.   (*Two* commas are needed to separate the interrupting expression *of course* from the rest of the sentence.)

   The sales representatives and the district managers, *naturally,* are very happy with the new commission schedule.   (Again, *two* commas are needed to separate the interrupting expression—in this case, *naturally*—from the rest of the sentence.)

2. Do not separate a subject from its predicate by one comma.

   Please submit your application and your résumé to our recruiter.   (No comma needed.)

   Please submit your application and your résumé, *as well as your references,* to our recruiter.   (*Two* commas set off the interrupting phrase *as well as your references.*)

EDITING PRACTICE 2

Correct any errors in the following sentences.

1. Although the estimated cost was $13500, the actual cost was only $9850.
2. Janet said, "I think that using radio commercials to promote these products is a very very good idea!"
3. Our duplicating expenses for the months of July and August totaled $1900; travel expenses $3750; entertainment expenses $1155; and miscellaneous expenses $750.
4. The new room is only 22 feet, 8 inches long by 15 feet, 6 inches wide, but it should serve our purposes well.
5. The comprehensive bibliography (see pages 1,180 through 1,192) will be helpful to anyone who wishes to find out more about this topic.
6. One well-respected accounting firm with specific experience in hotel-motel finances is LaCross, Pennyworth, Dixon, & Shapiro.

COMMUNICATION LABORATORY

APPLICATION EXERCISES

A. Practice applying the comma principles presented in this unit. On a separate sheet of paper, indicate where you would place or remove commas and explain why. Write *OK* for any sentence that is correct.

1. Marsha's thorough report which has been distributed to the Executive Committee will be discussed at Friday's meeting.
2. We are confident, that we can reduce the production costs and make this project profitable.
3. Only Roberta Cohen who is in charge of the Records Retention Department has the authority to destroy old files.
4. Danielle Lancer, a partner in the firm of Simms, Oates, & Godfrey, will speak to our accountants at 4 p.m.
5. We have prepared Room 2,143 for her presentation, and we will serve refreshments immediately after she has finished.
6. By December 31 144 representatives will have submitted their estimated budgets for the coming year.
7. The total weight of the envelope is only 3 pounds, 4 ounces.
8. Paula's idea, in our opinion, was innovative, very innovative.
9. Ms. Whitter's final proposal which we received only Friday afternoon has not been thoroughly reviewed yet.
10. All the contracts, checks, and other valuable documents were given to Sandra Ryan who is a corporate executive.

11. The insurance company's check for $321,754 is incorrect; the correct amount is $231754.
12. Merrill Lynch Pierce Fenner, & Smith is one of the large brokerage firms that will be in the new building; Dean Whitter Reynolds is another.
13. We need several large, glass, containers with spillproof lids to store these strong chemicals safely.
14. Payroll deduction provides a safe convenient method to save money.
15. In February we received many, many orders to install these machines; in March, only two or three orders.
16. Is the correct address 1,372 Rockaway Parkway, or is it 1,732 Rockaway Parkway?
17. Be sure to remember that the maximum cargo for each trailer is 12500 pounds.
18. Please add the ZIP Code number to this address card: 10,723.
19. Ask Claire whether that company is in Springfield Illinois or Springfield Massachusetts.
20. We are very, very happy with the two, 30-second commercials that Karen and Andy developed.

B. Correct each error in the following sentences. Write *OK* on your paper for each correct sentence.

1. Have you seen the new, executive offices on the ninth floor?
2. Ruck, Moser, Naldi, Hancher & Torella is one of the foremost consulting firms in the state; we have made an appointment with one of the senior partners from Ruck, Moser to discuss ways to improve our public image.
3. To receive your $5 rebate complete the enclosed card and return it to us before March 19.
4. If you had joined the retirement plan when you began working here you would probably have earned several thousand dollars by now.
5. Mr. Winchester do you want to have the entire order shipped to your warehouse?
6. Francine wants to hire part-time help but David strongly believes that we should ask our own staff members to work overtime.
7. Our manager decided consequently to reassign some of our long-term projects.
8. Yes, John, I seen Ms. Haliburton in the lobby just a few minutes ago.
9. If you wish, of course, you may use the overhead projector which is in the stockroom, I believe.
10. Her husband who is also an audio technician works for another radio station.
11. The engine, the transmission, the air conditioner, etc. are covered for five years or 50,000 miles under the terms of this warranty.

12. The model that she ordered is now out of stock but we can probably get it for her within the week.
13. Century Motors, Inc. provides all the vehicles for our sales representatives and our executives.
14. We should review the major features of these products, before the meeting begins.
15. Before the meeting begins, we should review the major features of these products.

C. Make the following message clear by correcting all the errors that you find.

> Our experience with Lindeman Motors, Inc., has shown that, we can expect fair prices and excellent service on all the vehicles it sells or leases. Our experience with Centurion Auto Sales and Rentals on the other hand has been almost entirely negative. Although Centurion has a reputation for very low prices it also has a reputation for poor service and for hidden costs. When our current lease agreement with Lindeman expires next month therefore we recommend renewing the lease, for an additional 24 months. The 10 percent increase in our total monthly payment (to $15550) will we believe be well worth the small additional price as compared with Centurion's slightly lower price for the same autos ($14995).

VOCABULARY AND SPELLING STUDIES

A. These words are often confused: *manner, manor; emanate, eminent, imminent.* Explain the differences.

B. For each sentence identify the meaning of the word in italics.

1. Unfortunately, Gerald works with customers in a *perfunctory* way. (*Perfunctory* means (a) secretive, (b) exhaustive, (c) mechanical, (d) hasty.)
2. With her knowledge of our procedures, Helen can help you to *expedite* the process. (*Expedite* means (a) cancel, (b) accelerate, (c) understand, (d) reverse.)
3. Angela did a *prodigious* amount of work in a very short time. (*Prodigious* means (a) sloppy, (b) overwhelming, (c) formal, (d) financial.)

C. Rewrite the following paragraph, correcting spelling and punctuation errors as you do so.

> Our supervisor, Jim Gormly is teaching a short coarse on the basics of word procesing begining next Wendesday. Sponsored by the corporate training program this course will be offerred again in the spring.

COMMUNICATING FOR RESULTS

Attendance on the Job. Matt Chesterton, one of your coworkers in the Word Processing Center of a large corporation, often calls in to say that he is sick and cannot come to work. In fact, Matt is out about three days a month on a regular basis.

Today Matt confides in you and tells you that he is not really sick when he calls; he just takes a day off when he is in the mood to do so—especially on days when he knows there will be a heavy work load. What advice would you give to Matt?

U · N · I · T
29
Semicolons, Colons, and Dashes

Semicolons, colons, and dashes have specific uses within the sentence. Knowing these uses will improve your reading skill, and applying them properly will distinguish your writing from the ordinary.

The Semicolon

The semicolon announces a partial stop somewhat stronger than a comma. Thus a semicolon, not a comma, is often required to join the independent clauses in a compound sentence. In addition, a semicolon is often needed before explanatory or enumerating words and in a series of items that already have commas within them.

In Compound Sentences. Before we see how semicolons are used in compound sentences, let's review what a compound sentence is: *A compound sentence is a sentence with two or more independent clauses.* Remember that an independent clause is one that can stand alone *and still make sense.* A compound sentence, therefore, is a sentence with two such clauses (or more than two).

The clauses in a compound sentence (1) may be joined by a comma plus a conjunction, (2) may be joined by a semicolon without a conjunction, or (3) may be written as two separate sentences.

Jane now works in our headquarters office, but she has also worked in some of our district offices. (Two independent clauses joined by a comma plus the conjunction *but*.)

Jane now works in our headquarters office; she has also worked in some of our district offices. (Two independent clauses joined by a semicolon. A comma is not strong enough to join these two clauses.)

Jane now works in our headquarters office. She has also worked in some of our district offices. (Two independent clauses written as two separate sentences.)

Now that you have reviewed the compound sentence, study the three uses of semicolons in compound sentences.

1. *To Join Clauses Without Conjunctions.* A semicolon is strong enough to join two independent clauses without a conjunction. A comma cannot do so.

The committee decided to cut total expenses by 20 percent; the advertising budget was reduced more than others. (No conjunction joins the two independent clauses—just a semicolon. A comma is not strong enough to join these clauses.)

2. *To Join Clauses With Transitional Expressions.* When the second independent clause includes a transitional word or phrase, a comma is not strong enough to join the clauses. They must be joined by a semicolon.

Benjamin approves all large purchases for the entire division; however, he is now in Europe on business. (A semicolon is needed to join these independent clauses. A comma is *not* strong enough to do so.)

3. *To Prevent Misreadings.* If a compound sentence contains commas in either or both clauses *and* a strong break is needed to make the message clear, use a semicolon to separate the clauses even if a conjunction is used. If no misreading is likely, use a comma.

Among the topics to be covered today are general sales techniques, our discount policy, and commissions; and the incentive compensation plan will be discussed next week. (The semicolon provides the break needed to ensure that the reader pauses after *commissions*.)

Before Explanatory or Enumerating Words. Use a semicolon before words and phrases such as *for example, for instance, namely, that is*, and *that is to say* when they introduce an independent clause, an enumeration, or an explanation that is not essential to the rest of the sentence.

Ms. Hagen asked the managers to report any planned personnel changes for next year; *namely*, she is interested in knowing of any staff additions planned for next year. (*Namely* introduces an independent clause.)

There are several qualified candidates for the product manager position; *for example*, Elizabeth Bancroft, Mel Trainor, Sid Ford, and Anne Marie Wilson. (*For example* introduces an enumeration.)

In a Series. Series of items that contain internal commas (such as commas in city and state names or in certain company names) should be separated by semicolons instead of commas to prevent misreading.

Those district offices now participating in the experimental study are in Bloomington, Minnesota; Kansas City, Kansas; Albany, New York; and Seattle, Washington.

NOTE: A semicolon, not a comma, precedes the conjunction before the last item in a series containing internal commas.

CLASS PRACTICE 1

In each of the following sentences, choose the correct punctuation mark within parentheses and explain each of your choices.

1. Several well-known speakers are on the program tomorrow, including Marcia Q. Steinbeck(, ;) director of marketing for Panorama Tours(, ;) Adrian Welch(, ;) publisher of several magazines(, ;) and Jeffrey C. Ulster(, ;) senior designer for Phelps & Morris Clothing.
2. Our warehouse is closed for inventory during the next two weeks(, ;) consequently(, ;) we cannot ship this order until April 20.
3. Any questions concerning the purchase of this property should be addressed to Ms. Lewis, Mr. Judd, or Mrs. Kalbach(, ;) and Mr. Cuomo should be given copies of all correspondence pertaining to the sale.
4. Sales of this particular model have increased steadily over the past five years(, ;) we sold approximately 25,000 units last year.
5. Mr. Ober suggested several ways to test the idea(, ;) for instance, we can survey all our credit card customers.
6. One executive in the group questioned the necessity of what she called "extraordinary" merit increases(, ;) all the other executives considered the raises fair and justified.

The Colon

A colon serves a specific function: It tells the reader "Listen to this," or "Here is something important." Study the following uses of the colon.

Colon Before a List. A colon is used to introduce a list within a sentence or a list that is tabulated. Before the colon appears, the reader is often given a hint that a list will follow by such words as *the following, as follows, this,* or *these.*

The total price of $1596 includes the following:

1. A 512K microcomputer
2. A disk drive
3. A monitor

4. A monitor stand
5. The disk operating system (DOS)
6. Four comprehensive system manuals
7. Accounting and word processing software packages

You may pay for your purchase in any of these convenient ways: by check, by money order, or by credit card.

Colon for Emphasis. A colon may be used to give added emphasis to a word, a phrase, or a sentence.

Our manager consistently stresses one aspect of our products: quality.   (Colon to emphasize a word.)

Allen explained the reason for his bonus program: to reward employees for superior efforts.   (Colon to emphasize a phrase.)

The supervisor of the Accounts Payable Department has a well-known rule: Compare each check with the purchase requisition before mailing the check.   (Colon to emphasize a sentence.)

When a colon precedes a complete sentence, as in the last example, the first word of the sentence is capitalized if the sentence states a formal rule or requires additional emphasis. However, if the sentence following the colon merely completes the main thought, use a lowercase letter.

Clarence has a good excuse for missing this workshop: he will be on jury duty all week.   (Lowercase letters because the second sentence completes the main thought.)

Remember: Every employee must wear his or her safety helmet before entering the plant.   (Capital letter for emphasis.)

CLASS PRACTICE 2

Make the correct choices for each of the following sentences.

1. Please type this code number on the order form(: . ,) A705-50.
2. Double-check your guest list, please, to make sure that the following clients are included(: . ,) Wendall Pomerantz, Estelle Raub, Sean McGeough, and Laura Ashley.
3. Only three performances will be given during the summer(: . ,) July 8, July 20, and August 5.
4. Caution(: . ,) Avoid getting the solution on your skin.
5. You may receive your free catalog by calling the following numbers(: . ,) Of course, if you wish, you may pick up your copy at any of our stores.
6. The sales pattern has been very predictable for the past few years(: . ,) Review these sales reports to see for yourself.

EDITING PRACTICE 1

On a separate sheet of paper, correct any errors in the uses of semicolons and colons in the following sentences. (HINT: Be sure to look for errors in the use of capitals following colons.)

1. Our direct mail campaign was most successful in these areas; Atlanta, Georgia, Memphis, Tennessee, and Louisville, Kentucky.
2. When you return damaged merchandise, be sure to include the following information. The manufacturer's name, the model number, the serial number, and the date of purchase.
3. The warranty expired last December, Mr. Spears: however, the cost of repairing your dehumidifier will be less than $15.
4. Be sure to specify where these items are to be shipped: The printer, to our Albany warehouse; the monitor, to our Manhattan district office; and the box of old files, to the Records Retention Center.
5. The conference features some excellent speakers, including the following well-known data processing experts. Clay Samuels, Wanda Heller, James Sampson, and Leonette Cummings.
6. Important. Make sure you enclose a packing slip with each order.

The Dash

The dash is an abrupt, emphatic punctuation mark that has a special impact on a sentence. The dash can often be replaced by a comma, a semicolon, a colon, or parentheses. But the dash has a few of its own unique uses. In any case it is a strong, forceful mark of punctuation and therefore must be used correctly—and sparingly.

As a Substitute for Other Punctuation. Although a dash can often be replaced by other punctuation, the emphasis of the sentence is weaker without the dash. For example, compare the following pairs of sentences, noting how much more emphatic the sentences with dashes are.

Commas vs. Dashes

One new supplier, Acme Typesetters, is very conveniently located.

One new supplier—Acme Typesetters—is very conveniently located.

Semicolons vs. Dashes

The list price of the Electra stereo package is the highest; however, the quality of the Electra is also the best.

The list price of the Electra stereo package is the highest—however, the quality of the Electra is also the best.

Colons vs. Dashes

Buying from Jensen Audio has these advantages: reliable service, low prices, and a wide variety of name brands to choose from.

Buying from Jensen Audio has these advantages—reliable service, low prices, and a wide variety of name brands to choose from.

Parentheses vs. Dashes

Spectrum Appliances has three convenient stores (on Berkeley Avenue, in the Howard Mall, and on Sunset Road) for your shopping pleasure.

Spectrum Appliances has three convenient stores—on Berkeley Avenue, in the Howard Mall, and on Sunset Road—for your shopping pleasure.

NOTE: When parenthetical material appears at the end of a sentence, only *one* dash is needed to set off the words—as opposed to *two* parentheses.

For your shopping pleasure Spectrum Appliances has three convenient stores (on Berkeley Avenue, in the Howard Mall, and on Sunset Road). (*Two* parentheses.)

For your shopping pleasure Spectrum Appliances has three convenient stores—on Berkeley Avenue, in the Howard Mall, and on Sunset Road. (*One* dash to separate parenthetical copy at the end of a sentence.)

Before *These* or *All*. Use a dash to separate a list from the word *these* or *all* whenever *these* or *all* refers to the list.

Leadership, human relations skill, the ability to communicate well—*these* are the characteristics of the successful manager. (The word *these* summarizes the items listed before the dash.)

Safety, high yield, monthly dividends—*all* are available to you as a member of this municipal bond plan. (The word *all* refers to the list that precedes the dash. The dash provides the necessary pause.)

Before a Repetition or a Restatement. Use a dash before a repetition such as the one illustrated here:

Thelma did a superb job of planning and coordinating the entire week-long conference—a very fine job. (Dash before the repetition.)

With Afterthoughts and Contrasting Statements. Use a dash before a deliberate afterthought to give variety to your writing or to soften a strong statement.

All of us look forward to seeing you at next year's convention—sooner, we hope! (A planned afterthought.)

Your territory was about 15 percent under budget—but economic conditions, of course, seriously curtailed customer buying. (To soften the effect of the main thought.)

Likewise, to give special emphasis to a contrasting statement, use a dash to set it off.

Total revenue for the first quarter was $5.5 million—against a goal of $5.7 million—for all our subsidiaries. (Dashes set off the contrasting statement.)

Punctuating Material Set Off by Dashes. The words that are set off by dashes may be punctuated as described below.

At the End of the Sentence. Whenever "dashed" material ends a sentence, the second dash is omitted and the sentence then ends with the regular end-of-sentence punctuation.

We buy our supplies from Webster Stationers—*all* our supplies.   (This is a declarative statement.)

Who is the person standing at the podium—the woman with the briefcase?   (This is a question.)

What a tremendous value—a genuine bargain!   (This is an exclamation.)

Within the Sentence. Words within two dashes may end in a question mark or an exclamation point, when appropriate; a period is used only if the last word is an abbreviation that requires the period.

Her latest book—a certain best-seller!—is to be made into a movie.   (The words within the dashes are an exclamation.)

Analysts predict that Gold Label stock—do you know its present price?—may double by the end of this year.   (The words within the dashes are a question.)

We find that leasing equipment—such as cars, trucks, and vans—is less expensive in the long term.   (No period before the second dash.)

We find that leasing equipment—cars, trucks, vans, etc.—is less expensive in the long term.   (Period before the second dash only because of the abbreviation *etc.*)

Commas within dashes are used in the normal way, as are quotation marks:

Several agents—Carolyn, Frank, Leo, and George, for example—recommended that we review and update the commission plan for all insurance policies.

These executive cars—known in industry jargon as "brass hats"—are being sold at 25 percent below their original list prices.

CLASS PRACTICE 3

Where are dashes needed in the following sentences?

1. Take advantage of the discount nearly 10 percent by placing your order before November 15.
2. Are you planning to attend the Basic Finance workshop the one in Cleveland on February 9?
3. Tampa, Seattle, Detroit, Charleston these are the cities we are concentrating on.
4. Some of our service departments Customer Service, for instance eventually will be moved to our Henry Street building.

5. Everyone on the Search Committee agreed that Charles is well qualified very well qualified.
6. Charleston not Charlestown is the site of the new factory.

EDITING PRACTICE 2

Test your ability to use dashes by correcting any errors in the following sentences.

1. The liter, the meter, the gram,—these are the basic units for capacity, length, and mass in the metric system.
2. The Hazlett Paper Companies—have you bought supplies from them—submitted the lowest bid.
3. Discount prices, quality merchandise, excellent service,—all are yours when you buy from A-One Distributors.
4. We selected the 6:30 a.m. flight, not the 2:30 p.m. flight—because our meeting will start at noon.
5. Ms. Flowers has been the top sales representative for the past three consecutive years quite an accomplishment!
6. All of us, of course, are excited about the same thing the upcoming trip to Honolulu.

COMMUNICATION LABORATORY

APPLICATION EXERCISES

A. In the following sentences, parentheses indicate possible missing punctuation. On a separate sheet of paper, indicate the punctuation you would use for the parenthesis. Write *OK* for any sentence that requires no added punctuation.

1. Our Graphic Arts Department's latest video ( ) have you seen it ( ) has been nominated for a special award.
2. Inform the Legal Department of the subpoena ( ) do it immediately, Irwin.
3. Only one person in the company ( ) Ethel Pena ( ) has experience in this area.
4. The cancellation was based on one critical factor ( ) The project's total cost was more than 50 percent over its budgeted cost.
5. Among the items that were returned undamaged were these ( ) computer terminals, monitors, printers, and modems.
6. Computer terminals, monitors, printers, and modems ( ) these were among the items that were returned undamaged.

7. The primary thrust of the campaign is focused around radio and television commercials ( ) in addition ( ) of course ( ) we will also have many full-page ads in major big-city newspapers.

8. Remember ( ) If you feel that you have been treated unfairly, notify the Equal Employment Opportunity officer in the Personnel Department.

9. I'd like another copy of the procedures manual ( ) one that has illustrations of the newest forms.

10. At the end of the demonstration, you should do the following ( ) summarize the product's major features, repeat the low monthly payment, review our easy credit terms, and close the sale.

11. No, we have not been very satisfied with the service we have received from Dallas Central Distribution Company ( ) we have ( ) consequently ( ) begun searching for other potential suppliers.

12. Our survey supported the fact that our clients highly value ( ) our fast service, our cooperative sales representatives, and our low interest rates.

13. Our fast service, our cooperative sales representatives, our low interest rates ( ) these are the features that our clients rated most important in our recent survey.

14. Jim Smyth ( ) not Tim Smith ( ) is the director of sales.

15. Doris Markham ( ) is she still the senior vice president of marketing ( ) is one of the most respected authors in the area of business management.

B. On a separate sheet of paper, show your corrections for each of the following sentences. (Some sentences may have more than one error.) Write *OK* for any sentence that has no error.

1. Three of our plant managers—Beatrice Roland, Milton Fox, and Wayne Sockwell,—have requested additional funds for plant modernization.

2. As soon as Mr. Sills leaves his production meeting. Let's meet with him to discuss this contract.

3. Not surprisingly, the survey clearly stressed that customers value one factor more than any of the others, quality.

4. If you should need additional information just call our Human Resources Department.

5. Mr. Dennison asked us why the printing of the new catalog has been delayed?

6. The managers and their assistants emphasized throughout the meeting, that the production budget must be increased by at least $15,000.

7. Accounts Payable is now backlogged because of employee absence, three of four staff members have been out with the flu for the entire week.

8. Entertaining clients, car repairs, airline fares. These expenses comprise about 60 percent of the budget for travel and entertainment.
9. If Ms. Galway accepts the position in our headquarters office. She will become the youngest executive in the entire corporation.
10. Edwin Abernathy, Clark Simmons, Anthony Franks and Nicole Ruck, are permanent members of the Procedures Committee.
11. Needless to say, all of us were pleased to hear that our department had won the cash prize very pleased.
12. Our company has a well-established reputation for manufacturing goods such as: refrigerators, washers, driers, microwave ovens, and dishwashers.
13. Caution; Smoking is prohibited anywhere in the lab area.
14. Yes, the sale ends on Saturday, we will be open until 9 p.m. each evening until then.
15. Among the products that are especially popular according to our store managers are children's toys, adult board games, mystery books and smoke alarms.

C. Insert the correct punctuation marks in the places with parentheses.

After we review the entire February issue (   ) we should begin laying out our plans for succeeding issues (   ) at least for March and April (   ) How much ad space have we sold for the March and April issues (   ) How many pages will each issue be (   ) Such questions must be answered immediately (   ) In addition, I do not like the tentative feature story for March (   ) do you (   ) We should meet (   ) Alan, Evelyn, Bruce, and I (   ) before the end of the week to discuss all this.

VOCABULARY AND SPELLING STUDIES

A. These words are often confused: *peace, piece; stationery, stationary.* Explain the differences.

B. On a separate sheet of paper, write the singular forms of the following plural nouns.

1. parentheses
2. teeth
3. CPAs
4. Messrs. Parker
5. notaries public
6. secretaries

C. Column A on the next page lists six words containing prefixes, and Column B lists the meaning of many of the most commonly used prefixes. Match the words with the meanings that refer to their prefixes.

A	B
1. subway	**a.** before
2. contradict	**b.** against
3. postscript	**c.** around
4. inconvenient	**d.** between, among
5. antedate	**e.** one
6. interstate	**f.** beyond
	g. under
	h. above
	i. after
	j. not

COMMUNICATING FOR RESULTS

Being Blamed for Others' Errors. Your employer calls to your attention some errors in reports that she believes you prepared. The reports in question are not yours. What should you say or do?

U · N · I · T

30

Periods, Question Marks, and Exclamation Points

A famous pitcher, known to be a man of few words, was asked to comment on his last game. He was quoted as replying ".". History records a few other examples of similar replies. For example, one famous author wrote to his publisher to find out how his book was selling. He simply wrote "?" The book had indeed been selling very well, so his publisher replied "!"*

The period, the question mark, and the exclamation point are the marks used to end sentences. Obviously these are very familiar punctuation marks and easy to master. This unit will review their basic familiar uses and will discuss the few problem areas in using these marks.

* Adapted from *Wordwatching*, Vol. 5, No. 10, September 1982, copyright © by Kay Powell.

The Period

The most commonly used mark of punctuation is the period. You already know the essential uses of the period. Let's review when to use a period and when not to use a period. Then we will review some common pitfalls.

Use a Period. After declarative and imperative sentences, after indirect questions, and after requests phrased as questions, *use a period.*

After Declarative and Imperative Sentences. A declarative sentence makes a statement, and an imperative sentence is an order or a command. Use a period after each.

Ms. Morehead wants to attend the word processing workshop.   (A declarative sentence—it simply makes a statement.)

Give Ms. Morehead some information about our upcoming workshops.   (An imperative sentence—a polite command. In this construction the subject *you* is understood.)

After Indirect Questions. An *indirect question* is really a statement, because it simply rephrases a question in statement form. Use a period after indirect questions. Of course, use a question mark after a direct question.

"Does anyone know," James asked, "when the revised manual will be distributed?"   (James' actual words are in quotation marks. His actual words comprise a question and require a question mark.)

James asked whether anyone knows when the revised manual will be distributed.   (This is not James' original question; it is a restatement of his original question. This restatement is an indirect question and requires a period.)

After Requests Phrased as Questions. Sometimes a request is written in question form. Use a period when such requests clearly indicate that an answer or an action is expected. (Requests that end with a period are called *polite requests.*) Use a question mark when such requests require a "yes" or a "no" answer (as, for example, for favors).

Will you please send us your payment.   (An action is being requested. This is simply a polite way of saying "Send us your payment.")

Will you be able to ship the merchandise in time for our Fourth of July sale?   (A genuine question—*can you* ship it in time?)

CLASS PRACTICE 1

Which of the following sentences should end with periods?

1. Will you send us a copy of your latest catalog
2. Will Mr. Andre be available this afternoon for the marketing meeting
3. May we have your check by March 30
4. A sales representative asked when the new price list will become effective

5. Will you please credit our account for the damaged merchandise we returned

6. Leroy wants to know when the final payment is due

Do Not Use a Period. There are a few instances in which writers confuse the rules concerning the uses of periods. Do not use a period after (1) numbers or letters in parentheses, (2) headings or titles that are on separate lines, (3) roman numerals (except when followed by titles, as in outlines), (4) even amounts of dollars, and (5) abbreviations that already end in periods.

> The supervisor cited three reasons for the delay: (1) the recent strike, (2) the backlog in shipments during summer, and (3) the time needed to check customers' credit accounts. (Not (1.), (2.), ...)

> Summary

> BIBLIOGRAPHY

> Endnotes   (No period after headings that appear on separate lines.)

> Mark Wyne III will be the new CEO.   (Not *III. will be* . . .)

> Ms. Tyson suggested $20 as a fair list price for our new computer game.   (Not *$20. as a* . . . .)
> Store hours are from 9 a.m. until 8 p.m.   (Not *8 p.m..*)

In addition, do not use a period after items in a list unless the items are long or are essential to complete the sentence that introduces the items.

> Nancy discussed three problems:

> 1. The profit margin
> 2. Increased competition
> 3. Government regulation

Now notice how the items in the following example *are* needed to complete the introductory sentence:

> Nancy discussed:

> 1. The profit margin.
> 2. Increased competition.
> 3. Government regulation.

EDITING PRACTICE 1

Find and correct any errors in the following sentences.

1. Using the various controls on this word processor, you may delete (1.) a single letter, (2.) an entire word, (3.) an entire line of copy, and (4.) an entire paragraph.

2. Tell Andrew to ship this order to Ms. Jackson c.o.d..

3. Because it exceeds $500., this expense must be approved by Mrs. VanHalen.
4. Sandra identified the following possible sites for the distribution center:
   a. Jackson, Mississippi.
   b. Hot Springs, Arkansas.
   c. Mount Hood, Oregon.
5. Is it true that Edward Sloan III. has been appointed to the board of directors?
6. The lowest estimate (only $2500.) was submitted by United Tool Company Inc.

Period Pitfalls. One of the common errors in using periods is to use a period *before the end of the sentence*, thereby stranding a group of words and creating a fragment.

> Next April we will launch an advertising campaign for our new video recorders. The most expensive and extensive campaign we have ever developed. (You should quickly see that the second group of words makes no sense unless it is joined to the first sentence. See the next example.)

> Next April we will launch our advertising campaign for our new video recorders, the most expensive and extensive campaign we have ever developed.

A second common error related to period use is to use a comma where a period (or a semicolon) should be used. In other words a sentence that should end with a period is instead joined by a comma to another sentence.

> The company is now negotiating leasing agreements with two well-known firms, Standard Motors has proposed an especially attractive arrangement. (A period or a semicolon should follow *firms.* Two sentences have been joined—incorrectly— by a comma.)

EDITING PRACTICE 2

Find the errors in the following sentences and explain why they are errors.

1. All of us expected the price of computer equipment to drop this year, we deliberately delayed last year's purchases to take advantage of the price reduction.
2. Our plan calls for heavily increasing our radio advertising. In an effort to reach young adults.
3. Leonia generally conducts the sales training classes, she has been a successful agent for more than 15 years.
4. These new products are selling better than we had expected, sales are now about 25 percent over estimates.
5. Ella will be in charge of the department. While Mr. Paulson is on vacation next week.
6. Place all these documents in the safe before you leave, they should not be left lying on your desk overnight.

The Question Mark

The question mark is used after a direct question. Note that it is also used after a short direct question that follows a statement.

Who has the order from Owens Chemicals?   (Direct question.)

Why did Mr. Haney decide to buy from Newton Falls Plastics?   (Direct question.)

This disk drive is expensive, isn't it?   (The sentence begins as a statement and ends as a question. Use a question mark.)

All these word processors come with a one-year warranty, don't they?   (Use a question mark because a question is joined to the statement.)

When a series of questions is included in one sentence, use a question mark after each question.

Is she still planning to travel to England? to Japan? to Germany?

CLASS PRACTICE 2

In the following sentences indicate whether a period or a question mark is needed at the point marked by parentheses.

1. Lynn and Susan have already submitted their reports to the committee, haven't they(   )
2. Will you please send one copy of the discount list to each of the district managers(   )
3. Did Mr. Quentin say that we should get revised bids from all the suppliers—Rainey Plastics(   ) Jenks & Bond Inc.(   ) National Wholesalers(   )
4. Yes, Ms. Diaz wants to know if the discount applies to all orders placed during the month of March(   )
5. Eleanor Whitney is the head of the Art Department, isn't she(   )
6. Will you have sufficient brochures for all our sales representatives(   )

The Exclamation Point

To express strong feeling, use an exclamation point after a word, a phrase, or a sentence. But do not overuse the exclamation point—especially in business correspondence.

Congratulations! Henry and I are delighted to hear that you have been promoted to assistant marketing director.   (Exclamation point after a word. Note that the sentence that follows is punctuated in the usual way.)

Another best-seller! How happy I am to hear that your second book . . . .   (Exclamation point after a phrase.)

Why didn't we think of this sooner!   (Exclamation point after a sentence.)

Note that the need for the exclamation point must often be determined by the writer. For example, the last sentence could also have been written as a simple question:

Why didn't we think of this sooner?   (Now the sentence does not show as strong emotion as with the exclamation point.)

CLASS PRACTICE 3

Indicate the punctuation at the point or points marked with parentheses in the following sentences. Explain your choices.

1. Another promotion( ) All of us congratulate you( )
2. What a surprise( ) I am very happy to know that you have returned to Chicago( )
3. My sincere appreciation to you for all your help( ) Thanks( )
4. I cannot believe it( ) Did you hear that Stephanie and Bridget are opening another store( )
5. What a record( ) Your sales for July set a new company record, and we congratulate you for your achievement( )
6. Whose idea was this( )

COMMUNICATION LABORATORY

APPLICATION EXERCISES

A. At the point marked by parentheses, indicate the correct punctuation for the following sentences. If no punctuation is needed, write *OK.*

1. Will you please call me as soon as Bob Webber arrives( )
2. Are you aware that Accu-Plus products—unlike most others—are warranted for a full five years( )
3. Congratulations( ) All of us hope that your new business is a smashing success( )
4. Harry, do you know when the messenger is scheduled to arrive( )
5. Have you had the opportunity yet to visit our Dallas office( ) our Tampa office( ) our St. Louis warehouse( )
6. Jerry is now seeking another bonded mailing house( ) Freehold Mail Service is now out of business( )
7. Will you please give my assistant a copy of the minutes of the last status meeting( )
8. We just heard the good news( )
9. Has Elana spoken with you yet about the upcoming sales demonstration( )
10. Stephen has already completed the first draft for this speech, hasn't he( )

11. As you know, Carla is in London( ) her assistant Edward is handling her projects.
12. No, these goods are not duty-free if they are purchased in the U.S.A.( )
13. To understand these concepts clearly, reread Chapters III( ) and IV( ) of this text.
14. Have you registered for the July accounting workshop yet( )
15. The actual price for the computer, the keyboard, the monitor, the printer, the modem, and two disk drives was only $2500( )

B. On a separate sheet, correct the following sentences and explain your reasons for making each correction. If a sentence has no error, write *OK*.

1. John, between you and I, I seriously doubt whether this project will ever be approved.
2. You may use the calculator on Tom's desk, he will be out until at least next Tuesday.
3. Call the messenger quickly, we must ship these cartons to Chicago as soon as possible.
4. What an incredible story.
5. No. We have no plans to close the Ames Street warehouse.
6. Did you know that the Kubick's own only about 4 or 5 percent of the stock in Kubick Industries?
7. Her assistant and me quickly discovered the reason for these errors.
8. Edna has been the supervisor of the Word Processing Department since 1984, she will probably be named an assistant vice president soon.
9. Tell anyone who needs more of them forms to call the Tax Department.
10. Several of the executive's have already commented on the improved service since we installed the new equipment.
11. An additional discount of $10. will be given to anyone who orders before December 31!
12. Has he took all the cartons to the Accounting Department yet?
13. Yes, there are rumors that Bell Fuel, Inc. will merge with McKinnon Oil, but the rumors are unsubstantiated.
14. Ellen, Steve and Pearl are the three most likely people to be asked to conduct the training sessions.
15. Dr. Fred Ausiello, a noted expert on nuclear energy will give the lecture this evening.

C. Is the punctuation correct in the following paragraph? Correct any errors as you copy the paragraph on a separate sheet of paper.

Congratulations. Your hard work throughout last year has certainly paid off. Your total sales for the year were 155 percent of budget. Everyone here in the headquarters office applauds you for this superb achievement. What do you have planned for *this* year.

VOCABULARY AND SPELLING STUDIES

A. These words are often confused: *expand, expend; interstate, intrastate.* Explain the differences.

B. By adding a prefix to each of these words, change the word to give it a negative meaning.

1. normal
2. engage
3. proper
4. noble
5. literate
6. enchanted
7. reasonable
8. likely
9. understood
10. achiever
11. order
12. embark
13. essential
14. popular
15. convenient

C. How are the following pairs of words spelled when *ing* is added to each?

1. hop, hope
2. plane, plan
3. mop, mope
4. dote, dot
5. bar, bare
6. pine, pin

COMMUNICATING FOR RESULTS

The Last Minute. Audrey is an administrative assistant for Kent and Roberta. All three are highly skilled, experienced workers with a positive attitude, and all three enjoy working with one another. One problem, however, is that Kent often—almost always—waits until the last minute to give Audrey his work. For example, yesterday at 4:45 he gave her a rather lengthy report that was due to be submitted to the vice president on the same day. Audrey worked until 6:15 to complete and submit that report. What should Audrey do?

31

Quotation Marks

Punctuation marks are signals that help the reader interpret a message correctly. Quotation marks, for example, tell the reader, "These are the exact words spoken or written by a person." In addition, quotation marks have other related uses, all of which are discussed in this unit.

Direct Quotations

Use quotation marks to record the precise words of a speaker or a writer. As you will see below, a comma helps to separate the quotation from the rest of the sentence.

> Mr. Peters said, "All supervisors and managers are invited to attend an excellent workshop on interpersonal relations." (Note that the period at the end of the sentence is inside the second quotation mark.)

> "In our opinion this workshop will help middle-management personnel communicate more effectively with clients and with coworkers," Mr. Peters continued. (Note that the comma after *coworkers* is inside the second quotation mark.)

For long quotations (for example, quotations longer than one sentence), use a colon instead of a comma to introduce the quotation.

> During our monthly divisionwide meeting, Mr. Peters said: "All supervisors and managers are invited to attend an excellent workshop on interpersonal relations. In our opinion, this workshop will help . . . ."

Because quotation marks identify the exact words someone said or wrote, they must be placed around the quoted words only, even when the quotation is interrupted.

> "All supervisors and managers," Mr. Peters said, "are invited to attend an excellent workshop on interpersonal relations."

Terms and Expressions

Writers use quotation marks to give special significance to certain terms and expressions. In the following discussion note how quotation marks are used for explanations and definitions, for unfamiliar terms, for slang and humorous expressions, and for translations of foreign words.

Explanations and Definitions. Use quotation marks to give special significance to expressions introduced by *marked, entitled,* and *signed.*

> Please be sure to clearly mark each container "Caution: Hazardous Chemicals."

> The candidate's campaign theme, entitled "Prepared for Today—Planning for Tomorrow," was certainly effective.

Definitions of words or phrases are also enclosed in quotation marks. Note that the words that are defined are printed in italics (in typewritten copy, underscoring is the equivalent of italics).

> The abbreviation *cps* means "characters per second" and refers to the speed with which a word processing printer prints copy.

> The abbreviation cps means "characters per second" and refers to the speed with which a word processing printer prints copy. (Note that underscoring is the same as italics.)

> As used in word processing, the word wraparound means "the ability to automatically start a new line of copy."

Unfamiliar Terms. Technical terms and other terms that may be unfamiliar to the reader are generally placed in quotation marks.

> Whichever plan you select, you will enjoy additional savings because all our plans are "no-load funds." (The technical term *no-load fund*—a mutual fund that charges no commission—may be unfamiliar to readers.)

Slang and Humorous Expressions. When slang and humorous expressions are used in writing, they are enclosed in quotation marks.

> Henry explained that within the next two or three years all these old-fashioned machines would "bite the dust."

> When we asked her for the summary, she told us it "ain't ready yet." (Quotations show that the deliberate grammatical error is intended to be humorous.)

Translations. Foreign words and phrases are underscored in typewritten copy (set in italics in print). Their translations are placed in quotation marks.

> The corporation encourages staff members to work *pro bono publico*—that is, "for the public good"—and gives employees time off for charity work.

EDITING PRACTICE 1

Correct any errors in the following sentences by adding quotation marks. Can you explain your reason for each correction? Write *OK* for any sentence that has no error.

1. Early in September, Ms. Everhart said, we will mail this new brochure to all clients.

2. Ms. Hammond specifically said, I want all travel budgets frozen until the first of January.
3. No, I did not know that the French term *par avion* means "by airplane."
4. Agnes, please take all the folders marked Confidential to Ms. Alsop before the end of the day.
5. If you prefer, Helene explained to the customer, we can bill you next month.
6. She defined *ad valorem tax* as follows: the tax on the price or the value of a commodity.

Titles

Use quotation marks to enclose the titles of parts or chapters of books, but underscore book titles.

> Make sure that you read carefully Chapter 4, "Estimating Income Taxes," in Personal Finance.   (Quotations for the chapter title; underscoring or italics for the book title.)

Also use quotation marks for the titles of lectures, essays, sermons, articles, mottoes, paintings, poems, and sculptures.

NOTE: Underscoring and italics are used for the titles of *separately bound works* such as magazines, newspapers, long poems, movies, operas, plays, and, of course, books.

> Last July she wrote "Stretching Your Personal Income," an article that appeared in The Wall Street Journal.   (Article title in quotations; newspaper title underscored for italics.)

> You will definitely profit from reading Part 3, "The Successful Business Attitude," in his new book, How to Reach the Top of the Corporate Ladder.   (Quotations for the title of part of a book; underscoring for italic for the title of the book itself.)

EDITING PRACTICE 2

Correct any errors in the following sentences by adding quotation marks or underscores as needed.

1. Among the magazines that we read regularly is U.S. News & World Report.
2. Our company sponsors an employee theater group, which is now working on a production of Cats.
3. Myron is planning to give a speech, Your Future in the World of Advertising, to the students at Wilson High School.
4. For an overview of the word processing programs that are most popular today, read Chapter 3, Using the Microcomputer for Word Processing.
5. Gloria Lenhart, a well-known investment adviser, writes a weekly column entitled The Most for Your Money.

6. There are, as you know, variant spellings for certain words; for consistency, the spellings in this text are based on Webster's Ninth New Collegiate Dictionary.

Quotation Within a Quotation

Use single quotation marks (on a typewriter, the apostrophe key) to set off a quotation within a quotation.

"Tell the Shipping Department manager to be sure to label each carton 'Fragile,' please," said Vernon.

The instructor said, "A wise consumer is not fooled by exaggerations such as 'once-in-a-lifetime offers.' "

Punctuation at the End of Quotations

The positioning of other punctuation marks inside or outside the ending quotation mark sometimes causes confusion. Yet the rules governing such cases are few and easy to understand. Study the following three principles:

1. *Periods and Commas.* Always place periods and commas *inside* the second quotation mark.

"As you predicted," said Ms. Coleman, "our retail sales have exceeded $1 million this year." (Note the position of the comma and the period *inside* the second quotation mark.)

2. *Colons and Semicolons.* Always place colons and semicolons *outside* the second quotation mark.

Notice these charts in the article "Tomorrow's Interest Rates": Chart 1.4, Chart 1.9, and Chart 2.5. (Colon *outside* second quotation mark.)

For quantity orders the sales agent promises us a "very special deal"; however, we have no room for storing large inventories. (Semicolon *outside* second quotation mark.)

3. *Question Marks and Exclamation Points.* If the words within quotations make up a question or an exclamation, then the question mark or exclamation point belongs *with* those words—that is, it belongs *inside* the second quotation mark.

Lavar asked, "What is the latest interest rate on Treasury bills?" (Are the words within quotations a question? Yes. Therefore, the question mark belongs *inside* the second quotation mark.)

We all shouted, "Congratulations, Bob!" (Are the words within quotations an exclamation? Yes. Therefore, place the exclamation mark *inside* the second quotation mark.)

On the other hand, if the quoted words are just *part of* a question or an exclamation, then the question mark or exclamation point belongs to the entire sentence, not just to the quoted words. In such cases place the question mark or exclamation point *outside* the second quotation mark.

Have you read her column, "The Most for Your Money"?   (Here the words in quotations are *part of* the question; thus the question mark is placed *outside* the second quotation mark.)

According to the agenda this meeting was supposed to be "a short question-and-answer session"!   (The quoted words are not an exclamation; they *belong* to an exclamation. Thus the exclamation point is placed *outside* the second quotation mark.)

EDITING PRACTICE 3

On a separate piece of paper, correct any errors in the use of quotation marks in the following sentences. Write *OK* if there are no errors.

1. "When Louise went to the airport," said Anthony, "she did remember to take all the signed contracts, didn't she"?
2. Did Francine say, "Set up an appointment with Mrs. DePinta?"
3. Ben yelled out, "Congratulations on your promotion, Wendy"!
4. Although the cartons were marked "Fragile," several items were damaged.
5. "According to the builders," said Mr. McKay, "we can move into our new offices on Thursday, March 15".
6. Jim asked, "Who has the most recent chart on mortgage rates"?
7. "Can you explain," asked Dina, "why these folders are marked 'Confidential,' William?"
8. Ms. Fordyce specifically said that she wants applicants "with plenty of experience;" therefore, I will share these résumés with her.

COMMUNICATION LABORATORY

APPLICATION EXERCISES

A. On a separate sheet of paper, correct any errors in the use of quotation marks and related other punctuation. Write *OK* if there are no errors.

1. Ms. Askins specifically said, "Deliver each contract by messenger".
2. Did she say, "Deliver each contract by messenger?"
3. Yes, Time is published by Time Inc.
4. I can hardly believe that Mr. Simms called it "a slight disagreement over money!"
5. Do you know the meaning of the French expression faux pas?
6. Doesn't that expression mean "a social blunder?"

7. In the column marked "Number," please enter your social security number.

8. Her latest article, 'Taking Advantage of Opportunities During Inflationary Times,' has stirred quite a controversy.

9. Each container must be labeled as follows: "Poison—Do not Swallow".

10. The text clearly distinguishes between principle, which means "rule," and principal, which means "chief or primary."

11. Post these Thank You for Not Smoking signs along the corridors, please.

12. Do you think it's true, asked Fred, that these bonds will soon be selling at a premium?

13. Were the envelopes that contained the contracts marked Confidential?

14. Irene asked, "Do you think that Barbara and Audrey would like to attend the Software Products show next week"?

15. We were surprised to hear Ms. D'Amato say that our design shows "energy, vitality, and creativity"!

B. Find and correct any errors in the following sentences. If a sentence has no error, write *OK* on your paper.

1. Most of us believe the packaging costs are excessive, Tim and Jocelyn certainly do.

2. The net operating profit (NOP) for our consumer products division was $1.2 million; our industrial tools division, $2.75 million; and our leasing subsidiary, $2.2 million.

3. The logotype that Carl designed was creative very creative.

4. Yes, Frances will audit the Des Plaines Illinois warehouse before she returns.

5. Checks are accepted, the identification requirements are printed on these notices.

6. Several items have not yet been delivered, agendas, seating arrangement charts, name tags, handouts, and product brochures.

7. The cost may be slightly over $750 but it should not exceed $1000.

8. Dennis, Janice and Mark will be coordinating all the details of the sales conferences.

9. The dies should be completed by Friday but Phyllis suspects that there will be a short delay.

10. The dies should be completed by Friday Phyllis however suspects that there will be a short delay.

11. Paula Chin one of the distributors in the Midwest suggested an alternative procedure for setting goals.

12. As soon as she entered the room, we all shouted "Congratulations!"

13. We realize that the initial expense for the machinery is high, we know however that we will save money in the long run.

14. Ideally, we would like to find a sales representative who: is a self-starter, enjoys traveling, and has graphic arts experience.

15. Mr. Carney has already posted the salary level for the new position, he listed the salary as $35,000 a year.

C. Edit the following paragraph.

Please update the attached budget forms and return them to the district office by November 15. As you will see these forms are different than the ones we had been using. For example, one new column ("Percent Change") requires you to compute the change for each budget item as compared with last years' budget. We have enclosed a brief description, of all the changes in the new form to simplify your understanding of the new procedures. Please be sure, to read the entire description before proceeding. If you should have any questions just call the district office at 555-8429. Remember, that the enclosed materials are marked Confidential and should be locked in a safe place at the end of each day.

VOCABULARY AND SPELLING STUDIES

A. These words are often confused: *human, humane; forgo, forego.* Explain the differences.

B. In the following sentences match the letter of the correct term with the definition in italics.

1. *One who is being taught a job* is (**a**) an instructor, (**b**) an understudy, (**c**) a trainee, (**d**) a jobber.
2. *One who has the authority to represent another in a business transaction* is (**a**) a notary public, (**b**) an agent, (**c**) a financier, (**d**) an author.
3. *One to whom a debt is owed* is (**a**) a creditor, (**b**) a cashier, (**c**) an auditor, (**d**) a referee.

COMMUNICATING FOR RESULTS

Gossip in the Reception Area. In the reception area of your office, there are chairs for visitors who are waiting for various people. As you walk by this area, you have often noticed employees gathered in twos and threes talking about personal aspects of business—gossip, really—while visitors can clearly overhear their conversations. The nature of the talk often concerns dissatisfaction with a supervisor or with the company in general or similar negative topics.

What effect do you think such talk will have on visitors? Do you think that your coworkers should participate in such gossip—especially within hearing of others? How do you think such talk affects the work of employees?

32

Parentheses and Apostrophes

Two more signals, parentheses and apostrophes, will help you improve the effectiveness of your messages. Study their uses in this unit.

Parentheses

Like commas and dashes, parentheses may be used to set off words that give additional information. What, then, are the differences among these three punctuation marks?

Parentheses for Additional Information. While dashes emphasize the information that they set off, parentheses *de*emphasize the words that they enclose. Commas are generally used to set off additional information that flows smoothly into the sentence—information that does not require the stronger break of dashes or parentheses. The following examples show typical uses of parentheses, dashes, and commas to set off additional (or parenthetical) information.

> The winner of the sales contest—the prize is a remote-controlled VCR!—will also receive a special bonus. (The dashes help provide emphasis for the words *the prize is a remote-controlled VCR!*)

> For the month of June this Silver Star television and VCR will be on sale for only $795 (plus shipping and tax). (Parentheses deemphasize the words *plus shipping and tax.*)

> The sale on all Silver Star products, as our store manager explained, will be for the entire month of June. (The words separated by commas flow smoothly into the sentence and do not require the stronger break that parentheses or dashes would provide.)

Other Uses of Parentheses. Besides their task of setting off additional information, parentheses are also used to enclose (1) references or directions, (2) numbers or letters in enumerations, and (3) repetitions of dollar amounts in legal writing.

> A chart of interest rates (see page 343) is provided to simplify your computations. (Reference.)

> Since 1983 Addison Appliances has paid its monthly balance promptly (see the annual credit reports attached). (Direction.)

For your convenience we have enclosed (1) our latest brochure, (2) a handy order form, and (3) a credit application form.   (Numbers in an enumeration.)

EDITING PRACTICE 1

Insert parentheses wherever they are needed in the following sentences.

1. Add state tax see pages 313 through 363 to the sale price.
2. Call the Personnel Department 555-7000 to discuss these benefits.
3. The main items on the agenda concern 1 the new security system, 2 records retention policies, and 3 merit-increase guidelines.
4. The cost of raw goods usually only 5 percent of total costs is expected to rise dramatically over the next five years.
5. We arrived at the airport on schedule our plane landed precisely at noon but were delayed by local traffic.
6. The low rate of inflation only 5 percent for the past year has helped us keep our prices competitive.

Parentheses With Other Marks of Punctuation. Parentheses can be used (1) to enclose words within a sentence or (2) to enclose a sentence that stands alone. Let's look at each category separately.

To Enclose Words Within a Sentence. Follow these rules when the words enclosed in parentheses are *part of* a sentence.

1. Do not use any mark of punctuation *before* the opening parenthesis.

   If we are able to ship your order before July 18 (and we sincerely hope that it is possible to), we will call to inform you of the new date.

2. After the closing (or *second*) parenthesis, place any punctuation that the sentence ordinarily would require.

   Before we discuss hiring policies (see item 4 on the agenda), we must review these guidelines.   (The normal punctuation after *Before we discuss hiring policies* is a comma. Therefore, place the comma after the second parenthesis.)

   Should we use the same price list (see the attached sample)?   (After *Should we use the same price list,* what punctuation would you use? A question mark, of course. Place the question mark after the second parenthesis.)

   For a true comparison, we used unit sales, not dollar sales (see Column 1); as a result, we noticed the following changes in buying trends.   (The semicolon that would ordinarily be placed after *dollar sales* must be placed after the closing parenthesis.)

3. Place *inside* the closing parenthesis the following marks only:

   a. A question mark (if the words within parentheses form a question).

Bernice said that the standard discount is 25 percent (or did she say 35 percent?).   (Are the words within parentheses a question? Yes. Place the question mark inside the closing parenthesis.)

b. An exclamation point (if the words within parentheses form an exclamation).

We may be eligible for a substantial discount (perhaps as much as 50 percent off!).   (Because the words within parentheses are an exclamation, the exclamation point is placed before the closing parenthesis.)

c. A period (if the period belongs to an abbreviation).

Mark left early to meet a client at the airport (his client will arrive at 7:45 a.m.).

4. Do not capitalize the first word within parentheses (unless that word is a proper noun). This rule applies even if the words within the parentheses are an independent clause because the entire parenthetical element is *part of* a sentence.

Yesterday our new front-wheel-drive vehicles arrived (have you seen them yet?), but they will not be displayed until September 23.   (Lowercase for *have*.)

You will find this reference helpful (Chapter 8 especially).   (Capital for *Chapter* because it is the title of a specific chapter.)

To Enclose a Sentence That Stands Alone. When the words enclosed in parentheses are not *part of* a sentence but are entirely independent, the first word is capitalized and the end punctuation is placed *inside* the closing parenthesis.

It is essential, of course, for every manager to adhere strictly to the corporate guidelines for interviewing and hiring personnel. (Please read the enclosed booklet, and discuss any questions with someone in the Personnel Department.)

Our marketing strategies are based on the plan that the Executive Committee approved last March. (See the minutes of the meeting of the Executive Committee dated March 21, or call Amanda Whitman for a copy.)

EDITING PRACTICE 2

Apply the punctuation principles you have just learned. Insert punctuation marks in the following sentences.

1. In such cases be sure to 1) send a copy of the customer's letter to the Legal Department and 2) include a draft copy of your reply.
2. Do you agree that the best sites for such stores are malls and major shopping centers (for example, the Pheasant Run Mall?)
3. She suggested spreading the costs over a three-year period. (I prefer amortizing the costs over a five-year period, don't you)?

4. Ms. Goode will not be able to attend the workshop (she will be attending an engineering conference in Detroit) however, her assistant manager will be available.
5. Will the container hold at least 2 liters (about 2 quarts?)
6. One suggestion was to invest in very conservative bonds (for example, Treasury bills;) however, Treasury bills are too short-term for our goals.

The Apostrophe

The primary use of the apostrophe is in forming possessives of nouns. In addition, the apostrophe is commonly used in contractions. Less often, the apostrophe is used to form "special" plurals and to show where numbers have been omitted.

In Possessives of Nouns. As you already learned, the apostrophe is used to indicate the possessive forms of nouns.

Noun	Possessive Form
attorney	my *attorney's* office
attorneys	our *attorneys'* offices
assistant manager	the *assistant manager's* decision
assistant managers	those *assistant managers'* decision
Mrs. Ford	*Mrs. Ford's* invoice
the Fords	The *Fords'* invoice

In Contractions. Contractions are shortened forms of words, such as *won't* for "will not," *shouldn't* for "should not," *isn't* for "is not," and *aren't* for "are not."

The results of the survey *aren't* what we anticipated.   ("Are not.")

In "Special" Plurals. The apostrophe is *not* generally used to form plurals; however, an exception is the plural form of a letter or of a word that might otherwise be confusing without the apostrophe.

For some strange reason this printer is printing i's and a's very sloppily.   (Without the apostrophes the plural forms of the letters *i* and *a* might be misread as the words *is* and *as*.)

The apostrophe is not necessary for the plural forms of most capital letters (of course, the plurals of *A*, *I*, and *U* are exceptions). But plurals of lowercase letters (*t's* and *h's*, for example) and lowercase abbreviations (*f.o.b.'s*) could easily be confused without apostrophes.

To Show Omitted Numerals. The apostrophe is used in year numbers such as *'79* and *'84* to show that the first two numbers—*19*—have been omitted.

EDITING PRACTICE 3

Practice what you have just learned by inserting apostrophes as needed in the following sentences.

1. Lets discuss two of our best sales years—85 and 87.
2. Only Joels careful proofreading saved us from a costly error.
3. Havent you sent your forms to the Personnel Department yet?
4. Have you heard about Daniels winning the Most Valuable Employee Award?
5. Did you get your supervisors approval to change your vacation schedule?
6. No, you certainly shouldnt leave negotiable instruments lying around the office.

COMMUNICATION LABORATORY

APPLICATION EXERCISES

A. On a separate sheet of paper, indicate the correct punctuation for the following sentences. Write *OK* for any sentence that has no error.

1. No, Ms. Quinn, theres no extra discount for purchasing large quantities.
2. A $10,000 prize (can you imagine that) will be awarded to the winner of the sales contest.
3. You must complete and submit the following forms (all are available from the Personnel Department) a tax-withholding form, a life insurance form, and a medical insurance form.
4. As soon as shes ready, we will go to the ticket counter to confirm our reservations.
5. Expenses for the first quarter were down—a decrease of nearly 20 percent!—according to our comptroller.
6. Call Johns office 555-7500 to confirm our afternoon meeting.
7. Use the listing of authorized agents (its printed at the back of this booklet) to find out more about this once-in-a-lifetime offer.
8. Because the cost of tin has risen drastically (almost 30 percent over the last two years) we are now looking for a substitute metal.
9. As you know, 50 percent of the employees arent eligible for this expanded medical coverage.
10. Ms. Rosenblatt and I went to the same college; she was a member of the Class of 83.
11. If youd like to attend the Computer Show, call Mike Walsh for a ticket.
12. Has Ms. Fishers agent returned my call yet?
13. The radius of the gear is only 25 centimeters (10 inches,) according to the specifications sheet.
14. By Friday we must 1) submit a rough budget for travel and entertainment, 2) total all expenses for the first quarter of the year, and 3) update the production schedule for our top-priority projects.
15. His managers instructions were to send all check requests and petty cash vouchers to Ms. Shapiro.

B. Find and correct any errors in the following sentences. Write *OK* for any sentence that has no error.

1. Send the original photographs to the Graphic Arts Department (it's still on the fifteenth floor, isn't it).
2. The winner of the first prize for management effectiveness was Eleanor Chang, second prize, Bert Palmer, and third prize, Dina Clancy.
3. Ms. Tyson spent the first few minutes as you know singling out all the staff members who deserved extra credit.
4. The deadline for submitting the completed forms is Friday at 6 p.m..
5. Is the deadline next Friday at 6 p.m?
6. Bob is the director of marketing, Nancy is the chief product manager for our industrial products division.
7. "The primary concern" she continued, "is the safety of all employees in each of our plants".
8. Mr. Crosby considered all three estimates "too costly", he asked us to get three additional estimates from different suppliers.
9. Please be sure to complete this form. Before you attend next week's seminar.
10. She simply replied "Is there any reason for not canceling this agreement?"
11. Thanks to Donnas extra efforts, we were able to complete the prototype in time for the shareholders' meeting.
12. Submit your product specifications and prices by March 15. If you want to list your new products in the fall catalog.
13. Has Eileen reviewed the advertising campaign that Jerry and Leonia are developing.
14. Amanda wants to discuss these issues with the head of the Electrical Engineering Division but Amanda has been in Europe for the past three weeks.
15. Develop an agenda and send it to the committee members. Before the next committee meeting on Friday, November 12.

C. Edit and revise the following rough-draft paragraph.

The enclosed booklet discusses business ethics for all Blanton employee's. The book clearly tells you, what you can expect of Blanton and what Blanton expects of you. As you will see among the topics covered are conflict's of interest, the rules governing outside employment, handling confidential information, relations with suppliers, and your responsability to report any violations of this code. Blanton Manufacturing has a worldwide reputation for integraty. All of us make every effort to mantain this reputation.

VOCABULARY AND SPELLING STUDIES

A. These words are often confused: *access, excess; maybe, may be.* Explain the differences.

B. Use your dictionary to look up the two different meanings and pronunciations of each of the following words: *consummate* (adjective and verb), *invalid* (noun and adjective), *refuse* (verb and noun), and *entrance* (verb and noun). Next to each word write the part of speech, the pronunciation, and the meaning for that particular word.

C. Fill in the blanks with *y*, *i*, or *ie*, whichever is correct.

1. bus__ness
2. dr__ness
3. occup__ing
4. rel__ance
5. territor__s
6. attorne__s

COMMUNICATING FOR RESULTS

Using References. On her first day on the job, Carla was shown her new office and was given the free time to arrange everything in it to her liking. On the shelves Carla has found a dictionary, a thesaurus, a ZIP Code directory, an atlas, an almanac, and a business writer's handbook. Carla does not have much shelf space, so she decides to put these books in the storeroom. She asks you if you think that is a good idea. What advice would you give to Carla?

U · N · I · T

33 Capitalization

Capital letters make words distinctive. Because they help words to stand out, capitals are used in special cases—for example, to show the reader where a new sentence starts or which words in a title are the most important words. Writers, therefore, must use these special signals correctly. In this unit you will review some of the well-known basic uses of capital letters. In addition, you will learn to avoid some of the common errors writers make with capital letters.

First Words

One of the routine uses of capital letters is to set off first words. Examples follow.

1. First word in a sentence or a group of words used as a sentence:

In 1986 we sold the warehouse on Elm Street and leased space on Grand Avenue. (*In*, a word that is not ordinarily capitalized, *is* capitalized when it begins a sentence.)

Vera asked us whether we are going to the seminar. *Of course!* (Although *of course* is not a complete sentence, it is treated as a complete sentence and *of* is capitalized. Reason: *Of course* is considered a short way of saying, *Of course we are going to the seminar*—a full sentence.)

2. First word in a direct quotation:

Barry asked, "Shouldn't we send these original photographs by messenger?" (The quotation is part of a sentence, yet the first word of the quotation is capitalized. The first word of a quotation is capitalized *only* if it is a complete sentence or it begins with a proper noun.)

3. First word in a question within a sentence:

All of us are wondering, *Will* this equipment be shipped on schedule? (An independent question is included within the sentence, and the capital letter for the first word of that question helps set it off.)

4. First word of each entry in a list or an outline:

The first mailing will include:

1. *A* cover letter explaining the special offer we are making.
2. *A* brochure illustrating the entire product line.
3. *Our* credit-application form.
4. *An* order form.
5. *A* service contract form.
6. *A* reply envelope.

Names of Persons

Names of persons are proper nouns and must be capitalized. The capital letter tells the reader that this is the name of a specific person.

Because there are so many similarities in the spellings of names, be especially careful to follow the exact spelling of a person's name. Note, for example, the following common, similar names:

Steven, Stephen
Carol, Carroll, Caryl
Allen, Alan
Clark, Clarke
Kelly, Kelley
Smith, Smithe, Smyth
Macmillan, MacMillan, McMillan
Van Horne, VanHorne, van Horne

CLASS PRACTICE 1

Provide capitals for the following sentences. Be sure to explain why each of your choices must be capitalized.

1. have jim mcmann and catherine bentley been invited to attend?
2. do you think that you and i can complete all the invoices by friday?
3. perhaps the most important question is, what effect will this have on employee morale?
4. be sure to call mr. carver's office to reschedule our appointment.
5. she distinctly asked, "what is the source of the statistics?"
6. can we process all the invoices by next week? definitely!

Names of Places

These few rules will help you to capitalize place names correctly:

1. Capitalize the names of countries and major geographic areas, streets, parks, rivers, shopping centers, buildings, and so on.

United States	Canada
Georgia	Ontario
Augusta	Toronto
Fourth Street	Blake Avenue
Raritan River	Modesto Park
Willowbrook Mall	Sears Tower

2. Capitalize the word *city* only when it is part of the official name of the city: *Kansas City* and *New York City*, but *the city of Provo.*
3. Capitalize the word *state* only when it follows the name of a state: *Pennsylvania State*, but *the state of Pennsylvania.*
4. Capitalize the word *the* only when it is part of the official name: *The Dalles* (a city in Oregon), *The Hague* (capital of the Netherlands).
5. Capitalize *North, South, East,* and *West* when they are used to refer to specific sections of the country.

   Our headquarters office is in the *South*. We plan to open our first district office in the *North* by next September.   (Referring to specific sections.)

   But do not capitalize such names when they are used simply to indicate directions:

   The warehouse is about 6 miles *east* of Albany and 2 miles *south* of our store.

CLASS PRACTICE 2

Which place names should be capitalized in the following sentences?

1. Our offices in canada—we have one in toronto and one in montreal—submitted the most innovative suggestions.

2. After we attend the conference in st. louis, we will inspect sites in springfield and joplin.
3. Only one store in the pheasant run mall (computer city inc.) has opened so far.
4. A new restaurant in wilkes-barre, pennsylvania, has been selected for our banquet.
5. Do you know where the mayville park section of town is located?
6. Two of our offices in the south—the one in lake city, florida, and the one in new orleans, louisiana—are recording excellent sales.

Names of Things

You have already seen how some proper nouns (the names of specific persons and places) are capitalized. To complete your understanding of when to capitalize proper nouns, you will now learn when to capitalize the names of specific *things*.

Organization Names. Capitalize the names of specific companies, associations, societies, commissions, schools, political parties, clubs, religious groups, and government agencies and bureaus.

> Time Inc.
> United Van Lines
> Warner Communications

Many organization names are equally well known by abbreviations that are written in all-capital letters with no periods. Abbreviations will be discussed in greater detail in Unit 34.

> Radio Corporation of America (RCA)
> Securities and Exchange Commission (SEC)
> Society for the Prevention of Cruelty to Animals (SPCA)
> University of Southern California (USC)

Names of specific departments or divisions in a company or an organization are also capitalized.

> Send these copies to the Payroll Department.   (A specific department.)

> Send copies to every manufacturing division in the corporation.   (Not a specific title.)

Product Names. Capitalize the names of commercial products such as *Coca-Cola*, *Kleenex*, and *Ivory Snow*. But do not capitalize the common nouns that identify the general class of the product.

> Ivory soap
> Kleenex tissues
> Xerox machines
> Zenith televisions

Historical Events and Documents. Capitalize the names of historical events or historical periods, specific treaties, bills, acts, and laws.

> the Vietnam War
> the Bicentennial
> the Medicare Act
> National Secretaries Week

Holidays, Months, and Days of the Week. Capitalize the names of holidays, months, and days of the week.

Veterans Day	Christmas
Passover	Thanksgiving
Memorial Day	Fourth of July
September	October
Monday	Friday

Do not capitalize the names of the seasons—*winter, spring, summer,* and *fall.*

CLASS PRACTICE 3

Which words in the following sentences should be capitalized? Which words should not be capitalized?

1. Write to the united states government printing office for these free brochures.
2. ms. lee, the owner of hillside fashions, attended elgin high school and emory university.
3. She made a large donation to the museum of modern art.
4. During the intermission we served coke, coffee, and tea.
5. Our next meeting is scheduled for monday, october 9, at the lynchburg supply company.
6. Jack Malone, who also works in the purchasing department, is a member of the rotary club.

Proper Adjectives

Because proper adjectives are derived from proper nouns, proper adjectives are also capitalized.

Mexican art	Chinese dialects
German food	Italian operas

Headings

In headings and in titles of books and articles, capitalize the first and last words and all major words. Consider as major words all words except:

1. The articles *a, an,* and *the.*

   How to Become an *Expert* in the *Stock Market*   (Book title.)

2. Conjunctions with fewer than four letters, such as *and, but, or, nor, as,* and *if.*

"Stocks *and* Bonds *and* You"   (Article title.)

3. Prepositions with fewer than four letters, such as *at, for, out, up,* and *in.*

Life *in* the Twenty-First Century   (Heading.)

"Investment With Potential *for* the Future"   (Article. *With* is capitalized because it has four letters.)

"What Are We Waiting *For?*"   (Article. Note that *for* is capitalized because it is the last word in the title.)

For hyphenated words treat each part of the compound individually.

"An Up-to-Date System for Controlling Inventories"

First-Class Travel on a Second-Class Checkbook

CLASS PRACTICE 4

Correct any errors in the use of capitals in the following sentences.

1. If you would like to read an interesting article, read "In The Beginning Was The Company."
2. Her first article, "A Day In The Life Of An Ad Writer," described the zany goings-on in the world of advertising.
3. The soon-to-be-available french, italian, and spanish editions are expected to sell well.
4. Ms. Jacorek, a yugoslavian citizen, currently works for an asian exporting company.
5. The 10 percent discount is limited to General Electric Products only.
6. For a good laugh be sure to read "A Woman's View Of The World Of Television."

Personal and Official Titles

Whenever a person has a title that is written before his or her name, capitalize that title.

Professor Eunice P. Ringenbach
Major Peter Ford MacDonald
Reverend A. J. Loomis

Titles that are written after names are not capitalized unless:

1. The title is that of a high government official.

Among the scheduled speakers is Gerald Weems, a *Senator* who is a leader in environmental protection.   (*Senator* is considered a high official.)

2. The title appears on a displayed line or is being described as part of a displayed line.

Roseanne Ausiello, Treasurer   (The signature line of Ms. Ausiello's letters.)

Ms. Roseanne Ausiello, Treasurer   (The first line of an inside address or an envelope address.)

Send your résumé in confidence to Ms. Roseanne Ausiello, Treasurer, Columbia Productions Inc., 200 Meadowbrook Parkway, Acton, Massachusetts 01720. (Description of a displayed line.)

In all other cases do not capitalize a title that follows a person's name. In addition, do not capitalize *ex-* and *-elect* and *former* and *late* when they are joined to titles (unless, of course, they begin the sentence).

The story about *ex-*President Richard M. Nixon will appear in the March issue.

Mayor-*elect* Farley said that she would appoint a special commission to enforce these regulations.

Is *former* Governor Noonan one of the guest speakers?

Miscellaneous Rules

Short Forms. Do not capitalize short forms such as *company, corporation,* and *college* when they are used in place of full names.

Edna plans to attend Del Mar College beginning next fall. As you know, the *college* is in Corpus Christi, Texas.

Tom and I work in the Research Department. The *department* is now conducting some interesting studies, the results of which should aid the general welfare.

However, capitalize short forms that refer to major government bodies, prominent national officials, and well-known places.

Capitol Hill has been Rosemary's beat since she became a reporter. After several years she has earned the respect of everyone on the *Hill.*

Other short forms that are capitalized are the *Bureau* (referring to the Federal Bureau of Investigation), the *House* (for the House of Representatives), and the *Coast* (for the West Coast).

Letter Parts. Capitalize the first word and any title in the salutation of a letter (and any proper names, of course). Capitalize only the first word in a complimentary closing.

Dear Ms. Sinclair:
Dear Margaret:

Sincerely yours,
Cordially yours,

Family Titles. Capitalize words denoting family relationships only when they are used as a part of a person's name or as a substitute for a person's name.

Mother	BUT:	my mother
Aunt Bernice		your aunt

School Subjects. Capitalize the names of languages and of specific numbered courses. Do not capitalize the names of subjects (proper nouns or adjectives are exceptions).

French	Italian
Accounting 101	mathematics
history	business English

COMMUNICATION LABORATORY

APPLICATION EXERCISES

A. On a separate sheet of paper, indicate the correct capitalization of words in the following sentences.

1. Mr. Chesterton, the Comptroller of the Company, must approve all purchases over $5000.
2. We generally begin planning the ads for our Spring styles in september or october.
3. Send a copy of these forms to the Manager of the purchasing department.
4. Leslie Warner, formerly with our London Office, has joined the executive staff here at our Headquarters.
5. Here is a very informative article: "How To Get The Most From Your IRA."
6. Connie Daniels, the supervisor of the Credit Department, does volunteer work for the democratic party, doesn't she?
7. The store in the oakdale mall offers plenty of space, but the lease agreement is too restrictive.
8. Edna and I enjoy traveling in the south—especially in the Atlanta Area.
9. Can we complete this project by the end of the week? absolutely!
10. When the senator arrives (she's our Keynote Speaker), please seat her at this table.
11. In his latest News Conference the president announced his plans for increasing employment throughout the Country.
12. Dr. Graham certainly proved to be a superb speaker; he was recommended by the Boston chamber of commerce.
13. Sheila began working for the Company after she was graduated from Iowa central community college, which is in fort Dodge, Iowa.

14. Her speech, "The Secret To A Successful Career On Wall Street," was greeted with loud applause.
15. The site for the annual sales convention is selected on a rotating basis: one year, in the south; the next, in the east; and so on.

B. Correct any errors in the following sentences. Write *OK* for any sentence that has no error.

1. If he had wrote to the client sooner, he would have settled this claim by now.
2. Because Chicago Illinois is the most convenient site for our Sales Representatives, we generally hold our major meetings there.
3. Did you say that Joan Tiller will chair the committee.
4. Wesco Drug Company is one of the leading manufacturers of vitamins, Wesco has been our major supplier of nutritional products since 1973.
5. When he was graduated from Business School in 1985, Howard started working in the security department in our main building.
6. If you would like any more of them booklets for the employees in your Department, Ms. Bentley, please let us know.
7. Yes, the Personnel Department will be able to provide you with part-time help. If you call in advance to discuss your specific needs.
8. Of course, if Marsha wants Annette and myself to coordinate all the workshops, we will be glad to do so.
9. Because Ms. Grayson flight to Amsterdam was canceled, she was able to attend our monthly production meeting.
10. Since he been in charge of the Graphic Arts Department, Elrod has introduced many timesaving and money-saving procedures.
11. Yes, I am sure that the idea of reorganizing the entire division was her's.
12. Among the successful new franchises on the east coast is the one in Lowell, Massachusetts.
13. John Williams who is considered an expert in this field has reviewed the proposal and has submitted his detailed critique to the Executive Board.
14. The person who is considered an expert in this field is John Williams.
15. Ms. O'Connor has been busy researching materials for an article she is writing, "How To Manage You're Time Effectively."

C. Most of the errors in the following paragraph are capitalization errors—but not all. Find and correct each error.

The keynote speaker for next saturdays' dinner meeting of the Glenwood civic association will be Dr. Vanessa Gravilek, a Former Professor of Psychology. The title of Dr. Gravileks' speech is "The Need for Improved Productivity among Office Workers." Admission is free to Members.

VOCABULARY AND SPELLING STUDIES

A. These words are often confused: *credible, creditable; metal, medal, meddle.* Explain the differences.

B. Identify the synonyms in the following groups of words.

1. imminent, professional, volatile, approaching
2. genuine, spacious, commodious, infantile
3. superficial, ridiculous, shallow, serious
4. prestige, fairness, renown, panorama
5. disparage, value, discredit, distrust

C. What is the correct plural form for each of the following nouns?

1. runner-up
2. agenda
3. handful
4. bill of sale
5. go-between
6. analysis
7. agency
8. attorney
9. decision-maker
10. layout

COMMUNICATING FOR RESULTS

Telephone Effectiveness. You overhear your coworker Edward answering the phone one day. The conversation goes like this:

> Edward: Hello.
> Caller: Who is this?
>
> Edward: Whom do you want to speak to?
> Caller: I was trying to reach someone in the Trust Department.
>
> Edward: This is the Trust Department. May I help you?
> Caller: Yes—Is Ronnie Lipton there?
>
> Edward: Yes.
> Caller: May I speak to her, please?

How effective do you think this conversation is? Suggest some ways that it could be improved.

34 Abbreviations and Symbols

If you look closely at the way we speak and write, you quickly see that Americans certainly enjoy taking shortcuts! Perhaps the most obvious indicator of our preference for shortcuts is our use of abbreviations. *CRT* (for "cathode-ray tube"), *EFI* (for "electronic fuel injection"), and *WP* (for "word processing") are just a few of the abbreviations that have been coined in the recent past and are already becoming common.

As with all the other tools of writing, abbreviations are indeed helpful, but there are rules for their use. As you study this unit, you will master the correct ways to use abbreviations and symbols in your writing.

Personal Titles

Because we are so accustomed to using abbreviations such as *Mr., Mrs.*, and *Dr.*, we may be tempted to abbreviate all titles with names. However, as you will see below, not all titles should be abbreviated.

Titles After Names. Always abbreviate the following titles when they are written after a name:

> Jr. (for "Junior")
> Sr. (for "Senior")
> B.S. (for "Bachelor of Science")
> Ph.D. (for "Doctor of Philosophy")
> D.D. (for "Doctor of Divinity")

Likewise, abbreviate all other academic titles that follow a name.

> Andrew P. Young Jr., D.D.S.
> Clarissa Melon-Ross, M.D.

Titles Before Names. Always abbreviate the following titles when they are used before personal names: *Dr., Mr., Messrs.* (the plural of *Mr.*), *Mrs., Ms.,* and *Mses.* or *Mss.* (plural forms of *Ms.*). The titles *Miss, Misses,* and *Mesdames* are complete words and are not followed by periods. Note how the singular and the plural forms of these titles are used before names.

Singular	Plural
Miss Clara P. Dubois	the Misses Dubois
Ms. Jane Carlton	the Mses. Carlton
Mrs. Samantha Graye	the Mesdames Graye
Mr. Paul Dunham	the Messrs. Dunham

In general, spell out all other titles used with personal names.

Professor Harris P. Truscott	Mayor DeMaria
Senator Weinberg	Representative Murdock
Governor McKinley	Officer Jenkins

Military Titles. In formal correspondence spell out long military titles. In informal correspondence and when space is limited, abbreviate long military titles.

Brigadier General Clay B. Flagg   (Formal)

Lt. Col. Marilyn C. Hoolihan   (Informal)

Titles of Respect. *Reverend* and *Honorable* are titles of respect used in addressing the clergy and government officials of certain rank. In formal usage spell out these titles and use the word *the* before them. In informal usage omit the word *the* and use the abbreviation *Rev.* or *Hon.* if you wish.

the Reverend James K. Filbert   (Formal)
Rev. James K. Filbert   (Informal)

the Honorable Clarissa J. Fenimore   (Formal)
Hon. Clarissa J. Fenimore   (Informal)

Organization Names

The name of an organization should follow its *official* spelling, punctuation, and capitalization. Thus, if a company uses an abbreviation such as *Co.* or *Bros.* or a symbol such as & or / in its name, use the abbreviation or symbol when writing the name.

Aetna Life & Casualty

Humphrey Bros. Inc.

R. W. Randall Jr. & Associates

Linda Caldora, Ph.D., P.A.   (*P.A.* means "professional association.")

Larkin/Justin/Brown Advertising

As you saw in Unit 33, many organizations are as well known by their abbreviations (usually all-capital abbreviations) as by their full names. Except in the most formal writing, using abbreviations such as the following is correct.

AT&T	American Telephone and Telegraph
AMA	American Medical Association
YWCA	Young Women's Christian Association
IRS	Internal Revenue Service
NLRB	National Labor Relations Board
AFL-CIO	American Federation of Labor–Congress of Industrial Organizations
AAA	American Automobile Association
WABC	(Radio station call letters)
CORE	Congress on Racial Equality
NASD	National Association of Securities Dealers

If your reader might not know the meaning of the abbreviation, spell out the full name followed by the abbreviation in parentheses.

Among the bidders was National Cash Register (NCR). In our meetings with representatives of NCR, we discussed all our various requirements for a computerized billing system, and NCR's engineers are now studying our needs.

CLASS PRACTICE 1

Which words should be abbreviated in the following sentences, and which ones should be spelled out? Write *OK* if no changes are needed.

1. Please ask Mister Friedlander to attend this afternoon's meeting, Sara.
2. Does Joanne still work for the IRS?
3. Have you already interviewed Wm. LeBaron for the open marketing position?
4. Among the major manufacturers of computers are AT&T, IBM, and NCR.
5. One investment that our analysts favor is stock in Control Data Corporation (CDC). The reasons for recommending CDC stock follow.
6. Yes, Sen. Lloyd is a former partner in this firm.

Other Abbreviations

As you read the following discussions, remember that the "general rule" is to spell out terms and expressions in the body of a business letter or memo. However, when the writing is considered "technical," abbreviations are acceptable because they can often save time without sacrificing clarity. On the other hand, abbreviations are not only acceptable but often *mandatory* on business forms and in charts and tables because of severe space restrictions.

General Terms and Expressions. Spell out most general terms and expressions in business letters and memos.

1. When the days of the week or the months of the year *must* be abbreviated (for example, in charts and tables and on business forms), use the following abbreviations:

Sun.	Thurs.
Mon.	Fri.
Tues.	Sat.
Wed.	

Jan.	Jun.	Oct.
Feb.	Jul.	Nov.
Mar.	Aug.	Dec.
Apr.	Sept.	

Do not abbreviate *May*.

2. Always abbreviate *a.m.* and *p.m.*, but use these abbreviations only when preceded by figures.

The meeting is scheduled for 10 a.m.   (Note that writing *10:00* is unnecessary.)

Let's begin this project in the morning.   (Not *in the a.m.*)

3. Abbreviate expressions such as the following only on forms and in charts or tables where space is restricted. In all other cases write out the full word or words.

ea.	each
doz.	dozen
acct.	account
chg.	charge
ASAP	as soon as possible

For a complete listing of commonly used abbreviations, refer to a business writer's handbook or a dictionary.

Mailing Addresses. Spell out all parts of street addresses (except numbers, of course). When space is limited, use the following abbreviations:

N.	North	St.	Street
S.	South	Ave.	Avenue
E.	East	Rd.	Road
W.	West	Blvd.	Boulevard
		Pkwy.	Parkway

961 East 96 Street

10 North Willow Avenue

110-75 S. Martin Luther King Jr. Blvd.   (Limited space.)

The words *Post Office* may be spelled out or abbreviated in box numbers.

Post Office Box 789 *or* P.O. Box 789

On the last line of a mailing address, either spell out the state name or use the appropriate two-letter abbreviation (see page 313). In either case, however, do *not* use a comma before the ZIP Code number.

Bryan, Ohio 43506

Bryan, OH 43506

Do not abbreviate any part of a city name except *St.* in cities such as *St. Louis* and *St. Paul.*

ABBREVIATIONS OF STATES, TERRITORIES, AND POSSESSIONS OF THE UNITED STATES

AL	Alabama	Ala.	MO	Missouri	Mo.
AK	Alaska	. . .	MT	Montana	Mont.
AZ	Arizona	Ariz.	NE	Nebraska	Nebr.
AR	Arkansas	Ark.	NV	Nevada	Nev.
CA	California	Calif.	NH	New Hampshire	N.H.
CZ	Canal Zone	C.Z.	NJ	New Jersey	N.J.
CO	Colorado	Colo.	NM	New Mexico	N. Mex.
CT	Connecticut	Conn.	NY	New York	N.Y.
DE	Delaware	Del.	NC	North Carolina	N.C.
DC	District of Columbia	D.C.	ND	North Dakota	N. Dak.
			OH	Ohio	. . .
FL	Florida	Fla.	OK	Oklahoma	Okla.
GA	Georgia	Ga.	OR	Oregon	Oreg.
GU	Guam	. . .	PA	Pennsylvania	Pa.
HI	Hawaii	. . .	PR	Puerto Rico	P.R.
ID	Idaho	. . .	RI	Rhode Island	R.I.
IL	Illinois	Ill.	SC	South Carolina	S.C.
IN	Indiana	Ind.	SD	South Dakota	S. Dak.
IA	Iowa	. . .	TN	Tennessee	Tenn.
KS	Kansas	Kans.	TX	Texas	Tex.
KY	Kentucky	Ky.	UT	Utah	. . .
LA	Louisiana	La.	VT	Vermont	Vt.
ME	Maine	. . .	VI	Virginia Islands	V.I.
MD	Maryland	Md.	VA	Virginia	Va.
MA	Massachusetts	Mass.	WA	Washington	Wash.
MI	Michigan	Mich.	WV	West Virginia	W. Va.
MN	Minnesota	Minn.	WI	Wisconsin	Wis.
MS	Mississippi	Miss.	WY	Wyoming	Wyo.

Use the two-letter abbreviations on the left when abbreviating state names in addresses. In any other situation that calls for abbreviations of state names, use the abbreviations on the right.

Letter and Memo Notations. A few "specialized" abbreviations serve unique functions in letters and memos. One is *cc:* (or *cc,* without the colon), which indicates that a *c*arbon *c*opy or *c*ourtesy *c*opy will be sent to the person or persons listed.

cc: Myron Schwartz
    Helen P. Boynton

The abbreviation *PS:* is used to indicate a *postscript*—an addition to the body of the letter positioned at the end of the letter.

PS: Why not use the enclosed coupons to get a 25 percent discount on your next purchase!

The word *Enclosure* is usually spelled out on letters but may be abbreviated *Enc.* on memos. The purpose of the enclosure notation, of course, is to indicate that something is included with the letter or memo.

See Units 40 to 49 for examples of the above notations.

Units of Measurement. In technical writing units of measurement are abbreviated. However, in a letter or memo in which a measurement is given only once or twice, spell out the measurement.

The desktop model is only 14.1 in long, 15.5 in deep, and 7.4 in high; it weighs 35 lbs; and it handles standard 8½- by 11-in paper.   (Technical copy.)

The new model handles both 8½- by 11-inch paper and 8½- by 14-inch paper.   (Spell out *inch* in nontechnical copy.)

The abbreviations of some customary and metric measurements are listed below. Note that the same abbreviation is used both in singular and in plural constructions.

Customary Measurements		**Metric Measurements**	
in	inch(es)	mm	millimeter(s)
ft	foot, feet	cm	centimeter(s)
yd	yard(s)	m	meter(s)
mi	mile(s)	L	liter(s)
oz	ounce(s)	mg	milligram(s)
pt	pint(s)	g	gram(s)
qt	quart(s)		
gal	gallon(s)		
lb	pound(s)		

For a comprehensive listing use a general or a technical dictionary or a business writer's handbook.

Forming Plurals of Abbreviations

The plurals of abbreviations may be formed in various ways. Read the following general guidelines, but refer to a writer's handbook or a dictionary whenever you are in doubt.

1. For all-capital abbreviations, as well as mixed abbreviations that end in a capital letter, add *s* to form the plural:

CPA	CPAs
Ph.D.	Ph.D.s

2. For most abbreviations that end in a period, add *s* to form the plural, as follows:

No.	Nos.
dept.	depts.
mo.	mos.

3. However, for abbreviations that consist of individual lowercase letters separated by periods, add *'s* to form the plural:

f.o.b.	f.o.b.'s
c.o.d.	c.o.d.'s

4. For the plurals of abbreviated personal titles, follow this list:

Mr.	Messrs.
Ms.	Mses. or Mss.
Mrs.	Mesdames
Dr.	Drs.

5. For abbreviations of units of measure, use the same form in both singular and plural constructions:

1 kg	4 kg	27 kg
1 yd	7 yd	87 yd

6. In references, for the plural of *p.* ("page"), write *pp.*; for the plural of *l.* ("line"), write *ll.*:

(See pp. 356–357, ll. 120–158.)

As you can see from the number of variations above, it is essential to check a writer's handbook whenever you are in doubt.

CLASS PRACTICE 2

Are abbreviations used correctly in the following sentences? Should any additional words be abbreviated?

1. Because Mister Janusck is now out of town, we are canceling our 3 PM production meeting.
2. We should require about three or four yds of fabric, according to Henry.
3. On Tues. or Wed. of next week, let's review all these accts.
4. Has Doctor Demerest arrived yet? Is she scheduled to be here this a.m.?
5. Do you know the current value of I.B.M. stock, Mister Gregus?
6. Send copies of these price lists to our Tex. office and our Fla. office, please.
7. A lens of about 135 mms is what we need.
8. When are you leaving for Saint Louis?

COMMUNICATION LABORATORY

APPLICATION EXERCISES

A. On a separate sheet of paper, make any corrections needed in the following sentences. Write *OK* for each sentence that has no error.

1. Alicia P. Stephenson, PhD, one of the senior members of the Research Department, has developed this customer survey questionnaire.
2. Ellen suggested that we update the listing of chg. accts., and I fully agree with her.
3. The 20-second commercials on W.Q.X.R. and W.N.C.N. have been the most effective, according to this report.
4. Ron is now working toward his M.B.A., which he expects to complete next June.
5. One of the largest manufacturers of computer components is the Anderson Electronics Corporation in Ft. Washington, PA.
6. The messenger service will not pick up cartons weighing more than 70 lbs.
7. Of course, Mr. Rubin, we will try to replace the damaged equipment ASAP.
8. The I.B.M. technician has already repaired this machine, Mister Kline.
9. Doctor Samuelson has submitted his research study to the A.M.A., hasn't he?
10. Sales for the first three mos. of this year have exceeded estimated budgets by more than 15 percent.
11. In Jan.—certainly no later than Feb.—we will have the new system in operation throughout the comp.
12. We need about a gal of this special glue for photographs.
13. According to this catalog, the price is only $15 ea. when purchased in quantities of a doz. or more.
14. The chairperson said, "We are running late; I suggest that we continue this discussion in the a.m."
15. The directions recommend mixing about an oz or so of the powder in a pt of the liquid.

B. Find and correct all the errors in the following sentences. Write *OK* if a sentence has no error.

1. She asked, "Does Ms. Christenson and Mr. Levesque have any additional information on the status of the union negotiations?"
2. Anne Simpson, who has been heading a committee to study hiring practices throughout the corporation will deliver the speech at this evening's meeting.

3. All the managers agree that we must improve our order-fulfillment services, however, we do not consider a new computer system the answer to all our problems.

4. The new plant is on Kennedy Blvd., not W. Hanson Rd.

5. Let's take these packages to the P.O. as soon as possible, Carole.

6. Please note that the first package is addressed to Albany, GA, and the second one is addressed to Albany, NY.

7. If you would like to increase your life insurance for just pennies more each month. Complete the enclosed form and return it with your next premium.

8. Because this is a rush project, we will try our best to complete it by Thurs. or Fri.

9. Betty said "Anyone who wants to apply for either of the two supervisory positions that are now open should contact Ira Gregorian in the Personnel Department."

10. Because we were temporarily out of stock on Model X100 microwave ovens. We were instructed to substitute Model X250, which sells for about $50 more.

11. Most of the representatives in this district has already taken the Telephone Techniques workshop.

12. One of the foremost ad agencies in this city is Trent/Hood/Reynolds Associates.

13. Alvin and Yolanda have been assigned to work on the revision of the procedures manual, they have more management experience than anyone else in the company.

14. As a result of the commercials on WRKO, we gained three new accts. in just two days!

15. After you read Chapt. 3, you will better understand how to identify and reach a target audience.

C. Revise the following paragraph.

The personal computer market is growing tremendously each year. I.B.M., Radio Shack, Apple, and other companies, are predicting increased sales of personal computers for this year and the next. We have decided, therefore, to study the potential of a new magazine for owners of personal computers, we have tentatively called this magazine The Home Computer. The Harrison Agency will conduct a feasibility study to determine the potential, of such a magazine. By September 30 we expect to have, all the information necessary to make our decision.

VOCABULARY AND SPELLING STUDIES

A. These words are often confused: *continual, continuous; magnificent, munificent.* Explain the differences.

B. For each of the following words name an *antonym*—a word that is opposite in meaning.

1. different   4. objective
2. complicated   5. receive
3. sensible   6. careful

C. Add *el* or *le* to each of the following words.

1. lab___   4. nick___
2. mod___   5. pick___
3. gigg___   6. whist___

COMMUNICATING FOR RESULTS

Pompous Prose. A coworker wrote the following paragraph, copying the style she had read in an old report. How would you rewrite this to make it sound clear and natural?

Henry Marcusi terminated his employment with our organization as of the first day of August, A.D. 1983, citing as his reason the acquisition of another position with a firm also headquartered in this city. The same Mr. Marcusi performed exceptionally well in his position here, which was as media planner in our advertising department. In his tenure with our firm (the extent of which was precisely three years six months), he always achieved the established goals within budget and on schedule. Our consensus is that we would consider reemploying him if he were to apply to us at some future time for a position with us.

U · N · I · T

35 Numbers

Numbers provide our communications with specific information—quantities, dollar amounts, percentages, measurements, dates. The importance of numbers and the precision with which they are used are obviously critical to accurate communication. Begin, then, to study when to write numbers in words and when to write them in figures.

Numbers Written as Words

Generally, numbers are expressed in figures in business correspondence. However, there are occasions when numbers are written in words.

Numbers From 1 Through 10. When used in isolated instances, the numbers from 1 through 10 should be written in words.

Each of the *four* speakers has *one* hour to complete his or her presentation.

Of the *nine* proposals that were submitted to the panel, only *five* were accepted.

Numbers That Begin Sentences. Write in words any number that begins a sentence. Rephrase the sentence if the number is too awkward to express in words.

Thirteen districts have reported that this new product line is a smashing success.

Two hundred sixty-three sales representatives have attended the Telephone Techniques seminar.   (Awkward.)

The Telephone Techniques seminar has been attended by *263* sales representatives.   (Rephrased sentence is not awkward.)

When spelling out large numbers (numbers over 1000), use the shortest form possible.

Fifteen hundred orders were received in the first week of the sale!   (Not *One thousand five hundred.*)

Twenty-four hundred samples have been distributed to qualified buyers throughout the area.   (Not *Two thousand four hundred.*)

Fractions Standing Alone. Write in words a fraction that stands alone without a whole number.

Approximately *one-half* of the responses commented favorably on the new billing system.

Ages. Ages are spelled out unless they are considered significant statistics or technical measurements.

Caryn Johnson has been appointed director of sales. Caryn began working for Logan Industries at the age of *nineteen*, when she joined our sales staff in Ames, Iowa.   (A general reference to age.)

Only employees who will have reached age 55 by January 1 of next year are eligible for this new policy.   (A significant statistic.)

Periods of Time. General periods of time are usually written in words.

Although these ads were created about *fifteen* years ago, they are still effective among young adults.

CLASS PRACTICE 1

Find and correct any errors in the following sentences. Write *OK* if there are no errors.

1. 19 applicants called for appointments within the past hour.
2. Perhaps we should appoint a panel of 3 or 4 people with production experience to study these issues.
3. The board of directors has voted against the mandatory retirement age of seventy.
4. If you or your staff members need 2 or 3 of these helpful manuals, call Nancy Dobson in the Personnel Department.
5. Mr. Hammond, who has managed our Chicago regional office for the past twelve years, will be appointed to the new position.
6. The margin on these products, as Ms. Wilson explained, is about ½ more than the margin on those products.
7. Kay asked whether we will be able to send her 10 or 12 brochures.
8. One thousand five hundred employees have signed up for the payroll savings plan as of this morning.

Numbers Written as Figures

Writing numbers in figures is generally preferred in business writing because figures are emphatic and specific. Below are the instances in which numbers should be written in figures.

Numbers Higher Than 10. You already saw that numbers from 1 through 10 are written in words. Numbers above 10 are written in figures.

We requested bids from *16* suppliers that were approved by the committee.

Sherry estimates that from *200* to *250* employees will opt for the additional coverage.

Sums of Money. Write sums of money in figures.

According to this estimate, the printing cost for each manual will be $2.43.

A 4-ounce bottle sells for $6; an 8-ounce bottle, $10.   (Note that the additional zeros in *$6.00* and *$10.00* are not necessary.)

Amounts smaller than $1 are expressed with the word *cents*.

Although the estimated savings is only *12 cents* an issue, the total savings at the end of the year is several thousand dollars.

Amounts in millions and billions are written in figures, with the word *million* or *billion* spelled out.

The "asking price," according to industry experts, will exceed $3.6 million.   (Also acceptable: *3.6 million dollars*.)

Time. Use figures with *a.m.* and *p.m.* Use either words or figures with *o'clock:* words for greater formality; figures for less formality.

Her estimated time of arrival is *9:45* p.m.

We will leave for the airport at 9 o'clock.

We invite you to be our guest at the banquet, which will begin at *nine* o'clock. (More formal than *9 o'clock.*)

House, Street, ZIP Code Numbers. House numbers (except for the number *one*) are always written in figures. Note that the abbreviation *No.* or the sign # should not be used with house or box numbers.

The new address is *One* Wall Street.

Mail her correspondence to her home address: *191* Central Avenue, East Peoria, Illinois 61611.

Send the package under his name to Box *8989*, Indianapolis, Indiana 46227.

Spell out street names from *1* through *10.* Use figures for numbered street names over *10.* When figures are used, the ending *st, d,* or *th* may be omitted if a word such as *East* or *West* separates the house number from the street number. If there is no such word between the house number and the street number, use the original ending to prevent misreading.

1212 Fourth Street
350 West 67 Avenue
767 23d Street

Use one space before the ZIP Code number; use no punctuation after the ZIP Code in an address block.

Ms. Elana Howard
1125 22d Avenue
Grand Rapids, MI 49502-0000

Decimals. Decimals are always expressed in figures: *5.7, 11.45, 9.6454.* For clarity use a zero before the decimal point when there is no whole number: 0.25.

Mixed Numbers. Write a mixed number (a whole number plus a fraction) in figures, except at the beginning of a sentence.

The cost of the project was 2½ times higher than had been estimated.

When spelling out a mixed number (for example, at the beginning of a sentence), use the word *and* to separate the whole number from the fraction.

Three *and* one-half times more orders came in in July than in June.

Numbers in Series; Related Numbers. When one number in a series must be written in figures, write all the numbers in figures.

Our department consists of *one* manager, *two* secretaries, and *six* ad writers.

BUT: Our department consists of 2 managers, 5 secretaries, *12* media buyers, and *13* ad writers.   (Because the numbers *12* and *13* are above *10*, they must be expressed in figures; likewise, all other numbers in the series should be expressed in figures.)

Related numbers are numbers that refer to the same kinds of things. Treat related numbers similarly—write them either in figures or in words.

Kenneth mailed *32* brochures to his special customers and has already received *8* orders in just two weeks!   (Ordinarily, *8* would be spelled out; here, however, it is related to the figure *32* and must be expressed similarly—in figures. Note that *two* is not related to the other numbers and is therefore correctly spelled out.)

Percentages. Use figures with the word *percent*.

Last week the interest rate was about *8* percent; this week the rate is fluctuating between *9* and *10* percent.

The symbol % is generally used in technical writing and in tables and invoices, not in general correspondence. Always use figures with the symbol %, with no space between the figure and the symbol: *3.2%*, *6.75%*, and so on.

Weights and Measures. Use figures to express numbers in weights, measures, and distances.

We need several *3*-gallon containers of this lubricant.

Each solution has precisely *4.5* grams of solvent.

Miscellaneous. When a number is considered "significant," it is generally expressed in figures, even when the number is under 10.

We allow *5* days for a check to clear; for out-of-town checks we allow *6* days.   (Here, the numbers *5* and *6* are significant; they deserve the special emphasis that figures provide.)

Consecutive numbers (as in *100 twenty*-cent stamps) deserve special attention. To avoid the possibly confusing *100 20-cent stamps*, write the smaller of two consecutive numbers in words, even if that number would usually be written in figures.

CLASS PRACTICE 2

Check how well you understand the rules for writing numbers in figures. Correct any errors in the following sentences. Write *OK* if there are no errors.

1. Edison Plastics will move to its new offices at 1 Willow Grove Boulevard in September.

2. Predictably, nine of the 12 word processing operators preferred the same equipment.
3. Significantly, the average inventory level last year was nine days; this year, the average has been 12 days.
4. Sales through the month of August have exceeded our estimate for summer sales by five percent.
5. We taped two 14-column sheets to create this chart.
6. This building is now worth one and a half times its value when we purchased it just three years ago.
7. The records of all four hundred and fifty accounts are filed on this diskette.
8. We plan to hire three sales representatives for our New York office; 11 for our Seattle office; and 14 for our San Francisco office.

Ordinal Numbers in Dates

Numbers such as *1st, 2d, 3d, 4th,* and so on, are called *ordinal numbers.* Follow these rules for using ordinal numbers in dates.

1. Do not use an ordinal ending for the date when the day follows the month: *April 1, September 3, October 13,* and so on.
2. Use an ordinal number when the date precedes the month: *the 1st of April, the 3d of September, the 13th of October,* and so on.

COMMUNICATION LABORATORY

APPLICATION EXERCISES

A. Can you find all the errors in number expression in the following sentences? On a separate sheet of paper, correct any errors. Write *OK* for any sentence that is correct.

1. 350 of the employees in the Wilkes-Barre factory are enrolled in this special program.
2. Please have a messenger take this envelope to Mr. Kinoy's office—his address is 1,301 Vernon Boulevard.
3. Based on your experience, would you say that $500.00 is a fair price?
4. Let's take advantage of the discount—order 250 5-pound boxes.
5. 10 good reasons for starting an IRA are discussed in this informative booklet.
6. Daily compounding increases the effective rate of interest to as much as 11% annually.
7. The dimensions are five and a half inches long by four inches deep by two inches high.
8. All the screws required (6 3-inch flathead screws and 9 1½-inch roundhead screws) are included in the kit.

9. No more than four and a half grams of fat are included in an average serving.
10. Next year's research budget is the highest ever—$2,500,000.
11. Write the deadline date on your calendar: March 30th.
12. Surprisingly, only ⅓ of the shareholders voted in favor of the merger.
13. The total price (which includes six percent sales tax and all shipping charges) is only $1965.75.
14. Although the quality of this paper is far superior to the paper we used for the last printing, the additional cost is only $.09 an issue.
15. Tomorrow at 10:00 a.m. we will discuss the policy in question: No. 189-876-4301.
16. Angela Whitmore, age 42, was identified as the executive vice president's successor in the newspaper reports.
17. If you need only 2 or 3 blank forms, you may take these; if you require more, you may pick up blanks at the IRS office nearest you.
18. If we begin now, we can discuss both issues in about 1 hour.
19. Did you know that Mary Clanton won 1st prize in the monthly sales contest?
20. Copy this address for future reference: Ms. Leonora Martin-Ford, 16,075 Halsey Street, Flagstaff, Arizona 86,001.

B. Find all the errors in the following sentences; write your corrections on a separate sheet of paper. Write *OK* for a sentence that has no error.

1. The list price of this modem is $295.00, but the discount price is only $195.00.
2. The directions suggest mixing five grams of powder in one and a half liters of water.
3. Harry been to one of our regional marketing meetings, hasn't he?
4. Gregory asked whether we had any copies of the affirmative action plan?
5. The increase in the unit cost with the new packaging material is only $.29; however, multiplied over a one-year period, the increase alone totals more than $20,000.
6. The President's goal, as stated in this memorandum to all employees, is to reach ten million dollars in annual sales by the year 1994.
7. 22 of our auditors will be working on this project by the month of July.
8. Please order 12 14-column accounting pads for Jim and I.
9. The entire balance is due in thirty days, as stated in the enclosed copy of the original agreement.
10. So far, we have interviewed eight executive assistants, fourteen recruiters, and twenty-five managers.
11. Frances and her assistant, Ken Thompson, is responsible for all the photography.
12. Be sure to send duplicates to Mr. Rose and I.

13. Only Ms. Cranston, Dr. O'Riley and Mrs. Filbin are scheduled to speak at tonight's banquet, according to this program announcement.
14. One of the primary reasons for appointing a special panel, is to study and improve safety measures in each chemical-producing facility.
15. Karyn is rather eager to start her new job, she will head the Salina, Kansas, district office as of next January 1.

C. Edit the following excerpt from a memorandum.

At Ms. Vernon's request we are scheduling a meeting for the 10 of July. The purpose of the meeting is to discuss sales strategies.

As you know, sales for the first ½ of the year are down about 25%. Among the topics we plan to discuss are, the ways in which we can cut our expense budgets by a total of four hundred thousand dollars. In addition, we will explore some of the reasons we predicted sales so poorly.

VOCABULARY AND SPELLING STUDIES

A. These words are often confused: *deceased, diseased; risky, risqué.* Explain the differences.

B. Among the following words are some of the words most frequently misspelled in the business office. Which words are misspelled?

1. refered
2. sincerly
3. intrest
4. applicible
5. aproximately
6. conveniance
7. comittee
8. reccomend
9. statment
10. aggreement

C. In an effort to save space and at the same time attract attention, vendors often take shortcuts in writing copy for signs. Check the following signs for correct use of numbers. Are there any errors?

1. Special Sale—½ Off!
2. 1 Day Only!
3. All 1-of-a-Kind Bargains!

COMMUNICATING FOR RESULTS

An Honest Error. You proofread twice the letter that was printed for a special mailing to customers. Now, while you are looking at one of the printed copies, you spot an error—a misspelled word that you missed for some reason. Now this error appears on all the several thousand copies that were printed!

What should you do? No one knows about the error but you. Should you tell your supervisor? If so, when?

Chapter

6

Even in this era of automated communication technology, the written word has survived. It is still the basic tool with which ideas, especially in business, are presented. Whether you are writing in longhand or keyboarding on a word processor, you must give life to your ideas. Knowing how to use the principles of effective writing will help you to accomplish this.

The techniques mastered by successful business writers apply to all written forms of communication—especially letters, memos, and reports. Given a situation that requires writing in business, you will be able to do the following when you master the units in this chapter:

1. *Use words, phrases, and clauses so that your messages will be interpreted correctly.*

2. *Avoid stiff and outdated phrases that communicate little information and detract from a positive, conversational tone.*

3. *Use balanced words, phrases, sentences, and paragraphs.*

4. *Apply the techniques for effective sentence and paragraph writing to your messages.*

5. *Develop your written message so that each idea flows smoothly into the next.*

U · N · I · T

36

Using Words Effectively

The extent of your vocabulary is obviously one important factor in your ability to communicate. However, aside from any technical language used in your industry, most of the words you will use in your letters, memos, and reports will be rather common words, everyday words that business people will be familiar with. Thus your ability to write effective business communications is not dependent on your knowledge of fancy, complex terms. Your ability *is* strongly dependent on your skill in selecting the *right words* from among common, everyday words.

Effective business writing, then, is simple and straightforward, not fancy and overly complex. The impact of your written messages—and your *spoken* messages too—will depend strongly on your ability to use conversational words appropriately, to choose positive words, and to achieve variety through your use of synonyms. Your writing success will also depend on how expertly you avoid words that are unnecessary, biased, obsolete, and overused.

Finding "Double Agents"

The meanings of words determine how we react to them. The meanings found in dictionaries are called *denotations*. These are the factual, objective definitions of words.

But many words have additional meanings, secondary meanings that result from personal reactions. These meanings are called *connotations*. For example, would you feel the same about paying "a $5 charge" as you would feel about paying "a $5 *penalty*"? Probably not. Although the amount is the same in both cases ($5), most people bristle at the word *penalty* because it has a strong negative connotation. As consumers we know that we must pay "charges" and we accept them, but no one accepts *penalties* ungrudgingly!

Some words are "double agents"—they have two opposite connotations. Workers may react favorably to *labor union*, for instance, but members of management may not. Likewise, reactions to *Republicans*, *Democrats*, and *strike* will vary, depending on which team one favors. The successful writer is keenly aware of each reader's potential reaction to his or her message and therefore selects words carefully. The successful writer has developed a sensitivity to possible interpretations by the reader. As you choose the words that will make up your message, be sure to watch for "double agents."

Adopting a Conversational Tone

As they keyboard or dictate messages, many business people feel the sudden impulse to impress their readers with an extensive vocabulary. In a telephone or a face-to-face conversation, for example, a person says:

> We need these supplies in our warehouse no later than May 4.

But in a letter that same person might write:

> It is imperative that the complete shipment be received at the above-mentioned address by the fourth of May.

Not only are the words *imperative* and *above-mentioned* a bit showy, but the sentence itself would sound self-important even if these words were replaced. Furthermore, the sentence is several words longer than necessary.

Routine business messages are not opportunities to display the richness of your vocabulary. They are business assignments that require writing clear, direct messages—and such messages are best achieved through the use of a *conversational tone*. Of course, your tone will vary depending on how well you know the reader. Writing to a business associate whom you've known very well for several years, you might say:

> Dear Marisa:
>
> Thanks for sending me the purchase order for the additional brochures you requested. Because you called me quickly, I was able to change the printing quantity before the job reached the Production Department. Anyway, you will have your brochures—all 25,000 of them!—by Friday, June 6.
>
> By the way, Marisa, ...

On the other hand, if you do not know your client very well, you might write:

> Dear Ms. Stein:
>
> Thank you for sending us the revised purchase order for 25,000 of your full-color sales brochures. As you originally requested, all the brochures will be delivered to you on Friday, June 6.
>
> Ms. Stein, you may be interested in . . . .

There is an obvious difference in the style of each excerpt. The very informal, friendly approach of the first example begins with the salutation, *Dear Marisa,* and continues throughout the letter. The second example is more formal. However, both examples use a conversational tone. Despite their differences, neither is stiff or pretentious.

Before you begin writing, then, consider the reader. How well do you know her? What must you tell her? How would you talk with her if she were face-to-face? Consider such questions as you write and you will develop a conversational tone and a degree of formality that are appropriate for that particular reader.

Whether you know the reader well or not at all, you should avoid the terms listed in the left column below and replace them with other more conversational terms, such as those suggested in the right column.

Avoid These Expressions . . .	Instead, Say . . .
1. *Acknowledge receipt of*	1. *Thank you for* or *I received*
"This is to acknowledge receipt of your letter."	"Thank you for writing me about . . . ."
2. *Advise*	2. *Say, tell, let us know*
"Please advise us of your intended delivery date."	"Please let us know when you will deliver the order."
I cannot advise you as to when the contract will be ready."	"I cannot tell you when the contract will be ready."
3. *Am (Are) in receipt of*	3. *Thank you* or *I have received*
"We are in receipt of your check for $81.20."	"Thank you for your check for $81.20."
	"I have received your check for $81.20 and appreciate . . . ."
4. *As per*	4. *As* or *according to*
"We are crediting your account as per instructions."	"As you instructed, we are crediting your account."
	"We are crediting your account, according to your wishes."
5. *At an early date*	5. *Soon* (Or give a specific date.)
"You will hear from us at an early date."	"I will write you soon about . . . ."
	"You will hear from me by August 15 about the new delivery date."
6. *At this time, at present, at the present writing*	6. *Now* (Or omit entirely.)
"My opinion at this time (or *at present*) is that the meeting will take place."	"I now think that the meeting will take place."
	"I believe that the meeting will take place."
7. *Attached hereto*	7. *Attached, here, enclosed*
"Attached hereto is the agreement for your signature."	"Attached is the agreement for your signature."
	"Here is the agreement, which I hope you will sign."

Avoid These Expressions . . .	Instead, Say . . .
8. *Beg*	8. *Ask, request, hope,* and so on
"I beg your indulgence in this matter."	"I request a 30-day extension." "I hope you will allow me another month in which to pay this bill."
9. *Due to the fact that*	9. *As, because, since*
"Due to the fact that our factory is on strike, we cannot . . . ." "You have been placed on our preferred list of customers due to the fact that you always pay promptly."	"Because our factory is on strike, we cannot . . . ." "Since you always pay your bills promptly, we are pleased to list you as a preferred customer."
10. *Duly*	10. Do not use. Superfluous.
"I received your February 8 order, which I duly acknowledge."	"I appreciate your February 8 order."
11. *Enclosed please find*	11. *Enclosed* or *here*
"Enclosed please find your copy of the minutes of our last meeting."	"Enclosed are the minutes . . . ." "Here are the minutes . . . ."
12. *I have before me*	12. Do not use. Superfluous.
"I have before me your reminder of the deadline for my article."	"I am grateful for your reminder of the deadline for my article."
13. *Herewith*	13. Do not use.
"I am sending you a duplicate bid herewith."	"Enclosed (or *attached*) is a duplicate bid."
14. *In re*	14. *Regarding, concerning, as to*
"In re the freight charges, I believe they are high."	"Regarding the freight charges, I believe they are high."
15. *In the event that*	15. *In case* or *if*
"In the event that you cannot arrive on Tuesday evening, I will schedule the conference for Wednesday."	"If you cannot arrive on Tuesday evening, I will schedule the conference for Wednesday."
16. *In this matter*	16. Do not use. Superfluous.
"I will await your action in this matter."	"I will await your action."

Avoid These Expressions . . .	Instead, Say . . .

17. *Kindly*

"If our substitution is not satisfactory, kindly let us know."

17. *Please*

"If the substitution we are sending is not satisfactory, please let us know."

18. *In the amount of*

"Our money order in the amount of $6 is enclosed."

18. *For*

"Our money order for $6 is enclosed."

19. *Party* (referred to a person)

"According to another party in your firm, our record is satisfactory."

19. *Person* (Or use a name or title.)

"According to your credit supervisor (or *another person*, or *Mrs. Black*), our record is satisfactory."

20. *Same*

"I have received your letter and thank you for same."

20. *It, they, them,* or omit.

"Thank you for your letter."

21. *State*

"In response to your inquiry, I wish to state that we can furnish you with the items you specified."

"In your letter you state that you want a ripple finish on the letterheads."

21. *Say, tell,* or omit.

"We can furnish you with the steel plates you need."

"In your letter you say (or *you mention*) that you want a ripple finish on the letterheads."

22. *Take the liberty of*

"I am taking the liberty of sending you the beige, rather than the desert tan, drapery material."

"May I take the liberty of telling you how much we value your business."

22. Omit.

"Therefore, I am sending you the beige, rather than the desert tan, drapery material."

"Many thanks for your business."

23. *Thank you in advance*

"Thank you in advance for any courtesies you can extend Mr. Phillips."

23. Do not use. It is presumptuous to thank a person in advance.

"I would appreciate any courtesies you can extend Mr. Phillips."

24. *The writer*

"The writer wishes to acknowledge receipt of the book."

"Please send the samples to the attention of the writer."

24. *I, me, my*

"Thank you for sending me the book."

"Please send the samples to me."

Avoid These Expressions . . .	Instead, Say . . .
25. *Trust*	25. *Hope, know, believe*
"I trust my suggestion will be satisfactory."	"I hope my suggestion will be satisfactory."
"I trust you will agree with the action I have taken."	"I believe you will agree with the action I have taken."
26. *Under date of*	26. Omit.
"I have your letter under date of May 1."	"I have your May 1 letter."
27. *Under separate cover*	27. *Will send, am sending,* and so on
"I am mailing the back issues under separate cover."	"I will send the back issues to you today."
	"The sample you requested was mailed this morning."
28. *Up to this writing*	28. *So far* or omit.
"Up to this writing I have had no word from the Wilson Company."	"So far I have had no word from the Wilson Company."
	"I have not heard from the Wilson Company."
29. *Would ask, would remind, would say*	29. Do not use *would* in this way.
"I would ask that you bear with us on your delayed order."	"I hope you will understand why your order will be delayed."

Creating a Positive Atmosphere

When you greet someone face-to-face, the words you use help create a certain atmosphere. Your listener will quickly detect—and react negatively to—words that are cold or unpleasant and, as a result, will not feel comfortable. On the other hand, warm, friendly words will put the listener at ease.

When you greet someone in writing, your choice of pleasant, positive words will help make your reader ready to listen to your message. Even when the actual content of your message is negative (for example, when you must return damaged goods to a supplier or reject someone's offer), using cold, irritating words such as the following will only make the problem worse:

blame	delay	fault
careless	dissatisfied	inferior
complaint	error	mistake
defective	failure	negligence

Words like these make readers defensive because they accuse the reader, and accusations are seldom effective. Imagine, for instance, including this sentence in a letter to a supplier:

Because the *defective* motor that you sent us *failed* to work properly, we are of course *dissatisfied* and are returning the *faulty* motor.

Remember the discussion on the word *penalty?* Just as no one likes to be penalized, no one likes to be accused of wrongdoing. Instead, the writer will get better results by choosing words that create a positive atmosphere:

All the Allied products that we have purchased in the past ten years have performed very well. However, the on/off switch for the Allied motor that you recently shipped us has not worked as it should.

Without accusing, without putting the reader on the defensive, the writer builds a case for returning the motor by creating a positive atmosphere.

Cutting Unnecessary Words

Most people value their time—and rightly so. Thus people become annoyed when they are forced, for example, to wait on line for more than a reasonable amount of time or to listen to a 30-minute speech that could have been completed in 10 minutes.

In the same way, readers become annoyed when they are forced to read a letter that is twice as wordy as it should be. The business writer has an obligation to economize by pruning unnecessary words from letters, memos, and reports. Note, for instance, how the wordy examples below can be rewritten concisely.

Wordy	Concise
check in the amount of $5	$5 check
at this point in time	now
I wish to take this opportunity to thank you for	Thank you for . . . .
at all times	always
for the period of a year	annually

Note, too, that each concise example conveys the same message. The meaning is not diluted by the shorter expression. The concise term does the same job but does it more quickly.

Avoiding Biased Terms

America's work force consists of men and women. In all businesses, at all job levels, in all regions of our country, we find both women and men at work, and our language must reflect this reality.

Terms such as *businessman* and *salesman* do not reflect this reality. Worse, such terms completely overlook both the existence of women in the work force and their contributions to government, business, and industry.

As a result business people are careful to avoid biased terms, such as those listed below.

Instead of . . .	Use . . .
fireman	firefighter
mailman	mail carrier
insurance man	insurance agent
foreman	supervisor
stewardess	flight attendant
policeman or policewoman	police officer
businessman	business person, business worker
businessmen	business people, business workers
salesman	sales representative, salesperson, salesclerk

Note that even when a bias-free term such as *sales representative* is used, the rest of the sentence may still betray bias:

Every sales representative in the country will improve *his* effectiveness by completing this sales techniques seminar.

Is "Every sales representative in the country" a man? No. Therefore, change the pronoun *his* to *his or her*. Or change the sentence to the plural form.

All sales representatives in the country will improve *their* effectiveness by completing this sales techniques seminar.

Adding Extra Interest Through Synonyms

Word *variety* contributes to successful writing. Colorless words and overused words are about as interesting as the tenth rerun of a mediocre TV series. Overused words include the following:

good	awful	little	big	think	fix	fantastic	bad
fine	know	lovely	say	come	go	great	super

Overused does not mean "wrong," of course. But when you want to describe something special, overused words just won't do.

To introduce your new products, Ms. Robertson, we plan to develop a *good* television-advertising campaign. We will begin the campaign with *great* commercials aired during prime time. Our *fine* artists will develop *fantastic* graphics that will do a *really good* job of attracting viewers' attention.

Of course, there is nothing negative about *good, great, fine,* and so on. Quite the contrary! But will Ms. Robertson consider this campaign "special"? Will she willingly spend perhaps millions of dollars of her company's money on this *good* campaign? Will she easily be convinced that your *fine* artists will be successful? All too common and overused, these words no longer convey any special meanings.

Instead, consider these substitutes:

a *unique* or an *extraordinary* campaign

eye-catching, spell-binding, or *viewer-oriented* commercials

Our *talented, creative, and experienced* artists

will develop *startling computer-age* graphics

will do an *especially effective* job

If you were Ms. Robertson, which campaign would you rather pay for?
Here are some additional examples of overused words and suggested substitutes:

Instead of . . .	Consider . . .
a *bad* forecast	an *inaccurate* or a *misleading* forecast
a *good show*	a *compelling performance* or a *dramatic reenactment*
a *nice* supervisor	a *considerate,* a *well-respected,* or a *well-liked* supervisor
an *awful* record	a *deplorable* or an *inconsistent* record
clean offices	*spotless* offices

Develop an awareness of colorless words that you may tend to overuse.
Remember that such words are not "wrong," but they are often not very
effective either.

COMMUNICATION LABORATORY

APPLICATION EXERCISES

A. Practice your ability to distinguish between the denotation and the
connotation of words. For each of the following words, write the dictionary
definition (the word's denotation) on a separate sheet of paper. Then write
your personal reaction to each word (its connotation).

1. summer
2. home
3. baseball
4. teapot
5. apple
6. beach
7. chalkboard
8. poodle

B. Give at least one synonym for each of the following italicized words.
Consult a dictionary or a thesaurus if you need help in finding a good word
to substitute.

1. This thermometer takes very *exact* measurements.
2. The company *commemorates* the anniversary of its founding every year.

3. Every manager must *defend* his or her budget.
4. A salesperson must always *keep* a positive attitude.
5. Andrea offered a new *slant* on our sales problem.
6. *Speed* is to be avoided on some jobs.
7. We must all work together to *shape* a new advertising campaign.
8. Ms. Cellars likes her computer assistants to *test* every program.
9. Is there really a *choice?*
10. The company's decision to cut prices was *brave*.

C. Substitute a more precise adjective for the overworked *little* in these examples.

1. a little town
2. a little locomotive
3. a little mind
4. a little kitten
5. a little matter
6. a little portion
7. a little wire
8. a little build
9. a little computer
10. a little issue

D. Change the following negative statements into positive statements.

1. Do not forget the sales meeting at the end of the month.
2. Don't fail to ship this order by airfreight.
3. You forgot to provide a delivery date.
4. We cannot deliver your order because our plant is closed until July 15.
5. Do not lower the product's quality.
6. Don't anger customers by being late for an appointment.
7. We cannot act on your request at this time.
8. We will not forget your special request.
9. We won't know our prices until April 1.
10. Never forget a customer's preferences.

E. Rewrite the following sentences to eliminate outdated or unpleasant expressions.

1. Kindly favor us with a note if we can help.
2. We are in receipt of your order of May 5, and we thank you for same.
3. Your shipping department's blunder caused us unbelievable trouble.
4. As per our recent discussion, attached hereto is our latest price list.
5. I have your letter under date of August 27.
6. Please be so kind as to find a photocopy of my canceled check.
7. We are forwarding the book you ordered under separate cover.

8. The order will arrive late due to the fact that the railroad is on strike.
9. This is to acknowledge the receipt of your reservation.
10. We are crediting your account as per your wishes.

VOCABULARY AND SPELLING STUDIES

A. In each of the following groups, three of the four words have similar meanings. Which word is the intruder?

1. impartial, fervent, unbiased, objective
2. offend, entreat, beg, implore
3. blossom, bloom, forbid, flower
4. fabricate, fashion, shape, dodge
5. meddle, invent, interfere, tamper
6. revise, denounce, correct, remedy
7. coarse, gross, refined, crude
8. guarded, wary, watchful, open
9. exception, principle, rule, regulation
10. routine, customary, irregular, uniform
11. speculate, theorize, guess, validate
12. hide, disclose, communicate, tell
13. knowledge, learning, fiction, information
14. significant, meaningful, unimportant, serious
15. complicated, elementary, basic, pure

B. These words are often confused: *morning, mourning; hail, hale.* Explain the differences.

COMMUNICATING FOR RESULTS

Gobbledygook. High-sounding words and phrases cloud the meaning of your writing and speaking. For example, "Consumers purchase when they possess sufficient funds" means, in everyday language, "People buy when they have enough money." Rewrite the following example of gobbledygook so that it is easy to understand.

The values of equities have constantly eroded over the recent past. Nevertheless, the long-term economic prospects appear positive. We therefore suggest that long-term investors retain their positions in sound equities. Those who have additional funds to commit and those who have refrained from a commitment should buy on weakness. These investors should search out sound equities that combine secure current yield with the likelihood of future price appreciation.

37

Writing Effective Sentences

In Unit 36 you learned how word choice contributes to the effectiveness of a sentence. In fact, the words selected in any particular sentence are the most important factor in communicating accurately. In addition, correct grammar and spelling are critical factors. But word choice, grammar, and spelling are not the only factors that determine whether a sentence is, or is not, effective.

In this unit you will study sentence structure, tone, emphasis, length, and other factors that contribute to the effectiveness of sentences, including advanced techniques that professional writers use to ensure the success of their messages.

Varying Sentence Patterns

Imagine a letter constructed of only *simple* sentences:

> We received your purchase order this morning. Thank you for ordering from us. We will give you the usual 25 percent discount. We will deliver the merchandise to your store on May 3. We will charge the entire cost to your account . . . .

Boring, isn't it? This short message contains no grammatical errors, and all the words are spelled correctly. However, a message in which every sentence follows the same pattern is certain to be lackluster and dull—or worse, childish. Using a *variety* of sentence patterns, on the other hand, helps keep the reader in step with you. The above message, for instance, could easily be revised as follows:

> Thank you for your purchase order, which we received this morning. As usual, you will receive a 25 percent discount, and the total cost will be charged to your account. On May 3 we will deliver the merchandise to your store.

Although few words have been changed, the use of different sentence patterns in this example helps stimulate reader interest. Now the first sentence expresses two ideas. The first is "Thank you for your purchase order," which is expressed as an independent clause. The second idea, "which we received this morning," is a dependent clause joined to the main clause.

The second sentence is a compound sentence. It joins two independent clauses of equal value: (1) "you will receive a 25 percent discount," and

(2) "the total cost will be charged to your account." To provide further variety, the writer begins this compound sentence with an introductory phrase, "as usual."

In the third sentence, the words *on May 3* are positioned at the beginning of the sentence for added emphasis. A minor change, but it is effective because it, too, contributes to the variety of sentence patterns in this short message.

As you continue reading this unit, you will learn how to employ such techniques so that you will be able to write a variety of sentence patterns in your business messages.

Emphasizing Key Words

When speaking face-to-face with someone, we can gesture, raise or lower our voices, point, and otherwise emphasize what we are saying. In writing, as you know, different techniques must be used for emphasis. Visual devices include underlining and using all-capital letters or boldface type. In addition to visual emphasis, experienced writers use more advanced, less obvious techniques to provide emphasis within a sentence.

One way to emphasize is to control the structure of the sentence carefully so that a natural stress falls on the desired words. Depending on their objective, experienced writers can provide emphasis anywhere in the sentence. For example, in an effort to grab the reader's attention immediately and convince her or him to read on, the writer of this sentence decided to emphasize the first words:

> A *special 45 percent discount*—that's what you will receive, Mr. Stetson, on your next order for Mercury office furniture.

The writer uses several techniques to draw attention to the words *a special 45 percent discount*. Positioning the key words at the beginning of the sentence and separating them from the rest of the sentence forcefully stresses these words. The dash signals a pause, and the pause, in turn, leaves the key words on stage by themselves, getting all the attention.

Did you notice that the sentence is not in normal order? (Normal order is "You will receive a . . . .") By detouring from the normal sentence order, the writer makes the key words stand out all the more. Furthermore, the italics (especially at the beginning of the sentence) have the effect of bright red paint.

More often, however, the emphasis falls naturally at the end of the sentence.

> The committee members considered the experience of the candidates, evaluated the management potential of each man and woman, analyzed the ability of each to work harmoniously with coworkers, interviewed each candidate twice, and agreed unanimously that the best person for the position is Samantha Edwards.

The sentence is deliberately long. The lengthy sentence mirrors the lengthy process of choosing the right candidate. Also, the length of the sentence helps build suspense and, consequently, gives added emphasis to the final words, the name of the person selected. The reader discovers the "answer" only at the end of the sentence.

Tomorrow's discussion will focus on the most important reason for accepting Ford Distribution's proposal: a *guaranteed* profit.

In this example, once again, the emphasized words are at the end of the sentence. The colon adds to the emphatic effect by deliberately pointing to (and therefore highlighting) the key words.

Coordinating and Subordinating Ideas

A sentence may present one main idea, or it may contain two (or more) ideas. If the ideas are of equal importance, the writer indicates their equality by using a coordinating conjunction (*and, or, but,* or *nor*) to join the ideas. REMEMBER: A coordinating conjunction joins elements of equal rank.

We must review this proposal, *and* we must complete our inventory analysis.

Harriet is scheduled to speak at the sales meeting in Denver, *but* Martin is scheduled to attend a seminar.

Each example lists two ideas that are equal in strength. The first sentence simply joins the two ideas with the conjunction *and*. The second sentence joins and contrasts two equal-weight ideas with the conjunction *but*.

An alternative way of expressing equal ideas is simply to join the two clauses with a semicolon (and no conjunction), as follows:

We must review this proposal; we must complete our inventory analysis.

Harriet is scheduled to speak at the sales meeting in Denver; Martin is scheduled to attend a seminar.

In some sentences, of course, the two ideas are not of equal weight. In such cases the writer must clearly label the subordinate idea by using a subordinating conjunction such as *because, since, when,* or *although*. (See page 234 for a list of subordinating conjunctions.)

After we left the seminar, we discussed the negotiations with Ms. Halpern.

The subordinating conjunction *after* clearly labels *we left the seminar* as the subordinate clause. The main clause is *we discussed the negotiations with Ms. Halpern*. The conjunction *after* does more than merely *join* the clauses, however; it also specifies a certain *time relation* by telling what happened first.

The opposite time relation could have been indicated by using the conjunction *before*.

Before we left the seminar, we discussed the negotiations with Ms. Halpern.

In either case, with *after* or with *before*, the subordinating conjunction tells the reader "This is the subordinate clause." To understand better how subordinating conjunctions work, let's use the conjunction *and* to join these same clauses.

We left the seminar, and we discussed the negotiations with Ms. Halpern.

The *and* indicates that the two clauses are of equal weight—no time relation is expressed. Let's look at another example:

Because the deadline is March 15, Harold has been working diligently on the inventory report.

The subordinating conjunction *because* shows a cause-and-effect relationship between the subordinate clause, *the deadline is March 15*, and the main clause, *Harold has been working diligently on the inventory report*. In other words the conjunction *because* tells the reader *the reason why* "Harold has been working diligently on the inventory report." It establishes a cause-and-effect relationship—something that the conjunction *and* cannot do satisfactorily:

The deadline is March 15, *and* Harold has been working diligently on the inventory report.

Is there any valid *connection*, any special *relationship*, between these two clauses? Apparently not, because the writer merely strings them together with the conjunction *and*.

In the following examples the subordinating conjunctions are italicized. As you read each sentence, try to determine the specific relationship that the subordinating conjunction indicates. Do you see why the writer did not use *and, or, but,* or *nor* to join these clauses?

Since we bought this high-speed duplicator, we are saving about $250 a month.

Although Marion was attending the shareholders' meeting, her assistant gathered the information for Ms. Haskells.

If I receive another discount coupon, I will share it with you.

Achieving a Conversational Tone

In the previous unit you learned that pleasant, conversational words help foster positive business relations. Now you will see that word choice alone cannot guarantee a conversational tone; other factors, too, must be considered.

Active Voice. Writers generally prefer active voice to communicate their thoughts directly and forcefully. In the active voice the subject is doing, has done, or will be doing the action. In the passive voice the action is being done to, has been done to, or will be done to the subject.

Mel is coordinating the distribution of these materials to the committee members.

The subject *Mel* is doing the action expressed by the verb *is coordinating.* This sentence illustrates the use of active voice.

The distribution of the materials to the committee members is being coordinated by Mel.

Now the subject is *distribution,* and the verb is *is being coordinated.* Note that the main verb is a past participle with a "being" verb helper. It is, therefore, passive voice.

Read aloud the two sentences above to convince yourself that the first example is much more direct, more straightforward, more natural than the second example. Then, for additional examples, compare the following pairs of sentences.

Our supervisor prefers getting three estimates for all expenses over $1000.   (Active voice)

Getting three estimates for all expenses over $1000 is preferred by our supervisor.   (Passive voice)

Ms. Hahn conducted a comprehensive survey of all employees to get their responses on such issues.   (Active voice)

A comprehensive survey of all employees was conducted by Ms. Hahn to get employees' responses on such issues.   (Passive voice)

Most employees indicated a willingness to pay an additional premium for extended medical and dental coverage.   (Active voice)

A willingness to pay an additional premium for extended medical and dental coverage was indicated by most employees.   (Passive voice)

In each of the above examples, the active voice is the better choice. You may wonder, Is the passive voice ever useful? Answer: Yes! For instance, many consumers would react negatively to the following sentence:

We will charge you a $10 fee for late payments.

This sentence stresses a negative idea, almost a threat that "we" will perform. A writer who is aware of the reader's potential reaction would never write such a threatening-sounding statement. And admittedly, the following passive-voice rephrasing is no better:

You will be charged a $10 fee for late payments.

Now, instead of the negatives that "we" will do, the sentence emphasizes the negative that will happen to *you.* But there is another, better passive-voice alternative:

A $10 fee will be charged for late payments.

Because it is less personal—no *we,* no *you*—this statement is neither threatening nor negative. It is merely factual. For this reason passive-voice statements are often employed in reports in an effort to strip the report of any personal bias, as in this sentence:

> It was concluded that charge customers who participated in the survey strongly prefer changing the present credit policy.

Thus, as you see, passive voice *does* serve a useful purpose.

Direct Address. In an earlier unit you were introduced to *direct address*, citing the name of the person you are speaking to. What better way to make sentences sound "conversational" than to include the reader's name!

> If you order 100,000 or more imprinted envelopes, *Ms. Johanson,* you will qualify for the quantity discount and for free storage in our warehouse.

> Whenever you would like to meet with one of our representatives, *Tyrone,* please let us know.

> Of course, *Mr. VanNostrand,* we will be glad to schedule an appointment at your convenience.

Not surprisingly, in each case direct address contributes strongly to the conversational tone. Because you are including your reader's name in the sentence, direct address is an almost foolproof method for making sentences conversational. As a general rule, however, be sure to limit the use of the reader's name. Using the reader's name more than once in a paragraph is usually unwarranted and will often appear phony.

Controlling Sentence Length

There is no "correct" or "ideal" length to set as a goal for sentences. A 10-word sentence is too long if it contains unnecessary words. A 50-word sentence is too short if it omits important information. As a result, the careful writer checks every sentence in an effort to cut any repetitive or unneeded words.

> All of us here at Quality Crafted Products Inc. sincerely thank you for placing your order with us for an Allied Quality Crafted motor.

This type of sentence may often appear in business letters—that is, in *poor* business letters. To begin, the words *here at Quality Crafted Products Inc.* and *with us* are clearly extra and should be cut. The words *All of us* are not wrong, but they could easily be replaced by a straightforward *We* ("We sincerely thank . . ."). In fact, the writer could simply say, "Thank you for . . ." without seriously affecting the courteous tone or the meaning of the sentence. Also, how about replacing the words *for placing your order . . . for* with "thank you *for ordering*"?

As you can see, the example sentence could be shortened—without loss of meaning—as follows:

> Thank you for ordering an Allied Quality Crafted motor.

Let's look at another example:

When we meet with the managers of our branch offices from the Eastern Region, we must be sure to elicit from them as part of our discussion what they think is the best way to improve productivity.

Compare the above sentence with the revision that follows:

When we meet with the Eastern Region branch managers, we must elicit their suggestions to improve productivity.

The goal is not to write the shortest sentences possible. The goal *is* to eliminate unnecessary words, words that add nothing to the meaning and the impact of the sentence. The goal is to control sentence length and offer a variety of not-too-long, medium-length, and short sentences.

The length of a sentence can be deliberately long or deliberately short to create a special effect. For example, as you learned earlier, the writer may use a longer sentence to help emphasize key words that are positioned at the end of the sentence. Another device used for emphasis is to position a very short sentence after one or more rather long sentences—or vice versa. Examples of both these techniques are discussed in the next unit.

Balancing Sentence Parts

Various elements within a sentence must be treated in parallel fashion—they must be *balanced*. Imagine, for example, writing the numbers *1, 2,* and *III*. A striking imbalance results because two arabic numerals are mixed with a roman numeral. Like elements should be treated in a like manner. To be balanced, all three numbers should be consistent (either all arabic or all roman).

Balancing Articles. In a series the article *a* may be expressed only once (before the first item) but "understood" before each subsequent item.

We need the approval of *a* branch manager, regional manager, or vice president.

It is not necessary to say "*a* regional manager, or *a* vice president." Expressed before the first item, the *a* is understood before the other items in the series.

However, only *a*—not *an*—is "understood."

We need the approval of *a* branch manager, *a* regional manager, or *an* assistant vice president.

Because *both* articles, *a* and *an*, are required, the correct article must be expressed before *each* item in the series.

Similarly, repeating the article *the* is sometimes essential to the meaning of a sentence:

She already has the approval of the vice president and general manager.

She has the approval of *one person:* that person is "the vice president and general manager." To indicate that *vice president* and *general manager* are *two* different people, repeat the article *the* before *general manager:*

She already has the approval of the vice president and *the* general manager.

Balancing Verbs. The verb phrases *will go* and *will attend* share a common element, *will.* In the following sentence note that *will* is expressed only once, in the first verb phrase, but it is understood in the second verb phrase: "and (*will*) attend."

Ms. Hennessy *will go* to Seattle and *attend* the computer conference.

Now note this common trap:

We never have, and probably never will, recommend such investments.

The sentence attempts to shorten "We never have recommended, and probably never will recommend, such investments." However, the verb phrases do not share any common elements. The first phrase is "have recommended"; the second is "will recommend." By omitting *recommended,* the writer falls into the trap and forces the first phrase to share an element from the second. The result is "We never have . . . *recommend,*" which is obviously wrong.

Balancing Prepositions. You have already learned the need to team certain prepositions with certain words. In Unit 24, for example, you learned the distinction between "waiting *for* someone" and "waiting *on* a customer."

Two other examples are "respect *for*" and "belief *in.*" Watch what happens when the writer tries to share *one* preposition for both purposes:

We have great respect and belief in that organization's policies.

What happened to "respect *for*"? By dropping *for,* the writer forces *in* to substitute so that "great respect *in* . . ." is understood. But *in* is wrong. The sentence, of course, should be:

We have great respect *for* and belief in that organization's policies.

Here's another example:

Each executive should strive to listen and work closely with his or her staff.

The meaning is "should strive to listen *to* . . . his or her staff." By dropping *to,* the writer incorrectly forces *with* to substitute. Be sure to balance prepositions precisely.

Balancing Comparisons. Words are just as frequently omitted in comparisons. As a result, lopsided sentences occur:

Our vice president appreciates your efforts just as much, and maybe more, than I do.

The sentence *should* say "just as much *as* . . . I do." But by dropping *as*, the writer creates "just as much . . . *than* I do," and this of course makes no sense.

Whenever you see comparisons using *as* or *than*, be alert for such possible omissions.

The following sentence is correct. Can you identify which word in this sentence is expressed once and is then "understood" later in the sentence?

Her manager attends more sales conventions than my manager.

The verb *attends* is understood at the end of the sentence, after "than my manager (*attends*)." But note that *attends*—and only *attends*—can be "understood."

Her manager attends more sales conventions than the other managers.

Now the sentence reads "than the other managers (*attends*)," and the understood verb is wrong. The plural *managers* now requires *attend*.

Her manager attends more sales conventions than the other managers attend.

The "understood" verb in such sentences must be the *same* verb that is expressed, not a form of that verb.

Balancing Clauses. In clauses imbalances may occur either as a result of omissions or as a result of careless positioning of words—sometimes resulting in ludicrous sentences.

Did Martha lose the check or her supervisor?

Ask Bill if he can handle this project or his assistant.

The first sentence asks, "Did Martha lose . . . her supervisor"! And the second sentence questions Bill's ability to "handle . . . his assistant." Neither sentence is correct. Possible revisions include:

Did Martha lose the check, or did her supervisor lose it? *or:* Did Martha or her supervisor lose the check?

Ask Bill if he or his assistant can handle this project.

Avoiding Common Errors

To close this unit on effective sentences, let's review some of the most common problems that trap business writers—even *experienced* business writers.

Indefinite Pronouns. Although the *writer* always knows what his or her pronoun references should refer to, the *reader* is sometimes puzzled by an *it* or a *they* that appears without a clear prior referent. For example:

Ms. Blair said to call Personnel and ask *them* for a copy of the report.

The sentence contains no plural word that *them* could correctly refer to. For clarity, say instead:

Ms. Blair said to ask someone in Personnel for a copy of the report.

Let's look at another example:

We have been working on the annual inventory report and the product catalog since January, and *it* is very difficult.

What does *it* refer to? The inventory report? The catalog? January? Perhaps the sentence should be:

We have been working on the annual inventory report and the product catalog since January, and handling both projects at once is very difficult.

In the following example note how *this* betrays fuzzy thinking on the writer's part:

When our primary supplier is out of stock, we now order from another source. *This* had caused us problems in the past.

What does *this* refer to? Here is one way to avoid the *this* confusion:

When our primary supplier is out of stock, we now order from another source. In the past, waiting for the primary supplier caused us problems.

A very common error, especially in speaking, is illustrated below:

They say that the market for personal computers will increase drastically next year.

Who is *they?* Such statements bear no weight and have no merit. Instead, cite a specific source, one that will lend credibility to the statement.

Industry analysts (*or* computer experts *or* salespeople *or* manufacturers) predict that the market for personal computers will increase drastically next year.

That and Which Clauses. A *that* clause presents essential information and is therefore *not* separated from the rest of the sentence.

The district *that* is first in sales this year is the Dayton office.

The clause *that is first in sales this year* is critical to the meaning of the sentence. Rather than provide extra information, this clause identifies *one* district out of several possibilities. The clause is essential, therefore, to understanding the sentence. Remember, then, not to separate essential clauses from the rest of the sentence.

Which clauses are *non*essential and *are* separated (by commas) from the rest of the sentence.

Next Monday my supervisor and I will visit our Dayton office, *which* is the number-one district in the country, to discuss the new strategy.

Which refers to *Dayton office;* because the *which* clause presents non-essential information, it is separated by commas from the rest of the sentence.

Also, be sure to avoid using a *which* clause to refer to an entire sentence or an entire thought.

> The high estimated retooling cost will be addressed in our meeting on Thursday, *which* is of major concern to all of us.

The position of the *which* clause might mislead the reader into thinking that *Thursday* (or even *the meeting on Thursday*) "is of major concern to all of us." But the "concern" is really for the *cost:*

> The high estimated retooling cost, which is of major concern to all of us, will be addressed at our meeting on Thursday.

COMMUNICATION LABORATORY

APPLICATION EXERCISES

A. Rewrite the following sentences. As you do so, be sure to vary your sentence patterns, provide emphasis as needed, and coordinate and subordinate ideas properly. (Add any details needed to make your answers realistic.)

1. The Seattle store now leads all our other stores in total sales. The Seattle store opened only last year.
2. Ms. Breskin joined our staff in April 1985. Ms. Breskin had been a manager for Stearns, Markham & Ulster. Stearns, Markham & Ulster is a well-known accounting firm.
3. The first training session will be held on March 19, and the second training session will be held on August 3. The lecturer for the first session will be Jay Haggerty, and the lecturer for the second session will be Pamela Claye. The first session will be held in Room 2205, and the second session will be held in Room 2360.
4. You placed an order for 50,000 envelopes. We received the purchase order yesterday. You specified that you need these envelopes by April 5. We will ship the entire order to you by truck no later than April 1.
5. We now have more than 300 orders to be processed. Bill and Jane are both on vacation this week. Dan has the flu. He has been out of the office too. That leaves only six order processors handling the entire load. We need part-time help.
6. We must complete this inventory analysis by March 30. Our manager needs the inventory information for her report due April 4.
7. The panel recommended Ellen Simon as a consultant. Ms. Simon is a well-respected attorney. Her office is in Rochester, New York.

8. I want to attend the Chicago sales meeting. Evelyn wants to attend the Denver sales meeting.

9. Frank received an excellent raise. He is responsible for winning the Henderson account.

10. We have planned our project carefully. We are confident that we will finish the project on schedule.

B. Rewrite the following sentences to make them conform to the principles you learned in this unit. (Add any details needed to make your answers realistic.)

1. The review of the estimates for accuracy will be handled by me.
2. Per your recent request for an updated new catalog of our products, enclosed please find same.
3. It is suggested by me that we place a classified ad for an experienced consultant, a man who knows about computer training.
4. They say that this new product will more than likely be a big success.
5. At the present time, plans for revising the procedures manual have not been formally approved by the company's Policy Committee.
6. One of the sessions at the upcoming conference—time management—is especially interesting to me because it is a really important topic to everyone in business.
7. If you need help with this computer software, ask someone in the Finance Department. They will be glad to help.
8. John never has, and probably never will, learn to keyboard accurately.
9. Emily and I have no appreciation or interest in highly speculative investments.
10. Ask one of the product managers if they can help us complete these product analysis forms.
11. Finally we found the memo that she had written on the floor.
12. Barry and Helen conduct more training sessions than she.
13. Do you know whether Ms. Owens went to Albany or Mr. Barkley?
14. If they are interested in this new service, a customer should call this toll-free number.
15. Due to the fact that the invoice date was labeled incorrectly, one of our fellow employees in the Accounts Payable Department rejected the aforementioned invoice and returned it to us for approval.
16. All of us want to improve the efficiency of this department's handling of schedules, which is our goal.
17. It is strongly recommended, Mr. Gibson, that you consider our service contract before the expiration of your warranty, which is certainly a bargain at only $25 a year.
18. An eagerness to begin the challenging project was evident among the employees with whom I work.

19. A reply from you before the ninth of next month as to your ability to accept our invitation will be most appreciated.

20. We are now studying several discount policies that we consider attractive to customers, because it will mean more business for us.

VOCABULARY AND SPELLING STUDIES

A. How are the following words spelled when the suffixes indicated are added?

1. direct- or
2. mile- age
3. prefer- ed
4. perform- ance
5. sunny- er
6. shake- y
7. jealous- y
8. true- ly
9. forget- ing
10. know- ledge

B. Which words in the following groups are misspelled? Respell them correctly.

1. ment, apply, sought, sord
2. ferce, gallon, chanel, panel
3. lawyer, maner, wisper, tennis
4. ballance, relief, secure, acept
5. document, difficult, paralel, citys
6. atractive, storege, reveal, similar
7. grammar, iner, conect, admire
8. suggest, discus, oppose, confus
9. shalow, polish, selfish, sesion
10. decrese, obtain, occupy, ocur

C. Add a suffix pronounced *shun* to each of the following.

1. miss_____
2. men_____
3. mo_____
4. cau_____
5. satisfac_____
6. affec_____
7. instruc_____
8. except_____
9. explor_____

D. Choose *ize, ise,* or *yze* to complete each of the following.

1. notar_____
2. anal_____
3. advert_____
4. adv_____
5. disgu_____
6. rev_____
7. critic_____
8. organ_____
9. exerc_____

E. How are the following spelled when the *uhble*-sounding suffix is added?

1. respons_____
2. cap_____
3. imposs_____
4. vis_____
5. wash_____
6. pass_____
7. sens_____
8. lov_____
9. reli_____

F. Which of the following words ending with the sound of *seed* are misspelled? Spell them correctly.

1. proced	6. intercede
2. succeed	7. conceed
3. exced	8. secede
4. receed	9. superceed
5. sede (yield or grant)	10. acceed

COMMUNICATING FOR RESULTS

Write as You Talk. Saying something aloud before writing it often helps to make your expressions more natural. Rewrite the following paragraph as you would *say* it. See how much your writing can be improved.

In compliance with the regulations governing such matters, your recent complaint about the malfunctioning of your kitchen appliance has been referred to our engineering staff. It is currently being analyzed. After the analysis has been concluded, one of our engineering representatives will contact you directly.

U · N · I · T

38 Joining Sentences Into Paragraphs

In Unit 36 you analyzed techniques that will enable you to choose words appropriately for any given sentence. Then, in Unit 37, you learned to construct sentences effectively by controlling length, structure, emphasis, and so on. Now you will concentrate your attention on ways to join sentences into effective paragraphs.

Paragraph Guidelines

Just as words are combined to form a sentence, so, too, are sentences combined to form a paragraph. A *paragraph*, therefore, is "a group of related sentences joined for a specific purpose and separated from the rest of the message." The key words, which you will see as we proceed, are *related* and *specific*.

To begin, note that there are no rules concerning paragraph development—only *guidelines*. For most routine business letters, memos, and reports, try to:

1. Control—and *vary*—paragraph length.
2. Use each paragraph as a vehicle to carry related sentences and convey one specific part of the intended message.
3. Link sentences within each paragraph in a deliberate, logical sequence.
4. Use transitional devices as necessary to strengthen the link from one sentence to another.

Let's review each of these guidelines.

Paragraph Length

There is no "correct" or "ideal" length for an effective paragraph. Successful writers deliberately manipulate paragraph length, just as they manipulate sentence length, in an effort to create certain effects. As a result, a "good" paragraph may be 10, 15, or more lines long, or it may be only 1 line long. More often, of course, a paragraph is neither extremely long nor extremely short. Whenever possible, try to limit the maximum length of a paragraph to about 8 lines.

Before we discuss the *content* of the paragraph, let's look more closely at the *visual effect* of paragraphs. The length of each paragraph in a letter, memo, or report contributes to the impact of that message on the reader. Compare, for example, the three letters illustrated on pages 354–356. The content of all three letters—both the wording and the sentence sequence—is the same. Only the paragraphing of each letter is different. As a result, the visual impact of each letter differs.

The first letter (page 354) consists of two long paragraphs—two solid blocks of copy that certainly do nothing to encourage the reader to continue. The paragraphs have a forbidding look. For most readers this letter will be as inviting as a *very* long book on a *very* dull subject. Such solid blocks of copy have a negative effect on the reader.

At the other extreme is the message illustrated on page 355. Instead of just two overly long paragraphs, the same sentences are now divided into too many paragraphs. Perhaps the writer, in an effort to avoid scaring the reader with solid blocks of copy, overcompensated.

Whatever the reason, the result of too many short paragraphs is just as disastrous as the very long paragraphs. Broken into so many small pieces, the letter has a choppy appearance. It has all the visual appeal of a shopping list. The content, too, suffers: Rather than presenting related ideas logically, the letter challenges the reader to make sense of the message, as if it were a puzzle. There is nothing wrong with a short paragraph, even a one-sentence-long paragraph. But several or many consecutive short paragraphs give the message a fragmented appearance.

**Family
Investments Inc.**
1200 Broad Street
Santa Maria, California 93454
(800) 555-6000

March 15, 19--

Ms. Thelma P. Mancuso
1200 North Sheridan
Valencia, California 91355

Dear Ms. Mancuso:

Finding and choosing the "right" investment may be a tough
decision for you. After all, you work hard for your money,
and you want to invest it wisely. Safety, of course, is an
important consideration. A <u>very</u> important consideration!
But at the same time, you'd like to get high interest on
your investment. You'd also like to take advantage of some
of the tax-free investments that you keep hearing about, but
how do you go about choosing the municipal bond that is best
for you? Do you simply select the highest interest rate?
Or do you choose the bond with the highest rating? Should
you simply keep your money in a savings bank, despite the
low interest rates? Or should you . . . .

Yes, there <u>are</u> many options available. Since 1955, nearly
375,000 investors like you have opted to place their savings
in the Watson Prime Reserve Bond Fund. The Watson PRB Fund
has consistently yielded high interest rates and has met the
highest safety standards for preserving investors'
principal. In fact, the Watson PRB Fund has set several
"records" in the investment community for high yields and
safety. In addition, the interest earned from the Watson
PRB Fund is completely tax-free. Suddenly, making the
"right" investment decision is as simple as calling us
(toll-free) for a free information packet: (800) 555-6000.

Sincerely,

Janet P. Hare

Janet P. Hare
Vice President

JPH/rw

**Two solid blocks of copy have a negative effect on the reader. Compare the visual
effect of this letter with the appearance of the letter on page 356.**

The paragraphing of the third letter, illustrated on page 356, is certainly
an improvement. It offers no solid block of copy to scare away readers.
Instead, the letter is divided into several paragraphs, each presenting one
part of the total message.

Note that this letter contains two very short paragraphs, each one sentence
long. The writer deliberately uses these short paragraphs to create a special

**Family
Investments Inc.**
1200 Broad Street
Santa Maria, California 93454
(800) 555-6000

March 15, 19--

Ms. Thelma P. Mancuso
1200 North Sheridan
Valencia, California 91355

Dear Ms. Mancuso:

Finding and choosing the "right" investment may be a tough
decision for you.

After all, you work hard for your money, and you want to
invest it wisely. Safety, of course, is an important
consideration. A _very_ important consideration!

But at the same time, you'd like to get high interest on
your investment.

You'd also like to take advantage of some of the tax-free
investments that you keep hearing about, but how do you go
about choosing the municipal bond that is best for you?

Do you simply select the highest interest rate? Or do you
choose the bond with the highest rating? Should you simply
keep your money in a savings bank, despite the low interest
rates? Or should you . . . .

Yes, there _are_ many options available. Since 1955, nearly
375,000 investors like you have opted to place their savings
in the Watson Prime Reserve Bond Fund.

The Watson PRB Fund has consistently yielded high interest
rates and has met the highest safety standards for
preserving investors' principal.

In fact, the Watson PRB Fund has set several "records" in
the investment community for high yields and safety.
In addition, the interest earned from the Watson PRB Fund is
completely tax-free.

Suddenly, making the "right" investment decision is as
simple as calling us (toll-free) for a free information
packet: (800) 555-6000.

Sincerely,

Janet P. Hare

Janet P. Hare
Vice President

JPH/rw

Too many short paragraphs give this letter a choppy, fragmented look. Compare the visual effect of this letter with the appearance of the letter on page 356.

effect. The first, "Yes, there *are* many options available," is positioned between the two longest paragraphs in the letter. Sandwiching this one-sentence paragraph between the two long paragraphs has a double effect: (1) the short sentence enhances the visual impact of the letter, and (2) it also emphasizes the content of this important sentence by placing it on center stage.

Family Investments Inc.
1200 Broad Street
Santa Maria, California 93454
(800) 555-6000

March 15, 19--

Ms. Thelma P. Mancuso
1200 North Sheridan
Valencia, California 91355

Dear Ms. Mancuso:

Finding and choosing the "right" investment may be a tough decision for you. After all, you work hard for your money, and you want to invest it wisely.

Safety, of course, is an important consideration. A <u>very</u> important consideration! But at the same time, you'd like to get high interest on your investment. You'd also like to take advantage of some of the tax-free investments that you keep hearing about, but how do you go about choosing the municipal bond that is best for you? Do you simply select the highest interest rate? Or do you choose the bond with the highest safety rating? Should you simply keep your money in a savings bank, despite the low interest rates? Or should you . . . .

Yes, there <u>are</u> many options available.

Since 1955, nearly 375,000 investors like you have opted to place their savings in the Watson Prime Reserve Bond Fund. The Watson PRB Fund has consistently yielded high interest rates and has met the highest safety standards for preserving investors' principal. In fact, the Watson PRB Fund has set several "records" in the investment community for high yields and safety. In addition, the interest earned from the Watson PRB Fund is completely tax-free.

Suddenly, making the "right" investment decision is as simple as calling us (toll-free) for a free information packet: (800) 555-6000.

Sincerely,

Janet P. Hare

Janet P. Hare
Vice President

JPH/rw

The last paragraph also consists of only one sentence. It is especially effective because its wording reminds the reader of the first sentence of the letter ("Finding and choosing the 'right' investment . . ."). Together, the paragraphs in the third example contribute positively to the visual appeal of the letter.

As you see, from analyzing these three letters, paragraphing affects both the visual impact and the content of your message. For polished writing, control the number and the length of paragraphs in your letters, memos, and reports.

Writing 50-Word Messages at the Computer. Although the preceding rules on paragraph length are certainly effective in writing typical business messages, they do *not* apply to electronic messages—short notes written on and relayed by a computer. Let's see why.

In today's office, as well as today's home, many business people communicate their messages by computers *networked* (connected) to other computers. Their electronic messages are exchanged from computer to computer—and therefore to other *people*. The "other people" may be on the same floor as the sender or (thanks to the use of telephone lines) may be thousands of miles away. The messages are most often interoffice memos that are read *on screen*—they are not typewritten and printed.

For many reasons electronic messages are brief. Among the factors that contribute to their brevity are these:

1. First of all, the purpose of electronic messaging is direct, straightforward communication, and direct communication is best achieved through brevity.
2. Electronic messages are almost always interoffice memos, written from one employee to another. Less formality is required for interoffice communications.
3. Computer time is valuable. Shorter messages require less writing time and less reading time, freeing the computer for other uses and promoting greater office productivity.
4. Screen space is limited to a certain number of characters across the screen and a certain number of lines down the screen. As a result, just as "paper efficiency" in the office requires that routine memos be written on *one* page, "computer efficiency" demands that electronic messages be written on *one* screen.
5. Many electronic messages are relayed over telephone lines, and telephone time is costly.
6. Electronic messages usually *stay* "electronic." Although they can be printed and filed, they usually are not. As a result, electronic messages *very* strongly emphasize the need to communicate specific information very directly, very quickly.

For these reasons, then, electronic messages are usually one paragraph long—in fact, most are no longer than 50 words. To see the specific differences between paper memos and electronic messages, read this memo, which was prepared and distributed manually, without networked computer equipment:

INTEROFFICE MEMORANDUM

TO: District Managers   FROM: Georgine Klein
    Regional Managers   Sales Information Department
    Product Managers

SUBJECT: July Sales Report   DATE: July 21, 1989

    I know that all of you are eager to see the July sales report for several reasons. First of all, sales for our two new stores will be included. Furthermore, July is always our greatest revenue month. Moreover, our Fourth of July sale is our biggest of the year.
    In an effort to provide you with printouts of the July sales report before the usual date (August 15), we will assemble all the data, print the report, and distribute copies by August 7. I know that some of you are busy working on your sales estimates for next year. If you must have a hard copy of the July report before August 7 to finish your estimates, please call my assistant, Abigail Fromme. Abigail will try to provide you with a hard copy. By the way, while the copies are being printed and distributed, you can call the Sales Information Department for any specific sales data you may need.
    Call me or Abigail if you have any question or problem. We will be glad to help.

                    GK

This memorandum was prepared and distributed manually, without networked computer equipment.

When Georgine wrote and distributed this memo, her company had not yet installed its sophisticated computer system. Now, when Georgine needs to communicate essential information to people within her company, she writes an electronic message—a *short* electronic message. Today, Georgine would write that same message as follows:

```
The printouts of the July sales reports
will be distributed no later than August 7.
If you must have a hard copy before then,
call Abigail Fromme in Sales Information
(Ext. 4670). If you need specific data
without hard copy, boot up "JulInv"
for the data you need. (48 words)
```

This memorandum was prepared and distributed electronically. Because of the nature of electronic transmission, this message must be brief, direct, and to the point.

Because of the nature of electronic transmission, Georgine's message is short—under 50 words. She can transmit this message from her computer terminal to the terminals of the 34 other people in her company who need this information. Most of the other people are located in the same building; the rest are located in branch offices throughout the country. The computers that are in the same building are directly wired to Georgine's computer. The computers located in the branch offices use telephone lines to relay messages.

If this sounds "futuristic," it is *not*. Many companies and many individuals are now sending messages by computer, as Georgine now does.

Here is another example of a typical electronic message:

```
The August 19 meeting of the Budget Committee
has been rescheduled to 9 a.m. on September 7
in Conference Room 45. Notify Jorge Diaz
ASAP if you cannot attend.
```

REMEMBER: When writing messages that will be transmitted electronically, keep it short!

Related Sentences

Earlier we mentioned that a paragraph consists of *related* sentences. Read, for instance, the following letter—a direct, straightforward response to a request. As you do so, note how sentences within each paragraph are related.

Dear Ms. DePalma:

Thank you for calling for information on Federal Savings & Loan's new Home Equity Loan Service. We have enclosed the application forms required.

Ms. DePalma, only Federal S&L can boast that it has approved more home-equity loans than any other bank in Greene County. In fact, in the past twelve months Federal S&L has approved more than $23 million in home-equity and home-improvement loans to your neighbors here in Greene County. That's why our motto is "Helping Our Community."

As you complete the application forms, please call me if you should need any information or have any questions. I will be delighted to assist you.

Sincerely,

Enclosure

Most straightforward, direct letters such as this one follow a three-paragraph plan: The first paragraph is an introduction. The second paragraph discusses business details. The third paragraph is the close.

Now let's look more closely at the contents of each paragraph.

1. In the opening paragraph the first sentence identifies the purpose of the letter (to respond to the reader's "calling for information"). The second sentence informs the reader that the application forms she wants are enclosed. Thus both sentences are related.

   (Technically, the first paragraph gives the reader all the information she requested. But the writer wants to do more than send the reader her forms. The writer wants to take advantage of this opportunity to sell the reader—to convince her to deal with Federal S&L. The writer devotes the entire second paragraph to this purpose.)

2. The sentences in the second paragraph are also related. Each sentence gently "sells" the reader on the benefits of getting a home-equity loan from this particular bank.

3. In the third paragraph both sentences combine to strengthen the image of Federal S&L as a friendly, helpful bank. Together, these two sentences provide a goodwill statement to end the letter.

What if the reader had called for information on *two* subjects—say, a home-equity loan *and* interest rates on certificates of deposit (CDs)? The writer would then create a separate paragraph (devoted to CDs, of course) positioned *before* the closing paragraph.

Sequence of Sentences

A sentence in which the words are jumbled presents the reader with a puzzle:

For Allied Industries I have for ten years worked.

With little effort we can easily assemble the pieces properly to form "I have worked for Allied Industries for ten years." The difficulty of solving such puzzles depends on the number of words and how jumbled they are. This puzzle was rather simple.

Whether the puzzle itself is difficult to unravel or not, any sentence with jumbled words is rather easy to *identify* because the resulting sentence always sounds awkward. But when sentences within a paragraph are out of sequence, readers may not realize that they face a puzzle. Consequently, the effect of jumbled sentences is worse because readers may not quickly *identify* the problem.

In the following paragraph, for example, the sentences are related. However, the impact of the message is flawed. Do you see why?

> One service contract covers the cost of both parts and labor for two full years. The other service contract covers only the cost of labor, not of parts, and costs $50 a year for each pump. The fee for the parts-and-labor contract is $100 a year for each pump. Ford Pumps Inc. offers two service contracts, both of which are optional. By the way both contracts include free annual maintenance.

Obviously, *something* is wrong. The sentences are related, but they are jumbled. In developing a plan for the message, the writer assembled related sentences but did not put the sentences in logical sequence, as follows:

> Ford Pumps Inc. offers two service contracts, both of which are optional. One service contract covers the cost of both parts and labor for two full years. The fee for the parts-and-labor contract is $100 a year for each pump. The other service contract covers only the cost of labor, not of parts, and costs $50 a year for each pump. By the way both contracts include free annual maintenance.

As you see, then, writing and assembling related sentences within a paragraph does not guarantee effectiveness. Even if all sentences are related, the sentences must be arranged in a logical sequence—in the order that will best communicate the intended message. For most routine messages the best arrangement results from the *direct approach.*

The Direct Approach. In a paragraph organized according to the *direct* approach, the first sentence opens immediately with the main idea, and the following sentences then present supporting facts.

> We are seeking authorization to hire (before May 15) at least three additional full-time clerks in the Order Department. As you know, the Order Department now processes an average of about 4000 orders each month—25 percent more than last year. Furthermore, during our busy summer season we receive as many as 5500 orders each month. Moreover, the Order Department now employs fewer full-time clerks (only 14) than were on staff last year (17). To handle both our present high volume and the expected increase in volume, we will surely need additional clerical help.

The approach is obviously straightforward. Using the direct approach, the writer (1) bluntly states the request first and then (2) provides the supporting details, the reasons for the request. Of course, busy executives prefer receiving memos that are direct and factual.

Sometimes, there is no "main" sentence. For example, if you were explaining how to assemble a motor, you would follow a direct approach; each sentence in the step-by-step sequence would be equally important. Likewise, in the following chronological arrangement of sentences, there is no main sentence:

As the enclosed agenda shows, the workshop will begin at 8:45 a.m. Mona Roberts, my assistant, will introduce the speakers, beginning with Claire Reynolds, who will discuss "Time Management" from 9 a.m. until 10:30. After a 30-minute refreshment break, William Cohen will discuss "Project Planning Techniques" from 11 a.m. until 12:30. Then, from 12:30 until 2 p.m., during the luncheon, we will . . . .

Unless you have special objectives, using the direct approach generally results in the most effective organization for routine business letters, memos, and short reports.

The Indirect Approach. For certain sensitive writing assignments (saying "no" to a request, for example), the direct approach will be too tough—harsh enough to lose a customer or annoy a coworker. Beginning the main paragraph with a sentence that says "No, we cannot grant your request" is seldom the best way to gain new and keep old clients!

Using the indirect approach, the writer (1) discusses the relevant facts first and then (2) announces the final decision—the reverse of the direct-approach pattern. By leading up to the sensitive part of the paragraph, the writer softens the blow. Further, by citing the supporting details first, the writer shows that the decision follows logically and naturally from the facts presented.

The July issue of *Consumers' Monthly* said that B&G Electronics "has the best returns policy in the electronics industry." Indeed, most stores accept returns on merchandise purchased within 30 days, but B&G accepts returns *within 90 days*. Because you purchased your Masters VCR more than ten months ago, Mr. Hastings, we cannot accept this return. Fortunately, however, since your VCR is still under the manufacturer's warranty, you may send it to the authorized Masters service center nearest you.

If the paragraph opened bluntly with "No, we will not allow you to return the VCR," B&G Electronics might have lost a customer (however unreasonable his request). Instead, the writer develops a reasonable argument, listing first "the reasons why," then announcing the decision. Note how the argument gains momentum with each sentence until, finally, the last sentence tells the reader he has only one recourse: return the VCR to the manufacturer.

When faced with sensitive issues (whether the reader is wrong or not), use the indirect approach. Doing so will help you maintain good customer and coworker relations!

Transitional Expressions

The basic goals of paragraph development are to separate messages into manageable parts, each part consisting of related sentences arranged in a logical sequence. But whenever you separate a written message into parts, you must help the reader see how those parts are related.

Certain words and expressions provide bright beams of light to show the reader specifically how parts are related. We call these special tools *transitional words and expressions.*

A *transition* is "a word or a phrase that serves as a special connective between two things." Thus a transitional word or phrase is a signal light that shines on the writer's map, leading the reader smoothly from one place to another. Without transitions the reader travels in the dark!

Among the many transitional words and expressions that are popular and effective are the following:

accordingly	first	nevertheless
after all	for example	on the contrary
again	for instance	on the other hand
also	further	otherwise
as a result	furthermore	similarly
at the same time	however	still
besides	in addition	then
consequently	meanwhile	therefore
finally	moreover	yet

As you will see, transitions are indeed important to clear writing. Transitions can be used to show a sequence of steps (*first, then, finally*), to contrast thoughts (*however, on the other hand, nevertheless*), to add emphasis (*again, in addition, moreover*), and so on.

Below you will see how transitions work. Because they carry the reader smoothly from one idea to another, transitions are useful (1) within a sentence, (2) between sentences, and (3) between paragraphs.

Within a Sentence. Read the following sentences—then *re*read them without the italicized transitions. When the transitions are dropped, do the sentences convey the same message?

The entire staff worked overtime; *nevertheless,* we were unable to process all the backorders.

She discussed the causes of the problem; *then* she explained the reasons for each.

The estimated cost was exceptionally high; *therefore,* we decided to scrap the project.

Ms. Gelden prefers using the same marketing strategy; *on the other hand,* Mr. Forster strongly advocates changing our policy.

Our supervisor is reviewing our travel-expense budgets; *similarly,* she is checking estimated costs of all major projects.

Without the transition each sentence is still grammatically correct; however, without the transition each sentence seems to be "missing something." The transition serves to bridge the two ideas expressed in each sentence.

Between Sentences. Transitions work the same magic between sentences:

> The committee members carefully analyzed the problem. *First,* we asked all sales representatives for their suggestions. *Then,* we scheduled meetings with each branch manager. *Finally,* we developed a questionnaire for our customers.

First, then, finally—these three words provide excellent transitions from one sentence to the next.

Between Paragraphs. Paragraphs are the major subdivisions of the typical letter, memo, or short report. The relation between paragraphs, too, must always be clear to the reader.

> Last July the Research Department conducted a survey of all charge-card customers. One surprising result of that survey was the discovery that nearly 72 percent of our customers labeled our returns policy "unfair."
>
> *Naturally,* all of us are concerned that so many valuable customers have clearly indicated such a negative response to our long-standing policy against returning any merchandise 30 days or more after the purchase date. *Consequently,* a special committee was appointed to review the problem and submit recommendations for solving customers' dissatisfaction.
>
> *As a result,* effective next January 1, Smithson Discount Stores' returns policy will be changed as follows: . . . .

The italicized transitions here plainly label the relationship between sentences and paragraphs. Let's look at how each transition accomplishes its task.

1. *Naturally* carries the reader smoothly from the end of the first paragraph to the beginning of the second. Note how *naturally* provides the perfect bridge between these two statements: (1) "our customers labeled our returns policy 'unfair,' " and (2) "all of us are concerned . . . ." (The words *of course* could have done the same job.) In other words *naturally* helps show a cause-and-effect relationship between the statement at the end of the first paragraph and the statement that begins the second paragraph. It shows that it is *natural* to be "concerned" in such a situation.
2. The transition *consequently* bridges two sentences. Like *naturally,* this transition also shows a cause-and-effect relationship: we were "concerned" about "a negative response"; *as a consequence of this concern,* "a special committee was appointed . . . ."
3. The third paragraph begins with *as a result,* which is really a short way of saying "as a result of the special committee's review." Thus *as a result* includes some understood words. It also tells the reader, "the committee's recommendations will follow."

Did you notice that the above transitions are economical? Each says quite a lot—but does so succinctly.

COMMUNICATION LABORATORY

APPLICATION EXERCISES

A. Select an appropriate transitional word or expression from the choices in parentheses.

(Consequently, As you know, Moreover,) the BSI Salary Administration Committee recently completed a year-long study of industry salaries. (Meanwhile, Naturally, As a result,) last month Benson Services Inc. announced a new salary schedule for all graded employees.

(Therefore, Also, On the other hand,) the Salary Administration Committee recommended that an incentive-compensation plan be established for all employees. (Naturally, However, Furthermore,) company executives were interested in the details of the plan and reviewed it carefully.

(As a result, For example, Besides,) we are pleased to announce that as of next January 1, a new incentive-compensation plan will be in effect. The details of this plan are explained in the enclosed booklet.

(Meanwhile, Of course, Accordingly,) BSI's employees are its most valuable asset. (Therefore, Yet, Still,) we are very pleased to offer this special compensation plan in an effort to reward our employees for their hard work, creativity, and dedication.

B. Provide acceptable paragraph breaks for the following lengthy block of copy. Also, add transitions as necessary. Use a separate sheet of paper.

Last July we commissioned Fullmer Marketing Consultants to conduct a study of businesses in our area. The specific goals of the study were (1) to determine the number and the size of local businesses that are interested in and have a need for hotel services and (2) to identify the specific hotel services that will best satisfy their needs. Last week FMC submitted its report, which offers valuable information and interesting statistics that will be helpful to us as we plan our future marketing strategies. The report shows that 275 new businesses were established here in Greene County during the past five years. Most (182) of these new companies are firms having between 50 and 125 employees—an ideal market for our hotel services. The report lists the kinds of hotel services that these businesses identified as "most helpful," with "complete conference facilities" heading the list. The report contains very valuable information and must be studied carefully. Because the report is so important to our future marketing objectives, we have invited Leonia Fullmer, who conducted the survey and wrote the report, to meet with us for a full-day session during which we will review in detail both the findings and their potential impact on our strategies. We are asking you and your staff members to set aside Tuesday, December 3, for this meeting with Ms. Fullmer. We know that all of us will benefit from this session.

C. Read the following memorandum. Then (1) place sentences in a logical sequence and (2) group the sentences into acceptable paragraphs. Use a separate sheet of paper.

As you know, we have several important decisions to make concerning this year's sales meeting, and we will need ample time to prepare for the meeting, which is scheduled for August 15. First of all, we must begin the site-selection process. Please plan to meet with us on Tuesday, January 9, from 9 a.m. until noon, in Conference Room B, to begin planning this year's meeting. Next, we must develop a theme for the meeting. As you can see, then, we have plenty of work ahead of us! In addition, we must assign the development of the product-information brochures to product managers, and we must select speakers to present each new product. To save time, please review the enclosed materials before we meet on January 9. As you will see, the materials include suggestions for the site for and the theme of this year's meeting as well as some valuable comments on last year's session.

D. Rewrite the following paragraph so that it flows smoothly.

Last year we closed four branch offices to conserve funds. This decision saved about 8 percent on our operating budget. Sales decreased by 14 percent. A large portion of this decrease can be traced to the closing of the offices. A portion is due to the general decline in the economy. I would suggest that we reopen these offices. Their closings cost us more than we saved.

VOCABULARY AND SPELLING STUDIES

A. These words are often confused: *threw, through, thorough*. Explain the differences.

B. Three of the four words in each line below are synonyms. The fourth is an antonym. Spot the intruder in each group.

1. frighten, calm, alarm, terrify
2. conform, correspond, deviate, match
3. enthusiasm, eagerness, zeal, indifference
4. happy, miserable, distressed, pitiable
5. forceful, weak, strong, mighty

C. Complete the following by adding *ar*, *er*, or *or*—whichever is correct.

1. supervis___
2. lawy___
3. regul___
4. direct___
5. monit___
6. sweep___

COMMUNICATING FOR RESULTS

"Prepositionitis." "Prepositionitis" is the trap of using too many prepositional phrases, thereby making sentences long and unwieldy. Some prepositions, of course, are necessary. Rewrite the following sentences, eliminating unnecessary prepositional phrases.

1. The supervisor of our branch office in St. Louis has asked for additional workers for the summer.
2. The efficient use of our computer equipment depends upon careful scheduling.
3. At the meeting of our Ohio representatives held in May, we decided upon a special promotion for that territory.

U · N · I · T

39

Designing the Final Message

Imagine approving a house design one room at a time. Without ever seeing an overall design that shows *all* the rooms together on one sheet, you would surely have trouble seeing exactly how the parts of the house are interrelated. As a result, you would have trouble ensuring that the final product, the finished house, will meet your specifications and fit your needs.

In a similar way, you cannot ensure that your final letter or memo, the one you are about to send a client or a coworker, meets your specifications unless you carefully review the entire finished letter. Whether you dictate to a machine or to a stenographer, type your own letters and memos, or keyboard your messages on a word processor or personal computer, you must review the final message to make sure that it:

1. Creates a favorable impression.
2. Appeals to the reader's point of view.
3. Is correct in every detail.
4. Is courteous, friendly, and sincere.
5. Promotes goodwill.
6. Is clear and complete.
7. Is concise.
8. Maintains a smooth flow.

In this unit you will learn how to evaluate each of these qualities of business messages.

Create a Favorable Impression

Will your reader *want* to read the letter or memo you are sending? Is it sloppily typed? Is the ink smudged? Do the margins seem to run over the end of the page? If so, would *you* want to read the message? Probably not!

If the message is worth writing, it is worth your effort to ensure that the stationery is neat, the ink is not smeared, the margins are "standard," and so on. Each message, whether it is the first one you are writing to someone or the hundredth letter to the same person, requires *care*. Take the time to impress your reader with the looks of your message. If the looks are impressive, the reader will continue *willingly*. Attractive stationery, neat typing with standard margins, unnoticeable corrections (if any)—these are sure to impress your reader.

REMEMBER: A prestigious-looking message is a reflection on *you*.

Appeal to the Reader's Point of View

When writing a sales letter, the goal is to make the reader act—to buy a specific product or service. The most important technique in writing a good sales letter is to *appeal to the reader's point of view*. By putting themselves in the reader's place, sales writers produce action-getting letters. For example, read this beginning of a sales letter:

Your $22 check will give you 12 informative issues of *Financial Planning*.

One can almost imagine hearing the reader's reaction: "Ho hum." If, instead, the writer had considered the reader's point of view, perhaps the letter would have begun like the following letter:

You can *save more than $20* on a year's subscription to *Financial Planning* and enjoy the most highly respected investment advice and money-saving tips.

Now the writer tries to see the offer from the reader's point of view and, as a result, writes a better opening sentence.

This technique, however, is not limited to use in sales letters. In fact, appealing to the reader's point of view makes good sense in *all* letters and memos. Note, for instance, how the writer addresses the reader in the following memo:

Please note that your supervisor has registered you for the Production Workshop here in our headquarters building on August 9 and 10.

A polite way of saying "You *must* attend!" If you were the reader, wouldn't you prefer receiving the following memo instead?

As a manufacturing professional, you will surely enjoy participating in the Production Workshop for which your supervisor has scheduled you on August 9 and 10 here in our headquarters building.

The writer of the second memo appeals to the reader's professionalism, whereas the writer of the first memo simply wrote from the *writer's* point of view, not the reader's.

Be Correct in Every Detail

When a reader finds, for example, a letter dated "September *31*" instead of "September *13*," will the reader suspect that there are other errors in the letter? Of course!

The reader who finds one error almost automatically starts searching for others. Even if the reader finds no other errors, he or she may still suspect that there *are* other errors. The unit costs in the body of the letter, the scheduled project-completion dates, the catalog numbers—these kinds of data can no longer be trusted once the reader has found an error.

A business message must be correct in every detail. Incorrect dates, poor spelling and grammar, code numbers, prices, discounts, and so on, cause problems both for the reader and the writer. Even if the reader knows the right answer, as in the "September *31*" example above, the reader will have a negative impression of the writer.

In the final business document, check for the following common error categories:

Spelling and Grammar Errors. As you reread the message, do you find any errors in spelling, grammar, punctuation, number use, or capitalization? Check for all the kinds of errors you studied earlier in this text.

Statistical Errors. An error in spelling is often obvious if the message is carefully reread. But is the code number *K132-673* correct? You cannot be sure; you must check it against a source document to be sure. A *source document* is a price list, a catalog, a computer printout, or any similar document that is *known* to be correct.

Inconsistencies. Does the letter say *Ms. Alexis* in the salutation and *Dr. Alexis* elsewhere? Either *Ms.* or *Dr.* can be correct, of course, but only one should be used, not both. Check the letter—and *all* business documents—for such inconsistencies.

Format Errors. Does the final message follow a standard format for letters, memos, and reports? Are the margins correct? Are the spaces between letter parts and the spaces between paragraphs correct? Check all such details carefully. You will learn more about formatting letters and memos in Unit 40 and formatting reports in Units 51 and 52.

Content Errors. Did you write "Jane Gibson" when you really intended "Jan Gibbons"? Did you unintentionally ask to have a package sent to you when the package should be sent to the warehouse? Did you say that you would send the rest of the materials "within a few days" when you really don't know when the rest of the materials will be ready? Correct such errors!

Miscellaneous Errors. Does the body of the message state that a copy of a report "is enclosed" but the letter shows no enclosure notation? Were copy notations omitted?

Indeed, many kinds of errors are possible. Avoiding them requires careful attention both during the writing process and after the message has been typed.

Be Courteous

Would you continue shopping in a store where your patronage was not appreciated? A famous chain of stores displays this sign at all cash registers: "Your purchases are free if we fail to say 'thank you.' " The owners claim they have never lost any money but have won thousands of friends. They show their customers *courtesy*.

Of course, good manners are not reflected merely in a "please" or "thank you." The *way* in which you say or write "please" or "thank you"—the tone—makes the difference. The tone of your message tells many things about you—your attitude, your sense of fair play, your desire to be of service. Such expressions as the following help to give your message a desirable tone:

> "You were very kind to . . . ."
> "We are most grateful for . . . ."
> "We very much appreciate your . . . ."
> "We were very happy to know that . . . ."
> "We value your . . . ."
> "You are entirely correct in saying . . . ."

These phrases do not in themselves make a courteous letter. Your letter must "talk to" and treat the reader like a guest in your home.

Be Friendly

Friendliness is an important writing quality. *Friendliness* and *courtesy* are related terms, but they are not synonymous. You may use courteous words and yet not be very friendly. For example, the person who wrote the following was not actually discourteous. But the letter does not sound very friendly, does it?

> We can't do a thing about your request for a discount. Our special discount offer expired a month ago. Please send us a check for an additional $11.50.

You can inject warmth into your messages by writing as you talk, by keeping the reader's point of view, and by using friendly-sounding words and expressions. Now let's try to inject a friendly tone into the previous message:

> We wish we could honor your request for a discount. However, our discount offer expired a month ago. Since the merchandise currently available was manufactured at a higher price, we must reluctantly ask you to send us your check for an additional $11.50.

Be Sincere

Sincerity in your messages shows a genuine interest in your readers. False sincerity, however, will show through. If you are sincere, customers will recognize your desire to be of service. Your sincerity will make them feel that they will benefit by acting as you request. When you are sincere, you mean what you say and your message reflects this feeling. To write a sincere message, you must believe in people, in your company or organization, and in yourself. You must talk *with*, not *at*, people. Following are examples of expressions that reflect sincerity:

"You are correct. We did send you the wrong . . . ."
"Please accept our apology for the delayed shipment."
"Our mistake is very embarrassing to us."
"We would like very much to help you; however, we . . . ."
"I will be happy to explain the situation."
"You have a right to better service, and we have an obligation to provide it."
"You are right in saying that three weeks is a long time."

Promote Goodwill

Goodwill is the positive feeling about and attitude toward a firm by the general public, by customers, and by suppliers. It is *very* highly valued. Every letter you write should help to promote goodwill for your firm, because goodwill is considered one of the major purposes of all business messages.

Goodwill results from:

1. Good products or services.
2. Ethical conduct.
3. Superior service to customers.
4. Prompt attention to details.
5. Effective communication.
6. Friendliness.

Remember that every message you write *is* the company insofar as the reader is concerned. Your message sells—or unsells—the reader on your firm.

When you write messages, you should have a thorough knowledge of your company and of its goods or services. You also should have loyalty toward your company; you should believe in it and its goods and services. If you are sincere in this belief (and also a good business writer), then your faith will show in your letters. Goodwill must necessarily follow.

One secret for building goodwill is to provide prompt action. When an order comes in, fill it immediately. When a request comes in, answer it within 48 hours. If a customer has a complaint, attend to it without delay. Failure to reply quickly to a letter is a sure way to destroy goodwill. Even if you are unable to answer all the writer's questions within 48 hours, you should write anyway, giving what help you can and indicating when the remaining questions will be answered.

Be Clear and Complete

Have you ever received a message that you did not understand? How did you feel—confused, and maybe a little angry? What kept the message from being clear? Was something left unsaid? "Let's meet on Wednesday to discuss these surveys," Jim writes. But Jim doesn't tell you *when* on Wednesday or *where*. So his message is not clear because it is not complete. You can see, then, that completeness contributes to clarity in letter writing and that a clearly written message is vital if your letter is to achieve its purpose. You can't meet Jim if you don't know when and where to meet him.

And Miller Supplies can't fill your order for widgets if you don't tell them the size you want. Incomplete messages can be costly, for they lead to errors, often cause delays in filling orders, and call for other letters of clarification to be written. With the cost of today's typical business letter running over $25, it is necessary to make the *first* letter get the job done successfully.

Clarity also depends on the words you use and the way you use them. First, you must have a clear idea of what you want to say. Then you must decide how you are going to say it. In general, use the simplest everyday expressions—those the reader will surely understand. Contrast the following:

POOR: It is absolutely essential that all delinquent payments be forwarded within 15 days to avoid substantial penalty charges.

BETTER: Please pay overdue bills within 15 days to avoid added charges.

Be Concise

A concise message—a message that covers the subject in the fewest words possible—is more certain to be understood than a rambling, wordy message. But do not think that *concise* and *brief* mean the same thing; brevity is only a part of conciseness. To be concise, a message must be *both* brief and complete. Look at the following request:

Please send me four of the shirts that you advertised in yesterday's *Seattle Times*. My check for $32 is enclosed.

This request certainly meets the test for brevity, but could the order be filled? No; the size (and perhaps color) desired has not been specified. Brevity is desirable, but it must not be achieved at the expense of clarity or completeness.

Conciseness means saying all that needs to be said and no more. In business, time is money—and few business people have time to read irrelevant details.

Maintain a Smooth Flow

You have already learned how to create paragraphs of *related* sentences and how to join paragraphs with transitional devices—important techniques for maintaining a good flow in a business message. Perhaps the first and most important step in maintaining a smooth flow, however, is to *plan* the message before writing. You will learn more about planning techniques in Unit 41.

When rereading your finished message, again put yourself in your reader's place. Does the message flow smoothly? Will the reader get *the message you intended?*

COMMUNICATION LABORATORY

APPLICATION EXERCISES

A. Rewrite each sentence below from the reader's point of view.

1. I would like to work for your company because of your fine benefit plans.
2. Your immediate order would allow us to reduce inventories.
3. We need your reservation by the middle of the month to avoid problems with our bookkeeping.
4. Your early confirmation will make it easier for us to hold your room.

B. The following sentences do nothing to build goodwill. Rewrite them.

1. Please submit your order again; we can't seem to locate the original.
2. You made an error in not advising us of your room preference.
3. A careful customer would have brought this complaint to our attention much earlier.
4. You should have completed a credit application.
5. It is far too late for you to receive our special discount.
6. Because so many people fail to pay promptly, we do not ship merchandise until we receive their check.
7. Your order will be delayed because your size is so unusual.
8. All our other watch purchasers are completely satisfied.
9. It can't possibly be that we sent you the wrong batteries.
10. Our careful order clerks never make that kind of mistake.

C. Each of the following messages lacks some important information. Rewrite the message, providing the information that will make it clear and complete.

1. We would like to introduce our new line of sweaters to you at the Colony Hotel.
2. I would like to receive a copy of your schedule of upcoming events.
3. Please send six of your best white shirts to me at 81 Exeter Drive, Sunderland, Missouri 63042.
4. Would you like to attend our meeting at 10 a.m. tomorrow morning?
5. When does the plane leave?

D. Rewrite the following message. Paragraph it correctly by applying the principles you learned in Unit 38. Add connecting words as necessary.

We received your order today for three dozen Holt portable AM/FM radios. We welcome this opportunity to serve you. There has been such a great demand for Holt radios. We are temporarily out of stock. This fine product will again be available in eight days. Our plant is working overtime. Your order will be shipped very soon. Once again, we very much appreciate your order. We are convinced that the quality of Holt products will make up for the slight delay.

VOCABULARY AND SPELLING STUDIES

A. These words are often confused: *deprecate, depreciate; bow, beau, bough.* Explain the differences.

B. Many of our most frequently used words are derived from Latin or Greek roots. Using the root in the first column, add two or more words containing this root to each word in the third column.

Root	Meaning	Words Built From Root
1. dict-	say	predict
2. fer-	carry	transfer
3. scrib-	write	describe
4. geo-	earth	geography
5. voc-	call	vocal

C. Change the present tense forms of the verbs within parentheses to the past tense forms.

1. The clerk (tear) the invoice by mistake.
2. We (see) the new word processing system last week.
3. She (begin) the meeting on time.
4. The rest of our group (catch) the last plane for Chicago.
5. Our general manager (send) invitations to all our loyal customers.
6. Clarissa (write) a letter that explained the delay.

COMMUNICATING FOR RESULTS

Getting Away. Assume that you are a sales representative for a large manufacturer. You are visiting Mr. Dennis Bronson, the purchasing agent for one of your key accounts. Within the hour Mr. Bronson has placed a sizable order with you. Since it is close to lunchtime, he suggests that the two of you dine together. However, you have an appointment with a customer whom you have been trying to develop into an even larger account. It will take you approximately forty-five minutes to travel to your appointment. Suggest ways in which you can make your important second call without antagonizing Mr. Bronson.

In your job you will quite frequently have to deal with business letters. Business letters are perhaps the most common form of written communication. They are so common that at one time or another you, like everyone, will be asked to write one. To do so, you need to know something about language structure, psychological principles, writing techniques, and different kinds of letters.

Because there are different kinds of letters, you will need some guidelines on how to write them. The message plans in the following units include these guidelines. They are simple, logical, easy to follow, and easy to remember. In fact, you will find that you automatically think of these guidelines when you plan and write your business letters. Given a situation that requires you to write business letters, you will be able to do the following when you master the units in this chapter:

1. *Select which of the three letter-writing plans best helps you organize your ideas.*

2. *Place letter parts appropriately, classify kinds of business letters, and plan and dictate business letters.*

3. *Write routine letters that request, transmit, acknowledge, or respond.*

4. *Write letters that request favors or donations.*

5. *Write letters with unpleasant news or refusal decisions but still maintain goodwill.*

6. *Write effective claim and fair adjustment letters.*

7. *Write credit and collection letters with the help of paragraph libraries.*

8. *Write persuasive sales letters and attention-getting public relations letters by developing shell documents.*

9. *Write thoughtful social-business letters.*

40

Selecting Letter Format and Style

Many things that we use in our society are available in a wide variety of models and styles. Consider, for example, the different kinds of motor vehicles at your disposal. Not only may you choose from automobiles, trucks, and vans but also each of these classifications offers you a variety of models and styles. Automobiles are available in sedan, coupe, or sports models; they range from small economy cars to giant gas guzzlers. You may select from literally hundreds of designs and their variations. The car or other vehicle *you* select, though, is one that best meets your needs and that reflects you.

The same is true of styles for business letters. There is no standard by which the appropriateness or inappropriateness of a specific style can be firmly established. However, some companies adopt one particular style, and employees are expected to use that style. In all other situations the choices are for you to make from the styles discussed in this unit.

Since the differences among formats and styles concern the placement of letter parts, you will first review the various parts of business letters; then you will review the different arrangement styles of letters. In this way you will be better able to present your ideas within an acceptable framework, leave the reader with a positive impression, and keep the reader's goodwill.

Letter Parts

The letter writer works with many letter parts: the address, the salutation, the message, and the complimentary closing, to mention some. These parts must be arranged in a sequence that will make the letter meaningful and will contribute to attaining the purposes of the message. See, for example, the letter on page 379.

Usually a letter is divided into four sections. These sections, each of which contains several essential and a few optional parts, are the following:

1. The heading
2. The opening
3. The body
4. The closing

The Heading. Except in unusual situations—when proof of the mailing date is important, for example—envelopes are not retained and filed in business

Letterhead: The company's printed name and address.

the energy concern

840 DALTON ROAD
MIDDLETOWN, N.J. 07748
(202) 555-3900

Date Line: The date (month, day, year) starts between lines 12 and 15.

March 17, 1989

Inside Address: The name and address of the person to whom you are writing.

Mr. Sidney Afton
832 Laverne Place
New Brunswick, NJ 08903

Salutation: An opening greeting.

Dear Mr. Afton:

Subject Line: Indicates what the letter is about.

Subject: Saving Money and Energy

We very much appreciate your recent phone call. We value every customer inquiry and are always happy to explain how our services and products can make your home more energy-efficient, thereby saving your hard-earned dollars.

Message: The text of the letter; paragraphs are typed single-spaced.

As you requested, Paul Rasmussen, one of our energy consultants, will arrive at your home at 2 p.m. on Saturday, March 25. Paul will conduct an energy audit of your house, using the latest and most sophisticated survey tools. After the audit, Paul will send you a computer printout like the one enclosed that will tell you precisely how financially advantageous our various products and services will be. There is no charge for this survey, and of course you are under no obligation whatsoever.

Thank you for giving us the opportunity to be of service.

Complimentary Closing: A parting phrase.

Sincerely,

Company Signature: Emphasizes that the writer is acting on behalf of the company.

THE ENERGY CONCERN

Valerie C. Esterbrook

Writer's Identification: The signer's name or title or both.

Valerie C. Esterbrook
Sales Manager

Reference Initials: The initials of the writer and/or typist.

lms

Enclosure Notation: A reminder that the letter has an enclosure.

Enclosure

Copy Notation: The names of those who will receive copies of this letter.

cc: Paul Rasmussen

The parts of the business letter must be arranged in a sequence that will make the parts meaningful.

offices. Therefore, the information that the reader needs to answer a letter must be included in a *letterhead* and *date line*. These are the essential heading parts referred to when the reply is written and, frequently, after the letter has been filed.

The Company or Organization Letterhead. Almost every company uses high-quality stationery with its name, address, and telephone number printed on it. These identifying items, and often such additional data as the names of the company's top executives, its slogan, and so on, are referred to collectively as the letterhead. Some examples are shown below.

In addition to providing identification of the writer's company, the content and design of the letterhead help to project the company's image. Although the reader is primarily interested in getting to the writer's message as quickly as possible, the letterhead is almost sure to be glanced at first. An opinion of the company may be formed (perhaps subconsciously) because of its letterhead: It's old-fashioned or it's modern; it's futuristic or it's ultraconservative; it's middle-of-the-road or it's progressive; and so on.

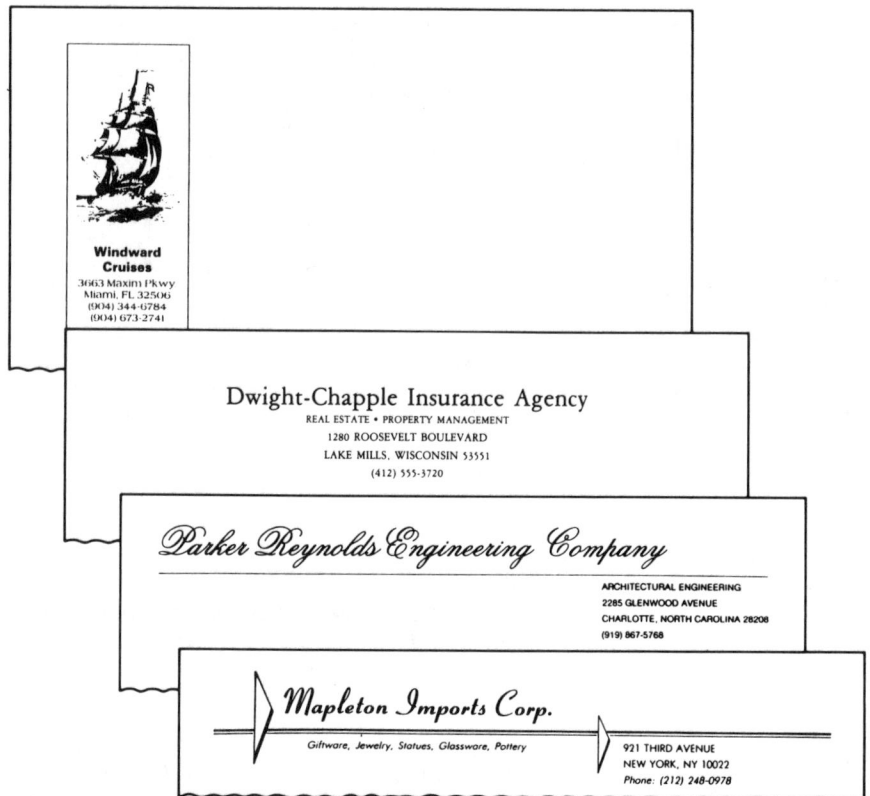

Windward Cruises
3663 Maxim Pkwy
Miami, FL 32506
(904) 344-0784
(904) 673-2741

Dwight-Chapple Insurance Agency
REAL ESTATE • PROPERTY MANAGEMENT
1280 ROOSEVELT BOULEVARD
LAKE MILLS, WISCONSIN 53551
(412) 555-3720

Parker Reynolds Engineering Company
ARCHITECTURAL ENGINEERING
2285 GLENWOOD AVENUE
CHARLOTTE, NORTH CAROLINA 28208
(919) 867-5768

Mapleton Imports Corp.
Giftware, Jewelry, Statues, Glassware, Pottery
921 THIRD AVENUE
NEW YORK, NY 10022
Phone: (212) 248-0978

The content and design of a company's letterhead identify the company and project the company's image.

the most favorable impression that it can—even if only for a fleeting second in a reader's mind.

The Date Line. Knowing when a letter was written is often *very* important—important to both the reader and the writer. With the flood of mail that every business office receives and sends, business writers would be unwise to assume that they or their readers will remember the exact order of events related to a particular matter. Every letter should therefore carry a date line consisting of the month, day, and year. Position the date somewhere between lines 12 and 15 on the letter.

There are two widely used date line styles—one for general business correspondence and one for military correspondence. In neither style is it acceptable to use a number to indicate the month—even if the letter is written to a military organization or an individual. Do not use *st, nd, rd, th,* or *d* after the day of the month.

Business	Military
April 15, 1989	15 April 1989
September 7, 1989	7 September 1989

Personal or Confidential Notation. A personal or confidential notation is typed below the date at the left margin to indicate that a letter is of a private nature. The notation may be typed in all-capital letters or initially capped and underscored.

PERSONAL OR Personal   CONFIDENTIAL OR Confidential

The Typed Heading. Office people become so accustomed to using printed letterheads, which contain return addresses, that they sometimes forget to type this information when they write personal business letters on plain paper. A personnel manager once remarked: "I received a splendid letter of application today. I'd certainly hire that woman if only I knew her address."

For a typed heading, use one of the following forms:

> 333 Blaine Street
> Missoula, Montana 59801
> May 18, 1989

OR:

> BRENDA I. WEAVER
> 333 Blaine Street
> Missoula, Montana 59801
>
> May 18, 1989

The Opening. The functions of the opening are to direct the letter to a specific individual, company, department, or other destination, and to greet the reader. The *inside address* directs the letter, as does an *attention line,* if used; and the *salutation* greets the reader. Both the inside address and the salutation are essential in the most commonly used letter styles.

From your point of view as the reader, the opening is assurance that the letter is intended for you and that the writer is thoughtful enough to say "hello" before beginning to talk business. In addition to serving a practical need, the opening serves the purpose of courtesy and helps establish the overall letter tone.

The Inside Address. The name of the addressee, which should always be preceded by a courtesy title (except when followed by *M.D.* or another abbreviation), is usually the first line of the inside address. Common courtesy requires including the person's job title when it is known—either on the same line as the name or on a separate line in the inside address. The name of the addressee's company; the street address; and the city, state, and ZIP Code number are also included. The following are examples of accepted inside-address styles:

Mr. Melvin T. Moss
Chairman of the Board
Continental Insurance Company
1300 Laurel Canyon Avenue
Ogden, Utah 84401

Ms. Linda R. Schur, Chairperson
Business Education Department
Laguna Hills High School
400 West Haskell Avenue
Milwaukee, Wisconsin 53203

Sarah R. Granados, M.D.
(or Dr. Sarah R. Granados)
8750 Griswoll Street
Albuquerque, New Mexico 87101

Mrs. Elizabeth Wong
46 Breighton Heights Way
San Francisco, California 94111

The Attention Line. When a letter is addressed to a company or to a department within a company rather than to a specific person, an attention line may be used to speed up handling of the letter. This line is typed below the inside address and above the salutation. The following are various styles of attention lines:

ATTENTION MS. JOYCE T. ARNTSON
ATTENTION GENERAL MANAGER

Attention Ms. J. T. Arntson
Attention General Manager

Notice that they are typed in all-capital letters or in underlined upper- and lowercase letters. Remember to use one of the following salutations with an attention line: *Ladies or Gentlemen:* or *Ladies and Gentlemen:*.

The Salutation. There are several accepted forms of salutations, and each form reflects a different tone. The following are examples of salutations and descriptions of their use:

Singular Form	**Plural Form**	**Use**
Dear Steve: Dear Angelica:		Used for informal busi- ness letters—implies a personal friendship.

Singular Form	Plural Form	Use
Dear Mr. Dixon:	Dear Messrs. Dixon and Brauman:	Used in routine business correspondence addressed to one or several individuals—formal but cordial.
Dear Mr. Brauman:		
Dear Ms. Stresino:	Dear Ms. Stresino and Mrs. Crosby:	
Dear Mrs. Crosby:		
	Ladies and Gentlemen:	Used for correspondence addressed to a company or to a group.
	Ladies or Gentlemen:	
Dear Madam:	Dear Mesdames:	Used only for *very formal* correspondence; avoid in most correspondence.
Dear Sir:	Dear Sirs:	
Dear Madam or Sir:	Dear Mesdames or Sirs:	
Madam:	Mesdames:	
Sir:	Sirs:	
Madam or Sir:	Mesdames or Sirs:	

If you know the name of the person to whom you are writing, then use the name in the salutation. This approach shows more consideration and meets the receiver's ego needs since we all like to see our name in print (spelled correctly of course). If you don't know the person's name, use an attention line with the person's job title (*ATTENTION PERSONNEL MANAGER*). Then use a salutation such as *Ladies and Gentlemen.*

The Body. The body of the letter is, of course, the most important section of the letter—from both the writer's and the reader's point of view. Here the writer makes every effort to get his or her thoughts effectively across to the reader. The important thing to remember is that the body of the letter consists essentially of the *message* and may optionally include a *subject line.*

The Subject Line. The writer can give the reader advance notice of what the letter is about by including a subject line immediately *below* the salutation (so that it precedes the message). Like the attention line, the subject line is typed in all-capital letters or in underlined upper- and lowercase letters. The word *Subject* may be omitted, but when it is used it is followed by a colon:

SUBJECT: ANNUAL STOCKHOLDERS' MEETING
Subject: Annual Stockholders' Meeting

In legal correspondence or when referring to policy or project numbers, the term *In re:* or *Re:* may be used in place of *Subject:*

The Message. The message is the "body and soul" of the whole letter—all the other parts are appendages, arms and legs, that support and help make the messaage work. By using the letter-writing principles discussed in Units 41–48, the writer gives the message a purpose that is meaningful to both the writer and the reader.

The message of every business letter usually consists of at least two paragraphs—even if the second paragraph is nothing more than "Best wishes to you," or something along that line.

The Closing. Just as a person usually says "Good-bye" when finishing a conversation, so a writer usually uses a *complimentary closing* in a business letter. The only thing that is different is the way in which the "Good-bye" is said.

The Complimentary Closing. Complimentary closings, like salutations, vary in form and tone. The important thing to remember is to match the tone of the complimentary closing with that of the salutation as closely as possible. *Dear Bob* and *Very truly yours*, for example, obviously would make a rather absurd combination in a letter. Forms that are commonly used are as follows:

Formal	Informal
Yours very truly,	Sincerely,
Very truly yours,	Cordially,
Very sincerely yours,	Sincerely yours,
Very cordially yours,	Cordially yours,
Respectfully yours,	Best regards,

The Company Signature. The company signature, the typed name of the company, is usually considered an optional part of the closing. Some companies prefer having their typewritten names in the closing on the theory that the company, not the writer, is legally sending the letter. Most companies, however, do not use a company signature.

When a company signature is used, it is usually typed in all-capital letters on the second line below the complimentary closing:

Sincerely yours,   Very truly yours,

PACIFIC INDEMNITY CORPORATION   LLOYD, HANSON & MOTT

The Writer's Signature. This is simply the handwritten signature of the person who has written the letter.

The Writer's Identification. In most instances the writer's name and job title (and/or department) are typed below the signature. Sometimes only the writer's title and/or department are used. Here are several examples of styles:

Ellen R. Reynolds, General Manager   William C. Carlton
                                                                    Executive Vice President
S. W. Whitcomb, Manager
Accounting Section   Assistant Manager
Agency Management Department   Service Department

Reference Initials. The reference initials serve an administrative purpose only. If the writer's name is included in the writer's identification, then his or her initials may be omitted in the reference initials. Remember that when used, the writer's name or initials are written first, followed by the typist's initials. The following are widely used reference-initials styles:

FCBorstal/laj	laj	(Three initials indicate that
FCB/LAJ	FCB	FCB signed the letter, crn
FCB/laj	FCB/crn/laj	wrote it, and laj typed it.)

Enclosure Notation. When something is included with the letter in the same envelope or package, this fact should be indicated by an *enclosure notation*. Such a notation helps writers, recipients, and secretaries confirm that all the enclosures are included when the letter is sent and received. The following are widely used enclosure notations:

Enclosure	Enclosure: Contract	Enclosures:
Enc.	2 Enclosures	1. Contract
Enclosures (2)	1 Enc.	2. Check
Enc. 2	2 Enc.	3. Envelope
		4. Memo

Mailing Notation. When some special postal service, such as *registered mail* or *certified mail*, is to be used in mailing a letter, a note indicating the special service should appear on all copies of the letter. Such notations are typed below the reference initials (or below any enclosure notations). A sample notation is shown in the letter on page 392.

Copy Notations. When the writer wishes to send a copy of the letter to one or more persons and wishes the addressee to know a copy is being sent, a *copy notation (cc)* is indicated on the original and all duplicate copies of the letter. The *cc* is typed in lowercase letters and it may be followed by a colon. Note that *cc* applies both to carbon copies and to copies that are duplicated photographically.

cc Public Relations Department   cc: Mr. Paul Raskin

Other acceptable copy notations are as follows: *c, copy to,* or *copies to.*

Blind Copy Notation. The *blind copy (bc) notation* never appears on the original copy of a letter. It appears only on copies and is used only when the writer wishes to send a copy to a person other than the addressee but does not want the addressee to know that a copy is being sent. For ease of location and referral, the blind copy notation is typed on the seventh line of the page at the left margin. All *cc* and *bc* notations should appear on the writer's file copy.

Postscript. The writer who has unintentionally forgotten to mention something in the message can add a *PS* rather than have the letter completely retyped. In fact, some writers deliberately add postscripts to draw the reader's attention to a particularly important point. A postscript therefore functions as part of the *body,* but it is always positioned in the closing section of the letter. The letters *PS* may be omitted, but when they are used, they are followed by a period or a colon. A postscript is illustrated in the letter on page 392.

Positioning of Letter Parts

The sequence in which the letter parts occur in a business letter follows the order in which they have just been discussed. Their horizontal positioning—whether typed to begin at the left margin or the center, for example—is determined by the letter's arrangement style, which will be discussed later in this unit. The vertical spacing of the letter parts, however, is relatively fixed.

The placement of the whole letter on the page can do much to enhance or destroy the impact of the message on the reader. If the left and right margins are approximately even, the letter looks balanced horizontally; if not, it looks as though it is ready to fall sideways off the page. The same is true of vertical placement. If the letter ends too high on the page, it looks as though it is hanging at the top of a cliff. If it ends too low, it looks as though it is sliding right off the page. The letter should be balanced visually.

To balance your letters visually on a page, you must set your margins according to the size of the type your typewriter has (pica or elite) and the size of the stationery you are using. *Pica* type fits 10 characters or spaces to the inch; slightly smaller, *elite* type fits 12 characters or spaces to the inch. The most commonly used stationery sizes are as follows:

Standard: 8½″ × 11″
Baronial: 5½″ × 8½″
Monarch: 7¼″ × 10½″

Knowing the size of type and the size of the stationery, then, you can determine your margin settings by using the chart below.

If the Stationery You Are Using Is . . .	Use Line Length of . . .	Set Margins at . . .*
	4-Inch Line	
Baronial	40 spaces (pica)	22-67
	50 spaces (elite)	26-81
	5-Inch Line	
Standard and	50 spaces (pica)	17-72
Monarch	60 spaces (elite)	21-86
	6-Inch Line	
Standard	60 spaces (pica)	12-77
	70 spaces (elite)	16-91

* The additional five spaces added to the right margin setting avoids overusing the margin release key on regular typewriters. For word processing programs with word wrap, deduct five spaces from the right margin.

Spacing. On standard 8½- by 11-inch stationery, the date may be typed on any line from line 12 to line 15, with the inside address typed five lines below it. One blank line is left before the salutation, each paragraph, and the complimentary closing. If an attention line or a subject line is included, one blank line precedes and follows these parts.

The writer's identification should be preceded by at least three blank lines to allow room for the signature, and at least one blank line usually separates the writer's identification from the reference initials. Generally, no blank lines are left to separate the reference initials from the enclosure and copy notations.

A postscript, if used, would be preceded by one blank line, and a *bc* notation would be typed about 1 inch from the top of the page or copies only.

All these parts except the blind copy notation are shown in the sample letters on pages 379 and 391–394.

ZIP Code. The postal ZIP Code follows the state in an address, with no punctuation preceding or following it. In the inside address, in a typed letterhead, on an envelope, and in running text material, the ZIP Code is preceded by only one space.

The state may be spelled out, or it may be abbreviated, using the official two-letter abbreviations recommended by the United States Postal Service.

Winston Tire Company
4800 Century Avenue
Oklahoma City, Oklahoma 73111-1131

Mr. Kurt Stadthaus
436 Greenview Place
Canton, OH 44708

Using these official abbreviations will aid handling by an optical character reader (OCR), which the U.S. Postal Service uses to process mail.

The Second Page

Sometimes letters cannot be completed on one page, and the message must be continued on a second, and sometimes even a third, page. When this happens, *plain* (not printed letterhead) paper of the same size and quality as the letterhead sheet should be used for continuation pages.

Side Margins. All continuation pages should have the same side margins as the first page. Since there would be over 200 words in the body of a two- or three-page letter, the right and left margins would be about 1¼ inches each.

Top and Bottom Margins. The top margin of a continuation page should be 1 inch (start typing on line 7). At least 1 inch—no more than 1½ inches—should be left blank at the bottom of each continuation page. The last page of a letter may, of course, have a much deeper bottom margin.

Continuation-Page Heading. A heading consisting of the name of the addressee, the page number, and the date should appear at the top of each continuation page. Two of the commonly used arrangements for such headings are illustrated below. Remember that three blank lines should be left between the last line of the heading and the first line of the continued message.

Ms. R. D. Norland   2   February 3, 1989

OR:

Ms. R. D. Norland
Page 2
February 3, 1989

When dividing a paragraph at the bottom of any page, leave at least the first two lines on the page and carry at least two lines to the continuation page. If this isn't possible, carry the whole paragraph over to the continuation page. Do *not* divide the last word on any page.

The Envelope

Envelopes should be of the same quality and color as the letterhead paper, as illustrated on page 389. Here are some points to remember when addressing envelopes.

1. On a small (No. 6¾, 7 or 5⅝) envelope, start the address on line 12 about 2 inches from the left margin; on a large (No. 10) envelope start the address on line 14 about 4 inches from the left margin.
2. Single-space all addresses and use block style.
3. Always type the city, state, and ZIP Code on the last line.
4. Leave one space between the state and ZIP Code.
5. Type the attention line or any personal notation below the return address. Begin on line 9 or on the third line below the return address, whichever is lower. Capitalize each word, and underscore the entire notation.
6. If special mailing services are required, type the service in all-capital letters on line 9 in the upper right corner of the envelope.
7. If the envelope does not contain a printed return address, be sure to type a return address in the upper left corner—it should not be typed on the back of the envelope.

Thee PRINTING Place

OFFSET PRINTING
COLOR XEROX
TYPESETTING
XEROX 9500

Thee PRINTING Place

OFFSET PRINTING • COLOR XEROX • XEROX 9500 • TYPESETTING
19559 PARTHENIA STREET, NORTHRIDGE, CALIFORNIA 91324

19559 PARTHENIA STREET • NORTHRIDGE, CALIFORNIA 91324 • (818) 993-8184

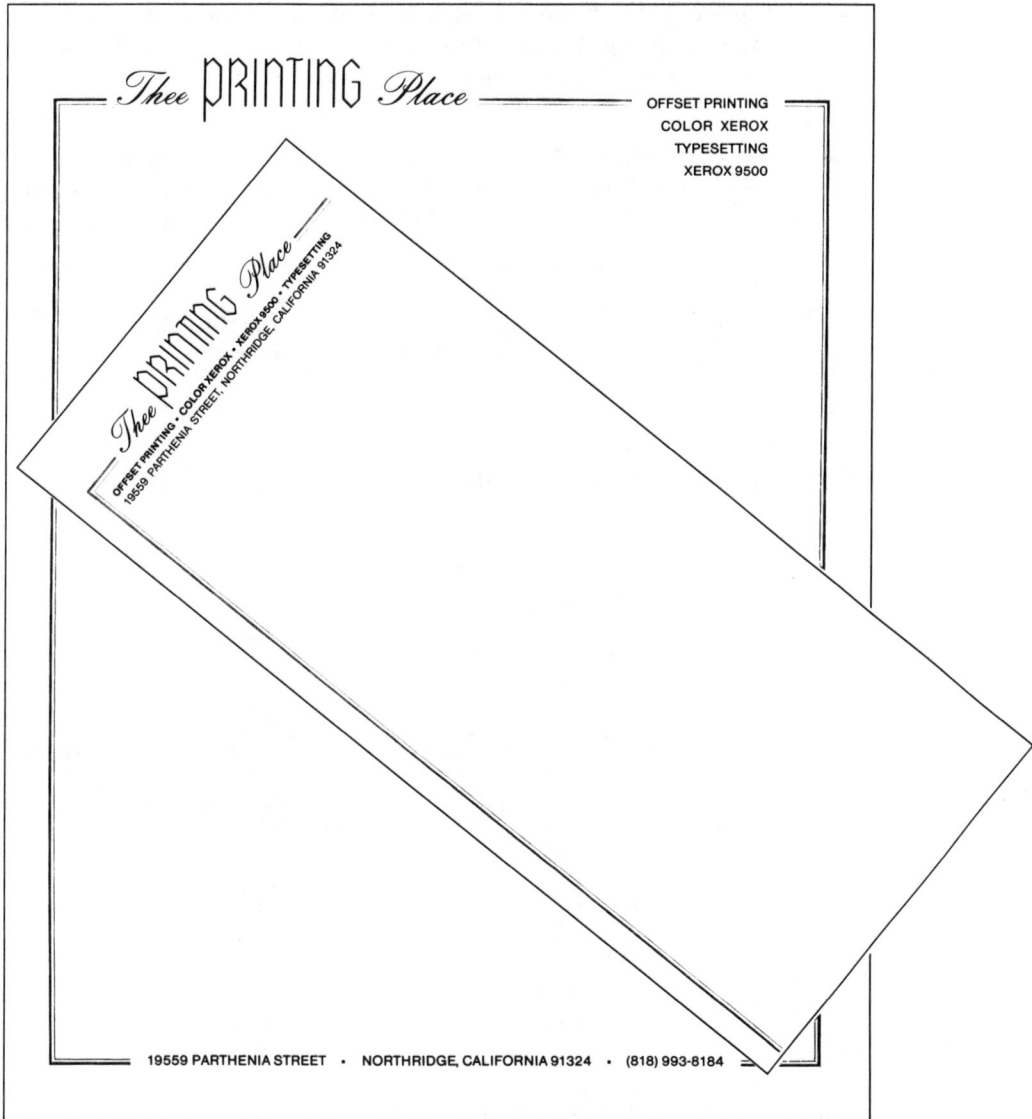

A company's envelopes should be of the same quality and color as the letterhead.

Arrangement Styles of Letters

The arrangement style of a letter depends upon the *horizontal* placement of the various letter parts. The order or sequence in which the parts are positioned is, as indicated in this unit, fixed in a logical pattern that is normally not altered to suit individual tastes.

Block Style. Letters in which *all* the parts begin at the left margin are written in block style. This style, which is illustrated below, saves typing time since the typist doesn't have to use the tabulator in setting up the letter.

Modified-Block Style. In arranging a letter in modified-block style, the typist usually changes only the position of the date line, the complimentary closing, and the writer's identification. All these parts generally start at the

OFFICE TECHNOLOGY NETWORKS, INC.

4833 Gateway Boulevard East
El Paso, Texas 79905
(713) 555-1348

February 6, 1989

Ms. Geneva Clauson
Investment Properties Company
708 Talton Avenue
San Antonio, TX 78285

Dear Ms. Clauson:

Subject: Form of a Block Letter

This letter style is fast becoming the most popular style
in use today. Efficiency is the main reason for its popularity. The typist can save time and eliminate the necessity
of working out placement. Some organizations are even designing letterheads to accommmodate this style. A few years
ago, some people felt the block style looked odd. That
complaint is seldom heard today, however. As more organizations use a block style, people have become accustomed to
its appearance.

This letter also illustrates the subject line and the
enclosure. A subject line may be typed with initial caps
or all in caps. It should start at the left margin. It
always appears after the salutation and before the body of
the letter. An enclosure notation starts at the left
margin and always appears on the line after the reference
initials.

Sincerely,

Annette G. Fuentes

Annette G. Fuentes
Manager, Customer Services

nkm
Enclosure

The block letter is the fastest one to type because each line begins at the left margin.

horizontal center of the page. However, the date may be aligned to end at the right margin, and the subject line may be centered or indented five spaces. A letter in modified-block style is illustrated below.

Modified-Block Style With Indented Paragraphs. These letters are exactly the same as the modified-block style except that the first line of each paragraph is indented five spaces. This style is illustrated on page 392.

OFFICE TECHNOLOGY NETWORKS, INC.
4833 Gateway Boulevard East
El Paso, Texas 79905
(713) 555-1348

February 6, 1989

Ms. Carla Furman
Steffins and Wasserman Ltd.
1382 Victoria Street
Toronto, Ontario
CANADA M5C 2N8

Dear Ms. Furman:

This modified-block letter style is still very popular for two reasons:

    1. Many people feel comfortable with the traditional appearance.

    2. The blocked paragraphs make it slightly more efficient to type than a letter with indented paragraphs.

Lists, quotations, and addresses may be indented on either side for a clearer display. If it is necessary to use more than one paragraph for a quotation, a standard single blank line is left between paragraphs.

Special mail service, such as special delivery or registered mail, is shown on the line below the reference initials. We do so only to record this information for our files.

When the letter is being sent to a foreign address, the country is typed in all-capital letters on a separate line, as CANADA is shown above.

                Sincerely,

                Annette G. Fuentes

                Annette G. Fuentes
                Manager, Customer Services

nkm
Registered

PS: We treat postscripts in the same way that we treat other paragraphs, except that we precede each postscript by <u>PS</u>: or <u>PS</u>.

The modified-block letter is very popular. Note that the mailing notation is below the reference initials and that all-capital letters are used for *CANADA* in the inside address.

```
                    OFFICE TECHNOLOGY
                    NETWORKS, INC.
                    4833 Gateway Boulevard East
                    El Paso, Texas 79905
                    (713) 555-1348


                                        February 6, 1989



        Banton, Turchon, and Vick, Inc.
        9004 18th Street NW
        Washington, DC 20009

        Attention:  Training Director

        Ladies and Gentlemen:

             The modified-block letter with indented
        paragraphs is still popular because of its
        traditional appearance.  The indented paragraphs give
        this style a distinctive look.

             This letter also shows an attention line.  Like
        the subject line, the attention line is typed at the
        left margin, but above the salutation.  It is usually
        typed with initial caps but may also be all in caps.

                              Cordially,

                              Annette G. Fuentes

                              Annette G. Fuentes
                              Manager, Customer Services


        nkm

        cc: Ms. T. Spock
            Dr. F. Mantel
```

In the modified-block letter with indented paragraphs, the first line of each paragraph is indented—usually five spaces.

Simplified Style. These letters are similar to block-style letters in that all lines begin at the left margin. However, the simplified letter has some additional features. The salutation is replaced by a subject line typed in all-capital letters. The complimentary closing is omitted, and the writer's identification is typed in all-capital letters on its own line. A simplified letter is illustrated on page 393.

OFFICE TECHNOLOGY NETWORKS, INC.

4833 Gateway Boulevard East
El Paso, Texas 79905
(713) 555-1348

November 1, 1990

Miss Sherry Weinstein
680 Forrest Road, N.E.
Atlanta, GA 30313

THE SIMPLIFIED LETTER

A number of years ago, a new letter format, called the
simplified style, was developed. The letter you are reading,
Miss Weinstein, is prepared in that style.

1. Its lines all begin at the left margin.

2. It omits the salutation and complimentary closing.

3. It uses a subject line, typed in all-capital letters and
    preceded and followed by two blank lines. (Note that the
    word Subject is omitted.)

4. It identifies the signer of the letter by an all-capital
    line that is preceded by four blank lines and followed by
    one blank line--if further notations are used.

5. It uses a brisk but friendly tone and uses the addressee's
    name at least in the first sentence.

Perhaps, Miss Weinstein, for the sake of efficiency, you might
like to use the simplified letter style.

(Mrs.) Annette G. Fuentes

ANNETTE G. FUENTES--MANAGER, CUSTOMER SERVICES

pw

The simplified letter is similar to the block letter, with some additional features. These features are illustrated above.

Social-Business Style. The social-business style differs from regular business letter styles in a number of ways. Instead of opening the letter, the inside address may be typed at the left margin five lines below the signature line. Reference notations, enclosure notations, copy notations, and often the writer's typewritten signature are omitted. Informal salutations, often followed by a comma instead of a colon, characterize the social-business style. Complimentary closings such as *Cordially, Regards, Sincerely,* and *Best wishes* also maintain the informality of this letter format. An example of the social-business letter style is shown on page 494.

Punctuation Style for Business Letters

The message part of the business letter is punctuated, of course, using the standard rules for punctuating sentences. Two parts that get special punctuation treatment are the salutation and the complimentary closing. The salutation traditionally ends with a colon, and the complimentary closing traditionally ends with a comma:

Dear Karen: Cordially,
Dear Mr. Larson: Sincerely,
Ladies: Yours truly,

All display lines in the other parts of business letters end with no punctuation unless, of course, the line ends in an abbreviation:

Mr. Bryon Landesman   Mrs. Mary Ann Biaggi
700 Gaston Ferry Road   Arcs Mortgage Company, Inc.
Hicksville, New York 11802   940 Harvest Avenue
                             Coventry, Connecticut 06238

Enclosure   Enc.

cc Miss Sharon Meister   cc Mr. Jeffrey T. Harris, Jr.

COMMUNICATION LABORATORY

APPLICATION EXERCISES

A. Many of the following letter parts contain errors. Rewrite each, correcting the errors wherever they occur.

1. Dear Ms. Montgomery,
2. Walter Drury
   429 Zelzah Avenue
   Columbia, MD 21045
3. 9/3/1989
4. lrc/PKW

5. Mr. William Schaefer
   9320 Independence Avenue
   Jericho, NY
6. A-1 Plumbing Supplies. Inc.
   1450 McClay Street
   San Fernando, CA 91340

   SUBJECT: YOUR ORDER NO. 123788

   Gentlemen:

B. Write the salutation and complimentary closing for each of the following.

1. A letter to a competitor, Ms. Lisa Stanfield, who has just received a promotion in her firm.
2. A letter to a state senator, Thomas Griswell, inviting him to speak at a monthly meeting of a trade association.
3. A letter to your state's department of economic development inquiring about plant sites.
4. A letter to a good customer, Mr. Kenneth Killion, that includes an invitation to a formal dinner party.

C. Bring to class some business letters that you or a member of your family has received. Be prepared to discuss the appropriateness of format, style, and letterhead for each letter.

VOCABULARY AND SPELLING STUDIES

A. These words are often confused: *pursue, peruse; populous, populace.* Explain the differences.

B. Which of the words that follow each of these sentences is nearest in meaning to the italicized word in the sentence?

1. We *partitioned* the office to give each worker some privacy. (**a**) restored (**b**) divided (**c**) examined (**d**) scattered
2. We developed a *calculated* plan for expanding our share of the furniture market. (**a**) secret (**b**) unusual (**c**) reckless (**d**) deliberate
3. I remained *composed* as the customer enumerated how inferior our product was. (**a**) distressed (**b**) intense (**c**) calm (**d**) defiant

COMMUNICATING FOR RESULTS

Work First or Plan First? Each morning before she begins working, Jennifer prepares a list of all the things she must do. She then numbers the items in the order of their importance and begins working on the first item. Ted, her coworker, thinks that Jennifer wastes valuable time organizing her day this way. He prefers to start working. With whom do you agree? Discuss.

U · N · I · T

41

Planning Your Letters

Using the formats and arrangement styles discussed in Unit 40, you will be sure to send letters that look attractive and modern. As inviting as your letters may look, however, they cannot be effective and promote goodwill if your writing is not well organized and your ideas are not well planned.

In this unit you will preview the major kinds of business letters and learn how to plan these letters from the reader's point of view. Three basic plans are offered that are sure to help you organize any kind of business letter—and write it effectively.

Kinds of Business Letters

Business employees write many types of letters—to ask for information, advice, or favors; to send information; to collect money; to apologize for a mistake; to refuse a request that cannot be granted; to apply for a job; or to sell the company's products or services.

Business letters, though, are written not only by the business employee. They are also written by others to conduct *personal* business. Parents, students, bill payers, and consumers are just a few of the others who have occasion to write personal business letters. A parent may write to the school board requesting better courses; a student may write to several colleges requesting catalogs; a bill payer may write to Mervyn's Department Store to clarify charges on the last statement; a consumer may write to an automobile manufacturer to request a new car adjustment.

One could hardly name all the kinds of letters written—the list is practically endless. However, the following are among those most frequently in use.

Request Letters. Request letters may also be called "please send me" letters. They are the simple requests for information, literature, favors, appointments, reservations, and so on. Secretaries and stenographers often write such letters for their employers.

Another type of request letter is written to order merchandise or services. It is commonly called an *order letter*. Many large companies use a form called a *purchase order* for this purpose, but thousands of small companies place orders for goods and services by means of letters.

Letters Answering Requests. Just as a business firm often writes letters asking for something from another organization, it also receives a great many letters of request. Form letters and postcards are often used to acknowledge routine requests if the reply does not require a personal message.

If a letter is needed to convey a personal message, it may not be so easy to write. You may sometimes have to tell a customer that the order will be delayed because the merchandise is out of stock, or you may have to refuse a customer's request for a special favor simply because you cannot possibly grant it. These letters require the utmost tact and courtesy.

Letters answering requests give the letter writer an excellent opportunity for making friends and building goodwill. They are, therefore, among the most important communications in business.

Claim and Adjustment Letters. However hard people try to avoid them, mistakes will occur in business. A furniture store receives a shipment of lamps and several are broken. A disappointed parent feels that the tricycle she ordered for her child does not look new—the paint has been scratched in several places. A shoe store manager receives too many shoes in size 6A and too few in size 7B. These are typical situations in which the person who has been inconvenienced or offended writes a letter in protest. Although these letters are called *claim letters*, they really are *complaint letters*. All businesses receive—and send—them.

Letters written in response to claims are called *adjustment letters*. When the adjustment asked for is not granted (it isn't always; the claim may be unreasonable or unjustified), you must write the claimant a letter refusing to make the adjustment. To retain goodwill, you must always give a logical reason for the refusal. Because adjustment letters are among the most difficult to write, they require special understanding of people, plus extensive knowledge of the company the writer represents.

Credit and Collection Letters. A large percentage of business transactions in this country are handled on a credit basis. Letters must be written in response to requests for credit. Usually, the responses are favorable: "We are pleased to welcome you as a new charge customer at Elliot's." Sometimes, however, requests for credit must be declined because the applicants are not good credit risks. These are perhaps the most difficult of all letters to write. People don't want to be told that they are a poor credit risk!

Collection letters are written because a very small percentage of those who are given the privilege of credit violate that privilege. Therefore, they must be reminded, reasoned with, and sometimes threatened before they will pay what they owe. Collection letters are among the most challenging to the letter writer—their effectiveness is measured by the amount of money they bring in from forgetful or careless customers.

Sales Letters. In a sense, every letter business people write is a sales letter because it automatically becomes a showcase for the writers and their firms. However, there are letters written for the specific purpose of selling a product or a service. You probably have received a great many of these. A publisher wants to sell you a subscription to a magazine; a record company tries to persuade you to join its record club; an insurance company asks you to buy a policy. Millions of such letters are written every year.

Other sales letters come under the heading of *promotion letters*. These don't attempt to make *direct* sales; their primary purpose is to make friends and to create a good feeling between the company and its customers. In the long run, of course, the desired outcome is an increase in customers—and in sales.

Employment Letters. Employment letters deal with getting a position. They are written by everyone, not only by those who expect to work in business. Employment letters include letters inquiring about a position, letters of application, letters thanking an employer for an interview, and letters of resignation.

Social-Business Letters. Many letters of a social business nature are written to maintain friendly relationships with customers and business acquaintances. Typical social-business correspondence includes letters of congratulation, letters of sympathy, invitations, letters of friendship, and thank-you letters. Since they show thoughtfulness on the part of the writer, social-business letters do a great deal to build goodwill.

Classifying the Kinds of Business Letters

No matter what kind of business letter you write, you must consider its effect on the reader's needs. How you put your ideas on paper and in what order you present your thoughts will in large part determine how your reader will react to your message.

Although there are many different *kinds* of business letters, these kinds of letters can be handled simply in terms of the reader's anticipated reaction. Three basic letter patterns enable the business writer to solve problems with request, order, claim, adjustment, credit, collection, sales, employment, and social-business letters. By putting ideas together according to the basic patterns, you can work within the framework of the reader's needs and minimize the possibility of creating ill will.

Everyday letters may be matter of fact or may share good news. Persuasive letters, on the other hand, attempt to convince the reader to do something not previously considered or something that might be inconvenient.

Letters that refuse (say "no") or convey bad news have the potential of alienating the reader. It is the business writer's task to transmit the bad news and still maintain the reader's goodwill. The following discussion of the three organizational plans will help you in planning your business letters. Each plan considers the reader's needs in presenting its message.

Everyday Letters. In your role as an effective writer, you will face a variety of communication situations. In some cases your writing tasks will be pleasant. You may tell a reader that the charge account she has requested has been opened; that your company will be able to donate 500 pens for a charity benefit; that you will be able to ship the requested merchandise today; that you will be able to attend the sales convention next week. These "yes" letters are easy to write because they tell your reader good news. The reader's needs are met in this type of correspondence by the positive answer that the request will be granted.

Other everyday letters include order letters, acknowledgments of orders, simple requests, simple claims, and friendly collection reminders. Because of their routine nature, everyday letters use a direct approach in conveying their messages. The business writer usually starts the letter by telling the reader the good news, by granting the request, or by stating the claim. After the opening statement come the necessary details and then a friendly statement designed to maintain or generate goodwill. The organizational pattern for everyday letters is outlined below.

1. Direct statement indicating purpose of the letter.
2. Necessary details (if any) to carry through the purpose of the letter.
3. Goodwill statement that brings the letter to a close.

If you wanted information from the Las Vegas Chamber of Commerce for a class report, you would organize your letter according to the plan for everyday letters.

1. Request information about the city of Las Vegas for class report.
2. Indicate specific kinds of information needed—population trends, industrial growth patterns, unemployment figures, building trends, and recreational facilities.
3. Close with a statement of appreciation for any help that can be given in gathering information.

Persuasive Letters. Everyday letters take a direct approach and are simple to write. More skillful writing techniques are needed, however, when you show Mrs. Fauria why she should purchase your product; when you convince the Yum Yum Candy Company that it should send you a complimentary display; when you ask Illuminaire Company to replace your flashlight because it is defective, or when you request Mr. Hanson to pay his past-due account of $248.23. What particular needs must be met for each situation? How can our ability to meet our reader's needs be stated so that the reader acts positively?

The organization of persuasive writing is important in getting your reader to act positively. By using an indirect approach in persuasive writing, you can show your reader *why* he or she should take a desired action before you actually ask that action to be taken.

Human needs for financial gain, status, health, security, family, leisure time, and comfort and convenience provide bases upon which to organize the persuasive letter. A general organizational pattern that incorporates satisfying human needs is presented below.

1. Attention-getting statement or device that encourages the reader to continue reading the letter.
2. Factual statements that demonstrate the writer's ability to meet the reader's needs.
3. Presentation of request in terms of how it will benefit the reader, if possible.
4. Request for action.

If your electric hair drier broke just two days after the warranty had expired, you might want to write a persuasive claim letter. In this case you would probably use the following organizational pattern:

1. Praise company for its reputation for quality and dependability.
2. Explain that the electric hair drier broke two days after warranty expired. Appeal to pride by indicating you know that this is not a usual occurrence with the company's products.
3. Indicate that you wish to have the hair drier repaired under terms of warranty.
4. Ask company to let you know if it will comply with your request.

Bad-News Letter. Probably the most difficult communication situation involves saying "no." But you must say "no" when you refuse requests, refuse adjustments, and refuse credit. Conveying bad news is just as difficult as saying "no." We find explaining order delays or announcing price increases difficult—especially while still trying to maintain the customer's goodwill. How can you avoid losing a customer when sending bad or negative news?

Like the persuasive letter, the bad-news letter should take an indirect approach. If you were to say "no" or relate the bad news in the opening sentence, you would immediately lose your reader.

To maximize the amount of potential goodwill in a bad-news situation, you should begin your letter with a neutral statement upon which both you and the reader can agree. Then you should present the reasons for the refusal (as positively, tactfully, and courteously as possible) before actually stating the refusal. Offer an alternative, if possible, and then close your letter with a goodwill-building statement. This organizational pattern for bad-news letters is outlined below.

1. Neutral opening statement upon which the reader and the writer can agree.
2. Reasons for the refusal stated in positive, tactful, and courteous terms.
3. Statement of refusal.
4. Suggested alternatives, if any.
5. Statement to retain goodwill of reader.

The bad-news letter organizational plan might be used to tell a customer that the bank for which you work is unable to lend him or her the $3000 requested:

1. Thank customer for the credit request.
2. Discuss the need for collateral. Discuss the income requirements for a $3000 loan without collateral.
3. Compare customer's qualifications with requirements and courteously refuse request (or combine refusal with alternative proposal).
4. Indicate amount you can lend, if any.
5. Indicate that you look forward to hearing from customer if the alternative is satisfactory *or* invite customer to take advantage of one of your other banking services.

Planning Leads to Better Results

If you were going to take a long trip, would you just get into your car and take off? Not very likely. Your car might break down shortly after you started, you might run out of money before you reached your destination, and you might waste much valuable time by traveling on the wrong routes. Many things could go wrong because you had not planned ahead.

A blueprint helps the carpenter build a house; a pattern helps the dressmaker make a dress. Without the blueprint and the pattern, the builder and the dressmaker would be lost. When you write a letter, your "blueprint" can be of great help to you, for an effective letter does not just happen—it combines knowledge, experience, and careful planning.

How to Plan. The first step in any planning process is to gather all the materials you will need to do the job. In writing a letter, these materials may include the letter to which you are replying, a good dictionary, and pertinent information, such as prices and delivery dates. Only when you have all the necessary tools and information at hand can you plan an effective letter.

Using this information, you may wish to make brief notes—either on a scratch pad or on the letter to which you are replying. From these notes you can prepare a rough draft of your letter.

First, however, you should prepare an outline of what you wish to say, for an outline will help you organize your thoughts. This practice will save you time and money, and it should prevent the necessity for writing follow-up letters to add information or explain something that was not previously stated clearly.

Using your outline, you should next prepare a rough draft of the letter. Then check this draft for correct spelling and grammar and for completeness and accuracy of details. You may wish to improve the wording or change the order of some sentences so that your meaning is clear, your words are vivid, and your ideas flow. This is the process of editing, as described in Unit 7.

Probably you will want to prepare another draft, and perhaps still another, before you arrive at a final draft. In each you will incorporate the changes made in the preceding draft. This procedure is time-consuming, but it results in a better letter.

As you gain experience in letter writing, you will find that you need to spend less and less time in detailed planning; in time many facets of the letter-writing process will become almost automatic.

A Successful Example. An outline for a letter quoting personal computers wholesale prices to a retail store might look like the one given below. Notice how this outline follows the organizational plan for everyday letters.

1. Send catalog of complete line of Computab computer products.
2. Appreciate interest in the Computab line.
3. Recommend economical Basic 4 model for Laramie Electronics' special anniversary sale.
4. Quote price of $539.95 each in lots fewer than 25 and $489.95 each in lots of 25 or more.
5. Promise delivery one week after order is received.
6. Reassure retailer that Computab products are good sellers because of their low prices and fine values.

Eventually, when you have had more experience in planning and writing business letters, you will need only brief notations to direct you. Your condensed outline then might look like this:

1. Send catalog; acknowledge inquiry.
2. Basic 4 model $539.95 each in lots fewer than 25 and $489.95 each in lots of 25 or more.
3. Delivery in a week.
4. Goodwill closing.

Here is the letter written from this outline:

Dear Mr. Meyer:

As you requested, here is the current Computab catalog that describes our complete line of personal computers and accessories. We appreciate the opportunity to acquaint you with our products.

For Laramie Electronics' special anniversary sale, we recommend the economical Basic 4 model that is described on page 7 of the catalog. The Basic 4 wholesales at $539.95 each in lots fewer than 25 and at $489.95 each in lots of more than 25. You can expect delivery one week after you place your order.

We predict that the Basic 4 will be a big seller for you. At its under $1000 retail price, the Basic 4 represents a superior value and meets the growing demand for this kind of equipment. Like many other retailers throughout the country, you will have great success with this fine product.

Sincerely yours,

Dictating Effectively	If you were scheduled to speak to a group of people on a certain topic, would you simply wait until you were standing before your audience to decide what you were going to say? Obviously not. You would certainly want to outline your message beforehand, gather any pertinent facts, estimate the length of your presentation, and so on. Only by planning your speech can you be sure that it will be effective. Dictating letters and memos also requires advance planning.

Whether you dictate directly to a secretary or use dictating equipment, you should plan a written or a mental outline of your letter, memo, or report and have at hand all the data you will need. As you dictate, be sure to do the following:

1. Speak clearly—enunciate each syllable.
2. Specify the spelling of any proper names, unusual words, and words that may be confused, such as homophones.
3. Indicate the beginning of each new paragraph and the placement of any tables or lists.
4. Include proper punctuation marks.
5. List specifically any enclosures to be included, copies to be made, or mailing service to be used.
6. Mention whether a rough draft is required.
7. State when the finished copy is needed.

In addition, when dictating to a secretary, ask the secretary to let you know whether you are speaking too quickly or too slowly. And be sure not to move around the room as you speak.

Before dictating to a machine, read the instructions for operating the machine. Then practice using it for a few minutes to make sure that your speech is clear and that your voice is neither too loud nor too soft.

Following these guidelines will help you not only to write more effective letters but also to save time and increase your productivity.

COMMUNICATION LABORATORY

APPLICATION EXERCISES

A. List all the types of letters that you have received during the past year.

B. List and describe the types of letters that the following people might write in a typical month:

1. Electronics store owner
2. Police chief
3. High school or college teacher
4. Automobile dealer
5. Librarian
6. Physician or dentist

C. Bring to class at least four examples of different types of letters that you are able to collect at home or from people in business. Be prepared to discuss:

1. The kind of letter.
2. The reason the letter was written.
3. The organizational plan used to write the letter.

D. For each of the following situations, tell the kind of business letter you would write. Then indicate which organizational plan you would use to write the letter. For example, if the situation is to replace a defective product, your answer would be an adjustment letter using the everyday plan.

1. To send a customer a requested price list.
2. To order 3000 pens imprinted with the company's name.
3. To request payment on a long overdue account.
4. To interest a potential vacationer in a resort.
5. To thank the Richmond Corporation for an interview.
6. To sell a lawn maintenance service.
7. To congratulate a competitor on a promotion.
8. To invite potential customers to a plant tour.
9. To complain about a long overdue shipment.
10. To reject someone who has applied for a job.

E. For each of the following situations, plan the letter you would write. Outline the letter, using one of the three basic organizational plans.

1. Kathy Chidester wants to attend Foothill College after she graduates from high school. In order to pay her tuition and expenses, she will need a part-time job on campus. Outline the letter Kathy would write to the Director of Financial Services at Foothill College requesting information about part-time clerical jobs on campus. Be sure to ask about the kinds of jobs that are usually available and about what the pay scale is. Kathy would like to have any available literature describing such jobs and whatever application forms might be required. She has enclosed a résumé.

2. Assume that you are the assistant to the Director of Financial Services at Foothill College. You have been asked to reply to Kathy Chidester's letter. Outline the letter that you might write in response to her inquiry. Be sure to answer all her questions.

3. Assume that Kathy Chidester has forwarded her completed applications to you. After reviewing them and noting that she has fine clerical and secretarial skills, you feel that, even though no full-time position is available, she would be qualified for a part-time position with one of the two companies near campus. She would have a better opportunity for

advancement and her rate of pay would be higher. Outline your letter telling Kathy that she would probably do better working off campus. Tell her about the two possibilities and provide her with all the information she will need to apply.

VOCABULARY AND SPELLING STUDIES

A. These words are often confused: *intense, intents; insoluble, insolvable, insolvent.* Explain the differences.

B. Use either *raise* or *rise* to complete each of the following sentences. (Some sentences require the past tense or past participle forms.)

1. You can be sure that those two members of the staff will always _____ objections to any new ideas.
2. If stock prices continue to _____, we may wish to reinvest these funds.
3. Because your rates have _____ so sharply, we must find another method for shipping our products.
4. How many students _____ their hands to answer the question?
5. Last year the cost of living _____ 3 percent.

C. Which of the following frequently used words are misspelled? Spell each correctly.

1. application
2. apointment
3. akward
4. necessary
5. lisence
6. posess
7. sincerely
8. unconscious
9. privlege
10. anual

COMMUNICATING FOR RESULTS

Correcting an Error. In checking a cash register tape, a food shopper notices that he has been charged $11.90 for a $1.19 item. The customer comes to you, the manager on duty. What will you say to the customer to correct the error and maintain his goodwill?

U · N · I · T

42

Everyday Letters

Most of the correspondence that flows into and from a business organization is made up of *everyday busines* letters. These letters are routine in nature. They ask for information, respond to simple requests, transmit documents, order goods or services, make reservations, request appointments, inform customers and clients, and further the simple, routine operations of a business organization.

Everyday business letters are considered routine because they have a neutral effect on the reader. Such letters are very common and do not present special problems. They do not attempt to persuade the reader to take an inconvenient action, nor do they refuse to grant a request. These kinds of letters usually grant requests graciously, provide needed information, or contain inquiries the reader is eager to answer. The positive or neutral aspects of the everyday letter are the basis for its routine handling.

Writing everyday letters is usually quite simple, but they are not unimportant and deserve no less attention than more difficult letters. Regardless of its purpose or length, every letter requires careful planning and thoughtful writing to do the job it is intended to do.

Characteristics of Everyday Letters

When writing a routine letter, ask yourself this important question: "What kind of letter would I like to receive if this letter were being sent to me?" You would probably decide that you would want the writer to be as *brief* as possible—to avoid wasting your time. On the other hand, you would want the writer to give you *complete* information so that you wouldn't need to write for more details. And you would probably expect the writer to be *courteous* and *tactful*. While these characteristics are applicable to any kind of business letter, they are especially important in routine letters where miscommunication can lead to additional cost and ill will.

Brevity. Some people are inclined to ramble in a simple letter. Consider the aimless verbiage in the letter that follows:

Ladies and Gentlemen:

I have been a subscriber of your magazine for nearly two years. Well, maybe it's been three years. During this time I have not missed reading a single issue, at least not that I can remember. Surfing is one of my favorite sporting activities so your magazine articles are of interest to me.

Anyway, I was wondering if I could take advantage of your offer to extend my subscription to Surfing Magazine for the next two years. I wish to take advantage of your special two-year rate so I am enclosing a check for $18 to cover the cost of this subscription for that period.

Please continue to send the magazine to me at the following address: Jeffrey Hunter, 460 Pacific Coast Highway, Malibu, California 91756.

I look forward to your renewing my subscription and to receiving my monthly issues of Surfing Magazine.

Sincerely yours,

Enclosure

Ridiculous? Of course it is. But the letter serves to illustrate the pitfall into which many writers fall: *going into unnecessary detail.* You have already seen that the entire first paragraph of this letter could have been omitted— with much better results! The remaining part of the letter could have been expressed in fewer words too.

Look at the following letter. Note that it says what needs to be said—no more, no less—and then stops.

Gentlemen:

I wish to take advantage of your offer to extend my Surfing Magazine subscription. A check for $18, your special two-year rate, is enclosed.

Please continue sending the magazine to me:

Jeffrey Hunter
460 Pacific Coast Highway
Malibu, California 91756

Sincerely yours,

Enclosure

Completeness. In striving for brevity, the writer should not overlook the need to give complete information. Business firms often receive letters that contain no return address (and frequently the writers of such letters are the most vocal about the poor correspondence habits of the firms to which they have written!). Other important information may be lacking too.

Suppose you were the reservations clerk of a hotel that received a letter requesting a room for June 24, but the letter did not indicate whether a single or double was needed. What if you were an order clerk who received a letter requesting a blue shirt, but no size was stated? No doubt in both situations another letter would be needed to gather all the necessary information. The cost of business letters is rising all the time. An incomplete letter only calls for another letter, which means more expense.

Tact and Courtesy. Pleasant words like *please, thank you, appreciate, pleasure,* and *grateful* do more to create goodwill than brusque statements and demands. These kinds of words set the scene for building a positive business relationship.

Place yourself in the reader's position. Write the kind of letter you would like to receive. Use positive words and pleasant expressions. Make your reader feel important and convince that person this letter was written with his or her needs specifically in mind. Although you may be writing a routine business letter, do not let your reader feel unimportant for even one minute.

Organization of Everyday Letters

Because most everyday letters are routine and tend to have a positive or neutral effect on the reader's needs, they take a direct approach. Therefore, their organization is patterned after the plan for everyday letters:

1. Direct statement indicating the purpose of the letter.
2. Necessary details (if any) to carry through the purpose of the letter.
3. Goodwill or other statement that brings the letter to a close.

Notice how the following letter uses the everyday letter plan outlined above.

Gentlemen:

Please send me the name of a dealer in the Seattle area from whom I can purchase your Delicate Rose bedroom suite.

After seeing your advertisement in this month's Decorator's World, I called several furniture stores in our area. None of them stock the Delicate Rose line.

I would appreciate receiving this information as soon as possible so that I may surprise my daughter with a new bedroom set for her sixteenth birthday. I have always enjoyed the luxury of your fine furniture and am looking forward to the possibility of owning some additional pieces.

Sincerely yours,

Organizational plans, such as the plan for everyday letters, help the business writer place ideas in a meaningful sequence. The organizational plan is only a guide, however, and the writer must tailor the letter to make sure that it will accomplish its purpose as simply, as clearly, and as completely as possible.

Sometimes a routine letter will not require a presentation of details to accomplish its purpose, so the second step in the organizational plan may be omitted. Other situations may occur when no goodwill closing is needed to carry out the sequence of ideas. In these cases the business writer may close with a statement relating to the contents. Notice in the following letter, for example, how the writer concludes courteously with a request for additional information.

Ladies and Gentlemen:

Please send me your complete portfolio of Italian, French, Spanish, and other furniture that you advertised in this month's issue of <u>Decorator's World</u>. Enclosed is my check for $3.

I would also appreciate receiving the names of furniture store dealers in the Chicago metropolitan area who carry your line.

Sincerely yours,

Enclosure

Routine Requests

Have you ever answered magazine or television advertisements that invited you to send for something free? If you yielded to those temptations, you probably wrote a routine request letter (unless you merely filled out a coupon). These routine request letters are letters that ask for something the reader is eager to give.

Many routine requests are written in every business. For example, an administrative assistant writes (1) to a supplier asking for a catalog or a price list; (2) to a publisher asking for reprints of an article or to be listed as a subscriber; (3) to a hotel asking that a conference room be reserved for a meeting or that reservations be made, and so on. All these routine requests follow the organizational plan for everyday letters.

Requesting Information, Literature, or Free Service. Most letters requesting information, literature, or free service are short. They should give only the information needed by the reader to fulfill the request. Of course, they should also contain a return address so that the recipient knows where to respond.

Ladies and Gentlemen:

Please send me a copy of <u>No-Fail Flowers to Plant Now</u> advertised in the February issue of <u>Home and Family</u>. I am also interested in receiving a booklet you published several months ago, which I recently saw at a friend's home. It is titled <u>Not All Roses Are Red</u>. Do you have a copy to send me?

I have learned a great deal about gardening from your various publications, and I, as well as my friends, appreciate this wonderful service.

Sincerely yours,

Often a postcard will serve as well as a letter in making routine inquiries; in fact, many companies prefer postcards.

Dear Mr. O'Brien:

Please send me <u>Solving Your Copier Problems</u>, the booklet advertised in this month's <u>Office Management</u> magazine. My address is 8320 Corbin Street, S.E., Atlanta, Georgia 30317.

I certainly appreciate your distributing this valuable publication.

Sincerely yours,

Ordering a Product or a Service. Most business firms of medium and large size use a purchase order form when ordering goods. Such a form centralizes in the hands of one department the responsibility for ordering merchandise and helps to eliminate the possibility of employees' ordering goods on their own initiative. Also, a purchase order form is quicker to prepare than a letter.

Orders may also be placed on an order blank supplied by the company from which goods are being bought. Some companies supply such order forms.

A third way of ordering merchandise, used widely in small companies and by individuals, is through letters and postcards.

Accuracy is extremely important in preparing order letters. Figures and items must be checked and rechecked. To make an order letter easier to read and to check, the competent writer places each order item on a separate line in tabular form.

Ladies and Gentlemen:

Please send us the following daisy wheels for our Model 4050 International printers:

Quantity	Item	Price	Amount
2	No. 732 (Courier, 10 pitch)	$7.80	$15.60
4	No. 737 (Letter Gothic, 12 pitch)	7.80	31.20
1	No. 734 (Orator, 10 pitch)	8.30	8.30
1	No. 739 (Courier, 12 pitch)	7.80	7.80
Subtotal			$62.90
6% Sales Tax			3.77
TOTAL			$66.67

Our check for $66.67 is enclosed. Please let us know when we may expect delivery of this order.

Sincerely yours,

Enclosure

Every order letter must contain all the necessary information to process the order. Besides quantity, price, and amount, the order letter should pay careful attention to additional specifications. If applicable, is color and size information included? Has the method of payment been discussed? Is a specific date of shipment important? Are both the customer and the supplier in agreement on the method of shipment who will pay the freight charges? All these items need to be considered in composing the order letter.

Requesting Appointments. In business the usual practice is to make an appointment by telephone or letter when you wish to call on an individual at his or her office. Of course, if you are requesting an appointment with someone nearby, the use of the telephone is quicker and less expensive. Out-of-town appointments are often made by letter.

Dear Mr. Koltai: *Christmas and New Year in Florida*

I am planning to spend December 9 in Oklahoma City and would like very much to talk with you or one of your associates while I am there. We are setting up a profit-sharing program in our organization, and I have been told that you have a very effective plan at Walton Industries.

Would you find 10 a.m. on the 9th a convenient time to see me? An hour of your time should be sufficient and would mean a great deal to me.

Sincerely yours,

Making Reservations. While hotel reservations may be made by telephone, many persons prefer writing letters so that they are assured all the information has been conveyed correctly. What kinds of information need to be included? Of course, the dates of arrival and departure are paramount, but other kinds of information are important too. The hotel needs to know the name of the person who is to occupy the room. If there are other persons in the party, their names should be given too. Does the guest want a single room or a double room? What will be the arrival time? (Rooms are usually not held after 6 p.m. unless the person making the reservation asks that it be held for late arrival.) Is payment for the first night included to guarantee that the room will be held? Other information that might be given—although it is not always essential—is the guest's preference for a room location, the expected price, and any special required services.

Ladies and Gentlemen:

Please reserve a single room for Mrs. Frances Cates, national sales manager of Data Products, Inc., for March 23 and 24. Mrs. Cates will arrive at approximately 7:30 p.m. on March 23, so please hold the reservation for late arrival. If possible, Mrs. Cates would like to have a room facing Lake Michigan.

Please confirm this reservation and let me know if a deposit or credit card number is required.

Sincerely yours,

Letters of Transmittal

A check, a money order, or an important business paper sent by mail should always be accompanied by a letter. A letter helps to identify what is being sent so that the recipient knows exactly what you *intended* to send. The letter also provides a valuable record for future reference. When remittances or business papers are accompanied by a letter, the file copy answers the question: "I wonder whether I sent that magazine article to Bud Billings as I promised." or "How many copies of the Home Savings contract did I send to Edwards & Young?"

Good transmittal letters should be able to accomplish the following:

1. Identify *what* is being sent and *how many* (if money, the *amount*).
2. Specify any action necessary on the part of the recipient.
3. If transmitting money, identify the purpose for which the money is to be used—to apply on account, in payment of a certain invoice number, for services rendered, or for purchases made.

Note the following example:

Dear Professor Duffey:

Enclosed are the original and one copy of the contract for your manuscript, Breaking Through the Software Barrier. Please sign both copies, return the original to me, and retain the copy for your files.

The reviewers who critiqued your manuscript were very complimentary. Congratulations on preparing such an excellent manuscript. As you know, our target date for publication is January 1988. I'll be in touch with you when editing begins.

Sincerely yours,

Enclosure

Letters of Acknowledgment

A usual business practice—and always a very good one—is to acknowledge by letter receipt of any money, business papers, orders, favors, appointments, and oral agreements. Letters are important in acknowledging such business matters to avoid misunderstandings, to provide a record, and to show courtesy.

Letters of acknowledgment help avoid misunderstandings or mistakes. If you have received an order and will make shipment as soon as possible, the customer will want to know. If you do not acknowledge the order, the customer may assume that you did not receive it or wonder what you are doing about it if you did. A written acknowledgment should state that you have the merchandise in the requested quantity and tell the customer when you are going to fill the order. In this way misunderstandings and mistakes can be avoided.

Written acknowledgment letters provide a record, and records provide the internal control and memory of business. You would not want to trust your own memory as to the date on which you promised delivery of an order, especially if you are responsible for hundreds of orders. The copy of your acknowledgment, therefore, provides the information. A written record may also be needed for legal proof.

Courtesy builds goodwill in a business organization, and acknowledgment letters are one way to show courtesy. By reassuring the reader that you have received the order and are doing something about it, you show courtesy and build goodwill.

Acknowledgment letters, because they are routine letters, generally follow the everyday letter plan. After you have expressed appreciation for the reader's action, you may then supply the necessary details before giving your goodwill closing.

Acknowledging Receipt of Money. When money is received on a regular basis, such as monthly in the payment of an account, usual business practice calls for acknowledging the current month's payment on the next month's statement. Isolated payments or payments received· on an irregular basis, however, require individual attention and should be acknowledged through a form or letter. Remember these special considerations when writing letters that acknowledge the receipt of money:

1. Express thanks for the money, even though payment may be long overdue.
2. Be sure to mention the amount that is received. This letter provides a valuable record for the future. Rather than just saying, "Thank you for your check," say, "Thank you for your check for $123.50."
3. When appropriate, mention how the money is to be used—to apply on account, to be used as full payment for merchandise or services, or whatever the purpose of payment.
4. If you can think of something pleasant to say to the sender, do so. "We appreciate your prompt payment" or "Doing business with you is always a pleasure" or "I hope you will enjoy your new Cranston hardwood floors."

Following is a typical example of a letter acknowledging the receipt of money.

Dear Ms. Baca:

Thank you for your check for $87.50. This amount has been applied to your account, leaving a balance of $93.

We appreciate your promptness in making this payment, Ms. Baca, and we are always pleased to serve you.

Sincerely yours,

Acknowledging Business Papers. Important business papers—such as contracts, securities (stocks and bonds), notes, insurance policies, bids, and the like—should always be acknowledged promptly, since they are often just as important as money. In writing such letters, be specific as to just what was received and to any identifying numbers. If any action is required, your acknowledgment should state clearly that you have taken such action.

Dear Mr. Hedge:

Your life insurance policy, No. BFLS1003468, arrived today. As you requested, we will cancel the policy and send you the cash surrender value, $4312. You will receive a check within 30 days.

May we recommend, Mr. Hedge, that you consider the possibility of maintaining your current protection through the purchase of term insurance. Considerably less expensive than ordinary life, this kind of insurance would enable you to retain the same amount of protection with up to 70 percent less in premium payments.

If you are interested in looking into this program or if we can be of further service, please call Sylvia Padilla at 555-9875.

Sincerely yours,

Acknowledging Orders. Some business firms acknowledge all orders they receive for goods or services. Automation makes possible the easy use of form letters or postcards for this purpose. However, to welcome a new customer, to acknowledge an unusually large order, or to remind longtime customers how much you appreciate their business, individually written letters are much more effective. Customers, especially, appreciate the "extra touch" of a personal letter, such as the one illustrated on page 415.

Letters acknowledging orders follow the same plan as other acknowledgment letters. Because the customer is primarily interested in when the merchandise will arrive, this information is supplied in the opening sentence. Once you have expressed the main idea, you may then follow up with a statement of appreciation and other necessary details pertaining to the order.

Individually written acknowledgment letters provide the writer with an excellent opportunity to create goodwill. In the concluding sentences of the letter, you may reassure the reader that the purchase was a wise one. On the other hand, if your customer just purchased golf clubs, you might conclude the letter by giving a low-pressure pitch for your golf balls. Other kinds of goodwill closings might include a hearty welcome to a new customer or a statement of appreciation for the business given you by a longtime customer.

The general plan for organizing order acknowledgments includes the following:

1. A statement concerning the time and method of delivery.
2. A statement of appreciation for the business received.
3. Special instructions related to the order.
4. A goodwill closing.

FRANKLIN PORCELAIN
FRANKLIN CENTER, PENNSYLVANIA 19091
215-459-6553

January 24, 1984

Mrs. Claire Marcil
35 Foster Street
New Haven, CT 06511

Dear Mrs. Marcil:

I am very pleased to tell you that your porcelain
sculpture by Ronald Van Ruyckevelt, "The Queen Elizabeth
Rose," has been handcrafted to your commission and is
ready to be sent to you.

This original work of art is the premiere issue in
the Royal Horticultural Society's first collection of
flower sculptures in porcelain. And when you actually
have this exquisite work before you, I think you will
agree that it is a triumph of realism. Each of the 15
individual petals has been formed by hand and then assembled carefully by hand to form the complete flower.
And no fewer than 12 ceramic colors were hand-applied,
achieving a range of subtly beautiful, authentic shades.

When you entered your commission for "The Queen
Elizabeth Rose," you instructed us to bill you for the
deposit as soon as your sculpture was ready for shipment.
The invoice for that initial payment is enclosed, and the
balance will be billed in three equal monthly installments after your sculpture is sent to you.

We wish to thank you for commissioning this beautiful work. It is, I am sure, a work that will give you
much pleasure for many years to come.

If you wish to pay in full for this purchase, you
may do so by remitting the total order amount as shown
on the enclosed invoice.

Sincerely,

Jonathan Strauss

Jonathan Strauss

sm
Enclosure

Customers appreciate the "extra touch" of a personal letter of acknowledgment.

Notice how the general plan is put to work in the following letter:

Dear Mrs. Matsuyama:

Your Jet Stream outboard motor is being shipped today by prepaid freight. Thank
you for your order.

Would you do us—and yourself—a favor? Just as soon as your Jet Stream "Ultra Plus" arrives, please fill out the card attached to the motor and mail it back to us. Receipt of this card will tell us that the motor arrived in good condition and serve as a record of our special two-year guarantee.

We hope you have many happy hours of motor boating. Let us know if we can help you further. Incidentally, Playa del Rey Marina in Pacific Beach carries a complete line of parts and accessories for your Jet Stream "Ultra Plus."

Sincerely,

Confirming Appointments and Agreements. Appointments and agreements, whether made orally (in person or by telephone) or in writing, should be confirmed by letter. A letter will clarify any possible misunderstandings—especially for appointments and agreements made orally.

Dear Lisa:

I very much enjoyed meeting with you last Tuesday at the Professional Secretaries International meeting. Your method for handling correspondence procedures certainly seems efficient, and I gained a number of ideas from our discussion.

I was especially pleased when you suggested we get together for lunch on the 26th. Unless I hear from you, may I assume that our appointment is still on? I'll plan to arrive at your office about 11:45.

Sincerely,

Writing Acknowledgments While the Manager Is Away. When managers are out of the office, their administrative assistants or secretaries are expected to acknowledge important letters and explain any delays caused by the managers' absence. These acknowledgment letters are usually brief, courteous, and noncommittal. *Noncommittal* means that the administrative assistant or secretary should be careful neither to reveal private company matters in acknowledgments—not saying, for example, where the manager is—nor to commit the company in any way. For example, if a secretary works for a magazine publisher and receives an article in the editor's absence, the following letter would *not* be appropriate.

Thank you for sending us your article, "Choosing a Word Processing Program." It is extremely good, and I know Ms. Chu will want to publish it in the next issue of <u>Computer File</u>.

If the editor feels different about the article, this letter will put her in an embarrassing position. The noncommittal, but courteous, letter the secretary might write is as follows:

Dear Mrs. Berger:

Thank you for your article, "Choosing a Word Processing Program," which you wish to have considered for publication in an early issue of <u>Computer File</u>.

The editor, Ms. Eleanor Chu, is out of the office on a short business trip. When she returns, I will be sure to give her your article.

Sincerely yours,

Note that the secretary has said that Ms. Chu "is out of the office on a short business trip." It is usually best not to reveal more than this. Such information as "Ms. Chu is in Miami on vacation" or Ms. Chu is in Akron this week visiting a new printing plant" would not be appropriate. The safest phrase, when in doubt, is "Ms. Chu is out of the office this week."

When the employer is away and the correspondence cannot wait, letters are often referred to another individual in the company. Before referring letters to another person, however, the administrative assistant or the secretary must be sure that it is permissible to do so. Only the urgent or highly important letters will usually deserve this action.

Dear Mr. McIntyre:

Thank you for your November 5 letter to Mrs. Oliver.

Mrs. Oliver will be out of the office for about two weeks, so I am referring your letter to our sales manager, Mr. T. J. Loring. You will be hearing from Mr. Loring just as soon as he has had an opportunity to study your proposal.

Sincerely yours,

Simple Responses

There is nothing that says "we are interested in you" better than a prompt reply to an inquiry. For this reason some companies insist that all mail be acknowledged within 48 hours after it is received; others set 24 hours as the maximum. Although simple letters of response may be a daily routine in many offices, such letters should not be handled in a routine, mechanical fashion. Each inquiry should be given individual attention to ensure that all questions have been answered and that the inquirer's goodwill has been retained.

Businesses that receive many inquiries of the same type usually develop a form letter (either printed or typed and stored on a word processor or computer) to send to all those who request information. In addition, to save money and to present the product in the most favorable light, the company will probably prepare special booklets containing photographs, descriptive information, and sales features. Some type of letter, however, is needed to accompany the booklet. Even if generated on automated equipment, the more personal the letter can be made to look, the more successful it will be.

Many inquiries, of course, cannot be answered by a form letter or a postcard. And even if they could, some companies consider inquiries important enough to deserve individually written replies. Routine letters of response fall under the classification of everyday letters. Letters telling the reader that you can accept an invitation to speak at a banquet, that you can provide favors for the charity bazaar, or that you can attend a 9 a.m. Wednesday morning meeting are treated like all other everyday letters. Because they convey the good news the reader is waiting for, these letters of response use a direct organizational plan. Like other everyday letters, the routine answering letter grants the request or provides the important information in the opening sentence because the answer is what the reader wants most. Details related to the main idea and a goodwill closing follow.

Notice how the everyday letter plan is used to accept an invitation.

Dear Mr. DeLeon:

Yes, I will be able to speak to the Indianapolis chapter of the Medical Administrators' Association on Tuesday, October 30.

As you requested, the presentation will be a 45-minute address dealing with techniques for improving communication skills. I will speak on "Impact or Impediment—What Is Your Effect in the Medical Environment?" slanting the presentation toward what medical administrators can do to improve communication among the diverse groups of employees on a hospital staff.

The $200 honorarium you suggested is appreciated. I am looking forward to attending your meeting, Mr. DeLeon. When you have confirmed the details concerning the time and place, please let me know.

Sincerely yours,

The following response was written as the result of an inquiry. Mrs. Weston asked about replacement seats for her child's swing set. Notice how the everyday letter plan is used to answer Mrs. Weston's questions. In closing, the writer took advantage of this opportunity to introduce Mrs. Weston to another one of the company's products.

Dear Mrs. Weston:

Replacement seats for Gym Dandy swing sets are available in three sizes. The 18-inch bench sells for $5.60, the 24-inch bench sells for $7.80, and the saddle seat sells for $4.75. You have your choice of yellow or white molded plastic.

All orders should be accompanied by a money order. Also, please include a $1 handling charge for each seat requested. The new seats should reach you within three weeks after we receive your order.

Perhaps you might be interested in our new line of sandboxes, Mrs. Weston. As you can see by the enclosed brochure illustrating the various sizes and shapes, these sandboxes have been designed to complement your Gym Dandy swing set. Your local toy center has a complete display of this new line and would be pleased to help you select a sandbox for your child's enjoyment.

Sincerely yours,

Enclosure

COMMUNICATION LABORATORY

APPLICATION EXERCISES

A. In a magazine or a newspaper, find an advertisement offering a free pamphlet or booklet that you might like to have. Clip the advertisement. Then write a letter requesting the booklet or pamphlet and attach the advertisement to your letter. After your letter has been returned to you by your teacher, you may want to send for the booklet or pamphlet.

B. You have been offered a summer job with Dalton Community College, which you will attend in the fall. You will work in the student records office processing applications from entering freshmen. To get the job, you need three letters of reference. Your business English teacher, Dolores Tomlan, has moved to this address: 9432 Sunglow Street, Homestead Park, Pennsylvania 15120. Write Ms. Tomlan asking her if she would send a letter of recommendation to Mr. T. A. Caruana, Personnel Director, Dalton Community College, P.O. Box 749, San Diego, California 92109.

C. Assume that you are employed by a small legal firm and have been asked to investigate the possibility of computerizing its billing system. The firm presently owns an IBM Personal Computer that is used for word processing. While reading *PC News*, a national computer magazine, you notice an advertisement for a variety of software packages designed for the legal office—among which is a billing program. Write Legal Beagle Software Inc., 3854 Centinella Avenue, Topeka, Kansas 66604, to request information describing specifically the functions, contents, and features of its billing program. Inquire also whether the company has a booklet describing its other programs for the legal office. If it does, you would like to receive this information too.

D. Write a letter to the Del Coronado Hotel, Coronado, California 92118, to make a reservation for your five-day vacation. Request a room in the Ocean Towers at the lowest possible rate. You will need a room with two double beds. Because this hotel is in a resort area, a deposit is required; include with your letter a $100 check. Supply dates and other details.

E. You receive a signed contract from a client, John Plum, Flintridge Industries, 9300 Washington Boulevard, Detroit, Michigan 48233. The contract is to provide photocopying services (machines, maintenance, and supplies) to all of Flintridge's offices for the next two years, which makes Mr. Plum a major client. Acknowledge receipt of this contract and use this opportunity to generate continued goodwill for your company.

F. A regular customer, George Muhlhauser, writes to renew a contract with your company. Your supervisor, Alice Haberman, who is in charge of such contracts, will be out of town until October 5, and you have no authorization to renew contracts. Ms. Haberman has asked you to acknowledge receipt of all correspondence in her absence. Write a noncommittal letter acknowledging receipt of this customer's letter.

G. Donald Sampson, an industrial client whom your company represents, called to request a Tuesday, May 5, appointment at 9 a.m. He inquired as to whether you have a carousel slide projector available since he wishes to show the sales staff some slides illustrating the features of his new product line. Write a letter acknowledging the appointment and confirming the availability of the equipment. Mr. Sampson's address is 8750 Arminta Street, S.E., Portland, Oregon 97213.

H. Last week Mrs. Agnes Streebing, a counselor from nearby Los Altos Hills College, visited your school. Just as she was leaving, you managed to ask her for an appointment to see about enrolling at Los Altos Hills College. You will graduate from Kennedy High School in June and would like to continue your education in some field of business, possibly computers. Mrs. Streebing suggested that you drop by her office after school a week from Thursday to discuss Los Altos Hills' business curriculum and the possibility of your attending this college. Write the letter you would send to Mrs. Streebing confirming your appointment. Los Altos Hills College is located at 5600 Woodlake Street, Raleigh, North Carolina 27611.

I. Assume you work in the Visitors' Bureau of the Rocky Point National Wildlife Preserve, Rocky Point, North Carolina 28457. You receive a letter from Ms. Sally Abramowitz, Sarames & Abramowitz Travel Agency, 3575 Osborne Street, Huntsville, Alabama 35801. Ms. Abramowitz asks for literature and any other information needed to plan a trip through the preserve. Send her several pamphlets. In your letter point out that this preserve is one of the few places that has red-tailed twitter geese. The best time to visit the preserve is during the spring and fall. Food facilities are available, but she may also bring her own box lunches and take advantage of the picnic grounds or indoor dining facilities.

J. Assume you work in the offices of the Miami Chamber of Commerce. Kym Freeman, a student at Washington High School, has written a letter requesting information about Miami for her term report. She would like to have up-to-date information about population, industrial growth, housing, and recreational facilities. Answer Ms. Freeman's inquiry. Include various pamphlets published by the Chamber of Commerce and other civic groups. In your letter point out one or two interesting facts about Miami. Address the letter to Ms. Freeman at 1350 Shawnee Avenue, Des Moines, Iowa 50313.

VOCABULARY AND SPELLING STUDIES

A. These words are often confused: *elicit, illicit; key, quay.* Write each in a sentence that illustrates its meaning.

B. Are these statements correct?

1. Two adjectives that precede a noun are always connected by a hyphen.
2. In typewritten material words referred to as words are either underscored or enclosed in quotation marks.
3. Words that interrupt a direct quotation are also enclosed in quotation marks.
4. Slang is capitalized for emphasis.
5. Commas and periods are always placed inside, never outside, quotation marks.

C. In which of the following words should an *e* appear in the blank space?

1. d__scriminate
2. d__cribe
3. d__sease
4. exist__nce
5. restaur__nt
6. bull__tin
7. calend__r
8. materi__l
9. correspond__nce
10. __nquired
11. p__rsuade
12. memor__ndum
13. s__parate
14. listen__rs
15. d__stinctly

COMMUNICATING FOR RESULTS

Planning a Meeting. Your company has named you as head of a task force. Your job is to develop a plan for employees to spend one afternoon a month tutoring high school students who are having problems with certain subjects. Prepare a memo to the other task force members announcing the first meeting and listing a few of the items that will be discussed. Be sure to let them know that their ideas are needed and most welcome.

UNIT

43 Persuasive Request Letters

In most cases request letters can be handled routinely because they are everyday business letters. Order letters result in direct sales. A letter requesting information about a product or service may have money-making potential for a company. Likewise, written messages requesting hotel reservations improve the profit picture of the receiver. Even letters requesting appointments, although they may not directly result in sales, simplify the business operation from either a selling or a purchasing viewpoint. All these kinds of letters are eagerly awaited by the recipient. They improve the recipient's position and lead directly to goal fulfillment.

Other request letters, however, do not directly benefit the receiver. In fact, these requests may cause an inconvenience, cost money, or take up valuable time. How, then, can the business writer expect the receiver to comply with his or her request? While some request letters (and other types of persuasive letters) may attempt to spur an action that the reader is not necessarily inclined to pursue, the well-written persuasive request shows how this action will benefit the reader. If no direct benefit can be seen, the successful persuasive letter appeals to pride, fair play, fear, recognition, or self-worth—any of the motivators that stimulate human responses.

The job of the persuasive letter is to convince the reader to take an action that on the surface is not directly self-serving. To achieve its goals, then, a letter designed for action should be based on the psychology of communication discussed in Units 2 and 3.

Qualities of Persuasive Requests

Request letters, especially those persuasive in nature, need to be planned carefully. Close attention must be given to the reader's needs, and any attempt to relate the reader's needs to the request will bring the writer a step closer to accomplishing the purpose of the letter. By placing yourself in the reader's position, you can more easily see how the request could fulfill one of the reader's personal needs.

The request letter should be exceptionally well written, with ideas stated in as little space as possible. At the same time, the ideas should be presented completely and clearly. The writer must also be courteous and tactful—and

422

definitely make it as easy as possible for the reader to carry through the desired action.

Be Concise. Have you ever received a letter that just rambled on and on? What did you do with it? More than likely you glanced through it briefly and set it aside. Most other readers would do the same.

A letter that is written to persuade a reader to take an action must be worded so that the reader has no opportunity to become bored. Each word must contribute to the meaning of the message and hold the reader's attention. Only by making every word count can you accomplish this goal.

To achieve conciseness, avoid the needless repetition of words and ideas. Make sure that every sentence in your letter contributes specifically to accomplishing its purpose. Avoid including any unnecessary ideas that do not contribute to the reader's understanding of your request.

Develop Ideas Clearly and Completely. To promote understanding, you need to develop your ideas clearly and completely. The reader needs to be taken step by step through your reasoning process. Be sure that each idea follows logically from the previous one. Incoherent writing places stumbling blocks in the path of the reader and makes it difficult to interpret your request.

Test your own writing for coherence. If you were to remove a sentence, would the paragraph still make sense? If it would, your writing is too wordy. Another test for coherence is to assess the availability of all the necessary information. Have enough details been supplied to give a vivid, concrete picture persuasive enough for the reader to take the desired action? Omissions of important information and descriptive words provide a dull perspective. Test the following for coherence:

> Please attend a retraining session on Friday at 9 a.m. The session will end by noon.

Some concrete information has been supplied here: the type of session the reader is being asked to attend and the time during which the session will take place. But what concrete information is *missing?* The reader may want to attend the retraining session but should be told the following: What is the retraining for? On which Friday will it take place? And, most importantly, where is the session being held?

Idea development should not revolve around the needs of the writer, but instead should take into consideration the needs of the reader. For example, in writing to alumni of the local high school to request donations for a gymnasium, appeal to their sense of pride in their alma mater. Offer them recognition for their tax-deductible contributions of $100 or more by having their names appear on a plaque.

Request letters can very often offer psychological or other nonmonetary rewards for compliance. But these compensations must be presented from the reader's viewpoint and carefully woven into the persuasive request.

Where possible, the request should be paired with the psychological appeal. Notice how the following appeal to pride is used to solicit a donation from alumni.

> To keep your alma mater the best in the city, send your tax-deductible contribution in the enclosed envelope while this letter is before you.

Be Courteous and Tactful. If you have a special request, write to a particular individual, if possible, rather than to a company. Using a person's name makes your letter more personal and starts you off properly with the person whom you are addressing.

Be sure you have spelled all names correctly and have written them exactly as the addressee prefers to have them written. Correct titles and proper spelling get your letter off to a good start and set a receptive stage for your special request.

If you do not know the name of the person who would handle your request, you can at least speed up its handling by indicating the department you think will respond. For example, if your letter concerns employment, you would address the personnel department; if it concerns an order, you would address the sales department; if it concerns advertising or customer relations, you would probably address the advertising department or public relations department.

Expressions of appreciation are always in good taste, but do not write "Thank you in advance" or, worse yet, "Thanking you in advance." You cannot be sure that the reader will take the action you request. To thank in advance takes the reader for granted and may be the phrase that defeats the purpose of your letter. Here are some expressions, though, that exhibit tact and courtesy when used with requests:

> "May I please . . . ."

> "I will be grateful if you would . . . ."

> "Will you please . . . ."

> "I would appreciate having . . . ."

> "Please send me . . . ."

Expressions of expectation such as the following are appropriate in anticipating a favorable response to a special request.

> "I hope that we can count on your cooperation."

> "Your suggestions would be genuinely appreciated."

> "I would appreciate this help."

> "We will be grateful for this special service."

Make It Easy to Respond. Courtesy copies are frequently used to make it easy for those who receive them to grant favors. Of course, a self-addressed, stamped envelope should be enclosed too. For example, in a letter requesting a company to participate in a word processing survey, a copy may accompany the original so that the recipient may simply check and return the copy. Following is an example of a letter that was accompanied by a courtesy copy.

Dear Mr. Sirakides:

Have you had the time, along with your other duties as information processing manager, to keep abreast of all the new developments in word processing during the last year? Have you wondered what other companies are doing to upgrade their equipment and procedures?

If so, you are among hundreds of other information processing managers throughout the country. That is why the Executive Board of the National Data Management Association has undertaken as its major project for this year a research study to assess the status of information processing in business, government, and industrial organizations in the United States.

You will receive a copy of the research results to provide you with an up-to-date picture of information processing installations throughout the country. But before we can send you this data, we will need you to spend approximately an hour filling out a questionnaire about information processing equipment and practices in your company. This data, as well as data from other leading organizations, will be used as the basis for this study.

May we count on your assistance to complete this project? For your convenience I am sending you an extra copy of this letter. Please indicate your answer in the space provided and return the copy to me in the enclosed envelope.

Sincerely yours,

Janet Horne
Project Director

mf
Enclosure

Please
Check (✔)

1. Yes, I will participate in the research project; please send me the questionnaire. As soon as the results have been compiled, I wish to receive a copy of the study. _____
2. I personally am unable to complete the questionnaire. Please contact (Name) _____, (Title) _____, of our company, who may be able to assist you. _____
3. Our company is unable to participate in this research project now. _____

The courtesy carbon is just one mechanism to induce favorable responses. Stamped return envelopes and postcards also make it easier for the reader to say "yes." Separate response forms that are easy to fill out and return are another kind of convenient mail reply. Where faster or more personal replies are desired, invitations to call a certain number, collect if toll charges apply, simplify even further the response process.

Organization of Persuasive Requests

Before actually writing a persuasive request, you must determine the approach you will take. First of all, ask yourself, "In what way *will* or *can* my request benefit the reader?" Look at your request from the reader's viewpoint to determine whether it can benefit him or her in any way.

Do not limit your analysis to profit motives, but view your request in terms of satisfying one or more of the reader's psychological needs. Fulfillment of the need for recognition (having one's name appear on a plaque) or the need for self-actualization (keeping up to date on developments in one's field) or one of the other psychological needs is a powerful motivator. Therefore, develop your persuasive request around fulfilling the needs of your reader, and write the letter as much as possible from the reader's viewpoint.

The organizational plan for persuasive letters assists in developing a letter that will present your request in its most favorable light. Once you have gained your reader's attention with a stimulating or provocative opening, you continue to build interest by relating the discussion of your request to the reader's needs. Then, by allowing the reader the opportunity to respond easily, you have used the appropriate motivational techniques to stimulate your reader to take the desired action. Specifically, the persuasive organizational plan uses the following outline to accomplish its purpose.

1. Attention-getting statement or device that encourages the reader to continue reading the letter.
2. Statements that (a) present facts or (b) meet the reader's needs.
3. Presentation of request in terms of how it will benefit the reader, if possible.
4. Request for action.

Notice how the letter on page 427 uses the persuasive letter plan to accomplish its purpose. As an attention-getter, a real X ray was enclosed with the letter.

Kinds of Persuasive Requests

Among the array of persuasive letters are sales letters to prospective customers, the first several collection letters in a series, persuasive claims, job application letters, requests for donations, letters requesting favors, and responses to inquiries with sales potential. Each of these types of letters attempts to convince the reader to take a specific action, one toward which

University of Illinois at the Medical Center, Chicago

UNIVERSITY OF ILLINOIS COLLEGE OF MEDICINE

Office of the Executive Dean
1853 West Polk Street, Chicago, Illinois 60612
(312) 663-3500

You're a physician . . .

can you look at this X ray and

tell what's wrong with this young man's heart?

You can't. Even if you could examine every detail of John Williams' heart
with an X ray . . . you still couldn't <u>see</u> the problem. Why? Because John's
heart condition is much like the one <u>you</u> experienced when you first realized
you had to become a physician. And that type of heart condition must be <u>felt</u>
to be diagnosed.

It's an ache. A longing. And while you fulfilled your ambition at the
University of Illinois College of Medicine . . . John's chances are slim.
John, like hundreds of other qualified applicants, is being held back because
of our limited instructional space--limited equipment and teaching aids--
limited number of faculty.

Right now, we're actively seeking funding for the basic instructional necessities from the Legislature. But to maintain <u>high-quality</u> standards in the
face of expansion calls for support in areas not covered by state financing.
We also need funds to provide flexibility of program planning, adaptation of
technological advances to education, and scholarships.

You can help us fulfill, with unequaled excellence, the heart's desire of
hundreds of young people by making a gift of $50, $100, $500, or $1000 to the
unrestricted <u>Granville A. Bennett Dean's Fund</u>.

Your gift, today, will give someone else the opportunity to earn the title you
proudly possess . . . Doctor.

Sincerely yours,

William J. Grove, M.D.
Dean, College of Medicine

Courtesy of University of Illinois College of Medicine.

**This persuasive request letter uses a human-interest appeal to encourage the reader
to respond.**

the reader presently has a neutral attitude or one that may cost money,
require time, or result in inconvenience.

Sales, collection, claim, and application letters are all covered in detail
in separate units. Requests for donations, letters requesting favors, and
responses to inquiries with sales potential are described in the remaining
part of this unit.

Requests for Donations. Donations of money, products, and time for worthy causes are often solicited through business letters. These letters generally use the persuasive letter plan, since their purpose is to motivate the reader to take an unselfish action. See how the following letter attempts to secure a food donation for a function to benefit senior citizens.

Dear Mr. Cardini:

Just as your commercials advertise, "All family members—from toddler to grandpa—love the smooth, zesty flavor of Coria's spaghetti with meat sauce." And Coria's is easy to prepare too, either for lunch or for dinner.

Many of us in the Chicago Area Youth Association are big eaters of your pasta platters, and that is why we thought of Coria's in connection with our forthcoming Senior Citizens Festival on September 9. CAYA, a nonprofit community youth group, is sponsoring a festival for 50 less fortunate senior citizens who reside in convalescent homes in our city. We plan to transport the senior citizens to our center, serve them lunch, and then provide a show with old-fashioned "big band" music and entertainment.

CAYA is financed solely through contributions from community members; therefore, our budget is quite limited. To provide a delicious and nutritious lunch for the senior citizens, we are asking manufacturers like you to donate sufficient quantities of their food products. Would you be able to send us 12 spaghetti with meat sauce platters to help highlight an afternoon in the lives of these individuals?

Of course, your contribution is tax-deductible. Special thanks will also be given to Coria's in our monthly newsletter, which is distributed to over 1000 families in the Chicago area.

May we count on you to help brighten the day for 50 less fortunate senior citizens? I would appreciate receiving your answer by August 6 so that we can confirm our menu plans.

                                        Sincerely yours,

Letters Asking Favors. Another type of persuasive letter that sometimes must be written is one requesting a special favor. Of course, these letters should have the same characteristics as any other persuasive letter, and they are organized according to the same letter plan.

Dear Ms. Sarver:

Your very interesting article in the November issue of The Administrative Assistant magazine prompted me to write you.

The Denver chapter of PSI is having its annual Administrator-Secretary Night on Thursday, January 18. Our members and their administrators (we expect about 80 people in all) have expressed a particular interest in hearing a lively talk on letters secretaries can send in their administrators' absence. We are especially interested in having our administrators hear something about what the secretary can do to help the employer with communication problems. Our program calls for a 30-minute presentation from the speaker.

Would you be able to address our group on January 18? You can build your speech along the same lines as your article, if you wish. As you know, this night is the highlight of our year's meetings, and we would be pleased to have you as our guest speaker.

I hope you can accept this invitation, Ms. Sarver. If you can, I will write you again giving you all the details—time, place, and complete program plans.

Sincerely yours,

Responses to Inquiries With Sales Potential. One of the main purposes of advertising is to get readers and listeners so interested in a product that, if it isn't readily available, they will make a trip to their dealer for a closer look or they will write a letter asking for more information. Inquiries received as a direct result of advertising have a great deal of sales potential. Therefore, when a writer shows interest, some companies respond with a polished sales promotion letter instead of a simple response to an inquiry.

Letters of response with direct sales potential need to show the reader *why* the desired action should be taken—that is, why the product should be purchased. Persuasive letters written from the reader's point of view stimulate action—to purchase the new car, the aluminum siding, the air conditioner, or the stereo. Therefore, the persuasive letter plan is used in responding to inquiries with sales potential.

Notice how the first two paragraphs of the following letter get the reader's attention and develop interest. The presentation of the request and the request for action are carried out in the concluding paragraph.

Dear Mr. and Mrs. O'Reilly:

Naturally, we are delighted that you are interested in the Sphinx. Thank you for giving us a chance to tell you more about this captivating new model that has just received Sports Car International's sweepstakes award.

The enclosed booklet, Continental Sports Cars, was prepared especially for you and others like you whose taste runs to the bold, the daring, the unusual—the discriminating. Only in the Sphinx does the true sports car lover find the ideal ride. You will be thrilled with its sleek lines, its handling, its economy.

May I suggest that you visit your local dealer, Andre's Sports Car Village, to test-drive the new Sphinx. Only when you get behind the wheel of the Sphinx can you fully appreciate the sensational advantages of this little masterpiece.

Sincerely,

Enclosure

Here is still another example of how a response to an inquiry can be used to bring a potential customer closer to the sale.

Dear Miss Jacobs:

We are so pleased that you thought of the Fireside Lodge for the annual awards dinner of the Dallas chapter of the National Management Association.

We have two excellent private dining rooms—the Regency Room and the Garden Court—ideal for a group the size of yours. Each banquet room seats 100 to 125 people and is equipped with a loudspeaker system, a piano, and a movie projector and screen. The Regency Room also has a raised dais where the speaker's table may be placed. Both rooms are still available for May 18.

The decor of both the Regency Room and the Garden Court will give you a delightful, absolutely private dining atmosphere. Each is air-conditioned and sound-conditioned. As you know, the Fireside Lodge has an excellent reputation for the finest meals and service. I am enclosing our banquet menu, featuring full-course dinners ranging from $15.25 to $24.95.

I would be happy to show you these two lovely dining rooms, Miss Jacobs, when it is convenient for you to visit the Fireside Lodge. Would it be possible for you to have lunch here with me one day next week? Just telephone me at 555-2491.

                                        Sincerely yours,

Enclosure

COMMUNICATION LABORATORY

APPLICATION EXERCISES

A. Assume that you have just accepted a position as an administrative assistant at the American Institute for Cancer Research in Washington, D.C. One of your first tasks is to critique the following letter and make suggestions for improving its effectiveness in raising funds for cancer research. This letter will be sent out nationally by direct-mail advertisers to potential contributors.

Make a list of suggestions your administrator may give to the person responsible for writing the letter.

Dear Friend,

The American Institute for Cancer Research (AICR) is now conducting its Annual Fund Drive.

During this time tens of thousands of Americans will make their annual contribution to fight cancer through AICR.

In the next several weeks I will be meeting with several members of the AICR Board of Directors to plan our coming year's budget. During these meetings it would be a big help to know what programs we will be able to afford next year.

So if you could please use the enclosed postage-paid envelope to make your contribution to fight cancer, it would be greatly appreciated.

I want you to know that we look forward to counting you among our friends and supporters in the coming year.

Sincerely,

J. Richard Nicklin, M.D.
President

pr
Enclosure

PS. If you make only one contribution to fight cancer every year, please use the enclosed postage-paid envelope to make your gift now during our Annual Fund Drive.

B. Your immediate supervisor, Louise Peebles, is the convention chairperson for the National Information Management Association convention to be held in Madison, Wisconsin, from April 4 through April 7 at the Remington Arms Hotel. You expect nearly 1200 people—word and information processing managers and supervisors—from throughout the United States to attend this convention. For many of these people, this will be their first visit to Wisconsin.

Ms. Peebles would like to provide as favors at the April 5 banquet samples of various Wisconsin cheeses. A small (perhaps 1-ounce) individually wrapped packet to be placed at each seat would suffice. Write the Wisconsin Cheese Manufacturers Association requesting it to donate 1200 packages of cheese. One of your members in Madison would be able to pick up the cheese several days before the convention. Of course, you would publicize that the cheeses were donated by the Wisconsin Cheese Manufacturers Association. Address your letter to Mr. James Reikl, Director of Public Relations, Wisconsin Cheese Manufacturers Association, 780 Adams Boulevard, Madison, Wisconsin 53701.

C. For one of your classes, assume that you have been given the assignment of interviewing a person who presently is working in an occupation in which you are interested. To complete this assignment, you will need to inquire about duties, qualifications, educational background, opportunities for employment, salary, benefits, work schedules, and opportunities for advancement. Such an interview could take from 45 minutes to an hour, since you need to obtain a comprehensive picture of the position for a report you must write. Select an individual whom you might like to interview and write him or her a letter requesting an interview.

D. Assume that you are employed by the American Kayai Motor Co., Inc. The company has developed a questionnaire it wishes to send to those people who have purchased a new Kayai within the last five years. Even if the buyer no longer owns the Kayai, you wish to learn how well that car met the buyer's needs.

Your company is committed to satisfying its customers—and improving its products and service. That is why you need to hear from experienced Kayai car owners. Write the cover letter to accompany the questionnaire, persuading the reader to fill out and return the questionnaire.

E. Answer the following letter of inquiry. Use this letter as an opportunity to persuade the reader to purchase and install your Carson authentic oak kitchen cabinets. Address the letter to Mr. Edward Young, 3129 Miller Road, Flint, Michigan 48507.

Gentlemen:

Please send me a copy of your pamphlet <u>Modern Kitchenry</u>, which was advertised in <u>Decorator's World</u> magazine. I am interested in replacing my present kitchen cabinets with Carson authentic oak cabinets.

While I am at it, I am also thinking of having my kitchen floor recovered. Do you have any suggestions for colors that would blend with authentic oak?

Sincerely yours,

F. You are employed by Crickton Realty, 1732 Henway Drive, Des Moines, Iowa 50318. You receive a letter from Henry T. Bonner, 2231 Treadway Street, Los Angeles, California 90069, requesting information about available housing in Des Moines for a family of six. Respond to his letter, referring to an enclosed list of suitable dwellings. You would very much like to sell Mr. Bonner a house, so make your letter as friendly and persuasive as possible.

VOCABULARY AND SPELLING STUDIES

A. These words are often confused: *raise, raze, rays; costume, custom.* Write each in a sentence that illustrates its meaning.

B. Indicate the prepositions that should be used in these sentences.

1. The contract states that our salary increases are retroactive _____ January 1.
2. The office is adjacent _____ the elevator.
3. This computer table is identical _____ those I ordered.
4. Did Mr. Rodriguez give his approval _____ the new sales campaign?
5. Ms. Otabe was not satisfied _____ the last shipment.
6. *Rug* is synonymous _____ *carpet.*

C. Add an *e* to the end of the following:

A Word Meaning:	To Result in a Word Meaning:
1. Pertaining to or characteristic of people	Kind, merciful, tender
2. Relating to a choir or chorus	A simple tune sung in unison
3. Ethical	A confident state of mind
4. Melodious, harmonious	A social entertainment featuring music
5. Characteristic of cities	Smoothly polite

COMMUNICATING FOR RESULTS

Say it Better. Rewrite the following letter. Simplify the content and keep it friendly.

> Some time ago we were forced to discontinue Wearwell tires as a stock item in our inventory owing to the dissolution of the Wearwell Company last month and are therefore unable to fill your kind order for four of them. In consequence of this, therefore, we regretfully return your check made in our favor for $168.35 and request that you write us again.

U · N · I · T

44

Refusal Letters

As a business writer you have a relatively easy job when you are sharing good news with customers. After all, there is little or no danger that such letters will alienate customers or will cause them to take their business elsewhere. All you need do is tell the customers exactly what they want to hear.

Sometimes, however, you cannot comply with a request because some information you may need is missing, the request is unreasonable, a product is sold out, or other circumstances prevent your granting the request. In situations like these you must write refusal or bad-news letters—letters that say "no."

The word *no* can cause more ill will than any other word in the English language. Therefore, letters that refuse requests or convey bad news are very difficult to write. Care must be taken not to offend readers when you are unable to satisfy their needs. Customers must be led to understand the logic behind and the reasons for the refusal. Every letter you write has as its secondary purpose the promoting or retaining of goodwill. But the ill-will potential of a refusal letter is so great that only by drawing on your knowledge of human behavior can you write a "no" that gives your reader the feeling of "yes."

Qualities of the Refusal Letter

All the principles of good business writing are essential in writing letters that say "no." The following four guidelines, however, are of particular importance to bad-news and refusal letters.

Be Prompt. As you learned in Unit 41, most firms consider answering letters of inquiry within 48 hours good business practice. Whether the letter carries good or bad news, this policy should be carried out. Delayed negative responses can only offend the reader even more and lessen your chance of retaining goodwill. Of course, to avoid writing the refusal letter by handling more pleasant duties instead is tempting. But the longer the letter is delayed, the more difficult it will be to write and the more likely you are to compound the problem.

Be Positive. Avoid using negative words such as *fault, refuse, unfair,* and *unreasonable.* Maintain a positive tone in your writing and use words that convey pleasant images. Always try to phrase your refusal in a positive way by emphasizing what you *can* do for your readers instead of what you cannot do. Notice how much more positive it is to say, "Your order will be shipped in two weeks" than "Your order will be delayed for two weeks." "We sell only through authorized dealers" is more friendly than "We refuse to sell directly to the public."

Be Helpful. In writing a refusal or bad-news letter, you can occasionally provide an alternative solution. Although you cannot comply with the original request, you may be able to suggest some other plan that may help the reader. For example, if you cannot accept an invitation to speak at a certain meeting, you may recommend someone who can. Or if you cannot accept an appointment for June 17, you may suggest the reader see you on June 19. When possible, you should try to help the reader by providing a substitute plan.

If you had to refuse to donate door prizes to the Little League's fund-raising breakfast, you might include the following sentence in your letter to give it a "yes" slant.

We will, however, be glad to support your project by displaying your poster in our store window.

Or when refusing to arrange space in your store for the sampling and promotion of a new delicatessan item, you might be able to offer an alternative date.

> We would be pleased to speak with your demonstrator, Ms. Marcus, sometime in January to arrange for a promotion early in the spring.

Be Tactful. While the inquirer's request may be unreasonable or the tone insistent, always respond with a tactful letter. Do not insult the reader or indicate that the request is unreasonable. Avoid accusations and other discourtesies in writing your letter. Be careful to explain the circumstances fully and in such a way that the reader accepts the refusal or bad news as being necessary. Study these pairs of tactless and tactful responses.

> ABRUPT: We cannot send you the personnel information breakdown requested in your April 3 letter. The time and money involved in preparing such a pamphlet would be prohibitive, a fact that you, as a manager, should have taken into consideration before making your request.

> TACTFUL: We wish we could send you the personnel information breakdown requested in your April 3 letter, but we do not have the data readily available. As a manager, you can see that the time and money involved in preparing such a pamphlet would be prohibitive.

> SARCASTIC: Surely you cannot seriously expect us to accept return of the clothing you purchased from us on January 4 of last year. We are sending the items back to you today and will notify you whenever we decide to go into the used-clothing business.

> TACTFUL: We would like very much to accommodate you by accepting the return of the clothing purchased from us on January 4 of last year, but we are unable to do so. To protect all our customers who may purchase returned merchandise, we place a two-week limit on the return of all wearing apparel.

Organizing the Refusal Letter

Because refusal letters contain information antagonistic to the reader's needs, the writer must take care not to alienate the reader and thereby lessen the chance of retaining goodwill. If readers can be shown why you must refuse the request, delay the order, or refuse the invitation *before* they are told "no," they may be more tolerant and understanding. Their self-images may not be as threatened since they have been taken step-by-step through the reasoning process that led to the refusal or bad news. Consequently, the following indirect organizational plan should be used for refusal letters and letters conveying bad news:

1. Neutral opening statement upon which both the reader and the writer can agree.
2. Reasons for the refusal stated in positive, tactful, and courteous terms.
3. Statement of refusal.

4. Suggested alternatives, if any.
5. Statement to retain goodwill of reader.

Notice how the bad-news organizational plan is used to refuse the following request:

Dear Mr. Wong:

Your new line of heavy-duty machinery is certainly of interest to me. I appreciate your contacting me about an appointment to discuss how this equipment can improve our production and increase sales.

On Monday, April 25, I am scheduled to fly to Boston for a two-week sales conference. Consequently, I will not be able to meet with you on April 27. Perhaps you might be free on Tuesday, May 10, and could come to my office at 10 a.m. that day.

I look forward to hearing from you as to when we might get together to discuss your new machinery.

Sincerely,

Explaining Refusals and Delays

Many kinds of requests are directed to a business organization. People ask for appointments, special favors, literature, service, information, and jobs. Sometimes you must ask for additional information before complying with a request. At other times you must refuse the request completely, as in the case in the letter illustrated on page 437.

Refusing Orders. The primary purpose of any business is, of course, to sell goods or services for profit. Usually nothing makes a business happier than to receive an order. Under some circumstances, however, orders must be refused. Sometimes customers have poor credit ratings or do not have the legal qualifications to purchase the product sold. In other cases the product has been discontinued. The most common instances involve consumers who try to purchase directly from a wholesaler or manufacturer. The wholesaler or manufacturer must, of course, refer them to a retail store. This type of letter is not so much a refusal as it is an explanation and a referral.

Following is a typical letter refusing an order. The letter was sent by a national manufacturer to a customer who ordered directly from the warehouse. Notice how the letter uses the bad-news plan to achieve its goal.

Dear Mrs. Hezzelwood:

We appreciate your interest in Global products and are pleased that you wish to order our Spacesaver Deluxe microwave oven. Global does indeed live up to its motto, "A satisfied customer with every purchase."

Since we distribute our products through local dealers only, we are unable to serve you directly, Mrs. Hezzelwood. I am pleased, however, to refer you to

Carnation

World Headquarters

5045 Wilshire Boulevard
Los Angeles, California 90036
Telephone: (213) 932-6000

August 9, 1985

Mr. David Avila
3519 Carlson Boulevard
El Cerrito, CA 94530

Dear David:

Thank you for taking the time to meet with us regarding career opportunities with Carnation Health and Nutrition Centers.

While we are impressed with your background and believe that you have a great deal to contribute to an organization, the limited number of available positions forces us to select only a relatively small number of the many talented applicants we see. Unfortunately, we cannot offer you a position at this time.

We appreciate your interest in Carnation Health and Nutrition Centers and wish you much success in whatever career you select.

Very truly yours,

Roseann B. Perrotti

Roseann B. Perrotti
Director of Store Operations
Health and Nutrition Department

lg

Courtesy of Carnation Company—Health and Nutrition Division.

The letter of refusal must be written in such a way as to retain goodwill.

the Biltmore Appliance Center at 220 West Main Street in Firebaugh. The Biltmore people will be delighted to demonstrate our complete line of microwave ovens and many other unrivaled Global appliances.

I am returning your check for $225.95 and hope that you will make a trip to Biltmore Appliance Center right away for your new Global microwave. You will find our Spacesaver Deluxe to be one of the wisest investments you have ever made.

Sincerely yours,

Enclosure

Why not take this opportunity to build goodwill with the retail store? Send Biltmore Appliance Center a copy of the letter so the Biltmore management will (1) know you are living up to your agreement of selling only on a wholesale basis, (2) appreciate your effort in helping make the sale, and (3) contact the customer about the specific merchandise.

Refusing Unreasonable Requests. Businesses sometimes receive requests for information that must be refused. The request may be unreasonable or the information sought may be confidential. For example, a physician or a hospital employee cannot divulge medical information about a patient; a bank will not give information regarding a depositor except to those authorized by the depositor to receive such information. Letters refusing to give information follow the bad-news plan. Study the following example:

Dear Ms. Mellert:

I appreciate your letter in which you ask for information concerning markup rates on drug products sold in our store. Because markup rates vary considerably, Ms. Mellert, a figure that would apply to all drug products does not exist. Putting together detailed information would require more time than we can afford just now.

May I refer you to Service Bulletin 16, Markups in the Drug Industry, issued by the State Bureau of Commerce and Industry. This 50-cent booklet contains markup rates for the drug industry as a whole, and I am sure it will be helpful to you. You can obtain a copy by writing to the State Bureau of Commerce and Industry, 3001 Central Avenue, Hartford, Connecticut 06103.

Sincerely yours,

Refusing Invitations. A business organization and its employees receive numerous invitations to participate in exhibits, to speak before groups, to take part in various kinds of community activities. Most business executives feel that to participate in these affairs is wise—they help to build goodwill for the business. However, not all such invitations can be accepted because of time or financial limitations. In writing a letter refusing an invitation, you may adapt the bad-news plan to include the following three points:

1. Express appreciation for the invitation.
2. Give a logical reason for having to refuse.
3. Keep open the possibility of accepting a similar invitation in the future (if desirable).

Note the following example of a letter refusing an invitation to speak:

Dear Mr. Scott:

I was pleased and complimented by your invitation to speak at the February meeting of the San Dimas Rotary Club.

Because I plan to be out of town during the last week in February, I am unable to accept your invitation. An important company business trip is scheduled for that time and it cannot be postponed. I am genuinely sorry that I cannot be with you.

If you wish, I would be pleased to address the San Dimas Rotary Club on the topic "S-t-r-etching Your Investment Dollar" at a later date. Just let me know at least a month in advance.

Sincerely,

Delays in Filling Orders. Delays generally occur because the customer has not given you enough information to fill the order or because the goods ordered are temporarily out of stock. In either case, be sure to open your letter with a statement of appreciation for the customer's order.

When writing letters concerning delays because you are temporarily out of stock, explain why the merchandise is not being shipped immediately and tell the reader when the order will be delivered. For both the incomplete order and the out-of-stock acknowledgment, conclude with a statement designed to reinforce confidence in your company and its products.

In the following example notice how the bad-news plan described on pages 434 and 435 is used to tell a customer about a shipping delay.

Dear Mr. Dietsch:

We appreciate receiving your order for Butler-in-a-Box that was featured in the April issue of Computerworld. Apparently a good many others saw the article also because we have been swamped with orders for this new little effort-saving sensation.

I am sending you today two complete component units; the remaining four will be shipped on Monday, June 14. I regret, Mr. Dietsch, that you should be inconvenienced on your very first order, but I hope you will understand that we were not prepared for the large quantity of orders received. You may be sure that our factory is now geared for round-the-clock production to keep all our dealers supplied.

I hope you find keeping Butler-in-a-Box in stock just as hard as we do—they are becoming increasingly popular! We look forward to doing business with you on a regular basis and promise our usual prompt service on your next order.

Sincerely yours,

In writing letters of this type, observe the following rules of tact, courtesy, and goodwill:

1. Always tell the customer first what you *can* do; then what you *can't* do. ("We are sending two of the units now; the rest will have to be sent later.")

2. Keep the tone positive. Even though you must apologize for the delay, don't overdo it. Assume that the customer understands. ("This rush of business naturally caught us unprepared.")

3. Reestablish customers' confidence in your firm by encouraging them to place additional orders. ("We look forward to future business. We will give you our usual prompt service.")

Delays Caused by Incomplete Requests. Suppose you receive the inquiry shown on page 441. Obviously, this letter is neither clear nor complete. When possible, try to answer the customer's inquiry on the basis of your first letter. Sometimes you can answer it by providing more information than the customer needs. To answer this letter, you would have to know the kinds and quantities of gifts the customer desires; and the customer may not be able to answer these questions until you send the prices. In this case the entire price list should be sent to the customer with an everyday covering letter. Naturally, you could conclude such a letter with a sales appeal urging the customer to visit your shop.

Other inquiries may not be handled so easily, however. Any attempt on your part to answer some letters on the basis of the initial inquiry would probably fail to satisfy the customer. What you must do, then, is write the customer to ask for the information you need. Such a situation must be handled tactfully, without giving correspondents the impression that they were negligent or careless. If the order is incomplete, ask the customer in a positive way for the additional details. A statement such as "Before we ship your order, Mr. Jones, would you please tell us whether you prefer your shirt in white or blue?" tactfully indicates to the reader that he did not provide you with sufficient information.

Make replying easy for the customer so as to increase your chance of completing the sale. Consider, for example, the following reply to a letter requesting a copy of a company's "booklet on gardening."

Dear Mrs. Geiberger:

We appreciate your interest in our service publications on gardening. At present we publish over 300 booklets on every aspect of home gardening. In this way we hope to help our customers solve their special gardening problems.

Enclosed is a complete list of our publications. Just check the ones you want and mail your list in the enclosed stamped envelope. Please include a postage and handling fee of 50 cents for each booklet requested (no cash or stamps, please).

If you will let us know which booklets are of interest to you, we will forward them to you immediately.

Sincerely yours,

Enclosure

November 4, 1989

Ladies and Gentlemen:

I would like to buy some unusual gifts for the holidays. I am unable, however, to come to Tampa until late this month, and I would like to know in advance of my trip how much the gifts would cost.

Sincerely yours,
John R. Lyons

A letter that is unclear and incomplete may lead to a delay in fulfilling a request.

COMMUNICATION LABORATORY

APPLICATION EXERCISES

A. Assume that you are the editorial assistant to Ms. Sharlene Pollyea, executive editor of Wentworth Publishing Company, a small textbook publisher of high school and college mathematics textbooks. Lester Winters, the high school supervisor of mathematics for the Los Angeles Unified School District, 450 North Grand Avenue, Los Angeles, California 90007, writes Ms. Pollyea requesting Wentworth to purchase exhibit space at a conference being planned for mathematics teachers in the Los Angeles high schools. Because you have a limited budget for purchasing exhibit space, you must confine your participation to large regional, statewide, or national meetings. Write the letter Ms. Pollyea will send. Refuse the request politely, keeping in mind that the Los Angeles Unified School District does purchase some of your books.

B. The Nashville Center for Handicapped Children, 5900 Jackson Highway, Nashville, Tennessee 37205, requests a donation from your company for a minibus to transport wheelchair-bound children. Your company, Customline Vans, makes a large donation each year to the Nashville Community Fund for distribution. You cannot possibly make donations for all the requests you receive. Write a tactful refusal letter. Suggest that the Nashville Center for Handicapped Children contact the Nashville Community Fund. Write the letter so that the Nashville Center for Handicapped Children will not be offended; the center is highly respected in the community.

C. What is wrong with the following letter? Note specific errors; then rewrite the letter.

Dear Ms. Atkinson:

We are returning your check for $119.90. We stopped carrying Neato lawn trimmers when the manufacturer went out of business last year.

Yours truly,

D. You are employed in the Denver supply center of MBI, a major manufacturer of computers and other office machines. Your company's latest computer printer, the SilentWriter, has been such a best-seller that you are now completely out of stock on ribbons for this printer. You expect to be able to replenish your stock by March 10. Write a form letter to be sent in response to the many orders you are receiving for SilentWriter ribbons.

E. You are a public relations associate at Shaw Electronics. You receive a request from Ms. Ellen Togo, a career counselor at Chatsworth Hills High School, 430 East Mountain Avenue, Kansas City, Missouri 64141, for a plant tour. Your plant is not set up to give tours, mainly because of safety regulations. However, you do provide speakers—accompanied by a slide presentation and free literature—for young people's groups on the topic of careers in electronics. Your company will even provide refreshments after the presentation. Write a letter refusing the request for a plant tour but retaining Ms. Togo's goodwill.

F. You work for Brereton's Discount Appliances, 845 Lindley Avenue, Columbia, South Carolina 29208. You receive an order from Mark Luers, 1821 Aldea Street, Greenville, South Carolina 29611, for the compact-size Minisnack Model 6 office refrigerator. This model had a lock. The manufacturer found there was not enough demand for this model and discontinued it. You now carry Model 8, which has no lock but is 15 percent larger than the Model 6 and sells for the same price ($135). You also have a Safe-Guard

Model 21A refrigerator that has a lock. Although this refrigerator is the same size as the former Model 6, it sells for $155. Recommend the Minisnack Model 8 if he doesn't need a lock; the Safe-Guard 21A if he requires a lock.

G. You are employed by LTU Precision Valves. You receive an order from Vandock Oil Tools, 1200 Elmer Street, Missoula, Montana 59801, for 125 No. 81A7 valves. You welcome the business; but unfortunately, because of a recent steel strike, you are out of stock on these valves. About ten days will be needed to fill this order. Write the kind of letter you would like to receive if you were the company that had placed the order.

H. You are the purchasing supervisor at The Gourmet Pantry, 1115 Parkway Plaza, Minneapolis, Minnesota 55455. Mrs. Gertrude Weber, 540 Clearbrook Road, Rochester, Minnesota 55901, sends you an order for a Culinary Art food processor. You carry several models with different-sized feeder tubes, blades, and container capacities. The accessories that accompany each model differ also. Send her a pamphlet that illustrates the models of Culinary Art food processors you have available. Provide her with an easy way to reply.

VOCABULARY AND SPELLING STUDIES

A. These words are often confused: *appraise, apprise; pretend, portend.* Write each in a sentence that illustrates its meaning.

B. Correct the capitalization in these sentences:

1. The president left the white house on Wednesday.
2. The Bordens will celebrate their Tenth Wedding Anniversary at Rick's steak house.
3. She is qualified to take accounting II next Semester.
4. He enjoyed his Tour of the west.
5. Have you read *Better Health through exercise?*

C. What are the plurals of the following?

1. business
2. century
3. 1980
4. deer
5. a
6. handful

COMMUNICATING FOR RESULTS

Getting the Facts. John Rickert, a customer who is behind in his installment payments, has been threatened by letter with repossession of his furniture.

He comes to you, a credit clerk at the company, waving the letter and shouting, "You can't take my furniture back unless you return the $150 in payments I've made." His installment contract reads: "I, the lessee, hereby rent from the Ace Furniture Company the goods listed above . . . . The lessors agree that, if at the end of the term of the lease, the lessee has fulfilled all covenants, they will convey a free and clear title to the above articles to the lessee." You are an experienced credit clerk and have dealt with this kind of situation before. Because of this you know that you should select your words carefully. What will you say to this customer? Be sure you understand the contract. HINT: Your company does not want to take back the furniture.

U · N · I · T
45
Claim and Adjustment Letters

Mistakes will happen—no matter how efficient a business firm tries to be. A customer may receive the wrong merchandise, slow service, invoices or statements that contain errors, or even discourteous treatment at the hands of employees. Letters in which complaints are expressed—that is, letters in which customers make a claim against the company—are called *claim letters.*

The company for which you work undoubtedly will receive some claim letters; in turn, the company will have occasion to write claim letters to those from whom it buys. As a consumer you will also have many opportunities to write such letters. Therefore, to promote the company's and your own best interests, you need to be familiar with claim situations and with the principles of writing effective claim letters.

Preparing to Write Claim Letters

People writing claim letters are interested in one thing: *satisfaction.* If the merchandise is faulty, they want it replaced at no cost or inconvenience to themselves. If the service is poor, they want an apology and assurance that service will improve; they may even want some compensation for the inconvenience caused them. If an error has been made, they want it corrected.

To get satisfaction, claimants must present their cases carefully and thoughtfully to the people they feel are at fault. Suppose you ordered a gold identification bracelet from a mail-order house, specifying that the bracelet be engraved with your name. When the bracelet arrives, you are disappointed to find that a silver bracelet was sent. You become quite upset and a little angry. "How could they make such a stupid mistake?"

How would you begin your letter? In the first place, you should not write the letter while you are angry. Cool off first. You can do a much more convincing job when you are calm and can see the situation in a reasonable light. The mistake was not intentional; mistakes never are. If your letter were written in anger, it might begin like this:

> Somebody was certainly careless to send me a silver bracelet when I asked for a gold one. Don't your order clerks know how to read? I simply do not understand . . . .

Such a letter might do more harm than good.

You would surely get much more willing cooperation from the seller if you had been courteous. Imagine how much sympathy you would get from the order clerks with your insulting remarks! A letter like the following would accomplish your purpose and do it much more successfully.

> Ladies and Gentlemen:
>
> Today I received a silver identification bracelet (your Invoice 753291) instead of the gold identification bracelet specified in my May 25 order, a copy of which is enclosed.
>
> I am returning the silver bracelet to you in a separate mailing. Please substitute a gold one with the name "Karen" engraved in script.
>
> The quality of these identification bracelets is superb, and I am looking forward to receiving my gold bracelet as soon as possible.
>
> Sincerely yours,

Writing Claim Letters

When writing a claim letter, remember to explain *carefully* and *tactfully* what is wrong. Avoid negative accusations or threats such as "I demand," "I must insist," "you will have to," "unless you," "why can't you," and so on. Discourteous statements such as these only tune out the reader. In addition, they lessen the likelihood of your obtaining the best possible service that you could possibly receive.

Avoid lecturing the reader about the ethics of the situation. You can't change the reader's values in one letter. And you only add more words. You want readers to read the specific points of your claim—not to be distracted or to begin skimming the letter because of words that seem to have no bearing on the specific situation from the reader's point of view.

So that your claim can be processed quickly, be sure to include any details necessary for identifying your claim—dates, catalog numbers, styles, order numbers, invoice numbers, and so on. If appropriate, also indicate the loss or inconvenience you have suffered—but, by all means, don't exaggerate!

Another important consideration in stating your claim is to let the company know specifically what you wish it to do about the situation. Remember, though, do not be unreasonable in your request. If the electric toothbrush you received as a gift breaks a month before the one-year warranty expires, don't ask the company to send you a new toothbrush. All you can expect is a repair of the one you have.

All the considerations described in the preceding paragraphs are important in writing a successful claim letter. The way you present your ideas in the letter, however, may vary. The nature of the claim itself will determine whether you will need to write a simple or a persuasive claim letter.

Simple Claims. Companies recognize that errors will occur occasionally, and they are prepared to handle them to the customer's satisfaction. Therefore, most claim letters may be written using the everyday letter plan. A simple and tactful statement of the situation in the opening paragraph gets the claim letter off to a direct start. Details needed to process the claim and the specific action the customer desires should follow the direct statement. Of course, skillful letter writers will conclude their letters with a statement that builds goodwill or one that shows they anticipate satisfaction of the claim. Notice how the everyday letter plan (see Unit 42) is used in the following letter:

Ladies and Gentlemen:

The china platter I ordered from your Christmas catalog arrived broken. Apparently, too little packing had been placed in the box before it was sent from the warehouse.

This platter is Item B-1087347 on page 48 of your catalog. It was purchased on October 16 and charged to my VISA account under your Shipping Invoice PL5387895. I am returning the broken platter to your store and would appreciate your replacing it with a new one in the same size and pattern.

The platter is to be a Christmas gift, so I would appreciate receiving the replacement by December 15.

Sincerely yours,

Persuasive Claims. Occasionally, claim situations may not be so obvious. If your travel alarm clock stops working two weeks after the warranty expires, you may wish to convince a reputable company that it should repair the clock free of charge. After all, you used it on only one vacation! Or you may wish to return clothing you purchased over a month ago because it shrank when you washed it, even though the tag is marked "Machine

Washable." Many situations require an explanation before requesting an adjustment, and for these situations you must write persuasive claim letters.

Like other persuasive letters, the persuasive claim begins with an attention-getting statement. In some cases this statement may begin to explain the situation; in other cases it may relate to the good reputation of the company or ask a question to stimulate the reader's interest. Then a presentation of facts and details leads the reader to the request for an adjustment. A closing that anticipates receiving the adjustment rounds out the persuasive claim letter. Notice how the following letter uses this approach.

Ladies and Gentlemen:

Seagel's has always represented quality service and quality merchandise. That is why I know you will be interested in this letter.

Last month I purchased, through your fall catalog, a Menning sweatshirt (your sales check 8739261 dated October 9) and charged it to my Seagel account. The luxury and durability of my other Menning sweatshirt prompted me to purchase this one.

Because of the red-and-white color combination, I decided to hand-wash the sweatshirt in cold water, in spite of its machine-washable label. Much to my dismay, though, the red color ran and turned the white color to pink. I know you will agree that the colors in a Menning garment should not bleed, especially when it has been carefully hand-washed. Therefore, I am returning the sweatshirt to your store and would appreciate your crediting my account for $31.25.

Since Seagel's always stands behind its reputation for quality, I look forward to receiving credit for this merchandise.

Sincerely yours,

Preparing to Write Adjustment Letters

In writing answers to claim letters, you are on the other side of the fence. Your customers wish to present a claim, and they write to you. They may be dissatisfied with your merchandise, your service, or your general efficiency. You will respond to their claim with an *adjustment letter*.

Opportunity to Remedy Faults. A good company welcomes customer comments because they create opportunities to identify and remedy faulty products or poor services that may exist. Your job is to see that customers receive fair treatment—fair to them, of course, but also fair to your firm. Since adjustment letters sell satisfaction too, they are really *sales* letters.

Policies Differ. Most firms have established broad policies for making adjustments. Some are very generous and practice the motto "The customer is always right." Others are not so eager to please customers, especially if the customer is wrong. Even in the most generous organizations, there will be numerous occasions when claims cannot be granted.

Regardless of the fact that established policies exist for most adjustment situations, there will always be exceptions. For example, an old customer who has dealt with a firm faithfully over the years is likely to receive a little more consideration than a new customer who is merely shopping around for the best buy.

Many factors enter into the decision as to whether or not an adjustment will be granted. Often there is simply no policy to cover an adjustment situation, so letter writers must weigh all the evidence and then do what they think is fairest to their customers and to their employers. However, the writer must have or must get authority for an adjustment that is out of the ordinary.

Writing Adjustment Letters

When writing adjustment letters, under all circumstances be patient, tactful, and diplomatic. Always be sure to observe these four principles:

1. Reply promptly.
2. Show the customer that you understand the problem.
3. Tell the customer exactly what you are going to do about the problem.
4. Avoid negative words and accusations.

Reply Promptly. The longer customers wait for replies to their claims, the angrier they get and the harder soothing their feelings becomes. Show customers that they are important enough to warrant your immediate attention to their problems and that they are getting fast action.

"Right after I finished reading your June 10 letter, I looked into the matter of . . . ."

"We lost no time tracing the discrepancy in the invoice you wrote about . . . ."

"Good news! The lawn mowers arrived this morning, and they are already on their way to you."

"To make sure that there would be no slipup this time, I personally saw that your order . . . ."

"Your letter arrived this morning, and we have already put a tracer on your shipment."

Show Understanding. Those who make claims want, first of all, to have someone understand why they feel as they do. Your letter will be more effective if it expresses empathy.

"We can imagine how you feel about . . . ."

"You are entirely right about . . . ."

"Indeed, we can understand that . . . ."

"Your point is well taken, and . . . ."

"We ourselves have been in the same situation, and . . . ."

"Surely you have a right to feel that . . . ."

Be Exact. Tell customers exactly what you are going to do about their claims. If you are in a position to grant an adjustment, say so immediately and describe how you are going about it.

"Our check for $78.62, which is a refund on Invoice A1428, will be sent to you this week."

"Within a day or two, you will have your new green blanket to replace the blue one you returned . . . ."

"You have been given $184 credit for the eight dead batteries. Although these batteries were carefully inspected before they left our warehouse, they . . . ."

"We are pleased to replace the plastic hose on your Loyal vacuum cleaner with a new 'Tite-Nit' hose made of nylon."

"You are entirely right. The discount to which you were entitled was not shown on your February statement. You may be sure, however, that . . . ."

Even if you are not able to grant the claim, you should be exact in telling the customer why.

"We wish we could offer you an adjustment on this clothing, but our inspection shows that the suit has been worn several times and is soiled. You can understand, of course, that . . . ."

"Time slips by so fast that we can understand how it happened that your May 8 check contained a discount deduction of $32.70—although the 10-day discount period had expired. Would you like to send us a check for $32.70, or should we add this amount to your next statement?"

"Nothing would please us more than to accept your Bernardo guitar for a refund, but we are bound by the terms of the guarantee that you received with your instrument."

Avoid Negatives. Negative words tend to put an unhappy claimant in an even more irritable frame of mind. On the other hand, positive, pleasant words help to soothe the claimant's irritation. Thus you should try to conclude your letter with a positive statement that will build goodwill. In the following examples notice the difference in tone between the positive statements and the negative ones.

NEGATIVE: We have received your complaint of June 3.

POSITIVE: We appreciate receiving your helpful June 3 letter.

NEGATIVE: We are sorry to hear of the unfortunate delay in the delivery of your Purchase Order 4286.

POSITIVE: We are glad that you called our attention to the late arrival of your Purchase Order 4286.

NEGATIVE: Your July 8 criticism has been received.

POSITIVE: Thank you for the friendly suggestion made in your July 8 letter.

NEGATIVE: Please accept our apologies for sending you unsatisfactory goods.

POSITIVE: We will check all your future orders even more carefully than usual.

NEGATIVE: Because of your failure to give us your house number, our driver had to bring back the parcel, thus delaying delivery for three days.

POSITIVE: Our driver returned your parcel to our store because the house number was omitted from the address.

Kinds of Adjustments

Adjustment letters answer claim letters. As the writer of adjustment letters, you may grant fully the requests of the claimant or reject totally the writer's proposals. Many times you may not grant the claim as the writer suggested, but instead you may seek to rectify the situation through an alternative procedure. Whatever method of adjustment you choose, you must organize your response carefully and seek to retain, as much as the circumstances permit, the goodwill and future business of the claimant.

Full Restitution. Full-restitution adjustment letters are easy to write because they do exactly as the claimant asks. These "yes" letters follow the everyday letter plan to solve the problem described in the claim. Each begins with a statement granting the adjustment. Only the details in subsequent paragraphs vary, depending on whether the seller is at fault, the fault is divided, or the customer is at fault but the claim is granted to retain goodwill.

Seller at Fault. If you are the seller of goods or services and you are entirely at fault in a claim situation, you will usually, of course, grant an adjustment. And you should do so willingly. Just as you have greater respect for persons who readily admit their mistakes, your customer will respect your company when it cheerfully fulfills its responsibilities without quibbling. When you must grant an adjustment because your company is at fault, follow an outline such as this:

1. Tell the customer the good news immediately—preferably in the first sentence.
2. Explain how the mistake happened (if you have an explanation). Don't be afraid of embarrassment—it is folly to try to save face when you are unquestionably wrong.
3. Express appreciation for the customer's understanding, and tell the customer that you will do your best to ensure better treatment in the future.

The letter might read:

Dear Ms. Goldman:

This Friday we will send you by parcel post, special handling, 200 "Cougar" pennants to replace those that were printed in white instead of yellow. There will be, of course, no additional charge for these.

We have tried to find out what caused the confusion, but we have no explanation— or excuse. The only possible reason we can offer is that two members of our production department were ill last week, and we had to use inexperienced help for two or three days.

Please excuse us this time, Ms. Goldman. To help give you better service in the future, we have started a new training program for all those who are likely to be called into emergency service in the production area. We expect that this precaution will help us give you better service.

You may dispose of the 200 pennants that you received. It is not necessary to return them to us. Thank you for giving us an opportunity to serve you.

Sincerely yours,

Fault Is Shared. Occasionally, the seller and customer share the responsibility for error. For example, the customer may have misunderstood your policy because it was not stated clearly or because the sales representative gave the wrong impression. In another case one of your products may have malfunctioned and been damaged even further because the customer attempted to repair it. Of course, you should cheerfully acknowledge your part of the blame. At the same time you may try to convince the customer to share some of the responsibility too. The following letter uses a form of the everyday letter plan to accomplish this purpose:

Dear Mr. Tranner:

Your Creative Creations pinball machine has been restored to working order and is being returned to you today by parcel post.

The trigger device jammed because one of the bolts holding it in place had come loose. To prevent this situation from recurring, we have used special lock bolts to hold the trigger in place.

We replaced the spring-feed mechanism. Apparently a screwdriver or other sharp instrument had been used in an attempt to free the jammed trigger. Instead, the spring feed was bent so severely that it was no longer operable. Although there is no charge this time for this replacement, please understand that such repairs are not included under the terms of the warranty. May I suggest that in the future any needed repairs be left solely to our well-trained service staff.

Enclosed is a copy of our latest catalog describing the newest in Creative Creations electronic games. See for yourself the additional hours of enjoyment you can receive from these exciting, challenging entertainments.

Sincerely yours,

Enclosure

Goodwill Adjustment. You will sometimes grant an adjustment as a goodwill gesture, even though the customer is clearly at fault. The risk of turning down a good customer may be too great, or the amount in question may be so small that refusing to make the adjustment would be poor business. In such a case you should take full advantage of the opportunity to give in gracefully and build goodwill.

Dear Mrs. Ruis:

The Constellation stereo recordings that you returned on January 18 arrived yesterday. I am sending you a replacement for the first record; our inspectors found the other two to be in perfect condition, so they are being returned to you.

Upon examination of the records, our inspectors discovered that both sides of the first record had apparently been played with a blunt needle. May I suggest that you change the needle of your stereo before playing any other records. A record is only as good as the needle playing it, and a blunt needle will continue to damage your recordings.

The enclosed booklet describes the various needles recommended by Constellation—available at any record dealer that sells the Constellation line.

Sincerely yours,

Enclosure

Partial Adjustment. Sometimes customers may request adjustments that are unreasonable or that are not covered under the warranty agreement. Instead of refusing the adjustment, you can reach a compromise by attempting to meet the customer halfway.

For example, suppose a customer returned to you a piece of luggage that was badly scratched and requested a replacement under the terms of the warranty. "After all," states the customer, "you guarantee this luggage against damage." You guarantee the luggage against *breakage,* not necessarily damage, under normal travel conditions. Although you cannot replace the luggage, you can repair the scratch so that it will not be noticeable.

What if a customer writes you that one of your Lastever tires is threadbare after only 24,000 miles of service? Your 40,000-mile warranty does not guarantee the customer a full refund or even a new tire, as the claim letter suggested. You can, however, prorate the cost of the tire and issue a credit toward the purchase of a replacement.

Situations such as these two require partial adjustments. Since you are not doing exactly what the customers requested, you are in fact writing a bad-news letter. The task of the effective communicator is not to convey the bad news, but to present the circumstances in such a positive, thoughtful light that the customer is able to understand and accept graciously the partial adjustment.

Adapt the bad-news plan to the writing of partial adjustments. Use the following outline to organize your ideas:

1. Refer to the claim and its circumstances in a neutral manner.
2. Explain the circumstances for refusing the requested adjustment; tactfully weave in the refusal with the explanation.
3. Present your alternative for rectifying the situation.
4. Close with resale of your company or its products.

The following claim letter was received by a mail-order nursery. The warranty on the bulbs had expired. How would you handle this claim?

Ladies and Gentlemen:

The catalog you mailed to me last spring attracted my attention. Excited about the beautiful photos, I purchased an order of begonia tubers.

Even though I did everything the planting and caring manual prescribed, all I got were some sad-looking plants, without even a trace of a flower. Since my garden is landscaped with plenty of trees and an excellent sprinkling and misting system, I know that the begonias didn't bloom because of a lack of water or shade.

I relied on Spring Valley's Triple-Tested Seal of Approval, which ensured that the begonias would grow and bloom to my full satisfaction. I have great confidence in Spring Valley and would like to maintain it. Therefore, would you please stand behind your guarantee and refund to me the purchase price of these begonias—$23.82. A copy of my credit card statement is enclosed.

Sincerely,

Ella DeHass

Enclosure

The company that received this letter chose to make a partial adjustment. Notice how the bad-news plan was used to retain the business and goodwill of this customer.

Dear Ms. DeHass:

We appreciate hearing from you about your experience with our begonia tubers.

The guarantee period for the plants you purchased expired on August 1. Although we are unable to grant a refund after the guarantee period, we do wish to make an adjustment. Because we value you as a customer, we are enclosing a gift certificate for $23.82 for use on your next order.

You should be receiving our new spring catalog within the next six weeks. In it you will find many beautiful selections for the planting season, which is rapidly approaching.

Sincerely,

Enclosure

Adjustment Refusals. In many instances the customer's request for an adjustment is not justifiable and you must refuse the claim. Of course, this fact must be established conclusively before a letter is sent. You cannot automatically *assume* that the customer is wrong; therefore, all the facts should be obtained and weighed carefully. "Make sure you are right, and then go ahead" is good advice in writing letters of this type.

Even though you know you are right and the customer is wrong, however, this type of letter is still one of the most difficult to write. Somehow you must convey to the customer the idea that you are following the only course open to you and that, as a reasonable person, the customer will agree with you. You will have to rely on your best skills as a business writer!

Nonreturnable Merchandise. Suppose a customer writes wanting to return for credit some items of merchandise purchased several months ago. The reason given for the return is that the merchandise received was not that specified in the order. Of course, you are immediately skeptical. Why did the customer wait so long before reporting the error to you? After looking up the original order, you find that the correct merchandise was definitely sent; the bill was even paid. You conclude that the customer is merely trying to unload some unwanted stock and may be trying to take advantage of your company's very fair adjustment policies. In this particular case you cannot accept the merchandise for credit.

In writing the reply to this claim, use the bad-news letter plan, which may follow an outline like the one shown below:

1. Thank the customer for writing you, restating the adjustment he or she believes should be made.
2. Explain why granting the adjustment is not possible.
3. Offer helpful advice, if possible.
4. Assume that the customer accepts your position as fair, and close the letter on a friendly note.

The letter might read:

Dear Mrs. Murillo:

We appreciate your writing to us about the MiniCold bar refrigerators that you wish to return for credit.

Immediately after receiving your letter, I rechecked your January 11 order. The order specified 12 MiniCold bar refrigerators in wood-grain finish; the bill of lading matches your order in every respect. In fact, you have already paid the invoice for this shipment. Under the circumstances we are unable to accept these refrigerators for credit.

The MiniCold model was discontinued by the manufacturer in April. Several of our dealers, however, reported considerable success in moving the MiniCold model. Premier Furniture, in Austin, found that instead of advertising them as bar refrigerators, they sold much faster when billed as the "perfect size for your room in the college dorm." You might consider running such an ad on these refrigerators in connection with your summer furniture and appliance clearance sales.

Several new appliance designs and colors for fall have arrived. Particularly exciting is the new line of computerized kitchen appliances designed by Damaco. Look over the enclosed folder describing some of these "space age" marvels. This line promises to be one of the best sellers we have ever had.

Sincerely yours,

Enclosure

Buyer at Fault. Sometimes you must refuse to grant an adjustment because the product is no longer under warranty or it has been abused. Customers may request unwarranted repairs, replacements, or refunds. In any of these cases, the effective communicator must show the claimant why the request is not justified and minimize any resulting ill will.

Suppose a customer returned to you a microcomputer that "will not boot up *any software*" (customer's emphasis) and asks that it be repaired under the terms of the 90-day guarantee. You find that a power surge had apparently damaged the A disk drive; such repairs are not covered under the terms of the guarantee. You would need to write this customer a refusal letter using the bad-news letter plan.

Dear Ms. Gajewsky:

Your Computex microcomputer, along with your letter, arrived at our repair center yesterday. We appreciate your concern about its not booting any of your program disks.

Upon the arrival of your Computex, it was checked by one of our repair supervisors. Apparently a power surge has damaged the A disk drive and rendered it inoperable. Since your computer is guaranteed against defects in parts and work quality only under normal-use conditions, the needed replacement is not covered under the terms of the warranty.

We can, however, replace your A disk drive and restore your Computex to working order for $243, which is the actual cost of parts and labor. May we suggest that you also purchase a surge protector for an additional $23 so that this kind of damage does not occur again.

Please let us know if you wish us to make the replacement and whether or not you wish to purchase a surge protector. A postage-paid card is enclosed for your convenience in replying.

Sincerely yours,

Enclosure

Unearned Discounts. Occasionally customers may figure the discount on a bill incorrectly or may attempt to take advantage of a discount when they are not entitled to it. The company may do one of three things:

1. Return the remittance and request a check for the correct amount.
2. Accept the remittance and ask for an additional remittance to make up the difference.
3. Accept the remittance and add the difference to the customer's next bill.

In any event a letter must be written to the customer. Under no circumstances should the situation be ignored. In fairness to other customers who abide by the rules, the business cannot afford to make exceptions. In writing to customers, point out the error tactfully and appeal to their sense of fair play—but do both without offending them.

Dear Mrs. Cerola-Brown:

Thank you for your check for $1960 in payment of your June invoice. We appreciate the many opportunities you have given us to serve you.

We notice that in the past you have always paid your invoices within the discount period to take advantage of the saving. As you know, we can afford to give this discount because prompt payment enables us to make a similar saving on our purchases.

When a customer does not make payment within the discount period, we do not make any saving either. In the case of your June invoice, 18 days passed before we received payment. Of course, this is 8 days beyond the 10-day period allowed.

Because you are a good customer and because this is the first time you have gone beyond the discount period, we would like to allow the discount. However, if we did so, we would be unfair to our customers who pay within the 10-day period. They would lose confidence in us—and so would you.

Therefore, Mrs. Cerola-Brown, would you please send us with your next remittance the $40 remaining on your account.

Very sincerely yours,

Third Party at Fault. Quite often the roots of a claim lie neither in the customer's nor in the seller's actions but in the carrier's. Since the carrier assumes responsibility for safe delivery of any shipment accepted, the customer's claim for damaged or lost merchandise is usually against the carrier rather than against the seller. The seller should have a receipt showing that the merchandise was in good condition at the time it was released to the carrier. When a shipment arrives in damaged condition or is "short," the company to whom the claim is made may do one of two things:

1. Take the responsibility for the adjustment; then make a claim against the carrier.
2. Suggest that the customer enter a claim with the carrier, since the matter is really between the buyer and the carrier.

Following is an example of a letter from a supplier to a dealer who received a badly damaged television set. The bad-news letter plan is used to write this kind of adjustment letter.

Dear Mr. Nesbitt:

We appreciate your calling to our attention the damage done to the Magnaworld television that you ordered from us recently.

When the television left our Toledo warehouse, it was in perfect condition, as substantiated by a signed receipt from the Ohio Western Railroad. Evidently the television was damaged in transit, and your claim is with the railroad. The shipment was fully insured, so you should have no difficulty recovering the cost of the set.

Would you like us to send a duplicate shipment to replace the television damaged in transit? If so, please sign and mail the enclosed postcard and we will ship the replacement immediately.

Sincerely yours,

Enclosure

COMMUNICATION LABORATORY

APPLICATION EXERCISES

A. Assume that you had bought a set of tires from your local service station. You paid for the tires in six equal installments that were added to your monthly gasoline bill. Even though you have paid all six installments in full, your monthly bills continue to reflect these installment payments. So far, you have received two such "extra bills." Write to the Wilshire Oil Company, P.O. Box 170, New York, New York 10004, requesting that the company (1) stop billing you for the tires and (2) write you confirming that your credit rating has not been damaged.

B. Now suppose you work for the Wilshire Oil Company (see Exercise A). You are asked to write the adjustment letter in response to the claim. Address the letter to Frances Mullens, 350 Weddington Road, Macon,

Georgia 31206. After checking, you find that Ms. Mullens has continued receiving a bill because of an accounting error. Tell Ms. Mullens that you have corrected the error, apologize, and assure her that her credit rating is unchanged.

C. Suppose you had purchased a General Products portable cassette recorder from your local discount department store. Naturally, you filled out and sent in the card warranting your purchase for 90 days. After you had used the recorder for two months, it failed to record properly—all you get are muffled sounds. You wish to send the recorder to the General Products Repair Center to be repaired under the terms of the warranty. Write the claim letter to accompany your recorder. Address it to General Products Repair Center, 4830 Sherman Way, Pittsburgh, Pennsylvania 15229. Ask General Products to repair your recorder under the terms of the guarantee.

D. Assume that you are answering the claim in Exercise C. Because the recorder had been loaded improperly, its magnetic recording head had been damaged. You can repair the recorder, but not under the terms of the guarantee. Your guarantee warrants only defects in materials and workmanship. Write a refusal letter to Christopher Savage, 1210 Monogram Avenue, Santa Fe, New Mexico 87501. Tell him you can repair the recorder for $12.50; make it easy for him to reply.

E. A box of oranges you ordered from All-Sweet Oranges, Route 6, Fort Lauderdale, Florida 33314, arrives with some of the fruit spoiled. The oranges were crated poorly and were marked "Keep in a Cool Place." Write a letter making your claim.

F. Compose the adjustment letter you would write if you were employed by All-Sweet Oranges, who found that the Laraway Shipping Company was at fault in carelessly transporting the oranges (see Exercise E). Address the letter to yourself.

VOCABULARY AND SPELLING STUDIES

A. These words are often confused: *disposition, deposition; disprove, disapprove.* Write each in a sentence that illustrates its meaning.

B. Substitute the correct forms for any incorrect number style in these sentences. Write *OK* for any sentence that has no error.

1. The company retirement fund now has over two million dollars.
2. This historic oak tree is 10½ feet high.
3. The candidate needs only ⅔'s of the vote.
4. Aviation has changed our lives during the 20th century.
5. 32 tons were shipped yesterday.

C. Should one or two *l*'s be used in the blank spaces in these words?

1. ba__istics
2. cau__iflower
3. co__ection
4. cu__ture
5. mai__able
6. mi__eage
7. para__el
8. we__come

COMMUNICATING FOR RESULTS

A Delivery Error. You place an order by telephone to a local stationery store for ten columnar pads of a particular size for use by the accounting staff. Two weeks later a messenger brings in ten *cartons*, each carton containing ten pads. Of course, it is a mistake, but you know the messenger is not to blame—the delivery ticket shows ten *cartons*. How would you handle this problem?

U · N · I · T

46

Credit and Collection Letters: Using Paragraph Libraries

Today millions of Americans enjoy credit privileges. Perhaps the house you live in, the family automobile, your television set, and much of your clothing were purchased on credit. A conservative estimate reveals that a majority of all business in the United States is transacted on credit. The consumer buys merchandise on credit from the retail store; the retail store purchases its stock on credit from a wholesaler; the wholesaler buys on credit from the factory; the factory purchases its raw materials, also on credit, from various suppliers. The chain is almost endless, and the use of credit continues to grow. Many Americans travel, dine, and obtain hotel accommodations on a credit basis merely by producing a convenient credit card.

Even though millions of dollars' worth of business is done on credit each year, the losses from bad debts are surprisingly small. Most businesses estimate that of their total charge accounts, fewer than 1 percent will be uncollectible. One reason for this small percentage of "bad debts" is that credit privileges are not granted in a hit-or-miss fashion. Before businesses grant credit, they make reasonably sure that they will be paid for the goods they sell. Thus each prospective charge account customer is investigated carefully before credit is extended. Another reason for the small number of uncollectible accounts is, of course, that most people are honest.

Credit Letters

A person wishing to establish credit will usually go to a firm's credit department or will write or telephone for a credit application form. Such an application is illustrated on page 461.

Investigating the Applicant. When the store receives a credit application, the credit manager will begin immediately to investigate the references that have been supplied or in some cases will ask the local retail credit bureau to investigate. When asking for a reference from stores where the applicant has been a credit customer, the credit manager will usually use a form letter like this:

Dear _____:

_____(Name and Address)_____, has requested credit privileges from us and has given your firm as a reference.

We would very much appreciate your answering the following questions about _____:

1. How long has the applicant had an account with you? _____

2. Was there a credit limit? _____ If, so, how much?_____

3. Did the applicant make payments according to your terms? _____
   _____ Always   _____ Usually   _____ Irregularly

4. Does the applicant's account have an outstanding balance? _____ If so, how much? _____

5. Overall, do you consider the applicant:

   _____ An excellent credit risk?

   _____ An average credit risk?

   _____ A poor credit risk?

A stamped return envelope is enclosed for your convenience in replying. Of course, any information you give us will be kept confidential.

Sincerely yours,

Enclosure

Preparing the Response. All credit applications, of course, require responses. As credit has emerged as the basic medium for conducting business, firms have increasingly been required to welcome new credit customers or deny credit privileges to more and more applicants. Advances in office technology have permitted the mechanization of credit responses without

JCPenney Charge Application

Signature		For Office Use Only
Your Signature(s) mean(s) that you have read and agree to the terms of our Charge Account Agreement.	Applicant's Signature *Sarah Brown* Date 2/16/89 Co-Applicant's Signature Date	Store Number 196901 Account Number

General Information — (Please Print All Information)

Type Of Account You Want (Check One) ☑ Individual ☐ Joint

Have You Applied For A JCPenney Account Before? Applicant ☐ Yes ☑ No Where ___ When ___
Co-Applicant ☐ Yes ☐ No Where ___ When ___

Name Of Applicant To Whom Our Billing Statements Should Be Sent
(First) SARAH (Initial) (Last) BROWN
Social Security Number 054-19-8718 Date Of Birth 5/22/51 No. Of Dependent Children 0

Name Of Co-Applicant (If Joint Account Requested)
(First) (Initial) (Last)
Social Security Number Date Of Birth / / Relationship To Applicant

Name And Relationship(s) To Applicant(s) Of Any Other Person(s) You Will Allow To Charge Purchases To Your Account
(First) (Initial) (Last) (Relationship)

Information About Applicant To Whom Our Billing Statements Should Be Sent | Information About Co-Applicant (If Joint Account Requested)

Present Residence Address—Street 1131 S. PRINCE ST.
City, State PALMYRA, PA Zip 17017 18
Area Code & Phone Number (717) 555-9811 How Long At This Address Yrs. 8 Mos. 2 Monthly Mtge./Rent $450
Do You ☑ Own ☐ Rent ☐ Own Mobile Home ☐ Live With Parents ☐ Other (Please Specify)
Former Address — Street 338 W. 77th ST. How Long 5 YRS
City, State NEW YORK, NY Zip 10024
Employer (Give Firm's Full Name) WILSON + WILSON, INC. How Long 5 YRS
Employer's Address (Street/City/State) 2 MAIN ST., HARRISBURG, PA Business Telephone 555-1144
Type Of Business STEEL MFG Present Position EXEC. SECRETARY Monthly Salary $1,250

Present Residence Address—Street
City, State Zip
Area Code & Phone Number ( ) How Long At This Address Yrs. Mos. Monthly Mtge./Rent
Do You ☐ Own ☐ Rent ☐ Own Mobile Home ☐ Live With Parents ☐ Other (Please Specify)
Former Address — Street How Long
City, State Zip
Employer (Give Firm's Full Name) How Long
Employer's Address (Street/City/State) Business Telephone
Type Of Business Present Position Monthly Salary

You Need Not Furnish Alimony, Child Support Or Separate Maintenance Income Information If You Do Not Want Us To Consider It In Evaluating Your Application

Other Income — Source(s) NONE Amount (Monthly)
Other Income — Source(s) Amount (Monthly)

Bank Accounts (Include Co-Applicant's. If Joint Account Requested)

Bank — Branch	Account In The Name Of	Checking & Savings	Checking	Savings	Loan
1 PENN STATE NAT'L	SARAH BROWN	☐	☐	☐	☐
2		☐	☐	☐	☐

Credit References (Include Co-Applicant's. If Joint Account Requested)
Credit Cards (Include Loan Or Finance Companies)

Firm Name	Location	Account/Loan Number	Account/Loan In The Name Of
1 MASTERCARD	PENN STATE NAT'L	8766000698338765	SARAH BROWN
2			
3			

Personal Reference
Name Of Person Not Living At Address Of Applicant Or Co-Applicant RONALD J. STOKES Relationship To Applicant SUPERVISOR Present Residence Address (Street/City/State) 42 DEVON ST., ICKESBURG, PA

JCP-6600 (Rev. 5/82) After completing application, detach at perforation, fold down from top, moisten flap, fold and seal. Postage paid by JCPenney.

Courtesy of JC Penney Company, Inc.

A credit application usually requests personal as well as business information.

having these letters lose their personal touch, thereby containing costs and generating customer goodwill.

Computerized word processing equipment enables business writers to store form paragraphs to cover a number of circumstances. These form paragraphs even make allowances for inserting variables, such as different dates or different amounts of money. Letter writers need only to select the appropriate paragraphs, designate the correct sequence, supply individual variables, and instruct the word processing operator to prepare the letter. In just a matter of minutes, a beautifully typed, personalized document appears.

Because the process for preparing credit responses has been streamlined, you probably think that there is little reason for you to learn how to write credit letters. On the contrary! Keep in mind that *someone* has to write those form paragraphs for the computerized paragraph library; *someone* has to select and organize the paragraphs to compile an effective letter; and *someone* has to revise continually the paragraph library so that it reflects accurately your business policies and practices. Picture yourself as that *someone* as you continue your study of this unit.

Although most credit letters are written using automated procedures and equipment, some small businesses today find it necessary to continue writing such letters on an individual basis. Also, some credit situations may be unique and not lend themselves to correspondence prepared through a paragraph library. These situations require your individual handling and your expertise as a writer of credit letters. As you study the following guidelines for the preparation of various kinds of credit letters, remember that these standards apply whether you are writing individual letters, creating paragraph libraries, or originating letters using a paragraph library.

Letters Granting Credit. If the decision regarding an applicant's request for credit is favorable, the letter writer faces a pleasant writing task—that of telling the customer the welcome news. The following outline, using the everyday letter plan, may be used as a guide in writing letters granting credit.

1. Welcome the customer, expressing your wish for a pleasant association.
2. Describe the special privileges available.
3. Explain the terms of payment.
4. Encourage use of the new charge account and offer any special assistance.

Dear Mrs. Easton:

We take great pleasure in opening a charge account at Braddock's in your name. I feel sure that this will be the start of a long and mutually pleasant association.

As a charge customer you will enjoy a number of conveniences at Braddock's. For instance, using your credit card will simplify purchasing—no more delays writing checks, showing identification, and obtaining purchase approvals. You will receive advance notices of special sales so that you may take advantage of these bargains before they are offered to the general public. You may also use your charge card at our Terrace Restaurant, in our Fur Salon, or for our Special Service Shopper. Your charge card is accepted for all our services!

By the 10th of each month, you will receive an itemized statement of your purchases made through the last day of the preceding month; purchases made after the last day appear on the following month's bill. Payments are due by the 1st of the following month, and a monthly charge of 1½ percent will be made on the balance remaining at that time. The enclosed brochure explains in detail the terms of your account.

We hope you will make regular use of your charge account. You may charge up to $1000 on this account without obtaining any prior credit approval. Brochures for our July sale should reach you within the next week; perhaps you will want to inaugurate your account by taking advantage of the bargains available during this sale.

Sincerely yours,

Enclosure

Many stores notify acceptance of applications for credit by a printed announcement card.

Letters Refusing Credit. If the credit manager determines from the information gathered that an applicant is a poor credit risk, a letter turning down the request must be written. No other letter is more difficult to write. Regardless of the wording, the writer is in effect saying the customer does not warrant the seller's faith. A letter refusing credit must be very tactful, as is the one on page 464. Remember, you want the customer to continue buying from you on a cash basis.

To write a letter refusing credit, use an indirect approach that follows the bad-news plan. Notice how the following letter leads the reader on a step-by-step basis to the refusal and then offers the alternative plan of purchasing on a cash basis.

Dear Mr. McBurney:

You have paid us a compliment by requesting credit privileges at Wilco's. Thank you for submitting your application.

As in the case of all those who apply for credit, we have made a careful investigation of your resources and credit obligations. Since you have a number of loan commitments, may we suggest that you continue to allow Wilco's to serve you on a cash basis until such time as you are able to reduce your present obligations.

You may be sure, Mr. McBurney, that we will welcome the opportunity to consider your application again when circumstances are more favorable toward your receiving additional credit.

Sincerely yours,

Letters Stimulating Credit Business. Business firms welcome the opportunity to grant credit to the right people—those who will use it wisely. In fact, because they know that credit customers are bigger buyers and generally more loyal customers, stores often put on special campaigns to encourage credit customers to make more frequent or larger purchases. These letters are combined sales-goodwill letters because they stimulate both interest in and sales for the firm.

Retail stores will often invite steady cash customers to open charge accounts on the theory that they will like the convenience of shopping in this manner and will, of course, be encouraged to make more frequent purchases. The following letter, using the everyday letter plan, encourages a cash customer to avail herself of a charge account.

fitzgerald's
& you
2451 East Main Street
Danville, Illinois 61832
(217) 555-8128

November 8, 1990

Mr. Alan Beardsley
1421 North Logan Avenue
Danville, IL 61832

Dear Mr. Beardsley:

Thank you for requesting a credit account with Fitzgerald's &
You. Fitzgerald's & You believes that people who have not yet
established credit certainly deserve the opportunity to do so,
and we would like to help you.

To establish your first credit account, then, we suggest
that you ask someone to act as a cosigner with you on the
credit application. Perhaps one of your relatives or
friends who has already established credit would be willing
to help you do this.

As soon as you and your cosigner have completed the enclosed
form, please return it to us, and we will reevaluate your
request.

All of us at Fitzgerald's & You are eager to welcome you to our
store again--soon!

Sincerely,

Brian Lavoie

Brian Lavoie
Credit Department

nw
Enclosure

A letter refusing credit should be tactful.

Dear Ms. Conners:

Hundreds of our customers enjoy the convenience of a charge account—you are cordially invited to join this group of privileged clientele.

Our charge customers are able to shop without having to carry large sums of money or suffer through the delays of paying by check. Often, too, they enjoy the convenience of shopping more easily by mail or by telephone. Merchandise that you really need can be purchased now, and you will not have to defer the pleasure of using it.

Rose and Decker pampers its charge customers in many ways, and you will be delighted with the personal attention you will receive. Why not come in and let us show you how easy it is to open an account—and begin using your new account immediately.

Sincerely yours,

Collection Letters

Most of the people who have been granted credit are conscientious and pay their bills on time. Some people, however, need to be reminded when their accounts are past due. The person who writes collection letters must assume that customers are fundamentally honest and fair and intend to pay their bills. This attitude is necessary to maintain the basic principle of credit—mutual faith. Therefore, the experienced credit manager assumes that "the customer is trustworthy until proven otherwise."

Collection-Letter Series. Collection letters are often written in a series. There may be as many as six letters in a series, beginning with the first reminder and ending with the final ultimatum. Many large department stores and mail-order houses have developed several series of collection letters—as many as five or six different sets. Each series may be independent of the others, or letters in one series may be used interchangeably with one or more in the others.

Collection-letter series are usually duplicated form letters; the typist merely fills in the date, inside address, and salutation. Some firms, however, prefer to give their collection letters a more personal touch (these command more attention) by having them typed on computers or word processing equipment. Each letter in a series is given a code number, and a careful record is kept of those that have been sent to the customer.

Other companies have automated their "personalized" collection series by using form paragraphs to construct letters. A variety of form paragraphs are stored in the computer, and correspondents merely select from the paragraph library to construct their letters. These paragraphs enable the business writer to shape each letter so that it conforms to the situation and conveys a personal semblance. Variables such as dates, amounts, items, and credit terms are easily inserted to personalize the letter even further.

As with paragraphs in a credit-letter paragraph library, *someone* must write and revise the form letters or paragraph library used in a collection series. Correspondents also need to know how to select and compile letters appropriate for a variety of collection situations. The principles discussed here will assist you in selecting, compiling, or writing collection letters.

The Collection Process. Most businesses send out statements each month to those who have charge accounts. These statements serve as reminders to pay. At the same time they furnish customers with a record of their purchases.

At one time charge customers looked upon the statement as a *dun*—a demand for payment. Today, however, we expect to receive a statement of our account each month and use it as a basis for payment.

A statement of account is all that most people need to pay their bills. No additional reminders are necessary. But sometimes statements are mislaid or forgotten. If the business does not receive payment within a specified number of days after the statement is sent, it may simply send a second statement and hope this will be sufficient. On the other hand, the second reminder may be a form letter or a card reminder, such as the one shown on page 467.

You will notice that form reminders are very impersonal and very gentle. There is a good reason for this. At this stage of collection, the credit manager doesn't want the customer to feel singled out. Otherwise, the customer's attitude may be "Why are they picking on me? I'm only a few days late." Because of this possible attitude, a personalized message in this situation is not so effective as a printed notice or a form letter.

If the various notices just discussed do not bring results, additional reminders will be necessary. The procedures to be followed from this point depend greatly on the customers. If their credit records are good, the store may continue reminding them with gentle hints that use the everyday letter plan. If there is some past history of tardiness in paying, the next reminder may be more persuasive. If the store suspects, because of past dealings, that a customer will be difficult to collect from, stiffer reminders may be written earlier. Also, the number of days allowed between reminders will depend on the store's experience with the customer; quick-paying customers are usually given more time between reminders. There is no standard pattern for all customers or for all businesses; many factors determine the frequency and the types of letters sent to collect past-due accounts. A typical pattern in a collection system may be as follows:

Step	Number of Days After Regular Billing
1. Reminder	30
2. Inquiry letter	45
3. Mild appeal	60
4. Strong appeal	75
5. Ultimatum	90–100

To illustrate a collection situation, let us assume that Marla Reynolds has a charge account with Fitzgerald's & You Department Store. Fitzgerald's & You records show that Ms. Reynolds has had an account for about a year. She has made frequent purchases during that time and has always paid her

AN OPPORTUNITY . . .

TO THANK YOU FOR YOUR BUSINESS AND TO REMIND YOU
OF THE BALANCE (SHOWN ON THE ENCLOSED STATEMENT
FOR YOUR CONVENIENCE) FOR YOUR RECENT PURCHASES.

IF YOU HAVE SENT US YOUR PAYMENT WITHIN THE LAST
FEW DAYS, PLEASE ACCEPT OUR THANKS. IF YOU HAVE
NOT, PLEASE TAKE THIS OPPORTUNITY TO DO SO.

HYLAND'S

The second reminder that payment is due may be in the form of a printed card.

bills, but several times reminders were necessary before the account was
paid.

During September Ms. Reynolds purchased a set of Willowbrook china
and a 40-piece set of Reed stainless steel flatware. The amount of her
purchase was $214.73. A statement was sent on October 1.

The Reminder Stage. Because Ms. Reynolds did not pay the $214.73
statement sent to her on October 1, a routine reminder form was mailed
on November 1. If Ms. Reynolds does not respond to this routine reminder,
the credit manager may choose to send her a more personal reminder or
advance to the next stage of collection, depending upon what kind of
customer he or she judges Ms. Reynolds to be.

If the credit manager considers her merely careless or forgetful, rather
than deliberately slow, the manager will send a second, more personal
reminder, somewhat like the one on page 468. Care will be taken not to
offend Ms. Reynolds since she is still considered a profitable customer. The
letter to Ms. Reynolds may sound something like this.

Dear Ms. Reynolds:

Haven't you overlooked something? According to our records, you received a
statement of your account in early October. On November 1 we sent you a
reminder that your balance of $214.73 had not been paid.

This matter is probably an oversight and you plan to mail us your check right
away. Better still, why not come to the store in person to take care of the account.
While you are here, stop in our Housewares Department to see all the new

merchandise we have received for the holiday season. We are especially pleased with our line of Colby stemware.

Cordially yours,

Notice that this letter uses a variation of the everyday letter plan and gently chides the customer for her oversight. Note, too, that she is indirectly

THE WALL STREET JOURNAL.

DOW JONES & COMPANY, INC. Publishers.
THE WALL STREET JOURNAL • BARRON'S

THE EDUCATIONAL SERVICE BUREAU
200 Burnett Road
Chicopee, Massachusetts 01021

Myrtle White
Manager, Subscriber Services

October 20, 1986

Mr. George Vandenburg
15 Summit Avenue
Providence, Rhode Island 02906

Dear Mr. Vandenburg:

We know how busy college life can be, with classes, studies and extracurricular activities. So we'd like to remind you that we have not yet received payment for your <u>Wall Street Journal</u> subscription. Here is a second copy of the invoice for your convenience.

No doubt by now you've had an opportunity to become familiar with <u>The Journal</u>, to use it as an adjunct to your studies, and to recognize what an important part of the American business scene it is. We hope you'll come to find, as many students have, that <u>The Journal</u> provides indispensable information for the campus and the business communities alike.

Your invoice is made out for the term you selected. If you chose less than a year, you can take this opportunity to extend your subscription to a full year and save even more at our special educational rate. Simply check the appropriate box on the invoice and enclose your payment.

To make sure you don't miss a day of your subscription, we are always happy to accept changes of address, whether on or off campus. Just give us two weeks' notice.

Thank you.

Sincerely,

Carole Brinkman

Carole Brinkman
Subscriber Services

an
Enclosures

PS: If you've sent payment, please excuse this request. Your payment and our letter probably crossed in the mail.

Credit managers may send a personal reminder letter to customers whose failure to pay may be accidental rather than deliberate.

complimented by the implication that there is no cause for worry on your part—you know she will pay. The letter ends with a sales message because at this stage you wish merely to plant an idea, not to offend the customer by overemphasizing your plea.

If this letter does not get results (but in most cases it will), you will have to use a different approach. Again, the time elapsed between the letter just illustrated and the next one will depend upon the customer and the store. In most cases the time between letters grows progressively shorter. If there is a problem in receiving payment, the store does not wish to drag the matter out; the customer may get the impression that prompt payment really isn't important.

Inquiry Letter. If Ms. Reynolds still does not pay, you begin to suspect that something is wrong—and that is exactly the approach you take in the next collection stage. The inquiry stage still assumes the customer wishes to pay but that something is preventing his or her prompt payment.

Reasons people hold up payment may be that they are dissatisfied with the merchandise, the service has been unsatisfactory, or they are in temporary financial difficulty. Whatever the case may be, you wish to take this opportunity to say, "Let's sit down and talk about it." Of course, if there is no such problem, you wish the customer to send a check for the overdue balance to clear up the account.

Dear Ms. Reynolds:

You have always in the past paid your account promptly. That is the reason we cannot understand why we have not received your check for $214.73 or an explanation why your account remains unpaid.

Is something wrong? We have no reason to believe anything other than that you are completely satisfied with the Willowbrook china and Reed stainless steel flatware. Perhaps there is some other reason that prevents you from sending your payment for these purchases. Whatever the circumstances may be, please let us know. We would like to work out a solution with you. However, we cannot do so unless we hear from you.

Write me personally, Ms. Reynolds, or give me a call at 555-8733 to discuss this situation. I am eager to hear from you. However, if there is no reason for nonpayment, won't you please take a moment now to write a check for $214.73 and mail it so that your account can be marked "paid in full."

Sincerely yours,

Mild Appeal. There are several appeals the store may use in writing the next letter if the "let's-talk-about it" approach does not get results. Since most people like to have others think well of them and are uncomfortable if their image is in danger of blemish, the appeal to pride is often successful. "We are confident your reputation for prompt payment and fair business practices will not allow you to permit this balance to remain unpaid any longer" says what is needed to implement this mild appeal.

The one most often used mild appeal is the appeal to fair play. This appeal tells the customer, "We have kept our part of the bargain—now won't you keep yours?" The appeal to fair play uses the persuasive letter plan to convince the reader to pay, as illustrated in the following letter.

Dear Ms. Reynolds:

Suppose a good friend of yours wanted to borrow your new china and flatware for a holiday party she was giving. Because you like her and wish her party to be a success, you gladly consent—even offer to help her move the china and flatware to her house for the occasion. Of course, you both understand that these items will be returned promptly after the party.

How would you feel if your friend kept the china and flatware and said nothing about returning them? If she even ignored several reminders from you that they should be returned? My guess is, Ms. Reynolds, that you would be somewhat bewildered—and a little annoyed.

We find ourselves in a similar position regarding your account. We granted you credit because we felt you would not abuse the privilege. Yet you have not paid for your September purchases, and you have not responded to the four notices we have sent you. We are naturally curious to know why. We sold you the china and flatware in good faith, and we have tried to see that you were pleased in every way. But we believe you also have a responsibility to show us that our faith in you was justified.

Won't you use the enclosed envelope to send us your check (the amount is $214.73) right now—this minute, while the matter is fresh in your mind. This will substantiate our faith in you.

Sincerely yours,

Enclosure

Strong Appeal. If this appeal to the customer's sense of fair play does not bring the desired results, the credit manager has reason to be worried about the intentions of the customer. What will the next step be? If the firm's collection policy permits (some firms have more lenient collection policies than others), a second appeal may be made before sending the customer a "pay-or-else" ultimatum. The second appeal letter, which also follows the persuasive letter plan, may make a strong appeal to fear.

Fear of losing one's credit rating and fear of losing one's credit privileges are the main motivators in this appeal stage. The resulting letter is positively worded but firm in its position. Sentences such as "To protect your credit rating, your account must be cleared up immediately" and "You would not want to lose your credit privileges by allowing this account to go unpaid" are typical statements that might appear in the strong appeal letter. The following letter illustrates fully how the appeal to fear can be carried out in the persuasive letter plan.

Dear Ms. Reynolds:

If we received an inquiry concerning your credit, we would like to say, "Of course, Ms. Reynolds is an excellent charge customer. She always pays her account and, what's more, she pays on time." If we received such an inquiry today, however, we unfortunately would not be able to be so positive.

You have been a good Fitzgerald's & You customer, Ms. Reynolds, and we value your friendship. But we do have some question about your intention of settling your current account. Frankly, we cannot imagine what is wrong.

Please help us to help you. Your credit reputation is a valuable asset, and we do not want to see it damaged. Your credit reputation is in danger, however, unless you send us your check immediately. The amount is $214.73.

Sincerely yours,

"Last-Chance" Ultimatum. If the appeal letters do not elicit immediate payment, the credit manager has no alternative but to assume that the customer does not intend to pay. Usually, however, the customer will be given one last chance before the matter is placed in the hands of a collection agency or an attorney, who will bring suit against the customer. (A collection agency is an organization whose business is to collect delinquent accounts for other firms. The agency makes its income by retaining a percentage of the money it collects on each account. Therefore, to recover the full amount due it, a store or other business may sue the customer for the amount of the account *plus* collection costs.) This "last chance" is a letter of ultimatum. It is courteous, but quite matter-of-fact and to the point. A letter of this type, which follows the everyday letter plan, may read as follows:

Dear Ms. Reynolds:

Would you please mark the date of January 15 on your calendar. This is an important date to you because unless your account is paid by that time (the amount is $214.73), we will be forced to place your account in the hands of a collection agency. I am sure you realize that this is a drastic step, and it is taken only when we have reason to believe that a customer does not intend to pay his or her account.

Of course, such a step will damage your credit reputation, so we hope it will be unnecessary. There is only one way you can stop us: send us your check immediately, or at least let us know your intentions. This is the last notice you will receive from us.

Sincerely,

Acknowledging Payment. When a customer responds to a collection letter by making full payment, some businesses write a special thank-you letter.

Dear Ms. Reynolds:

I was pleased to receive your check for $214.73. It has been credited to your account, which is now completely clear.

All of us at Fitzgerald's & You appreciate your cooperation, Ms. Reynolds. We hope you will continue to let us serve you in every way we can.

Sincerely yours,

Sometimes a customer sends only a portion of the amount due. This payment should be acknowledged by letter. At the same time the customer should be asked very tactfully when the balance may be expected. Since the partial payment indicates a willingness to pay, drastic steps should not be necessary to recover the remainder due.

Dear Ms. Reynolds:

Thank you for your check of $100 to apply on your October statement for $214.73.

Your account has been credited for $100, leaving a balance of $114.73. We hope you will send us your check for this balance very soon. Would you let us know when we may expect it.

Sincerely yours,

Sometimes recipients of collection letters admit frankly that they cannot pay. Of course, the credit manager is not greatly concerned about retaining such customers but is very much interested in getting the money due. Writing an angry response to such an admission will have no positive results. Bringing suit will be costly and unpleasant. The only other alternatives are either to grant a delay and request small weekly or monthly payments or to have the customer sign a note for the amount due. Sometimes both are demanded. The following is an example of such a letter:

Dear Ms. Reynolds:

Thank you for writing us about your inability to pay your $214.73 account. I appreciated your being so frank with us.

I know you are sincere in wanting to meet your obligations, and I want to be just as sincere in helping you do so. We can arrange for you to make monthly payments of $60 until your account is settled in full. If you will sign the enclosed 120-day promissory note, we will set up your account in four monthly payments— three for $60 and one for $34.73.

Just return the signed note in the enclosed envelope and send us your first payment by January 1.

Sincerely yours,

Enclosure

COMMUNICATION LABORATORY

APPLICATION EXERCISES

A. You work in the credit office of Broadway Department Store. You have been granting credit to customers simply by mailing them a card with a form message. Your manager has decided that a more personal approach should be used. Design a letter granting credit that the store could have typed on word processing equipment and personally signed for each new credit customer.

B. You are credit manager for Ashland Industries. Home Builders Supply, 1800 Parthenia Street, St. Paul, Minnesota 55106, requests $5000 credit. After checking the store's credit references, you find that the owner, John Keyes, is very slow in paying bills and is considered a poor risk. In fact, one of the credit references indicated that this store appears to be having severe financial difficulties. You decide to refuse the credit request. Write a letter to Mr. Keyes; try to persuade Home Builders Supply to buy from your company on a cash basis.

C. Ashland Industries has received three substantial orders from Builder's Emporium, 1200 Lankershim Boulevard, Lincoln, Nebraska 68509, for metal kitchen cabinets. You know that the Builder's Emporium chain is well established and has an excellent reputation. You would like to add this company to your list of charge customers. Write a letter to Charles Holt, the vice president, acknowledging his latest order and inviting Builder's Emporium to open an account with you.

D. You work for A-V Electronic Networks, a local retail store that specializes in the sale and repair of televisions, radios, stereos, video and cassette recorders, video games, electronic calculators, and microcomputers. Bruce Roberts, 410 Yolanda Avenue, Denver, Colorado 80205, purchased from you a video recorder for $689. He paid $239 down and promised to pay the rest in six monthly installments of $75 each. Mr. Roberts paid the first two installments but has not made any further payments. He is presently two payments ($150) behind. You have sent two reminders and a letter of inquiry. Now write a letter appealing to his sense of fair play. Try to collect the $150 past due and remind him about his next payment, which is due early next week.

E. Ashland Industries has received a $500 check from Ms. Cynthia Cordeau, owner of Avante-Garde, an interior design center, in partial payment of a long overdue account for $1250. Write Ms. Cordeau, 800 Beverly Boulevard, Beverly Hills, California 90049, thanking her for the check and inquiring tactfully when you may expect to receive the balance.

VOCABULARY AND SPELLING STUDIES

A. These words are often confused: *conscious, conscience; cereal, serial.* Write each in a sentence that illustrates its meaning.

B. For what words or phrases do the following frequently used abbreviations stand? Be sure to consult the abbreviations section of your dictionary or reference manual if necessary.

1. bal.
2. Ltd.
3. nt. wt.
4. Inc.
5. EST
6. ft
7. ETA
8. kg

C. The following "words" appear as they are pronounced. How are they spelled?

1. ruf
2. stā
3. wimin
4. rīt
5. līt
6. nē
7. nok
8. lēv

COMMUNICATING FOR RESULTS

Obtaining Information. As assistant manager of a hotel, you are responsible for authorizing all checks cashed for guests. The cashier has sent Mr. Lester to you. He wishes to cash a personal check for $50. What questions will you ask Mr. Lester before you approve his check for payment? With another student enact the scene as you think it might happen. Remember, you must get the information you need yet retain the goodwill of the guest.

47

Sales and Public Relations Letters: Developing Shell Documents

All business letters have something to sell—whether it is merchandise, service, a point of view, an idea, or simply goodwill. When you write a letter telling your customers how much you appreciate their business, you are selling goodwill. When you write collection letters, you are hoping to sell the customers the idea of paying their accounts. A letter explaining why you cannot grant a request sells a point of view. Even a letter applying for a job is a sales letter—the writer is selling abilities.

Usually, however, the term *sales letter* is used in connection with selling merchandise or service. "Experience the thrill of stepping from your bath and wrapping yourself in a luxuriously fluffy, absorbent Fieldtex towel" and "Your family is in safe, reliable hands when you trust your insurance program to Atlantic Mutual" are typical of the sales statements you are accustomed to hearing or reading. As you study this unit, which emphasizes the writing of letters selling merchandise or service, you should keep in mind that many of the same principles apply to writing letters that sell ideas, goodwill, or points of view.

Effectively written sales letters help convince the reader to buy, but they are not the only letters that help to make sales. Alert businesses use letters to build public relations—and good public relations ultimately create sales. Although the underlying motive of *public relations letters* is to increase sales, they do not "push" a product or service. Instead, they act subtly to build goodwill. The writer hopes to impress the firm name and its product or service on the mind of the reader so that when the need arises for this product or service in the future, the customer will think of the writer's firm.

Few sales and public relations letters are individually prepared in this day of mechanization and office automation. In fact, most sales letters are printed and sent by direct-mail firms. Public relations or business promotion letters, too, are often printed and distributed in this manner.

For those companies that still believe the "personal" touch is a more effective means of generating sales, the *shell document* has proved useful in sending large numbers of personalized sales and public relations letters. Letter writers create a document containing information that is to be sent to all names on a mailing list; this is known as the *shell document*. They then prepare a list of variables for each name—items such as name, address, city, state, ZIP Code, and salutation—that is to be used to prepare the final letter.

Computerized word processing equipment *merges* the shell document with the lists of variables in such a way that the recipients believe they have received an individually prepared letter. And in many ways they have! Variable lists in conjunction with the shell document can instruct the computer to call people by name within the letter or can supplement sections of the shell document to reflect their personal circumstances.

You may easily find yourself in the position of writing sales or public relations letters using shell documents, especially if you are employed by a small- or medium-sized business. As you study this unit, which emphasizes the writing of letters selling merchandise or service, you should keep in mind that many of the same principles apply to writing letters that sell ideas, goodwill, or points of view.

Sales Letters

A sales letter is effective if it achieves its purpose. The purpose may be to get prospects to come to your place of business, to think of your firm when they are in the market for your product, or to get them to place an order by return mail. In any event, the effective sales letter requires careful planning. In planning a sales letter, you should:

1. Determine your market—the people to whom you are writing. Are all your readers office workers, or do they represent all types of occupations?
2. Determine the aim of your letter. What do you want the reader to do?
3. Select the appeals that are appropriate to your readers. Why would people want to buy your product? What will it do for them?
4. Organize the facts according to a logical, effective, clear, and easy-to-follow plan.

Determine Your Market. For whom is the sales message intended? A mass audience—*all* the people in a particular area, regardless of occupation, income, and educational background—or a selected audience whose tastes and interests are known to be similar? The kind of person who will receive and read the sales letter should determine to a large extent the kind of letter you will write. If you are selling air conditioners, are you selling them to consumers who want the comfort and convenience of air conditioners, to retailers who want to make a profit in reselling the air conditioners, or to industrial users who may be more concerned with the economies to be effected by using your particular brand of air conditioner? The same sales letter could not be used very effectively for all three groups, even though the product is the same. Therefore, the first step in the sales process is to identify the people to whom the letter is to be sent.

Determine Your Aim. Why are sales letters written? Sales letters are written because face-to-face selling is not always necessary or possible. A sales letter may be written to accomplish any one of four purposes:

1. To get new customers to buy your product now.
2. To develop an interest in your product that will induce customers to buy later.
3. To get customers to visit your place of business.
4. To get customers to try your product or ask questions about it.

Once you have determined the market for your letter, you must decide which of these purposes you would like your sales letter to accomplish—and build your letter around this one purpose. A letter that tries to accomplish too many things at the same time usually winds up accomplishing nothing. If the aim is to get a customer to buy now, you will build your letter around the idea of getting the customer to take *immediate* action.

Select Appropriate Appeals. Once the writer has determined the purpose of the letter and the market to be reached, he or she must then determine the appeals the product will have for the reader. Although the air conditioner discussed in the following letter will do the same thing for everyone who uses it, different people will buy it for different reasons. The home consumer probably is concerned primarily with comfort and relaxation; the office or industrial user, with increased employee efficiency. Some appeals, however, are effective for every kind of audience. Most people like to save money, so the thrift of operation of the air conditioner may appeal to both the home consumer and the office or industrial user.

A sales letter for air conditioners sent to home consumers might read like the following letter. Notice that several appeals—pleasure, comfort, health, and thrift—are used in this letter. The central or main appeal, though, emphasizes the comfort of the prospective buyer.

Dear Mrs. Hollingsworth:

Do you remember the prolonged heat and humidity of last summer? For five nights in a row, the temperature did not go below 87 degrees!

Another "long, hot summer" is coming, bringing with it many uncomfortable days and nights. But this year you don't have to let the hot weather get you down. Relax and enjoy life this summer!

The new Comfort-Zone air conditioner has just arrived at our store. It is not only beautiful—but also beautifully cool! The 2-ton model will comfortably cool the average five-room home, providing 24 hours of relaxing comfort and permitting restful sleep. In addition, you breathe pure air, free of the dust and pollen to which so many of us are allergic. Its quiet operation and low-voltage consumption makes the Comfort-Zone a pleasure to own.

Why sacrifice comfort when for a few cents a day you can own and operate the Comfort-Zone? Come in today. You'll want to see and try the Comfort-Zone, the ultimate in modern air conditioning.

Sincerely yours,

From the appeals used to sell a product, buying points must be developed. Notice how in the previous letter an appeal was used to develop a buying point.

Appeal	Buying Point Developed
Comfort	Helps you to get a restful night's sleep
Pleasure	Helps you to relax and enjoy your home
Health	Purifies your air; especially helps people with allergies
Thrift	Costs you little to own and to operate

A letter attempting to sell air conditioners for office use might read this way:

Dear Ms. Keith:

How would you like to increase the efficiency of your office staff by 8 percent this summer?

Tests in over 150 business offices using Comfort-Zone air conditioners have proved that worker efficiency increased 8 percent after the Comfort-Zone was installed. Since increased worker efficiency means greater profits for your organization, the Comfort-Zone will pay for itself in just a few short years. And if you would like to spread the cost, you have 36 months in which to pay.

Improvements in the new model make your operating costs even lower. A 3-ton unit consumes only $9.80 worth of electricity each working day. Isn't that a small sum to pay for the comfort and increased working efficiency of your employees?

Won't you call and ask us to send our engineer to determine the air-conditioning needs of your office? Each day's delay costs you money.

Very sincerely yours,

Notice that the emphasis here is upon increased worker efficiency, low initial cost, and low operating cost. Since one primary purpose of a business is to make a profit, increasing worker efficiency and keeping costs low contribute to this profit motive. The following buying points are developed by these appeals:

Appeal	Buying Point Developed
Thrift	Low initial cost
Thrift	Low operating cost
Profit	Increased worker efficiency

The writer of sales letters has a choice of many different appeals. Those used depend upon the aim of the letter, the nature of the product, and the market—the people who will receive the letter. People usually spend their money for these reasons:

For comfort (air conditioner)	To be attractive (jewelry)
To make money (real estate invest-ments)	To be adventurous (travel)
To save money (home insulation)	To attract the opposite sex (cologne or perfume)
To save time (microwave oven)	To escape physical pain (aspirin)
To imitate others (designer clothes)	To be entertained (electronic game)
To be different (unique hat)	To protect family (smoke detector)
For health (toothpaste)	To be in style (new shirt or dress)
For enjoyment (videocassette re-corder)	To avoid trouble (casualty insurance)
For cleanliness (soap)	To take advantage of opportunities (clearance sale)
To avoid effort (power lawn mower)	To enhance reputation (charitable contribution)
To be popular (health and fitness salon)	To satisfy appetite (candy)
To safeguard possessions (home se-curity system)	For beautiful possessions (crystal stemware)

Of course, some products may be used to satisfy a number of desires. For example, a down coat has several appeals—to keep warm, to appear attractive, to be in style, and to impress others. Health insurance may be sold to satisfy the multiple needs for financial security, good health, and peace of mind, as in the letter on page 480.

Organize the Facts. You are now ready to begin composing your sales letter. You must, therefore, gather all the facts about your product and the various appeals that may be used and organize them according to the persuasive letter plan. This plan, as adapted to the sales message, calls for four steps, the ABCDs of sales letters:

Attracting attention
Building interest and desire
Convincing the reader
Directing favorable action

Let's take a look at what is involved in each of these steps.

Attracting Attention. A sales letter can attract the reader's attention even before it has been removed from the envelope. The envelope may be a color instead of the traditional white. It may have a thought-provoking question or statement printed on the outside. Or it may contain a logo or a picture, as does the one shown on page 481.

CAL FED ENTERPRISES

September 5, 1989

Ms. Jean McGrory
5902 Franklin Avenue
Los Angeles, California 90028

Dear Ms. McGrory:

We've seen it happen so many times. A family invests money with us, starts to earn more money, and then--suddenly--all their savings are gone.

Why? An unexpected illness has placed a family member in the hospital and created a severe family financial burden on the others to meet the sudden overwhelming expenses of a hospital stay.

That's why we decided to recommend the Group Hospital Cash Insurance Plan enclosed with this letter. Underwritten by Continental American Life Insurance Company, this benefit guarantees all of our customers supplemental hospital cash protection at economical rates.

With hospital costs rising faster than ever, the insurance you now own is probably not keeping pace. This Group Hospital Cash Insurance Plan was designed with these additional hospital expenses in mind.

As a customer of California Federal Savings, you are guaranteed acceptance. You will not be turned down.

We feel that our most valuable asset is you, and that's why we are pleased to announce this important service for our customers. Please read the enclosed material immediately. It provides complete details on how you can take advantage of this exclusive offer.

And remember . . . your acceptance is guaranteed.

Sincerely,

Peter D. Singer

Peter D. Singer
Customer Representative

ls
Enclosure

5670 Wilshire Boulevard / Los Angeles, California 90036
An Affiliate of CALIFORNIA FEDERAL SAVINGS AND LOAN ASSOCIATION

Courtesy of California Federal Savings & Loan Association.

The writer of a sales letter has a choice of many appeals, depending on the aim of the letter, the nature of the product, and the people who will receive the letter.

When the letter has been removed from the envelope, it can continue to attract attention through these devices:

1. Tinted stationery.
2. An unusual or clever letterhead design.

THE CYCLE SHOP
4100 Graham Boulevard, Houston, Texas 77052

Mr. Daniel Lockhart
1130 Willow Lane
Euless, TX 76039

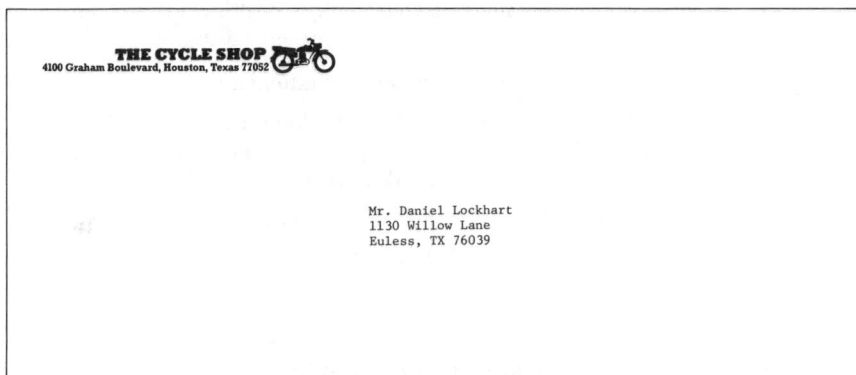

A sales letter can attract attention even before it is opened if the envelope containing it is creative and colorful.

3. A colored typewriter ribbon or print.
4. An unusual style of type, such as a script type.
5. A "gimmick" to step into the letter.
6. Placing certain words or sentences in all-capital letters.
7. Underscoring, boldfacing, or italicizing key words or phrases.
8. Using dashes or exclamation points for emphasis, such as "Call us today—tomorrow may be too late!"
9. Including an elaborate, graphic-filled descriptive brochure.
10. Designing of relevant and interesting graphics, perhaps in the margins or in the body of the letter.

All these devices are aimed at attracting attention. However, be sure not to "gimmick" the letter to the extent that these eye-catchers get in the way of the message.

The opening paragraph of the letter—in fact, *the very first sentence*—should excite curiosity, start a train of thought, attract attention in some way that will make the reader continue reading the letter. These opening sentences may be either questions or statements, and they should be original and concise. Questions should not be phrased so that they can be answered by a mere "yes" or "no." Statements should contain a startling new, interesting, or different fact that leads the reader to the major buying point. Here are some examples of opening sentences that have proved effective in sales letters.

Pertinent Questions

"How can you become the most fashionably dressed individual in Pittsfield?"
"Where can you save 8 cents on each gallon of fuel oil you buy for your home?"

"How much is your family's health worth to you?"
"If you lost your job today, how would you pay your bills?"

Startling or Significant Statements

"They said it couldn't be done, but *we* did it!"
"Word processing equipment can increase production up to *40 percent!*"
"You can*not* afford to be without one!"
"Three out of four families use hospital services at least once each year."

To select which device would best attract attention, the writer should consider one or more of these factors:

1. The kind of firm sending the letter.   (Is it a conservative bank? a store selling gardening supplies?)
2. The nature of the product.   (Is it a religious book? a lawn mower?)
3. The kind of audience to receive the letter.   (Are they nurses? electricians?)

Building Interest and Desire. When you have succeeded in getting the reader's attention, you must hold that attention. The best way to hold it is to build interest—by vividly describing your product so that your readers can virtually experience it. With colorful, descriptive words and expressions like those listed below, you can make readers feel, taste, or smell your product as well as see it—and you can also make readers "see" themselves using your brand and getting satisfaction from it. To stimulate readers to buy your product, you must use descriptions that will activate their emotions.

Objectives	Suggested Descriptions
To sell no-wax flooring	"It's a bright shine. A tough shine. An easy-to-wipe-up shine."
To sell canned frozen oyster stew	"Savory oyster stew with plump, pampered oysters."
To sell laundry detergent	"Softness—you can feel it in the *powder* . . . feel it in the *clothes!*"
To convince readers to send for a catalog from a plant nursery	"Lifelike illustrations you can almost smell and touch!"
To sell oranges	"Big, plump wedges . . . ."
To sell hardwood paneling	"The soft beauty and warmth of fine hardwoods."
To sell porcelain bathroom fixtures	"The porcelain finish is glass-smooth."
To sell small cars	"The driver who is fed up with bigger, thirstier cars switches to ____."
To sell air travel	"For travel elegance, fly with ____."
To sell electronic typewriters	"Letters that are a pleasure to type, a pleasure to sign, a joy to read."

Objectives	Suggested Descriptions
To sell soft drinks in cans	"And cans chill so fast, keeping the flavor fresh and full of zip."
To sell a station wagon	"From a frisky, sturdy little work-horse to the jauntiest little sedan of them all!"
To sell a soft drink	"You'll really welcome the cold, crisp taste that so deeply satisfies . . . the cheerful lift that's bright and lively."
To sell a deodorant	"New spray-on deodorant with staying power."
To sell an air deodorant	"Makes air smell flower-fresh."
To sell mustard	"A mustard that is shy and retiring is no mustard at all; a great mustard should manage to be a delightful contradiction of emphatically hot and delicately mild."
To sell fruit punch	"The circus-red color, the candy-and-ice-cream taste."
To sell shampoo	"Hair so satin-bright—airy-light!"

Suppose you write a letter to sell stereo tape decks. You attract the reader's attention in the first paragraph by asking, "How would you like to bring the concert hall into your living room?" You hope that the reader is interested—or at least curious enough—to find out how this can be done. So you vividly describe your product, appealing to the desire for relaxation. You continue your letter as shown:

> You have just come home after an exhausting day at the office. You relax your body in the comfort of your favorite chair. But you must relax your mind, too, freeing it of the many tensions of the day. You flip the switch on your Magnatone stereo. Suddenly the room is filled with the soft tones of your favorite music. You are carried away to the concert hall—every note, every tone is as clear as though the orchestra were performing in your living room. Soon both your mind and your body are completely at ease, and the cares and tensions of the day are forgotten.

Notice how the paragraph builds interest by emphasizing the desire for relaxation.

Convincing the Reader. If you have done your work well to this point, the reader is already strongly interested and partially convinced. The readers who really want to buy can certainly find reasons for doing so. Nevertheless, you must still convince readers that Magnatone ownership is an advantage. In fact, you must be able to convince them that they really cannot afford *not* to buy it. Therefore, you are ready now to bring out other features of the product that will convince them.

You have attempted to sell readers on the beautiful performance they can expect from the Magnatone and the effect that performance will have on their pleasure and relaxation. Now, what other features might appeal to them? They certainly would like to have a piece of furniture that will enhance the beauty of their living room and win praise from others, so you tell the readers:

> Your guests, too, will appreciate the true state-of-the-art sound when you invite them to your home for an evening of listening pleasure. You will win praise for the sleek styling of the unit. Both inside and out you will own the finest stereo tape deck anywhere at this low price.

Now some readers may think, "Well, this Magnatone is going to cost more than I can afford." You must convince them that this is not so. Therefore, your letter might continue:

> The magnificent Magnatone can be yours for only $200 down and $50 a month for 24 months, and your monthly payments will not begin until August.

Directing Favorable Action. You have now reached the point where if each of the preceding steps has accomplished its purpose, you must move the reader to act. Some action-getting suggestions that you might use are these:

1. Enclose a return envelope or postcard.
2. Imply that the reader "act now before it is too late."
3. Offer special inducements for prompt action.
4. Briefly repeat the advantages to the reader.
5. Mention that many others have taken advantage of the offer.

The letter you write to sell the Magnatone stereo tape deck, therefore, might conclude as follows:

> If you act before May 15, you may select $25 worth of tapes from those we have in stock as a FREE addition to your music library. Won't you come in today and listen to the Magnatone?

Public Relations Letters

The term *public relations* is a difficult one to define. In essence, a firm has created good public relations when its customers and clients think highly of it—highly enough to feel that the firm is more interested in a satisfied customer than it is in just making a sale. A business that has conveyed this feeling to its customers does not have to worry about sales. Public relations letters, then, such as the one shown on page 485, are letters written to show the firm's concern for its customers and for people in general.

Xerox Corporation
Warner Center
5901 De Soto Avenue
P.O. Box 2850
Woodland Hills, California 91365
818-999-6201

XEROX   February 14, 1986

Dr. Lyn Clark, Kathy Basil,
Ellen Anderson, and Dr. Caruana
Pierce College
6201 Winnetka Avenue
Woodland Hills, CA 91371

Dear Ladies:

I would like to take a moment to thank you for the time you gave to me
out of your busy schedule to show you a demonstration of the Xerox 1038Z
Marathon copier.

Though I am not the Representative to handle your account, it still meant
a great deal to me.

I hope that you have been taken care of fully. If I can ever be of any
assistance to you or any of your friends, please do not hesitate to call on
me.

Again, thank you.

Sincerely,

Sonja L. Freebairn

Sonja L. Freebairn
Marketing Representative
(818) 702-8147

SLF:kjk

Official Sponsor
1984 Olympics

Courtesy of Xerox Corporation, Warner Center, Woodland Hills, California.

Public relations letters are written in a friendly style and do not "push" the reader in any way. Their aims are usually good customer relations and possible future sales.

Public relations letters (sometimes called *business promotion letters*) are a special type of sales letter that sells indirectly. In fact, the chief difference between public relations and sales letters is that public relations letters *seem* to be selling nothing at all. Instead, they are written with an eye to the future; that is, with the thought that if you treat your customers well today, they will perhaps buy from you tomorrow.

Public relations letters are generally written to accomplish one of the following purposes:

1. To express appreciation to customers for their business. ("Thank you for your business during the past year.")
2. To capitalize on some special occasion—a holiday or a birthday, for example. ("We wish you and your family a joyous holiday season.")
3. To offer service to the customer. ("We have opened a branch bank in your neighborhood, and you will find that banking with us will be even more convenient.")
4. To show concern not only for customers but also for people everywhere. ("We have invested over $50,000 in new antipollution equipment this year.")

Expressing Appreciation. You may not feel that you are accomplishing much when you write to thank a customer for business. However, a courteous "thank you" serves as a gesture of goodwill and paves the way for future business with the customer. Don't you like to feel appreciated? When someone thanks you for something you have done, don't you feel an inner glow of satisfaction? So it is when a firm takes the time to thank you for your patronage; you certainly feel more kindly toward that firm. The next time you need its type of product or service, you will be more likely to think of dealing with this firm than with any other.

How do you think the recipient of the following letter might react to it?

Dear Mrs. Cunningham:

As another year draws to a close, Zigfield's feels very grateful for having customers like you.

Thank you for the business you have given us during the past year. We certainly appreciate your friendship and hope that you have derived much satisfaction from your purchases.

Please remember that we are here to be of service to you. During the coming year we hope that you will continue to give us the opportunity to serve you.

Sincerely yours,

A letter such as this will not sell a specific item, but it will certainly cement good relations. Notice that the letter is written in a friendly style and does not "push" the reader in any way. The letter illustrated on page 485 is written in the same spirit and looks to possible future sales.

Capitalizing on Special Occasions. A holiday, the beginning of a new season, a birthday or an anniversary, the arrival of new merchandise, a new type of product, a new service, or some other special event—any of these may prompt writing a letter to customers. Of course, in letters of this type you do not attempt to sell a specific item. However, by making customers aware of the new service or product—or by calling attention to some special event—you may be indirectly stimulating their desire to buy. In these letters you are attempting to give customers the impression of doing them a favor rather than of trying to sell them something.

Note, for example, the following letter announcing a sale especially for charge customers.

Dear Mr. Lombardi:

Badillo's is now preparing for its annual summer clearance sale. As you can see by the enclosed brochure, all our summer merchandise—women's dresses, men's sportswear, children's play clothes, patio tables and chairs, and a host of other merchandise—has been drastically reduced.

Before we offer these bargains to the general public, however, Badillo's wishes to say "Thank you" to our charge account customers by giving them an exclusive opportunity to take advantage of these savings. On Monday, August 30, our store hours will be extended from 6 p.m. to 10 p.m. This extra time will give you and our other special customers an opportunity to shop before the general sale begins on August 31.

Just give the enclosed ticket to our representative at the door, who will admit you to Badillo's special preview. If you wish to take advantage of these bargains, though, do plan to come early, as many sizes, styles, and colors are limited.

Sincerely yours,

Offering to Be of Service. Offering to be of service to the customer is another important function of the public relations letter. Whereas the sales letter says "Buy," this letter says "Let us be of service to you."

When a new family moves into the community, some progressive businesses send a welcome to the new residents and offer to be of service. If the service is not a costly one, an invitation to try the service with no charge or at a reduced cost is not an uncommon gesture. For example, here is a letter written by a dry cleaning establishment to new residents who move into the community it serves:

Welcome to the Garceau family . . .

It is a pleasure to have you as residents of St. Louis, and we hope you enjoy the community as much as we do.

Will you give us an opportunity to show you the excellent dry cleaning, pressing, and laundering service we make available to St. Louis residents? And at low cost too! Our courteous drivers will pick up and deliver your clothing, or you may prefer to bring it to any one of our twenty stores in your area. All twenty have convenient drive-in windows, so you don't need to get out of your car—and you save 10 percent by using our cash-and-carry service.

We are enclosing an introductory card that entitles you to a 50 percent discount on your first order—no matter how large or how small. Won't you come in to see us and let us give you a personal welcome to St. Louis?

Sincerely yours,

Enclosure

Showing Concern for People. All businesses must make a profit in order to survive. Besides their profit goals, however, most organizations also establish "people goals"—to provide equal employment opportunities for all, meet employees' needs, treat customers honestly, provide safe products and services, support projects that improve the quality of life in their communities, and so on. They know that their concern for people not only will help their employees and their customers but also will improve their productivity and profitability. Thus organizations use a variety of means to let the public know about their people-oriented activities. One of the most commonly used—and most effective—means is the public relations letter.

The following public relations letter offers to be of service. At the same time it might attract good future employees and more customers because it shows concern for people.

Dear Mrs. Morris:

As principal of Polytechnic High School, you have a great responsibility for the education of our youth. Raj Industries thanks you for your efforts.

We hope the following invitation will help you give students more insight into how products are manufactured, packaged, and distributed to dealers. You are invited to send your senior class to spend the day with us. We will plan a full schedule of activities for them and have them as guests for lunch in our cafeteria. You may choose a date that is most convenient for you.

Please call Ginger Campbell, our public relations director, at 555-3434 to make arrangements.

Sincerely yours,

COMMUNICATION LABORATORY

APPLICATION EXERCISES

A. For each reason for buying given on page 478, name at least one other product or service that might be bought.

B. Bring to class ten different sales letters or magazine advertisements. Identify the sales appeal used in each letter or advertisement and evaluate the effectiveness of the appeal.

C. Assume that you have been asked to work on the school football program committee and have been placed in charge of getting advertisements from local businesses. Half-page ads sell for $25; full-page ads, $50. Proceeds from ads are to be used partially for financing the cost of the program and partially for student transportation to out-of-town games. The ads will be read by all the high school students, as well as by many of their parents. Since the community really turns out for games, the ads will be seen by many people. Write a shell letter that can be sent to the businesses in your community, requesting that they purchase an ad in your school football program. If they consent to purchase an ad, tell them a student will call to arrange a visit to obtain information regarding ad content and layout. Be sure to make it easy for the business to give a "yes" response.

D. Suppose that you work part-time for a photographer in your community. Marcy Studios, your employer, specializes in wedding photographs. For storage in your computer, write a shell letter that is to be personalized and sent to women who have announced their engagements in your local newspaper. Sell them on having Marcy Studios take their wedding pictures.

E. Choose a product (such as a clock radio, a camera, a video game, a set of cookware, a video recorder, a home computer, or an electronic calculator) and gather sufficient information to write a sales letter. Define the group to whom you will write, select an appeal for that group, and write the appropriate letter.

F. Assume that you work for Bouquet Florists. At the end of each year, you mail a calendar to all customers who have ordered flowers from you that year. Write a letter of transmittal to accompany these calendars. Use this opportunity to build goodwill for Bouquet Florists by making this transmittal letter a public relations letter.

G. Assume that you work for Gelson's Country Store, which will open a specialty and gourmet foods department next month. This department will offer imported teas, fresh pastries, and exotic fruits. Write an appropriate letter telling Gelson's customers about the enlarging of the store and the new department.

H. As an employee of your county library, write a letter to welcome new people who move into your growing community. Enclose a card that lists library hours, information services, and activities for children.

VOCABULARY AND SPELLING STUDIES

A. These words are often confused: *detract, distract; carton, cartoon.* Write each in a sentence that illustrates its meaning.

B. Should *a* or *an* precede these words?

1. opposite
2. half
3. appetite
4. egg
5. ulcer
6. harvest
7. entry
8. highway
9. underdog
10. indication

C. Which of the following commonly used words are misspelled?

1. canidate
2. omitted
3. liesure
4. anilize
5. occasionally
6. seperate
7. bullitin
8. accommodate
9. calander
10. attornies

COMMUNICATING FOR RESULTS

A Club Project. The Community Service Club in your company plans to take orders for Christmas trees from employees in the plant. The proceeds are to be used for food baskets to be given to needy families. Write an announcement to go into your monthly employee magazine describing the why, what, where, when, how, and who (make up your own set of circumstances) for purchasing a tree. Appeal to the employees to purchase their trees from the club. Do this by describing the plight of the needy in the community, citing statistics about their number, and emphasizing their needs. Remember, however, to be tactful about the needy in the community. Be sure to include all information that the employees will need to purchase a tree from your club.

U · N · I · T
48

Social-Business Letters

The use of social-business correspondence has become increasingly important in today's business world. No longer do people think that social life should be distinctly separate from business life. In fact, many times the social lives of business and professional people closely involve their customers, vendors, associates, and even competitors. Social relations contribute to the success of a business by fostering a warm friendship and developing goodwill between the company and its public. Social-business letters are frequently the means by which friendship and goodwill are created.

Why Social-Business Correspondence?

If a friend invites you to spend a weekend, you write a thank-you note upon returning home. When someone presents you with a gift for your birthday, Christmas, graduation, or some other special occasion, you always write a letter of appreciation. Likewise, acts of kindness while you are hospitalized or during periods of personal grief are always acknowledged by letter. If someone helps you obtain a job, secures hard-to-get concert or theater tickets, or goes out of the way to be thoughtful, you write a letter of appreciation. Yes, you already know that all special favors should be acknowledged by a personal letter. In business the same courtesies should be shown.

Business executives receive invitations from business associates outside the company to attend social functions. They also receive favors or gifts from close business friends. From time to time they hear of promotions or special honors awarded to other executives or of personal tragedies (serious illness, an operation, or a death in the family) that strike them. These situations call for letters to be written and provide opportunities for building friendly relations.

Social-business letters are just as appropriate as letters to your personal friends who have been especially thoughtful. Business people who take the time to write social-business letters will be remembered, and their letters will add to their personal credit. They will undoubtedly also build goodwill for their company, even though this is not the underlying purpose of social-business letters.

Kinds of Social-Business Letters

Many executives who every day write effective business letters dealing with business matters find it difficult to compose social-business letters. As a correspondent you may be asked to write some of these social-business letters. Here is an excellent opportunity to reveal your abilities.

Although any acceptable letter style may be' used for social-business correspondence, many such letters call for the social-business format discussed in Unit 40. In this letter style the inside address may appear at the bottom of the page, and the signature lines and reference notations are usually omitted. Also, a comma rather than a colon is often used after the salutation. Other kinds of social-business correspondence—such as announcements, invitations, and replies to invitations—may take a printed or handwritten formal format.

Letters Expressing Thanks. People in business who receive gifts or are granted special favors should acknowledge the gifts or favors and express their appreciation. The following are examples of the kinds of thank-you letters frequently written by business executives and other employees. Note the direct approach used in each of these examples, as well as the brevity of the letters.

For a Gift

Dear Karen,

I was pleased to receive the Fontainbleu prints you so generously sent me. They are going to be framed for my office and will look very handsome with the new oak paneling.

Thank you for your generosity. The next time you visit us, you can see to what good use I am putting your gift.

                              Cordially,

Ms. Karen Freeman
Continental Portrait Company
7400 Lassen Court, Suite 280
Muskegon, Michigan 49445

For a Favor

Dear Bill,

I appreciate very much your thoughtfulness in getting tickets for Catherine and me to The Jazz Kid. We enjoyed this musical enormously—and the seats were just perfect.

Thank you for helping to make our visit to New York this Christmas an enjoyable one.

                              Cordially,

Mr. William Paige
41 White Oak Road
Somers, CT 06071

For Business Referrals

Dear Ann,

Thanks for telling Hank Wu of United Savings and Loan Association how pleased you are with the computer system we installed for your company. He called me last week, and we met today to discuss the possibility of installing a similar system at United.

I certainly appreciate your referring a new business prospect our way. If at any time we can help you in a similar way, we will do so.

Sincerely,

Ms. Ann Brower, Manager
Accounting Department
Lincoln Thrift and Loan
2800 Canoga Avenue
Dallas, Texas 75225

Letters of Congratulation. As with all social-business letters, the style of a letter of congratulation is designed to make the letter warm and personal, as is the one shown on page 494. The following are also examples of letters of congratulation. This kind of letter is usually written by the person who is to sign it, especially when the writer is a personal friend of the individual who is being congratulated.

To a Business Acquaintance

Dear Joanne,

I was pleased to hear that you have been promoted to national sales manager of Harris & Braun Enterprises. Congratulations! Harris & Braun is certainly fortunate to have such a dynamic and hardworking person in charge of its marketing operations.

If ever I can be of assistance to you in making contacts on the West Coast, please let me know.

Sincerely,

Whenever business executives take the time to recognize a milestone in the career of one of their employees, the thoughtfulness is certain to be rewarded in terms of a more productive employee. How do you think Ted would react to the following letter from his employer?

To an Employee

Dear Ted,

During the ten years you have been with Martell's, you have seen our company grow from a small local factory to a nationwide organization. Responsible for this remarkable growth are highly productive and loyal employees like you. I am pleased to write this congratulatory letter on your tenth anniversary, for it gives me an opportunity to thank you for your contribution to our success.

THE DAILY POST

230 West Superior Street
Duluth, Minnesota 55802
(612) 555-2135

May 3, 1989

Dear Louise:

Congratulations on being named State Journalist of the Year by the State Association of News Journalists. All of us at The Daily Post agree that your superb coverage in our weekend magazine section of the construction of the new State Center deserved the Association's top honors. We know that this is just the first of many awards that you will receive for your outstanding creative work.

To celebrate your winning this award, we'd like very much to have you as our guest for dinner on June 5. Will you be free?

Cordially,

Dick O'Hara

Dick O'Hara
Managing Editor

Ms. Louise Flores
2160 Trinity Road
Duluth, Minnesota 55811

nw

As with all other social-business letters, a letter of congratulations should be warm and personal.

As supervisor of our data processing staff, you have set up a highly flexible and effective system for handling the increasing volume of documents. I am sure you have heard the often-repeated statement around the office. "If you don't know, ask Ted." This statement is indeed a tribute to your efficiency.

I look forward to working with you in the years ahead. When I think of the slogan "Martell's is people," I can't help calling to mind a picture of you and all those like you who help to make our firm the congenial, effective group it is today.

Sincerely yours,

Formal Invitations and Replies. Occasionally business people receive formal invitations—to an open house, to a special party honoring a distinguished person, to a special anniversary celebration, or to a formal social gathering. These invitations, such as those shown on page 496, are usually engraved or printed and are written in the third person. When these invitations are handwritten, however, they are placed on plain white notepaper.

Replies to formal invitations are often requested by stating *Please reply* or *R.S.V.P.* (an abbreviation of the French *Répondez, s'il vous plaît*, which means "Please answer"). Even if such a notation is not placed on the invitation, there is an unwritten obligation to respond. If the invitation is written in the third person, the reply is also written in the third person and follows the wording and arrangement of the invitation, as shown in the replies on page 496. If the invitation includes a formal reply card and return envelope, the reply card may simply require a check (✔) to indicate whether the receiver will attend.

Announcements. Many companies send printed announcements to business associates to publicize the affiliation of a new partner or executive. Companies also use these notices to inform customers or potential customers of new sales representatives. Formal announcements also publicize new services, new branch offices, new locations, and company mergers. A typical announcement is shown on page 497.

Letters of Condolence. Letters of condolence are among the most difficult letters to write. Such letters should be brief and dignified. Obviously, the writer should not be depressing or recall too vividly the grief recently suffered. These letters should be written by the person signing them—not by a secretary or an assistant. Following is an example of a letter of condolence:

Dear Cheryl,

Please accept my sincere sympathy in the passing of your mother last week. I understand the difficult time you are going through since I, too, lost my mother last year.

My thoughts are with you and your family in this hour of grief.

Sincerely,

For a more personal touch, the letter should be handwritten rather than typewritten. However, except in the case of a close personal friend, a typewritten message is acceptable.

The Local Bank Tellers Club
requests the pleasure of your company
at a tea
in honor of
Nancy Fitzgerald
on Saturday, May the sixth
at four o'clock
Suite 13 of the Howard Building
Please reply

Formal invitations

Mr. and Mrs. John Shensa
request the pleasure of the company of
Mr. and Mrs. Barry Greenberg
at dinner
on Monday, the fourth of April
at eight o'clock
8106 Keats Road

R.S.V.P.

Mr. William Gregory
accepts with pleasure
the kind invitation of
The Local Bank Tellers Club
to attend a tea on
Saturday, May the sixth
at four o'clock
Suite 13 of the Howard Building

Formal acceptance

Mr. and Mrs. Barry Greenberg
regret that a previous engagement
prevents their accepting
the kind invitation to dinner
at the home of
Mr. and Mrs. John Shensa
on Monday, the fourth of April

Formal refusal

Formal invitations and replies may be handwritten, printed, or typed.

Creative Travel Planners
is pleased to announce the opening of our new
computerized business / vacation travel department.
Ms. Vi Brown, a travel industry veteran, will assist
you or your company with personal, professional travel
planning. Stop by our Warner Center offices
or give Vi a call.
Creative Travel Planners, Inc.
5855 Topanga Canyon Boulevard
Suite 540
Woodland Hills, California 91367

(213) 704-7033

Monday - Friday
9:00 a.m. - 5:00 p.m.

Many companies send printed announcements to publicize new services.

COMMUNICATION LABORATORY

APPLICATION EXERCISES

A. While driving to work one day, you see a good customer, Lynn Merrick, having car trouble. You take Ms. Merrick to a nearby service station for help. Three days later you receive a letter thanking you and saying that arrangements have been made for you and a guest to have dinner at a very fine restaurant. You have a delicious meal and a delightful evening at the restaurant. Write a thank-you letter to Ms. Merrick, Merrick's Personnel Agency, 12 Hunter Avenue, Memphis, Tennessee 38122.

B. Police Sergeant Marie Hannah spoke to your Employees' Service Club on the topic "Making Your Home Burglarproof." Write Sergeant Hannah a thank-you letter. Two employees have mentioned to you that Sergeant Hannah's advice may already have saved their homes from being robbed.

C. You read in the paper that a friend of yours, Chris Adams, is being given a three-month leave of absence from work to help with the summer job program for underprivileged youth. Write a letter congratulating your friend and offer your help.

D. You read in your association newsletter that your friend Carmen Gee has been promoted and is now a word processing supervisor in the Los Angeles offices of Atlantic-Ridgefield Company (ARCO). Write Carmen a congratulatory letter.

E. Carl Irwin's father passed away yesterday. Carl works in your department. Write him a letter of condolence.

F. You are employed by Reed, Barton & Howe, an insurance and investment counseling firm. Prepare a formal announcement about Michele Allen's joining your firm. The announcement will be sent to Ms. Allen's prospective clients and friends.

G. Prepare a formal invitation to attend a reception honoring the new president of Los Angeles Pierce College. The reception is being sponsored by the Pierce College Foundation. Invitations are to be sent to all community service organization members.

H. You have received a formal dinner invitation for the Saturday after next. Either accept or reject it. Supply all the necessary details.

VOCABULARY AND SPELLING STUDIES

A. These words are often confused: *liable, libel; ingenious, ingenuous.* Write each in a sentence that illustrates its meaning.

B. Which of the three words following each of these phrases is closest in meaning to the italicized word in the phrase?

1. *Provincial* attitude. Positive, elevated, narrow.
2. *Minute* detail. Tiny, simple, unnecessary.
3. *Volatile* temper. Violent, changeable, stable.
4. *Unobtrusive* lighting. Precise, regular, unnoticed.
5. *Articulate* speaker. Distinct, humorous, controversial.

C. Where are apostrophes needed in the following sentences? Write *OK* for any sentence that is correct.

1. Whose pen is this?
2. Theres a three-week trial period before the warranty goes into effect.
3. Theyre all taking their books. Where are yours?
4. Our photocopier has been broken since last week, but its scheduled to be repaired tomorrow.
5. Theres no way we can believe that the estate is completely theirs.

COMMUNICATING FOR RESULTS

Safe-Driving Course. You have been asked to arrange a safe-driving course for all interested employees in your company. Make a list of the information you will need to give and receive as you telephone the local automobile association to ask for an instructor.

Letters are only one of the many documents that you will need to write on the job. Many situations call for formal documents, circulated only among the members of the same company. These interoffice documents are called *memorandums*, or *memos*.

Information about meetings, sales strategies, product competition, and personnel matters are among the many topics you will write about in a memo. Memos are often addressed to one or more of your company colleagues and more often than not are sent traditionally. They are also telecommunicated to other colleagues—wherever their offices are—for their files.

You will often find yourself writing memos on matters of common interest to you and your company colleagues. Given a situation that requires writing memos, you will be able to do the following when you master the units in this chapter:

1. *Design interoffice memorandums in a commonly accepted business format.*

2. *Identify the major parts of the interoffice memo.*

3. *List the differences among routine, informational, and analytical memorandums.*

4. *Write routine memos.*

5. *Write informational memos.*

6. *Write analytical memos.*

7. *Use the techniques for tailoring memos for special purposes.*

49 Planning Routine Memos

Letters in business are used to communicate with customers, vendors, competitors, government agencies, or anyone else outside the company. When you wish to write to someone *within* your own company, however, you will send a memorandum. Memos are used to communicate with other employees, regardless of where they may be located—whether in the same office, in the same building, or in a branch office many miles away.

Because interoffice correspondence circulates only among individuals within the same company, the formality of an inside address, salutation, and complimentary closing is unnecessary. Instead, most companies have printed interoffice memorandum forms that save time and effort in the preparation of internal messages. In other aspects, however, memos and letters have a great deal in common, as you will see from the following discussion.

Memorandum Format

There are usually two main parts to a memorandum:

1. The heading
2. The message

Occasionally, when official approval or authority is required, the memorandum may be concluded with a line for the signature of the person originating the correspondence.

The Heading. The heading of a memorandum is usually printed and contains the identification labels *To:*, *From:*, *Date:*, and *Subject:*. Companies generally print above the heading their logo and/or name with the phrase "Interoffice Memorandum." A typical heading example is shown on page 503.

Routing Instructions. In the *To* and *From* sections the business title of each person is often included, particularly when the memorandum is being sent to a person whose office is in another city. A courtesy title—*Mrs., Ms., Mr., Dr.*—is sometimes included in the *To* section; however, in the *From* section the writer does not use a courtesy title. (Note how this principle also applies when you introduce yourself to someone: "Good morning, Ms. Conrad—I'm Felix Torti.")

TO: Mr. Richard Ahrens, Vice President, Personnel

```
┌─────────────────────────────────────────────────────────────────┐
│                                              COPIES TO:           │
│                   LITTON SYSTEMS, INC.                            │
│         FILE:      OFFICE CORRESPONDENCE                          │
│                                                                   │
│         DATE:                                                     │
│                                                                   │
│         SUBJECT:                                                  │
│  ───────────────────────────────────────────────────────────     │
│                                                                   │
│         TO                                                        │
│                                                                   │
│         FROM                                    LOC        EXT     │
│                                                                   │
│                                                                   │
│                                                                   │
│                                                                   │
│                                                                   │
└─────────────────────────────────────────────────────────────────┘
```

On some interoffice memo forms, the company's logo—as well as the standard heading—is printed.

FROM: Kathryn Daruty, Manager, Accounting Department

The memo forms used in large companies may also include *Department* and *Location* sections to expedite communication among coworkers in various branches of the firm. These sections need not be filled in if both the reader and the writer work in the same location or department.

The Date. Complete dates are just as important on memos as they are on letters. Dates are necessary for future reference to prevent oversights and miscommunication. Begin the date with the month followed by the day and the year. Some organizations prefer, however, to use the military style for expressing dates.

TRADITIONAL STYLE   DATE: January 15, 1989

MILITARY STYLE   DATE: 15 January 1989

The Subject Line. The subject, a brief statement telling what the memo is about, helps the reader to prepare for the contents and aids in filing the correspondence for future reference. The subject line is not a complete sentence but rather a concise phrase that includes some specific information. For example, the subject may read:

SUBJECT: Relocation of Midwestern Warehouse

The Message. The message follows directly after the last line of the heading, separated from the subject line by only two blank lines. By moving directly into the message contents, after presenting the essential information in the heading, business writers save both the readers' time and their own time.

Typewritten or computer-generated memorandums placed on standard 8½- by 11-inch forms are usually prepared with a left margin set two spaces

Company Logo

Allied Insurance
——and——
Affiliated Companies

Heading

Interoffice Memorandum

TO: Thomas Pearson   **FROM:** Elizabeth Genet

SUBJECT: Loss From December Storm   **DATE:** February 9, 1989

Message

The analysis of the company's losses as a result of the storm that hit the northeast states on December 11 and 12 of last year is now complete. This is the study that you requested in your memo of January 19.

As you are aware, most of the damage was suffered by the coastal New England states. This is the one area of the country where our company has relatively few policies in force. Our approximate losses in each of the states affected by the storm are given below:

Massachusetts	$1,025,800
Connecticut	723,100
Rhode Island	324,000
New Hampshire	182,300
	$2,255,200

Very slight losses were also sustained in eastern Vermont and southern Maine, but the total for these states is insignificant. Of the total amount of our New England loss, 82 percent comes from wind damage claims under the "Extended Coverage" provision of our standard homeowner's policy. The balance comes from claims filed by owners of marine policies.

Since some policyholders are late in filing claims, the above total could rise by as much as 10 percent. I will provide you with a final report in three months.

EG

mn

The parts of an interoffice memorandum are illustrated here. Note the format of the heading and the message.

after the longest identification label in the heading. The right margin is set so that it contains approximately the same number of spaces as the left one. Paragraphs are blocked and single-spaced with only one blank line separating them. Note the formats of both the heading and the message in the memorandum illustrated above.

The Tone of Memorandums

When setting the tone of the memo, effective business writers must evaluate the topic under consideration, their relationship to the reader, and the personality of the reader. All these factors govern the formality of the message presentation.

Topic Covered. In most companies and organizations, memorandums, like letters, are written in the first person. The trend is decidedly away from a stiff, formal writing style. However, some judgment must be exercised. Obviously a person writing to a company official to report the results of a financial audit will be more formal than a person writing a coworker about the company bowling league. Effective memo writers must use their decision-making skills here. They must match the formality of their tone to the organizational impact of the topic under discussion.

The Relationship to the Reader. The tone of the memo is influenced by the writer's relationship to the reader. Business writers who send messages to organizational superiors would probably adopt a more formal tone than if they were communicating with peers or subordinates—unless, of course, they were on a first-name basis with those superiors. In most cases using a formal tone with peers and employees whom you supervise would sound awkward and stilted, especially if you work closely with these individuals.

The Personality of the Reader. Another important factor in setting the tone of the message is the personality of the individual receiving the memorandum. As in most situations, stereotypes may not apply. For example, the president may insist on informality, whereas a peer might like a formal, impersonal tone. Make it your business, as an effective memo writer, to know your reader's personality and preferences in writing.

When Are Memorandums Written?

Many business firms tell their employees to put in writing all important information that crosses their desks. Written records help to do the following:

1. Determine responsibility.
2. Clear up inconsistencies.
3. Record needed information.

If you are sending important papers or documents to another person, for example, transmit them by memorandum so that if they become lost, there will be a record—your file copy—proving when they were actually sent and recording exactly what they were.

If you inform other employees of new telephone procedures, put this information into a written memo. This way, the employees who need to use these procedures have easy access to them and can refer to them when needed. Memorandums describing policy or procedural changes provide a permanent record for continual referral and clarification.

Discrepancies in records or accounts can be corrected through memorandums. Written evidence of needed changes provides a basis for amending company records or accounts. Documenting changes with a memorandum "paper trail" saves other employees from wasting time and duplicating work already done. For example, if you find that one of the computer operators in your department unintentionally added an extra $52 charge to nine accounts, you might write the accounts supervisor for these accounts to let that person know this error will be corrected on the next billing. You might further inform the accounts supervisor that each customer has been notified about the error—and your remedy.

Memorandums support and record the inner operations of a business. They are to a business what the news media is to history—both serve as a record of past occurrences and provide a basis for future analysis and decision making.

Message Organization

The presentation of the routine memorandum message usually follows either a *deductive* or an *inductive* organizational plan. These organizational patterns closely resemble the ones you studied to arrange ideas in business letters.

Deductive Design. A *deductive* plan moves from the general to the specific. Like business letters, most memos follow this direct organizational plan. These messages present the main, or general, idea in the first paragraph and then follow with the necessary, or specific, details to support the opening statements. Finally, the memo concludes with suggestions for future action or requests guidance on future action.

As you can see, the deductive design for memorandums parallels closely the everyday letter plan for message organization. Notice how this deductive design is illustrated in the following example:

DATE: August 3, 1989

TO: Peggy Moffat

FROM: Gordon Hammer

SUBJECT: Home Burglar Alarm Effectiveness Report

The Home Burglar Alarm Effectiveness Report that you asked to see is attached.

I would appreciate your returning it to me within ten days. Incidentally, Ms. Dalton has requested that the report not be circulated outside the company until its reliability can be checked.

If you have any questions about the report or need any additional information, please let me know.

Ohio River Valley Advertisers, Inc.

1845 North High Street
Columbus, Ohio 43210
(614) 555-9000

INTEROFFICE MEMORANDUM

DATE: November 28, 1990

TO: Charles Werner

FROM: Cynthia Lewis

SUBJECT: Earned Vacation Time for 1990

This year I have been involved in a number of crucial advertising contracts that simply did not allow me to take all my earned vacation time. I had hoped to squeeze in the two weeks owed to me this month, but filming delays in the Zip-a-Cola account have made that impossible. We are now running three weeks behind! If we ever hope to catch up, I will simply have to stay with it.

I am aware of the company's policy that vacation time be taken between January 1 and December 31 in the year that it is earned. Because of my unusual work load this year, however, I am requesting permission to carry over into next year the two weeks of my vacation time that remain for this year. Kathy Lambert, my manager, is aware of this request and has acknowledged her support of it.

I would appreciate your considering my request and look forward to receiving your answer.

CL

pm

This memorandum uses the inductive plan. It presents the specifics first and then leads the reader to the general point.

Inductive Design. Occasionally you may find you need to write a persuasive memorandum or one that conveys unfavorable ideas. Rather than take a deductive, direct approach, you are likely to be more successful if you use the inductive method to organize your message. The above memorandum uses the inductive plan.

An *inductive* plan moves from the specific to the general. Present the details (the specifics) first, such as reasons for the conclusion, and lead your readers on a step-by-step journey through your reasoning so that they proceed logically into your general message—the request or adverse news. In this way the readers are more likely to finish reading the memo and accept the conclusion you offer. By allowing them to see the specifics of your reasoning, you are better able to persuade them to see your general viewpoint and thus maintain good relations.

Notice how the memorandum on page 507 uses the inductive plan to persuade the reader to make an exception in the company's vacation policy.

COMMUNICATION LABORATORY

APPLICATION EXERCISES

A. You are the secretary of your school club, Future Business Leaders. Gloria McKimmey, a partner in a local accounting firm, has accepted an invitation to speak to your club about job opportunities in the accounting field. She is a knowledgeable and effective speaker and has a genuine interest in informing others about her field. Prepare a memo that will be posted in each classroom announcing Ms. McKimmey's speech, "Accounting—A Field of Opportunity." The program is scheduled for 3:15 p.m. on March 19 in Room 101.

B. A friend who works for another firm has shown you a copy of a new monthly magazine called *Office Automation Update.* Since the publication features the latest advances in office products and procedures, you believe it would be useful to several people in your office. Write a memo asking your supervisor for permission to subscribe to the magazine in your company's name. It is issued monthly and costs $28 for 12 issues.

C. Write a memo to Adela Garcia, your supervisor, asking for funds to attend a weekend communication conference in a city 150 miles away from your own. The conference, which will be held on October 18 and 19, will focus upon ways of improving employee efficiency through better internal communication. The conference leaders are people of established reputation in the field. Your estimate of the cost is about $330, an amount that includes mileage allowance, a hotel room for one night, meals, and a $150 registration fee for the conference.

D. Employees have been using the office postage meter as well as pre-stamped envelopes for personal correspondence. Write a memo to employees explaining that postage and stationery costs have risen greatly and that personal correspondence simply cannot be paid for by the company.

E. John Franz, one of your sales representatives, has been with a customer all morning. Two recent orders from this customer have been poorly handled and have arrived very late. John has spent the morning soothing the customer and promising that service will improve dramatically. John is not the only one of your salespeople who has had problems with slow deliveries from the warehouse. Write a memo to Bob Lyons, manager of the warehouse, explaining the situation and inquiring whether steps can be taken to speed up deliveries.

F. A long-time employee, Evan Maas, from a nearby branch office has requested information about early retirement. He would like to know what his monthly combined pension and social security payments would be if he retired at age 62 instead of age 65. He would also like to know how much notice the company needs if he plans to take an early retirement. As assistant personnel manager, respond to Mr. Maas with a memo that includes a booklet on retirement benefits. The company requests that employees provide three months' notice before retirement. Your department also has a retirement counselor who works individually with employees who are considering retirement. By making an appointment with Robyn Hatcher, Mr. Maas can obtain firsthand information specific to his circumstances in terms of monthly income, medical benefits, and life insurance.

VOCABULARY AND SPELLING STUDIES

A. These words are often confused: *marital, martial, marshal; charted, chartered.* Use each word in a sentence that illustrates its meaning.

B. Match each definition in the left-hand column with a word in the right-hand column.

1. a travel schedule	**a.** delete
2. showing great abundance	**b.** profuse
3. sturdy	**c.** subvert
4. to remove	**d.** itinerary
5. to overthrow	**e.** stalwart
	f. vivid
	g. derive

C. What are the superlative forms of the following adjectives and adverbs?

1. clear
2. complicated
3. good
4. less
5. carefully
6. few

COMMUNICATING FOR RESULTS

Former Supervisor. You have been promoted to the position of sales correspondent. In this position you work closely with 15 sales representatives in coordinating their schedules, making many of their appointments, providing sales support materials, tracking all advertising and promotion for their products, and writing letters to customers and potential customers. Before your promotion you were secretary to the employee benefits supervisor, Ms. Carla Newhouse, who trusted your judgment and who relied upon you completely. She always praised your work and had supported your promotion. In fact, your working relationship was so close that she still comes to you for help and advice several times a day. This takes up time you really don't have and also interferes with your transition to the new job and your relations with your new supervisor. You do not want to offend Ms. Newhouse, for whom you have great respect, or your supervisor, with whom you are trying to establish an effective relationship. You realize that you must do something before the situation becomes worse. What should you say or do?

U · N · I · T

50 Tailoring Memos for Special Purposes

In Unit 49 you learned that memorandums are the primary means for sending written messages within an organization. Routine memorandum messages comprise the majority of internal communications. Although these short, one-page memos that transmit, inform, and request are the most common written internal messages, the expert communicator needs to be skilled in writing specialized memorandum messages as well.

Memorandums tailored for special purposes are generally longer than routine memorandums—ranging anywhere from two to seven or eight pages. Because of the nature of their topics, these memorandums take on the characteristics of a *memorandum report*. Their writing style and tone are a compromise between the conversational informality of letters and the structured language of a formal report. Devices such as enumerations, headings, tables, and other graphics are used to break up text, to improve readability, and promote understanding.

Memorandums designed for special purposes use the same heading and message format as the routine memorandum. The organization of ideas in the message differ, though, depending upon the intent of the memo. *Analytical* memorandums differ from *informational* memorandums as *recommendation* memorandums differ from *progress* memorandums. *Proposal* memorandums require still another method of ordering ideas. Each of these special-purpose memorandums is described and illustrated in the following pages.

Sending Information

The *informational memorandum* presents facts or data on a single topic. This special-purpose memorandum differs from the routine memorandum only in complexity and length.

Consider, for example, the plant manager who wishes to inform all the staff about new safety requirements. He or she may need to discuss hazardous zones, various kinds of safety equipment, issuance of safety equipment, care of safety equipment, safety procedures, and emergency procedures. All this information needs to be spelled out carefully in detail for present reference and future referral. Informational memorandums such as these set policy and govern action.

Informational memorandums use a direct approach. Begin by telling your readers what your topic is. Then organize your ideas logically and provide your readers with the necessary details under each idea. Be careful to take your readers smoothly through each concept and, more important, from one concept to the next. An example of an informational memorandum appears on pages 512 to 514.

Analyzing Data

The *analytical memorandum* defines the problem for the reader, indicates the means by which the writer gathered and analyzed the data, shows the reader how the writer arrived at conclusions, and presents recommendations based on the conclusions drawn.

Suppose your supervisor asked you to investigate a series of group medical insurance plans. The purpose of your investigation is to select several options from which employees in your company may elect plans to suit their needs. You would need to respond to your supervisor's request in the form of an analytical memorandum, but first you would need to plan your study.

After gathering information about available medical insurance plans, you would need to establish a set of criteria by which you would be able to *evaluate* each option. For example, you might wish to consider, among

Central Bank

INTEROFFICE MEMORANDUM

DATE: March 14, 1989

TO: Estate Planning Staff

FROM: Steven P. Drengson

SUBJECT: GUIDE FOR ADVISING PROSPECTIVE CLIENTELE ON ESTATE PLANNING

A number of staff members have inquired about guidelines for advising clients in the development of their estate plans. Many clients request information about the kinds of people who should be selected as guardians for minor children. Should the same people have guardianship over the resources? What is the difference between a guardian, a trustee, and an executor? The following information may prove helpful to you in educating clients on these matters.

Guardians

Clients who have minor children are concerned about trying to select guardians for them. You may wish to provide them with the following guidelines in making their selection.

First of all, advise them to think of other couples most nearly like themselves. Often such couples are found among brothers and sisters, but not always and not necessarily. Good friends may be the best choice. Tell them that the ideal couple will have most or all of the following characteristics:

1. Their financial situation will be similar to the clients'. The clients should make sure that their children, through life insurance and other means, wouldn't become a financial burden.

2. They will be experienced parents. They will have children of their own, preferably a little older than the clients' so that any chance of rivalry will be reduced if the clients' children move in with them. The clients' children and their children should know and like one another.

3. They will profess the same religious faith as the clients do, especially if the clients want their children raised in that faith.

4. They will live in the community where the clients live so that the clients' children would be able to keep their old friends and wouldn't have to change schools.

The informational memorandum presents facts or data on a single topic. It differs from the routine memo only in complexity and in length. This informational memorandum is three pages. It begins above and continues on the next two pages.

other things, the following: illnesses or injuries covered, specific exclusions, dollar allowances for coverages, selection of doctors and hospitals, annual cost per employee, and maximum benefits. Your goal would be to select options that provide the greatest insurance value for the dollar amount invested and at the same time furnish employees with a broad coverage.

Estate Planning Staff   2   March 14, 1989

   5. Their educational level is the same as the clients'; they
       will share the clients' views about higher education.

   6. They will have room to house <u>all</u> the clients' children.
       Separation can be very hard on children, especially in
       time of loss.

   7. They will be willing, even honored, to have the job. This
       may be a matter of the clients' willingness to take on the
       guardians' children.

As the last point implies, clients should never name people as guardians
without talking to them about it first. There is no place for surprise
in this area. In many states minors aged 14 or older have the right to
pick their own guardians, so children should be included in the selection of their guardians.

Advise the clients not to name either of their parents as guardians.
Although they did a good job in raising the clients, there's an old
saying about grandparents: The joy of having the grandchildren come to
visit is exceeded only by the joy of having them leave. Child-rearing
is a young person's business; the fifty-year-old grandmother will be in
her late sixties when Johnny is in high school.

Usually the same person serves as "guardian of the person" and "guardian
of the property." However, if the child has a large estate not protected by a trust, it may be wise to appoint a trust company to serve as
guardian of the property. Thus the personal guardian won't have responsibility for managing the estate and can concentrate on raising the
child.

<u>Trustees</u>

Trustees, either persons or organizations, hold title to property for
the benefit of someone else. A trustee's duties fall into two categories: dispositions and administration. The former identifies the
beneficiaries and specifies when and if income and principal are to be
distributed as well as when the trust terminates. Administration per-
tains to investment, accounting, and tax decisions.

The skills needed to handle dispositions are quite different from those
needed for administration. Some trustees can do both--but some can't.
Provide clients with the following examples:

   1. A trustee's discretionary right to spend trust income for
       children's education and living requirements takes
       detailed knowledge of the children and their needs.
       Perhaps such a trustee should be the same person who is
       acting as guardian.

The informational memorandum (page 2).

Your memorandum not only would present the results of this analysis but
also would show *how you arrived at your conclusions*. The organizational
plan may be outlined as follows:

1. Description of the problem analyzed or the task assigned.
2. Procedures used for gathering the data.

Estate Planning Staff   3   March 14, 1989

2. A trustee's management of trust property requires investment skills and, if the property consists of an operating
   business, a thorough knowledge of the business. This may
   call for use of a trust company, perhaps with the guidance
   of managers of the business.

In some cases it is better to have two trustees rather than just one.
In this respect picking trustees is something like picking guardians:
one for the person and one for the property.

Clients sometimes have difficulty deciding whether to use an individual
or a trust company as a trustee. Both have advantages and disadvantages:

1. An individual may take a more personal interest in the
   beneficiary's welfare--but individuals die, get sick, take
   vacations, etc. Trust companies don't and can always be
   reached when needed.

2. Individuals are sometimes thought to be more imaginative
   investors than trust companies and therefore able to get
   better results. Remind clients that imagination is a two-
   edged sword, and many trust companies have excellent
   investment track records.

3. Fees and expenses are likely to be the same. An individual
   may charge a lower fee but may incur accounting expenses
   built into a trust company's fee.

Executors

An executor's basic tasks are very much the same as the trustee's: to
administer a decedent's property and dispose of it according to the
decedent's will. For that reason there is rarely any reason for the
client not to name the same person or institution as executor and as
trustee.

In considering an estate plan, clients should first consider naming a
trustee and _then_ naming the same individual or organization as executor.
The tail shouldn't wag the dog. The trustee's job is likely to be long-
lasting, perhaps for the lifetime of the trust beneficiary. The
executor's work, which ends with the distribution of the estate assets
to the heirs or to trusts for their benefit, normally lasts only 12 to
24 months.

                                    SPD

des

The informational memorandum (page 3).

3. Criteria established for analyzing the information.
4. Analysis of the data.
5. Conclusions based upon the analysis.
6. Recommendations for implementation.

Recommending New Ideas

Recommendation memorandums are used to suggest new ideas designed to streamline procedures, institute new products, lower operating costs, increase efficiency, or improve the company operations in some other way. These memorandums take a direct approach by telling the reader what the idea will do for the company and then following this disclosure with the necessary details.

Suppose you work in the offices of a large metropolitan insurance company. Everyone crowds into the elevators to arrive at his or her desk by 8 a.m., and people are often late because they have to wait 10 or 15 minutes for an empty elevator. The company cafeteria, too, is almost unbearable because everyone breaks for lunch between 12 noon and 1 p.m. Unless you are first in line, you can count on spending almost the whole hour getting through the serving line. A repeat performance of the morning rush at the elevators occurs each afternoon at 5 p.m. as people leave the building for home. In fact, some people have been known to leave early to avoid the rush.

You believe that efficiency could be increased if employees worked in staggered shifts. By having half the staff work from 7:30 a.m. until 4:30 p.m. and the other half work from 8 a.m. until 5 p.m., the company could cut down on lost time because of tardiness and early departures. Likewise, if the lunch hour was staggered into two shifts—11:30 to 12:30 and 12 to 1—congestion problems in the cafeteria could be reduced. Your coworkers encourage you to share your idea with management, so you decide to write a recommendation memorandum.

Your first step would be to summarize your recommendation in the opening paragraph. Indicate that because of the crowded conditions prevailing in the morning, at the noon hour, and in the afternoon, you recommend a staggered work schedule for employees in your company. Follow the recommendation with specific details:

1. Explain in detail the circumstances that prompted your recommendation.
2. Outline specifically all aspects of your recommendation. Be sure to include suggestions for implementing your ideas.
3. Show how the company will benefit from adopting your recommendation.
4. Offer to answer any questions or supply additional information, if necessary.

Reporting Progress

Progress memorandums provide an update on projects presently under way. They furnish management with information regarding the status of a long-term activity.

Suppose your company was converting its manual accounting procedures to a computerized system over a three-month period. Management would certainly want to know whether the conversion procedures were being implemented according to the projected timetable. If your company was building a new branch office that was scheduled to open on August 1, management would assuredly wish to know whether the building plans were progressing as scheduled. If your consulting firm had promised a procedures manual to a client by the end of January, management would undoubtedly want to keep tabs on its progress to ensure that the manual was delivered by the date promised. All these situations present good cases for writing progress memorandums. Those people charged with the development of projects find themselves in the position of having to write this type of memorandum.

Progress memorandums cover the developments and advancements made on a particular project for a specified period. Let us examine more closely the company that is converting its accounting from manual procedures to computerized procedures over a three-month period. The first progress memorandum may have been written after the project was under way thirty days; the second, after sixty days. These memorandums report in detail the advances made for a definite time period.

Begin the progress memorandum by identifying the project and briefly describing the expected outcome. Summarize the progress reported previously before providing a detailed presentation of the activities, accomplishments, and setbacks for the specific period under consideration. Organize the information for the current period by topic or in chronological order, depending upon the complexity of the project. Conclude your progress memorandum with a projection for future developments and a timeline for completion. An outline for this organizational plan follows:

1. Identify the project by name and describe briefly its objectives.
2. Summarize the progress reported in previous memorandums.
3. Provide a detailed presentation of activities, accomplishments, and setbacks for the specific period covered by the progress memorandum. Use one of two presentation methods:
   a. Presentation by topic
   b. Chronological presentation
4. Project future progress in terms of a completion timeline.

Making Proposals

Before funding seemingly costly programs, educational institutions, government agencies, and businesses require that prospective recipients submit proposals. These proposals provide reasons for funding the project, the project objectives, methods of implementation, costs of implementation, and procedures for evaluation and follow-up.

In most cases proposals are submitted to outside agencies and are prepared in a formal report format or a format prescribed by the outside agency. For proposals within the company, however, the proposal writer will write a proposal memorandum in memorandum format.

Suppose you were employed by a school district that had just received $100,000 to be used for computer education. You believe the Business Department could use a portion of this money to establish a computer laboratory—a proposal memorandum would certainly be in order. If you worked for a state agency that had received a sizable federal grant for studying the needs of the elderly in your state, a proposal memorandum on your part might initiate action on an aspect that you view as being crucial. As an accounting supervisor for a furniture chain, you may wish to write a proposal memorandum to convert your manual inventory records to a computerized system.

Proposal memorandums must be organized inductively so that the reader can be led step-by-step through the process of understanding the need for the project and its expenditures. In terms of business investments, the reader must also be made to understand how the company will benefit financially in both the short term and the long term.

Steps for organizing and writing the proposal memorandum are outlined below:

1. Statement of the circumstances or problem prompting the proposal.
2. Description of the objectives to be attained that will alleviate the problem.
3. Discussion of procedures for implementing the objectives.
4. Presentation of costs; presentation of savings or earnings, if applicable.
5. Explanation of procedures to be used to evaluate and follow up on objectives.

Displays for Readability

A lengthy memorandum containing a considerable amount of information and detail will be more effective if the writer arranges the information attractively and uses displays to categorize and introduce ideas. Enumerations, tables or other graphics, and headings enable the reader to understand more easily the thoughts contained in the memorandum.

Enumerations. A great many details will be easier to read if each point is numbered in 1-2-3 order, each number starting a new paragraph. A common format used for enumerations is illustrated in the memorandum shown on pages 512 to 514. Enumerations also help readers refer by number to specific points when they are replying.

Tables and Other Graphics. When the memorandum contains statistical matter, the writer should display this material in tabular form for easier reading, as in the memorandum shown on page 518. When there is a full page or more of detailed material, it may be displayed on separate pages.

Outside sources of information used for preparing tables or other graphics should be specifically and completely identified so that the reader could go back to the original source if necessary. Complete and accurate source identification enhances your credibility and helps your memorandom gain acceptance.

TRICOUNTY AIRLINES

MEMORANDUM

TO: Benjamin Spitzer   FROM: T. A. Arthur

SUBJECT: Monthly Boardings for Last   DATE: January 9, 1989
Year: Cranston-Titusboro

Following are the monthly boarding tables for last year
on all our flights operating between Cranston and
Titusboro. As you will recall, we begin this service
on January 1. The seat-occupancy rate, which is based
on the total of 1000 seats that are available monthly
between these two points is also included.

Month	Number	Occupancy Rate
January	362	36%
February	427	43%
March	512	51%
April	598	59%
May	673	67%
June	718	71%
July	640	64%
August	639	64%
September	720	72%
October	810	81%
November	830	83%
December	710	71%
TOTAL	7639	AVERAGE 64%

As you can see, this service has grown steadily since
we began it, largely as a result of our effective
promotion in the area. Since the break-even point for
our aircraft is 42 percent, it has been a profitable
service as well. The only decrease in growth came in
July and August, when many of our business passengers
were on vacation. The December decrease was due to the
storm at the beginning of the month.

These figures do not report on the increase in our
service between Titusboro and Wheeling, which is
obviously affected by the Cranston-Titusboro route. I
am gathering this information, and you shall receive it
within ten days.

                                        TAA

wp

When a memorandum contains statistical material, the writer should display this material in tabular form for easier reading.

Headings. Headings enable the reader to see the thought groups the writer had in mind as the report was prepared. These "signals" prepare the reader for the information that is to follow and break up the material into digestible units. Headings also give the reader a chance to pause and take a breath before beginning to read another section. These labels give the memorandum greater appeal and invite the reader to continue reading.

Headings consist of a word or phrase that describes the content that follows. One format is illustrated in the memorandum on pages 512 to 514. Notice that the heading is placed at the left margin. The main words are capitalized, and the entire heading is underlined. Two blank lines precede the heading, and one blank line follows it.

Multiple-Page Formats

Memorandums longer than a single page require headings for the second and succeeding pages. Such headings include the name of the person to whom the memo is addressed, the page number, and the date. This information appears 1 inch from the top of the page and may be shown horizontally or vertically. For horizontal placement begin the name of the recipient at the left margin, center the page number, and end the date at the right margin, as shown in the following illustration.

Robert Parker   2   October 8, 1990

Multiple-page headings shown vertically begin the name of the recipient, the page number, and the date at the left margin. The following example illustrates this format.

Robert Parker
Page 2
October 8, 1990

In preparing memorandums that extend beyond a single page, be sure to place at least two lines of a paragraph at the end of a page and carry over at least two lines of a paragraph to the following page. "Orphan" lines (the beginning line of a paragraph) and "widow" lines (the last line of a paragraph) may not appear by themselves on a page.

COMMUNICATION LABORATORY

APPLICATION EXERCISES

A. Assume that you are the administrative assistant to William Norlund, manager of the Mail Services Department at Transcontinental-America, a major insurance company. Mr. Norlund is concerned that many employees seem to be unfamiliar with how to use the mail services of the U.S. Postal Service. Domestic letters are often marked "Airmail" or "Priority Mail"; packages are marked "Second Class"; or items that should be sent "Certified" are marked "Registered."

Prepare an informational memorandum for Mr. Norlund's signature that describes the various classes of mail and the special services offered by the U.S. Postal Service. Direct the memorandum to *All Department Heads* and request the heads to distribute copies to members of their departments who use mailing services. Include in your memorandum information about the following classes of mail: first class, priority mail, second class, third class, and fourth class (parcel post). Also, provide the readers with information about priority mail, certified mail, registered mail, insured mail, and special delivery. To assist you with preparing this memorandum, consult your local post office for up-to-date booklets and brochures describing these mail classes and services.

B. As sales manager for Rathbourne Pharmaceutical Company, you have been requested by the vice president of marketing, Joshua Ravetch, to select a car to be issued to all salespersons. Your salespeople require a medium-sized vehicle that is sturdy and dependable. The trunk must be large enough to accommodate catalogs, samples, literature, and in some cases customer orders. You are to base your recommendation on initial price, cost of operation, and estimated maintenance expenses.

Consult recent issues of *Consumer Reports* to begin your research. Select several cars to research further based on the facts contained in *Consumer Reports*. Obtain additional information about these cars from dealerships and brochures, and prepare an analytical memorandum to send to Joshua Ravetch upholding your choice.

C. Suppose you are employed in a legal office. Your office prepares many repetitive documents that require only minor changes in wording or documents that use many of the same kinds of paragraphs; for example, wills, contracts, leases, adoptions, divorces, and so on. You feel that the computerized preparation of these documents would reduce costs, hasten preparation, and improve quality. Write a recommendation report to purchase a computer, printer, and word processing program for your office. Address your memorandum to Rosalyn Kalmar, the senior partner of the firm. Gather any additional information you may need to justify your recommendation.

VOCABULARY AND SPELLING STUDIES

A. These words are often confused: *ensure, insure; continual, continuous.* Define each word; then write each one in a sentence that illustrates its meaning.

B. Select from the words in parentheses the correct plural form of each noun.

1. What (criteria, criterions) were used to select the new plant site?
2. (Cargoes, Cargos) from both ships were seized by the port authorities.
3. Neither of the (attornies, attorneys) has indicated a willingness to compromise.

4. Last year Mr. Fry turned over the business operations to his (son-in-laws, sons-in-law).
5. None of the (companies, companys) on this list have received our new sales catalog.

C. Here are 12 words that you are likely to encounter frequently. If you prepare documents with either a typewriter or a computer, you must know the correct points at which to divide these words in order to make line-ending decisions. Words may be divided only between syllables. Without consulting your dictionary, indicate the syllable divisions. Then, using the dictionary, check the accuracy of your choices.

1. congratulate
2. accumulate
3. inadequate
4. repetition
5. privilege
6. obstacle
7. surprising
8. acquaintance
9. conscious
10. visible
11. utilize
12. similar

COMMUNICATING FOR RESULTS

Eager Receptionist. Marcy Andrews, the receptionist in your office, has been with the company for nearly two years. When Marcy first began her job, she directed customer inquiries to salespeople in the office, as she was requested to do. Now that Marcy has become better acquainted with the firm, she has taken upon herself the task of answering some inquiries, often giving out incorrect information. You do not wish to quell Marcy's enthusiasm or initiative, but this situation cannot continue. Both customers and salespersons have complained about this problem. As office manager, what steps would you take to correct this predicament?

You have seen from your reading of Chapters 7 and 8 that different situations on the job call for different records. Sometimes you will have to write a response letter. Sometimes you will have to write a routine memo. Other times you may be called upon to write a longer, more formal document, called a report.

Effective business writers must be ready to write appropriate documents on the job. Given a situation that requires writing business records, you will be able to do the following when you master the units in this chapter:

1. *Write informational and analytical reports.*

2. *Write news releases.*

3. *Write minutes of meetings.*

4. *Use telephone messages and routing slips effectively.*

5. *Select appropriate telegraphic services.*

51

Informational and Analytical Reports

Owners or managers of small businesses are able to keep in touch personally with everything that goes on in the firm. Whenever executives of a small company need information, they can go directly to the appropriate person and ask, "Carmen, will we be able to fill the Jackson order by April 10?" Carmen could probably base her answer on readily available data.

In larger businesses, however, the owner, manager, or president cannot personally keep in touch with all operations of the company. Even department heads in very large operations are not able to supervise directly all the activities under their direction. Many businesses are so large and complex that a firm may be scattered throughout a particular section of the country or throughout the United States. In fact, many businesses now operate worldwide. Therefore, when business executives need information, they often ask for a written report.

The Need for Business Reports

Business reports are written to communicate facts and ideas to others. Without facts and ideas, without data on costs and expenses, and without statistics that indicate trends, businesses could not operate. The flow of information and ideas is necessary for business executives to make their decisions. The quality and accuracy of their decisions determine the future of the company. To make successful decisions, executives, managers, and supervisors rely heavily on the information that is reported to them.

Information is reported on all levels of business. The board of directors studies the reports from presidents and vice presidents, who in turn rely on reports from their department heads and assistants. Managers and supervisors rely on reports from their sales staff, their accounting department, and so on. The information reported may be complex and detailed, or it may be simple and straightforward.

A complex and detailed report may be written to explain the results of a lengthy study on topics such as (1) whether the company should close its three outdated plants and open one modern plant, (2) whether the company should expand its product line, or (3) whether the company should merge with another firm. Reports that require a long period of research and investigation to analyze a major topic in depth are called *analytical reports*. The format and the language used for such a report are usually formal.

Most of the reports written in business are simpler and more straightforward than analytical reports. They are called *informational reports* because their purpose is to communicate facts, ideas, statistics, or trends in a direct manner. Informational reports are less formal than analytical reports—in fact, as you learned in Unit 50, informational reports are generally typed on standard memo paper or on printed forms.

Informational Reports

The informational memorandum you studied in Unit 50 is considered to be a kind of report. The average business worker writes many, many informational reports like these each year.

For an informational report the writer will generally have to gather and organize facts and figures and perhaps make recommendations. The report, prepared in memorandum format and illustrated on page 518, was written to inform the company's president of the flight boardings on an airline's new route. The writer of the report, the marketing director, will prepare similar reports for other routes that the airline flies. These are likely to be issued at regular intervals.

Periodic reports, reports that are submitted at regular intervals, are common in business. Sales representatives may submit their sales reports on a daily basis. Production managers may submit their reports on a weekly basis. Executives usually submit their expense reports on a monthly basis or upon the completion of a major trip. For an example of a common periodic report, see the completed expense report form on page 526.

In addition to periodic reports, other informational reports are frequently submitted. If you were asked, for example, to provide estimates of the cost of janitorial and maintenance services for a new building and warehouse, you might submit an informational report, prepared in a memorandum format, such as the one on page 527.

Writing Informational Reports. Like a business letter—like *all* business messages, in fact—an informational report must be clear, complete, correct, and concise. However, the wording of an informational report will be different from that used in a business letter. The wording for an informational report follows the style used *for any other memorandum*—that is, it is direct and to the point. The following paragraph, for example, might be used in a business letter informing a customer that a product that was ordered is no longer available.

We were most happy to receive your May 10 order for 50 ten-gallon oil drums. Since the Axton Oil Company is always working to improve its products, we no

Expense Report Summary

Name___Sara Cohen___
Division_____
Department_____
Location_____

Period Ending___December 30___ 19_88_

THIS REPORT IS DUE **15 DAYS** FOLLOWING PERIOD ENDING.
Advance privileges will be suspended, if Report is not submitted
WITHIN 45 DAYS following Period Ending.

Last Month's Closing Balance	DUE CO.	DUE ME
Last Month's Closing Balance		46 95
Error Corrections: Use this line only when notified		
Cash Advances or Travel Orders Date 12/2/88	50 00	
"		
"		
"		
Transportation Advances Date		
"		
"		
"		
Travel Refund		
Month's Expenses		162 71
Amount Surrendered to Cashier		
Amount of Remittance Enclosed	50 00	
Total Each Column	50 00	209 66
Insert Difference Between Totals Above into Proper Box	DUE CO.	DUE ME
CLOSING BALANCE ▶		159 66

I certify this report to be correct: *Sara Cohen* 12/30/88
(Date)
Dept. Head Appr. *Mark Chung* 12/30/88
(Date)
Add'l Appr. *Angela Martino* 12/30/88
(Date)
Add'l Appr. _____
(Date)

ENTERTAINMENT and MISCELLANEOUS EXPENSE RECORD

Date	Place	Misc.—Explain Expense Entertainment—List Guests & Affiliation	Business Purpose & Business Discussion	Total Expended
12/2	Pierre's	Luncheon with Graff of	Annual budget for	39 60
		advertising department.	advertising and promotion.	
12/10	Hungry Lion	Dinner meeting with Mr.	Discussion of marketing	81 15
		and Mrs. Jason Cukor,	program for Cukor	
		clients.	Department Stores.	
12/15	Hotel Ashe	Cocktails with Morton	Discussion of plans for	41 96
		Giles and Martin Tor.	next local community	
			affairs meeting.	

If this space is insufficient, use a plain sheet of paper and staple to this form.

TOTAL FOR PERIOD ▶ 162 71

Periodic reports such as this expense summary are usually prepared at regular intervals. They are usually completed on printed forms.

longer manufacture this container. It has been replaced by a seamless aluminum container with a special no-spill top. This container sells at retail for only 3 percent more than our former model and wins immediate customer approval everywhere.

In a report the same information would be worded in a more straightforward style, as follows:

Axton Oil Company no longer manufactures its former line of gasoline containers. Here is a list of our discontinued models and the improved models that we suggest as replacements.

WILCOX CORPORATION

Interoffice Memorandum

TO: Corinne Calvert   FROM: Henry Bester

SUBJECT: Maintenance Estimates--   DATE: September 27, 1988
St. Louis Branch Office

At your request, I asked the Purchasing Department to
secure estimates from outside suppliers to provide
janitorial and maintenance services for our new
St. Louis office building and warehouse. The
estimates are based upon the service specifications
that were drawn up by our purchasing staff. They
match in all essential respects the specifications
established for our home office facility.

Supplier	Monthly Cost	Yearly Cost
Aspen Cleaning	$10,632	$127,584
Rogers Associates	11,812	141,744
Republic Services	9,112	109,344
Wheelwright Company	12,005	144,060

In spite of the fact that the Wheelwright Company's
bid is the highest, the Purchasing Department is
recommending that we contract with that firm.
Sources in the area that are known to us are
enthusiastic about their services, which are reported
to be superior. The firm is well established and
most reliable.

Please let me know if you agree with the Purchasing
Department's assessment. If you do, I will advise
Purchasing to enter into an agreement with them.

HB

rd

An informational report must be accurate and complete, but also direct and to the point. It is usually prepared in an interoffice memorandum format.

Discontinued Models	Suggest Replacement
2-721—25 gallon	A-802
5-722—50 gallon	A-805
10-723—100 gallon	A-810

The replacements are superior to the discontinued models and retail for almost the same price. I have enclosed a copy of our current catalog.

Analytical Reports

An analytical report (1) defines a problem, (2) presents relevant data to analyze the problem, (3) draws conclusions from the data, and (4) makes recommendations based on the conclusions. Since it is a thorough, extensive report, it may take months (even a year or more) to complete the research, investigation, and analysis for the report and to submit it. In fact, because of the importance and the scope of such a report, several people may be asked to contribute to its preparation.

Obviously, an analytical report is not an everyday task for most business workers. It will be required only for special projects—projects that deserve detailed research, investigation, and analysis. Any company that is considering an expensive proposal (such as the possibility of installing a computer system or of opening a new branch office) or a major change (such as expanding its line of products or reorganizing its accounting system) will ask for an analytical report to help make a sound decision. A company specializing in market analysis (product testing, plant location, advertising media, and the like) has need for many analytical reports. Actually, the report is the end product of the business. Chemical, petroleum, drug, and similar manufacturing companies require analytical reports from research and laboratory personnel who are conducting experiments on new products.

Writing Analytical Reports. The pattern of the analytical report varies with the type of business for which it is prepared. Memorandum forms (such as those discussed in Unit 50) may be used for reports as long as five or six pages. Longer reports will require a more formal format.

Many companies adopt their own standard pattern for reports. The longer report will usually contain the following parts:

1. Memo or letter of transmittal
2. Summary
3. Body
4. Conclusions and recommendations
5. Appendixes

Letter of Transmittal. Since longer reports are more formal, a memorandum or letter of transmittal usually accompanies the report. The letter of transmittal serves several purposes:

1. It tells why the report is being submitted. The report may be the result of a project that was assigned several months earlier. Therefore, readers should be reminded of the reason for the report.
2. It identifies the report. Since executives receive many reports, it is important to identify each one so that it is easily recognizable.
3. It acknowledges sources of information and help. The people who helped gather and analyze data for the report should be acknowledged, of course.

Summary. Reports are presented to busy executives who will make decisions based on them. Many executives will not read an entire report.

Since they are interested in getting directly to the heart of the material, they will be favorably impressed with the writer who provides a well-done summary. A report that does not contain a summary is not a welcome sight to a busy executive!

The summary includes (1) the purpose for writing the report, (2) the methods for collecting data, (3) the conclusions based on the data, and (4) the recommendations based on the conclusions. Some executives prefer a summary that begins with the recommendations. As a general rule of thumb, the summary is about one-tenth the length of the body of the report.

Body. The body begins with a brief introductory paragraph stating why the topic is of interest. Then the main sections of the body (in order of appearance) are labeled as follows:

1. Purpose—explains what the writer hopes to accomplish.
2. Scope—tells what the report does include and what topic areas are to be covered.
3. Limitations—tells what the report does *not* include; usually specifies geographic locations and dates on information that is included.
4. Justification—lists those who will benefit from the report and explains why.
5. Related Publications—lists any articles the writer may have read before gathering the data.
6. The Present Study—presents the pertinent facts that have been gathered for this particular report.

In the "Related Publications" section, the writer will probably summarize the most relevant points of published articles on the subject. By showing what experts have said on the subject, this section adds credibility to the entire report. More important, these readings often provide direction for the writer in gathering and analyzing data. Report writers generally find appropriate articles in trade magazines, professional journals, newspapers, and periodicals. A complete bibliography of the articles should appear at the end of the report for those who are interested in reading more on the subject.

The facts offered in "The Present Study" section must be carefully assembled and clearly presented. Since there is no excuse for carelessness in a written report, the writer must be sure of the accuracy of the data presented. Careless errors will damage the writer's reputation for accuracy.

Conclusions and Recommendations. Up to this point the writer has explained why the report was written and what was discovered. Sometimes this is all that is required, and the writer's conclusions and recommendations may not be necessary. In some cases, however, the report may be incomplete without conclusions—especially if the report writer has been asked to include them. By asking for the writer's conclusions and recommendations, the executive is showing (1) faith in the writer's judgment and (2) interest in what the writer will say. The writer's conclusions and recommendations should be based strictly on the "Related Publications" and "The Present Study" sections of the report. Writing the "Conclusions and Recommendations" section gives the writer a prime opportunity to show his or her ability to think. In fact, good writing ability combined with the skills to prepare a successful report have in many cases brought the writer favorable attention and promotions.

Appendix. The appendix may include working papers that show statistical computations; graphics and visual aids (tables, pie charts, trend lines, maps, graphs) that were too numerous to include in the body; and computer printouts—in other words, any kind of material that supports the report. A report may have a relatively short body with a long appendix. If the appendix is very long, it may be divided into sections, each with its own title page. The appendix material should be fully identified in the table of contents. A good appendix can lend much credibility to a report.

Writing Headings and Subheadings

Headings and subheadings are important communication tools—especially in reports. They (1) form an outline for your report, (2) improve your organization, (3) prepare your readers for the next topic, and (4) help readers to keep on track. Like signs on freeways, headings and subheadings help readers proceed smoothly to their destination. Within a chapter the wording of headings should be balanced; the wording of the subheadings below each heading should be balanced; and so on.

Choosing the Right Tone

Shorter reports—those submitted on memo forms (see Unit 50)—use a conversational tone. Longer analytical reports generally adopt a formal (but not a stiff) tone. Contractions and the personal pronoun *I* are avoided, although they may be used correctly in other kinds of writing. Avoiding *I* gives the report a certain objectivity. For example, "I gathered the following evidence as I conducted a survey of . . ." sounds too much as if the report is based on the writer's personal feelings. Instead, "The evidence gathered during the survey proved that . . ." makes the report objective—based on facts, not on personal opinions.

Using Graphics

Statistical information should be presented as graphics, which are visual aids—tables, charts, graphs, trend lines, and so on, such as the table on the next page. Statistical data is much easier for the reader to comprehend when in visual rather than in paragraph form. Since graphics are usually grouped in the appendix, they should be mentioned in the report body. However, do *not* repeat all the data in the body; emphasize only the most significant points.

ANNUAL ABSENTEE RECORD OF OFFICE EMPLOYEES IN BRANCH OFFICES AS OF DECEMBER 31, 1988

		MONTHS OF SERVICE				
LOCATION	**TOTAL EMPLOYEES**	**OVER 240**	**OVER 180**	**OVER 120**	**OVER 60**	**FEWER THAN 60**
Boston	40	15	18	24	16	30
Detroit	20	8	10	12	11	12
Fort Worth	25	9	12	14	15	16
Las Vegas	10	4	5	6	8	10
Los Angeles	50	16	18	21	21	30
Totals	145	52	63	77	71	98

When developing the kinds of graphics just listed, be sure to follow these guidelines:

1. Label all graphics. Use a title that is clear and complete. The graphic should be able to stand alone—away from the report—and still be understandable. See, for example, the table shown above.
2. Identify the original source of the data. Give the full source for each graphic. List whatever information would help the reader identify and find the graphic: author's name, publisher's name, place of publication, date of publication, volume number, and page numbers for magazines, books, and periodicals; dates, locations, and names for interviews; and so on.
3. Explain the meaning of any typographic or artistic device such as colors, shaded areas, and stick figures. For example, in a graph comparing expenses for three different years, three different lines may be used to identify the years. The reader must therefore be told that the dotted line represents 1986, the solid line represents 1987, and the wavy line represents 1988. If a graphic device has a specific purpose, be sure to let the reader know that purpose.

Typing Analytical Reports

Expert typing and setting up of a report will increase the forcefulness of the communication by helping the reader to absorb the main points quickly. The long analytical report usually consists of the following parts:

1. Cover
2. Title page
3. Letter of transmittal
4. Table of contents
5. Summary
6. Body
7. Conclusions and recommendations

8. Bibliography
9. Supplementary material or appendix

Reports should be typed on plain white bond paper, 8½ by 11 inches. Each page should be typed on only one side of the sheet. All reports should be double-spaced, and each page after the first should be numbered. A left margin of approximately 1½ inches should be allowed for the binding. Top, bottom, and side margins of all but the first page should be 1 inch.

Most analytical reports require a title page. The illustration on page 533 shows the title and contents pages for a report on advertising needs.

Typing Headings and Subheadings. In typing headings and subheadings, observe the following points:

1. Use the same typing format for each level of headings.
2. Main headings are usually (a) typed in capital and small letters, (b) underscored, and (c) displayed on separate lines. Two blank lines are used above main headings and one blank line below them.
3. Subheadings, a secondary level of headings, are typed at the left margin in all-capital letters. They are not underscored. Two blank lines are used above these headings and one blank line below them. However, if a main heading directly precedes the subheading, then only one blank line is used above the subheading.
4. If a third level of heading is needed, the headings are usually run in with the text. They are (a) indented (like paragraphs) five spaces from the left margin, (b) typed in capital and small letters, (c) underscored, and (d) followed by a period (or a question mark or exclamation point, if appropriate). Two spaces are used after the period.

If all three levels of headings are required in a report, the headings would then be structured as follows:

Main Heading

SECONDARY HEADING

    Third-Level Heading. Text copy follows this run-in heading.

NOTE: Some writers prefer typing the main heading in all-capital letters and the secondary heading in capital and small letters. The main heading would still be centered (but not underscored), and the secondary heading would still be typed at the left margin. In either style the heading typed in capital and small letters is underscored; the heading typed in all-capital letters is not.

Binding the Report. When the report is completed, it may be bound at the side with staples (usually three vertical staples close to the left edge) or fastened at the top with a paper clip. Some reports are placed inside a special folder made for the purpose; others are bound by special backing paper of a heavy stock.

SURVEY OF CUSTOMER RELATIONS

TO THE KELSEY COMPANY

MARKETING PROGRAM

Prepared for Marco Sanchez
Director of National Sales

October 31, 1990

CONTENTS

A title page (left) and a table of contents (right) are standard parts of any analytical report.

COMMUNICATION LABORATORY

APPLICATION EXERCISES

A. Assume that you have been asked by your supervisor, Carol Crumley, to prepare a report on the types of telephone calls placed by your firm. She would like to know the weekly number of local calls placed and the weekly number of long-distance calls placed (station-to-station and person-to-person by direct dialing and with operator assistance, collect calls, conference calls, and international calls). Ms. Crumley would like to know the number of directly dialed calls versus those requiring operator assistance. She would also like suggestions for cutting the cost of telephone calls.

1. Prepare an outline for the proposed report, even though you will not actually gather the information.
2. Describe the procedures you would use in gathering the information and preparing the report.
3. List the sources of information that you would use.

B. Your supervisor has asked you to investigate the methods used to conserve energy in five firms in your area. Assume that you have interviewed five employees of different firms. Prepare a report of your findings.

C. Survey your class or a group of 25 students to determine their after-graduation plans. If students plan to attend college, determine which colleges and what they expect to pursue as their major fields. If students expect to apply for a job, determine the types of jobs for which they plan to apply. Prepare a graphic—a table, a chart, a graph, or a trend line—that would display your data most effectively. Discuss the information revealed by the visual aid.

VOCABULARY AND SPELLING STUDIES

A. How would you edit the following phrases to eliminate the redundancies?

1. at about
2. up above
3. add up
4. and etc.
5. pay out
6. repeat again
7. both alike
8. new beginning
9. same identical
10. connect up

B. On a separate sheet of paper, write the corrections you would make in the following sentences.

1. We chartered each salesperson's sales for the week.
2. The computer has all ready prepared the printout.
3. This typewriter has required a great deal of maintainance.
4. The work will be divided between Robert and I.
5. Its a great pleasure to have you as a customer.
6. I can not understand two aspects of your report.
7. Will you interduce me to your employer?
8. I spent many hours in the liberry yesterday.
9. The goverment changed its policy.
10. 10 of the employees were absent today.

COMMUNICATING FOR RESULTS

Writing a Public Announcement. Each Monday morning students announce upcoming events over the school's public address system. Write a 1-minute announcement about the monthly meeting of the school's Junior Achievement Club. The club will use this meeting to introduce several local business people, who will speak on topics relevant to starting a new job in their respective businesses. The club would like a large attendance at such an important and useful meeting. Tell when and where the club will meet and who the special guests will be.

U · N · I · T

52 Minutes, News Releases, and Other Form Messages

In business you will probably have frequent opportunities to attend meetings. Whether a meeting is formal or informal, a written record of the meeting will usually be prepared and distributed to everyone who attended the meeting and, perhaps, to other interested people as well. This written record, called the *minutes* of the meeting, is discussed in this unit.

This unit will also introduce you to news releases—a form of business communication that has a very special purpose.

Preparing Minutes of Meetings

In a typical business many committees and task forces operate within the company. The purpose of committees is to discuss various problems and to make recommendations to management. A *standing committee* is one that operates permanently year after year, although its members may change. A *task force* is a group of people who are appointed to solve a specific problem; when they make their recommendation on the "task" assigned to them, the task force is disbanded. Each department may have several committees that meet periodically—usually once a week, every two weeks, or monthly. If you are working in a sales department, for example, there may be committees on advertising, sales conferences, commissions, forms control, product development, public relations, and so on.

Minutes of Informal Meetings. The written record of the proceedings of a meeting is called the *minutes* of the meeting. Since most meetings in business are informal (that is, do not follow the rules of parliamentary procedure), the minutes are also informal. The minutes usually include the date, time, and place of the meeting; the name of the presiding officer; a list of those present (and frequently those absent); and the time of adjournment. Discussions are usually summarized.

Usually the minutes are signed by the person who took them and sometimes by the presiding officer as well. Minutes are usually duplicated, and copies are sent to each person present at the meeting and to other

```
                    The Market Focus Investment Group

                      MINUTES OF MONTHLY MEETING

                            May 15, 1989

    Presiding:   Herman Samuels

    Present:     Andrew Bolivero          John Levering
                 Sara Dorman              Barbara Oliverio
                 Mark Habib               Jane Masters
                 Joseph Hernando          Frederick Noonan

    Absent:      Lily Fields              Helen Tiller
                 Irene Isaacs             Donald Westin

    After calling the May 15 meeting to order at 4 p.m., the
    president requested the treasurer's report.  The treasurer
    distributed to each member a statement that indicated each
    member's present investment in the club's holdings.  The
    treasurer noted that a single share is currently worth $24.50
    and that this month's contribution plus accumulated dividends
    amount to a total of $450 that the club may invest.

    The president asked Joseph Hernando, chairperson of the
    investment committee, for the committee's recommendation.
    Mr. Hernando said that the committee has recently studied the
    stocks of computer manufacturers.  He reported that the
    committee believed that the present depressed market would
    improve in the next two years, which would result in
    improvement in the stock.

    Mr. Hernando said that his committee had located two companies
    whose shares were presently quite low and would probably
    benefit from a rebound: the Thibault Computer Manufacturing
    Company and Compuset, Inc.

    The president asked Mark Habib of Bennett, Duffy & Rooney, the
    club's broker, to comment.  Mr. Habib agreed with the
    committee's analysis and suggested Thibault as the best buy.
    He noted that the firm had assets that were underevaluated and
    that the 6.4 percent dividend is quite secure.  Ms. Dorman then
    moved that Thibault be purchased.  Mr. Noonan seconded.  The
    motion was approved unanimously, with one member abstaining.

    Mr. Samuels announced that the club's annual picnic is
    scheduled for Saturday, July 3, at Walker Park in Afton.  Each
    member may bring one guest.  More details will be mailed to
    each member next week.  The meeting was adjourned at 5:05 p.m.

                                    Respectfully submitted,

                                    Barbara Oliverio

                                    Barbara Oliverio, Secretary
```

The minutes of an informal meeting include the following information: summaries of discussions, the date, the opening and closing times, the names of presiding officers, and the names of present and absent members.

designated officials. The minutes of a meeting of an investment club committee are shown above.

Minutes of Formal Meetings. Minutes of meetings that follow parliamentary procedure are somewhat different in form from the informal minutes illustrated here. Formal minutes do not include discussions. Only motions,

```
                    The Historical Society of Kansas City

                    MINUTES OF THE MONTHLY MEETING

                         April 17, 1988


TIME AND       The regular monthly meeting of the Historical Society
PLACE          of Kansas City was called to order by the president,
               Walter Accaro, on April 17, 1988, at 7 p.m. in the
               Eisenhower Room of the Hartley Hotel.

MINUTES        The minutes of the last meeting were read and approved.

TREASURER'S    The treasurer, Victoria Angelini, gave the following
REPORT         report:

               Balance on hand, March 15, 1988         $2,500.00
               Cash received March 15-April 15            750.00
                   Total                               $3,250.00
               Paid out March 15-April 15                475.00
               Balance on hand, April 15, 1988        $2,775.00

               The treasurer's report was accepted.

OLD            It was moved, seconded, approved unanimously that a
BUSINESS       leaflet be printed to solicit new membership.  This
               leaflet would be distributed to local chambers of
               commerce and PTAs (Thomas Rooney, Lloyd Ulery).

NEW            After some discussion about improving communication
BUSINESS       between the club and the local media, the chairperson
               appointed a committee to report on this topic at the
               next meeting.  The committee will be:  Sandra Peebles,
               chair; Ronald Wallen; and Gladys Robbins.

PROGRAM        Walter Accaro introduced Marvin Esterman, an
               archaeologist at the University of Kansas.  Dr.
               Esterman's topic for this evening was "Improving
               Historical Site Selection in Kansas City."  His
               remarks are briefly summarized here:  "It is necessary
               to establish a list of criteria for site selection,
               based upon investigation and research.  Such criteria
               might be based upon what other historical societies
               are doing, as well as recommendations from the
               national society."  These recommendations were
               discussed in detail by the speaker and by several
               members of the audience.

ADJOURNMENT    The meeting was adjourned at 9:05 p.m.

                    Respectfully submitted,

                    Lawrence Chrisman

                    Lawrence Chrisman, Secretary
```

The minutes of a formal meeting do not include summaries of discussions leading up to votes.

resolutions, committee assignments and reports, and other specific accomplishments are included. Note in the example above how topical headings are used for easy reference and how the recorder has briefly summarized a speaker's remarks. Note, too, that motions should be worded specifically as shown and should be followed by the name of the person who made the motion and the name of the seconder.

RESOLUTION

WHEREAS our beloved colleague Carl Schultz passed away on June 6, 1988 and was one of the most sympathetic and hardest-working members of the Toledo Lions Club; and

WHEREAS his wise counsel and unselfish services will be missed not only by the members of the Toledo Lions Club but also by the community at large; therefore be it

RESOLVED, that we, his fellow Toledo Lions Club members, take this means of expressing our deep appreciation for his untiring and unselfish service to the organization and to the community, be it

RESOLVED, further, that we extend our sincerest sympathies to his widow, Mrs. Anna Strong Schultz; to his son, Mr. Victor Schultz, of Dayton, Ohio; and to his sister, Mrs. Maria S. Kraft, of Portland, Oregon; and be it

RESOLVED, further, that a copy of this resolution be included in the minutes of the Executive Committee of the Toledo Lions Club; that a copy be sent to the members of the immediate family, and that a copy be supplied both to the local press and television station.

ADOPTED, unanimously, by the Board of Directors of the Toledo Lions Club, this twelfth day of June, 1988.

Marvin Bradley
Marvin Bradley
Chairman

Ralph Farnsworth
Ralph Farnsworth
Secretary

The form of a resolution follows a definite pattern, including the use of the words WHEREAS and RESOLVED.

Resolutions. Resolutions to express sympathy, appreciation, congratulations, and the like, are often passed at formal meetings. The form of resolutions follows a rather definite pattern, as illustrated above.

Notice that the paragraphs giving the reasons for the resolution are introduced by the word *WHEREAS* (followed by a comma) and the paragraphs stating the action to be taken are introduced by the word *RESOLVED* (also followed by a comma).

News Releases

All businesses are eager to get as much favorable publicity as possible in newspapers and magazines, on radio or television—wherever there is a reading or listening audience. Larger businesses—even colleges—employ publicity directors whose job is to attract favorable public attention to the organization. The old saying attributed to a movie star, "I don't care what you say about me as long as you spell my name correctly," indicates how valuable publicity is to some people. Businesses, however, want only stories that show them in a favorable light, for public confidence is at stake. Unfavorable publicity can lose customers and lower stock values.

The physical form in which the planned news or publicity is given to news outlets is called a *news release*. Any subject that the business executive thinks may be of public interest or may bring the company name before the public may be the basis for a news release. It may be an announcement of a new product or service, the promotion of a major executive, a retirement, a death, an honor for an employee, the election of employees to civic posts, company anniversary celebrations, and so on. News releases are usually written, or at least approved, by one executive in an organization. In larger firms a public relations department or publicity department handles such releases. In smaller firms releases may be written by various executives. To prevent inaccurate or conflicting information from leaking out, however, these releases are usually channeled through one executive.

The purpose of the news release is to get a story into print or on the air. Newspaper, magazine, radio, and television editors receive hundreds of news releases every day from all types of businesses and individuals. The editor appraises these releases by one basic rule: "Is this item of current, specific interest to our readers or listeners?"

Form of the News Release. The style in which releases are written is highly important. Since news editors cannot accept for publication every news release they receive, everything else being equal, they will usually choose those that require the least amount of additional checking and editing. Therefore, a release should give complete information and follow as closely as possible the newspaper style of writing, as does the one on page 540.

News releases must be typed and reproduced (usually by stencil or photo-offset). Carbon copies should never be sent to an editor. Releases should be kept as brief as possible—rarely should they be more than a page and a half. The shorter and more interesting the news release, the better its chance of getting into print.

```
                                    Blessings Hospital
                                    Indianapolis, Indiana 46206
            N E W S   R E L E A S E  Release:  Immediate

                                    From:     Orville Conway
                                              Public Relations Director

        HIDEHIRO NAKAMA NAMED CHIEF ADMINISTRATOR OF BLESSINGS HOSPITAL

            INDIANAPOLIS, May 1--Hidehiro Nakama has been appointed chief

        administrator of Blessings Hospital of Indianapolis, according to

        the announcement made yesterday by Frances Howe, president of the

        Hospital Association of Indiana.

            Dr. Nakama succeeds Hector Bowman, who retired April 10 after

        26 years of service.

            The new hospital administrator joined the hospital staff in

        1981 as second assistant administrator of the children's wing.  In

        1983 he was appointed as first assistant administrator of the

        hospital.

            Dr. Nakama lives in the Cheshire Apartments with his wife,

        Uchii, head nurse at Suburbia Hospital in Indianapolis.  The Nakamas

        have two children, both of them enrolled at University Medical

        College.

            In commenting on his new post, Dr. Nakama paid tribute to the

        fine work done by his predecessor.  "I shall try to continue the

        fine program established by Dr. Bowman and to develop the fine

        reputation for quality care and service that has been built over the

        last thirty years." (END)
```

Any subject that a business thinks may be of public interest or may bring the company name before the public may be the subject of a news release.

Companies that issue a great many news releases have special forms on which to write them. Reporting a story on a special news release form is much more effective than writing a letter. Editors like to be able to read quickly; they cannot waste time going through the formalities of a letter. Like a letterhead, a news release form usually contains the name, address, and telephone number of the company. This information, however, may be placed at the bottom of the form. In addition, the name of the person who issued the release is included so that the editor can call for more information.

When writing or issuing news releases, be sure to observe all the points outlined here:

1. Always double-space the news release. Double-spacing is a must for all news releases so that the editor has room to make changes in the copy.
2. Use generous side margins and leave plenty of space at both top and bottom. This permits room for the editor to add typesetting instructions.
3. At the beginning of the story give a brief headline so that the editor may learn quickly what the release is about; for example, "New Plastic Office Accessories Announced" or "New President Appointed" or "Printing Press Handles Sheets 110 Inches Wide." (Editors will nearly always write their own headlines; nonetheless, news release writers should include a suggested headline.)
4. At the top of the form indicate when the news release may be made public. "For Release Upon Receipt" means that the story may be printed immediately upon receipt. Sometimes a news release may be issued several days in advance of the time it is to be used, in which case it will be marked, "To Be Released on July 1" or "Not to Be Released Before July 1."
5. Indicate the end of the release by typing the word *END* in parentheses or by typing three *x*'s: —*xxx*—. (The three *x*'s stand for "30," the signal telegraphers once used to signify "the end.")
6. If there is more than one page, add the word *more* in parentheses at the end of each page except the last page.
7. If the news release is long, insert subheads between paragraphs of the text to help break the monotony of type.

Writing the News Release. Whether your story heads for the wastebasket or the composing room may depend upon the words you use in your first paragraph. The first paragraph should summarize the basic idea of the story. It should stand by itself if need be, giving the *who, what, why, when,* and *where,* as stories appearing in newspapers generally do. Some examples follow:

> Appointment of Edith Wilson as comptroller of the law firm of Austin, Lavalle, and Gentry, Bergen, New Jersey, has been announced by Garrett Austin, president.

This release may be revised by the editor of the newspaper or magazine as follows:

> Edith Wilson has been named comptroller of Austin, Lavalle, and Gentry, a legal corporation of Bergen, New Jersey.

In any case, the news angle to the story is Ms. Wilson's appointment, rather than Mr. Austin's participation. Put the accent on Wilson; don't write as follows:

Mr. Garrett Austin, president of Austin, Lavalle, and Gentry, a legal corporation of Bergen, New Jersey, has announced the appointment of Edith Wilson as comptroller.

After the lead paragraph is written, move on to the background facts:

She succeeds E. Arnold Rooney, who retired July 1.

Additional background worth noting may then be given:

The new comptroller joined the firm in 1982 as an auditor. In 1983 she was made accounting supervisor and in 1984 was appointed assistant comptroller.

A well-written news release follows all the guidelines on the previous pages.

Routing Slips

Routing slips are sheets of paper that are used to send materials to several people. The routing slip may be a small (3- × 5½-inch) sheet that lists the names of the people who are to get certain articles or magazines. The routing slip is stapled to the first page, and after each person reads the material and crosses out his or her name, the magazine or article is passed on to the next person on the list. See the example illustrated on page 543.

A routing slip may also travel along with an important document—a contract, for example—that must be approved by several people. As each person approves the contract, he or she initials and dates the routing slip. The completed routing slip is filed as a one-page record showing that everyone did approve the document.

Routing slips that are used frequently may have names printed on them and a standard instruction at the bottom: "Return to P. Daniel, 29th Floor" or "Return to Library" or "Return to _____." Of course, a routing slip may also be individually typed as the need for one arises.

Obviously routing slips can save much time and money by reducing the need to duplicate the same information over and over again and by ensuring that all the people who *must* see a document or a magazine *will* see it.

Message Forms

Message forms allow people to take complete, accurate messages for others quickly. Thus they help us and our coworkers to build goodwill with customers and to work more efficiently with one another.

Since the forms usually include printed guide words (*To, Phone No., Date,* and so on) and easy-to-check boxes, the person who takes the message

From: Office Technology Library

Please read this publication promptly, cross through your name and send to next person on list.

If you cannot read immediately, place your name at end of list. Thank you.

Name	Floor	Department
J. Dale	10	Advertising
M. McColgan	9	Sales
I. Singh	5	Production
T. Sands	7	Legal
P. Schwartz	7	Legal
V. Rinaldi	4	Purchasing

Last person on list please return to
Office Technology Library — 11th Floor

Routing slips are helpful when material must be sent to several people.

To: *Harvey Lentz*
Here is a Message for You

Helen Sturgis
of *Sturgis + Wells*
Phone No. *555-7229* Ext. ___

☑ Telephoned ☐ Will-Call Again
☐ Returned Your Call ☐ Came To See You
☑ Please Phone ☐ Wants To See You

She wants to inform you of the progress made on the Fuller case.

Taken By *Andy* Date *10/28* Time *3:40 p.m.*

Message forms help people take complete, accurate messages.

writes very few words. In the example above, note that the check-off boxes make this form useful both for telephone messages and for messages from visitors.

Mailgrams and Other Telegraphic Services

Telephone and telegraph companies offer several services for sending messages. Perhaps the best known is the telegram, a fast (but costly) way to send a message anywhere in the world. To send a telegram, you can call Western Union, give the name and address of the person who is to receive the message, and dictate an exact message. Western Union will send your message by teleprinter to the branch office that is closest to the recipient, and the branch office will then deliver it. The cost of the telegram, which is based on the number of words in your message and its destination, can be charged to your telephone account.

Businesses today often use teleprinter equipment to communicate directly with branch offices or divisions. For example, a company with branches in San Francisco, Dallas, Chicago, and New York can facilitate communications among its branches by installing a teleprinter in each location. Two such services offered by Western Union are called *TWX* (teletypewriter exchange service) and *Telex*.

Western Union also offers Mailgram service, which is actually a joint service of Western Union and the United States Postal Service. Western Union wires a Mailgram message to the post office that is closest to the person who will receive the message. Since the post office gives Mailgrams special delivery service, they are usually received the day after they are sent. Mailgrams can be used successfully for advertising campaigns and for other volume mailings when special effect is desired, because their distinctive blue-and-white envelopes command the readers' attention and the telegraphic format impresses readers.

COMMUNICATION LABORATORY

APPLICATION EXERCISES

A. Prepare a set of minutes for either a class session or a meeting of a club that you belong to. Use the informal form discussed in this unit.

B. Prepare a formal set of minutes for an actual meeting that you have attended. The minutes might come from a club meeting or from the meeting of a local governmental agency. If you have not attended such a meeting, you may make up the necessary information.

C. Prepare a news release for your school or for a club or group that you belong to. If the release is for your school, it might announce a graduation, an athletic schedule, special student awards, or an annual play. If the release is for a club or group, it might announce an important upcoming meeting, a special activity or speaker, or a fund or membership drive.

D. Write a congratulatory message that your regional manager can send as a Mailgram to all sales personnel in the region. It has just been announced that the revenue budget has been exceeded by 23 percent. The message should contain 50 words or fewer.

E. A long-time employee from a branch office has called for information about early retirement. He would like to know what his monthly combined pension and social security payments would be if he retired at age 62 instead of age 65. He would also like to know how much notice the company needs if he plans to take early retirement. Leave a telephone message for the personnel director.

VOCABULARY AND SPELLING STUDIES

A. These words are often confused: *suit, suite, sweet; bearing, baring, barring.* Explain the differences.

B. Substitute a modern word or phrase for each of the following trite expressions:

1. At an early date
2. Kindly advise us
3. We trust
4. We beg to remain
5. Under separate cover

C. Three of the four words in each of the following groups are synonyms. The fourth word is an antonym. Underline this intruder.

1. attach, add, append, detach
2. start, begin, commence, terminate
3. conscious, asleep, awake, alive
4. invalidate, verify, authenticate, confirm
5. unskilled, expert, efficient, able
6. lively, dull, animated, alert
7. instantly, immediately, now, later
8. factual, true, correct, wrong
9. virtually, almost, every, nearly
10. objective, biased, just, fair

COMMUNICATING FOR RESULTS

Solving a Customer's Problem. Jason Hidalgo is a sales representative for an electronic parts manufacturer. As part of his normal customer contact program, he visits Henri Asche, the owner of an electronic parts retail outlet. Mr. Asche is very happy to see him. He tells Jason that he is in the midst of a special promotion and that his sale still has a week to go. Unfortunately, he is virtually out of one of Jason's line of chips that has been selling better than expected. He begs for an immediate shipment from a nearby warehouse and wants to order three times his normal amount. Jason realizes that supplies of the product have just about vanished and will not be available for another month. The only way that he can supply the amount that Asche needs is to deliver to him three smaller orders already promised other customers.

What should Jason say to Mr. Asche?

Your listening and speaking skills are always being put to use. At home, at school, at social activities, at work, *what* you hear, *what* you say, and *how* you say it are equally important. You want to be sure to communicate verbally and nonverbally in such a way that your receiver understands your messages without the benefit of a written record.

It is easy to see how effective listening and speaking skills influence business situations. Given a situation that requires listening and speaking skills, you will be able to do the following when you master the units in this chapter:

1. *Take brief—but complete—written notes at meetings, demonstrations, and lectures and of telephone instructions.*

2. *Remember more of what you hear and the names of people to whom you are introduced.*

3. *Eliminate the common misunderstandings that can result from spoken conversations.*

4. *Improve your ability to follow instructions on the job.*

5. *Address an audience confidently.*

6. *Learn to use the telephone efficiently.*

7. *Plan and manage successful meetings.*

53 Analyzing Effective Listening

Communication is a two-way process: *sending* a message and *receiving* a message. The sending device may be written words (written communication) or spoken words (oral communication). In written communication the *writer* is the *sender* and the *reader* is the *receiver*. In oral communication the *speaker* is the *sender* and the *listener* is the *receiver*. In both written and oral communication, there is no communication unless the message has been received. A letter that has been lost in the mail does not communicate. The best speech communicates nothing to you if you do not listen to it. How many lost messages have resulted in lost benefits to you?

The effectiveness of every communication depends first upon the proper functioning of the sending process and then upon the proper functioning of the receiving process. This unit stresses the importance of the receiving process in oral communication—listening—because listening skill is too often taken for granted and ignored.

How Listening Differs From Hearing

People often think that listening and hearing are the same thing, but they are really quite different. Hearing depends upon the ears, but listening uses the mind as well—and may even require the eyes. The ears permit you to hear sounds; the mind enables you to interpret these sounds, to recognize some of them as words, and to fashion the words into thoughts or ideas. With your mind you are able to determine that an oral message is important, interpret the message, and react to it.

Interpreting the message is a *thinking* act. It is dependent on both the listener's vocabulary and attitude. The listener must *want* to grasp the meanings of the words.

You may not have considered the eyes to be an important tool in listening. Yet what you see when a person is speaking is sometimes as important as what you hear. A smile, a quizzical glance, the appearance of boredom or exhilaration—all the facial expressions and mannerisms of a speaker may alter the meaning of the message.

The problem of improving listening is not one of improving the physical tools. Rather, it is a problem of improving the use of these tools so that they become more effective in receiving messages.

Why Improve Listening Efficiency?

Surveys have shown that listening occupies more time than any other communication activity: we spend more time listening than we spend talking, reading, or writing. Obviously, then, we can greatly improve our ability to receive communications by improving our listening skills.

The rewards of listening are great: they include increased knowledge, broadened experience, more and deeper friendships, increased job opportunities and promotions, development of facility in using language, and an increased appreciation of the spoken word.

On the other hand, ineffective listening may have a disastrous effect on any of these rewards, resulting in disappointments and failure. Frequently, potential school dropouts fail in their studies not because they can't learn but because they don't know how to listen. Snobs or bores may not want to be unfriendly; perhaps they just haven't mastered the listening requirements necessary for successful social relations. Employees may be fired not because they are unable to perform their jobs well but because they don't know how to listen to instructions.

Tests have shown that immediately after most people have listened to someone talk, they remember only about half of what they heard. Two months later, they remember only about a fourth of what was said. In other words the average person is only 25 percent efficient in listening skills. This fact means, then, that the average person has the potential for greatly increasing listening efficiency.

What does all this mean to you? Well, suppose you are one of these "average" persons. But, through instruction and practice, you are able to double your listening efficiency. You become 50 percent efficient in listening rather than just 25 percent. Consider what this improvement will mean in relation to your learning, your social life, your job. Consider how this improvement will increase your pleasure when you are with other people.

Listening and Your Social Life. Improved listening is certain to pay dividends in your social life. We find it easy to listen attentively to a good conversationalist, but courtesy demands that we *always* be good listeners. We should listen to others not only out of courtesy but also so that we can understand *what* the speaker is saying and *why*. In this way good listeners gain new friends and enrich and deepen their existing friendships.

Listening and Your Education. In high school today, many class hours are devoted to lectures and discussions, so doubling your listening effectiveness would greatly increase your learning productivity. It might eliminate "burning the midnight oil" when you cram for exams. Efficient listening—resulting in improved learning and remembering—also would give you more time for other subjects and for extracurricular activities.

Listening and Your Job. The rewards of improved listening are more tangible when you have a job, for often the rewards are in money. Beginning employees must listen to instructions and directions from their supervisors and coworkers. They must listen to suggestions and criticisms in order to improve their job performance. To advance in a job, they must have an awareness of what's going on in their department and in the company, and this awareness results in part from intelligent listening. You can easily see that improved listening will enhance your chances of success in business.

The Effect of Listening on Other Communication Skills

Each medium of communication can reinforce the other media to produce a higher degree of learning. For example, listening can be reinforced with reading, with speaking, and with writing to produce understanding and longer remembering.

Listening and Reading. Listening, like reading, is a message-receiving skill. But listening is more difficult than reading because, generally, you cannot relisten to a spoken message as you can reread a written one. You must get the message right the first time or you lose it.

Reading about a topic in advance will enable you to listen more effectively to the speaker's message because you bring more knowledge to the topic and thus derive greater benefit from it. When planning to attend an important committee meeting, if you examine the agenda and reread the minutes of previous meetings beforehand, you will be able to listen much more effectively during the meeting.

Listening and Speaking. Speaking reinforces listening in various ways. Good listeners repeat to themselves the speaker's important points, and they mentally rephrase these points in their own words; this process adds to the listeners' understanding. In addition, good listeners ask questions to clarify what a speaker is saying.

Speaking is often an aid to memory, thus helping the listener to remember. When you are introduced to people, for example, you will be more likely to remember their names if you repeat the name orally and use the name as much as you can in talking with the person or in talking with others about the person.

Listening and Writing (Note-Taking). Writing, perhaps more than any other communication skill, contributes to good listening. Frequently, the listener must take written notes in order to retain for future reference the information he or she hears. The student attending a lecture, the secretary taking a telephone message, and the accountant receiving oral instructions from a supervisor are but a few of the persons who write notes to reinforce their listening.

However, notes should be made with discretion. A listener who spends too much time taking notes may miss the heart of the message. A listener who is too dependent upon note-taking may be using these notes as a crutch to avoid real listening rather than as a reinforcement to listening. In the next unit you will be given specific suggestions for note-taking.

Listening and Job Success

Habits of efficient listening contribute greatly to one's success in all areas of life, but particularly in business and industry. So important are habits of good listening that many large corporations—American Telephone and Telegraph, General Electric, and General Motors among them—provide listening training for many of their executives and supervisory personnel.

Supervisors Must Know How to Listen. These corporations know that management must be able to listen properly if it is to be effective. They know that successful supervisors or managers don't just give orders; they also do a lot of listening. They listen to their employees to find out what they think so that management can help to settle grievances and establish good employee relationships. They also listen to their employees because they know that their employees often contribute timesaving and money-saving ideas to those employers who prove to be sympathetic and appreciative audiences.

All Employees Must Know How to Listen. Listening is extremely important at all levels of employment. Many employees in business and industry rely on listening skills to help them carry out their daily assignments. The telephone operator must listen carefully in order to handle the requests of hundreds of calls. The salesperson must listen just as carefully to determine the wishes of customers.

One large retailing organization found that two out of every three former customers had taken their business elsewhere because its sales personnel were indifferent to customers' needs. Moreover, the organization found that much of the indifference was expressed through poor listening.

All of us have had experiences like this one. In the sweater department of a store, you ask the salesclerk to show you a large brown cardigan sweater. The clerk appears to have heard correctly since there were no questions asked regarding your request. The clerk returns in a few minutes with blue and green pullover sweaters, one a medium and the other an extra large. You try to hide your annoyance and explain once again to the clerk what it is that you want. Poor listening habits have caused you unnecessary delay and have made extra work for the clerk. Such incidents are much too frequent in business.

Among others greatly dependent upon effective listening to succeed in their jobs are service department managers in all types of businesses. When a customer takes a car into an automobile service center, the service manager must listen carefully and record what the customer wants done with his or her car. The service manager must listen to the motor for clues to any difficulty. Then the manager must listen carefully to learn when and where the repaired vehicle is to be delivered. After the completion of the work, the manager must listen to the mechanics to determine what repairs have been made and whether they have been made satisfactorily. The success of all service department managers, therefore, depends greatly upon how well they listen in their roles as liaisons between customers and the mechanics making the repairs.

All employees who provide service of any kind—and that includes most—are partially, if not mainly, dependent upon their listening ability to carry out their duties. No one in business and industry is immune to the need for effective listening. Every worker—every secretary, accountant, shipping clerk, machine operator, maintenance person—receives much information and many instructions orally from coworkers, from supervisors, and from customers. Failure to listen results in errors and misunderstandings, and these are costly in terms of time, money, and goodwill.

Because effective listening is so important to you in every aspect of your life—social, school, and work—you should be eager to begin the listening improvement program suggested in the next unit.

COMMUNICATION LABORATORY

APPLICATION EXERCISES

A. Do you know how much listening time you spend during a typical school day? Guess the total time in hours and minutes. Then keep an hour-by-hour log of the actual time you spend in listening activities. Total the actual time and compare it with your estimated time. Members of the class will then compare their listening times with each other, noting the lowest and highest amounts of time used. Discuss the possible reasons for the differences.

B. Select a business position you might someday like to hold. In a brief paragraph list the activities of that position that require effective listening.

C. Try this listening activity that involves making introductions, an activity in which everyone has to engage sometime and in varying degrees. Divide the class into groups of five or six persons each. Each person is to prepare on a card or slip of paper a fictitious name and business title that he or she is to assume. Each person is then to introduce himself or herself to the others in that group. After all introductions have been made, determine whether each person in the group can introduce the others in that group by name and title. Missing one name in the group is acceptable. If you miss more than one, you aren't listening carefully enough. On other days during the week, the same exercise may be repeated by changing the group members in each of the groups.

D. In groups of two classmates each, plan a 1-minute skit to enact in class. In this skit two friends are conversing. One is a poor listener who wants to do all the talking, while the other is obviously annoyed. Write a script and perform it as written. Then enact the skit again, showing both persons as considerate and attentive conversationalists.

E. Prepare another listening skit to be enacted for 2 minutes. In this skit you are a job applicant discussing a position with a personnel supervisor. You show obvious signs of being a poor listener: instead of listening to a description of the job duties, you are thinking about what you are going to ask or say; you interrupt the speaker; you fiddle with your hands and pencil; you look everywhere but at the speaker. The skit ends when the supervisor tells you that you will be notified if the company wishes to hire you and then escorts you to the door. After each skit has been performed, list specific listening techniques that you *should* have used during the interview. Then reenact the scene, practicing sound listening techniques for a job interview situation.

VOCABULARY AND SPELLING STUDIES

A. In each of the following sentences, choose the word in parentheses that correctly expresses the meaning.

1. The new policy will (effect, affect) all our employees.
2. In what (addition, edition) did the computer article appear?
3. There is no logic in that (inane, insane) remark.
4. I have just signed a (partition, petition) against the tax.
5. We have seats for the match on the upper (tier, tear).
6. When the lunch hour was increased, the (moral, morale) improved.
7. The judge asked two (disinterested, uninterested) parties to settle the dispute.
8. The (trial, trail) was scheduled in Judge Rosen's court.
9. (Immortal, Immoral) books should be in all libraries.
10. A large (amount, number) of customers bought the new product.

B. The following words appeared in this unit. Read through the unit, locate each word, and guess its meaning from the way in which it is used in its sentence. Check the meaning of the word in a dictionary. Then use each word in a sentence of your own.

1. device
2. interpret
3. quizzical
4. disastrous
5. dividends
6. attentively
7. reinforce
8. indifferent
9. immune
10. aspect

COMMUNICATING FOR RESULTS

Vocabulary Game. Usually it is better practice to *know* a great many big words than to *use* them. For example, consider the following: "Homo sapiens who inhabit dwellings composed of translucent or transparent silicate materials should refrain from hurling concretions of earth or mineral matter." This statement, more simply put, means that people who live in glass houses should not throw stones.

This game of changing ordinary sayings into difficult-to-understand sayings by substituting complicated words for common words is fun and will improve your ability to recognize words. Use a dictionary or thesaurus to find more difficult and uncommon synonyms for words in three popular sayings or proverbs similar to the one used here. Try them out on your class. Discuss why it may be a good idea to know words that are not in your everyday speaking vocabulary, even though you may not use them frequently.

U · N · I · T
54
Improving On-the-Job Listening Skills

Our ears are assaulted with sounds continually. We *hear* these sounds, but we don't *listen* to all of them. We can't; we would be overrun with sound if we did. In self-defense we block off many sounds from our consciousness— we "tune out" unwanted sounds.

Blocking off sounds is a useful device, as it often aids concentration. But too often we also block off sounds to which we *should* be listening. Most of us have acquired bad habits of nonlistening, even when we are with our best friends, and these habits are very hard to break.

Fortunately, they can be unlearned and replaced by good listening habits. The first step in this process is to become *aware* of your deficiencies in listening and of your need for good listening habits. When you have made this awareness a habit, you will be well on your way to becoming a good listener.

How to Prepare for Listening

In order to prepare yourself for listening, you should follow these guidelines:

Determine Your Purpose. We have said that the chief difference between hearing and listening is that listening involves both the mind and the ears. Another way of expressing this difference is to say that *listening has a purpose.* This point is important because different purposes in listening imply different *kinds* of listening.

Your purpose in listening may be to act friendly and sociable, as would be the case in a party conversation; to obtain information, as in listening to a lecture; or to analyze critically, as in listening to a political debate.

Listening to a pep talk at a football rally is not the same as listening to a formal speech. Listening to a friend introduce you to someone is not the same as overhearing a conversation on a bus. In an introduction you would want to listen carefully for the person's name, as well as make note of any specific details that you can use as a basis for conversation. When listening to a speech, you would listen for main ideas and supporting facts. Because it is different from a formal speech, in a pep talk you would listen for the general tone of the meeting, which you could easily anticipate, and you might want to tune out the overheard conversation after a few minutes.

Listening in each situation calls for different skills and for different degrees of attentiveness. In each situation the demands are different because the purpose is different, so you must decide on your purpose for listening in every listening situation. You will be a better listener as a result of knowing *why* you are listening.

Get Ready to Listen. Good listening implies a *readiness* to listen. This means that you prepare yourself for listening—physically, mentally, and emotionally. Literally turn your back on distracting sights and sounds, if necessary, and always give yourself maximum opportunity for listening by sitting near enough to the speaker to see and hear easily. If possible, read about a topic in advance, because the more you know about a topic, the more interested you will be in what the speaker has to say about it. Mental preparation, because it invariably supplies you with a purpose for listening, automatically leads to emotional involvement. And this involvement, in turn, increases your readiness to listen.

Accept Your Share of Responsibility. Too often listeners approach speakers with an "I dare you to interest me" attitude. Such an attitude is tough on the speaker and is obviously discourteous. Remember that you, as a listener, share the responsibility for communicating with the speaker and therefore must be courteous to the speaker. By doing so, you will notice that the quality of your listening can affect the speaker's talking—it may even control it!

The reason is simple: we all crave good listeners, and we react accordingly. For example, imagine for a moment that you are in the midst of telling an interesting story. One of your "listeners" is flipping the pages of a magazine;

two others are whispering to each other; another is openly yawning. How would you react? Would you go on with your story? As you can see, then, an audience can influence the delivery, and even the length, of a speech.

How to Listen— Basic Rules

Listen With Understanding. Be sure you understand the speaker's ideas fully and completely; don't jump to conclusions about a false or half-true idea. To understand the speaker's ideas, you must listen *carefully*. If necessary, ask questions to clarify anything that is vague.

Listen With an Open Mind. Keep your mind open when you listen. Forget your biases and prejudices for the moment, and be ready to receive new ideas. Don't refuse to listen to new ideas just because they may *conflict with* those you believe. Hear the speaker out; don't tune in only what you want to hear. Of course, it is possible that your point of view may be changed somewhat as a result, but you should be courageous enough to take that chance. After all, the change may be for the better.

Listen Actively. Listening actively implies work on your part. Primarily, it means three things: concentrating, relating what you hear to what you already know, and reading between the lines.

To concentrate, you must be selective about the sounds you hear. Focus your attention on what a speaker is saying and disregard the noises coming from the street outside. Being an active process, concentration takes both willpower and energy.

Relating ideas and facts just heard to your existing store of knowledge means that change will take place. No change, no learning. And naturally, learning takes concentrated effort.

Reading between the lines—or sensing the implications of a speaker's message—is another rule of good listening. The good listener analyzes the speaker's word choice and observes closely the speaker's posture, facial expressions, tone of voice, manner, general appearance, and so on.

Listen With Empathy. Listening with empathy means putting yourself in the speaker's place—making an extra effort to understand the speaker's point of view. Naturally, such listening requires imagination. However, because it results in attentiveness that is very flattering to most speakers, listening with empathy serves to draw them out and to help eliminate any shyness, suspicion, or hostility they may have. Thus listening with empathy aids communication and usually results in many rewards for the listener.

How to Listen Critically

Critical listening is a special kind of listening—listening with a view toward analyzing and evaluating what speakers say and how they say it. It involves all the basic rules of listening, plus a few others: listening for main ideas and supporting details; reviewing points already made and anticipating what is coming next; and finally, analyzing the evidence and accepting or rejecting the speaker's conclusions on the basis of this evidence.

To listen critically may seem to be a large order given that you are expected to listen intently at the same time. However, good listeners do both all the time. They use their *spare listening time* to reflect on the words they have just heard.

All of us have this spare listening time because we think at a much faster rate than the average speaker talks. The rate of speech for most Americans is around 125 words a minute, but we think at a rate four or five times that fast.

The half-listener or nonlistener generally uses this time to daydream or to turn his or her attention elsewhere. Although you do have spare listening time, using it to daydream will not work out well. The reason is that daydreamers usually find their attention focused more on distractions than on the words of the speaker. By missing certain portions of the speech, the listener becomes less interested in the topic and more interested in the distractions, making the speech harder and harder to follow. Finally, the listener gives up completely and tunes out the speaker.

Good listeners, on the other hand, use their spare listening time to engage in thought processes that are closely related to what the speaker says; in other words, they listen *actively*. Such active listening results in increased understanding and longer remembering. Following are some rules for using your spare listening time.

Note Major Points. A well-prepared speech usually consists of a few major points. Often a good speaker may indicate these points near the beginning of the talk.

Suppose the speaker says the following:

> In the world of word processing in the past ten years, there has been a major revolution both in equipment and business practices that makes many traditional practices obsolete. Today we shall deal with the effects of word processing in the business classroom. We shall discuss this technological upheaval as it relates to the preparation of young men and women to work in the automated world of work. In our discussion of desirable changes in this preparation, let us consider three principal topics. First, the power of computerized word processing in changing the way the work is performed. Second, the changing purposes for preparing people for work in the computerized world. And third, the changing classroom methods required to teach young people to learn.

Thus the speaker actually reveals an outline in the presentation, and you should grasp this outline by noting these three principal points:

1. The changing methods of working
2. The changing purposes of education and training
3. The changing methods of teaching

Recognize Details. As soon as you grasp the speaker's major ideas, you should recognize that everything else that is said is, or *should be,* designed to support these main ideas. The details will help you to fill in the structure of the speech and lead you to a better understanding of the speech as a result. Details will also tell you a lot about the way a speaker thinks.

In the following portion of a speech, note that while the sidelights add color and interest to the main idea, they are not separate ideas in themselves; the main idea is comprised of only the italicized words.

> *One of the major factors in locating manufacturing sites today is the availability of trained personnel.* For example, Beverly Township in the eastern part of the state would be a suitable site for our new computer manufacturing facility except for one factor: lack of educational facilities. There is no university in the area producing engineering and administrative personnel. There are no technical institutes or training schools. The high schools in the vicinity lack both comprehensive vocational training programs and developed business courses. Although transportation facilities are ideal, taxes are low, land is inexpensive, and the climate is outstanding, it would be extremely difficult to staff such a facility in this location. Our only choice would be to institute our own training programs, and to do so would be extremely expensive.

In the preceding paragraph note the words *for example.* Speakers often provide the listener with cues to indicate whether an idea is a new one or whether it merely adds support to an idea already presented.

Rephrase and Review. The effective listener works to retain the message of the speaker in two ways: by *rephrasing* silently the speaker's words and by *reviewing* the major points of the speech from time to time. Using both methods will reinforce your understanding of the speech and help you remember the principal ideas.

The rephrasing process is similar to taking notes, except that you rephrase mentally: you concentrate on main ideas and summarize them as briefly as possible. You must practice the rephrasing process again and again so that you can master this listening skill. Note in the following illustration how you can mentally rephrase a speaker's words:

WHAT THE SPEAKER IS SAYING	WHAT YOU ARE SAYING TO YOURSELF
An ideal salesperson tries to ascertain a customer's real needs and then attempts to meet those needs. A successful salesperson usually tries to figure out what the customer really	The ideal salesperson meets the customer's real needs. Once a customer lets it be known that he or she would really like something, the salesperson does everything possible to make it

WHAT THE SPEAKER IS SAYING	WHAT YOU ARE SAYING TO YOURSELF
desires—a factor that often escapes the customer. Yet the good salesperson is able to bring these desires out into the open. For example, a person looking for a computer might very well put price above everything else, because we are all conditioned to be careful about money. However, the skillful salesperson soon determines that the customer really wants those additional options that add "something" to the computer. For example, the customer may say, "It would be nice to have color, but I don't think it is worth an extra $1000." Realizing what the customer *really* wants, the skillful salesperson says, "You know, in the final analysis, it really costs very little, since it will add to the value of your computer should you want to sell it or trade it in for another model. It will add about $600 to the value of your computer and, therefore, really cost you only $400. If you keep the computer for only two years, that's about $200 a year, or only about 60 cents a day." The salesperson is not being dishonest but merely is helping the customer get what he or she really wants.	appealing. The good salesperson fulfills the customer's needs and desires.

Detect Bias and Determine Motives. A biased viewpoint is a partial, or prejudiced, viewpoint. In business bias and preconceived opinions are natural because a company wants to sell its product or service; this desire then becomes its primary motive. But the critical listener must learn to recognize this bias and this motive.

For example, people who sell automobiles may focus all their attention on the favorable features of a particular make of car; it is natural to do so. But you, as a good listener, must recognize this bias and also the fact that what you hear from the seller may not be the whole truth. Automobile salespeople would be foolish to let you know all the weaknesses of their cars, since their motive is to sell them; nor would they rave about other cars.

The customary warning *caveat emptor*, which means "let the buyer beware," applies as well to listeners: let the listener beware of the words of biased or emotional speakers.

Take Notes. Note-taking should be used as an aid to remembering, not as a substitute for listening. When listeners spend too much time taking notes, they miss the heart of the message. Therefore, notes should be made with caution. Here are specific suggestions for note-taking:

1. Have plenty of notepaper, a good pen, and an extra pencil or two.
2. Use an uncluttered writing surface that provides backing for the paper.
3. Label your notes for easy identification later.
4. Listen for such speaker's cues as "first," "second," and "third"; "another important consideration"; "finally"; "the most significant thing"; "on the other hand"; "in summary"; as well as questions posed by the speaker, pauses, changes of emphasis in voice, and gestures.
5. Flag important parts of your notes with brackets, underscores, arrows, or indentions.
6. Listen for special instructions.
7. Go over your notes promptly after the speech to fix the major points more firmly in your mind.

Practice, Practice, Practice. Efficient listening, like other communication skills, requires practice. To become a good listener, take every opportunity to put the techniques presented in this unit into practice. In other words— practice, practice, practice!

COMMUNICATION LABORATORY

APPLICATION EXERCISES

A. Certain words have an emotional effect on the listener, creating either a positive or a negative effect. For example, the word *happiness* might have a positive effect, while the word *poverty* might have a negative effect. Can you think of five words that might have a positive effect and five words that might have a negative effect? List these words under appropriate headings on a separate sheet of paper.

B. On a separate sheet of paper, answer each of the following numbered questions by writing *yes, sometimes,* or *no.* The questions are designed to help you evaluate your own listening habits.

1. For a class on a given topic, do you read and think about the topic before the class meets?

2. When your teacher or others are speaking, do you pay close and considerate attention to what they say?

3. When in class, do you alertly listen to and accurately follow all the instructions and directions of the teacher?

4. When you enter an auditorium to listen to a speech, do you deliberately seat yourself where you can easily see and hear the speaker?

5. When listening, do you carefully watch the speaker's facial expressions?

6. When you receive instructions or directions that must be carefully followed, do you write them on a piece of paper?

7. When another person is introduced to you, do you mentally practice saying and spelling the name to fix it in your memory?

8. Do you take notes during all class presentations and discussions?

9. As soon as possible after an introduction, do you use the new name when speaking to the person just met to help fix it in your memory?

10. When listening in class, do you mentally rephrase in your own words what you have heard?

11. Do you suspect that you have a hearing or vision problem that a physician should check?

12. When you do not understand what a teacher or another student has said in class, do you ask questions to make the message clear?

13. When speaking on the telephone, do you try to picture the other person's facial expressions in order to participate more fully in the conversation?

14. In listening to a speech or lecture, do you mentally repeat to yourself important points that the speaker makes?

15. Do you deliberately make a mental note of oral messages you need to remember?

C. Using your answers to the questions in the previous exercise, prepare a 200-word written analysis of your listening skills. Your analysis should focus on the following points: (1) your listening weaknesses and (2) what you can do to improve your listening.

D. Good listeners are able to distinguish facts from opinions. On a separate sheet of paper, indicate which of the following are facts and which are opinions.

1. It is two o'clock now.
2. We must wear neckties to the banquet tonight.
3. Neckties are uncomfortable.
4. Gasoline prices are too high.
5. You are sitting in my assigned seat.
6. The car you bought is the best on the market.
7. I enjoyed my vacation to Florida.
8. Too many people are downtown at lunchtime.

9. Your car is only worth $2000.
10. I will give you $2000 for your car.

E. Using the suggestions for taking notes (page 560), evaluate your own note-taking skills. In what specific ways can you improve your skills?

F. Write a 30-second radio or television commercial for a product or service. Present the commercial orally in class. Then lead a discussion of the commercial that analyzes the motives and biases of its sponsor.

G. Join with the other members of your class in developing a list of rules and sound practices that will promote good classroom listening.

VOCABULARY AND SPELLING STUDIES

A. Match each verb in the left-hand column with its correct synonym in the right-hand column. Use a dictionary to find the meanings of words you do not know.

1. *impede* progress	1. weaken
2. *scrutinize* a letter	2. cancel
3. *condone* an error	3. abandon
4. *defer* the work	4. inspect
5. *dilute* the benefits	5. postpone
6. *repudiate* the action	6. implant
7. *curtail* the work	7. waste
8. *revoke* the decision	8. allow
9. *instill* confidence	9. shorten
10. *squander* money	10. hinder

B. Use each of the following nouns in the sentence that it best completes: *bias, discretion, empathy, involvement, motivation, retention.*

1. My boss has a _____ against lazy workers.
2. We had much _____ for the famine victims.
3. The President was criticized for his _____ in foreign relations.
4. The _____ of personnel avoids expensive training programs.
5. At the supervisor's _____, we may get tomorrow off.
6. We question the employee's _____ in stealing from the company.

COMMUNICATING FOR RESULTS

Listening. Your teacher will read a short passage. Listen carefully and try to absorb every important detail. Be prepared to give an accurate oral summary of the passage.

55

Analyzing Effective Speaking

We all make some use of each of the means of communicating—reading, writing, listening, and speaking. However, we spend most of our time in communicating with our voices. For example, in school we ask and answer questions, we contribute to discussions, we participate in debates, and we give oral presentations. Those who are most successful in extracurricular activities often depend upon their ability to express ideas orally. In your relationships with your friends and family, social conversation plays an important role as you talk about the events of the day and your plans for the future. Whether you work in an office, a store, or a gasoline station, you certainly spend much time in talking—giving instructions or explanations, asking questions or answering them, promoting good business relations, selling ideas, or selling your personal qualities.

Since most of us talk much more than we write, we are judged more by our speech than by our writing. Speech is an important part of your personality—it is individually and particularly yours. To many people your speech is *you*. The words you use, the way you put them together, the sound of your voice (tone, pitch, volume, and rate), and your enunciation and pronunciation all add up to the *you* that others hear. You can't separate your voice from your personality; they contribute to each other in many ways. On the telephone, for example, your voice represents your entire personality. Therefore, you should be as concerned about speech improvement as you are about personality improvement.

Creating a Favorable Impression: Dress, Posture, Expression, Manners, and Mannerisms

Effective speech, whether in a formal or an informal situation, depends upon factors other than the words spoken. The setting, or atmosphere, in which words are used often determines how they are received by the listener. Just as a successful play or motion picture must have the proper setting, musical background, and costumes, so must successful speaking have the appropriate atmosphere. Therefore, before learning the elements of effective speaking, you need to learn how to create a favorable impression that will set the stage for the best reception of what you say.

An impression is the sum total of many factors. Each of these factors needs to be studied and mastered. After these factors are learned, they must be practiced. Among the elements that help a speaker make a favorable first impression are the following:

1. Appropriate dress and grooming
2. Good posture and carriage
3. Pleasant facial expressions
4. Good manners
5. Lack of distracting mannerisms

Appropriate Dress and Grooming. It is impossible to prescribe a set of dress standards that will apply to every business situation today. In recent years standards of acceptable dress and grooming have changed quite drastically. Indeed, by the time you read these words, they may no longer apply. Therefore, the best advice one can give is to suggest that you first determine who will be the judge of your dress and grooming in a particular situation and how important this judgment is to you. If the judgment is important to you, then determine what is acceptable in terms of dress and grooming to that individual or group and dress accordingly.

Although business dress standards tend to be somewhat conservative, many offices have relaxed these standards and permit employees to follow some of the current fads. However, extremes in clothing, hairstyles, or makeup are not likely to be acceptable to those businesses that wish to convey a feeling of conservatism to their customers. To determine what will be acceptable, you should observe other employees in your company and read employee manuals that describe dress and grooming codes.

Regardless of what dress standards are followed, two aspects of grooming that are always important are cleanliness and neatness. Your overall appearance makes a strong impression. If you are well-groomed and neatly dressed, your appearance will inspire a basic confidence in your work habits.

Both men and women in business should wear clothing that is becoming to their physical size and age. Accessories should harmonize with the rest of your outfit. You want to be attractive but not showy. Above all, you want to convey a certain amount of maturity and good judgment—and one way to do so is to show that you know how to dress for business, for work.

Lack of cleanliness is offensive to most people. Therefore, skin, teeth, hair, breath, fingernails, and hands should be checked frequently to see that they are as clean as possible. Clothing that is clean and pressed will help you to make a better impression too. Furthermore, your clothing should fit well and be in good repair. If your shoes have heels that are run down and you are wearing clothing that has holes or is torn, you will attract attention—but it will be unfavorable attention. Instead, your goal should be to do everything possible in terms of dress and grooming to create the best impression of yourself in the minds of those with whom you come in contact.

Good Posture and Carriage. The positive effect you wish to create by wearing carefully chosen clothing and practicing good grooming can be completely destroyed if you do not sit, stand, and walk correctly. The fit and the hang of an article of clothing are best when posture and carriage are good. Therefore, if you take pride in your appearance, you should analyze your sitting, standing, and walking habits and make any necessary improvements.

Your Posture Tells. The main reason for studying correct posture and carriage, however, is that the way you carry yourself seems to reveal traits of personality and character. Do you sprawl when you sit? Then you are lazy. When you stand, do you always rest all your weight on one leg and hip? Then you tire or lose interest quickly and have no drive. When you walk, do you shuffle along with your head down? If so, you must be the kind of person who does not work well with others, and you very definitely show that you have no force of character.

"Not so," you say? Well, perhaps the tales told by your posture and carriage are false. For instance, although you do have the habit of relaxing in the chair, you are not lazy. But such is the impression you give, and erasing the impression of laziness will be very difficult. Accordingly, you need to study the following discussion of good posture and carriage so that you will be able to make an impression that is favorable—and true!

When you get ready to sit, bend your joints and sit. Do not fall into a chair as a rag doll would. Once in the chair, sit up straight—not rigidly, but not slumped either. For correct sitting posture, the best practice is to be sure that the end of your spine touches the back of the chair. A little practice in taking a seat and in sitting correctly will pay dividends. And if you like to sit with your legs crossed, make sure that you do not look awkward.

Stand Tall, but Not Stiff. People who stand correctly stand tall and hold their heads up. Their shoulders are in line with the rest of their body—not far back, not caved in toward the chest. They hold themselves erect, but not stiff. They have formed the habit of standing with their weight distributed evenly on both feet to avoid having to shift position continually. Standing tall will make you look self-confident and will give others a good impression of you.

There are as many variations in the manner of walking as there are people. You will find that it is impossible to change completely your own distinctive style of walking. You can, however, learn just one thing that will help. With steps neither too long nor too short, neither too fast nor too slow, walk as though you have somewhere to go and you intend to get there without stopping at way stations! Walking purposefully, you will give an impression of being ambitious, industrious, and self-directing.

Pleasant Facial Expressions. Part of the education of an aspiring young actor or actress consists of practicing the different facial expressions that reflect various emotions—joy, fear, pleasure, sorrow, and so on. If, through intelligent practice, actors can change their facial expressions, you, too, can change yours if you so desire. First, of course, you need to know what kind of expression creates a favorable impression. You need some pointers on how to assume such an expression. You need, too, to know where your own shortcomings are. And you need to practice before a mirror.

Look Interested. A pleasant, interested, alive-looking expression is a winning expression. Even a hasty glance at an expression like this would generate a feeling of warmth, of liking. In an interview, a meeting, a conference, or any other working situation, pleasant facial expressions promote pleasant relationships. Fortunate indeed are those of you who naturally and habitually have this type of facial expression. You are the extroverts, the ones who are interested in and enjoy other people; and you let your interest and enjoyment shine through. However, you represent a very small minority of our population.

Too many persons tell a story of indifference, boredom, or discontent with their expressions. Possibly they tell nothing at all. Some very intelligent people are afflicted with shyness, which they try to hide behind a "deadpan" or a bored facial expression. These are the ones who will profit by a study of the following discussion.

The eyes are the focal point of facial expression, as you can prove by doing this: stand in front of a mirror and think of something very pleasant that has happened to you recently. See how your eyes light up your whole face? Now pretend that you are shopping for a car and a dealer is showing you some interesting models. If you are good at make-believe, your eyes will reflect your intense interest. With practice you will find that it is not necessary to smile or grin in order to look pleasant but that it *is* necessary to *feel* pleasant. However, if you have a warm, attractive smile, use it whenever you can.

Really Look at People. Suppose that you are shy and that you do not look at those who are talking to you. Since they cannot see your eyes, they are unable to form a favorable opinion of your personality and disposition, and you run the risk of being judged as undesirable. For instance, there are interviewers who will not hire an applicant who looks everywhere but at the interviewer. They think that this habit indicates that the applicant is shy and shifty. So after you have worked to acquire a facial expression that will contribute to your advancement, be sure to look at people. Otherwise, your efforts will have been wasted.

Learning to look pleasant, interested, and alert is purely an individual problem. Only you can study your own expression, and only you can put in the practice time necessary to achieve the results you wish. You are the one who must consciously assume the facial expression that produces a favorable impression. It is you who must remember to look at people when you talk to them. The rewards, also, are yours alone. One of the rewards is that in a relatively short time, your improved facial expression will become your habitual expression.

Good Manners. Another very important factor in creating a favorable impression is showing good manners. The atmosphere of polish created by those who do and say the correct thing at the correct time earns the respect and admiration of all. These models of good taste and breeding, however, did not reach the state of being natural without learning and practicing and without brushing up from time to time. Your own manners may be excellent, but even you may need to study the following discussion and the suggestions given.

The Basis Is Courtesy. The basis of good manners is courtesy, and the basis of courtesy is consideration for others. Without courtesy good manners are only a false front.

However, natural courtesy, while basic, is not enough for correct behavior. Do not minimize the importance of knowing and observing the rules of etiquette. You must know such things as how to make and acknowledge introductions properly. You should, in short, be familiar with all the rules that govern correct social and business relationships. This means that you need to know and to review periodically the contents of an etiquette book. There are some slight differences between social and office etiquette, and you can learn them by studying a book on business etiquette.

Introductions. There are many aspects of social correctness, but only two that are frequently important in business usage will be discussed—introductions and handshaking. Although numerous rules apply to making introductions, they may all be simplified by determining quickly which of the two or more people being introduced you wish to honor or which has the more important position. Then say that person's name *first.* By so doing, you will find your introduction procedures automatically correct. For instance, if you were introducing anybody at all to your mother, you would say, "Mother, may I present . . . ," "Mother, I'd like you to know . . . ," or "Mother, this is . . . ." If you wished to introduce your manager, Mr. Lane, and a young man who is with you, you would say, "Mr. Lane, this is . . . ." You might call this technique a Quick Trick that will prevent those first embarrassing moments of silence that occur while you are trying to remember the various methods of presentation.

The second suggestion is that you learn to shake hands in a manner that will give an impression of decision and determination, of having a mind of your own. Clasp hands firmly, and shake hands once, without overdoing the up-and-down motion. *Firmly* does not mean "bone crushing." You should use just enough hand pressure to show some strength. Your handclasp may be more important to you than you realize. You may be shaking hands with one of those people who believe strongly that a handclasp tells all about character and ability. If this act tells a story, let that tale be favorable to you.

Lack of Distracting Mannerisms. The person who sits at the desk next to yours may be first-rate in grooming, posture, manners, and pleasant facial expressions. But what about that annoying habit of knuckle cracking? And what about the person who comes to tell you something, stands behind you, and breathes down your neck? or chews gum? And so on. Often, ambitious young people may work very hard to improve themselves but are still defeated because they have overlooked some mannerism that will annoy others.

Logically, then, as a finishing touch to your study on creating a favorable impression, study your own mannerisms. To appear favorably to others, you must let nothing detract from the impression you have worked so hard to produce. You will find it quite difficult to study yourself because you may not realize that you have distracting or annoying habits. For best results first study the people around you. Watch to see whether they have any behavior quirks. Whenever you observe a mannerism that you think is objectionable, say to yourself, "Do I do that?" After you have had practice in looking for these faults in others, you will be more likely to see your own faults.

Studying your own personal mannerisms and eliminating any that are undesirable are necessary tasks if you wish to protect your position. There is little profit in presenting a fine appearance and in being polite and well mannered if you consistently do something that annoys your colleagues.

Factors of Voice Quality

How you say something can be as important as what you say and how you look while saying it. Your voice qualities play a very important role in determining how your words affect the listener. For example, your voice can soothe people or make them angry, thus helping or hindering a situation. The first time people hear you, they are likely to classify you as cheerful or solemn, interesting or dull, lively or lazy.

Since most people in business communicate more frequently by speaking than by writing, voice quality can work for or against you and your company. For example, what is the effect on public relations of a switchboard operator with a voice quality that is irritatingly loud? of a receptionist whose voice is so low that visitors cannot hear half of what has been said? of a salesperson who speaks so slowly that the listener becomes exasperated?

Voice quality is determined by four principal factors: volume, pitch, tone, and tempo. The effectiveness of your voice depends also upon enunciation and pronunciation, as well as upon breath control.

In order to improve your voice, you must be able to control your breathing. Breath control depends both on correct posture and on deep breathing. Good posture enables a person to breathe into the lungs the maximum amount of air and also to control the amount of air expended. Deep breathing adds to the resonance of your tones because you have more air with which to vibrate the vocal chords. Be sure to breathe from the diaphragm, the muscle partition that separates the chest from the abdominal cavity.

Volume. Intensity, force, and volume are all similar words that describe the quality in your voice that enables people to hear you. Speakers must be heard, or they will lose their audience. Since good breath control is so important in providing volume, you should practice correct breathing so that you will not have trouble being heard.

Pitch. Pitch refers to the degree of highness or lowness of a sound. A shrill voice is much too high. A moderately low voice is usually the most pleasing. If your voice is unpleasantly high, you can lower it by making a conscious effort to do so over a long period of time.

If possible, record your voice on a tape recorder and listen to it several times. Try to hear your voice as others hear it, and ask your friends or classmates to criticize it. Practice lowering your voice and then record the same material a second time to see whether there has been any improvement.

Tone. It is your tone that reveals your attitudes and feelings to your listeners. In business relations, as well as in social life, try to use a pleasant and cheerful tone whenever possible. However, variations in tone, as well as in volume and pitch, will add interest to your speech. Think about what you are saying when you are talking or reading orally; then adapting your tone to your meaning will not be difficult.

Tempo. The rate of speed at which you talk is the tempo of your voice. Since your tempo often determines whether your speech is understandable, you should speak at an appropriate rate of speed. Use pauses to stress major points, for they add variety to a speech and also give emphasis to the points you want the listener to remember. By speaking important words slowly and less important words or phrases more rapidly, you contribute to both variety and clarity in your speaking.

Saying Words Correctly and Distinctly

A person applying for a position may be carefully groomed and may give the outward appearance of being a promising employee. But faulty pronunciation and poor enunciation may cost the applicant the position, particularly if the job calls for frequent oral communication with the public, either in person or over the telephone.

Pronunciation means saying words *correctly*, while enunciation means saying words *distinctly*. Both are necessary if you are to be understood and wish to make a good impression on others.

To some of us English is a second language, for we were raised in an area where some other language was spoken primarily. Some of us were brought up in parts of the United States where the language pattern is different from that where we are now living. We should not be ashamed if we speak with an accent. An accent may add character to one's speech and make the voice more colorful and interesting to the listener. Remember that the principal purpose of communication—in whatever form—is to be understood by the person or persons with whom you are communicating. As long as the listener understands you, you are achieving this goal.

Even those brought up in an English-speaking environment make mistakes in enunciation and pronunciation, usually because of carelessness. So regardless of background, everyone needs to make every effort to improve the speaking voice, particularly in the enunciation and pronunciation of words.

Enunciation

Listen to yourself. Do you run words together, leaving out some sounds? Do you say "jeet" for *did you eat?* "hatta" for *had to?* "gonna go" for *going to go?* Poor enunciation results from running words together, from leaving out letters or syllables, or from adding letters or syllables. Let us look first at a group of useful and common words that are sadly mistreated when letters or even whole syllables are dropped.

Lost Consonants. The final consonants most often dropped are *t*, *d*, and *g* when they are in combination with some other consonant. Thus *tact* becomes "tac," *field* becomes "feel," and *being* becomes "been." The *wh* sound, too, frequently is carelessly pronounced; for example, "'wat" for *what*. Practice saying the following phrases aloud until you are sure you do not slight the sounds of the underlined consonants.

arranging pictures	library list
assisting and managing	lingering longingly
attempted bankruptcy	next payment
beyond and beyond	outstanding debt
collect payment	recognized candidacy
competent party	seemingly strict
consigning a consignment	test of strength
current asset	thirty-three
demand payment	threat and threatening
doing typing and working	three hundred
earned a discount	through thick and thin
factual matter	tourist list
first of February	trust fund
kept a strict accounting	while whistling and thinking
length and width	why white wheels

Lost Vowels. When two vowels occur together in a word, the sound of one often tends to be slighted. Thus *li-on* becomes an indistinct "line." A single vowel used as a syllable is frequently overlooked and not sounded. A careless person will say "captal," completely ignoring the single-vowel syllable *i*. Pronounce the word correctly: "cap-i-tal." In the list below be sure to notice each vowel, and be sure you do not lose any vowel sounds when you practice these phrases:

accurate and regular	original company
alphabetic list of liabilities	particularly quiet
cruel lion	popular battery
eleven manufacturers	positive verification
especially positive	ridiculous habit
excellent family	separate poem
family history	singular sophomore
federal cabinet	temporarily separated
generally separately	terrible and trite
indirect and indefinite	usually interesting
indirectly responsible	variable capital
ivory tower	variable regulation
metropolitan area	veteran general
municipal regulation	

Lost Syllables. People who drop consonant and vowel sounds often drop syllables from words too. Such a person "c'lecs stamps" instead of "collects." It is as though the speaker wishes to make a contraction (shortened form like *it's*) out of every word spoken. Try to avoid losing syllables as you practice saying these phrases:

perhaps (not *praps*)	five-year *guarantee* (not *garntee*)
little people (not *lil*)	detailed *itinerary* (not *itinree*)
laboratory technician (not *labatory*)	*generally* acceptable (not *genrally*)
just *obligation* (not *obgation*)	*occasionally* wrong (not *occasionly*)

Addition of Letters or Syllables. The frequent mistake of adding extra sounds is another enunciation fault. As you say aloud the following italicized words, listen carefully to see whether you ordinarily add extra incorrect sounds to them.

a fine *athlete* (not *athalete*)	pop *singer* (not *sing-ger*)
the *height* of fashion (not *heighth*)	fourth *finger* (not *fing-ger*)
across the street (not *acrost*)	*disastrous* results (not *disasterous*)
broken *umbrella* (not *umberella*)	*entrance* examination (not *enterance*)
one roll of *film* (not *filum*)	a *hindrance* to progress (not *hinderance*)
drowned duck (not *drownded*)	a *mischievous* child (not *mischievious*)
grievous fault (not *grievious*)	a good *preventive* (not *preventative*)
rhythm for dancing (not *rhythum*)	a *burglar* alarm (not *burgular*)

One remedy for these types of enunciation errors is giving attention to spelling. If you spell these words correctly, you will be more likely to pronounce them correctly and enunciate them distinctly. If you misspell them, you may also mispronounce them.

Some Troublemakers. Some words are more difficult to enunciate than others. They require an even slower rate of speech, to allow maximum use of jaw, lips, and tongue. You will be surprised to know that most of these words are short three- to five-letter words. They usually include one or more sounds that are difficult to distinguish. Thus, *ache* requires both the long *a* sound and a definite hard *k* sound.

Most of your practice so far has been with phrases and sentences. Now practice pronouncing the following words out of context so that each one of them is clear.

ache	corn	fine	kit	nap	peat	tang
at	darn	gas	kite	nick	race	tent
balk	earn	grow	lay	oils	scab	very
big	else	heed	map	our	sign	wag
climb	fill	jam	nab	path	tan	wield

Pronunciation

All of us learned to talk by imitating the speech of those around us: first, of members of the family; then, of neighbors and friends; later, of schoolmates, teachers, coworkers, and others with whom we came in contact. Of course, many of us have moved from one part of the country to another and have changed our original pronunciation and other speech habits to conform to those characteristic of the region in which we now live. Thus our present speech patterns reflect the wide variety of social, cultural, regional, and other influences to which we have been exposed.

Variations in Pronunciation. Who decides whether a particular pronunciation is correct? Your answer most likely will be "the dictionary." However, this answer is only partially correct.

As indicated in the preface of explanatory notes of the dictionary, it is impractical and unnecessary for a dictionary to show all the pronunciations that are in use for a particular word. Most dictionaries show only the one or two pronunciations that occur with the greatest frequency among educated speakers. Since all of us can understand those pronunciations and agree that they are not incorrect, even though many of them may not be the pronunciations that we ourselves use, all of us tend to view them as the standard, or correct, pronunciations.

Pronunciation Difficulties

In addition to regional and other differences in speech, certain types of incorrect pronunciations are quite common. They may be grouped according to the following categories.

Incorrect Vowel Sounds. Many words are not pronounced correctly because certain vowels are sounded wrong.

The Sound of Long U. The use of the ōō sound instead of the correct long *u* sound (heard in *human*) is a common error. It makes a decidedly unpleasant impression on listeners who are speech-conscious.

Read the following words aloud, concentrating on using the long *u* sound.

annuity	humor	New York
beauty	institution	numerous
culinary	latitude	revenue
dubious	longitude	student
due	multitude	substitute
duke	neuralgia	substitution
duly	neuritis	suitable
duty	neurotic	tube
futile	new	tutor

Troubles With A. In another group of words the sound of long *a* (the sound in *hate*) is incorrectly replaced by the sound of short *a* (the sound in *hat*).

The following words are typical of this group. Again, read the list aloud.

āviator	gāla	stātus
blātant	ignorāmus	tenācious
dāta	lātent	ultimātum
flāgrant	rādiator	verbātim

In the following words the short *a* should be used instead of the long *a*.

Ărab	păgeant	păgination
deprăvity	măltreat	Spokăne

Troubles With I. In some words the sound of long *i*, as heard in *wide*, is incorrectly replaced by the short *i* sound heard in *hit*.

alumnī	grīmy	stīpend

On the other hand, in the following words the short *i* rather than the long *i* should be used.

Ĭtalian	respĭte

Substituting One Vowel for Another. In another type of mispronunciation, an entirely different vowel is substituted for the correct one. In the following words the underscored letters are often replaced. Read the list aloud, clearly enunciating the underlined letters. If in doubt about any pronunciation, consult your dictionary. The mispronunciations involved here are often closely linked with misspellings.

acc<u>u</u>rate	d<u>e</u>spair	esc<u>a</u>lator
d<u>e</u>scription	d<u>i</u>vide	exist<u>e</u>nce

just	percolator	restaurant
mathematics	permanent	sacrilegious
optimistic	preparation	separate
particular	privilege	

Incorrect Accent. Many pronunciation errors are caused by placing the stress, or accent, on the wrong syllable of a word.

In the following words the accent should be on the *first* syllable.

'ad-mirable	'dic-tionary	'in-teresting
'am-icable	'for-midable	'pref-erable
'ap-plicable	'in-famous	'the-ater
'com-parable		

In these words the accent should be on the *second* syllable.

con-'do-lence	ir-'rev-ocable	om-'nip-otence
de-'mon-strative	ob-'lig-atory	su-'per-fluous
ex-'traor-dinary		

In these words the accent should be on the *final* syllable.

| automo-'bile | di-'rect | rou-'tine (*n.*) |
| bou-'quet | po-'lice | |

Silent Letters. Among the chief stumbling blocks to correct spelling are silent letters, which occur in many of our most frequently used words. Because we do not hear these letters, they do not constitute a serious threat to correct pronunciation. However, there are a few important words in which letters that should be silent are often sounded. As you read aloud the following words, make a special effort *not* to sound the letters that are underscored.

almond	mortgage	salmon	vehement
corps	often	salve	vehicle
indict	posthumous	sword	

Just Plain Tricky. Many words often mispronounced cannot be classified under any of the above listings. There is only one way of mastering the correct pronunciations of these offenders. Concentrate on each one, first looking up the word in your dictionary and then repeating the word many times. Here are sample words of this type.

absorb	association	clothes
absurd	attorney	codicil
apron	bona fide	column
associate	censure	congratulations

coupon	luxury	perspiration
deaf	martial	possess
denunciate	medieval	prerogative
err	mercantile	quay
gist	Nebraska	reservoir
homogenous	once	soot
hundred	partner	strength
library	preemptory	suppose
luxurious	perhaps	tremendous

Some Tips to Help You

These miscellaneous suggestions will help you in your battle against mispronunciation and poor enunciation.

1. Be especially careful in pronouncing personal names. People resent having their names mispronounced just as they resent having them misspelled. Make an effort to learn the correct pronunciation of a person's name and to follow that preference. Don't be afraid to ask people for the correct pronunciations of their names.

2. Likewise, be careful in pronouncing geographic names. Often, the spelling is no guide to pronunciation. If you are uncertain, check the gazetteer in your dictionary. Following are a few geographic names that bear watching. You may be surprised when you verify their pronunciations.

Abilene	Edinburgh	Lima (Peru)	Southampton
Worcester	Haverhill	Marseilles	Valparaiso
Cannes	Houston	Norfolk	Versailles
Cherbourg	Illinois	Salina	Ypsilanti

3. Be especially careful with foreign words and phrases. Some very amusing (and embarrassing) mistakes can be made by pronouncing them, especially French words, as they are spelled. The dictionary gives the closest approximation possible to the English sounds.

4. Guard against running words together, making such sounds as "wotcha doon?" (what are you doing?), "shoulda" (should have), "willyuh?" (will you?), or "jeet?" (did you eat?). Nothing more quickly brands a person as careless, if not illiterate, as does sloppy enunciation.

5. When you learn a new word, learn its correct pronunciation at once. In other words, when you look up the spelling and meaning of a word, notice also its pronunciation and practice saying it correctly.

6. When you speak to a group of people, speak more slowly than you do in ordinary conversation and enunciate carefully.

If you faithfully carry out the suggestions outlined in this unit, you will soon find that your improved speaking qualities will improve your relations with people.

COMMUNICATION LABORATORY

APPLICATION EXERCISES

A. Ask yourself the following questions to determine how you set your stage for speaking. Answer each question with *usually*, *sometimes*, or *rarely*. Compare your answers with other members of the class to see whether they agree with you. Then make a list of the items needing improvement.

My Personality

1. Do I like to be with other people and make the first move to gain other acquaintances?
2. Do I look for ways to say complimentary things about people to them and others?
3. Am I understanding of the ways other people act or think, and do I avoid direct criticism and argument?
4. Am I positive and optimistic instead of gloomy and pessimistic when presented with a new problem or situation?
5. Do other people like to be in my company because I am likable and friendly?

First Impressions

1. Do I try to find ways of being helpful to other people and sympathetic to their problems?
2. Do I steer clear of controversial topics when I enter into a conversation with a new acquaintance?
3. Do I consciously think about other people's interests and their comforts when I converse with them?
4. Do I take the first step to meet, greet, and introduce strangers?
5. Do I avoid talking about personal problems, strong personal likes or dislikes, rumors, and personal prejudices when I first meet someone?

My Personal Appearance

1. Do I know what appropriate dress is?
2. Am I careful about cleanliness and good grooming?
3. Do I usually feel well dressed?
4. Are my clothes clean, pressed, and in good repair?
5. Do my personal health habits contribute to my appearance?

My Facial Expressions

1. Do I avoid showing indifference or nervousness toward others in my facial expressions?

2. Do I refrain from allowing my facial expression to reflect my personal problems or sad feelings?
3. When I first meet people, does my facial expression reveal genuine interest?
4. Do my facial expressions reveal the way I want to be understood?
5. Am I willing to allow my facial expression to reflect how I think instead of remaining deadpan and noncommittal?

My Mannerisms

1. Does the way I move about suggest alertness rather than lack of interest?
2. Is my posture straight without being stiff?
3. When I walk, is my weight well distributed on both legs?
4. Do I control meaningless gestures when I talk?
5. Do my movements suggest control rather than uncertainty, fright, and nervousness?

B. Conduct an informal survey of persons you know who are employed in business offices. In your survey you would like to determine:

1. Whether there are dress and grooming rules enforced in their offices.
2. What rules there are for men.
3. What rules there are for women.
4. How strictly these rules are enforced.
5. What happens if someone does not abide by the rules.

Be prepared to contribute your findings in a class discussion and to indicate your feelings regarding these regulations.

C. In pantomime express before the class some mannerisms (walking, hand movements, facial expressions) that would distract and limit communication. Then express the opposite positive characteristics. Was the class able to identify the points you were trying to make?

D. Your supervisor, upon his return from a three-day business trip, requests a list of the people who have telephoned the office during his absence. As you read the following names and telephone numbers, remember to make maximum use of your jaw, lips, and tongue in pronouncing each name. You may want to spell difficult names. For example: "Agawam Shoe Company (Agawam A-g-a-w-a-m) of Springfield, Massachusetts. Ms. Lillian Bohack (B-o-h-a-c-k), the sales manager, would like you to telephone her at (617) 555-9765."

Company and City	Person Calling	Telephone Number
Clauswitz and Cox Associates Haverhill, Massachusetts	John Clauswitz	(617) 555-7312

Company and City	Person Calling	Telephone Number
Gurson & Byron P.C. Elko, Nevada	Cecil Byron, Auditor	(702) 555-6453
Marketing Assistance Co. Oswego, New York	Joseph Wilton	(315) 555-7815
McElkiney Corp. Severna Park, Maryland	Judson Sims	(301) 555-2777
Excello Corporation Olympia, Washington	Barton Brandt	(206) 555-3004

E. In assisting with inventory taking in your firm, you are responsible for reading the quantities and stock numbers of some of the merchandise remaining on the shelves. Work with a partner. One of you reads from the previous inventory list, while the other checks the merchandise. Make certain you speak clearly. Be sure that the two lists agree, noting any errors in numbers or quantities of merchandise as you read the following information.

From the Inventory List		Merchandise on the Shelf	
Quantity	*Stock Numbers*	*Quantity*	*Stock Numbers*
6 cartons	73X1177	70 yards	91X3613
70 yards	91X3614	25 feet	11XR9197
12 dozen	73X6621	12 each	1SX6216Y
25 feet	11XXR9197	12 dozen	73X6621
10 each	1SX6215Y	6 cartons	73X1177

F. Each of the following words means one thing when accented on the first syllable and something else when accented on the final syllable. Write definitions for the words in each pair and then indicate the part of speech of each word.

1. absent	4. combine	7. object
2. project	5. progress	8. extract
3. digest	6. contract	9. contest

VOCABULARY AND SPELLING STUDIES

A. These words are often confused: *wave, waive; later, latter; biannual, biennial.* Explain the differences.

B. Which of the following place names are misspelled?

1. Poughkeepsie, New York
2. Eerie, Pensylvania
3. Cincinati, Ohio
4. DeMoines, Iowa

5. Huston, Texas
6. San Fransisco, California

C. What letter(s) should appear in the blank space in each of these words?

1. g__rd
2. ex__ust
3. fr__d
4. ex__rbitant
5. facil__tate
6. perform__nce

D. A letter or syllable has been either added or dropped from each of the following words. Spell each word correctly.

1. labratory
2. strenth
3. brillant
4. probly
5. temperture
6. surender
7. canidate
8. suprise
9. paralel

E. Match the definitions in the left-hand column with the foreign words and phrases in the right-hand column. Then look up the pronunciation of each of the foreign words or phrases.

1. troika
2. ennui
3. ingenue
4. ne plus ultra
5. junta
6. cognoscenti
7. hoi polloi
8. a priori

a. the common people
b. an actress who plays a naive young girl
c. the best possible
d. boredom
e. a council that governs
f. presupposed through experience
g. the knowledgeable
h. three who govern

COMMUNICATING FOR RESULTS

Making Decisions. Mr. Alberts, your employer, has just left the office to keep an appointment with a customer. The customer telephones the office and says: "Please tell Mr. Alberts that my wife has been in an automobile accident, and I won't be able to keep our appointment. I will telephone tomorrow to reschedule." Mr. Alberts is by now at the airport, getting ready to board a plane leaving in 55 minutes for Sacramento, where the meeting of the two was to take place. How would you get in touch with Mr. Alberts so that he will not take the flight unnecessarily?

U · N · I · T

56 Giving a Talk

You will probably have to talk before an audience sometime, if you have not already done so. Does this idea bother you? Many people have a fear of getting up before a group of people and giving a talk. Instead, they should feel complimented by any invitation to speak. The very fact that you are asked to give a talk indicates that someone believes that your ideas or experiences will be of interest and value to others and that you will do a good job.

The length and nature of talks vary. You may be asked for some brief remarks to introduce another speaker, or you may be asked to be a member of a panel discussion group. On the other hand, you may be invited to give a five- or ten-minute talk or even to present a longer speech at a meeting. Your success in any one of these roles will depend upon how carefully you plan your presentation. Only with careful planning will you be able to develop the feeling of confidence that will enable you to communicate your ideas to others, for an effective talk is the result of more than just knowing your subject. Not only do good speakers know what they are talking about, but also they know how to prepare and deliver the speech. Effective speakers have learned the best techniques of preparing and giving a talk, the techniques that you will learn in this unit.

Guides to Effective Preparation

Every good talk requires careful preparation. The speaker-to-be must be ready to cover the subject thoroughly and must carefully organize the presentation. Use the following guidelines to help you prepare your talk.

Determine Your Purpose and Topic. First of all, you must know the purpose of your talk. Are you going to inform, explain, convince, entertain, or combine two or more of these purposes? Only when you know *why* you are going to talk will you be able to select the subject of the talk. Ask yourself these questions:

1. Why was I asked to speak to this audience?
2. What is the occasion and reason for this meeting?
3. How long am I expected to talk?
4. What does the group expect to gain from listening to me?

5. Am I personally in harmony with the interests and background of this group?
6. How can I capture the audience's interest?

The answers to these questions will guide you in selecting a topic that will be timely and interesting.

Adapt Your Talk to the Audience. Who is your audience? What is their age range, sex, educational and social background, economic status, experience? What are their interests? A talk presented before one group may have little appeal for another group. For example, a discussion of modern office design that would be exciting to office workers might cause a group of athletes or truck drivers to go to sleep. Failure to know and to consider the audience can destroy the effectiveness of the talk.

Limit Your Subject. Don't select a two-hour subject for a ten-minute speech! It is better to make two or three specific points in a talk—and do the job well—than to ramble on about too broad a topic. The secretary who talked about "The Computer in Today's Office" would have presented a more interesting talk on a more limited topic, such as "How I Use Word Processing." Limit your subject so that you can emphasize two or three important points in the time allotted to you.

Collect and Organize Your Materials. Collect much more information about your subject than you will use. Use 3-by-5 cards to jot down ideas. Use your own personal experiences; talk with people who can help you; read newspapers, magazines, and books. Take good notes from as many sources as you can. As you organize the material you have collected, you will be able to select the most important ideas to include in your outline.

If the use of visual materials (transparencies, for example) or handouts (duplicated materials) will make your presentation more effective, carefully prepare these materials and determine at what point they may best be used.

Prepare Your Outline. A good outline is a "must" in preparing a talk. Prepare notes on cards first. Then arrange and rearrange them according to major ideas and order of importance. In the following example note that only important ideas are included in the outline.

DETERMINING CAREER AVENUES

I. Introduction:
    A. Thank chairperson for complimentary introduction.
    B. Explain personal interest in topic.
    C. Explain importance of topic to all young people.
    D. Preview the major points to be made:
        1. Do an inventory of interests and abilities.
        2. Learn about jobs that are of interest.
        3. Observe people doing these jobs.

   II. Take an inventory of interests and abilities:
     A. Indoor person or outdoor person?
     B. Working with people or alone?
     C. Concentration or action?
  III. Learn about jobs that are of interest:
     A. Read about the jobs.
     B. Talk with people who do such jobs.
  IV. Observe people doing these jobs:
     A. Ask to be an observer.
     B. Observe a typical day.
     C. Ask questions.
     D. Honestly judge your reactions to what you saw.
   V. Conclusion of presentation:
     A. Summarize principal points.
     B. Express appreciation for audience attention.

Arouse and Hold Interest. The success of your talk will depend on how well you are able to arouse and hold the interest of your audience. Make sure that you have variety and pep in your talk. Insert an amusing story here and there. Emphasize new ideas. You can hold interest by using personal experiences and examples. Your talk should have a certain element of suspense as the plot unfolds. Complicated ideas, such as figures or statistics, should be omitted, simplified, or supplemented by charts and graphs. As you prepare your talk, consider carefully how you will arouse and hold the group's interest.

Talk; Don't Read or Recite. How should you prepare your talk? Should you write your speech word for word? use only your outline? use notes on 3-by-5 cards? plan to talk without notes? These methods are all used by speakers to prepare their talks. Some people prefer not to speak from a written manuscript because they feel that their talk will sound stilted. Whatever method you select, be sure that your talk will sound natural—not like an oral reading or a class recitation.

    A written talk will be of value as you practice your presentation. It will enable you to fix each idea in your memory and to time your delivery. Having memorized the *what* and *how* of your talk, you can then use brief notes when you deliver it.

Practice, Practice, Practice. As you practice, try to anticipate the conditions of the actual talk. Imagine your audience in front of you. Stand tall and look at the audience. Talk loud enough for the person in the farthest corner of the auditorium to hear you. Make slow and deliberate movements. Use hand gestures sparingly, and then only if they seem natural to you. If a mirror is available, practice your talk in front of it. The person you see there should be the severest critic of your facial expressions and your platform appearance. Perhaps you can enlist the help of family and friends, too, to listen and offer suggestions. Don't be satisfied with your practice until the talk flows along from idea to idea without the aid of a written script.

Guides to Effective Delivery

Now that you have planned and practiced your talk, are you ready to deliver it to the audience? Study the following tips carefully. These pointers will help you present most effectively the thoughts and ideas that you have so carefully prepared. They represent the principles of effective speaking to groups; and if you know them and use them, your audiences will say, "What a fine speaker!"

Hide Your Nervousness. Face the fact that you will be nervous as you wait for your introduction. But remain confident, knowing that you have carefully prepared your talk. If you find that you have stage fright, take a deep breath before opening your mouth. The deep breath will help relax your vocal cords. Speakers who are not at all anxious are either those who give talks often or those who do not know enough to be nervous. Controlled nervous anticipation is good for you. It will key you up and give your delivery some sparkle and liveliness.

Check Your Volume. You know how annoyed, disinterested, and bored listeners become if they can't hear the speaker. Don't create this problem for your audience. If possible before the meeting, check your volume in the room where you are to speak. Have someone stand in the back of the room to tell you whether you can be heard perfectly. If you cannot make this test or if you sense that the audience cannot hear you, ask at the beginning of your talk whether everyone can hear; then adjust your volume accordingly. If a microphone is used, be sure you know how to use it.

Keep Your Head Up. Good speakers hold their heads high. This position gives an appearance of authority and helps the speaker project the voice better. Your words are more likely to reach your listeners instead of being lost as they fall to the floor.

Use a Conversational Tone. Remember that you are talking to an audience, not giving an oration. Your voice should reflect the warm, easy, conversational tone that you would use if you were talking to a group of your very good friends. Also, remember that you will destroy any warmth created by your tone if you allow a critical, scolding, or sarcastic note to creep in.

Look at Your Audience. An audience responds favorably to a speaker who seems to be talking directly to each person in the audience. One way of making your listeners feel that you are talking to each one individually is to look directly at the assembled people. Look at those in the middle section, then those to the right, and then those to the left. As you look, you may see nothing but a blur, a mass of faces. Let your eyes rest on different sections of the blur, and the audience will feel that you are giving a person-to-person talk. And, with experience, you will begin to see the faces and expressions of individual listeners. Find a focus point and use it.

Stand at Ease. How you stand and what you do with your hands will help or hinder your presentation. If possible, stand behind a lectern (a speaker's stand). The lectern will provide a place for you to put your notes. Avoid holding them, for nervousness may cause the papers to rattle like leaves in a storm. To keep your hands from getting in the way, grasp the lectern on each side or occasionally hold your hands behind your back. If you shift your weight from one hip to the other when you are nervous, train yourself to stand with your weight evenly distributed on both feet.

Avoid Mannerisms. Mannerisms such as playing with objects, clearing the throat or wetting the lips, repeating "uh" or "and" frequently, and overusing slang expressions are objectionable to audiences. If you do not know whether you have such mannerisms, ask some of your friends to watch and listen and report any they observe. A speaker with even one annoying habit cannot give the best possible talk, for mannerisms distract the audience and obstruct the thoughts the speaker is trying to convey.

Use Only the Time Allotted. If you are asked to talk for five minutes, don't talk for six minutes. A program with several speakers is usually timed to the last minute; anyone who does not keep to the time limit forces other speakers to shorten their talks. Not only are long-winded talkers thought inconsiderate; they are also marked as egotistical. They think that what they have to say is so important that the other speakers can be disregarded. To avoid going over the time limit, you might ask the presiding officer of the meeting to give you warning when you have only one minute left.

Observe Audience Reaction. You can and should train yourself to watch the audience as you speak and to be sensitive to its changing moods. If, as you talk, you see blankness or boredom on the faces before you, this signal tells you that your listeners need perking up. You might then tell one of the amusing stories you keep in reserve. Remember, however, that jokes are only effective if used intelligently.

If your audience seems tired, if the hour is late, or if the previous talks have been overlong, you have two choices: accept the situation as a challenge and give such an interesting and sparkling performance that everyone perks right up, or have pity on your audience and cut your talk to the bare essentials. Sometimes it is better to omit part of a speech rather than give it before a weary audience.

Carefully Select the Closing Words. Inexperienced talkers often give themselves away by lowering their voices as they say the last few words or by dashing off the ending in a hurried rattle. Of course, a beginner is happy to see the end in sight and is eager to get the ordeal over. What a pity, though, to spoil the effect of an otherwise fine talk with a poor ending!

Remember to keep your pitch up and to observe good timing to the very end.

COMMUNICATION LABORATORY

APPLICATION EXERCISES

A. From the following job titles, select one in which you are particularly interested. Collect information about the job, particularly the duties performed by someone in that job who has the skills that the job demands. Prepare an outline for a 5-minute talk. Prepare your talk and present it in class. (If none of these titles appeals to you, select your own job title.)

Accountant or auditor   Administrative assistant   Paralegal
Sales representative   Computer programmer   Bookkeeper
Teacher   Word processing operator   Receptionist

B. The following major topics were taken from notes for a talk entitled "Effective Business Speaking." Assume that you are going to give the talk. Arrange the notes in order of increasing importance, placing the least important idea first and the most important idea last. Be prepared to justify your selection of the three least important ideas and the three most important ideas.

The good speaker can motivate others; the good speaker can avoid mistakes and misunderstandings; good speaking skills impress customers; the good speaker gains personal satisfaction by being listened to; the good speaker can easily explain to coworkers what has to be done; the ability to express oneself brings one to the attention of management; a good speaker can get others to act on his or her ideas; the good speaker can help the company make a favorable impression upon the public.

C. List the three most important topics you selected in Exercise B. Then explain how you would go about preparing information that would allow you to develop each point.

VOCABULARY AND SPELLING STUDIES

A. These words are often confused: *censor, censure; read, reed, red.* Explain the differences.

B. Use either *sometime, some time,* or *sometimes* to complete each of the following sentences.

1. _____ next week I will complete the project I started.
2. I have already spent _____ working on it.

3. _____ he is late arriving at the office.
4. Do you have _____ to devote to helping me?
5. All workers need _____ for relaxation.

C. Correct the error in the use of the underscored word in each of the following sentences.

1. Jamie Lee is the soul owner of this business.
2. You have no rite to question my integrity.
3. The payment on your note will soon be overdo.
4. How will the new policy effect your salary?
5. All your efforts to change his thinking were in vein.

COMMUNICATING FOR RESULTS

Storyteller. A good conversationalist has a knack for relating an incident that is of interest to listeners: a strange or unusual happening, an embarrassing moment, a humorous occurrence, a recounting that sheds some light on human nature. From your own personal experience, select one such event to describe to your class. Limit yourself to 1 minute.

U · N · I · T

57
Speaking With and Without Electronic Equipment

In the office of yesterday communication was limited to face-to-face communication, pen and pencil, the typewriter, the telephone, and recording devices. Today's office still uses these methods, but it has expanded their use and added new ones. Today's offices have rightly been referred to as "electronic" offices.

As a prospective business employee, you have already learned the importance of oral communication in both the internal and the external affairs of a successful business operation. However, you must be aware of how various improvements in technology affect the communication process of today's business world. The basic elements of effective communication still apply, and will always apply, regardless of the technological improvements that are taking place daily. Effective communication must still be complete, clear, concise, correct, and courteous. And, above all, the human relations techniques must still be applied in all our dealings with people, regardless of their roles either inside or outside the business itself.

Almost all business employees have some contact with the public, either face-to-face or by telephone. As a business employee, you undoubtedly will meet and talk with the public frequently—to make reservations for travel; to receive money from, or to disburse money to, banks and business; to receive or place orders for services or repairs; to receive complaints and make adjustments; to provide or obtain information; and so on. Millions of people earn their livings primarily by meeting the public in person or on the telephone. Your first step in preparing yourself to meet the public is to give careful attention to the basic rules for dealing with callers. In addition, you need to learn how these rules may be applied to meeting a caller in person and to meeting the public by telephone.

Basic Rules for Meeting the Public

The rules for meeting the public—in person or by telephone—are based on courtesy, consideration, and friendliness. These are the same qualities that make a visitor in your home feel welcome, comfortable, and at ease. Applied specifically to business callers, the rules include those discussed below.

Give Prompt Attention to Callers. A caller's presence should be recognized immediately. Telephones should be answered promptly, before the second ring if possible. Have you ever waited and waited for a telephone call to be answered? Have you ever had to stand and wait for someone to attend to you in a store and felt completely ignored? If so, you know that you became increasingly uncomfortable, even angry, as you waited. You hung up the telephone, or you turned on your heel and walked out of the store. In a well-run business this does not happen. Salespeople, for example, are trained to recognize a caller immediately. A clerk busy with one customer will glance and nod at a waiting customer or say pleasantly, "I'll be with you in a moment." Then callers know that they are not being overlooked. As you meet the public, you must follow the same procedure and give prompt attention to all callers.

Greet Callers Pleasantly. The tone of voice you use to greet people should be cheerful and friendly. Even an angry caller will feel better hearing your pleasant, "Good morning, Mr. Kenney. How nice of you to call." Of course, if you don't mean what you say, it is best not to say it; your tone of voice and your facial expressions will often reveal that you are not sincere.

If possible, vary your greeting to fit the visitor. Treat all visitors as though they were special in some way—as they are! Try also to make the greeting fit the occasion. For example, a car dealer approaching a customer behind the wheel of a new demonstrator might say, "It's a comfortable feeling to sit behind the wheel of a new car, isn't it?" One of the following greetings may fit other situations: "Good morning." "What may I show you?" "Whom do you wish to see?" "How may I help you?" "What a pleasant surprise!" "We were expecting you." "How nice of you to call." "How are you today?" Just adding the name of the person, if you know it, will tailor the greeting for each caller. Often, too, the same words may be varied by a change in emphasis or in the way they are said.

Treat All Callers as Honored Guests. Be friendly and courteous to everyone. Never let a caller's voice or appearance influence what you say. Some very important people do not dress expensively, and not everyone has had the advantage of voice training. All callers deserve the same courteous and considerate treatment.

Prepare yourself for an occasional irritable or even rude caller. Treat such people with an understanding smile and gloss over their discourtesies. You represent the firm, and these people are your guests. If you must make some response, express sympathy: "I'm sorry you feel that way." Your own graciousness will often soften the caller's anger and might even make the caller friendly again towad you and your company.

Obtain Needed Information. Before you can refer a caller to someone else, you must find out the caller's name and the reason for the call. You can then relay this information to your boss, who will determine specifically who will handle the call.

Because people sometimes resent being asked about their business, you may need a lot of tact to get the needed information without harming pleasant relations. To a telephone caller you might say, "May I tell Miss Chan who is calling, please?" When greeting a caller in person, you might point a pen over a pad and say pleasantly, "Your name is . . . ?" And, as you write the name on the pad, you will probably repeat, "Oh, yes, Ms. Olga Komorov." Next you would ask, "And you would like to see Mrs. Nevsky about . . . ?" and also write her answer on your pad. Filling in a leading question is a natural thing to do, so your caller usually will freely and willingly supply the information you need.

Save the Caller's Time. Let callers know if they have to wait. On the telephone, if the wait is to be longer than two or three minutes, it is usually better to take the number and call back. You can say: "I'll have to get the information from the files, Mr. Fosse. It will take about five minutes to do so. May I have your number and call you back?"

Let callers know how long they must wait, even if it is a relatively short time. You might say: "I'm sorry, but Mr. Stavas will not be available for at least another hour. Would you like to make an appointment for later?" or "Mr. Stavas is in a meeting but should be free in about five minutes." Callers will appreciate this courtesy.

Be Discreet. Protect your employer in what you say—and in what you don't say. If your manager is late in arriving at the office, for example, don't say, "Mr. Greenberg has not come in yet this morning." The tactful thing to say is: "Mr. Greenberg is not in the office just now. I expect him in a few minutes." Make certain that your remarks reflect favorably on your employer.

Protect your employer's business, also. Certain business information is confidential, and you must keep it so. Imagine what a visitor would think of your company (and you) if you were indiscreet enough to say, "Business is so poor that Mr. Greenberg had to let some workers go last week." A prospective customer would not be favorably impressed! So be discreet in what you say on the telephone and in person.

Keep Within Your Authority. Know the limits of your authority and don't exceed them. If you think your company will replace a defective part, for example, but it is not your responsibility to make adjustments, don't say: "Certainly we'll replace this for you. Just take it to the service manager." Both you and your company will be embarrassed if for some reason the service manager is unable to make the adjustment. Keep within your authority by saying, "Why don't you talk with Ms. Courtney, the service manager?" Be sure you know the names of the people in your company who are authorized to make various kinds of decisions. You can then help callers by referring them to the appropriate person, and you will be keeping within your authority.

Say "No" Gracefully. Some decisions you must convey to callers will be unfavorable to them. Be pleasant but firm. Your knowledge of how to say "no" in a letter will help you. Review Unit 44 so that when you must refuse a caller, you can do so without losing goodwill.

Show a Genuine Desire to Serve. An extra courtesy or some thoughtful touch should be extended to guests to make their visit memorable. In business, too, you should be on the lookout for the little extra that makes the difference. Think, for example, how much an out-of-town visitor might appreciate your offer to reconfirm a returning flight. "While you're talking with Mr. Lugo, I'll call the airline to reconfirm your reservation." This kind of added service helps to make new customers and helps to keep current customers coming back.

With these basic rules in mind, you are ready to receive the public—in person or by telephone. When greeting callers, however, you need to know certain additional techniques.

Telephone Techniques

Telephone techniques differ somewhat from techniques for greeting callers in person because of the nature of telephone conversation and the technical equipment used.

A telephone caller is unable to see the other person's facial expressions or surroundings and must depend entirely upon the voice at the other end of the line. In voice-to-voice meetings, therefore, you should remember the following guidelines.

Identify Yourself Immediately. Callers cannot see you. They need to know whether they have the right number, company, or person. A switchboard operator usually identifies only the firm's name: "Ashe and Levin" or "This is Trend Office Supply Company." In answering an office or departmental telephone, identify both the office and yourself. You might say: "Dr. Gold's office, Joan O'Loughlin speaking"; "Personnel, Arthur Oliver"; or "Good morning. This is the Advertising Department, Morton Damson speaking." "Accounting, Bromberg" is technically correct, but the abruptness of the identification might confuse some people, and the purpose of this identification is to indicate who you are. Whatever greeting you use, remember that on the telephone you must identify yourself at once.

Keep the Caller Informed. Telephone callers can't see what is happening, so you must tell them. If you must leave the line to get some information, excuse yourself, saying, "I can find that information in just a few moments, if you wish to hold the line." Of course, all delays must be explained, and best business practice requires that you report to the caller every minute. You can make an appropriate remark, such as "We're still trying to locate Mrs. Leland" or "I'm sorry, Mrs. Leland is still talking on the other line. Do you wish to wait, or shall I have her call you?"

You must also let your callers know that you are following what they are saying. In person you might nod your head; on the telephone your voice must do the notifying. You can show that you are listening attentively by simple responses such as "yes" or "I see."

Be Ready to Write Information. Have pencil, paper, and message forms ready for use near the telephone. Then you won't delay the caller with, "Will you wait while I get a pencil?" Be sure, too, to verify the message. For example, after taking the message "Wants refrigerator serviced free under CS contract—wants service *today*," you would verify the information by saying: "You would like Mr. Ortega to call you regarding free servicing of your refrigerator under our company service contract, Mrs. Spanswick— and you want service today. Let's see, you spell your name S-P-A-N-S-W-I-C-K? And your number is 555-6212? Thank you. Good-bye."

How to Use the Telephone. The telephone is a sensitive instrument. Knowing how to use it correctly will enable you to greet telephone callers courteously and efficiently. Follow these suggestions:

1. Hold your lips about an inch from the mouthpiece. Don't let the mouthpiece slip down under your chin, and don't cut off your voice by holding your hand over the mouthpiece.

2. Adjust your voice to the equipment. Remember, you don't have to shout over the telephone. Use your natural voice. But enunciate clearly so that you will be understood.

3. Transfer calls efficiently and quickly. To transfer a call from the outside to another extension within the company, say to the caller, "If you will hold for just a moment, I'll have your call transferred." How you get the attention of the operator depends on the phone system in your company. Usually you should simply depress the cradle button once—firmly. When the operator answers, say, "Please transfer this call to Ms. Andrews on Extension 4893."

4. Avoid irritating mechanical noises. If you must leave the line, place the receiver on a book or magazine. The noise made when the receiver is bumped or dropped on a desk is magnified over the wire and will not be appreciated by the caller. At the completion of a call, place the receiver gently in the cradle. Of course, the courteous person will allow the caller to replace the receiver first.

Voice Input for Electronic Devices

The modern office frequently makes use of dictating and transcribing equipment in place of face-to-face dictation methods because of the many advantages of using such equipment. Among these advantages are the following:

1. Stenographers can save time from usual shorthand dictation. If a stenographer is a rapid and accurate typist and a good proofreader, these skills are all one must have for transcribing dictation from a dictating machine.

2. Writers of letters and reports can dictate their materials at any time or in any place rather than waiting for the availability of a secretary or stenographer to take the dictation. Even at home, after regular working hours at the office, or "on the road," preparation of letters and reports need not be delayed while awaiting the physical presence of an individual to take dictation.

Computers and Voice Input. A great deal of today's office activity involves the use of computers for communicating the written word in networks (groups of computers within one business organization) or with data banks (sources of all types of information stored on large computers at another location) or with other computers outside the business organization originating the communicating (from one business to another business).

Until recently this communication has been limited to the typed word. However, today computers may be activated by the human voice (called "invoice input") and material inserted into the computer with oral commands. The voice input is able to tell the computer what to do and how to do it. Furthermore, the voice input can provide the information that is to be transcribed into a written document—a letter, a memorandum, a report, or some form of telecommunication. In other words, with voice-activation computer software, you will be able to dictate a letter to the computer and tell it what style to use, how many copies to make, and how the letter is to be sent. It may even do the actual transmitting. As voice activation for computers is further developed, effective oral communication will become more and more important.

Guidelines for Voice Input

Whether the voice is to be used for dictation face-to-face or to a dictating machine or to activate and instruct a computer, there are certain guidelines that must be adhered to if the finished product is to be acceptable.

1. Plan in advance what you want to say—how the job is to be performed, what you want to include in the document to be prepared, and the general details regarding its preparation.
2. Practice using the equipment—the telephone, the dictating equipment, the computer—correctly and efficiently. The instructional manual that accompanies the equipment is one important source that should be consulted.
3. Give the individual or machine the necessary instructions for performing the job to be done.
4. Speak clearly and slowly and at a pitch that will not distort the voice. This action involves enunciating each syllable and correctly accenting and pronouncing each word. (See Unit 55.)
5. Specify the spelling of any proper names, unusual words, and words that may be confused, such as homonyms.
6. Indicate the beginning of each new paragraph and the placement of any tables or lists that are to be inserted.
7. Include proper punctuation marks, since machines do not know how to punctuate and all individuals do not always agree on what is necessary punctuation.
8. List specifically any special instructions regarding the number of copies required and the method of transmitting, as well as any enclosures to be included.

COMMUNICATION LABORATORY

APPLICATION EXERCISES

A. Your office manager asks you to write a one-page memo that summarizes the correct procedures to be followed by all office workers who receive telephone calls. As you plan your memorandum, give special attention to the following points:

1. Be prompt in answering calls
2. Get and give proper identification
3. Treat callers as honored guests

4. Establish ways to handle delays
5. Obtain needed information from callers

B. Assume that you work as an assistant to the sales director of a large firm. Your job is to contact dealers in order to assess customer response to new products. You visit the large dealers in person. You contact the smaller dealers by phone. Discuss the different techniques you would use in gathering reactions—by telephone and in person.

C. Mrs. DiSantis has told her staff that she must complete a very important report and is not to be disturbed by anyone under any circumstances. But in the middle of the morning, a Mr. Walter Kester telephones and insists, "I must talk with Mrs. DiSantis immediately about an important contract, for which the bids are closing at five o'clock this afternoon." What would you say to Mr. Kester? Would you use any of the following responses? Why or why not? Indicate your response and defend it in a paragraph.

1. "I'm sorry. I simply cannot disturb Mrs. DiSantis."
2. "Mrs. DiSantis is not in the office today."
3. "Please give me a telephone number where I can reach you within an hour. I will get your message to Mrs. DiSantis."
4. "If it's important, I'll connect you right away."

D. Select one of the following situations to enact in front of the class. Decide how you would communicate the unfavorable decision to the caller. Write a script for your skit.

1. The caller's application for a mortgage has been rejected because the down payment was too small.
2. The caller's bid to supply portable computers to your firm has been rejected in favor of another's, which was 15 percent lower.
3. Your employer does not wish to see a caller because the caller has provided poor service to your firm on several prior occasions.

VOCABULARY AND SPELLING STUDIES

A. The following words related to computer technology are used in this unit. Show that you understand the meaning of these words by constructing a sentence in which each word is used.

1. network
2. data bank
3. voice activation
4. software
5. telecommunication

Using your dictionary or another source, define the following computer terms:

   6. ergonomics
   7. robotics
   8. byte
   9. RAM
  10. ROM

B. Complete the following by adding *ary*, *ery*, or *ory*—whichever ending is correct.

   1. ev___
   2. cemet___
   3. vocabul___
   4. ordin___
   5. laborat___
   6. migrat___
   7. regulat___
   8. art___
   9. invent___
  10. station___ (letterhead paper)

C. Write the present participle form (ending with *ing*) of each of the following verbs:

  1. occur
  2. plan
  3. receive
  4. dine
  5. judge
  6. sell

COMMUNICATING FOR RESULTS

Handling a Difficult Caller. Mrs. Rico, a stockholder in the company for which you work, telephones and asks to speak with Mr. Angus, your boss and the company's public relations director. After you tell the caller that Mr. Angus is out of the office for the day, she explains her problem to you. She says that she has just been very rudely treated by the manager of your firm's retail store in Des Moines. She had tried to return some defective merchandise and was told that she has misused it. She characterizes the manager as "abusive," and she threatens not only to sell her stock but to tell all her friends and acquaintances about how she had been treated. You recognize that Mrs. Rico is highly agitated and needs to feel as if prompt attention to her complaint is assured. You want to preserve her goodwill in your response to her. Exactly what would you say to the caller? Write a summary of the conversation for your employer, so she will know how you handled the call.

58 Participating in Meetings and Conferences

Participating in group activities is good training for the person who hopes someday to be successful in business or industry. Therefore, you should make an effort to become active in one or more social, civil, religious, or school organizations.

More and more, in all walks of life, decisions are made as a result of group thinking. Many business groups and committees are organized to make the best use of the talents and ideas of employees. Often the work of each person in the group—participating members as well as leaders—is carefully considered by the people who help determine who should be promoted. Why? Management can observe how well a person works in a group and how well that person communicates with others—an important basis for advancement into leadership positions. Therefore, every person who plans to enter business should know how to participate effectively in a group.

The Group Member

For every leader in a group there are many more working members. You, therefore, will probably serve more often as a member than as a leader. Every person who is invited to join a group discussion has an obligation to contribute his or her best. Time and money are wasted when employees take meetings for granted and do not contribute their maximum efforts to the discussion.

Principles to Follow. Some rules for participating effectively in a group are discussed below. Knowing and practicing these rules will help you to be a valuable group member.

Respect the Opinions of Others. It is easy to respect the opinions of people whom you like and whose ideas agree with yours. Good group members, however, respect the opinions of all others in their group and are courteous to everyone, even though they may not agree with them.

Because good group members are open-minded, they listen attentively to each member of the group and respond with appropriate comments. Discourteous behavior—fidgeting, gazing into space, or trying to start an unrelated private conversation—marks the group member as a poor risk for promotion. The courteous person, on the other hand, is considerate of everyone at all times. You may have strong convictions, but you do not close your mind to a different point of view. You know that by considering the ideas and beliefs of others, you will grow and learn, you will gain a new respect for the thinking of others, and you will become a more effective person.

Use Only Your Share of Talking Time. Every member has a contribution to make to a group. Some people, however, have an exaggerated opinion of the value of their ideas, and they attempt to monopolize a meeting. Good group members know that everyone has an equal right and responsibility to talk. By limiting their own talking, they make sure that others are not robbed of their fair share of talking time.

Help to Harmonize Differences of Opinion. Good group members try to see the value in each opposing view and to balance these views to keep peace in the group. They recognize good ideas and encourage others in the group to make compromises that will help get results. Such a member might say, for example: "That's a good idea, and I can see how it would work under some conditions; but the other plan is good too. Shall we take the best from each?" Thus, by emphasizing the good aspects of all ideas, the effective group member is able to harmonize differences of opinion.

Help to Keep Discussion Relevant. Some members in a group easily let their talking wander from the discussion at hand. However, good group members stick to the subject and also help direct the ideas of others to the topic at hand. They may do so by reminding the group of their goal or purpose: "As I understand it, our purpose is to . . . ." Or when the discussion begins to wander, "Let's see now, what is it we hope to accomplish in this meeting?" Summarizing the progress made or pointing out stumbling blocks to reaching the goal may also help to keep group thinking on track. Thus the good group member takes action to let the group know whether it is reaching its goal.

Attitudes to Avoid. Of course, you probably realize that positive principles constitute good group membership, but just as important is for you to understand the attitudes and practices that *prevent* effective group work. An understanding of these attitudes and practices will help you avoid pitfalls and make you better able to harmonize differences of opinion and keep a discussion on the main track. The attitudes and practices of the following types of people hinder the smooth progress of a group.

Selfish-Interest Pleader. "I don't care what the rest of you think—what I want to see is . . . ," says the selfish-interest pleader. Martin has decided what *he* wants. Everything he says and does is intended to help him get his way despite the good ideas of others.

The Blocker. The blocker is opposed to every new idea. "That isn't the way to do it. Here's what we've been doing for years . . ." or "That's an idiotic idea. It won't work." Whatever the idea is, Ellen is against it. She often displays a negative, stubborn resistance. She opposes in a disagreeable manner and frequently without reason.

The Aggressor. The aggressor is usually unaware of the feelings of others. Dimitri may try to build his own importance by deflating the ego of others: "That's a silly thing to do. If I were doing it, here is how I'd go about it." But, alas, Dimitri usually avoids doing much! He may attack the group, its purposes, or the importance of the topic. He usually attempts to assert his superiority by trying to manage the group. As the name implies, the aggressor wants to take command.

The Sympathy Seeker. Alan, the sympathy seeker, may accept responsibility to do something for the group, but then he doesn't carry it through. He says: "I thought Fred was supposed to do that," or "I was just so busy that I couldn't get that done." Alibis, confessions of shortcomings, and exaggeration of personal problems are all used to gain the sympathy of the group. Such a person would like the group to compliment him for his weaknesses!

The Disinterested Bystander. Ursula, the disinterested bystander, may make a display of her lack of involvement. Through childish tactics, she may attempt to disrupt. Or she may patronize the group with a frozen smile that permits her to escape mentally from the boring proceedings.

Success as a Group Member. Study your role in a group. Make sure that you practice the principles that contribute to group success and eliminate all actions that might prevent you from being a good group member. Remember: A leader is usually selected from among the good group members.

The Group Leader

People who consistently block group action will not need to know how to lead a group. They won't be given the opportunity. However, people who know and practice the positive principles that help a group work together will soon be selected for a leadership post—an honor, but also a serious obligation. Before you take on the responsibility of chairing a group, therefore, make sure that you know the duties involved in planning and conducting a meeting.

Planning a Meeting. When you chair a group, you will usually plan all meetings—whether they are programs or business meetings. If the group does not have a constitution or bylaws to define your responsibilities, you can usually assume that you are responsible for all aspects of planning—place and time, publicity, pattern of the program, and speakers and other participants.

The Program. The first step is to write a plan for the program. This plan should answer the following questions:

1. What is the purpose of the meeting?
2. What theme or topic is to be considered?
3. Where and when will the meeting be held? Should reservations for a room or hall be made now?
4. Who will attend?
5. How many will attend?
6. What publicity will be needed?
7. How much money is available for speakers, arrangements, decorations, and so on?
8. What persons or committees should be appointed to make arrangements, sell tickets, publicize, act as hosts?
9. What form or pattern should the program take—speaker or symposium of speakers? demonstration? panel discussion? mock television or radio program? panel, with audience questions and answers? debate? small-group discussions? brainstorming? other?

Delegating Authority. At this point in planning you may feel overwhelmed by the size of the job ahead of you. Don't be, however, for an important characteristic of the leader is an ability to delegate authority. Specific tasks are assigned, usually in writing, to other people. Delegate as many details as you can, but be sure to follow up on each assignment. Carbons of letters of committee appointments or of letters written to the speakers can be used as a tickler (reminder) file. To avoid any last minute slipup, send reminders to all committees and speakers at least two weeks before the meeting. If you have carefully planned and effectively delegated responsibility, you can go before the group with a feeling of confidence that the meeting you conduct will be a good one.

The Agenda. In an agenda for a business meeting, like the one shown on page 599, the discussion items should be listed in the order of increasing controversy. For instance, the first item will be the one most likely to meet with almost total agreement. Next will come the item on which the leader expects less agreement, and so on. A sound psychological principle is behind this practice. If a group starts by agreeing, the members will be in a friendly and positive frame of mind that will carry over to succeeding discussion topics. Untrained leaders who start their meetings with the "big question"— the topic likely to provoke the widest difference of opinion—should not wonder why nothing is accomplished at their meetings.

Conducting a Meeting. You, the leader, set the tone for the meeting as you follow the agenda or program. If you are stiff and formal, the other people on the program are likely to be stiff and formal too. If you are natural and informal (but in good taste, of course), the others on your program will probably be natural and informal too. Most audiences today prefer a

```
                    APPLETON INSURANCE COMPANY

              Meeting of the Employee Welfare Committee

                    November 16, 1987, 4:30 p.m.
                      Executive Conference Room


                              AGENDA

        1. Call to order by Chairperson Reilly.

        2. Approval of the minutes of the October meeting.

        3. Approval of today's agenda.

        4. Announcements.

        5. Old Business:

             A.  Report of the subcommittee on employee rights
                 and duties.

             B.  Discussion of revision of awards standards and
                 procedures.

        6. New Business:

             A.  Plans for the annual Christmas banquet.

             B.  Discussion of the employee incentive plan.

             C.  Nominations for officers for 1988.

             D.  Other items.

        7. Adjournment.
```

In an agenda for a business meeting, the discussion items should be listed in the order of increasing controversy.

moderator who conducts an informal kind of meeting, whether or not parliamentary procedure is followed.

Parliamentary Procedure. The bylaws of most clubs state that business will be conducted according to Robert's *Rules of Order*. Robert's *Rules* are to parliamentary procedure what Emily Post and Amy Vanderbilt are to etiquette; and, as presiding officer, you will need to know some of the basic principles of Robert's *Rules* and how to apply them. For example, you should know how to call a meeting to order and how to determine whether a quorum is present; how to make and follow an agenda; how to recognize members who wish to make a motion; what an appropriate motion is and how it is seconded, amended, and voted upon; and how to adjourn a meeting. Most organizations will appoint a parliamentarian to help the group leader, but the leader who possesses a working knowledge of the rules is that much ahead.

Introducing a Speaker. An introduction should be short and simple and should include (1) some gracious remark that will make the speaker feel warmly welcome, (2) a statement of the speaker's topic, (3) a brief summary of the speaker's background or special interests, and (4) presentation of the speaker by name. The announcement of the name of the speaker is usually made last so that it serves as a signal for the speaker to come forward and begin the talk.

Responding to a Speech. The leader, of course, wishes the meeting to end on a high note. After an effective talk there is little to say. Even after a poor speech the leader shouldn't say too much. One or two comments about the importance of the talk or a short anecdote to leave the audience in good spirits is all that is needed. You should thank the speaker, express appreciation to those who helped plan the meeting, and adjourn.

COMMUNICATION LABORATORY

APPLICATION EXERCISES

A. Which of the following statements were made by people who practice principles of good group membership? Do any of the statements represent an attitude that is likely to hinder group progress? If you were chairperson, how would you respond to these negative statements?

1. "I don't think that this foolish scheme will work."
2. "I think there is a way to combine both ideas we have been discussing into one workable plan."
3. "My ten years at the Goldman Institute taught me that there is only one way to accomplish our goal."
4. "As far as I can tell, our purpose is simply to make a proposal, not to test its feasibility."

B. Write a plan for an important meeting of a group to which you belong. Include a speaker in the meeting plan. Use the questions on page 598 to guide your plan. Finally, write the introduction that you will use to present the speaker.

C. Write a letter to the person you have selected to be the speaker. Invite him or her to address the group. Be sure that the speaker gets all needed information, including a description of your group and its interests.

D. Write an appropriate thank-you letter to the speaker.

VOCABULARY AND SPELLING STUDIES

A. These words are often confused: *rout, route, root; incite, insight.* Explain the differences.

B. From each pair of words in parentheses, select the word that correctly completes the sentences.

1. I use (those, that) kind of disk in my computer.
2. Of the four printers available, I prefer the (smaller, smallest) one.
3. Jeremy was (real, really) happy to hear you were elected.
4. In order to get there on time, we must hurry (some, somewhat).
5. Mark is (sure, surely) acceptable as a candidate.

C. Choose the item that answers each of the following questions correctly.

1. Which one of the following expressions *should not* contain hyphens? first-rate opportunity, equipment that is up-to-date, high-quality merchandise
2. Which one of the following compound nouns *should be* hyphenated? notary public, vice president, trade in
3. Which one of the following words with prefixes *should not* be hyphenated? co-owner, non-neutral, ex-president, semi-independent
4. Which one of the following compound nouns *should not* be hyphenated? building-contractor, tie-up, follow-up plan

COMMUNICATING FOR RESULTS

Small-Group Discussion Technique. The small-group discussion technique is often used to solve problems. It is based on the idea that two heads are better than one. Here is the way it works. The class should be divided into small groups of four, five, or six. Then the members of each group should do the following: (1) Elect a presiding officer. (2) Agree quickly on a secretary or recorder who will take notes and later report the major points of the discussion to the entire class. (3) Make sure that everyone understands the problem you are to discuss. (4) Be sure that everyone enters into the discussion. When these activities are completed, the discussion process should be evaluated.

Each group should select one of these problems: (1) How can you improve your knowledge of career possibilities? (2) What kind of program can be established that would allow you to obtain actual work experience in interesting jobs?

Chapter

11

Effective communication skills will influence all aspects of your life, but never more so than when you get a job. Even the most basic business situations involve speaking, listening, reading, and writing.

Your command of communication skills will benefit you in a job situation. Given a situation that requires communicating on the job, you will be able to do the following when you master the units in this chapter:

1. *State your qualifications for employment in a complete, attractive résumé.*

2. *Complete employment application forms accurately and thoroughly.*

3. *Organize and write effective letters of application.*

4. *Prepare letters requesting others to serve as your references.*

5. *Write letters accepting or refusing positions offered to you.*

6. *Prepare yourself for a successful interview.*

U · N · I · T

59

Résumés and Job Applications

After the completion of your formal education, you will want to find a position in business that is suited to your training, interests, and career goals. This process of job seeking will call for your visiting a prospective employer's office and completing an application form. The employer may then make a decision regarding your employment on the basis of the information on your application form and through a personal interview. This process is probably the one most frequently used for obtaining a beginning position. Therefore, you should be prepared to put your best foot forward when preparing a job application form and participating in an employment interview.

Throughout your lifetime, however, you may find yourself in other job-seeking situations in an attempt to improve your position. As you gain experience, you are likely to become ambitious for better and better jobs. These better jobs very often call for written letters of application and summaries of your background and experience. Your writing skills may very well play an important part in obtaining the job you desire.

In any job-seeking situation, there are a number of ways you may use your writing skills: to complete an application blank, prepare a résumé (a summary of your qualifications), write an application letter, or write employment follow-up letters. To obtain your first job, you may need to complete only an employment application form. However, you may also need to prepare a letter of application and a résumé. As an ambitious job seeker, therefore, you should be able to prepare all the written material that will help you obtain the job you want.

What Abilities Do You Have to Offer an Employer?

You will be hired because you have a skill that an employer needs. Before you start your campaign for a job, you must decide for which specific jobs you are qualified and in which jobs you are interested. On the basis of your personal and educational background, you begin by listing specific skills and knowledge that would benefit an employer. Then you decide which specific job titles need the skills and knowledge you possess.

Which of the positions you have listed interest you most? Which ones interest you least? Direct your job-seeking efforts to the most interesting positions for which you are qualified.

604

For example, suppose your high school major is a general clerical program. Courses in the program may include typewriting, accounting, general business, business English and communication, filing, business mathematics, and office practice. At the end of your high school training, you will probably be able to type at least 50 words a minute, perform basic record-keeping functions, operate various calculating and duplicating machines, and compose business letters. Some of the job classifications for which you will have received preparation include clerk-typist, payroll clerk, teller, file clerk, general office clerk, correspondence clerk, or credit clerk.

Once you have assessed your skills and knowledge and determined the various jobs for which you are qualified, your most important decision involves selecting the job that interests you most. How can you locate such a position?

What Are Good Job Sources?

How do you find the job in which you are interested? Where do you look for the job for which you are qualified? Several employment sources may be investigated to find a job suitable for you.

School Placement Offices. Your school placement office may be a good place to begin looking for your first job. To employers, graduating seniors are a good source of personnel. If your school has established a reputation for providing training in occupational areas, then you may be able to obtain a job through your school placement office. In addition, your teachers may be able to supply specific names of employers who are looking for graduates in your particular field of interest.

Newspaper Advertisements. Newspaper advertisements placed by local businesses are a good source of employment opportunities. These advertisements may ask you to apply in person for the positions listed, or they may ask you to submit an application letter accompanied by a résumé.

Sometimes local professional journals or newspapers contain job listings. For example, the *Los Angeles Daily Journal*, a publication for the legal profession, is a good source of legal secretarial positions in the Los Angeles area.

Employment Agencies. Both state employment agencies and private employment agencies list job openings. Your local state agency places applicants in positions that have been referred to its office. Of course, this service is performed without cost to either the employee or the employer.

Private employment agencies charge either the employer or the applicant a fee for filling an opening that has been referred to them by the employer. Positions listed as "fee paid" are the ones employers pay for. Some companies prefer to refer all their openings to private employment agencies to save themselves the trouble and expense of screening applicants. In the long run it may prove less expensive for them to use an employment agency than to maintain their own personnel recruitment facilities.

Federal, State, County, and City Offices. Opportunities in civil service employment should not be overlooked, as salaries and opportunities for advancement are competitive with those in industry. Local federal, state, county, and city employment offices regularly publish announcements of job opportunities in their levels of government. Persons interested in working in civil service should consult local government employment offices to learn about the jobs available and to inquire about taking the civil service examinations for the jobs in which they are interested. Often, too, officials from various government offices will visit high schools to recruit qualified applicants and to administer civil service examinations right on campus.

College and University Offices. All institutions of higher education have business offices that employ many clerks, secretaries, managers, and administrators. Colleges and universities offer their employees some major advantages. Some institutions, for example, permit their employees to take one course during working hours. In addition, of course, employees have the advantage of working in a different environment—the college campus.

Individual Companies. Many companies do not actively recruit prospective employees through newspaper advertisements or employment agencies. Sufficient numbers of applicants present themselves to the company and directly request employment. While companies may not always have immediate openings in every area, a qualified applicant's résumé is usually filed for future reference.

Larger companies with hundreds or thousands of employees are constantly busy recruiting and placing personnel. Therefore, contacting these companies directly may often lead to obtaining employment.

The Résumé

Once you have decided what you have to sell an employer, you should prepare a written summary of your qualifications. This summary—called a *résumé*—is a description of your qualifications. It usually includes a statement of your education, your employment record (experience), a list of references, and other data that will help you obtain the job you wish.

A résumé is highly useful. You may use it to accompany a letter of application, present it to an employer at the interview, or use it to assist you in filling out an employment application form.

Since résumés are sales instruments, they must be prepared just as carefully as sales letters. They must present the best possible impression of you. The act of preparing the résumé is just as valuable as the résumé itself, for it forces you to think about yourself—what you have to offer an employer and why you should be hired. Thus it becomes a self-appraisal. Everyone brings unique talents to a position, but usually only after you prepare a résumé do you realize your true worth.

Make the Resumé Attractive. Because the resumé is a sales instrument, it should be as attractive as you can make it. Of course, it should be typewritten, perfectly balanced on the page, and free from errors and noticeable corrections. Resumés vary in length from one page to several pages, depending on how much you have to say about yourself. Your first resumé should probably fit on one page or at the most two, but as you gather experience and obtain more education, your resumé may get longer and more detailed.

Make the Resumé Fit the Employer's Needs. A resumé is tailored carefully to meet the employer's needs for the job for which you are applying. Thus it is an individual thing. Never try to copy someone else's resumé or use the same one over and over. You must find out what the job you are seeking demands and then tailor your resumé accordingly. For example, if you apply for a job where you will be required to take dictation at a high speed, you will want to emphasize your skill in shorthand. You will make absolutely sure that the employer knows you are a highly skilled shorthand writer and transcriber. On the other hand, if the secretarial job you want requires little in the way of shorthand but a good deal of talent in writing, you will mention your shorthand skill but emphasize your writing ability.

The Main Categories of a Resumé

The form of the resumé varies according to your individual taste and, more importantly, according to the job for which you are applying. If you are applying for a job with a bank or an accounting firm, you would probably want to use white paper and a conservative format. But if you were applying for a job with an advertising agency, you would probably want to exhibit creativity and might want to use a tinted paper and a more creative format.

The resumé illustrated on page 608 is an example of an effective arrangement. Notice that it contains four main headings "Position Applying For," "Experience," "Education," and "References." The information at the top of the form includes the name, address, and telephone number of the applicant. This is all the personal data needed here; you will supply other personal details on the application.

Position Applying For. The employer wants to know, first of all, the specific job for which you are applying. It is best to find out in advance whether there is a vacancy in the company and to specify that position by its correct title, such as "Secretary to the Assistant Credit Manager." If you don't know the specific job title, it is satisfactory to write "Payroll Clerk," "Sales Trainee," "Receptionist," and so on. Whichever resumé format you use— conservative or creative—be sure to include all the necessary details.

Experience. If you are a recent high school graduate, the employer will not expect you to have had a lot of experience that is related directly to the job for which you are applying. Employers understand that you have been in school and have used most of your summers for vacation. Nevertheless, any paid work experience, regardless of its nature, will impress an employer because the fact that you have worked reveals that you have some initiative. Therefore, be sure to mention such experience as temporary, part-time, after-school, Saturday, or vacation work—mowing lawns, baby sitting, delivering newspapers, and so on. Even volunteer typing or clerical work for a teacher or a community agency should be listed.

```
                            Marvin Hestenes
                          7639 Greentree Drive
                       La Jolla, California 92126
                         Telephone (603) 555-9876


        POSITION APPLYING FOR      Accounting Assistant


        EXPERIENCE                 Los Angeles Tire Manufacturers, Los
                                   Angeles, California.  June 1982 to
                                   present.  Assistant Bookkeeper.
                                   Supervisor: Ms. Marguerite Antony.
                                   Duties included preparing weekly
                                   payroll reports, distributing
                                   payroll, filing records of employees,
                                   monitoring use and service of all
                                   office microcomputers.

                                   Martin Manufacturing Company, La
                                   Jolla, California.  June 1980 to May
                                   1981.  Payroll Clerk.  Supervisor:
                                   Mr. Rico Vittori.  Duties included
                                   payroll preparation, typing, and
                                   banking activities.

                                   Meagen Department Store, San Diego,
                                   California.  Summer employment, 1978
                                   and 1979.  Supervisor: Mrs. Lillian
                                   Wellaman.

        EDUCATION                  San Diego Business College, San
                                   Diego, California.  Awarded
                                   certificate upon completion of
                                   ten-month accounting program in
                                   January 1979.  Skills: typewriting,
                                   70 words a minute.  Major subjects
                                   included advanced accounting, cost
                                   accounting, data processing, and
                                   Lotus 1-2-3.  Received Master of
                                   Accounting Award.

                                   La Jolla High School, La Jolla,
                                   California.  Graduated with honors in
                                   June 1978.  Served as Treasurer of
                                   the Bookkeeping Club in 1978 and as
                                   President of the Senior Class in 1978.

        REFERENCES                 Miss Theresa Alvarez, instructor, San
                                   Diego Business College, 983 Kester
                                   Drive, Point Loma, California 92126.

                                   Dr. Albert Kinter, Veteran Hospital,
                                   Victory, California 92128.

                                   Ms. Mona Murray, Principal, La Jolla
                                   High School, La Jolla, California
                                   92126.
```

A résumé should give specific details about the applicant's experience and education.

Include the following facts about your experience:

1. Name and address of your employer (including the telephone number is always very helpful).
2. Type of work you performed. Give not only the title of the position but also a brief description of the work.
3. Dates of employment. Employers usually prefer that you start listing your work experience with your *last* job and work back to your first job. When listing full-time experience by dates, it is important to leave no obvious unaccounted-for time gaps:

January 1985–September 1985	Did not work during this period; I cared for my mother, who was recovering from surgery.

OR:

August 1987–July 1988	During this period I was a part-time student at the Martin Business College. I was not employed.

If you have held one or more full-time positions prior to making the application, you may wish to state why you left each position. For example: "I left this position because I was needed at home."

Education. For most high school students, the education section of the résumé will be the most important, since work experience will at this point be limited. Therefore, give specific details about your training that qualify you for the position. Study the information presented in the résumé illustrated on page 608. Note that the courses emphasized are those that have particular bearing on the position being applied for. Note also that special skills and interests are described. Be sure, on your résumé, to list any honors you have received in school, even though they may not appear to be of great significance to you. Employers *are* interested.

Some people who take part in out-of-school activities mention their hobbies as indications of their broad interests. Mentioning outside interests is a good idea, especially if these hobbies give the prospective employer a clue to your personality and talents. For example, the hobby of working on cars will impress the manager of an automobile agency or an auto parts store. The hobby of reading will be of interest to a publisher. If art is your main hobby, this talent will appeal to a large number of employers.

References. At the end of your résumé, list the names of people whom the employer can contact for information about you. Common courtesy requires that you obtain permission before using a person's name for reference. (The letter requesting such permission is discussed in Unit 60.) Ordinarily, only three or four names need be listed, but others should be available to attest to your experience, education, and character. If possible, select your references according to the job for which you are applying. And let your references know what kind of position you are applying for so that they will be guided in their replies. If you are applying for a position as an accounting clerk, for example, a reference from someone in that type of work would be more appropriate than one from your family doctor. When you ask someone to write a letter of recommendation for you, include a stamped envelope to the prospective employer.

The following information should be given about each and every reference you include on your résumé:

1. Full name (check spelling) with appropriate/preferred title (such as *Ms.*, *Mr.*, *Miss*, *Mrs.*, *Professor*, *Dr.*).
2. Business title (such as *President, Director, Data Processing Manager*).
3. Name of company or organization and complete address.
4. Telephone number (with area code).

Filling Out Employment Applications

Most business firms like to have a standardized record for each employee. You will probably be asked to fill out the company's application form either before or after you have been hired. Frequently, personnel interviewers use the application form as they interview you. Since interviewers are familiar with this form, they can quickly select from it items about which to question you. The application form also provides a great deal of information about the applicant other than the answers to the questions asked—information regarding the legibility of handwriting, accuracy and thoroughness, neatness, and ability to follow written directions.

Here are some helpful suggestions to follow when you must fill out application forms:

1. Bring with you:
   a. A reliable pen. Many pens provided for public use are not dependable. An ink-blotched or unevenly written application form will reflect on your neatness.
   b. Two or more copies of your résumé, one or more for the interviewer and one for you to use in filling out details on the application blank.
   c. Your social security card.
2. Write legibly. Your handwriting does not need to be fancy, but it must be legible. You should take particular care that any figures you write are clear. If the interviewer has difficulty reading your writing, you will start your interview with one strike against you—that is, if you get as far as an interview!
3. Be accurate and careful. Double-check all the information you have included. Have you given your year of birth where it is asked for, and not this year's date? Are your area code and telephone number correct? Be careful to avoid any obvious carelessness.
4. Don't leave any blanks. If the information asked for does not apply to you, draw a line through that space or mark it "Does not apply."

5. Follow directions exactly. Since you have the opportunity to reread the directions to make sure you are completing the form correctly, reread them. If you ask unnecessary questions, you show that you cannot follow simple written instructions. The interviewer will then wonder how you would follow complicated oral instructions once you are on the job! If the directions say to print, then do not write. If the instructions call for your last name first, then do not give your first name first. If you are asked to list your work experience with your last job first, then be sure you do not list your first job first.

COMMUNICATION LABORATORY

APPLICATION EXERCISES

A. Investigate the kinds of jobs that are available in your community by studying the advertisements published in your local newspaper. List specific jobs that are of interest to you. Then list the kinds of jobs for which there are many ads.

B. Prepare a résumé that fits your qualifications. Assume that you will complete your high school training within the next few months.

C. Obtain application forms from two local business firms. Complete them just as you would if you were going to apply for a position. Be prepared to discuss in class the kinds of information that the forms required you to supply.

D. Exchange each of your application forms with other students in the class. Write a critique of each of the forms you receive.

VOCABULARY AND SPELLING STUDIES

A. These words are often confused: *born, borne; coarse, course; lesson, lessen.* Explain the differences.

B. What are the adjective forms of these verbs?

1. despair
2. investigate
3. spend
4. predict
5. harm
6. supplement

C. Add either *ant* or *ent* to each of the following to form a correctly spelled word.

1. ten___
2. eleg___
3. quoti___
4. defend___
5. solv___
6. independ___

D. Write the present participial form (ending in *ing*) of each of the following verbs:

1. believe   3. sit   5. duplicate
2. occur   4. develop   6. plan

COMMUNICATING FOR RESULTS

Innocent Bystander. You answer the office phone and hear the familiar voice of your manager's teenage son. The son calls frequently. Although he has a reputation in the office of being a "pest," your manager always loves to hear from him and seems to enjoy his calls. This is an exceptionally busy day, however, and your manager is working on a report that must be finished within hours. Your manager has given you strict orders not to be disturbed under any circumstances. You must honor your manager's wishes. What do you think you should say to her son?

U · N · I · T

60 Employment Letters

Your ability to write an effective employment letter will help you compete successfully against others who want the same job you want. At some point in your career, you will surely have occasion to write one or more of the following types of employment letters:

1. A letter of application. This letter may be written (a) in response to a newspaper advertisement; (b) at the suggestion of a relative, friend, teacher, or business acquaintance; or (c) on your own initiative, even though you do not know of a specific job opening in the business to which you write.
2. Letters to various persons requesting their permission to give their names as reference.
3. A follow-up letter to thank an employment interviewer for the time given you and to reemphasize some of your qualifications that particularly suit you for the job.

4. A letter accepting the position.
5. A letter refusing a position.
6. A thank-you letter to each person who helped you in your job-seeking campaign.

Letters of Application

Employers often receive hundreds of applications for one job, and they cannot possibly interview each person who applies. Therefore, the personnel recruiter uses the letter of application and other written documents as a basis on which to select those who will be called for a personal interview. An effective application letter can open doors to a bright future; a poor one could quickly close those doors. However, an application letter alone will rarely get you a job. Obviously, an employer needs more than your letter to decide whether to hire you. But your letter can make you stand out from other applicants. It can get your foot in the door—its main purpose.

Appearance. The appearance of your application letter gives the employer a first clue to your personality and work habits. A sloppy letter suggests that you may not be careful about your own appearance or about your work habits—and this is not the kind of impression you want your letter to make.

Appearances *do* matter. Imagine, for example, getting caught in the rain before you are to meet—for the first time—an important person. Even though you explain that you have been caught in the rain and are excused, your bedraggled appearance will create a negative first impression of you. Likewise, a sloppy letter will give a prospective employer an impression of you—but a sloppy letter cannot be excused. It says, "I didn't care enough to do it over." Employers are interested only in applicants who care enough to do the job properly.

Thus, in writing your application letter, you want the prospective employer to be favorably impressed and to grant you an interview. The physical appearance of your letter can do much to help create this favorable impression. Follow these instructions, therefore, in preparing your letter:

1. Use a good grade of 8½- by 11-inch bond paper (white). Be certain that it is clean and free from smudges and finger marks both before and after you write your letter. Be careful of paper that is specially treated so that it erases easily. "Erasable" paper is generally expensive. Moreover, you may be paying for extra smudges, because erasable paper tends to pick up old ink from your typewriter platen (roller). Since this paper erases so easily, you can blur the words merely by rubbing your finger across your paper. A good grade of bond paper is usually the best choice.

2. Type your letter of application. Here are some suggestions to follow when typing your letter:

    a. Make no strikeovers.
    b. Make very neat erasures. If an erasure can be detected easily, retype the letter.

  c. Use a black ribbon that is not so worn that the type is too light or so new that the type is too dark and smudgy.

  d. Balance your letter neatly on the page, allowing plenty of white space in the margins (at least 1½ inches all around).

  e. Clean your keys so that letters appear sharp and clear.

3. Address your letter to a specific person in the organization if it is possible to obtain his or her name.

4. Don't expect to get your letter exactly right the first time. Be willing to rewrite it until it represents you in the best possible light.

5. Never copy an application letter out of a book. Let your letter express your own personality.

Organizing the Letter. An application is usually accompanied by a résumé, such as the one illustrated on page 608. It is neither necessary nor desirable to describe fully your education and experience in the letter. This is the job of the résumé. The letter's main purpose is to transmit the résumé and to supplement it with a personal sales message:

> Can your business use a salesperson who is hard-working, conscientious, and ambitious? who understands human nature and who has the know-how of determining what people are seeking? who has a successful sales record even while going to school? who wants a career—not just a job—in your organization? If "yes" is your answer to all these questions, then I may be the very person you are looking for.

> Does your word processing personnel produce errorless copy hour after hour, documents that pass all tests for accuracy? I can—and I can verify this ability.

> Is there a place in your organization for an accountant whose work is accurate and meticulous and who accepts a demanding atmosphere as a challenge?

> Can you use a secretary who is a paragon of accuracy and who can take dictation at unusually high speeds?

Another good beginning for an application letter that sells is a summary statement of your special qualifications. This type of beginning gives the prospective employer an immediate indication of your ability and training. If these qualifications seem to be what is needed, the employer will read further. Here are some examples:

> My five years of marketing experience, plus my proven record of successful work with district sales staffs, should qualify me for the position of sales manager in your home office.

> A solid background in secretarial science at Kent High School, combined with over two years of experience in the Trust Department of the Avon Savings and Loan Institution, has given me both the knowledge and the experience to qualify me for the secretarial position advertised in the June 23 edition of the *News Mirror.*

My four years as receptionist for the Rittenhous Marketing Corporation has provided me with the experience of working with people that your customer service position requires.

When you have been told about a vacancy by another person—an employee of the organization or a friend of the person to whom you are writing or a teacher or guidance counselor—it is often effective to use that person's name (with permission) in your opening paragraph.

Ms. Audrey Campbell, a family friend, has told me that you need a reliable secretary. I have been an executive secretary for more than three years, and I believe that I have the qualifications you want.

Mr. Gerald Gilbertson, who is an order fulfillment supervisor, has informed me that you are looking for someone who is used to working with detail. Would over one year of experience as a statistical clerk in the U.S. Securities and Exchange Commission in Washington be of interest to you?

My accounting teacher, Dr. Alec Santini, has told me that you are looking for someone you do not have to train. I believe my qualifications would be of interest to you.

Developing the Body of the Letter. In the body of the letter, you should offer support for the statements made in the opening paragraph. Emphasize the highlights of your educational background and business experience that are specifically related to the job. You may also indicate why you would like to be employed by the firm to which you are applying. To impress the company favorably, get some of its literature and learn about its locations and activities. The *Funk and Scott Index* lists newspaper and magazine articles that have appeared about companies. Read some, and then you may be able to give specific reasons for being interested in a particular company. Following this suggested plan, the second paragraph of your application letter might read like one of the following:

I routinely take dictation at 140 words a minute. I can also operate a switchboard without becoming flustered during even the busiest hours of the day. I type accurately and rapidly and am able to compose routine letters. I also have a solid background in tax record-keeping procedures. Furthermore, I have practiced and sharpened all these skills for the last eighteen months in the offices of the law firm of Oak and Bucket, Inc.

My enclosed résumé sets forth both the training and the experience that I have had during my first two years in business. I believe that you will agree that my training and experience qualify me for the position of administrative assistant with your firm.

Concluding the Letter. A good conclusion in any letter tells readers what you wish them to do. In a letter of application you would like the reader to grant a personal interview. Therefore, ask for an interview and make your request easy to grant. Here are some suggested ways to accomplish this:

May I explain further during a personal interview my qualifications for the position? I can be reached at 555-1357.

I believe that I can tell you, in just a few minutes, why I am a likely candidate for the position you have available. May I have an interview with you? Just indicate a convenient date and time on the enclosed postcard.

To a prospective employer some distance away, the applicant may write:

I will be in the Baltimore area from July 1 to July 6. May I talk with you on any of these dates? My phone number is (203) 555-9876.

Sample Letters. The following letter of application for a position as secretary was written by a soon-to-be-graduated high school business student.

830 Jackson Boulevard
Pompano Beach, Florida 33062

June 24, 1987

Mr. Allen Burton
Director of Personnel
Carlton Electronics Company
876 Colina Parkway
Fort Lauderdale, Florida 33322

Dear Mr. Burton:

Ms. Mary Lynn, a business education counselor at Dale High School, has told me that your organization has an opening for a secretary. I would very much appreciate your permitting me to explain why I believe that I have the necessary qualifications for this position.

As the enclosed résumé points out, I have had two years of shorthand training and transcription at Dale High School and have developed a high rate of speed and accuracy in both shorthand and typing. In addition, for the last two summers I have had the opportunity to improve both skills as a full-time summer replacement at the main office of the Broward County Bank. This experience also served to acquaint me with the daily routine of a busy office. I have enjoyed both my training and my work experience and believe that I can satisfactorily fill the position that you have.

I can begin work anytime after July 10.

You can reach me at 555-4116 any day after 5 p.m. May I have a personal interview at your convenience?

Sincerely yours,

Enclosure

The following letter was written by a graduating student applying for an accounting position in reply to a blind newspaper ad:

876 Ibsen Place
Abbotsville, Minnesota 56321

June 1, 1987

The Times-Dispatch
Box No. 8798
Dales, Minnesota 56324

Ladies and Gentlemen:

Two years of high school accounting, supplemented by summer work at an accounting firm and strengthened by an evening program in accounting at the Downey Business College, have equipped me to handle the general demands of accounting work. I would therefore appreciate it if you would consider me for an accounting position in your firm.

I am presently employed as a tax clerk with the Imic Machinery Corporation. But I am looking for a position that would make greater use of my broad training. I would also value the opportunity to get into a more advanced phase of accounting. I plan to continue my accounting education through a night school program at our local community college.

The enclosed résumé summarizes my education and experience. It also includes the names of three people from whom you may obtain information about my character and ability.

I would very much like to talk to you in person. I may be reached by phone at 555-4200, Ext. 160, from 8:30 a.m. to 5 p.m. or at 555-1072 after 5:30 p.m.

Sincerely yours,

Enclosure

Letters Requesting References

Almost every prospective employer likes to have information regarding the character, training, experience, and work habits of job applicants. You may need to supply only the names, titles, and addresses of references, leaving to the interested prospective employer the task of obtaining the desired references. Under some circumstances you may request that the person speaking on your behalf write a letter of reference directly to the prospective employer. (In most cases a letter of reference that you carry with you is not too effective.)

Before using a person's name as a reference, you should request permission to do so. This permission may be obtained in person, by telephone, or by a letter such as the following:

Dear Mr. Lee:

I am applying for the position of order clerk currently available at the Grafton Mining Corporation in Alton.

As a student in your clerical practice class two years ago, I received the background that is needed for this position. I would like very much to use your name as a reference.

I have enclosed a return postcard for your reply.

Sincerely yours,

Enclosure

You might use a courtesy carbon and return envelope instead of the postcard.

If you are writing to request that a reference be sent directly to a prospective employer, you may say:

Dear Ms. Polanski:

I am applying for a position as assistant payroll clerk at Marvin's Department Store in Lincoln.

Since I worked under your supervision for two years in the Claims Department of the Southern Insurance Company, I believe that you are in a position to evaluate both my character and my ability. Would you be willing to send a letter of reference for me to Mrs. Bertha Williams, Personnel Director at Marvin's Department Store in Lincoln? I am enclosing a stamped and addressed envelope for your convenience.

Sincerely yours,

Enclosure

Follow-Up Letters

Application letters and letters requesting references are written before the interview with a prospective employer. After the interview there are several types of follow-up letters you may write. Here are some examples.

The Interview Follow-Up. If your application letter has succeeded in obtaining a personal interview for you, the next letter you should write will follow the personal interview. This letter may serve to satisfy one or more of the following purposes:

1. To thank the interviewer for the time and courtesy extended to you.
2. To let the interviewer know you are still interested in the position.
3. To remind the interviewer of the special qualifications you have for this particular position.
4. To return the application form that the interviewer may have given you to take home to complete.

5. To provide any additional data requested by the interviewer that you may not have had available at the time of the interview.

Notice how the interview follow-up uses the everyday letter plan by directly thanking the reader for the interview and then following up with details related to the interview.

Dear Mr. Agnew:

Thank you for discussing with me yesterday afternoon the position that you have available in your accounts payable office. You told me exactly what would be demanded of me in that position.

I am more interested than ever in this job. I believe that the position I have held for the last two years at Portland Container Corporation has given me the background I would need to perform the work required.

I have completed the application form that you gave me, and it is enclosed. I have asked my references to write to you directly.

I hope that you will look positively upon my application. Please let me know if I can supply you with any additional information.

Sincerely yours,

Enclosure

Letters of Acceptance. If you are notified by mail that you are being offered the position for which you applied, you should write a letter of acceptance. This letter does the following:

1. Notifies your employer-to-be of your acceptance.
2. Reassures the employer that she or he has chosen the right person.
3. Informs the employer when you can report for work.

The letter of acceptance, which follows the everyday letter plan, may read as follows:

Dear Ms. Carroll:

It is a pleasure to accept your offer of a secretarial position at Kinney Material Company, Inc. You can be sure that I will do everything possible to justify the confidence you have expressed in me.

Since June 30 is my graduation day, Monday, July 2, will certainly be a convenient starting date for me. I will report to your office ready to work at 9 a.m.

Thank you for the opportunity that you have given me.

Sincerely yours,

Letters of Refusal. Perhaps you have been offered a position for which you applied, but you have also received another offer that you believe is better. You should return the courtesy extended to you by writing a tactful, friendly letter of refusal. You may want to reapply to this same company in the future. Structure your letter according to the bad-news plan. Refuse the position only after you have expressed appreciation for being offered the job.

Dear Mr. Sawyer:

Thank you for offering me the position of inventory clerk at the Pacific Seas Company's warehouse.

It would have been a pleasure working with you and the other fine people at Pacific Seas. However, just two days before receiving your offer, I accepted a similar position at another company.

I very much appreciate the time that you gave me.

Sincerely yours,

Thank-You Letters. When you have obtained your position, remember that the people who have written reference letters for you undoubtedly helped you. You should be courteous enough to let them know that you have accepted the position. You might write a letter such as the following:

Dear Mrs. Torrington:

Thank you for the letter of reference that you sent on my behalf to the Porter Bank. You will be pleased to know that I have accepted the position of assistant treasurer of that bank.

I want you to know how very much I appreciate your support.

Sincerely yours,

Resignation Letters

Occasionally you may need to write a letter resigning from a position. (Of course, you should discuss your resignation with your supervisor before writing a letter.) Regardless of your reason for resigning, your letter should be friendly in tone and tactful. Someday you may want this employer to give you a reference, and you want the employer to remember you favorably. The following letter, which follows the bad-news plan, is a good example of a letter of resignation.

Dear Mr. O'Conner:

I want you to know how much I have enjoyed my last three years at the Baylor Tool and Die Company. I have learned a great deal here and have made many permanent friends as well.

Because I would like to make greater use of my sales background, I have accepted a position at the brokerage firm of Smythe and Dale. I would therefore appreciate it if you would accept my resignation effective August 15.

Thank you for all that you have done to make my work here both interesting and enjoyable.

Sincerely yours,

COMMUNICATION LABORATORY

APPLICATION EXERCISES

A. The following advertisements appeared in a recent edition of your local newspaper. Write a letter of application answering one of these advertisements.

> SECRETARY: Small office needs talented self-starter. Good position for the right person. Apply to Mr. Adam Colby, 162 Alston Avenue.

> ACCOUNTANT: Entry-level position for person with good training. Salary open. Apply to Box 78, *Daily Express.*

> TRAVEL COORDINATOR: Entry-level position. Work for a busy manufacturing firm with people who frequently must travel. Will teach the use of Official Airline Guide and routing maps. Much telephone work. No typing. Personnel Director, Stanton Company, Ventura Mall.

B. Write a letter to a teacher or an acquaintance requesting permission to use his or her name as a reference.

C. Assume that you have had a personal interview for one of the jobs in Exercise A. Write a follow-up letter to the person who interviewed you.

D. You have received a letter notifying you that you have been selected to fill the vacancy for which you have applied. Write a letter accepting the position.

E. Suppose that you have decided not to accept the position offered to you in Exercise D. Write a letter of refusal.

F. Write a letter to the person who wrote a letter of reference for you, notifying him or her that you have accepted a position.

G. You have been employed by World Travel Agency for three years. A friend who works for Pacific World Travel has told you of a vacancy in that firm. You have applied for, and been offered, that position. This position pays much more than your current salary; the opportunities for learning and advancing appear to be better; there are many more fringe benefits, including a college tuition plan and dental plan; and the office is much closer to your home. You decide to leave your current position. Assume that you have already discussed this new job with your supervisor. You must now put your resignation in written form. Write the appropriate letter.

VOCABULARY AND SPELLING STUDIES

A. These words are often confused: *breath, breathe, breadth; decent, descent, dissent.* Explain the differences.

B. From each pair of words within parentheses, select the one that correctly completes the sentence.

1. The usher kept the (isles, aisles) of the theater open.
2. The (lone, loan) reason for not going to the picnic is my mother's illness.
3. Webster has no (allusions, illusions) about the job.
4. A city (ordnance, ordinance) prohibits parking here.
5. You should (canvass, canvas) the class to see how they will vote in the election.

C. Remove the extra letter from each of the following words.

1. refferred
2. judgement
3. datta
4. picknic
5. choosen
6. acknowledgement
7. accommoddate
8. possitions
9. callendar
10. votting
11. envellope
12. corresppondence
13. offerring
14. writting
15. handicapp

COMMUNICATING FOR RESULTS

You Feel Responsible. Larry Clark, a close friend of yours, was looking for a job and asked you to speak with your supervisor about a data processing position with your firm. You spoke with your supervisor, Larry was interviewed, and he was eventually hired, partly because of your recommendation. He has been working in your department for about a month now. You have noticed that he is always late, both in the morning and after lunch. Moreover, he takes constant breaks during the day. Worst of all, he makes several mistakes that are due mainly to inattentiveness and lack of concentration. Because you helped him to get his job, you feel responsible for his performance. What, if anything, should you do?

In preparation for a class discussion of the problem, jot down some of the various things that you might do and identify what you believe would be the best course of action.

U · N · I · T

61

Employment Interviews

For any job opening, an applicant is required to have a personal interview. This interview may be the most important use you make of oral communication, for your future may depend upon your success in selling yourself during this interview. The employment interview is also one of the best examples of total communication because it is in the interview that job applicants reveal whether they possess the communication skills required for the position for which they are applying. Does the applicant *speak* well, *listen* attentively, *read* and follow instructions carefully, *write* an effective résumé?

Getting Ready for the Interview

An interviewer judges job applicants by the degree to which they know their own qualifications and the requirements of the job and by their ability to relate their qualifications to the requirements. Careful planning and preparation for the interview are required. Study the following suggestions thoroughly, for the way you apply them will be a big factor in determining your standing among the other applicants.

Know Your Qualifications. Before the interview be sure you have collected and reviewed the necessary information about your personal qualifications. If you wrote a letter of application (as discussed in Unit 60), refresh your memory about what you said. If you prepared a résumé (Unit 59), memorize the facts you included. It is a good idea to bring copies of your letter of application and extra copies of your résumé. Have a transcript of school credits at hand and review the names of subjects you have taken. Have available, too, a list of class activities in which you have participated, clubs and organizations to which you have belonged, honors you have won, and your hobbies and favorite sports. Know your school average and your attendance record. How embarrassing to be asked about your personal qualifications and not be able to remember exactly!

Interviewers will generally have on their desk your application letter or form, your résumé, school records, statements from previous employers, and letters of reference. Using these materials as a base, they will ask you questions. They may ask you to clarify or expand upon some information, and as you answer they will probably note how closely your reply agrees with the written records. Prepare yourself, therefore, by collecting and reviewing all the data on your qualifications. Have the information on the tip of your tongue so that you can answer questions readily and accurately.

Know the Job. Many employers advertise for experienced applicants to fill a position because they believe an experienced person is more likely to know the job—what is expected and how to perform. But the requirement of experience is not the handicap it may at first seem. An inexperienced applicant may be able to make up for a lack of experience by learning everything possible about that job. Thus prepared, the applicant can show the interviewer that a realistic understanding of what the job involves may make up for the lack of experience.

To learn about a job, you can talk with employees in that field. Before you leave school, you might ask a recent graduate who is now working in the company of your choice to talk about the job. If you have an opportunity to do so, take a field trip through the offices or plant. Read about the products manufactured or about the services or goods sold. Through friends, you may even be able to learn something about the people who own or operate the company and about the particular person who will interview you. The more you know about the job, the company, and the people you will meet, the better you will be able to relate your abilities to the specific job.

Match Your Qualifications to the Job. Well-intentioned, well-qualified applicants have been known to enter a personnel office with a general statement such as "I want to apply for a job." This shows lack of wisdom and immaturity. Such people might as well say that they have not considered what job they wish to apply for, what qualifications are needed, or how their own qualifications are related to the needs of the job. These applicants usually do not get past the receptionist. To avoid such a disappointment, you must prepare for the employment interview by considering how your abilities fit you for the specific job for which you are applying.

Conducting Yourself During the Interview

If you have prepared carefully for the interview, you should make a favorable first impression. Your dress and behavior will be correct for the situation, and you will appear self-confident and poised.

Your Appearance and Posture. Care in grooming, in the selection of clothing, and in the way you carry yourself, as discussed in Unit 55, is of major importance to every applicant. The clothing you wear to the interview should be neat, clean, comfortable, and, of course, appropriate. As interviewers talk with you, they will notice such details as your nails, teeth, and hair. A full night's sleep will contribute to your fresh, alert appearance. Any detail of appearance and dress that attracts unfavorable attention will count against you.

The ways that you walk and sit are clues to your personality and mental attitude. Walk with purpose and confidence; sit with composure and ease. Trained interviewers know that there is a direct relationship between personal habits and work habits—sloppy appearance, sloppy work; neat appearance, neat work. Therefore, make your appearance speak favorably for you at the interview.

Your Manner and Manners. Good manners are often taken for granted, but any lack of good manners is noticed immediately. Follow these tips on common courtesy and etiquette during job interviews.

Arrive on Time or Early. It is rude to be late for any appointment. If you are late for a job interview, you may make the interviewer wonder how often you will be late if you are hired. The interviewer might also conclude that you do not really want the job, since you are late. Rushing to arrive on time will leave you breathless, however; so start early enough to allow for any possible delays.

Meet the Unexpected With Poise, Tact, and Humor. If the interviewer is not ready to see you, take a seat and occupy yourself while you're waiting. Imagine the childish impression made by a person who says, "But Mr. Balducci told me that he would see me at eleven o'clock."

Follow the Interviewer's Lead. Remember that you are a guest. Shake hands if the interviewer offers to do so, and give a firm handshake. A limp handshake indicates weakness. Wait for an invitation before seating yourself, and let the interviewer tell you where to be seated. You are being a good guest if you follow the lead of the interviewer.

Be Tactful and Gracious in Conversation. Listen carefully. Don't interrupt, even if the interviewer is long-winded and you think of something to say right away. Follow the interviewer's conversation leads and show that you understand the importance of what has been said. Don't bore the interviewer with long, overdetailed answers; but do reply with more than a meek "yes" or "no" to questions. Never contradict the interviewer or imply that an error has been made, under any circumstances. Such lack of tact is rude and will do nothing to help you in the interview.

Show Appreciation for the Interviewer's Time and Interest. At the close of the interview remember to express appreciation, just as you would thank any host as you take your leave. Don't let the excitement and tension of the interview make you forget this courtesy. Failing to show appreciation could spoil an otherwise effective interview.

Your Speech and Conversation. The speech principles you have studied will aid you in demonstrating your oral communication. Have you worked to improve your voice? How is your enunciation? vocabulary and pronunciation? Do you still say "yeah" when you mean "yes"? If you have worked hard and applied all you have learned, your voice and speech will do you credit. You can concentrate on what you say.

What you say reflects your attitudes and tells what kind of person you are. During the interview, for example, if you betray that you are overly interested in salary, your lunch hour, vacation, sick leave, or short working hours, you may reveal that you are more interested in loafing than in working. Interviewers have a responsibility to employ people who want to work!

Typical Interview Questions. Understanding the intent of the interviewer's questions will help you answer more intelligently. Here are some typical interview questions, with the reasons behind them and suggestions as to what you might say in reply.

Why Have You Selected This Kind of Work? The interviewer wishes to know how interested you are in the work and what your goals are. An answer like "Oh, I just need a job" shows lack of purpose. Isn't the following a better answer? "I've wanted to be a secretary ever since I started school. That was my reason for taking the stenographic course. I believe I'll like this type of job too." This type of answer tells the interviewer that you know what you want from a job, that you have interest, and that you have a purpose.

If You Had Your Choice of Job and Company, What Would You Most Like to Be Doing and Where? Watch your answer to this question? The interviewer is trying to gauge just how satisfied you will be working in this job and in this company. The best answer, if you can truthfully say so, is: "Ms. Andersen, the job I want is the one for which I am now applying. The company? Yours. Before too long I hope to have proved myself and to have been promoted to greater responsibility."

What Are Your Hobbies? The interviewer is not interested in swapping information about your stamp collection. What the interviewer really wants to know is whether you have broad interests, for a person who has few outside interests is likely to become restless. Be ready to list briefly your major interests in hobbies and sports.

In What Extracurricular Activities Have You Participated? To what clubs do you belong? What offices have you held? What honors have you received? These and similar questions are asked to determine the scope of your interest in people—whether you are able to work with people and whether you have leadership qualities. These are the characteristics of a well-rounded, well-adjusted individual. In preparing for the interview, review your extracurricular activities so that you can give the facts without hesitation.

Would You Be Willing to Work Overtime? Employers like to see a willingness, even an eagerness, to perform well in a job. Overtime may be required seldom, but if it is, employers want to have people who will accept this responsibility. You would be entering a job with the wrong attitude if you were not willing to work overtime when necessary.

COMMUNICATION LABORATORY

APPLICATION EXERCISES

A. Make a list of your personal and educational qualifications to fill one of the following positions: receptionist, accounting clerk, secretary, word processing operator, clerk-typist, retail sales clerk. From the standpoint of an interviewer, make a list of qualifications for the job, including some that you may not currently have.

B. Make a list of your leisure-time activities. Include all extracurricular activities, clubs, offices held, and awards received. The completed list will include things that you might mention in an employment interview.

C. Make a list of grooming and dress standards that you might consult before going to an employment interview.

D. Assume that you are the personnel manager for one of the largest employers in your community. You have an opening for a general clerical worker. Make a list of questions that you might ask an applicant. Explain what each answer would tell you about the potential employee. In class use your questions to enact the interview in the form of a skit.

VOCABULARY AND SPELLING STUDIES

A. These words are often confused: *indignant, indigent, indigenous; imitate, intimate*. Use each word in a sentence that illustrates its meaning.

B. Select the word in parentheses that best completes each of the following sentences.

1. The suffix *-ist* in *pianist, journalist, economist,* and *specialist* gives these words the meaning of (one who, the study of, the science of, the act of).
2. The prefix *mis-* in *misguide, misstep, misuse,* and *misdirect* gives these words the meaning of (before, partly, wrongly, throughout).
3. The prefix *re-* in *reconsider, reunite, remit,* and *return* gives these words the meaning of (under, again, after, beyond).
4. The suffix *-ician* in *technician, electrician,* and *magician* gives these words the meaning of (the service of, the state of, the quality of, specialist in).

C. Replace the italicized words with correctly formed contractions.

1. You *would not* believe how many applied for the job.
2. Margaret *did not* carefully proofread the copy.
3. *It is* difficult to determine the cost of the work.
4. I can't be certain *who is* going to be assigned to that job.
5. *Let us* hear from you when you make your decision.

COMMUNICATING FOR RESULTS

Supervising People. You are a department head in a large firm. At salary-review time, you receive the following written report from one of your managers: "I cannot recommend either Ms. Lavin or Mr. Davies for the normal budgeted salary increases. For their first few months with the firm, they learned quickly and worked well and conscientiously. For the last few months, however, their work seems to have taken second place to long coffee breaks, lengthy personal visits with other employees, and continual inattentiveness. During this past week Ms. Lavin was unable to complete a five-page report. Mr. Davies fell further behind in the routine posting of invoices. I think you ought to talk with both of them."

You have asked each of these employees to come to your office. What will you say when each comes to see you?

REFERENCE SECTION

The following pages are a handy reference section on business-letter style. This material has been covered in the textbook, but it is organized here for easy use. Included on the inside back cover of this textbook are such useful items as proofreader's marks for rough drafts and revises and abbreviations of states, territories, and possessions of the United States.

OFFICE TECHNOLOGY NETWORKS, INC.
4833 Gateway Boulevard East
El Paso, Texas 79905
(713) 555-1348

February 6, 1989

Ms. Geneva Clauson
Investment Properties Company
708 Talton Avenue
San Antonio, TX 78285

Dear Ms. Clauson:

Subject: Form of a Block Letter

This letter style is fast becoming the most popular style in use today. Efficiency is the main reason for its popularity. The typist can save time and eliminate the necessity of working out placement. Some organizations are even designing letterheads to accommmodate this style. A few years ago, some people felt the block style looked odd. That complaint is seldom heard today, however. As more organizations use a block style, people have become accustomed to its appearance.

This letter also illustrates the subject line and the enclosure. A subject line may be typed with initial caps or all in caps. It should start at the left margin. It always appears after the salutation and before the body of the letter. An enclosure notation starts at the left margin and always appears on the line after the reference initials.

Sincerely,

Annette G. Fuentes

Annette G. Fuentes
Manager, Customer Services

nkm
Enclosure

The block letter is the fastest one to type because each line begins at the left margin.

OFFICE TECHNOLOGY NETWORKS, INC.

4833 Gateway Boulevard East
El Paso, Texas 79905
(713) 555-1348

February 6, 1989

Ms. Carla Furman
Steffins and Wasserman Ltd.
1382 Victoria Street
Toronto, Ontario
CANADA M5C 2N8

Dear Ms. Furman:

This modified-block letter style is still very popular for two reasons:

1. Many people feel comfortable with the traditional appearance.

2. The blocked paragraphs make it slightly more efficient to type than a letter with indented paragraphs.

Lists, quotations, and addresses may be indented on either side for a clearer display. If it is necessary to use more than one paragraph for a quotation, a standard single blank line is left between paragraphs.

Special mail service, such as special delivery or registered mail, is shown on the line below the reference initials. We do so only to record this information for our files.

When the letter is being sent to a foreign address, the country is typed in all-capital letters on a separate line, as CANADA is shown above.

Sincerely,

Annette G. Fuentes

Annette G. Fuentes
Manager, Customer Services

nkm
Registered

PS: We treat postscripts in the same way that we treat other paragraphs, except that we precede each postscript by PS: or PS.

The modified-block letter is very popular. Note that the mailing notation is below the reference initials and that all-capital letters are used for *CANADA* **in the inside address.**

OFFICE TECHNOLOGY NETWORKS, INC.

4833 Gateway Boulevard East
El Paso, Texas 79905
(713) 555-1348

February 6, 1989

Banton, Turchon, and Vick, Inc.
9004 18th Street NW
Washington, DC 20009

Attention: Training Director

Ladies and Gentlemen:

The modified-block letter with indented
paragraphs is still popular because of its
traditional appearance. The indented paragraphs give
this style a distinctive look.

This letter also shows an attention line. Like
the subject line, the attention line is typed at the
left margin, but above the salutation. It is usually
typed with initial caps but may also be all in caps.

Cordially,

Annette G. Fuentes

Annette G. Fuentes
Manager, Customer Services

nkm

cc: Ms. T. Spock
    Dr. F. Mantel

In the modified-block letter with indented paragraphs, the first line of each paragraph is indented—usually five spaces.

OFFICE TECHNOLOGY NETWORKS, INC.

4833 Gateway Boulevard East
El Paso, Texas 79905
(713) 555-1348

November 1, 1990

Miss Sherry Weinstein
680 Forrest Road, N.E.
Atlanta, GA 30313

THE SIMPLIFIED LETTER

A number of years ago, a new letter format, called the
simplified style, was developed. The letter you are reading,
Miss Weinstein, is prepared in that style.

1.   Its lines all begin at the left margin.

2.   It omits the salutation and complimentary closing.

3.   It uses a subject line, typed in all-capital letters and
     preceded and followed by two blank lines. (Note that the
     word Subject is omitted.)

4.   It identifies the signer of the letter by an all-capital
     line that is preceded by four blank lines and followed by
     one blank line--if further notations are used.

5.   It uses a brisk but friendly tone and uses the addressee's
     name at least in the first sentence.

Perhaps, Miss Weinstein, for the sake of efficiency, you might
like to use the simplified letter style.

(Mrs.) Annette G. Fuentes

ANNETTE G. FUENTES--MANAGER, CUSTOMER SERVICES

pw

The simplified letter is similar to the block letter, with some additional features. These features are illustrated above.

I · N · D · E · X

POINTS TO PONDER

- No matter what career you choose, you will spend a lot of time sending and receiving messages — *communicating*.
- Speaking, listening, writing, and using body language are all forms of verbal and nonverbal communication.
- Nonverbal communication — gestures, attire, grooming, facial expressions, posture, and body movements — contribute greatly to the meaning of a message.
- Whatever the communication situation — selling a product, asking for information, seeking a job — good human relations skills are a must.
- Most people who visit your business and with whom you correspond are customers or potential customers. Be sure to apply the essentials of goodwill-building when dealing with them.
- Teleconferencing makes it possible to send and receive voice, image, graphic, and written data anywhere, anytime.
- For business writers today, word processing — creating, editing, formatting, storing, retrieving, revising, and printing documents — has become a way of life.
- The point-of-purchase (POP) scanner in the supermarket is an example of information processing. Businesses use information processing to collect, organize, record, store, and retrieve sales, revenue, date-and-time, and inventory data.
- Business people read all types of materials — letters, memos, reports, articles, bulletins, and notices — to keep up to date and to perform their jobs well.
- Proofreaders compare prepared documents with input that is presumed to be correct, complete, and well written. Any differences are marked with proofreaders' marks.
- Editors must master grammar, punctuation, spelling, and vocabulary so that they can determine for themselves if a document is correct, complete, and well written.
- You can depend on your library to have the most up-to-date reference manuals to help you with your communication task.
- Many words are confused because they sound or look alike but have different spellings or meanings. Using your dictionary can help you locate the correct spelling and meanings of these words.
- Your mastery of grammar and punctuation provides the basis for good communication skills — skills that will help you succeed on the job.
- Even in this era of electronic communication, the written word is *still* the basic tool with which information — especially in business — is exchanged.
- Sentence structure, tone, emphasis, and length are among the many factors that make a written message effective.
- Effective business writers deliberately manipulate paragraph length to create a certain effect.
- Business documents are written so that records of decisions, meetings, and conversations can be made.
- Plan a written or mental outline before you dictate or write a business document.
- Business letters are so common that at one time or another you, like everyone, will be asked to write them.
- When writing a request letter, apply what you know about psychology and human relations. Ask yourself what kind of request *you* would like to receive if this letter were sent to you.
- The objective of a claim letter is *satisfaction*. To achieve this objective, you must present your case carefully, thoughtfully and tactfully.

- Credit letters, granting or refusing charge card privileges, can be written traditionally or electronically through the use of paragraph libraries.
- When personal selling is not possible, sales letters are written. In a sense *all* business letters have something to sell — merchandise, services, a point of view, an idea, and most of all goodwill.
- Social-business letters are goodwill-builders. These letters are written to acknowledge business-related social activities, such as awards presentations or retirement parties.
- Memos are written to communicate with fellow employees, regardless of where they may be located — in the same office, in the same building, or in a branch office miles away.
- Memos with a lot of data and detail will be clearer and easier to read if the writer uses graphics and other displays wherever possible.
- Business reports are written to communicate facts and ideas to others so that decision making can take place.
- Minutes are a written record of meetings. They are prepared and distributed to the meeting attendees and to other interested parties.
- Using message forms increases productivity. They allow us to take complete, accurate messages for others so that prompt responses can be made.
- The success of many daily activities on the job depends on expert listening skills.
- Listening is a difficult skill to master. You must get the message right the first time, or you will lose it.
- Your speaking skill is an important part of your personality — it is individually and particularly you. We are often judged by how we speak.
- Project a positive image as a speaker for your company by paying attention to attractive dress and grooming, good posture and carriage, pleasant facial expressions, and good manners.
- Every good talk requires careful preparation and polished delivery.
- On the job you will meet and talk with the public frequently.
- Whether you are recording in your office, speaking to a coworker, or making a presentation to a group, remember that your voice quality — your volume, pitch, tone, and tempo — can affect the meaning of your message.
- The most common electronic equipment for speaking is the telephone. When on the telephone remember that the caller cannot see you. Your voice represents not only you but *your company* as well.
- More and more, business decisions are made as a result of group thinking. Knowing how to participate in a meeting — as a leader or as a working member — will be an important part of your job.
- After completing your education, you will want to find a job that matches your training, interests, and career goals. Consult your school placement officers, newspaper ads, employment agencies, government offices, colleges, universities, and individual businesses to locate that job.
- When seeking a job you can use your writing skills a number of ways: to write an application letter, complete an application form, prepare a résumé, or write follow-up letters.
- Employers often receive many, many applications for a job. Make the employers notice you by carefully preparing your employment documents.
- Take the time to create a favorable first impression at your interview. Employers know that good *personal* habits usually mean good *work* habits.
- Your employment interview will test all your communication skills. You must speak well, listen attentively, read and follow instructions, and write effective employment documents.